LEGEND OF THE LANCASTERS

LEGEND OF THE LANCASTERS

The Bomber War from England 1942–45

Martin W. Bowman

Pen & Sword
AVIATION

First published in Great Britain in 2009 by
Pen & Sword Aviation
an imprint of
Pen & Sword Books Ltd
47 Church Street
Barnsley
South Yorkshire
S70 2AS

Copyright © Martin W. Bowman, 2009
ISBN 978 1 84884 017 1

A CIP catalogue record for this book is available from
the British Library.

Typeset in 11/13pt Plantin by Concept,
Huddersfield.

Pen & Sword Books Ltd incorporates the Imprints
of Pen & Sword Aviation, Pen & Sword Maritime,
Pen & Sword Military, Wharncliffe Local History,
Pen & Sword Select, Pen & Sword Military Classics,
Leo Cooper, Remember When, Seaforth Publishing
and Frontline Publishing.

Printed and bound in England by CPI UK

For a complete list of Pen & Sword titles please contact
PEN & SWORD BOOKS LIMITED
47 Church Street,
Barnsley,
South Yorkshire,
S70 2AS,
England
E-mail: enquiries@pen-and-sword.co.uk
Website: www.pen-and-sword.co.uk

Contents

Acknowledgements

John Aldridge; Frau Anneliese Autenrieth; Charlie 'Jock' Baird; Raymond V. Base; Jack Bennett; Maurice Bishop; Len Browning; Mrs Susannah Burr; Ronald J. Clark DFC; Allen Clifford; Oliver Clutton-Brock, Editor, RAF Bomber Command Association; Bob Collis; Fred Coney; Dennis Cooper; Coen Cornelissen; Leslie Cromarty DFM; Tom Cushing; Hans-Peter Dabrowski; Wing Commander S. P. 'Pat' Daniels; Frank Dengate DFC RAAF; Arnold Döring; Richard 'Ricky' Dyson GM; Ronnie H. 'Squiggle' Eeles; Howard 'Tommy' Farmiloe DSO; David G. Fellowes; John Foreman; Jim George; Group Captain J. R. 'Benny' Goodman DFC* AFC AE; Alex H. Gould DFC; Linda Greenacre; Charles Hall; Steve Hall; Brian 'Darkie' Hallows DFC; Roland A. Hammersley DFM; Jack F. Hamilton; Erich Handke; A. J. Stanley Harrison; Leslie Hay; Bill Hough; Maurice 'Frank' Hemming DFM; Ted Howes DFC; Zdenek Hurt; Ab A. Jansen; Mick Jennings MBE; Karl-Ludwig Johanssen; J. S. 'Johnny' Johnston; John B. Johnson; Les King; Wing Commander Rollo Kingsford-Smith RAAF; Brian Maidment, Air Research Branch; Larry Melling; Frank Mouritz; Maurice S. Paff; Simon Parry; Derek Patfield; Pathfinder Association; Wing Commander David Penman DSO OBE DFC; Bob Pierson; John Price; the late Bill Reid VC; Ernie Reynolds; the late Frederick Woodger Roots; Jerry Scutts; Wilhelm Simonsohn; Don L. Simpkin; E. N. M. Sparks; Max Spence; Bob Stainton; Dick Starkey; Maurice Stoneman; Frank Tasker; George Vantilt; Rob de Visser; Edwin Wheeler DFC; H. Wilde; John Williams.

I am extremely grateful to my friend and colleague Theo Boiten, with whom I have collaborated on several books, for all the information on the *Nachtjagd* or German night fighter forces contained herein.

Chapter 1

Under Cover of Darkness

The Germans entered this war under the rather childish delusion that they were going to bomb everybody else and nobody was going to bomb them. At Rotterdam, London, Warsaw and half a hundred other places, they put that rather naive theory into operation. They sowed the wind and now they are going to reap the whirlwind.

Air Marshal Sir Arthur T. Harris

On a warm July afternoon the dull throb of aircraft engines could be heard from high in the sky. At Mousehold aerodrome on the outskirts of Norwich no air-raid siren was sounded. At Barnards Iron Works, a collection of First World War hangars and outbuildings, there was no cause for alarm. It was Tuesday 9 July 1940. Although the Battle of Britain was about to start the cathedral city was not yet in the front line. When an air-raid warning was sounded, a young teenager, Derek Patfield, took his place as one of the pairs of spotters in the watchtower erected on the top of the Enquiry Office, watching for enemy attack using a pair of powerful binoculars. To relieve the boredom he often trained his binoculars on the young female employees walking between the workshops and offices. If he saw approaching enemy aircraft, or thought they identified one as enemy, Derek pressed the alarm siren which sounded all over the works resulting in the employees dashing to the air-raid shelters. Derek was a quiet lad with one hobby – aeroplanes. Flying was his only interest. In 1932 the Patfield family had moved from King's Lynn to Acacia Road at Thorpe-Next-Norwich near Mousehold aerodrome. Derek spent his spare time building flying models and on one occasion while doping the skin of a model, gave Mrs Hanson next door quite a scare as the smell of the dope was a strong pear drop, which she associated with a gas attack. She was most relieved when she saw young Derek in his garden doping a model. At Mousehold aerodrome he watched Professor Henri Mignet fly his home built aeroplane, *The Flying Flea* and he got Clem Sohn's autograph. Sohn, better known as, 'The Birdman' jumped out of an aeroplane and spread small under-arm wings and a

web between his legs to glide down, finally landing by parachute. Derek Patfield made a shaped pair of wings from garden canes and an old sheet and jumped off the coalhouse roof and finished up with a badly sprained ankle and a dressing down from his father for being so daft.

When the young spotters got fed up with the lack of aircraft activity during their two-hour shift, they would sound the siren, just for the hell of it, to see the panic it caused! False alarms were explained away as 'incorrect identification'. At 17.00 on the afternoon of 9 July when the two aircraft approached from the north-east, flying at about 600 feet, they made out the black markings in the shape of crosses on the wings and flung themselves to the ground. They were Dornier Do 17s. The factory site was hit by twelve 50kg high-explosive bombs. Three bombs, which failed to explode, were also dropped. The raid was all over in six long seconds. Two men who were working by the loading dock were killed and another threw himself to the ground 20 yards from where a bomb exploded but his only injury was a damaged toe, which later had to be amputated. One worker had a most remarkable escape when a bullet or bomb splinter went through his trouser-leg while others pierced the walls on either side of him. One of the aircraft was seen to bank away towards the centre of the city. At the famous Colmans' Mustard Works at Carrow, workers coming off shift poured through the main gates – jostling, laughing and bicycle bells ringing. As the Dorniers suddenly appeared overhead many of the women were pushing their bicycles up Carrow Hill. The Dorniers banked a little and dived and the sound of a whistling bomb rent the air. The older men, remembering the sound of falling bombs from the First World War, threw themselves to the ground at the same time shouting to the women, 'Down!' The women and girls did not immediately abandon their bicycles and they did not throw themselves to the ground. A bomb crashed through trees at the top of Carrow Hill and exploded at ground level. Four women were killed. Others were seriously injured and many suffered minor injuries.

On his 18th birthday Derek Patfield volunteered for the RAF as a fighter pilot but he was not quite tall enough. He was told to re-apply when he had managed to put on the extra inch. In the meantime his boyhood friend Joe Whittaker had become a sergeant air gunner on Wellingtons. When he was killed in action in 1942 on a raid on Saarbrücken, it was a pivotal moment for Derek and it set firm his determination to avenge his death. At last he got his call-up papers and AC2 Patfield set off for London, complete with small attaché case to get kitted out at Lord's cricket ground. His RAF uniform included a white flash on his forage cap denoting trainee aircrew, which made him very proud. On arrival AC2 Patfield asked the corporal in charge of recruits, 'What sort of aircraft do we fly? Where do we fly from?'

He replied, 'We haven't got any aircraft here. You've got to learn to march first.'

After lengthy spells training in England and Canada, two years later Flight Sergeant Patfield was beginning his tour as a bomb-aimer on Avro Lancaster bombers in RAF Bomber Command. This mighty four engined bomber could not have been more different from the twin engined Wellingtons that aircrew like Joe Whittaker had to fly during the first three years of the war when the aircraft was the mainstay of bomber operations from England.

Bombing German cities to destruction was not an entirely new concept. Ever since October 1940 crews were instructed to drop their bombs on German cities, though only if their primary targets were ruled out because of bad weather. During 1941 more and more bombs began falling on built-up areas, mainly because pinpoint bombing of industrial targets was rendered impractical by the lack of navigational and bombing aids. By 1942 the Air Staff saw the need to deprive the German factories of its workers and, therefore, its ability to manufacture weapons for war, and mass raids would be the order of the day or rather the night, with little attention paid to precision raids on military targets. However, RAF Bomber Command did not yet possess the numbers or type of aircraft necessary for immediate mass raids. All this would change under the

direction of Air Marshal Sir Arthur T. Harris CB OBE who, on 22 February 1942, arrived at High Wycombe, Buckinghamshire to take over as Commander-in-Chief of RAF Bomber Command. Harris was directed by Marshal of the RAF, Sir Charles Portal, Chief of the Air Staff, to break the German spirit by the use of night area, rather than precision, bombing and the targets would be civilian, not just military. The famous area bombing directive, which had gained support from the Air Ministry and Prime Minister Winston Churchill, had been sent to Bomber Command on 14 February, eight days before Harris assumed command. Harris warmed to his task and announced:

'The Germans entered this war under the rather childish delusion that they were going to bomb everybody else and nobody was going to bomb them. At Rotterdam, London, Warsaw and half a hundred other places, they put that rather naive theory into operation. They sowed the wind and now they are going to reap the whirlwind.'[1]

'Butch' or 'Bomber' Harris, as his crews were to call him, has been described by some of his 'old lags', as he fondly referred to them, as '. . . a rough, tough, vulgar egomaniac'. He was just what Bomber Command needed. He feared no foe, senior officers or politicians. He brooked no arguments from juniors and pooh-poohed any from those of equal or senior status who had a different opinion. Harris knew what he was going to do and proceeded to move heaven and earth to do it. Woe betide anyone who stood in his way. He was a firm believer in the Trenchard doctrine and with it he was going to win the war. According to Professor Solly Zuckerman, technical advisor to those responsible for the bombing policy, Harris '. . . liked destruction for its own sake'.[2] On taking up his position Harris had found that only 380 aircraft were serviceable and only 68 of these were heavy bombers while 257 were medium bombers. Salvation, though, was at hand.

In September 1941 the first of the new four-engined Avro Lancasters, a heavy bomber in every sense of the word, had been supplied to 44 (Rhodesia) Squadron at Waddington for service trials. In early 1942 deliveries began to trickle through to 44 Squadron and on the night of 3/4 March four aircraft flew the first Lancaster operation when they dropped mines in the Heligoland Bight. That same night Harris selected the Renault factory at Billancourt near Paris, which had been ear-marked for attack for some time, as his first target. A full moon was predicted so Harris decided to send a mixed force of 235 aircraft, led by the most experienced crews in Bomber Command, to bomb the French factory in three waves. It was calculated that approximately 121 aircraft an hour had been concentrated over the factory, which was devastated and all except 12 aircraft claimed to have bombed.[3]

During March the first *Gee* navigational and target identification sets were installed in operational bombers and these greatly assisted bombers in finding their targets on the nights of 8/9 and 9/10 March in attacks on Essen. On the latter date 187 bombers, including 136 Wellingtons, bombed the city which, without *Gee*, had been a difficult target to hit accurately. The first Lancaster night-bombing operation of the war was flown by 44 Squadron when two of its aircraft took part in the raid by 126 aircraft on Essen on 10/11 March. Despite the new technological wonder, the bombing was scattered on all three raids on the city, which was covered alternately by industrial haze and unexpected cloud. The same month 97 Squadron moved from Coningsby to Woodhall Spa, about ten miles away, to become the second squadron to convert from the Manchester to the Lancaster. But the early Lancasters gave some trouble, as 23 year old David 'Jock' Penman, 'a square, chunky' Scottish pilot,[4] recalls:

'Flight Lieutenant Reginald R. "Nicky" Sandford DFC of 44 Squadron flew a Lancaster in to convert a few pilots. Conversion consisted of one circuit by Nicky followed by one circuit each for the pilot to be converted. We then climbed into a Manchester and went to Woodford where we collected six Lancasters. I still remember with pleasure the surge of the four Merlins and the tremendous acceleration of the lightly loaded Lancaster after the painfully underpowered Manchester. Unfortunately the Lancaster had teething problems and the first was a main wheel falling off Flying Officer Ernest A. Deverill DFM's machine when he took off from Boscombe Down. Then an outboard engine fell off after a night landing on the grass at Coningsby. More serious trouble came [on 20 March off the Friesians] when six aircraft took off on the first operational sortie loaded with six 1,500lb mines. Returning over Boston 28 year old Flying Officer Eric E. "Rod" Rodley, who despite being one of the oldest on the squadron was the most youthful in appearance, looked out to see first one and then the other wing tip fold upwards. Even at full power he was descending but luck was on his side, as he dropped the aircraft in the sea without injuring the crew.[5] A second aircraft diverted to a strange airfield and, overshooting the runway, ended in a quarry. Engine trouble, maladjusted petrol cocks and upper wing skin buckling restricted flying but all were overcome in the end. The Lancaster was easy to fly and after the Hampden and Manchester it was like stepping from an ancient banger into a Rolls-Royce. After the wing tip failures, bomb load with full fuel was reduced from 9,000lbs to 6,000lbs and we stopped doing circuits and bumps with a full bomb load! It had always been customary to do night flying tests before operations with bombs on, though it was stopped on the Hampdens at Waddington when one enthusiastic low flyer skidded to a halt in a field with 4 × 500lb bombs on board.'

On 28/29 March 234 bombers, mostly carrying incendiaries, went to Lübeck, an historic German town on the Baltic, with thousands of half timbered houses and an ideal target for a mass raid by RAF bombers carrying incendiary bombs. Eight bombers were lost but 191 aircraft claimed to have hit the target. A photo-reconnaissance a few days later revealed that about half the city, 200 acres, had been obliterated. The increase in RAF night bombing raids in the more favourable spring weather met with a rapid rise in *Nachtjagd* victories. In March 1942 41 bombers[6] and in April 46 bombers,[7] were brought down by German night fighters. II./NJG 1, which had recently moved to St Trond, achieved its first six victories from this Belgian base during the month. On the night of 6/7 April, 157 bombers went to Essen but the crews encountered severe storms and icing and there was complete cloud cover at the target. Only 49 aircraft claimed to have reached the target area and there was virtually no damage to Essen. Five aircraft were lost.[8]

On the night of 8/9 April 97 Squadron operations finally recommenced in earnest when 24 Lancasters started up their 27-litre Merlin engines, took off and carried out a minelaying operation in the Heligoland Bight while the main Bomber Command thrust, by 272 aircraft, was aimed at Hamburg. Icing and electrical storms hampered operations. Although 188 aircraft claimed to have hit the target area, only the equivalent of 14 bomb loads fell on the city. Five aircraft failed to return, all seven Lancasters returning safely.

On 11 April 44 Squadron was ordered to fly long distance flights in formation to obtain endurance data on the Lancaster. At the same time 97 Squadron began flying low, in groups of three in 'vee' formation to Selsey Bill, then up to Lanark, across to Falkirk and up to Inverness to a point just outside the town, where they feigned an attack, and then back to Woodhall Spa. Crews in both the squadrons knew that the real reason was that they were training for a special operation and speculation as to the target was rife.

'Despite frequent groundings', recalls David Penman, 'training continued and early in April rumours of some special task for the Lancasters were confirmed when eight crews were selected to practice low level formation flying and bombing. The final practice was a cross-country at 250 feet for two sections of three led by Squadron Leader John S. Sherwood DFC* with myself leading the second section.[9] We took off from Woodhall Spa and were to rendezvous with 44 Squadron near Grantham but because of unserviceability they did not take off. We flew down to Selsey Bill and then turned round and headed for Inverness. Due to compass errors the lead section got off track and were heading into an area of masts and balloons. With no communication allowed I eventually parted company with the lead section and we did not see them again until we were bombing the target in the Wash at Wainfleet. Our low level flight up valleys to Edinburgh was exciting, but over the higher ground in the North we climbed to a reasonable altitude over cloud, descending in the clear at Inverness for a low level run. Once beyond Edinburgh, on the way back, we descended again to low level and, full of confidence, really got down to hedgehopping. Flying Officer Deverill on the left and Warrant Officer Thomas Mycock DFC[10] on the right maintained very tight formation and my only regret was the stampeding cattle when we could not avoid flying over them. Greater satisfaction came as we roared across familiar airfields a few feet from the hangar roofs and Waddington got the full blast of our slip stream as we rubbed in our success whilst they were stuck on the ground. A perfect formation bombing run with Sherwood's section running in behind completed a very successful day.

'A few days later I went to HQ 5 Group in Grantham with the Station Commander from Coningsby and Squadron Leader Sherwood. At 5 Group when the target was revealed, we were shattered and *suicide* was a common thought. However, the briefing was thorough with an excellent scale model of the target area and emphasis on low level to avoid detection, massive diversionary raids and little ack-ack or opposition at Augsburg. This briefing was only a day or two before the 17th and no one else was to be informed until the briefing on the day of the raid when take-off was to be 1515 hours. On Friday the 17th briefing was immediately after lunch with crew kitted ready to go. The scale model of the target was on display and the gasps as crews entered the room and saw the target were noticeable.'

At Waddington Wing Commander Roderick A. B. 'Babe' Learoyd VC, the 44 Squadron CO, began his address to the crews with, 'Bomber Command have come up with a real beauty this time' and added 'I shan't be coming with you. I've got *my* VC already. I've no desire to get another.'[11] At Woodhall Spa when the

curtain was drawn back at the briefing there was a roar of laughter instead of the gasp of horror. Before the laughter had died down, the 97 Squadron commander, Wing Commander Collier, entered and walked quietly forward to the front of the briefing room and mounted the dais. The crews came to order at once, listening intently. 'Well gentlemen', smiled the Wing Commander, 'now you know what the target is'.

The target was the diesel engine manufacturing workshop at the MAN[12] factory at Augsburg but no one in the room believed that the RAF would be so stupid as to send 12 of its newest four-engined bombers all that distance inside Germany in daylight. Crews sat back and waited calmly for someone to say, 'Now the real target is this' but Augsburg was the real target. Air Marshal Harris wanted the plant raided by a small force of Lancasters flying at low level (500 feet), and in daylight, despite some opposition from the Ministry of Economic Warfare, who wanted the ball-bearing plant at Schweinfurt attacked instead. Crews were ordered to take their steel helmets on this raid. Sixteen Lancaster crews, eight each from 44 (Rhodesia) and 97 Squadrons (including four 1st and 2nd reserve) were specially selected. Squadron Leader John Dering Nettleton, still on his first tour in 44 Squadron, was chosen to lead the operation. The 24 year old South African, who had been born at Nongoma in Natal and educated in Cape Town, had spent 18 months at sea in the merchant service before coming to England to join the RAF in 1938 to train as a pilot. Dark haired but fair-skinned, tall and reticent, grandson of an admiral, he was an inspired choice as leader.

Flying Officer Eric E. 'Rod' Rodley, the reserve pilot, who was known for his whimsical sense of humour, found nothing to smile about. He was appalled when the target was named but he and his crew of *F-Freddie* had clung to the hope that they were only the reserve. Rodley had been 'one of the lucky ones'; joining the RAFVR in 1937 and he already had instructing experience when war broke out. Consequently, he graced the first War Instructors Course at CFS in October 1939, after which he spent an exhausting and unrewarding year and a half in Training Command. Hence, by June 1941, he had over 1,000 hours in his logbook but he was '... quite unprepared for any wider aspects of the art'. A strange set of circumstances rescued him from the thraldom of instructing when 97 Squadron was re-formed and equipped with the Avro Manchester when all pilots had to have at least 1,000 hours under their belts. One of his contemporaries in 97 Squadron was Norfolk man, Flying Officer Brian Roger Wakefield 'Darkie' Hallows who, after flying three days of long formation cross-countries, was set to fly *B-Baker*[13] Like Rodley, Hallows had been an instructor before becoming a Manchester and then a Lancaster pilot.[14] It was his reputation for the use of R/T language 'which caused some watch tower WAAFs to giggle, some to blush'[15] and not for his jet black hair and full moustache that earned him his nickname 'Darkie'. When he had got lost and invoked the R/T get-you-home service of those early days, 'Darkie, Darkie' he, receiving no response, had tried again, but still no reply. Once more he had transmitted to the void: 'Darkie, Darkie – where are you, you little black bastard?'

Hallows recalls:

'Plenty was said about how important it [Augsburg] was and all that stuff. So we were obviously not intended to come back in any strength. Fighter Command had been on the job for several days, hounding the German fighters and when we were on the job we saw no fighters at all, all the way . . .' Just before the Lancasters took off 30 Bostons bombed targets in France in a planned attempt to force hundreds of German fighters up over the Pas de Calais, Cherbourg and Rouen areas. This was designed to draw the enemy fighters into combat so that the passage of the Lancasters would coincide with their refuelling and re-arming. Unfortunately it had the opposite effect and the incursion put the Luftwaffe on the alert. David Penman continues:

'Take-off was to be at 1515 hours with the two reserve aircraft taking off and dropping out when the two Vics of three set course.[16] We were to meet 44 Squadron near Grantham and then on to Selsey Bill, across the Channel, then down south of Paris before turning left and heading for Lake Constance. Take-off was on time, singly, with full fuel [2,134 gallons] and four 1,000lb RDX bombs with 11-second delay fuses to be dropped from 250 feet. Weather forecast was perfect with clear skies and good visibility all the way. I took-off and soon had Deverill on my left and Mycock on my right. We joined the lead section of Squadron Leader Sherwood, Flying Officer Hallows and Flying Officer Rodley. [As they had watched the other six aircraft starting up some of Rodley's crew had begun to have mixed feelings and almost wished now that they had got this far that they were going. Then *A-Apple* had a mag drop on No. 1 engine and Rodley's crew had fallen silent. Rodley thought of his wife in Woodhall Spa. She would probably guess what had happened. He took off with the others and moved into the No. 3 position, tucked in to port of Sherwood.[17]] Once again there was no sign of 44 Squadron near Grantham and we were never to meet. We maintained 250 feet to Selsey Bill and then

got down as close to the sea as possible for the Channel crossing. As we approached the French coast my rear-gunner informed me his turret was U/S and I told him it was too late to do anything about it and he would just have to do what he could with it. Crossing the French coast was an anti-climax as not a shot was fired and we flew on at tree top height to Lake Constance. We saw the odd aircraft in the distance but otherwise it was a very pleasant trip.'

Penman's Australian navigator, Pilot Officer E. Lister 'Ding' Ifould, who had joined the RAAF in 1940 and went to England in July 1941, saw frightened bullocks scampering across the furrows with their ploughs bumping along behind them. He saw French workers wave to them but usually only when they were working in secluded parts where their greeting would be un-observed. One greeting came from two or three workers deep in a quarry, down which Ifould had a momentary glimpse as his Lancaster flew over almost at tree-top height and again, in a wood, some charcoal burners stopped to give them a secret wave. The Lancs passed over no fewer than 27 German airfields almost at ground level and saw nothing except a few parked aircraft. This hedgehopping was a severe test of skill and endurance. Ifould's captain, Penman, had blisters on both hands when the job was done.[18]

Meanwhile 44 Squadron had not been as fortunate as 97 Squadron. Nettleton took his formation flying in Vics of three down to just 50 feet over the waves of the Channel as the French coast came into view. Five minutes later fighters intercepted Nettleton's first two sections in a running fight that lasted an hour. The Lancasters tightened formation, flying wingtip to wing-tip to give mutual protection with their guns, as they skimmed low over villages and rising and falling country-side. The Bf 109s of II./JG2 were forced to attack from above. Nettleton's No. 3, *H-Harry*, flown by Sergeant G. T. 'Dusty' Rhodes, was first to go down, a victim of Spanish Civil War veteran Major Walter 'Gulle' Oesau, Kommodore, JG 2.[19] None of the crew stood a chance at such a low altitude in an aircraft travelling at 200 mph. Nettleton recalled, 'I saw two or three fighters about 1,000 feet above us. The next thing I knew, there were German fighters all round us. The first casualty I saw was Sergeant Rhodes' aircraft. Smoke poured from his cockpit and his port wing caught fire. He came straight for me out of control and I thought we were going to collide. We missed by a matter of feet and he crashed beneath me. Two others went down almost at once and I saw a fourth on fire. At the time I was too much occupied to feel very much. I remember a bullet chipped a piece of Perspex, which hit my second pilot in the back of the neck. I could hear him say, "What the hell". I laughed at that.'

The whole of 44 Squadron's second 'Vee' was shot out of the sky. First to go was *V-Victor* flown by Warrant Officer J. F. 'Joe' Beckett DFM. His rear turret was out of action and this had attracted most of the enemy fighters. Hauptmann Heine Greisert of II./JG2 was later credited with shooting the Lancaster down. It crashed into a tree and disintegrated. The crew never stood a chance. *T-Tommy* flown by Warrant Officer Herbert V. Crum DFM, a wily bird, old in years and experience by comparison with most of the others, was next to go, shot down by Unteroffizier Pohl of II./JG2. 'Bert' Crum crash-landed his Lancaster in a wheat field at Folleville after two engines were set on fire. Fortunately, his second pilot, Sergeant Alan Dedman, had managed to jettison the bombs 'safe' before the crash. All the crew survived and six of them were taken prisoner. Sergeant Bert Dowty, the 19 year old front gunner was trapped in the nose turret until Crum attacked it with an axe and got him out. Crum split the petrol tanks with his axe and tried to set fire to the escaping petrol using a Very pistol but it would not ignite. Then one of the crew threw a lighted match into the petrol and soon the Lancaster was well alight. Breaking up into small parties, they set out to walk to unoccupied France but most never reached the Black Cat Café at Bordeaux. Dowty evaded capture and managed to hear all about the results of the raid on the BBC. He was caught on a train 16 days later near Limoges and was eventually repatriated at the end of the war. The Lancaster flown by Flight Lieutenant Nicky Sandford DFC, the leader of the section, faced the milling enemy fighters alone and forced his aircraft down even lower in a desperate attempt to shake off his pursuers. Suddenly ahead of him he saw a line of telephone wires. He held the nose down and flew underneath them but the FW 190s followed firing all the time. A little fellow with a pleasing personality, who was keen on music and who bought all the records for the Officers' Mess, he always wore his pyjamas under his flying suit for luck. This time Sandford was all out of luck. He finally fell victim to the guns of Feldwebel Bosseckert. With all four engines on fire, his Lancaster crashed into the ground in an inferno of flame.

Nettleton and Flying Officer John 'Ginger' Garwell DFM piloting *A-Apple* continued to the target alone, flying low in the afternoon sun across southern Germany until the South African sighted the River Lech, which he followed to the target. Over France Nettleton had noticed people working in the fields and cows and sheep grazing, and a fat woman wearing a blue blouse and a white skirt, and horses bolting at the roar of his engines, with the ploughs to which they were attached bumping behind them. But once in Germany nothing was to be seen. 'The fields appeared untenanted by man or beast and there was no traffic on the roads. But when we got near the target they started to shoot at us, but the heavy flak soon stopped – I think because the gunners could not depress their guns low enough to hit us. The light flak, however, was terrific. We could see the target so well that we went straight in and dropped all our bombs in one salvo.' Coming over the brow of a hill on to the target, the two Lancasters were met with heavy fire from quick-firing guns. The bomb-aimers could not miss at chimney-top height on a factory covering an area of 626×293 feet. Nettleton and 'Ginger' Garwell went in and dropped their bomb loads but Flight Sergeant R. J. Flux DFM, his wireless operator, yelled in Garwell's ear: 'We're on fire!'

Flux kept pointing over his shoulder and Garwell took a quick look behind him. The armour-plated door leading into the fuselage was open and he could see that the interior was a mass of flames. Garwell ordered, 'Shut the door' and saw Nettleton and some of his crew staring at his burning Lancaster. Garwell stuck his fingers up in a V-sign before turning to port into wind and putting *A-Apple* down in a field two miles west of the town. By now all five men crowded into the front cabin were coughing violently from the blinding, choking smoke and Flux opened the escape hatch over the navigator's table to try to get some air. A sudden down draught from the hatch cleared the smoke for a fraction of a second and Garwell could see a line of tall trees straight ahead. He opened up the engines and pulled back on the stick and flew into the ground at 80 mph. The Lancaster slid on its belly for about 50 yards and the fuselage broke at the mid-turret. Garwell, Sergeant F. S. Kirke DFM RNZAF and Sergeants J. Watson and L. L. Dando scrambled from the hatch but outside they found Flux, lying dead under the starboard inner engine. He had been thrown out on impact. His quick action had probably saved their lives. The two men in the fuselage perished.[20]

The second formation of six Lancasters in 97 Squadron had flown a slightly different route and had avoided the fighters in France. All they saw was a single German Army cooperation aircraft, which approached them and then made off quickly. Just inside Germany Flying Officer Ernie Deverill DFM at the controls of *Y-Yorker* noticed a man in the uniform of the SS who took in the situation at a glance and ran to a nearby post office where there was a telephone. Brian Hallows' crew in *B-Baker* shot up a passenger train in a large station and saw an aerodrome crowded with Ju 90s. South of Paris Flying Officer 'Rod' Rodley, flying *F-Freddie,* saw only the second aircraft he saw during the whole war. It was probably a courier, a Heinkel 111. It approached and, recognizing them, did a 90-degree bank and turned back towards Paris. Rodley continued flying at 100 feet. Occasionally he would see some Frenchmen take a second look and wave their berets or their shovels. A bunch of German soldiers doing PT in their singlets broke hurriedly for their shelters as the Lancs roared over. Their physical exercises were enlivened by a burst of fire from one of the rear-gunners and 'the speed with which they took cover did great credit to their instructor'. At a frontier post on the Swiss-German border an SS man in black uniform, black boots and black cap shook his fist at the low flying Lancasters. Crossing Lake Constance a German officer standing on the stern of one of the white ferry boat steamers fired his revolver at the bombers. Rodley could see him quite clearly, 'defending the ladies with his Luger against 48 Browning machine guns'. At Lake Ammer, the last turning point 10 miles south of the target, an old bearded Bavarian standing on the shores of the lake, took pot shots at them with a duck gun. One of the gunners asked his pilot if he could 'tickle' him.

'No, leave him alone' was the reply.

Accurate map reading, notably by Flight Lieutenant McClure and Pilot Officer D. O. Sands, Nettleton's navigator, in the first flight and Flying Officer Hepburn in the second, brought them to their destination.[21]

David Penman continues:

'Rising ground then forced us to fly a little higher and eventually we spotted our final turning point, a small lake. I had dropped back a little from Sherwood's section at this stage and mindful of the delay fuses on the bombs, made one orbit before turning to run in on the target. The river was a very good guide and the run in was exactly as shown in the scale model at briefing. A column of smoke beyond the target, presumably came from Garwell's aircraft and it was soon joined by another . . .'

Brian Hallows explained:

'The target was easily picked out – the situation of the factory in a fork made by the River Wertach and an autobahn made it easy to identify – and we bombed the hell out of it. The gunners were ready for us and it was as hot as hell for a few minutes.'

'Rod' Rodley recalled:

'We were belting at full throttle at about 100 feet towards the targets. I dropped the bombs along the side wall. We flashed across the target and down the other side to about 50 feet because flak was quite heavy. As we went away I could see light flak shells overtaking us, green balls flowing away on our right and hitting the ground ahead of us. Leaving the target I looked down at our leader's aircraft[22] and saw that there was a little wisp of steam trailing back from it. The white steam turned to black smoke with fire in the wing. I was slightly above him. In the top of the Lancaster there was a little wooden hatch for getting out if you had to land at sea. I realized that this wooden hatch had burned away and I could look down into the fuselage. It looked like a blowlamp with the petrol swilling around the wings and the centre section, igniting the fuselage and the slipstream blowing it down. I asked our gunner to keep an eye on him. Suddenly he said, "Oh God, skip, he's gone. He looks like a chrysanthemum of fire."'

David Penman watched as *K-King* flown by Sherwood also aged 23, received a shell through the port tank just behind the inboard engine and it crashed and blew up about 10 miles north of the town: 'Escaping vapour caught fire and as he turned left on leaving the target with rising ground, the port wing struck the ground and the aircraft exploded in a ball of flame. (I was sure that no one had survived and said so on return to Woodhall Spa but Mrs Sherwood would not believe it and she proved to be right.[23] I met Sherwood after the war and he had been thrown out of the aircraft, still strapped in his seat, up the hill and had been the sole survivor). As we ran in at 250 feet, tracer shells from light anti-aircraft guns on the roof of the factory produced a hail of fire and all aircraft were hit. Mycock's aircraft on the right received a shell in the front turret, which set fire to the hydraulic oil and in seconds the aircraft was a sheet of flame. It went into a climb and swinging left passed over my head with bomb doors open and finally burning from end to end was seen by my rear-gunner to plunge into the ground.'[24]

As soon as Ifould had let the bombs go, he heard Penman say: 'He's on fire!' Ifould looked over the side and saw flames streaming 10 to 15 feet behind Sherwood's Lancaster. Then he looked to starboard and saw that the other Lancaster (Mycock's) too was on fire. A second or two later the starboard side Lancaster dropped its bombs and dived like a stone to earth. Ifould learned later that it had been hit and set on fire when the Vee first got to the edge of the town, yet Mycock had carried on to the target and bombed. Penman's Lancaster, Ifould having dropped its bombs from about 300 feet, dived again to the safer level of the housetops and cleared the town safely. Seconds later they were overtaken by the port Lancaster in the Vee, in which the mid-upper gunner and wireless operator had gallantly succeeded in putting out the fire Ifould had seen streaming from it earlier. On only three engines, it seemed to overtake literally like a flash. As it passed Ifould caught a glimpse of a hole 6 feet by 4 feet wide in the metal of the fuselage, were the fire had burned through. The two men who had put the fire out later received the DFM for their bravery, which brought their aircraft safely home with no one hurt.[25]

A shell ripped the cowling of Penman's port inner engine and at the same time Deverill received a hit near the mid-upper turret and a fire started. Deverill told the mid-upper gunner to put it out. The starboard inner engine was pouring smoke and flame and Deverill fought to hold his position. Ron Irons, Deverill's wireless operator, left his set to help put out the fire. The oil recuperators had been punctured and burning oil was trickling down the fuselage into the well of the aircraft. 'Despite the distractions' recalls Penman, 'we held course and the front gunner did his best to reduce the opposition. My navigator was then passing instructions on the bombing run and finally called, "Bombs gone." We passed over the factory and I increased power and dived to ground level just as Deverill passed me with one engine feathered and the other three on full power. His navigator, Pilot Officer Butler, had managed to put out the fire near the mid-upper. I called Deverill and he asked if I would cover his rear, as his turrets were U/S. However, as my turrets were also U/S and Ifould had no wish to relinquish the lead, I told him to resume his position. Our attack had been close to the planned time of 2020 hours and as darkness took over we climbed to 20,000 feet for a straight run over Germany. It says a lot for Deverill's skill that he remained in formation until we reached the English coast and eventually landed at Woodhall Spa just before midnight.'[26]

It was close fighting; one rear-gunner spotted a German behind a machine gun on the roof and saw him collapse under his return fire. As the survivors turned westward, the light failed and the aircraft, led by Darkie Hallows flew back without any opposition under cover of darkness. Hallows noted. 'The quintessence of loneliness is to be 500 miles inside Occupied Europe with one serviceable turret! Time 8.15 hours.'

Hallows returned safely and was one of eight officers to be awarded the DFC for his part in the raid. Winston Churchill sent the following message to Arthur T. Harris: 'We must plainly regard the attack of the Lancasters on the *U-boat* engine factory at Augsburg as an outstanding achievement of the Royal Air Force. Undeterred by heavy losses at the outset, the bombers pierced in broad daylight into the heart of Germany and struck a vital point with deadly precision. Pray convey my thanks of His Majesty's Government to the officers and men who accomplished this memorable feat of arms in which no life was lost in vain.'[27]

Several days later Sir Dudley Pound, the Chief of Naval Staff, having waited for confirmation that the raid had been successful, wrote: 'I have now seen the photographs and assessment. I am sure this attack will have greatly helped in achieving our object. I much deplore the comparatively heavy causalities but I feel sure their loss was not in vain.'

Later, Hallows wrote in his diary:

'One event sticks in my mind. Over half the bombs dropped failed to explode!' Five of the 17 bombs dropped did not explode and although the others devastated four machine shops, only 3 per cent of the machine tools in the entire plant were wrecked. 'A bad way to spend an afternoon!'

Squadron Leader John Dering Nettleton, who landed his badly damaged Lancaster at Squires Gate, Blackpool 10 hours after leaving Waddington, was awarded the VC for his efforts. David Penman adds: 'Nettleton, it would appear, having increased speed to avoid fighters, bombed early and unable to cross Germany alone in daylight, turned back the way he had come. Due to navigational errors he eventually reached the Irish Channel and landed at Squires Gate. All surviving crews were grounded until a press conference, which I attended, was held at the Ministry of Information in London, when awards were announced.'[28]

The week following the Augsburg raid saw the third Lancaster squadron declared operational when 207 Squadron at Bottesford in Leicestershire joined the Battle Order as a series of raids on Rostock began. The Baltic coast port, with its narrow streets, was lightly defended and was the home of a big group of aircraft factories forming part of the great Heinkel concern on its southern edge. For four consecutive nights, beginning on the night of 23/24 April when just one Lancaster took part, Rostock felt the weight of incendiary bombs dropped by Bomber Command. The concentration was very heavy, all the bombs falling within the space of an hour. From about 0200 onwards, fires raged in the harbour and the Heinkel works, and smoke presently rose to a height of 8,000 feet. The navigator of the Lancaster arriving towards the end of the raid told his captain that the fire he saw seemed 'too good to be true' and that it was probably a very large dummy. Closer investigation showed that it was in the midst of the Heinkel works and the Lancaster's heavy load of high explosives was dropped upon it from a height of 3,500 feet. Damage to the factory was considerable. The walls of the largest assembly shed fell in and destroyed all the partially finished aircraft within. Two engineering sheds were burnt out, and in the dock area five warehouses were destroyed by fire and seven crates fell into the dock. By the end of the fourth attack two large areas of devastation had been caused in the old town. All the station buildings of the Friederich Franz Station had been gutted and the Navigational School and the town's gasworks destroyed. Photographs taken in daylight after the second attack on Rostock in which five Lancasters took part, including three from 207 Squadron, showed swarms of black dots near the main entrance to the station and thick upon two of its platforms. These were persons seeking trains to take them away from the devastated city. By the end only 40 per cent of the city was left standing though the contribution by the Lancaster squadrons was small; they flew just 3 per cent of the total number of over 500 sorties. Morale in Lübeck and Rostock fell to a very low level after the heavy and destructive attacks made on them in March and April. Evacuation of both towns was on a large scale, especially in Rostock.

In the Ruhr orders were issued forbidding workers to move more than 10 kilometres from their place of employment. In March and April the Ruhr newspapers published warnings against the spreading of rumours in which, they said, the number of air raid casualties was grossly exaggerated. It was the duty of every good citizen to refrain from such talk.[29]

Within a few days of the attacks on Rostock, Lancasters of 44 and 97 Squadrons had deployed to Lossiemouth in Scotland to take part in two attempts to sink the German battleship *Tirpitz* lying in Trondheim Fjord.[30] Then came raids on Stuttgart, carried out on 4 and 5 May where one of the main targets was the Robert Bosch factory. A total of 28 Lancaster sorties were flown without loss but the raids were not successful. On 8/9 May 21 Lancasters were included in a force of 193 aircraft that attacked Warnemünde, one of five towns listed in a directive that stressed the importance of bombing targets containing vital aircraft factories. The raid on the Heinkel factory near the Baltic town, just north of Rostock went reasonably well but 19 Lancasters, including four of 44 Squadron, were lost. These took the Rhodesia Squadron's losses to 10 Lancasters in just three weeks of operations. Although Mannheim was not one of the five suggested targets on the recently issued bombing directive, this city, the second largest inland port in Europe, was the target on the night of the 19/20 May. The docks were continually full of raw materials, tank parts, armour plating and other war supplies, which came to them down the Rhine from the Ruhr. There were also many industrial plants situated in or near Mannheim. In this attack Stirlings dropped more than 4,000 incendiary bombs, which left many fires alight. Next day Mr Justice Singleton, who had been asked to predict what the results of bombing 'at the greatest possible strength' would be during the next 6, 12 and 18 months would be, published his findings. Singleton concluded that overall accuracy had been low, except for a few exceptions and that electronic aids did not, as yet, appear to be having a significant effect. He considered that a trained target-finding force would greatly improve results. In the meantime attacks on easily located city targets with a concentration of bombers in a short a space of time, became the norm. Bombing specific targets was almost over although the Goodrich Tyre works at Gennevilliers near Paris was hit on 29/30 May. The Singleton Report had also considered that: 'The bombing strength of the RAF is increasing rapidly and I have no doubts that, if the best use is made of it, the effect on German war production and effort will be very heavy over a period of twelve to eighteen months and as such will have a real effect on the war position.'

Armed with this information on 30/31 May, Harris intended to strike a hammer blow against Cologne, a city of nearly 800,000 inhabitants and the third largest in Germany. In March and April Cologne was visited four times by a total of 559 aircraft. The hurt caused was considerable. By the end of April the Nippes industrial district, occupied by workshops, had been damaged. Heavy bombs had completely destroyed buildings nearby and the Franz Clouth rubber works had been rendered useless, much of the buildings being level with the ground. To the east of the Rhine a chemical factory, and buildings beside it, was almost entirely destroyed. Severe damage had also been caused to the centre of Cologne. Harris now had four Lancaster squadrons, with 83 Squadron at Scampton having taken part in its first sorties just two nights earlier. The raid on Cologne would also include the first Lancaster operations of 106 Squadron, the fifth Squadron to be equipped. At Coningsby 106 Squadron was commanded by 24 year old Wing Commander Guy Gibson DFC*, a leader who had already shown exceptional capabilities.[31]

'At six o'clock to the minute on that lovely May evening, the briefing-room was packed' recalls a contemporary account. 'Pilots, air-gunners, navigators, wireless operators and flight engineers squeezed into rows of old cinema seats, rescued months before from a blitzed London building. They stood in rows along the wall and they were crowded together at the rear of the room. They were cracking jokes and laughing and filling the room with din. They were happy. All day long they had known that something was in the air. Throughout the heat of the late morning and the afternoon of the 30th the ground crews had been working feverishly on the machines, testing, checking gauges and radio circuits, running in the ammunition, trundling out the bombs and setting fuses. There was every indication that a big show was on the slate. A door opened and the hubbub died. The station commander entered. He smiled as he held up a hand. For a moment he stood watching the concourse of eager young airmen, waiting for his words, words that would send them hurtling through hundreds of miles of space to attack an enemy that was beginning to feel the shock of retaliation. "Some of you have probably guessed that we've something special on the menu tonight," he said. "We have. We're bombing the Hun with over a thousand aircraft."[32] The announcement was received with cheers. Excitement ran like a fever among them, until checked once more by the commander's upraised hand. "I've a message for you from Air Marshal Harris." They waited and he read to them:

"The force of which you form a part tonight is at least twice the size and has more than four times the carrying capacity of the largest air force ever before concentrated on one objective. You have an opportunity, therefore to strike a blow at the enemy, which will resound not only throughout Germany, but throughout the world. In your hands lie the means of destroying a major part of the resources by which the enemy's war effort is maintained. It depends, however upon each individual crew whether full concentration is achieved. Press home your attack to your precise objective with the utmost determination and resolution in the fore knowledge that, if you individually succeed the most shattering and devastating blow will have been delivered against the very vitals of the enemy. Let him have it – right on the chin!"

The commander looked up as his voice added the final exclamation mark. The men broke ranks. Those seated rose to their feet. Arms lifted like lances in salute. The cheer broke in one vast wave. The briefing finished in an atmosphere of buoyant enthusiasm. The crews trooped out of the long room. Not a man of them but felt inspired by the words of the Commander-in-Chief... They knew they were flying that night to make history... They flew in the steely sheen of the midnight stars. Over the British coast and out across the darkness of the North Sea; south-east over the dykes and fields of the Netherlands; on over the banks of the Rhine towards the clustered pile of Cologne, ringed in red on the navigators' charts.'[33]

For 98 minutes a procession of bombers passed over the city and stick after stick of incendiaries rained down from the bomb bays of the Wellingtons to add to the conflagration. The Stirlings followed the Wellingtons closely. When the Halifaxes arrived, the raid had lasted for an hour and the fires then resembled 'distant volcanoes'. By this time Cologne was visible to latecomers 60 miles away, first as a dull red glow over a large area of ground. One captain reported: 'So vast was the burning that ordinary fires on the outskirts of the city or outside it, which I should usually have described as very big, looked quite unimportant. It was strange to see the flames reflected on our aircraft. It looked at times as though we were on fire ourselves, with the red glow dancing up and down the wings.' In one Lancaster that approached the target with a mixed bomb load the bomb-aimer, lying in the nose, jotted down his impressions of the kaleidoscopic scene. When later he got back to base he put those impressions on record:

'It looked as though we would be on our target in a minute or two and we opened our bomb-doors. We flew on. The glow was as far away as ever. We closed the bomb-doors again. The glow was still there, like a huge cigarette end in the German blackout. Then we flew into the smoke. Through it the Rhine appeared a dim silver ribbon below us. The smoke was drifting in the wind. We came in over the fires. Down in my bomb-aimer's hatch I looked at the burning town below me. I remembered what had been said at the briefing. "Don't drop your bombs," we were told, "on the buildings that are burning best. Go in and find another target for yourself." Well, at last I found one right in the most industrial part of the town. I let the bombs go. We had a heavy load of big high explosives and hundreds of incendiaries. The incendiaries going off were like sudden platinum-coloured flashes, which slowly turned to red. We saw their many flashes going from white to red, and then our great bomb burst in the centre of them. As we crossed the town there were burning blocks to the right of us, while to the left the fires were immense. There was one after the other all the way. The flames were higher than I had seen before. Buildings were skeletons in the midst of fires; sometimes you could see what appeared to be the framework of white-hot joists.'

Flying Officer Brian 'Darkie' Hallows DFC could still see the fires on his way out and they were visible at the Dutch coast on return.[34] One gunner said later that he could see the burning city from the Dutch coast too. 'It was a fiery speck in the darkness like the tail of a motionless comet' was how he described the scene of destruction. The *Daily Telegraph* headline the following day was: 'At a Bomber Command Station. Sunday. On the 1,001st day of the war more than 1,000 RAF bombers flew over Cologne and in 95 minutes delivered the heaviest attack ever launched in the history of aerial warfare.' The German defences were locally swamped by the mass of bombers, 30 of the 43 losses (only one of which was a Lancaster) estimated shot down by night fighters. These were mainly achieved on the return journey when the bomber stream had been more dispersed than on the way in. In all, 868 crews claimed to have hit their targets and post-bombing reconnaissance revealed that more than 600 acres of Cologne had been razed to the ground. The fires burned for days and almost 60,000 people had been made homeless. Of the area laid waste that night about half was situated in the centre of the city. The cathedral appeared to be unscathed except for damage to windows; but 250 factory buildings and workshops were either destroyed or seriously damaged. Photo reconnaissance revealed what appeared to be a dead city. An air-raid warning, which was doubtless sounded, would have cleared the streets while the photographs were being taken; but it was significant that there was absolutely no transport visible, no trains, buses or cars.[35] The Air Ministry reported after reconnaissance had been made. 'In an area of seventeen acres between the Cathedral and the Hange Brucke forty or fifty buildings are gutted or severely damaged. Buildings immediately adjacent to the south-eastern wall of the Cathedral are gutted. There is no photographic evidence of damage to the Cathedral, although the damage to the adjoining buildings suggests that some minor damage may have occurred. The Police Headquarters and between two hundred and three hundred houses have been destroyed in another area of thirty-five acres extending from the Law Courts and the Neumarkt westwards almost to the Hohenzollernring. An area of three and a half acres between St Gereon's Church and the Hohenzollernring has been completely burned out.'

Speaking for the whole nation, the Prime Minister gave his congratulations to Air Marshal Sir Arthur Harris, the Air Officer Commander-in-Chief, Bomber Command.

'I congratulate you and the whole of Bomber Command upon the remarkable feat of organization, which enabled you to dispatch over a thousand bombers to the Cologne area in a single night and without confusion to concentrate their action over the target into so short a time as one hour and a half. This proof of the growing power of the British bomber force is also the herald of what Germany will receive city by city, from now on. Winston Churchill.'

The Air Marshal's reply to the Prime Minister was succinct, but it contained a promise: 'All ranks of Bomber Command are deeply appreciative of your message. They will pursue their task with undiminished resolution and with growing means at their disposal until the goal is achieved.' The intensified effort, in the words of Sir Arthur Harris, caused the Germans 'to look back to the days of Lübeck, Rostock and Cologne as men lost in a raging typhoon remember the gentle zephyrs of a past summer'.[36]

Squadrons repaired and patched their damaged bombers and within 48 hours they were preparing for a second 'Thousand Bomber Raid', this time against the Ruhr town of Essen in the heart of 'Happy Valley' on the night of 1/2 June. 'To ride the Ruhr', one Canadian pilot explained graphically, 'on a night when Jerry's on his toes is to switchback round the edge of hell. They sure brighten up the party and sling their greetings around with a free hand!' And the guns and searchlights were not the only defences. In the Ruhr night fighters 'swarmed like wasps round a particularly sour dustbin'.

Electricians, fitters, riggers and armourers worked as never before. The ground crews worked 18 hours a day for five days, fitting and testing every detail – engines, armament, electrical gear, instruments and other equipment. Without their unremitting toil and that of the repair and maintenance parties provided by the firms, which built the aircraft, no bomber would have been able to take the air. Finally, a force of 956 bombers, 545 of them Wellingtons, was ready. Again the numbers had to be made up by using OTU crews and aircraft. No. 5 Group contributed 74 Lancasters and 33 Manchesters. Essen was the chief focal point of the attack, with the assault spreading over the continuous string of industrial towns, which merged their municipal boundaries above the richest deposits of coal and iron in Europe. Although seemingly lacking the concentration of the earlier raid on Cologne, the bombing nevertheless was effective enough to saturate the defences. One skipper went as far as to say that the fires were more impressive than those of Cologne had been. A belt of fires extended across the city's entire length from the western edge to the eastern suburbs. Many fires were also spread over other parts of the Ruhr. Of the 37 bombers lost on the raid, night fighters claimed 20 and just four of the losses were Lancasters – 5 per cent of the Lancaster force dispatched. After Cologne and Essen Harris could not immediately mount another 1,000 bomber raid and he had to be content with smaller formations. A force of just 195 aircraft, including 27 Lancasters, returned to Essen the following night with no more success. It was not until the night of 25/26 June when the number of Lancaster squadrons had risen to seven, that the third and final 'Thousand Bomber Raid', in the series of five major saturation attacks on German cities, took place. In total, 1,006 aircraft, including 472 Wellingtons and 96 Lancasters, attacked Bremen, the second largest port in the Reich and home to the Focke Wulf aircraft factory.[37] The overall plan was similar to those of the pervious 1,000 bomber raid except that the time over the target area was reduced to just over an hour. Once again instructors and OTU crews were pressed into the night action, as Squadron Leader David Penman, now an instructor at Waddington, recalls:

'On 25 June the operations board showed a "maximum effort" and much to my surprise my name was down to take Lancaster R5631 with Flight Sergeant Tetley, my student, as second pilot and five crew members I had never seen before. At briefing it was explained that this was to be a 1,000 bomber raid, needing all fit aircrew to get all the serviceable aircraft in the air for an attack on Bremen. With a number of different types taking part I was glad to be in a Lancaster. Briefing completed with six 1,000lb bombs aboard as well as three SBCs. The take-off was on time and we climbed and eventually levelled out at 16,000 feet with patchy cloud above, and enough gaps below, to see the target area. There was considerable flak and soon the evidence of night fighters in the area as aircraft caught fire and blew up. Forty-eight aircraft went down this night and I saw most of them. I was certainly glad to be in a Lancaster but sad to see so many aircraft on fire and exploding at lower levels. We were lucky with a suitable break in the cloud to enable the bomb-aimer to drop on target. With aircraft going down all round, we were glad to get clear of Bremen without being hit, and with all the weight gone made a very fast run back to Waddington. Total flying time, four hours twenty minutes. My visit to Bremen in a Hampden on 1 January 1941 had taken six hours ten minutes carrying only 2,500lb of bombs! This time the weight of bombs, and with the whole area on fire, the damage must have been dreadful. We lost a lot of aircraft and crews but the losses on the ground must have been very much greater. I felt sorry for the people on the ground who were being killed and injured and having their houses destroyed. Unfortunately it appeared to be the only way to bring the war to a close more quickly. It was a relief to transfer later in the war to Transport Command and do something constructive rather than destructive.'

The actual bombing operation was crowded into 1 hour and 15 minutes. The heavy bomber crews were given the opportunity of bombing the red glow of the fires, using *Gee* as a check, or proceeding to a secondary target in the vicinity of Bremen. The cloud conditions prevailed at many of the targets of opportunity and many crews, unable to bomb, brought their lethal cargoes home. The total of 48 aircraft lost was the highest casualty rate (5 per cent) so far, though only one Lancaster was lost. Large parts of Bremen, especially in the south and east districts were destroyed. The German high command was shaken but 52 bombers were claimed, destroyed by the flak and night fighter defences for the loss of just two Bf 110s and four NCO crew members killed or missing. A record 147 Bomber Command aircraft were destroyed by *Nachtjagd* in June.[38]

During the next few days three more raids were made against Bremen and the contribution made by the Lancaster rose to 20 per cent of the total effort. Twin engined types like the Wellington and, to a lesser extent, the Hampden still formed the backbone of Bomber Command but Harris was gradually building up his numbers of four-engined types. The number of Lancasters available on any given night was averaging over 50 and this figure would double by the end of July. On the 11th 44 Lancasters made a dusk attack on the U-boat construction yards at Danzig, a round trip of 1,500 miles, of which the first half was made in daylight. Only two Lancasters were lost when they were shot down by flak at the target. On 26/27 July, 403 bombers including 181 Wellingtons and 77 Lancasters were dispatched in full moonlight to Hamburg, which suffered its most severe air raid to date and widespread damage was caused, mostly in the housing and semi-commercial districts. The Fire Department was overwhelmed and forced to seek outside assistance for the first time. Some 14,000 people were made homeless, 337 lost their lives and 1,027 were injured. Damage amounted to the equivalent of £25,000,000. Twenty-nine bombers including 15 Wimpys (so called from the American Disney cartoon character 'J. Wellington Wimpy' in 'Popeye') and two Lancasters were shot down.[39] Bomber Command was stood down on 27/28 July but this was the full moon period and on 28/29 July a return to Hamburg was announced at briefings. Crews were told that the raid would be on a far bigger scale than two nights before, with nearly 800 bombers planned but bad weather over the stations of 1, 4 and 5 Groups prevented their participation.[40] For the next main force raid, on Düsseldorf on 31 July/1 August, Bomber Command's training units again helped swell the numbers with 630 aircraft, including over 100 Lancasters for the first time in the war,[41] being dispatched. Some extensive damage was inflicted but 29 aircraft, 18 of which were shot down by *Himmelbett* night fighters, were lost. So ended the month of July and the 'moon period'.

The inaccuracy of bombing at this time led, in August, to the Pathfinder Force being created, under the command of Air Commodore Donald Bennett, whose dynamic leadership of 8 (PFF) Group was destined to play a vital role in marking targets for the main force on operations from now on.

Bennett himself was a great civil pilot before the war. In 1938 he flew the *Mercury*, the upper component of the *Mayo* composite aircraft, from Dundee to South Africa, and established a long-distance record for seaplanes. He joined the RAAF as a cadet in 1930, and was commissioned in the RAF in 1931. He took a flying boat pilot's course at Calshot in 1932, transferred to the RAAF Reserve in 1935 and the eve of war found him in command of the *Cabot*, the big flying boat, which was to carry the mail from Southampton to New York. Soon after the Germans invaded Norway the *Cabot* and her sister flying boat *Caribou* were destroyed by the enemy in the Norwegian fjords. Bennett was among the founders of the Atlantic Ferry Service. He was re-commissioned in the RAFVR in 1941 and was called on for service on the active list. As captain of a bomber, Bennett, then a wing commander, won the DSO for courage, initiative and devotion to duty when, after being shot down during an attack on the *Tirpitz* in Trondheim Fjord, Norway on 17 April 1942, he and his second pilot, Sergeant N. Walmsley, escaped from the enemy to Sweden. It was soon after his return that Bennett became associated with the new Pathfinder Force, whose identification symbol, worn only when not flying, was a gilt eagle worn below the flap of the left breast pocket.[42]

Five Group was still the only group of Bomber Command with Lancasters except for the Pathfinders who were allotted 83 Squadron. Another significant happening was the first of the Lancaster specialist operations, which took place on the night of 27/28 August when nine Lancasters of 106 Squadron led by Wing Commander Guy Gibson DFC★ carried out a raid on the *Graf Zeppelin*, Germany's only aircraft carrier, berthed at Gdynia. The carrier, which was launched in 1938, had been photographed at Swinemünde on 22 April but PR photographs taken on 5 May showed that the carrier had moved (it had put to sea for trials in the Baltic). Intelligence reports were that it was complete and ready for commissioning. The Squadron had trained for this operation for several weeks to gain accuracy in planting their turnip-shaped 5,000lb 'Capital Ship' bombs on a range target. The Lancasters needed full fuel loads to return to base from their target, 950 miles distant, so that, together with the weight of the bombs, they took off at the unprecedented all-up weight of 67,000lb. Hitherto, 60,070lb had been the maximum permissible. Making his first operational trip since 1918 was Squadron Leader Dicky Richardson, an acknowledged expert on bombsights Unfortunately a haze over Gdynia reduced visibility to a mile and in spite of some Lancasters spending as long as an hour over the target, only two of the seven that reached Gdynia dropped their bombs and there were no reports to confirm any hits on the target.[43]

During September 86 heavies were shot down by night fighters. One of the worst nights was on the 10/11 September when training aircraft swelled the numbers in a 479-bomber raid on Düsseldorf. Thirty-three aircraft failed to return and the OTUs were hard hit. Many training aircraft from various OTUs and Conversion Units were included in the force of 446 bombers that attacked Bremen on 13/14 September when 21 aircraft were lost. On 23/24 September 83 Lancasters bombed Wismar for the loss of four aircraft. By the end of the month 5 Group could put a total of nine Lancaster squadrons in the air. The first time that they did was on 1 October when 100 of them flew in magnificent procession across England to drop practice bombs on the Wainfleet range, while fighters carried out mock attacks along the route. The reason for this practice became known to crews when, on the afternoon of 17 October, Wing Commander Leonard C. Slee DFC, commanding 49 Squadron, led a force of 94 Lancasters to the Schneider armaments factory at Le Creusot on the eastern side of the Massif Central, 200 miles south-east of Paris. To maintain secrecy the code name Operation *Robinson* was chosen; a rather allusive name if the popular mispronunciation of Creusot is considered.[44]

The Lancasters took off from their respective stations and joined up before heading south-west across Cornwall and then south for the Brest peninsula. Even over England the Lancasters flew low, so low that Sergeant N. J. Waddington RAAF, who was bomb-aimer in a leading Lancaster, noticed that their trailing aerial was taken off by a rock on the coast. The Lancasters crossed the French coast between La Rochelle and St Nazaire. Over France they hurdled telephone wires and houses while people opened their doors and windows and waved. He watched a horse with a plough bursting its way helter-skelter through hedges and ditches while the ploughman stood and waved. No. 50, the veteran RAF squadron that had played its part in the First World War as an interception unit in the defence of London, was in the centre of the raiding formation in the attack on Le Creusot. The Squadron's contingent included the famous 'Ye Olde Dingo Flyte' led by their Australian CO, Squadron Leader P. B. Moore DFC.[45] Forty-four miles from the objective the Lancasters fanned out and headed for the target as practised at Wainfleet. Pilot Officer A. S. Grant RAAF, Wing Commander Slee's navigator, was so accurate that the Lancs arrived over the vast armament factories at 1809, precisely to the minute ordered for the attack to begin. Within the next seven minutes 88 of the Lancasters got their bombs away over the 287-acre site. Six others of 106 Squadron, led by Wing Commander Guy Gibson DFC*, each carrying ten 500-pounders, bombed the Henri Paul transformer and switching station at Montchanin, which supplied the plant with electricity. Crews reported accurate bombing at Le Creusot and dropped almost 140 tons of HE and incendiary bombs from 7,500 to 2,500 feet. Damage to the armaments factory was not extensive however, as many of the bombs fell short and struck the workers' housing estate near the factory.

The return route was flown at tree top level with four aircraft being damaged by birds. The only aircraft lost was a 61 Squadron Lancaster flown by Squadron Leader W. D. Carr, which crashed into a building while bombing the transformer station. Carr attacked at such a low altitude that the Lancaster was either caught in the blast of its own bombs or flew into a building. The only other casualty was a Lancaster of 207 Squadron, which had turned back with an engine failure. While flying at 30 to 40 feet above the sea near Brest it was attacked by three Arado Ar 196 seaplanes. The rear-gunner got in a long burst at one Arado and it crashed into the sea. For a time the two other Arados kept pace with the Lancaster, slightly below it. Then one rose, fired and hit the bomber's ailerons. The Lancaster's front gunner replied, but a few seconds later the float-plane reappeared on the starboard and the two aircraft, bomber and fighter, turned in towards each other. The floatplane gunner fired a burst, killing the Lancaster's flight engineer. Sergeant J. H. Lovell, the Australian wireless operator/air gunner went on directing the fight from the astro hatch. Then the Lancaster's gunners fired again and like the first Arado, it went into the sea.

The third Arado made off at once and the Lancaster returned safely to Langar.[46]

With the coming of autumn weather and a decrease in Bomber Command activity on some nights the 'Happy Valley excursion' ceased running and targets alternated between Germany and Italy. On 22/23 October 112 Lancasters and the Pathfinders were sent to Italy to drop 180 tons of bombs on Genoa in a raid which was to coincide with the opening of the Eighth Army offensive at El Alamein. It was a perfectly clear moonlight night and the Pathfinder marking was described as 'prompt and accurate'. Out of the winter night dropped showers of flares and the scene below was suddenly lit up like a stage. One Lancaster pilot observed, far below him, the vapour trails spread by other aircraft going low to make their bombing run. It was a concentrated attack in the new style that had developed from the thousand-bomber experiments. The defences, for once, seemed to be caught on one foot and no Lancasters were lost. Huge explosions were seen and large fires spread and grew more angry in colour.

Major Johnny Mullock MC the 5 Group anti-aircraft liaison officer, who had flown as special observer with Bomber Command on its raids on Lübeck, Rostock and the Renault works, went on the 1,500 mile round trip to Genoa. He watched the raid from the fall of the early bombs to the fading out of the resistance from the shore gunners, and gave it as his opinion, when he returned, that the raid was the most concentrated made to that date. He saw only one stick of incendiaries miss the target area: 'As we came down the other side of the Alps the valleys were shrouded in mist and we were afraid that Genoa might be obscured. But over the plain the weather cleared again. From thirty miles away I could see the light of the flares dropping over Genoa. As we got nearer it looked as though the whole town was ablaze. There was a big oil fire, with flames spurting up into the air and clouds of black smoke on top of them – we circled round before making our bombing run, and I counted thirteen big fires, and innumerable little ones. Clouds of smoke were coming up. When we first came in there had been A.A. fire and a good deal of tracer. As the attack developed, the guns almost entirely stopped firing. I could see tracers coming from the sea; the ships in the bay were evidently firing.'

It was the 46th operational flight for one flight lieutenant and when he got back to base he enthusiastically announced that it was by far his most successful: 'As we crossed the Channel on the way out, we watched what was about the best sunset I have the ever seen. We never saw land until we reached the Alps. The clouds above France were lit by the sunset glow. When the sun went down on our starboard side the full moon came up on our port, and the clouds were still lit up. Up cuts of air were driving the clouds away as we got to the Alps, the mountaintops soared above the clouds in the moon. The mountains were glistening white and almost purple in the shadows. We saw a wide glacier. As we passed the Alps the clouds were disappearing and the moon shone down into the deep valleys. There was no mist or haze and we could see every river, lake and village. We were early on Genoa, so we circled the Mediterranean. I think that another bomber and us were the first to drop flares. They went down at the same time and showed up the harbour, lots of buildings and streets. At first I thought they were the shimmering white haze above Genoa, but it was only the whiteness of the town, which has a great many white buildings. After the flares came our bombs. When I had seen them burst on the target we came down to just above the sea to watch the main attack. We never saw a bomb wasted. Oil storage tanks blew up with a sudden red glow and gave off great volumes of smoke. We did a slow climb over the sea, and as we did so, we saw eighteen fires glowing in the target area. They were all well con-centrated and five of them were very large indeed. We saw one searchlight trying to find us, though it was in the midst of a bunch of fires.'[47]

On 24 October, 88 Lancasters were sent to attack Milan in daylight. This time a fighter escort of Spit-fires accompanied the force across the Channel to the Normandy coast. The Lancasters then split up and flew independently in a direct route across France, close together and very low, hedgehopping in the manner in which the Augsburg and Le Creusot raids had been made possible. Some crews went down as low as 200 feet and saw cars that had run off the road in some panic. One crew reported that a searchlight was switched on! Using partial cloud cover as their only protection, the Lancasters rendezvoused at Lake Annecy before crossing the Alps into Italy. At 1704, the first Lancasters nosed down through the heavy clouds and unloaded. They came in rapidly, pinpointing their targets and wheeling round. Mixed in the general delivery of HEs and incendiaries was a goodly pro-portion of 4,000 pounders, which rocked the city's industrial heart. Altogether, 135 tons of bombs fell on the city in 18 minutes. Some of the Lancasters went down to 50 feet to bomb their targets. One captain identified the town by the racecourse and was able to aim at the new railway station and marshalling yards, which were the specific target. The surprise was total and the warning sirens only sounded after the first

bombs exploded. Thirty large fires were started and over 400 houses were among the buildings destroyed or damaged. The Italians claimed that a Lancaster came down to rooftop level and machine-gunned people in streets near the church of St Christopher. A Fiat Cr.42 *Falco* biplane fighter attacked the Lancaster flown by Sergeant J. B. Cockshott of 61 Squadron but it did not close and he was able to bomb from 10,000 feet. A Maachi 202 *Folgore* (Thunderbolt) fired at another Lancaster. Anti-aircraft fire and Italian fighter defences were weak. One Lancaster was lost over the target and two were shot down by German night fighters over northern France on the way home in the evening, when darkness came down and afforded some protection. A fourth Lancaster, which was attacked over the Channel, crashed at Ford airfield in Sussex and all except two crew, one of whom died later, were killed. When the returning Lancaster crews landed, it was to hear news that brought ready grins to their faces. At the very moment they had touched down, Halifaxes, Stirlings and Wellingtons were en route to the targets they had left to drop more bombs.

Early in November Lancasters bombed Rommel's main supply base at Genoa again, as Allied troops prepared to invade North Africa. The night of 6/7 November was dark and a large number of flares had to be dropped by the Pathfinders to light up the port for the 72 Lancasters. Flak was heavier than before, especially from the dock area but the results obtained were described as 'very satisfactory'. Later it was found that most of the bombs had fallen in residential areas. Two of the Lancasters failed to return. The following night 175 aircraft, including 85 Lancasters, returned to the port in the heaviest raid on this city of the war. Weather conditions over the target were very favour-able for bombing, but all the way to the Alps the bomber crews had their work cut out. Rain and cloud brought visibility to only a few feet, while icing and sudden electrical storms gave the pilots some cause for anxiety. 'It was as if we were flying in the slipstream of another aircraft,' was the description given by a pilot later. One front gunner reported that, as his plane penetrated cloud, ice came crackling through the turret ventilators in handfuls, while currents threw the bombers about. Above the clouds when pilots climbed, the night was bitterly cold and thick hoarfrost coated the windscreens. Over the Alps snow was falling steadily. Ice flew in large chunks from the whirling airscrews, rattling against the windscreen like hail. PR photographs later confirmed returning crews' claims that this was a very successful and concentrated raid. Six aircraft, including one Lancaster, were lost.

On 13/14 November 67 Lancasters and nine Stirlings once more went to Genoa, which was becoming daily more and more important as a supply base for the Axis armies in North Africa. In the six days that had passed since that last full day's raiding on the port, many more guns and searchlights had been rushed to defend the port against the RAF's return. Flak-ships on the German model were stationed in the harbour. Among the individual targets attacked was the Ansaldo works, to the west of the port, which constructed naval armaments and marine engines. Night fighters were met going out and on the way back and over France one German machine was sent down in flames. The bombing force, for the second time, returned without losing a bomber during a raid on Genoa. 'Another pair of white gloves,' was how Sir Arthur Harris smilingly described the exploit when he received reports on the night's work.

A night passed and then to Genoa again flew Bomber Command to bring off a third 'white gloves' raid. It was actually the sixth attack on the port since the opening of the Mediterranean offensive. The raid by 40 Halifaxes, 27 Lancasters and 11 Stirlings was crowded into one furious spell of 25 minutes and in that time hundreds of bombs, of 1,000 pounds in weight or larger, were dropped over the target areas. Weather, again, was right for the intrepid bomber crews. There was a bright half-moon and visibility was good. Objects below were picked out with comparative ease and one observer, who had been told to look out for a statue of Mussolini in a new square, had little difficulty in pin-pointing it. The pilot of another bomber was fascinated by a fire, which he saw start at the end of a row of warehouses on a small peninsula extending into the inner harbour. The fire ran like liquid along the entire row. He also saw a stick of bombs straddle the western docks, where a large liner was berthed. On the way home Focke Wulf and Junkers night fighters engaged the returning bombers but no bombers were lost. Some days later a message was received in England from a man who had stood on a hill above Genoa and viewed the stricken port. On six nights the RAF had gone to the port, for the total loss of only 12 aircraft and the bombing had been concentrated into a period of no more than two and a half-hours. In that short space Genoa had been completely knocked out as an effective Axis supply base. 'The burned and destroyed areas in Genoa are so large and many that it is useless to attempt to give details of the damage,' wrote the eyewitness. 'Seen from a height, one has the impression that half of the town has been destroyed and in the port almost everything seems to be destroyed, burned or damaged. Among the

few exceptions in the port area are the silos where the grain for Switzerland was stored. Lack of small craft in the port, as a result of a large number having been sunk or severely damaged, is causing difficulties to the port authorities.

But Genoa was not to suffer devastation alone. Three nights after the third 'white gloves' raid, on the night of 18/19 November, a cargo of 4,000 pounders was delivered on the city centre at Turin and the Fiat motor factory by 77 aircraft. The raid went off with the customary precision. When the RAF bombers left, smoke from the blitzed Fiat works and other industrial targets drifted in a wide stream northwards across the town. All the aircraft got back to their Bomber Command stations. Back to Turin went 232 bombers, including 86 Lancasters, the next night. They found that German night fighters were posted far to the south, inland from the French coast, to attack the bombers should they return. A new Lancaster squadron became operational when 467 began operating Halifaxes but the Aussies re-equipped with Lancasters at Bottesford within a few weeks. One squadron of Lancasters for the first time had a number of encounters with the desperate German pilots. Their wing commander's aircraft was attacked three times. First he had to fight it out with a Ju 88 on the French side of the Alps. By diving the wing commander got below the Junkers and the mid-upper gunner got in a burst that sent the Ju 88 spinning away. It was shortly afterwards that a Bf 110 rushed in, with cannon blazing. The Lancaster gunners opened fire and the Messerschmitt disappeared. Later, on the way back, another Ju 88 approached the Lancaster but, by rolling off, into a patch of cloud an encounter was avoided. At the end of half an hour a good many fires were blazing furiously in Turin and there was one enormous fire pouring from a large warehouse. A column of smoke rose to 8,000 feet and one hovering Lancaster, seeking its own special target, flew right through the black cloud.

On the 28/29th of the same month Turin was attacked again, this time by 228 aircraft, 117 of them Lancasters. That night the city felt the weight of the RAF's new 8,000lb bombs when they were carried to Italy for the first time. A great many tons of high explosives and some 100,000 incendiaries were also dropped on the city's targets. Wing Commander Guy Gibson DFC* and Flight Lieutenant W. N. Whamond of 106 Squadron dropped the first 8,000lb bombs on Italy. Pilot Officer F. G. Healy had also set out carrying an 8,000lb bomb but as the Lancaster's undercarriage would not retract its bomb had to be jettisoned into the sea. Gibson gave it as his opinion when he returned that

Turin – 'had received a packet last night'. The packet was made up of three wide areas blazing from end to end. Huge fires raged in the locality of the Royal Arsenal, flames shot with bright reds and yellows and vivid greens. The way back was strewn with night fighters. One Lancaster crew sighted as many as 23 over northern France and had a running fight with eight, claiming one FW 190 shot down in flames.[48]

In December the RAF visited Turin three times to round off the work of reducing the armament industry of the city to near-impotency. On the night of 8/9 December 133 bombers and Pathfinders, including 108 Lancasters, were ready to be dispatched. While bombing-up at Syerston incendiary bombs fell from the racks of a 61 Squadron Lancaster, exploded and set fire to the aircraft. The inhabitants of Newark and district were able to hear for themselves the explosion of a 4,000lb bomb. Group Captain 'Gus' Walker, the Station Commander went out to the bomber on a fire tender and the Lancaster blew up killing two men and blew the Group Captain's arm off. 'Gus', who had played rugby for Yorkshire, Barbarians and England, returned and post war became Air Marshal Sir 'Gus' Walker. At Turin the fires raised by incendiaries and more 8,000 pounders were reflected on the white summits of the alpine peaks. There were only half-a-dozen searchlights flickering wanly and dispiritedly across the inferno, which engulfed the target area and only one Lancaster was lost. When 227 Bomber Command aircraft, 115 of them Lancasters, returned the following night, the inferno had not completely subsided. Fires were still sending up hungry tongues of flame and a pall of smoke still floated across the city. Again the fires left when the bombers started for home, revealed the alpine peaks silhouetted darkly against the roseate glow to the south after the aircraft had passed the range. Two Wellingtons and a Lancaster failed to return. This was a disappointing raid, with the Pathfinders unable to perform as effectively as the previous night.

On the 11/12th the 82 Turin-bound bombers, which included 20 Lancasters, flew through bad weather and a thick curtain of snow. One Lancaster captain said: 'Shortly after crossing the Channel we ran into thick cloud. The farther we went the worse it got. Then we struck an electrical storm. Vivid streaks of bluish light darted along the glass in front of my cabin and there were bright sparks between the barrels of the guns. At first we thought they were flashes of flak. The windows began to ice up and then we ran into driving snow. Very quickly the fronts of my windows and of the gun-turrets were covered with ice and snow, which also interfered with the smooth running of the engines. We began to lose height. Three of my engines cut out for short periods and for about ten seconds only one engine was working. The flight engineer got the engines running again but I had to decide not to risk crossing Alps. The weather was equally bad coming back.'

One Lancaster bomb-aimer reported: 'Only a small part of the glass of my compartment was clear of ice, and through it I searched for a gap in the clouds. Ice had formed all over the aircraft, and snow fell as we approached the Alps. When I went into the front turret after bombing I found several inches of snow behind the gunner's seat.' It was like flying through Arctic skies and more than half of the force turned for home before attempting to cross the Alps. Three Halifaxes and a Stirling were lost. Twenty-eight crews claimed to have bombed Turin but Italian reports indicated that only a handful of bombs had hit the city.

One of the heaviest attacks of December was on 20th/21st when Duisburg was the target. Two Lancasters were lost at the outset when a 9 Squadron machine, piloted by Sergeant L. C. Hazell, climbing for height, hit a 44 Squadron Lancaster being flown by Flight Sergeant A. C. Elger in mid air. They fell in Canwick Road, Bracebridge, two miles south of Lincoln with the loss of both crews. Altogether, 12 aircraft, including six Lancasters were lost this night. The turn of 1942–43 saw the introduction of new radio aids. *Oboe*,[49] which gave a sonic indication of when to bomb, was used for the first time on the night of 20/21 December by six Pathfinder Mosquitoes of 109 Squadron, in an attack on a power station at Lutterade in Holland near the German border. H_2S,[50] which gave a visual identification of the terrain below, was first used in January.

On the night of 21/22 December Lancasters bombed Munich and then 1942 operations ended with '*Gardening*' in enemy lakes. By the end of 1942, 5 Group's 10 bomber squadrons were completely equipped with Lancasters, while 1 Group was in the process of converting from Wellingtons to Lancs and two Lancaster squadrons equipped 8 (PFF) Group. In March 1943 115 Squadron began converting from the Wellington to become the first Lancaster unit in 3 Group, which had on strength six Stirling squadrons, all of which were gradually converted to the Lancaster.[51] The Lancaster (and Halifax) crews could fly up to 10,000 feet higher than those of the Stirling, which was slower and had to be routed independently to lessen the risk of being hit by bombs dropped by the other two types of aircraft. In April 1944 the changeover in 6 (Canadian) Group from Halifaxes to Lancasters began in earnest and, by May,

Bomber Command would have an operational strength of 1,100 aircraft of which 616 were Lancasters.

All this was in the future. By early 1943 the German night defences had reached formidable new levels and AI-equipped[52] night fighters were now capable of exacting a toll of up to 6 per cent bomber casualties on any deep penetration raid into the *Reich*. Thus, Bomber Command losses rose rapidly during the first few months of 1943, although in early January operations were, of necessity, on a limited scale, normally to the *U-boat* bases on the Atlantic coast, although on 10 January the Air Ministry announced: 'For the fifth time in seven days aircraft of Bomber Command raided the Ruhr last night, dropping many 4,000lb bombs and causing large fires. The principal weight of the attack was delivered on Essen, home of the Krupps combine of industries, which was said to employ 175,000 workers out of the town's population of 700,000.'

'Happy Valley was as spiteful as ever,' was the verdict of one veteran pilot who made the run.

Notes

1. 'Have you ever seen a map of London? It is so densely built that one fire alone would be enough to destroy the whole city, just as it did over two hundred years ago. Göring will start fires all over London, fires everywhere, with countless incendiary bombs of an entirely new type. Thousands of fires. They will unite in one huge blaze over the whole area. Göring has the right idea: high explosives don't work, but we can do it with incendiaries; we can destroy London completely. What will their firemen be able to do once it's really burning?' Albert Speer to Hitler at a dinner in the Reich Chancellery in 1940 imagining the total destruction of the capital of the British Empire.
2. *From Apes to Warlords* (London 1978).
3. It was reported that 300 bombs fell on the factory destroying 40 per cent of the buildings. Production was halted for four weeks and final repairs were not completed for several months. A post-war American estimate said that the production loss was almost 2,300 vehicles. Just one aircraft (a Wellington) was lost but 367 French people were killed, 341 were badly injured and 9,250 people lost their homes.
4. Later Wing Commander Penman DSO OBE DFC.
5. Rodley, lost in cloud took his Lancaster down through the gloom to observe his position. Unaware that the cloud base was so low he broke out at 200 feet in a shallow dive and he literally had to yank the control column to lift the nose clear of a row of houses at Boston. The starboard wing hit a roof and the wingtip broke away while the port wingtip, for no apparent reason, stuck upright at 90 degrees to the wing. Rodley skilfully put the Lancaster down near the beach at Frieston near Boston and all the crew were uninjured. The Lancaster was a little damaged and it was swamped by the incoming tide and written off, but not before technicians from Farnborough examined the aircraft. If nothing else the incident showed what would happen when a Lancaster was yanked out of a dive and modification action was taken to strengthen Lancaster wingtips on the production lines.
6. Including 27 by II./NJG 2 with six of these being credited to Oberleutnant Ludwig Becker and four each by I. and III./NJG 1.
7. Including 12 by II./NJG 2, 9 by I./NJG 1 and 4 by III./NJG 1.
8. Two of them Hampdens, a Manchester of 61 Squadron, a Stirling and a Wellington.
9. Squadron Leader 'Flap' Sherwood, fair-haired and aesthetic looking, only just 23. In his desire to infuse his crews with his own fanatical keenness he often tried to panic them into a sense of urgency, hence the nickname, 'Flap'. *Strike Hard, Strike Sure; Epics of the Bombers* by Ralph Barker (Chatto & Windus 1963/Pen & Sword Military Classics 2003)
10. Deverill was 26, an ex-apprentice with 11 years' service, recently commissioned and a veteran of over 100 operational flights. Mycock, slight and ginger-haired, had been awarded the DFC for a daylight raid on the *Scharnhorst* and *Gneisenau* in Brest. Barker, op. cit.
11. Learoyd was awarded Bomber Command's first VC of the war for his determined attack on the Dortmund-Ems Canal in a 49 Squadron Hampden on 12/13 August 1940.
12. *Maschinenfabrik Augsburg-Nurnberg Aktiengesellschaft.*
13. Hallows was 11 years at Gresham's School, Holt, where his father was proprietor of the old market town's Steam Laundry. Hallows later passed through Sandhurst and took a commission in the King's Liverpool Regiment, which he later relinquished to take up flying. In June 1938 he joined the RAFVR when he felt that a war was inevitable, so it was no surprise when all reservists were called to report to their units around the end of August 1939. Then followed a wait until October, when he began a 'Wings' course at No. 9 FTS, Hullavington. They were an unruly lot and finally the station commander got them all together and said that he was going to award them their wings and commission all sergeant pilots to acting pilot officers. He added that they were not fit to be senior NCO pilots – how right he was! Then it was off to Central Flying School, to become an RAF flying instructor, which had been Hallows' profession prior to August 1939. At CFS he won a trophy for 'Best all-round Cadet'.
14. At Hullavington he had been a Qualified Flying Instructor until, in June 1941, he had seen a 'rather odd' notice asking for experienced twin-engined pilots to join Bomber Command, to fly Manchester bombers. Little did any of them know what a killer the Manchester was. Anyway, it was off to Finningley, with not a Manchester to be seen – they were all grounded with engine trouble. Eventually, in September 1941, Hallows got to 97 Squadron at Coningsby, where he actually flew a Manchester.
15. *The Augsburg Raid* by Jack Currie DFC (Goodall Publications, 1987)
16. All 16 had taxied out so the second reserve cut their engines and watched the others leave and over Selsey Bill the first reserves swung round and returned to Lincolnshire, leaving 12 Lancasters flying low over the water.
17. Barker, op. cit.
18. *Royal Australian Air Force Overseas*(Eyre & Spottiswoode, London 1946)
19. Oesau had shot down 10 a/c in Spain and was the 3rd German pilot to reach 100 victories, on 26 October 1941. He was shot down and killed in air combat with P-38 Lightnings SW of St Vith, Belgium on 11 May 1944 in his Bf 109G-6. At the time

of his death, his score stood at 127 aerial victories, including 14 four-engined bombers.

20. All four men who were taken prisoner, were decorated, Garwell being awarded the DFC, Kirke a bar to his DFM and DFMs for Watson and Dando.

21. Sands, McClure and Pilot Officer Patrick Dorehill were awarded the DFC and the four sergeants on the crew each received the DFM.

22. L7573 flown by Squadron Leader J. S. Sherwood DFC*.

23. She shook her head and told Penman: 'I would have known if he'd died. I'm convinced he's all right. Don't worry'. He had suffered no more than minor burns.

24. R5513 was on fire over a mile from the target but Mycock continued on to drop his bombs on the factory and became enveloped in flames and crashed. There were no survivors. Mycock's navigator was an old school friend from his home town.

25. *Royal Australian Air Force Overseas* (Eyre & Spottiswoode, London 1946).

26. The aircraft was a complete write-off.

27. Of the seven crews lost, 37 men were killed and 12 men survived to be made POW; 36 men returned.

28. Although also recommended for a VC by Air Marshal Harris, Sherwood was awarded the DSO After a brief spell instructing with 1661 HCU and being promoted to wing commander, Nettleton returned to 44 Squadron as OC in January 1943. He failed to return from a raid on Turin on 12/13 July 1943. In addition to the awards already mentioned, Penman was awarded the DSO and Lester Ifould, Darkie Hallows, Ernie Deverill and Rod Rodley and Pilot Officer Hooey, Penman's second pilot, the DFC. Six sergeants on 97 Squadron each received the DFM.

29. The raids on the old Hanseatic port of Lübeck on 28/29 March and now Rostock prompted the Luftwaffe into reprisal, or *Baedeker* raids, after the German guide book to English cities, on Canterbury, Exeter, Norwich and York. At Lübeck 304 tons of bombs were dropped in 180 minutes. Soon after the attack began at 2230, one crew reported that there were a few small fires. Twenty minutes later others reported that the fires seemed to have spread right across the island on which the old part of the town is situated. The greater part of it was burnt to the ground. Great quantities of stores accumulated during the winter for use in the Russian campaign were destroyed.

30. Between 27 and 29 April a total of 23 Lancaster and 54 Halifax sorties were flown and these resulted in unconfirmed hits on the battleship. Six Halifaxes and one Lancaster were lost on the two raids.

31. Born on 12 August 1918 at Simla, the son of an official in [a Cornish mother] the Imperial Indian Forest Service, Gibson was educated at St George's School, Folkestone and St Edward's School, Oxford, before being commissioned into the RAF in 1937. His first posting was to 83 Squadron as a bomber pilot. He was awarded the DFC in July 1940. In August Gibson was posted to instruct at an OTU before transferring to 29 Squadron flying Beaufighter night fighters. Gibson claimed three enemy aircraft destroyed and one damaged flying Beaufighters on 29 Squadron, the first over the Humber on 1 February 1941 with Richard James on their first combat. James, writing in *We Will Remember Them: Guy Gibson and the Dam Busters* by Jan van den Driesschen with Eve Gibson, Erskine Press, 2004, 'knew very well that we actually shot down six and damaged two

more'. On 21 November 1940 Gibson, recently promoted to flight lieutenant, married Eve Moore, a stage actress, in Cardiff. Gibson was promoted to squadron leader with a bar to his DFC on completion of his second tour in 1941. After a short spell of instructing he had taken command of 106 Squadron.

32. One thousand and forty-seven aircraft including 602 Wellingtons, 131 Halifaxes, 88 Stirlings and 73 Lancasters of 5 Group.

33. Flight Lieutenant John Price, a pilot on the raid, recalled: 'The target area was the centre of Cologne and the map clearly showed the red crosses of every hospital in the city. I would have nightmares after the war thinking about all the women and babies we killed that night. It is now obvious to me that we in England were determined to save our land at whatever the cost and that killing the enemy, of whatever gender, was the only answer.'

34. Darkie Hallows flew his 27th and final trip on 9/10 January 1943 to Essen, 'a lovely night, clear and dark'. Fifty Lancasters of 5 Group and 2 PFF Mosquitoes bombed the city for the loss of three Lancasters. One hundred and twenty-seven buildings were destroyed or seriously damaged and 28 people were killed. Hallows noted: 'We pranged the flares. Flak very hot and too close too. Bombs seen burning in built up area. Time 4.00. Load $1 \times 4,000$ 12 SBC.' Hallows was then posted to ground duties and non-operational flying – Group HQ, two different Bomber Conversion Units (Stirlings and Lancasters) – instructing again until, in January 1945, he was posted to command 627 Pathfinder Mosquito Marking Squadron at Woodhall Spa, where he completed four operations. At the end of the war he was told that he was not needed for the Far East because he was on his second tour of operations and was sent on leave. He was then given a permanent commission in the RAF.

35. The raid destroyed 3,330 buildings, seriously damaged 2,090 more and lightly damaged another 7,420 dwellings. It was estimated that between 135,000 and 150,000 of Cologne's population fled the city after the raid. Between 11 May 1940 and 31 May 1942 RAF heavy bombers attacked Cologne on no less than 144 raids.

36. Between 11 May 1940 and 31 May 1942, of the principal targets in the Ruhr, Essen had been attacked 89 times, Duisburg 93 and Dortmund 33. Of the main German cities outside that great industrial area, Bomber Command had been to Cologne 144 times, to Mannheim 68, to Hanover 64 and to Magdeburg 26. The four German ports most directly concerned with the Battle of the Atlantic were Bremen, Wilhelmshaven, Kiel and Emden, while Hamburg, the second city in Germany, was a base not only for that battle but also for the Russian front. Targets in the first of these cities had been attacked 110 times, in the second 88, in the third 82, and in the fourth 82. Hamburg had been attacked 115 times.

37. This raid was the last flown operationally by Manchesters, after which the type was withdrawn.

38. At this time the only effective tactical measure available to counter the German night fighter defence was the saturation of the German GCI system by concentrating the bomber routes through relatively few GCI *Räume* (boxes) or through *Gebiete* (zones) in which, few or no GCI stations existed. In 1942, when the RAF began attacking targets within a period of 30 minutes, the narrow night fighter zone in the west was quickly penetrated and, at the same time, only a few fighters came into contact with the bomber stream. Flak, emplaced in single

batteries, was unable to cope with the concentrated attacks by the RAF. The carefully practised system of concentrating several batteries' fire on a single target broke down because so many aircraft appeared over the target at the same time. As a result the night fighter zone in the west had to be rapidly increased in depth and extended to Denmark in the north and to eastern France in the south. Operational control had to be developed whereby two or more night fighters could be brought into action in any night fighter area at one time. Also, bombers over the target were attacked by fighters as well as flak, which was consolidated into large batteries near the targets and concentrated at the most important targets. Above all, accuracy had to be increased by developing a large number of radar range finders.

39. 7.2 per cent of the total force dispatched – 181 Wellingtons, 33 Hampdens, 77 Lancasters, 73 Halifaxes and 39 Stirlings. Oberleutnant Lothar Linke of 5./NJG 1 shot down Lancaster R5748 of 106 Squadron and it crashed at Rottevalle in Friesland. Most of Bomber Command's inward and outward routes on raids against German targets were over the Netherlands and during 1941–1943 the night-fighting *Geschwader* NJG1 and NJG 2 were based at various airfields in the Low Countries. Operating from Leeuwarden II./NJG 2 destroyed an estimated 320 bomber aircraft. All Major Helmut Lent's first 65 night victories (May 1941-July 1943) were claimed while flying from Leeuwarden. Oberleutnant Heinz-Wolfgang Schnaufer claimed 32 of his all-time record total of 121 night victories while serving with the Leeuwarden *Gruppe*. Linke, with 24 night and 3 day victories was killed on the night of 13/14 May 1943. After shooting down two Lancasters (W4981 of 83 Squadron and ED589 of 9 Squadron) and Halifax DT732 of 10 Squadron over Friesland, he suffered an engine fire (Bf 110G-4 G9+CZ, Werke Nr 4857). He baled out near the village of Lemmer in Friesland but he struck the tail unit of his Bf 110 and was killed. Linke's *Bordfunker* Oberfeldwebel Walter Czybulka baled out safely.

40. Ultimately 256 aircraft – 165 of 3 Group and 91 OTU comprising 161 Wellingtons, 71 Stirlings and 24 Whitleys took part.

41. Three hundred and eight Wellingtons, 113 Lancasters, 70 Halifaxes, 61 Stirlings, 54 Hampdens and 24 Whitleys.

42. *Royal Australian Air Force Overseas* (Eyre & Spottiswoode, London 1946).

43. Subsequent photos showed no sign of activity and it was assumed, correctly as it turned out, that all work on the carrier's development had been abandoned. The Germans eventually scuttled the *Graf Zeppelin* in January 1945 to prevent it falling into Russian hands. Although the Russians raised it, the carrier sank while being towed to Leningrad in 1947. As the ship was completed in August 1942 but never went to sea, perhaps the Lancasters were successful.

44. *Lancaster – The Story Of A Famous Bomber* by Bruce Robertson (Harleyford Publications Ltd 1964).

45. 'Ye Olde Dingo Flyte' was founded in the First World War when 50 Squadron, then commanded by a Major Harris who later became Air Chief Marshal Sir Arthur Harris of Bomber Command, used the attack signal 'All Dingoes Run'. When the squadron re-formed a few years before the Second World War 'A' Flight commemorated the historic past and the old signal used in the defence of London by painting 'Ye Olde Dingo Flyte' above the door of the flight office. When the Second World War began, Moore was serving in the flight under Squadron Leader D. F. C. Good DFC of Adelaide, who was posted missing in April 1941. *Royal Australian Air Force Overseas* (Eyre & Spottiswoode, London 1946). In April 1942 Moore was posted to 455 Squadron RAAF as a flight commander but when that squadron was transferred from Bomber to Coastal Command he was returned to 50 Squadron and took command of 'Ye Olde Dingo Flyte'. He took six outstanding crews with him from 455 Squadron. These included several of the men who were subsequently decorated for their work in the raid on the Ruhr dams in May 1943.

46. Slee, and Grant, who later in the war added a DFC and Bar to his decorations, both received an immediate DSO for their part in the raid. On 19/20 June 1943 288 Halifaxes and Stirlings and two Lancasters bombed the factory and the Breuil steelworks, for the loss of two Halifaxes, as there was little German opposition. Twenty-six Lancasters of 8 Group were given a second target, the electrical-transformer station at Montchanin.

47. The night following, 122 Halifaxes, Stirlings and Wellingtons set out to bomb Genoa again but the target was almost completely cloud covered and it was later determined that Savona, 30 miles along the coast from Genoa, had been bombed.

48. Two Stirlings and a Wellington failed to return – one of the Stirlings being piloted by Flight Sergeant R. H. Middleton, who was awarded a posthumous VC.

49. *Oboe* was the most accurate form of high-level blind bombing used in the Second World War and it took its name from a radar pulse, which sounded like a musical instrument. The radar pulses operated on the range from two ground stations ('Cat' & 'Mouse') in England to the target. The signal was heard by both pilot and navigator and used to track the aircraft over the target, If inside the correct line, dots were heard; if outside the line, dashes, a steady note, indicated the target was on track. Only the navigator heard this signal. When the release signal, which consisted of five dots and a two-second-dash was heard, the navigator released the markers or bombs.

50. British 10cm experimental airborne radar navigational and target location aid.

51. By May 1945 No. 3 Group had 330 Lancasters in 11 squadrons on nine airfields.

52. Airborne Interception (AI)

Chapter 2

The Battle of the Ruhr

Just then another Lancaster dropped a load of incendiaries, and where, a moment before, there had been a dark patch of the city, a dazzling silver pattern spread itself a rectangle of brilliant lights – hundreds, thousands of them – winking and gleaming and lighting the outlines of the city around them. As though this unloading had been the signal, score after score of fire bombs went down, and all over the dark face of the German capital these great incandescent flower-beds spread themselves. It was a fascinating sight. As I watched and tried to photograph the flares with a cine-camera, I saw the pin-points merging, and the white glare turning to a dull, ugly red as the fires of bricks and mortar and wood spread from the chemical flares.

Broadcaster Richard Dimbleby reporting on the raid on Berlin
on 17/18 January 1943 for the BBC.

The sky was steel blue and everywhere below there was the restless crisscross pattern of long white beams. Sergeant Robert S. Raymond, one of a small number of 'Yanks' in Bomber Command and his crew, had never seen so many searchlights or so great a barrage, as over the Ruhr before. His second pilot, a new boy on 44 Squadron, who was there to get some experience, was on his first operational flight. The neophyte could not stop shaking but Raymond's boys, having made a few trips by now, were 'absolutely steady and normal under fire'. Raymond even found time to study the scene, which to him represented a 'marvellously beautiful picture' especially on such a night with a few scattered clouds and the moon in its second quarter.

On the night of 13/14 January, 66 Lancasters raided Essen. Two *Oboe* Mosquitoes had to return without marking and the sky markers of the third Mossie failed to ignite above the cloud, but the city was bathed in light. German aircraft even dropped decoy flares to try to distract the Lancaster crews. In the bomb bay Raymond's crew carried a 4,000 pounder and more than 1,000 incendiaries. Down they went, the cookie adding to the great red mushroom explosions of the other 4,000-pounders and the fire bombs stoking up the long strings of incendiaries being laid out in geometrical patterns among the buildings. It was destruction on a colossal scale and terrifying in its concentration and intensity.

Four Lancasters failed to make it back to their bases. Usually Raymond's Lancaster was among the last to return to Waddington because he and Griffiths, his flight engineer, believed in saving their engines. He was a miser with petrol, Raymond thought quite rightly, and the engineer's most famous remark was in crossing the Alps when the pilot asked for more power to gain height. Griffiths opened the throttles about half an inch and said, 'There, that's all you can have'. His knowledge of the Merlin engines, due to long experience, was amazing for a young man of 19 years. One of the Lancaster's engines overheated badly at more than half-throttle, so that it was not much help. Griffiths and his pilot talked over the possibilities and procedures in such cases by cutting other crew members off the intercom; otherwise they would have too much to think about. The air temperature was – 30°C and the North Sea was pretty cold at that time of year. But this was the shortest trip they had ever made, a fact, which would have been lost on the 'new boy' on the squadron who was still shaking after they landed back at Waddington. Interrogation after the trip was always a pleasant time for Raymond and the crew. It was carried out in the warm, brightly lighted Mess while they were eating. WAAFs moved about serving food. All of Raymond's own officers were around and usually a number from the Air Ministry looked on. There was much laughter and many enquiries among the crews about incidents en route. There was much kidding if a pilot did not land promptly when it was his turn. The whole scene was a complete contrast to that of half an hour earlier when most of them were stacked on the circuit listening to the others and the WAAF in the control tower, 'cursing like troopers if any stooge didn't land on first try'.[1]

On 16/17 January Berlin was bombed for the first time in 14 months by 190 Lancasters and 11 Halifaxes.[2] Air Marshal Sir Arthur Harris, C.-in-C. Bomber Command, sent them on their way with the words: 'Tonight you are going to the Big City. You will have the opportunity to light a fire in the belly of the enemy that will burn his black heart out.'

This raid marked the first use of purpose-designed Target Indicators (TIs) instead of modified incendiaries, which had previously been used.[3] Only one Lancaster was lost but the raid was a disappointment. Thick cloud en route and haze over the target caused problems and the bombing was scattered. The Berlin flak had proved light and ineffective and it was assumed that the greater altitude of the attacking force had surprised the German gunners. Harris repeated the raid on Berlin, sending 170 Lancasters and 17 Halifaxes back to the 'Big City' the following night, when the weather was better. Broadcaster Richard Dimbleby reported on the raid for the BBC, flying with Wing Commander Guy Gibson DSO DFC*, the CO of 106 Squadron at Syerston in a 9 hour 15 minute round trip. It was Gibson's 67th op.[4] Next morning British listeners tuning in to the BBC Home Service heard Dimbleby's broadcast on their wireless sets:

'The Berlin raid was a big show as heavy bomber operations go: it was also quite a long raid, and the Wing Commander who took me stayed over Berlin for half an hour The flak was hot but it has been hotter. For me it was a pretty hair-raising experience and I was glad when it was over, though I wouldn't have missed it for the world. But we must all remember that these men do it as a regular routine job. The various crews who were flying last night from the bomber station where I'd been staying had flown on several of the Essen raids. That means that night after night they've been out over one of the hottest parts of Germany, returning to eat, drink and sleep before going out again. That's their life, and I can promise you it's hard, tiring and dangerous.

'Four-engined Lancasters, Halifaxes and Stirlings roared out over the North Sea. We flew among them and, turning back from the cockpit to look into the gorgeous sunset, I counted 30 or 40 Lancasters seemingly suspended in the evening sky. They were there wherever you looked – in front, behind, above and below – each a separate monster, each separately navigated, but all bound by a coordinated plan of approach and attack. Up above the clouds, the dusk was short The orange and crimson of sunset died back there where the coast of England lay, and ahead of us the brilliant moon hung with the stars around her; below us, the thick clouds hid the sea. We were climbing steadily, and as it grew dark we put on our oxygen masks when the air grew too rarified for normal breathing.

'As we approached the enemy coast I saw the German Ack-Ack. It was bursting away from us and much lower. I didn't see any long streams of it soaring into the air, as the pictures suggest: it burst in little yellow, winking flashes, and you couldn't hear it above the roar of the engines. Sometimes it closes in on you and the mid- or tail-gunner will call up calmly and report its position to the Captain so that he can dodge it. We dodged it last night, particularly over Berlin: literally jumped over it and nipped round with the Wing Commander sitting up in his seat as cool as a cucumber, pushing and pulling his great bomber about as though it were a toy.

'We knew well enough when we were approaching Berlin. There was a complete ring of powerful searchlights waving and crossing, though it seemed to me that most of our bombers were over the city. Many of the lights were doused: there was also intense flak. First of all they didn't seem to be aiming at us. It was bursting away to starboard and away to port in thick, yellow clusters and dark, smoky puffs. As we turned in for our first run across the city it closed right round us. For a moment it seemed impossible that we could miss it, and one burst lifted us in the air as though a giant hand had pushed up the belly of the machine but we flew on.

'Just then another Lancaster dropped a load of incendiaries and where, a moment before, there had been a dark patch of the city, a dazzling silver pattern spread itself a rectangle of brilliant lights – hundreds, thousands of them – winking and gleaming and lighting the outlines of the city around them. As though this unloading had been the signal, score after score of firebombs went down, and all over the dark face of the German capital these great incandescent flowerbeds spread themselves. It was a fascinating sight. As I watched and tried to photograph the flares with a cine-camera, I saw the pin-points merging, and the white glare turning to a dull, ugly red as the fires of bricks and mortar and wood spread from the chemical flares.

'We flew over the city three times, for more than half an hour, while the guns sought us out and failed to hit us. At last our bomb-aimer sighted his objective below, and for one unpleasant minute we flew steady and straight Then he pressed the button and the biggest bomb of the evening, our 3½-tonner, fell away and down. I didn't see it burst but I know what a giant bomb does and I couldn't help wondering whether, anywhere in the area of the devastation, such a man as Hitler, Göring, Himmler or Goebbels might be cowering in a shelter. It was engrossing to realize that the Nazi leaders and their Ministries were only a few thousand feet from us, and that this shimmering mass of flares and bombs and gun-flashes was their stronghold.

'We turned away from Berlin at last – it seemed we were there for an age – and we came home. We saw no night fighters, to our amazement, nor did any of the flak on the homeward journey come very near us. We came back across the North Sea, exchanged greetings of the day with a little coastwise convoy and came in to England again, nine hours after we had flown out. There were so many machines circling impatiently round our aerodrome that we had to wait up above for an hour and twenty minutes before we could land and it was two o'clock in the morning when the Wing Commander brought us dawn to the flare path and taxied us in.

'We climbed stiffly out, Johnny from the tail turret, Brian who used to be a policeman from the mid-upper, Hutch, the radio operator, Junior the navigator – by far the youngest of us all. Then the Scots co-pilot, a quiet calm sergeant, and last the short sturdy Wingco who has flown in every major air raid of this war and been a night fighter pilot in between times. They were the crew – six brave, cool and exceedingly skilful men.[5] Perhaps I am shooting a line for them but I think somebody ought to. They and their magnificent Lancasters and all the others like them are taking the war right into Germany. They have been attacking and giving their lives in attack since the first day of the war and their squadron went on that show too. *Per ardua ad astra* is the RAF motto. Perhaps I can translate it 'Through hardship to the stars'. I understand the hardship now and I'm proud to have seen the stars with them.'[6]

In February attacks were made on German cities, on French seaports on the Atlantic coast and strikes were resumed against Italy. On 4/5 February Bomber Command returned in force to Turin. A total of 188 aircraft including 77 Lancasters made the trip while four Pathfinder Lancasters attacked the port of La Spezia with new 'proximity fuzed' 4,000lb bombs, which exploded between 200 and 600 feet above the

ground to widen the effects of the blast. Three PFF Lancasters dropped their bombs successfully and all returned safely. At Turin the flak was reported to be 'not up to the German standard' and a Canadian pilot quipped that he 'saw one night-fighter' and that 'he flew through the flak. I guess he knew Italian flak wouldn't hurt him.' Three Lancasters failed to return from the bombing of Turin, which caused serious and widespread damage. After a raid on Lorient on the 13/14th when seven aircraft were lost from the 466 dispatched, crews were 'on' again the next night to city targets. Some 243 bombers were sent to bomb Cologne once more and 142 Lancasters crossed the Alps again, this time to attack Milan. Their targets were 24 factories, three of them turning out war materials on the number one priority list. Fires could be seen from 100 miles away on the return flight. Only two Lancasters were lost on this raid. One Lancaster crew fought a memorable and gallant action. Sergeant Ivan Henry Hazard's crew in 101 Squadron had bombed and were on the home run when a Fiat Cr.42CN *Caccia Notturna* (night fighter)[7] made a diving attack on them. The Lancaster caught fire amidships almost immediately, one engine dead and two of the petrol-tanks were holed. Sergeant Leslie Airey the rear-gunner was wounded in the leg but he sat at his gun-button, waiting until the attacker was a bare 50 yards away, and then gave it a burst, which put its engine on fire. The mid-upper gunner, Flight Sergeant George P. Dove DFM who was from Redcar in Yorkshire, likewise remaining at his guns, waited while the flames lapped his turret and at the right moment gave the fighter another burst. This sent it whirling down out of control, flames from its engine spreading over fuselage and tail. Meanwhile the fire in the Lancaster was pronounced out of control and reluctantly Hazard gave the order to prepare to abandon the aircraft.[8] However, the inter-com system had been wrecked and the rear-gunner with his injured leg could not make a parachute descent so the captain decided to make a crash-landing. But before he could find a spot to land on Sergeant William E. Williams the navigator and Pilot Officer Frederick W. Gates the wireless operator, working like men possessed, got the flames under control. Dove, though burned badly about the face, hauled Airey out of his turret. Flight Sergeant Dove DFM recalled:

'My window was burned and ammunition began to explode. The smoke was so thick that I could scarcely see the fighter when I got him in my sights. Only one gun was working properly. I scrambled down and picked the rear-gunner out of his turret. But owing to the fire and a hole blown in the bottom of the aircraft by the explosion, I couldn't carry him forward to the bed, and I had to prop him up near his turret.'

Again Hazard revised his plan, determined to try to make his base on three engines. He got up to 15,000 feet, staggered over the Alps and, with his tanks practically drained dry,[9] at length landed at Tangmere. Gates, of Cheam in Surrey, said later:

'The pilot did a first-class job of work on that trip. He made three vital decisions in quick succession. After we were hit and set alight by the fighter the pilot put the aircraft into a spiral dive and pulled out about 800 feet from the ground. Bullets had hit incendiary bombs that were not released from our aircraft. We heard an explosion and in 15 seconds the fire was burning fiercely.'[10]

On the night of 16/17 February 327 bombers, 131 of them Lancasters, attacked Lorient again, mostly dropping incendiary loads in clear visibility for the loss of one Lancaster. The next main force raid was on 18/19 February when the target for 195 aircraft, 127 of them Lancasters, was Wilhelmshaven. Although the Pathfinders claimed to have marked accurately in clear visibility, most of the bombs fell in open country west of the target. Four Lancasters were lost. As the results were doubtful the bombers were detailed to return to Wilhelmshaven the following night. Crews never liked going to the same target two nights in a row. They always felt that the defences would be more alert and more practised the second time around. It seemed a good effort, though the resultant fires were subdued. The defences waited until they were sure that the target was marked before opening fire. The early Pathfinders had a relatively quiet reception but the second wave, carrying mostly incendiaries, was to start fires to illuminate targets for the 52 Lancasters following up with their 4,000lb 'blockbuster' bombs. Once they were sure that the target was identified, the German defences gave them all they had. German gunners were always more accurate and quicker at the beginning of a raid than later on. Crews bombed on Pathfinder Force (PFF) markers with a mixed bomb load. The PFF Force was the elite group in Bomber Command. It had the best crews and the latest and best equipment. Their mission was to mark the target with flares, either ground or air. Then the rest of the force bombed on those flares. This was to improve the bombing accuracy and it did. However, there were still many problems – most of them caused by the constant enemy, the weather. There was 8/10ths cloud and smoke over the target. Intense heavy and light flak was encountered.[11] Despite

the dreadful weather conditions, three experienced German night fighter crews had been given permission to take-off from Leeuwarden to try and intercept the returning Wilhelmshaven force. Oberleutnant Paul Gildner[12] and Unteroffizier Heinz Huhn, his experienced radar operator, were one of them. Huhn recalled in his diary:

'A thick layer of mist and bad ground visibility prevail. Enemy bombers are reported approaching Wilhelmshaven. We can't take-off. Still, Gildner wants to get after the bombers, if necessary he will fly the Dornier. The bombers fly back through the boxes in our area. We decide to take-off all the same. There's a full moon. The Dornier is not fitted with flame dampers, so from the engine exhausts long flames trail back. The radio and radar equipment of the aircraft is completely worn out. I switch off the *Lichtenstein* and we have to search without it. We immediately get a course to steer for a mission in box *Tiger*.[13] The first *Kurier* is a Halifax [sic]. Suspecting no attack, its crew must feel quite safe. Gildner attacks, the *Kurier* starts to burn and at 2105 hours it crashes into the North Sea. *Sieg Heil*.

'The reflector sight has broken down and only one cannon still fires. We are guided onto another aircraft. At 2110 hours we obtain visual contact; a Halifax [sic]. A giant pillar of smoke from our first kill rises from the water. An attack, the *Kurier* trails a long banner of smoke, it explodes and crashes into the sea. Time is 2116 hours. We are vectored onto another aircraft, this time we engage a Boeing [sic]. R/T connection is very bad, as a transmitter on the ground has broken down. I am dripping with sweat, have to switch all the time and tune the radio set. And my helmet fits miserably. Nevertheless, were still in business and remain in visual contact with the enemy bomber. We get into attacking position. Gildner opens fire; only three machine guns are still working. The aircraft is not burning yet. We charge in again and fire another burst, then have to turn away as a second *Kurier* is flying only 200 metres away from us. So, this one is getting away. We can only claim a damaged. Our own aircraft has been hit by return fire in the propellers. We immediately turn back for home and safely touch down. In the Operations Room we have a big party that same night with champagne and red wine. Jabs has shot down three bombers, all Short Stirlings. Our third probably didn't make it back home either as it sent off a SOS. In the afternoon of the 20th our lightning visit to Leeuwarden comes to an end and we fly back to Gilze.'[14]

During the 1943 strategic night bombing offensive the life expectancy of a bomber crew was between eight and eleven operations, whereas each crew member had to complete 30 'trips' before being sent on 'rest' at an Operational Training Unit. Flight Sergeant Maurice 'Frank' Hemming DFM, a flight engineer in 97 (PFF) Squadron flying Lancasters, recalls:

'The most frightening ops were those to the Ruhr (Happy Valley to the crews), these targets being heavily defended. The real danger was on the bombing run in, when the pilot had to fly straight and level under the bomb-aimer's guidance, for what seemed like forever. Our five trips to Berlin – "The Big City" to us – were no picnic due to night fighters. We certainly saw more of our bombers either shot down, or hit by flak and blown up than at other targets.'

February 1943 had been a month of hard operational flying for Bomber Command. Towards the end of the month round-the-clock bombing was inaugurated and the crews of Bomber Command, for their part of the schedule, had begun carrying a new 8,000lb cookie. This was the new era of cascade bombing and thunderbolt attacks. March 1943 came in with a roar, when, on the 1st, crews were briefed for Berlin. Just over 300 aircraft were dispatched and 17 bombers failed to return. The Pathfinders experienced difficulty in producing concentrated marking because individual parts of the extensive built up area of the 'Big City' could not be distinguished on the H_2S screens. Though the attack was spread over 100 square miles, because larger numbers of aircraft were now being employed and because those aircraft were now carrying a greater average bomb load, the proportion of the force, which did hit Berlin caused more damage than any previous raid to this target.[15]

After a break of one night the bombers returned to the *Reich* on the night of 3/4 March with a raid on Hamburg by 417 aircraft, 149 of them Lancasters. The raid was led by 14 H_2S equipped Pathfinders but six suffered radar failures including one PFF aircraft whose crew decided to 'press on regardless'. But the radar operator still managed to pick out distinctive features such as the Alster Lake in the centre of the city and the point where the Elbe narrowed at Hamburg. However, the tide was out and revealed extensive mud-banks, which on H_2S screens looked like a river narrowing several miles downstream of the city. It was not the Alster Lake that the H_2S operator had seen; it was the Wedel Lake, 13 miles downstream. The marker flares went down over the small town of Wedel where most of the bombing was concentrated, although in Hamburg a proportion of the bombing force did hit the city and the fire brigade had to extinguish 100 fires. Later

PR photos revealed that of the 344 crews who had confidently reported bombing Hamburg, only 17 had actually hit the city. To most Hamburgers it seemed that their city had largely escaped, for the time being at least. Prophetically, at a concert in a convent garden a blind woman singer leaning against a harpsichord sang, *Die schwere Leidenszeit beginnt nun abermals* – 'The time of suffering now begins once more.' That time was fast approaching.

On the night of 5/6 March it was Essen's turn when 442 aircraft, 157 of them Lancasters and *Oboe* equipped Mosquitoes, began what has gone into history as the starting point of the Battle of the Ruhr. The cascade that night included no less than 150 4,000-pounders and two-thirds of the bombs carried were incendiaries. For most of the way out the route was cloudy but 15 miles from the target the weather cleared although pilots reported valley mists were still seeping in from the river. The eight *Oboe* Mosquitoes marked the centre of the city perfectly with red TIs and the Pathfinder 'backers up' arrived in good order and dropped their green TIs blind on the target. Only if there were no reds visible were the main force to bomb the 'greens'. These were followed by the first cookies, which wailed down and then erupted with violence and flame and the raid was well under way. The valley mists and industrial haze did not affect the outcome of the raid, which was bombed in three waves with the Lancasters bombing last, the entire weight of the raid being concentrated into a volcanic 45 minutes. Fifty-six aircraft turned back early because of technical problems and other causes. Fourteen aircraft including four Lancasters were shot down and 38 other bombers returned with damage. Damage was modest but a week afterwards the Air Ministry announced that 450 acres of Essen had been designated a devastated area. Of the Krupps' plant alone, 53 separate large workshops were affected by the bombing. Thirteen of the main buildings in the works were completely demolished or seriously damaged. Over 470 people were killed on the ground and over 3,000 houses were destroyed, while over 2,100 were seriously damaged. The havoc was caused by nearly 1,000 tons of high explosive dropped by crews without them needing to see the target. 'Essen,' said the special Air Ministry announcement on 12 March, 'is now the second most blitzed town in Germany. Only in Cologne is there a greater area of devastation.'

When, on 9/10 March, 264 aircraft including 142 Lancasters set out for Munich the wind caused this raid to be concentrated on the western half of the city rather than in the centre but much damage was caused. Flight Sergeant Ken Brown RCAF's crew in 44 Squadron at Waddington flew their first operation as a crew after their 'settling-in period'. A few weeks earlier, on a clear, moonlit night in mid-February the 20 year old Canadian from Moose Jaw, Saskatchewan, and his English navigator Sergeant Dudley Heal, had flown a first operation over enemy territory, each with an experienced crew, to Wilhelmshaven. In 1939 Dudley Heal was an Assistant Preventive Officer in the Waterguard branch of HM Customs and Excise at Southampton Docks. As established civil servants he and his close friend and colleague, Les Twentyman – who had joined the service on the same day – 18 September 1936, were exempt from call up to the Armed Forces. Indeed, if they wanted to enlist they would have to obtain the permission of the Board of Customs first. When the Board announced in March 1940 that after a certain date in May no Customs staff aged 23 or over would be allowed to join the Armed Forces it made their minds up for them. They were both 23! Heal and Twentyman applied forthwith for permission to enlist in the RAF. But in the winter of 1940–41 their colleagues in the Waterguard were astonished to see them back at the dock gates once again, this time in RAF uniform with Special Police badges on their arms. Finally, after washing out of pilot training in Canada, Heal was sent to Pensacola in Florida in January 1942 and he came in the first six in the exams and was flown home in late May. At No. 3 Advanced Flying Unit, Bobbington, Shropshire, where eventually he was reunited with the rest of his course from Pensacola in the end of term exams, Heal came top with 93 per cent. His next move was to No. 19 Operational Training Unit, Kinloss where 'crewing up' with one or other of the pilots, bomb-aimers, wireless operators and gunners took place as he recalls:

'Your name Heal?' asked the pilot, a tall well-built chap.

'Yes', I said.

'Then you're going to be our navigator,' he said.

I looked questioningly at him. 'Who says so?' I asked.

'I've just been to the Navigation Office', he said. 'You were top of your course at AFU so we want you to be our navigator.'

'I looked at the other two who were obviously in complete agreement with him. I liked the look of all of them and if I considered it at all my reaction would have been that here was someone who was interested in survival, which couldn't be bad. I agreed to join them without further ado. Ken Brown was a Flight Sergeant and wore a crown over his three stripes while the rest of us were still sergeants. We shook hands; he introduced the bomb-aimer, Stefan "Steve" Oancia and the rear-gunner Grant MacDonald and off we went to the NAAFI for a cup of tea. We then acquired a wireless operator, "Hewie" Hewstone and from that time on, our being together as a crew was everything. Our next move, early in 1943, was to Wigsley in Lincolnshire where we converted firstly to the twin-engined Manchester and then the Lancaster. We acquired two new crew members, Basil Feneron, Flight Engineer and Donald Buntain, mid-upper gunner. Ken had difficulty accepting mine and Basil's Christian names and ended by calling us "D" and "Buzz" respectively. One memory of Wigsley is of arriving back from a cross-country flight to find the airfield swathed in fog. Rather than try and land somewhere else Ken had Steve drop navigation flares on a dummy run, after which we were able to land on the airfield.'

Navigation presented no problems for Dudley Heal on the operation to Wilhelmshaven but it was ironic that he and his crew should find Waddington swathed in fog and be diverted to Leeming in Yorkshire after returning. The Munich raid was Sergeant Dudley Heal's first opportunity to use *Gee*; 'that marvellous navigational aid', as he called it.

'We floated calmly down over Southern England, the Channel and Northern France, checking our position at intervals with *Gee*. I worked out the change of course for Munich and shortly afterwards took another fix. To my horror we were well south of where we should be (if the fix was correct) and I told Ken so, working out a new course as I did so. This would be a long flight and we could not afford to waste petrol so I aimed directly for Munich, Eventually we began to see the same sort of picture ahead that I'd seen at Wilhelmshaven and I knew we were on the right track. We arrived over Munich 45 minutes after we should have done and had the "flak" and searchlights all to ourselves. There did not appear to be any fighters about. (They were our main worry of course on a moonlit night) and I have always assumed that they had returned to base after the main force had turned for home and it was not considered worthwhile to get them airborne again for one bomber.

'For the return journey I chose the shortest possible route and we landed back at Waddington long after everybody else, having been airborne for eight hours and fifteen minutes. The following morning the Navigation Leader sent for me. Eyeing my chart from the previous night he said, "According to this you flew over every major city in the German Reich last night." Restraining the temptation to say, "Yes, that was how it felt to us,"

I told him what had happened and we tried to find some explanation for it. I dismissed the thought that I had given Ken the new course to turn on over Northern France and for some reason he hadn't done so. It seemed just as unlikely to me that I had worked out the new course and had not passed it on to him. Anyway, the Nav Leader arranged to have the aircraft compasses swung, a process carried out on the ground whereby they could be checked for accuracy. No fault was found and the mystery remains to this day.'

At the 6./NJG4 base at St Dizier on the night of 11/12 March Feldwebel Gerhard Rase and his radar operator Unteroffizier Rolf Langhoff and the other German crews went out to their Bf 110 night fighters. Rase and Langhoff were still waiting to achieve their first night *Abschuss*. On the other hand, their *Staffelkapitän*, Oberleutnant Hans Autenrieth, was almost into double figures. NJG 4's Bf 110 crews had been quite successful on the night of 9/10 March when they destroyed six *Viermots* over France. Three of them were Lancasters and Oberfeldwebel Reinhard Kollak destroyed two of these. Rase was no doubt anxious to emulate Kollak and his *Staffelkapitän* and the other high-scoring pilots in the *Gruppe*. There would be plenty of opportunities because over 300 Lancasters, Halifaxes and Stirlings were given Stuttgart as their target on 11/12 March. The main force would be led by a dozen PFF Lancasters, equipped with H2S and 16 'backers-up' whose task was to maintain landmark illumination in passing, along the route, Châlons-sur-Marne-Bischmiller-Stuttgart-Baden-Baden, and return.

At Wyton, one of the 'backers-up' in 83 Squadron was Acting Squadron Leader Norman A. J. Mackie DFC, a very experienced pilot who had begun his first tour with 83 Squadron at Scampton in May 1941. He flew 23 ops on Hampdens before converting to the Manchester and he finally completed his tour of 200 hours in March 1942. After a 'rest' instructing at 29 OTU in November Mackie rejoined his squadron at Wyton, which had re-equipped with Lancasters and had become one of the original five PFF squadrons. *F-Freddie* had been allocated to his crew when it arrived new on the squadron in November 1942. They had made 13 out of their 19 trips on this Lancaster and they 'loved it dearly'. However, *F-Freddie* was in for inspection on 11 March and since Squadron Leader John Hurry was on leave, Mackie was given his aircraft. Sergeant Ken Chipchase, aged 21, was the youngest of the crew and was the rear-gunner. At age 30, Flight Sergeant Alexander 'Jock' Lynch DFM, the mid-upper gunner, was the oldest member of the crew. Lynch had

been awarded the DFM for downing two night fighters on his first tour with 144 Squadron. Flight Sergeant W. E. Barrett DFM was the bomb-aimer. Pre-war, he had visited Germany where he had acquired a *Nazi* dagger with the inscription *Blut und Gott*, which he always carried in his flying boot when going on ops. Flight Sergeant L. E. J. 'Lew' Humber the W/Op always wore a forbidding pair of black gloves, which he said, brought him luck. The navigator was Flight Lieutenant A. M. 'Joe' Ogilvie DFC. The flight engineer this night was Sergeant R. Henderson, a new pilot on the squadron who was going on the trip instead of the regular flight engineer, Flight Sergeant Geoff Seaton, 'to get the feel of ops'. The CO, Wing Commander Gillman, conducted the briefing at Wyton at 14.30 hours. Zero hour was 22.45. The route appeared straightforward and the met forecast very reasonable and the crews were not at all unhappy with the target because, generally speaking, anything in southern Germany was preferable to the Ruhr, Hamburg or the 'Big City'.

After main briefing crews had their usual general 'crew chat' before dispersing either to the sections for a further specialist briefing or back to the Mess to rest up before their ops' meal of egg and bacon. Take-off was scheduled for about 20.00 hours and since Norman Mackie always liked to have plenty of time to dress and so on, he wandered down to 'A' Flight in good time. There followed the inevitable chat and wisecracks and then they were aboard the lorry for dispersal.

During the aircraft check Lew Humber discovered that his helmet headset was faulty and he had to make a mad dash to the engineer officer's van and he scrambled aboard the aircraft just in time. The ladder was quickly stowed, door closed and Mackie taxied out, the very last Lancaster, as the rest of the squadron were now well on their climb away from base.

As they proceeded to the target they could see small bursts of flak in different areas and the occasional searchlight, but nothing was near enough to cause any concern. The target lay only 40 miles from Baden-Baden and the usual searchlights and flak peppering the bombers ahead could be seen. The heavy flak was inaccurate and slight to moderate in intensity, with some light flak hosing up periodically a little way below. The raid was not successful. The first use by the Germans of dummy target indicators was reported, though the Pathfinders claimed to have marked Stuttgart accurately, but the main force was late arriving and most of the bombing fell in open country. Only the south-western suburbs of Vaihingen and Kaltental were hit.

After bombing, Mackie's crew set course for Baden-Baden where, with other PFF aircraft, they were to deposit their incendiaries to provide route-markers as a navigational aid to aircraft of the main force and so prevent them from straying over Karlsruhe or Strasbourg. Numerous searchlights were exposed at Karlsruhe and adjacent areas with some intermittent flak, which indicated that some aircraft had already wandered off track and were possibly being harried by night fighters. Norman Mackie could not help thinking it was rather cruel to set fire to an ineffectual little spa town like Baden-Baden but as Jock Lynch remarked: 'They would at least have some bloody water to put the fires out!'

Leaving Baden-Baden behind they set course for Châlons-sur-Marne about 180 miles distant at just below 17,000 feet. The crew's thoughts, as usual after leaving the target safely, were that another op was now thankfully under their belts. About eight minutes to run before reaching their turning point at Châlons-sur-Marne one of the Merlin engines was running a little rough with the revs tending to fluctuate from time to time. Suddenly, the Lancaster gave a violent shudder as cannon shells thudded into the starboard wing from below, shaving the canopy, as they whipped by in a reddish stream. The starboard engine burst into flames. Almost instinctively, before Jock Lynch yelled, 'Fighter – fighter, corkscrew starboard – corkscrew starboard' as he opened fire and the tracer ripped into the metal, Norman Mackie was diving to starboard but not quick enough to avoid being hit. Also, on seeing the starboard inner engine had caught fire he yelled at the flight engineer to take extinguishing action. At the same time Mackie realized that his dive to starboard was far too steep and, on trying to lift the wing up and roll into the corkscrew climb, the ailerons did not appear to be responding. Unfortunately, the flight engineer had mistakenly pulled back the starboard outer throttle and not the starboard inner as he should have done and was about to feather the good engine. Mackie knocked his hands away and powered the starboard outer engine to full boost and revs and quickly dealt with the starboard inner himself. All the cowlings had disappeared from the starboard inner engine, which was now enveloped in flames and belching smoke back in the slipstream across the wing. Although feathering had stopped the engine, the prop continued to slowly rotate and the controls felt very spongy. However, the wing had now started to come up and Mackie attempted to continue a corkscrew as best he could. He dived to about 11,000 feet and hoped that the change of altitude might lose the Bf 110, which was being flown by Gerhard Rase.

The Feldwebel, and Oberfeldwebel Kollak, began a second attack from the starboard quarter and Rase poured tracer into and around the Lancaster. Jock Lynch yelled 'corkscrew-corkscrew; I see the bastard' and the whole aircraft vibrated as he fired his guns. Mackie was now attempting to throw the Lancaster around using the throttles and flying controls as best he could, but the bomber continued to lose height, which he was powerless to arrest. Tongues of flame were licking around No. 1 tank, which still had a fair quantity of fuel and there was a horrible acrid smell wafting about in the aircraft. By the time the Lancaster was down to about 4,000 feet the whole aircraft started to vibrate badly and with the fire spreading along the starboard wing and licking around the cockpit Mackie ordered the crew to bale out. Before he left he knew that his altitude was about 2,500 feet and so he did not waste time before pulling the rip-cord.

Feldwebel Gerhard Rase and Unteroffizier Rolf Langhoff returned to St Dizier no doubt elated at gaining their first victory. The remains of the Lancaster they had shot down were damaged but recognizable and were sought out and photographed by Rase and his *Staffelkapitän*, Oberleutnant Hans Autenrieth, a few days later. None of the crew could be found at the site of the crash, so they assumed that they had baled out and subsequently escaped capture. Possibly, however, the dead crew members had been recovered and buried by the recovery team from the local *Luftwaffe* airfield sector. Operational units were never tasked with these duties as it was the policy to keep flying personnel away from the crash sites until any victims had been recovered and taken away, to spare the crews from the sight of the often gruesome scenes at these crash sites. In fact, Barrett and Humber had been taken prisoner. Lynch and Chipchase were killed and laid to rest in Sogny-en-l'Angle. Henderson and Ogilvie avoided being captured and they returned to the UK on 6 June 1943. Henderson was awarded the DFM on 23 July 1943. As captain of Lancaster JB424, he and his crew were killed in action during a Berlin raid exactly four months later.

Norman Mackie was captured by a *Wehrmacht* patrol on the second night after baling out and he was imprisoned alone in a room adjoining their control post with his flying boots removed. However, he forced a boarded-up window and escaped without raising the alarm. With the help of various French Resistance groups, he reached Switzerland in early April. At first he was imprisoned in the Prison de St. Antoine, Geneva but he was later released and classed as an internee. During the second half of 1943 he worked for the British Air Attaché before making a clandestine departure from Switzerland on 6 December 1943. He and his fellow escaper made it to Spain on 20 December. A short spell of imprisonment followed in Figueras but eventually Mackie was released and he reached England via Gibraltar on 17 January 1944. On return to the UK he briefly served as a Lancaster flying instructor at PFF NTU before he was appointed as Squadron Leader Flight Commander to form 571 Squadron in 8 Group on 23 April 1944. He went on to complete another 40 ops, being awarded the DSO before he was finally rested in December 1944.[16]

Meanwhile, on the night of 16/17 April Langhoff died in air combat over Châlons-sur-Marne. Rase survived the war with four *Abschusse* to his credit. On 11/12 March he and eight other crews in NJG4 claimed nine *Viermots* destroyed, plus two 'probables'. In all, 11 Bomber Command aircraft failed to return from the Stuttgart raid and two more crashed on return in England.

Beginning on 27/28 March, Berlin was attacked for two nights in succession. The first raid by 396 aircraft was a failure. The Pathfinders marked two areas but they were short of their aiming points by five miles. Consequently, none of the bombs came within five miles of the target area in the centre of the city. Nine aircraft were lost. When, on the night of 29/30 March, 329 aircraft of Bomber Command raided Berlin again[17] one of the aircraft was a 49 Squadron Lancaster[18] piloted by 26 year old Flying Officer George F. Mabee RCAF. He and his crew were flying their first operation since joining 'A' Flight at Fiskerton on 10 March. They were shot down by Leutnant Hans Krause and his crew in I./NJG 3 at Wunstorf near Hanover. Krause recalled:

'As on every night, a weather briefing took place in the crew room on 30 March at 18.00. According to the meteorologists, no operations could have taken place at all due to the miserable weather conditions; not because we could not have flown, as all-weather flyers we were able always to do that but because the enemy would not have been able to make out any target. The ceiling, as we were able to see for ourselves, was at about 500 metres, the tops at 7,000 metres and in between compact cloud. There was no enemy activity at first, only later were isolated targets reported over the North Sea and the Baltic, heading east. We knew that they would turn south at Stralsund or Greifswald and attack Berlin. Generally, bombs dropped through cloud always struck something but the air raid warning alone would disrupt traffic and production more than one would generally assume. Towards 02.00 the returning flights began, scattered over the entire area of northern Germany.

One of these returning enemy bombers set course for Hanover to set off an air raid warning and thus came into our area. Cockpit readiness had already been ordered; then take-off was ordered. At around 02.35 our Bf 110 thundered along the runway and into the pitch-dark night. Because of the risk of getting in each other's way in the clouds, the remaining aircraft stayed on the ground for possible operations later. I climbed in serpentines at two-three metres/second upward and it took an age before I came out of the clouds at 7,000 metres. But then we found the sky star-spangled and clear with a full moon making the cloud below appear like snow and visible afar. It felt like a bit of space opening up before our eyes.

'With the airfield below us, we flew a little to the east. The visibility was so good as to seem like daylight. After climbing another 400 metres we were able to observe an area of several kilometres around us. And then we saw him, the enemy bomber. He crept along looking like a fat beetle crawling over a ground-glass screen illuminated from below. We watched him for a while from a safe distance above and to his left. It was an Avro Lancaster. He flew on a westerly course and only a few metres above the bright layer of cloud, into which he would certainly disappear at any sign of danger. Otto Zinn, my radio operator, transmitted all the data to ground control and then ordered radio silence. We intended to attack shortly. The rear-gunner had his quadruple machine guns pointing aft and so we could assume that we had not yet been made out by him. With the moon behind us, I then dived at him like a falcon on his prey and commenced firing at about 200 metres, aiming at the port wing which caught fire at once. He did not have a chance. He dived into the cloud and into the void below, leaving a ghostly reddish glow behind him. We followed but in an orderly descent of about five metres/second.

'We were unable to observe the actual crash but certainly its bright glow, clearly visible even through the cloud, contrasting the dark of the night. We came out of the cloud at about 500 metres and were able to see the burning wreckage. The force of the impact had scattered burning pieces over several hundred metres. To our surprise the crash site was only about ten kilometres to the north-west of our airfield. We landed at 04.35 and drove to the crash site. The glow, visible from afar, gave us the direction. We were surprised to find so many people there already at such an early hour. Because of the still exploding ammunition and signal cartridges we parked the car at a safe distance in a country lane beside a flak colonel and his adjutant. Their conversation indicated that their flak battery stationed nearby would claim this *Abschuss* in order to paint another white ring on their gun barrels. But we had not seen a single burst of flak during our entire sortie. During our conversation the colonel thought he had the better argument. We left, certain that the decision would be made at a higher level.

'While looking at the burning wreckage, we heard calls for help, faint at first but then louder, from the bushes 150 metres away. Otto and I looked at each other in amazement. Perhaps a local farmer had paid for his curiosity with a splinter from an exploding cartridge? Whatever, help was needed and so Otto and I went along a furrow towards the coppice. To our surprise we soon made out the rear fuselage of the Lancaster which had remained hidden in the dark. The fuselage had become entangled in the dense branches of the trees. Then we saw a member of the British crew lying on a soft bed of leaves and moss. He had gone clean through the fuselage and was in a pitiful state. His legs and arms must have been broken in several places as they were at strange angles to his body. His face and hands were covered in blood. A faint "help" again came from his lips and also a call for "water" but even the lightest touch caused him to cry out with pain. We were convinced that our British aviator comrade would soon breathe his last but we decided, in spite of his screams of pain, to release him. We pulled and pushed, seeking cover in the furrows, as far as the track through the field. He lost consciousness. Without the terrible screams of pain, the rescue operation became easier. Further helping hands were able to lay him on an available farm cart, then, out of the blue, our ambulance appeared and we knew that our patient was in good hands with the local military medical officer Dr Wesendorf.

'I sent the usual operations report to the *Gruppe* at Vechta for further transmission to the commanding officer. Dawn was breaking before I was able to retire for a well-earned rest. It was almost midday when the telephone rang. Our medical officer asked me to go to see him at the sick-quarters. Expecting the worst, he led me to the sickroom. But I was pleasurably surprised to find a man [the Lancaster rear-gunner, Sergeant G. A. Jones] very much alive in the bed. Having been briefed by the medical officer, he knew who I was and we shook hands with a smile as is proper amongst flying comrades. The doctor had cleaned the patient's body of blood and abrasions, then set the broken limbs and put them in splints. A bullet had been removed from his buttocks which, in a macabre sort of way confirmed the *Abschuss* through night fighter and not flak. He was taken to hospital the following day where the doctor

expected him to have a good chance of recovery. Having exchanged home addresses, we parted with best wishes for the future. Unfortunately the address got lost in the turmoil of the war. He was the wireless operator, came from the Midlands and was 21 years old.'[19]

Altogether, 11 Lancasters failed to return from the Berlin raid. At Wickenby anxious eyes scanned the horizon for the return of Sergeant F. W. Pinkerton's 12 Squadron Lancaster. Pinkerton arrived over the target five minutes ahead of time before the flares had gone down. A Master held the Lancaster searchlight, which suddenly exposed the aircraft. Then a very large cone, estimated to be about 40 searchlights, picked it up. The aircraft at this time was at 19,000 feet. Flak began coming up about one minute after the aircraft had been coned and Pinkerton believed that they were hit, probably in the wings. He then jettisoned his bombs, lost height in his attempt to get out of the searchlights and finally escaped from them at about 3,000 feet. The four engines were running well and there was no damage evident in the aircraft, but the Lancaster would not climb above 15,000ft. Pinkerton found he could not get the rear-gunner on the intercom and sent the W/Op Sergeant F. Morton to investigate. After a quarter of an hour Morton returned saying that the rear-gunner's microphone was u/s. The flight engineer gave the W/Op his helmet to take to the rear-gunner. After another quarter of an hour the flight engineer complained of lack of oxygen (they were at 15,000 feet) and about 10 minutes later became unconscious. They now ran into more searchlights and flak, possibly at Bremen. Pinkerton altered course to 191 degrees in order to escape from this defended area. He also lost height to 3,000 feet to try and get the flight engineer round. The navigator and mid-upper gunner went back to look for Morton and found him dead with a broken neck near the step. Forty minutes after leaving the area, believed to be Bremen, Pinkerton discovered he was still on course 191 degrees and at once changed course to due west. After a while both starboard engines cut due to lack of petrol, but the navigator turned on other tanks and they started up. About two hours after leaving Berlin the starboard inner engine failed, not due to lack of petrol, and the propeller was feathered. The flight engineer now calculated that they had petrol for one hour's flying. After a time they crossed a flak belt, which they believed to be at the Dutch coast. The flight engineer now calculated that they had only 20 gallons left and just afterwards the starboard outer engine cut for lack of petrol. They were still at 3,000 feet. Pinkerton gave the order to bale out and he landed three kilometres from Rotterdam. He managed to evade capture and later returned to England. Four of the crew survived to be taken prisoner but Sergeant G. C. W. Warren's parachute failed to deploy and he was killed. When they baled out they had been flying for seven to eight hours. Pinkerton believed that he should have had petrol for about ten hours and he thought that the flak hit over Berlin must have caused him to lose some petrol.

A few nights later, on 2/3 April, another Dominion pilot, Warrant Officer Warren L. 'Pluto' Wilson, an Australian from New South Wales, and his crew in 467 Squadron RAAF at RAF Bottesford, flew their first operation when the targets this night were the strongly defended U-boat pens at St Nazaire and Lorient. His flight engineer was 18 year old Sergeant Charles A. Cawthorne, who had joined the RAF as a boy apprentice before volunteering for aircrew duties. Cawthorne recalls:[20]

'The Station Commander was a very experienced bomber pilot, Wing Commander Cosme L. Gomm DFC and the Squadron Commander was Squadron Leader David A. Green. Both men were keen to show the rest of 5 Group what an Aussie squadron could do and to this end were keen to build one of the highest totals of operational sorties within the Group.[21] The Squadron flew their first operational *Gardening* (minelaying) sorties on 2/3 January. These were quickly followed by an *Oboe* trial bombing operation against Essen in the Ruhr Valley. As we approached the target at St Nazaire, Harry Crumplin the navigator was persuaded to come forward into the cockpit to see the target area ahead all lit up with searchlights, TIs and the irregular flashes from exploding bombs and flak. He took one look, muttered, "Bloody Hell" and quickly disappeared behind the black curtain around his crew position. In complete contrast to this experience, less than 24 hours after facing the flak of St Nazaire, I accompanied our wireless operator, David Booth, to his wedding in Manchester. Our tour of operations progressed very satisfactorily and we soon found ourselves involved in what was referred to in the newspapers as The Battle of the Ruhr. Despite Bomber Command sustaining heavy casualties during this period, our crew remained relatively unscathed but nevertheless we were alarmed to find that every time we went on leave, another crew become a squadron casualty whilst using our aircraft.'

Essen, the home of Krupps, was bombed by 317 aircraft on 3/4 April and over 600 buildings were destroyed. Fourteen Halifaxes and nine Lancasters failed to return,[22] a 'chop rate' of 6 per cent. The next night, 4/5 April, the largest number of aircraft operated so far, 577, went to Kiel. It was a cloudy Sunday night with sky marking to bomb on; not much flak and no sign of fighters but the results were disappointing. Marking was difficult due to the cloud and strong winds and little damage was done to the major port and naval base. Twelve aircraft – just 2 per cent – were lost. After Essen one bomber pilot noticed that 'everybody said' that it was a 'piece of cake'. Nineteen bombers were lost on the Duisburg raid of 8/9 April from a force of 392 aircraft. The following night another eight Lancasters failed to return from a force of 104 Lancasters and five Mosquitoes that went to Duisburg.[23] Leutnant Oskar Köstler[24] and Unteroffizier Heinz Huhn were ordered off from Bergen in a Bf 110G-4[25] for a patrol in *Himmelbett* box '*Herring*'. Huhn recorded his experiences in his diary:

'Almost cloudless, moon, take-off at 21.50. To begin with flying on radio beacon. After an hour at last contact with *Lichtenstein* at 2.2 kilometres. Köstler: "I have him at 200 metres distance". Sitting below him. Halifax or Lancaster at forty metres. I have to call out the speed. At last! Attack! The cannons start firing. Suddenly a blow from ahead, bright as day, boiling hot. What was that? Have we been hit? No, Tommy's exploding. Splinters rain onto our machine. We are burning. In front of me flames, a bright flood. We are going down. Heat is beating into my face. Leutnant Köstler is silent. I reach for the cockpit roof jettison lever. Helmet is singed, have to close eyes. At last the handle! Roof flies away. I rise up and shove myself off. Get away. Machine going down, burning. I somersault, cannot find the rip-cord. At last, a jerk, I float. Around me burning parts. I find that I am over water. Unlock parachute safety catch. I believe to be carried further out to sea, so I pull the parachute lines. Parachute collapses, falls. Icy cold, hands freezing. I notice that I'm drifting towards land. How high might I be? Attack was at 5,500 metres, jumped at 5,000? I reach for the signal pistol but it is not secured and my hands are almost rigidly stiff.

'Am over land ... pain, hang uncomfortably in the 'chute. Hands are stiff and without feeling. I had lost my boots during the jump. Bright patch below me. A lake? Would I drown in a puddle after all this? But I'm still very high. Swinging violently. At last the earth is coming up towards me. Woods, trees. Splintering, I am hanging between two trees. Helpless. No strength left and my hands frozen stiff. Parachute straps cutting into my flesh. Must wait until my hands have warmed. Pain. At last feeling returns to my fingers. I swing myself towards a tree trunk, am about four-five metres above ground. I grip the trunk. Release straps! Won't work. Lock frozen? With a final effort I clamber a little higher. Fortunately there is a branch which gives support, otherwise no strength left and fall down. Not to break my neck now, after all this! A little higher. Straps loosening at last. Chest straps are free but leg straps still pulling me upwards. A little higher still. At last the leg straps are released too. Climb, slide, fall down the trunk. Moss at the bottom. Dinghy off. I feel faint. Struggle up. Limbs unharmed. Signal pistol and torch still there. Have three red cartridges left. Must not use them senselessly.

'Start walking through the forest. Fall down again, get up, stumble, lose signal pistol, search for it and find it again. Move on. Feet cold, socks wet through the damp ground. Face burning, skin singed. Find a track, then past a meadow, finally a good road. Tread on sharp metal fragments of the Tommy lying around on the road everywhere. March on, pass a lone building. Fire one red. See no telephone wire in the bright light, so carry on. After an hour a railway crossing. Change direction and follow the rails. Painful for the feet due to sharp stones. Half an hour's laborious tramping along the rails. No signal cabin. Suddenly a noise behind me: a train. Load the last red cartridge. A shot in front of the engine. Brakes squeal. Train stops. Flash SOS. Freight train. Have to identify myself, get aboard. Face burning, eyebrows crusted over. Try to phone from next station. No connection. Continue on train to Harderwijk. Get out there. At the unit there I hear: Leutnant Köstler dead. Call Bergen: they think I'm a ghost as I had been reported dead. Karl Vinke had shot down three this night. Then into sick quarters. Eat, ointment on the forehead, sleep. In the morning I was taken to the crash site. Had spoken during the night with Hauptmann Ruppel and made my report. At crash site. Bits from the Tommy strewn around for miles. Pieces of bodies everywhere. At the crash site of our machine also bits everywhere. Must have exploded in the air. Leutnant Köstler with open parachute dead beside the wreckage. The body whole, only the bloody head is put into the coffin. Then a car arrives from Leeuwarden to fetch the coffin. I go with it.'[26]

Sergeant Charlie 'Jock' Baird, a 19 year old Scot from Edinburgh, mid-upper gunner in 20 year old Warrant Officer Den Rudge's crew in 103 Squadron at Elsham Wolds, Lincolnshire, began his tour on 10/11 April.[27] He recalls: 'Being an all NCO crew bonded us all the more as we slept, ate, imbibed and flew together. Our pilot, an English lad, turned out to be a top grade pilot. Our second trip, to La Spezia in northern Italy on

13/14 April, lasted 9 hours 45 minutes.' Altogether, 208 Lancasters and three Halifaxes flew the 700 miles to the port and bombed the San Vito Arsenal, the shipyards and the submarine base area, causing heavy damage. Flying Officer V. A. Wilson, the captain of the last Lancaster to leave the port, saw the dockyards burning furiously: 'I could see below me the interiors of the buildings looking quite black but with the walls white-hot. And there were wide areas as red as the inside of a furnace.' There was not much flak and the searchlights, in the words of one pilot, 'waved hopelessly, like grass in the wind'. 'In fact,' Wilson continues, 'the only dangerous moment we had was when we were over the Alps. I was looking at the white caps of the mountains and the dark valleys when suddenly everything seemed to blur. I looked at my instrument panel and I could see only a luminous haze. I realized that I was passing out and made a quick check of the oxygen supply. Somehow or other we had developed a bad leak and there was no oxygen left. Clouds then came between the ground and us. I asked the navigator if it was safe to go lower. In a rather weak voice he said he didn't think it was. But by that time there was nothing else to do, as I knew I should become unconscious at any moment, so I put the nose down and hoped for the best. We lost 5,000 feet and then found we were just clear of the mountains and over France. We began to feel less 'muggy' and came home the rest of the way in good spirits.' Four Lancasters were lost and three more, which were either damaged or in mechanical difficulties, flew on to land at Allied airfields in North Africa.[28]

Den Rudge's crew in 103 Squadron started their third trip on 16/17 April and it had his crew wondering about their choice of going into action as 'Jock' Baird recalls:

'This trip was to the Skoda arms works at Pilsen in Czechoslovakia and we were warned to be extra careful passing Saarbrücken. We were well and truly coned by about 25 searchlights and we took a bit of a hammering before eluding them. On arrival at Pilsen a blue master searchlight caught us and was soon joined by many more. We copped an awful beating and the port outer petrol tank was holed in the process. I reported it as smoke but it was petrol. I alerted the skipper and our engineer did a quick transfer of fuel. This all happened rather quickly but it made my hair stand on end. We finally broke clear and headed for home where we found 74 small holes and one shell had gone clean through the wing, fracturing the port outer petrol tank. We were more than fortunate several times during this trip but it went a long way to cementing us together as a crew. W4845 never flew on ops again having been badly damaged this night. It was a 9 hour 50 minute trip and 54 aircraft were lost[29]

'Our tour of ops carried on through the battle of the Ruhr and we did 20 ops to that hotbed. Most evenings we were routed out over or between the Friesian Islands, Texel, Terschelling etc. and then into the German fighter belt. We had about eight encounters with fighters but I had keen eyesight and always picked them up quickly and we evaded them. My skipper was very much alert and he never lost even a split second when I gave him instructions on evasive action; a great guy. We were a very alert crew and spoke only when absolutely necessary. No idle chatting and our turrets kept moving from take-off to landing. This was a great comfort to our skipper. We finished our tour on 23/24 August to Berlin, when 58 aircraft went missing. Sadly we all had to part and go as instructors. Our skipper was awarded the DFC and navigator the DFM. Well earned; they were two fine men.'

On 20/21 April 339 aircraft, including 194 Lancasters, visited Stettin, an 8½ hour round trip over 600 miles from England and well outside the range of *Oboe*. It turned out as probably the most successful raid during the Battle of the Ruhr though Bomber Command still lost between 6–7 per cent,[30] which many old sweats saw as 'the going rate for the job'. No more main force operations were flown until the night of 26/27 April when the target was Duisburg again and 561 aircraft, including 215 Lancasters, 135 Wellingtons and 119 Halifaxes, were dispatched. Seventeen aircraft were lost, 10 of them to night fighters over the Netherlands. More than 30 tons of bombs a minute for a space of three-quarters of an hour rained down on the important inland port, the largest in Europe, which handled about 75 per cent of all the cargo passing along the Rhine. For two nights following, large numbers of aircraft carried out minelaying off the Biscay and Brittany ports and in the Friesian Islands and off Heligoland. The second of these *Gardening* operations, during which 593 mines were laid, cost 22 aircraft with 155 of their crews missing. It was the highest loss of the war on mine-laying, an unprecedented loss rate of 10 per cent for what supposedly were 'easy' operations. Low cloud over the German and Danish coast forced the minelayers to fly low in order to establish their positions before laying their mines and the losses resulted from light German flak. Minelayers were given a really hot time while they were within range of coastal batteries and night fighters too had special instructions to go in and engage them. A Lancaster minelayer was just leaving the Danish coast when a night fighter swept in to attack from astern. The German's fire was accurate and raked the bomber from nose to tail. The rear and mid-upper gunners were both wounded. Getting the shot-up Lanc back to Britain over 300 miles of open sea was no mean feat. Those of the crew who were able to work were struggling hard every minute of the way against the aircraft's tendency to slide down into the water. 'We heard the rear-gunner cry out,' the pilot related after landing, 'and the wireless operator went to see what had happened. On the way he found that the mid-upper gunner had been wounded and was lying on the floor of the aircraft. His seat had been shot away from under him. When the wireless operator got to the rear-turret he found that the doors were jammed and he had to break them down with an axe. Then with the help of the bomb-aimer he pulled the gunner out of the turret. They wrapped the two gunners in blankets and gave them orange juice and some morphia. Meanwhile, I was trying to get the aircraft under control. When the fighter hit us the Lancaster went into a flat spin. The port aileron had been shot away and we dived down nearly 9,000 feet before I could get the Lancaster under control. The flight engineer then came to my help and by heaving on the control column together we managed to right the aircraft. It was pretty exhausting work and we took it in turns to hang on to it. The flight engineer had to keep a check on the petrol-gauges, as two of the tanks had been holed and he was afraid that we might be running short of petrol. We found that we also had to keep the starboard rudder pushed hard forward. It was too much of a strain for me to hold it, so the bomb-aimer pushed it forward with a bar against a support and held it there.' It seemed a veritable miracle that the pilot, flying thousands of feet above the North Sea at night in an aircraft with its radio aerial shot away, its tail-wheel punctured, both turrets riddled like sieves, two fuel-tanks holed, fuselage shot up and port aileron missing, should have got home. But he did.

Bomber Command crews wondered if 'there were going to be any easy targets left?' On the last night of April, over 300 bombers headed for Essen again and dropped more bombs on its already devastated environs to take the figure to 10,000 tons which, at that time, was the heaviest weight of bombs dropped on any town in the world. Twelve aircraft failed to return. Night fighters inflicted half the losses. The world's press took notice of the performance of Bomber Command and the *New York Times* commented in its leader: 'Germany is apparently reaching the point where she cannot cope, materially or physically, with the effects of bombing. Her enemies did not wait to pummel her cities until the population was strained by years of war and the armies were scraping the bottom of the barrel for men and material. They waited because they were unable to hit sooner. But if Allied strategy had been dictated not by necessity but by a plan to reserve its full striking power until German force was spent, the results would be very much like what there are now.'

On 2 May Flight Sergeant Eddie Wheeler was delighted and excited when he and his crew were posted to 97 'Straits Settlement' Squadron in 8 Pathfinder Group at Bourn near Cambridge. The squadron was equipped with Lancaster IIIs and was commanded by Wing Commander R. C. Alabaster DFC, a superb navigator. Wheeler recalls:

'Apart from being an efficient CO, he was an absolute gentleman and was most caring for the crews under his command. Our living quarters at Bourn were pretty Spartan but we enjoyed the atmosphere of life on the squadron. Two days after arriving, we were called for our first operational briefing and the adrenaline started flowing again. We had during that morning undergone fighter affiliation with Thunderbolts based at Debden and we were amazed at the manoeuvrability of the Lancaster and with the fire power of the rear, mid-upper and front turrets we considered that we could face an adversary with greater confidence than ever before. We filed into briefing at 17.00 hours and saw that our target was Dortmund. We drew a gasp when we saw our bomb load totalled 12,000lbs, comprising a 4,000lb cookie, four 1,000lb and eight 500lb GP bombs. The all-up weight with our considerable fuel load was staggering and we wondered how we were going to get airborne on the comparatively short runway. At 21.30 hours we were aboard Lanc ED862 doing our pre-flight checks and then the four engines burst into life. The sense of power as 20 aircraft taxied in line from dispersal points to the take-off runway was frightening. When one thought of 240,000lbs of explosive power, line astern and in close proximity it needed only one aircraft to spark off a major disaster. At 22.10 hours the brakes were released and with all available power we surged down the runway. It seemed we would never lift off before we ran out of runway. At long last we were up – just! It appeared as if we were brushing the treetops and ascent was painfully slow but sure. "Hitch" [Flying Officer H. Hitchcock, navigator] called out a course to steer to reach our coastal rendezvous with the main force. I tuned the radio to the Group frequency ready to receive the Command half hourly broadcasts which, in code, would transmit any relevant information as to target alterations, recalls etc.

It was vitally important to listen to and log these transmissions as we were committed to radio silence except in the direst emergency. The German listening posts would pick up transmissions from the aircraft immediately and we would give them ample opportunity to have a "reception" party waiting for us.

'Over the sea, the gunners tested their guns after making a careful search for other friendly aircraft. This procedure had to be terminated after a time in view of the danger when forces became so concentrated. The gunners were always apprehensive at the thought that their guns would freeze up after flying at 20,000 plus feet. One normally had only a split second to act if attacked by an enemy fighter. The warmth of the cabin and the constant droning of the four engines had the effect of introducing drowsiness. To keep myself alert in between broadcasts I took a walk, positioned myself in the astrodome and peered into the blackness of the night – sometimes to see the red-hot exhausts of nearby aircraft or the tell tale vapour trails. Crossing the enemy coast brought the inevitable deep lines of searchlights and accompanying flak – that had not changed after two and a half years – I remembered it well! We got to the target and the Ruhr was solidly defended. It was a new experience for Peter [Pilot Officer H. P. Burbridge, bomb-aimer] as he took his position in front of his bombsight. After an initial "Bloody hell" he directed Johnny [Flight Lieutenant Johnnie Sauvage, pilot] on to the aiming point with his directions of "Left, left, steady" and it seemed an interminable period before he said "*Bombs gone.*" The uplift after release of our full load was very dramatic. After the photo of our bomb plot was taken, Johnny said: "Let's get the hell out of here," and promptly threw the Lanc around the sky to escape the accurate anti-aircraft fire. As I stood in the astrodome, the sight below was incredible. It seemed a sea of fire and I could imagine the hell being experienced by those poor unfortunates down there.

'The return flight was uneventful until we switched on our IFF equipment, which identified us as a "friendly" to UK defences. Listening in to the broadcast it was evident that the weather was deteriorating. A landing at base was considered out of the question and we were directed to divert to High Ercall. A landing at a strange aerodrome after six hours of tension was not good for morale – we just wanted to get back to our beds and relax. Not so, we had to wait our turn for debriefing, then to follow the Duty Officer to find available sleeping accommodation here, there and everywhere. But at least we had survived the first trip of our second tour safely. It was Bill's [Flight Sergeant William Waller, flight engineer] and Peter's first operation and I don't think they could sleep at all. They had both done their jobs competently and we were confident that they would prove to be valuable crew members. We flew back to Bourn the next day and found that there was a stand-down from ops, so we all went into Cambridge to celebrate – which we did, in fine style.'[31]

Squadron Leader Kenneth Holstead Burns, an American from Oregon, flew one of 97 Squadron's bombers to Dortmund but lost the use of one engine on the outward flight. To continue offered the prospect of having to jink from night fighters and flak with a lagging aircraft that might at any moment become completely unmanageable. Burns continued, got to the target, bombed it and returned to base, the dead engine still giving no sign of life. A few nights afterwards he flew to attack a target in Czechoslovakia and, when all of 200 miles distant from his target, ran into a thick curtain of flak. His aircraft was hit, and the air-speed indicator rendered unserviceable. Burns again went on, knowing he would have to come back over territory where gunners would be waiting for him. He again bombed his target 'vigorously' and got home. His actions earned him the award of a bar to his DFC.

Flight Sergeant Eddie Wheeler waited a week before being briefed for the attack on Duisburg-Ruhrort on 12/13 May when more than 1,500 tons of high explosives and incendiaries, more than was dropped on Cologne in the thousand-bomber raid, was dropped. Whereas the Cologne raid had taken 98 minutes, concentration at Duisburg-Ruhrort was so controlled that delivery was made in half that time. Zero hour was fixed for 02.00. The first flares and bombs went down dead on time. The last aircraft was winging home 45 minutes later.

'The flight was in bright moon with no cloud and excellent visibility. The target was clearly identified visually, which was a rarity. Our total bomb load of 11,000lbs went down at 2 a.m. and the glow of the fires was seen from 40 miles away. As usual, the flak was intense and accurate but we came away unscathed and landed at base without incident at 04.06 hours.'[32]

Then, on 13/14 May, 442 aircraft were sent to bomb Bochum, a smaller town than Dortmund lying at the eastern side of the central Ruhr but highly industrialized and an important transport centre for the entire region. On this attack and others made elsewhere during the night, Bomber Command broke the record it had set up only 24 hours earlier for the largest tonnage of bombs carried in a single night. Another 156 Lancasters and 12 Halifaxes set off on a long haul to bomb the Skoda

armaments factory at Pilsen in Czechoslovakia. Eddie Wheeler was one who was awakened at 11.00 with news that 'ops' were on again that night and an earlier briefing than normal gave the hint of a longer target.

'Bill Waller our flight engineer had to withdraw with a real stinker of a cold. Flying at 20,000 feet on oxygen would do him no good at all. His deputy had to be Sergeant Ken Fairlie. When we saw that the target was Pilsen in Czechoslovakia, we wished that we all had bad colds! We took off at 21.40 hours and we were not due back at base until approximately 05.00 next morning. In the bomb bays we carried a 4,000lb cookie and six 500lb GP bombs, not inconsiderable for the distance involved. It was bright moonlight again, visibility very good, but considerable ground haze. With such conditions, the gunners and lookouts had to be right on their mettle, we must have been so clearly visible to marauding fighters. A cluster of five red TIs went down as we did our bombing run at 13,000 feet and Peter saw our bombs going through the centre of the cluster A vague glow was seen through the haze as we turned for home. Seven and a-half-hours after take off we saw the welcome sight of Cambridge and landed safely at Bourn at 05.10 hours. By the time we had been de-briefed and devoured our eggs and bacon breakfast it was 09.00 and tired as we were, it was difficult to get a satisfactory sleep. Up again to lunch, we were delighted to learn that we were not required for "ops" and many "cat-naps" were taken in the Mess before embarking on another affray in Cambridge.'

The raids on Pilsen and Bochum cost 33 bombers. One of the Lancasters lost was ED667 of 57 Squadron piloted by Pilot Officer J. B. Haye, a Dutchman. He took off from Scampton at 11.37 hours to attack Pilsen, carrying one 4,000lb HC bomb and five 1,000lb bombs. After leaving England the engine temperatures were a little high and the aircraft was climbing badly with the result that the Dutch coast was crossed at 17,000 feet instead of 20,000 feet as intended. Apart from running a little warm, the engines appeared to he functioning perfectly. Just after turning into the second leg of the track and about five miles before crossing the coast of the Dutch mainland, Haye noticed a white flare shot up behind the Lancaster, to about the height at which it was flying. Flight Sergeant W. J. McCoombes RCAF the rear-gunner reported this. It was a very dark night with no cloud and after crossing the Friesian Islands Haye, as was his normal custom, flew on a weaving course of about 15 to 20 degrees each side of his track. But two or three minutes after midnight, just before crossing the German border, he flew straight and level to check his DR compass. When he had been flying straight and level for about two minutes Haye suddenly saw white tracer passing the nose of the aircraft from dead astern, about 30 degrees below level, and heard shells hitting the aircraft. He believed that the enemy aircraft, which was being flown by Hauptmann Herbert Lütje, *Staffelkapitän* 8./NJG 1, might have been following the Lancaster unseen all the way from the point at which the white light was seen. As soon as the bomber was hit Haye pulled back the stick to make a starboard peel-off, but almost immediately he felt the rudder bar suddenly go completely free and the rudder became unserviceable. He accordingly side-slipped out of the peel-off down to about 16,000 feet and then noticed that the aircraft was on fire and flames were coming from the underside of the fuselage and the bottom of the mainplanes below the inboard fuel tanks.

Lütje had fired only one burst and was not seen at all by any of the crew. Haye told the bomb-aimer to jettison the bombs at once and this he did but the fire continued just as fiercely as before. He then ordered the crew to abandon the aircraft. During this time the aircraft became very nose-heavy and Haye had to keep turning back the elevators. The aileron control alone remained unaffected. The intercom also gradually became unserviceable. The flight engineer handed Haye his parachute and he saw the bomber and flight engineer go past him and bale out. The navigator shouted something in the Dutchman's ear but he was unable to catch what he said and, as the aircraft was becoming more and more out of control, Haye waved to the navigator to get out at once. The navigator and W/Op then baled out. Meanwhile Haye had to keep turning back the elevator control and he noticed the mid-upper gunner standing behind him without his parachute. He shouted to him to get his parachute and get out. But by this time he had turned back the elevators as far as possible and the Lancaster suddenly went into a steep dive and the stick was useless. The fire had spread rapidly and the inside of the bomber was filling with smoke and flames. It was also blazing up round the engines, which, however, continued to run satisfactorily. The IAS was then 250 and rising and about two minutes after the Lancaster had been hit Haye was forced to abandon the aircraft, which was then at about 10,000 feet. Lütje claimed six victories this night, three Pilsen-bound Lancasters and three Halifaxes.[33]

Unteroffizier Karl-Georg Pfeiffer of 10./NJG 1 was another of the successful night fighter pilots this night. He recalls:

'We headed for night-fighting area *Löwe* (between Leeuwarden and Groningen). Very soon the *Jägerleit-offizier* (JLO, or GCI-controller) announced a *Kurier* flying over the Zuider Zee in a north-easterly direction. At last an incoming aircraft, which had not yet dropped his bombs. Ground control directed us to the target and Unteroffizier Willi Knappe my *Bordfunker* soon had it on his *Lichtenstein* radar. As we got closer, we noticed that the Britisher[34] was constantly altering his course. Obviously an old hand who knew that he was passing through the German night fighter belt. I placed myself exactly beneath him and tried to follow his regular weaving movements. That was no simple matter. At long last we were weaving in unison like dancers to music and the time had come when I had to pull up. My neck was almost stiff through constantly staring upward. I pulled up quickly and was no more than 25 metres below and behind his tail. Then I remembered that I had not armed the cannon. Down quickly and away. He had not noticed us and I was able with shaking hands to repair my lapse. Now the manoeuvre had to be done all over again. I followed his movements, climbed a little, pulled up and fired! I intended to make certain by cutting through the fuselage from front to rear, when I realized that he would still have all his bombs on board. On firing I gave a little left rudder and the projectiles did not strike the fuselage but the port wing with the two engines, which caught fire at once. That was enough. Now away to the side and down I went. As I turned I noticed that the bomb doors were open and the whole load went down, narrowly missing my Me 110. We saw the Lancaster burning brightly. One could already see through the skeleton of the fuselage and still it continued to fly. Did the crew manage to bale out? They certainly had sufficient time. Suddenly the aircraft exploded and the burning parts fell into the North Sea. We landed at about 04.37 hours after a half-hour flight and were glad that the night with its terrors was over. Once again all had gone well.'[35]

Flight Sergeant Ken Brown's crew in 44 Squadron meanwhile had flown to Essen, Duisburg and Berlin among other targets in that month of March. They were then completely taken aback to be told, early in April, that they were being posted forthwith to Scampton, a few miles north of Lincoln, and the base for 57 Squadron, to join a new squadron that was being formed. No other information was forthcoming, as Dudley Heal recalls:

'We were not told why we had been chosen. We were on our way within 24 hours. We found we were only one of twenty crews, which would arrive within the next few days to join Squadron "X".'

Notes

1. *A Yank in Bomber Command*, Robert S. Raymond, Pacifica Press, 1998.
2. The Stirlings were withdrawn from an original plan so that only the higher-flying heavies would participate and most of the force came from 5 Group.
3. There were eventually several types of TI from 250lb to the 'Pink Pansy' model weighing 2,300lb, which made use of a 4,000lb-bomb casing. It got its name from the red pyrotechnic added to the basic marker mixture of benzol, rubber and phosphorus. There were also TIs of good ballistic form arranged to eject coloured roman candles either in the air or on impact with or without explosives. A 250lb TI lit up a radius of 100 yards.
4. The award of the DSO had been made in November 1942 and a bar would follow in March 1943.
5. Gibson's crew consisted of Flying Officer 'Junior' Ruskell, Sub/Lieutenant Muttrie, Flight Lieutenant Oliver; Pilot Officer E. G. 'Bob' Hutchison, WOp/AG; Flying Officer Wickens and McGregor. R5611 went MIA on 14 May 1943. Gibson, who led the famous Ruhr dams raid in May 1943, was KIA in a Mosquito of 627 Squadron on 19/20 September 1944. Hutchison, who flew as Gibson's WOp/Ag on the Dams raid, was KIA on 15/16 September 1943 on the Dortmund-Ems canal raid.
6. Nineteen Lancasters and three Halifaxes were lost on the night of 17/18 January. The routes taken by the bombers to and from Berlin were the same as those followed on the previous night and German night fighters were able to find the bomber stream. On both raids the Pathfinders were unable to mark the centre of Berlin and bombing was inaccurate. The experiments with the Lancaster-Halifax force using TIs against the big city now ceased until H₂S became available. Thirty-five major attacks were made on Berlin and other German towns during the Battle of Berlin between mid-1943 and March 1944; 20,224 sorties, 9,111 of which were to the big city. From these sorties (14,652 by Lancasters), 1,047 aircraft failed to return and 1,682 received varying degrees of damage. Air Marshal Sir Arthur Harris said later: 'We can wreck Berlin from end to end if the USAAF will come in on it. It will cost between 400–500 aircraft. It will cost Germany the war.'
7. The CR.42CN was a night fighter version of the CR.42 *Falco* biplane fighter-bomber with exhaust flame dampers, radio and small underwing searchlights.
8. Pilot Officer Moffatt, the bomb-aimer, baled out.
9. After leaving his position to help with the fires, Sergeant James Fortune Bain, the engineer, returned to find the starboard tank holed and leaking. He turned on the balance cocks and manipulated the petrol system throughout the return flight with the greatest skill and on landing only 15 gallons of petrol were found still in the port inner tank. *In Action With the Enemy; The Holders of the Conspicuous Gallantry Medal (Flying)* by Alan W. Cooper, William Kimber, 1986.
10. A report on their Lancaster by the A. V. Roe Company stated, 'It was the severest fire damage ever seen to one of our aircraft and the Skipper has to be praised on his skill in getting it back'. Sergeants Bain, Airey and Williams were all recommended on 16 February for awards of the Conspicuous Gallantry Medal (CGM), Pilot Officer Gates the DSO, while Hazard and Dove were recommended for the Victoria Cross. These two latter recommendations went as far as the AOC of No. 1 Group, Bomber Command, who approved them but upon reaching the C.-in-C., were changed, on 11 March to immediate awards of the CGM. All five CGMs and the DSO to Gates were gazetted on 23 March. On returning after special leave Hazard was assigned a new Lancaster and on 20 March he took it up for an air test. He made a low pass over Hornsea beach but on pulling up at the end of his run, the tail wheel struck a concrete pill box on the beach. The impact caused the Lancaster to break up. All ten men including Hazard, Bain and Williams, were killed instantly. Cooper, op. cit. Pilot Officer Gates DSO died when the Lancaster in which he was flying, crashed when returning from Dortmund on 5 May 1943.
11. The Pathfinder marking caused the main force – 338 aircraft were dispatched – to bomb north of Wilhelmshaven. Later, it was discovered that the Pathfinders had been issued with out-of-date maps, which did not show up-to-date town developments.
12. Gildner, a Silesian by birth, had volunteered for the *Wehrmacht* in 1934 as an infantry officer but had transferred to the *Luftwaffe* and he became a *Zerstörer* pilot, joining *Nachtjagd* in July 1940. As the third *Nachtjagd* pilot Gildner had been awarded the *Ritterkreuz* on 9 July 1941 after his 14th *Abschuss*. After the death in combat of Reinhold Knacke on 3/4 February he had been given command of 1./NJG 1. Gildner's score stood at 38 *Abschüsse*, two in the Battle of France and 36 at night.
13. *Himmelbett* box on Terschelling.
14. Both 'Halifaxes' which Gildner claimed were Lancasters, of 156 and 467 RAAF Squadrons, both crashing into the North Sea, 20 and 15 km north of Vlieland respectively. The 'Boeing' was a Stirling, probably BK627 of 90 Squadron. (Altogether, 12 bombers failed to return and four of them were Lancasters). On 24/25 February Gildner, whose score stood at 44 victories, was killed when his Bf 110G-4 crashed on final approach to Gilze-Rijen following an engine fire. Heinz Huhn managed to bale out at low level.
15. Much damage was caused to the south and west of Berlin, 22 acres of workshops were burnt out at the railway repair works at Templehof and 20 factories were badly damaged and 875 buildings were destroyed. Some bombs hit the Telefunken works at which an H₂S set taken from a Stirling shot down near Rotterdam was being reassembled. The set was completely destroyed in the bombing but a Halifax of 35 Squadron with an almost intact H₂S set, crashed in Holland on this night and the Germans were able to resume their research into H₂S immediately. *The Bomber Command War Diaries* by Martin Middlebrook and Chris Everitt (Midland, 1985).
16. *Night Airwar: Personal Recollections of the conflict over Europe, 1939–45* by Theo Boiten (Crowood, 1999).
17. One hundred and sixty-two Lancasters, 103 Halifaxes and 64 Stirlings – 21 aircraft, including 11 Lancasters, failed to return.
18. Lancaster III ED469, which had taken off from Fiskerton at 21.45 hours.
19. Jones was repatriated in 1944. The Lancaster, Krause's 3rd victory, crashed in flames at Eilvese near Wunstorf. The other six crew perished. Hauptmann Hans Krause, who was decorated with the coveted *Ritterkreuz* on 7 February 1945 after his 28th victory and at the same time appointed *Kommandeur*, I./NJG 4 at Vechta.
20. *Thundering Through the Clear Air: No. 61 (Lincoln Imp) Squadron At War* by Derek Brammer (Tucann Books 1997).

21. Cosme Gomm was born in 1913 in Curitiba, an industrial town in Parana State, Brazil. Flying Whitleys, his first tour of 33 sorties ended in April 1941, the month when his DFC was gazetted. On completion of his tour Gomm was posted to 604 Squadron equipped with Beaufighter Is for night fighting and commanded by John Cunningham. Cosme Gomm flew 19 operational patrols and gained two, and one shared, victories. On 7 November 1942, his 29th birthday, Gomm arrived at Scampton with orders to form 467 Squadron RAAF. The new squadron moved to Bottesford just over two weeks later. His second bomber tour began on 16/17 January 1943 with a raid on Berlin. On 11 June 1943 Wing Commander Gomm's DSO was gazetted. See *Flying For Freedom: Life and Death in Bomber Command* by Tony Redding (Cerebus, 2005).

22. Oberleutnant von Bonin, *Staffelkapitän* 6./NJG 1 downed Lancaster ED694 of 9 Squadron at Stevensbeek. I./NJG 1 destroyed a Lancaster and four Halifaxes, three of them by *Gruppen Kommandeur* Major Werner Streib. Hauptmann Herbert Lütje, *Staffelkapitän* 8./NJG 1 claimed Lancaster ED334 of 83 Squadron at Winterswijk and a Halifax. Leutnant August Geiger and Unteroffizier Emil Henzelmann both of III./NJG 1 destroyed an unidentified Lancaster and a Halifax.

23. IV./NJG 1 destroyed five Lancasters, three of these credited to Oberfeldwebel Heinz Vinke. ED554 of 207 Squadron went down at Jisp; ED566 of 9 Squadron went down in the North Sea. Oberfeldwebel Vinke claimed ED724 of 103 Squadron destroyed over the North Sea west of Alkmaar. ED502 of 9 Squadron came down at Snelrewaard near Utrecht. ED724 of 103 Squadron, flown by Flight Lieutenant K. G. Bickers, which Oberfeldwebel Vinke claimed destroyed in the vicinity of Alkmaar limped back to England with Sergeant R. H. Howell (rear-gunner) dead. Attempting to land near Bodney airfield, the bomber was wrecked. Major Werner Streib of I./NJG 1 claimed Lancaster ED806 of 9 Squadron at Nistelrode. Oberst Werner Streib achieved 67 *Abschüsse* (including 30 *Viermots*) in 150 sorties with NJG 1 plus 1 as *Zerstörer* in I./ZG 1. He was awarded the *Ritterkreuz* with *Eichenlaub* and *Schwerter*.

24. Köstler and original *Bordfunker* Unteroffizier Völler were one of the newly-trained crews posted to 10./NJG 1 in summer 1942. They claimed their first victory on 1/2 March 1943. Völler had fallen ill early in April and was replaced by Huhn, whose two previous pilots were KIA.

25. G9 + CX (Werke Nummer (Serial) 4811).

26. There were no survivors from Flight Sergeant J. D. Steele RCAF and his 101 Squadron crew when Lancaster III ED618 exploded at 22.43 hours. Leutnant Oskar Köstler and Unter-offizier Heinz Huhn's BF 110 crashed a few km further north, at Elburg.

27. When a force of 502 Lancasters, Halifaxes, Stirlings and Wellingtons raided Frankfurt.

28. On the night of 14/15 April Bomber Command attacked Stuttgart with 462 bombers. 23 a/c failed to return including eight Stirlings. Again *NJG 4* was successful, 12 of its crews scoring 17 confirmed victories.

29. There were 197 Lancs and 130 Halifaxes 'on' this night. Thirty-six Lancasters and Halifaxes were lost on the Pilsen raid and 18 aircraft on Mannheim – 11 per cent of the force. These were the highest loss to date.. Pilsen should have been a 'piece of cake': a long flight into southern Europe well away from the heavy defences. Unfortunately it was a night of bright moonlight and the fighters got into the bomber stream early. From then on it was a fight for survival with mainly luck deciding who was caught. It was soon learned that the raid did not affect the Skoda armaments factory. The major damage was to a lunatic asylum seven miles away. All in all it was 'a terrible waste of crews'.

30. Twenty aircraft (13 Lancasters and 7 Halifaxes) failed to return from Stettin and eight Stirlings failed to return from Rostock.

31. Thirty-one aircraft or 5.2 per cent of the bombing force were lost. Another seven bombers crashed in England in bad weather. Lancaster III ED862 and Pilot Officer D. J. Marks DFM were lost without trace on 30 July 1943.

32. Five hundred and seventy-two aircraft attacked Duisburg. Twenty-four of these losses are attributed to night fighters of NJG 1. Thirty-four aircraft or 5.9 per cent of the force failed to return.

33. Lancaster ED667 of 57 Squadron went down at Albergen. Haye evadaed capture with the help of his Dutch compatriots and four of the crew were captured and taken prisoner. Two of the crew were killed in the night fighter attack. Ten minutes after shooting down ED667 Lütje claimed R5611 of 106 Squadron at Rossum/Weerselo. Lancaster W4305 of 44 Squadron went down between Bevergern and Hörstel. His six victories took Lütje's tally to 28. He was awarded the *Ritterkreuz* two weeks later and appointed *Kommandeur* of IV./NJG 6 in Rumania. Lütje ended the war as *Kommodore* of NJG 6 with 50 kills. In all the Bochum raid cost 24 aircraft and Pilsen, nine.

34. Lancaster W4110 of 44 Squadron.

35. It was Pfeiffer's 4th *Abschuss* and he was awarded the *EK I* (*Eisernes Kreuz I* or Iron Cross 1st Class) which a *Bordfunker* received after the 6th.

Chapter 3

Chastise

In the early hours of this morning a force of Lancasters of Bomber Command led by Wing Commander G. P Gibson DSO* DFC* attacked with mines the dams of the Ruhr Basin. Eight of the Lancasters are missing . . .

BBC Home Service 17 May 1943

Flying Officer Joseph Charles 'Big Joe' McCarthy DFC RCAF, a burly 23 year old, 6 feet 3 inch Irish-American from New York City, had just beaten the odds by completing his first tour with 97 Squadron at Woodhall Spa, on 11 March 1943. A few days later he received a telephone call from Guy Gibson. The 24 year old Wing Commander told him, 'I'm forming a new squadron. I can't tell you much about it except to say that we may only be doing one trip. I'd like you and your crew to join us.' It was on 17 March that 'Squadron X' was formed, at Scampton in Lincolnshire. McCarthy, who was fascinated by all things aeronautical was a favourite of his fellow pilots and was known on the squadrons as 'the big blond American'. On his uniform he wore dual shoulder flashes 'USA' and 'Canada'. Born in St James, Long Island, on 31 August 1919, Joe McCarthy was raised in Brooklyn. His family had a summer home on Long Island where one of his summer jobs was as a lifeguard at Coney Island, the money helping to pay for private flying lessons at Roosevelt Field where, in 1927, Charles Lindbergh had taken off on his epic solo New York to Paris flight. In 1940–1941 McCarthy tried three times to join the US Army Air Corps but he never heard back from them! One of his neighbourhood lifelong friends was Donald Joseph Curtin who suggested that they enlist in the Royal Canadian Air Force. Because of the war, Curtin had been laid off from his job as a cruise director with the Holland America Steamship Company. McCarthy and Curtin boarded a bus and headed north for Ontario. They crossed the St Lawrence River by ferry and the Canadian Customs helped them get a connecting bus to Ottawa. They spent the night at the YMCA and the following morning, 5 May 1941; they proceeded to the recruiting office. However, they were told to return in six weeks. The two Yanks told the officials that they did not have the money to come back so if the RCAF wanted them they had better decide that day! The Warrant Officer in charge took a second look at the two American volunteers, changed his mind and had them sign enlistment papers.

Pilot Officer Curtin went on to fly Lancasters at Syerston with 106 Squadron and he was awarded the DFC after his first sortie in July 1942 and a further award of a bar to his DFC was approved in January 1943. During the period Curtin was with 106 Squadron Guy Gibson was his commanding officer. It was during a visit to see Curtin at Syerston that McCarthy first met Gibson. He remembered him as one of those men to whom leadership came as naturally as breathing; autocratic and impatient at times, yet commanding instant respect. It was a foregone certainly that Curtin would have been invited to join Squadron X if he and his crew had not been lost in a Lancaster over Nuremberg on the night of 25/26 February. Don and his crew were buried in the War Graves Cemetery in Dumbach, Germany.

All but one of Joe McCarthy's crew of six eventually decided to follow their aircraft captain to Squadron X. Sergeant George L. 'Johnny' Johnson his bomb-aimer, almost did not make it as he was due to get married on 3 April and his bride to be had warned him that if he was not there on that date then he 'needn't bother to come at all'. McCarthy with his customary directness told Gibson that they had finished their tour and were entitled to leave. They got four days' leave and Johnson made it to the church on time.

From 97 Squadron there also came other pilots like Flight Lieutenant David J. H. Maltby DFC and Flight

45

Lieutenant J. L. 'Les' Munro RNZAF. Maltby, born at Baldslow near Hastings in May 1920, had trained as a mining engineer before the war and he had joined the RAFVR in 1940, winning the DFC with 106 Squadron on Hampdens. He had flown a total of 28 ops on Hampdens on 106 Squadron, and Manchesters and Lancasters on 97 Squadron. Maltby's new crew, all sergeants, arrived at Woodhall Spa on 18 March prior to beginning his second tour. They were posted to 617 Squadron a week later. Three of them had yet to fly on operations; Bill Hatton, the flight engineer, had flown two ops, and John Fort, the bomb-aimer, had flown just one while at OTU. On 7 May Victor Hill, who had flown 22 ops on Lancasters, including the raid on the Schneider works at Le Cruseot, joined Maltby's crew as the replacement front gunner.[1] Maltby has been described as 'large and thoughtful, a fine pilot.' Like many pilots he was superstitious, always taking his oil and grease stained field service or 'fore and aft' hat on every op and even on parade. Les Munro on the other hand has been described as, 'a most charming fellow with an excellent operational record'. He too had discussed with his crew the question of whether they should volunteer or not. Pilot Officer Warner Ottley DFC, born in 1923 in Battersea and growing up in Herne Bay, had joined the RAF in 1941 and trained in England and Canada before serving with 83 and 207 Squadrons. Flight Lieutenant Robert N. G. Barlow DFC RAAF, 32, originally from St Kilda, Victoria, who had joined the RAAF in 1941, arrived from 61 Squadron at Syerston. Sergeant Cyril T. Anderson and 22 year old Flight Sergeant William Clifford Townsend DFM were from 49 Squadron. Bill Townsend had joined the Army in 1941 but soon transferred to the RAF. At Bottesford in Leicestershire Sergeant Frank Heavery DFM's crew in 467 Squadron RAAF were given the choice by their CO, Wing Commander Cosme L. Gomm DFC, who asked if they wanted to transfer to the special duties squadron being formed at Scampton. Heavery, who had flown a dozen ops with the Empire Squadron, said that he would like to talk it over with the rest of his crew.[2] Heavery polled his six crew members about moving to Scampton and put it to the vote. Two of the crew were in favour but three of the crew said that they preferred to stay with 467 Squadron. Heavery held the casting vote and he decided that they would stay as they were. Selected in their place were Vernon W. Byers RCAF who, at 32, was older than most Lancaster captains, and his crew. Born in Star City, Saskatchewan he had joined the RCAF in 1941, training in Manitoba before coming to England and joining 467 Squadron RAAF in February 1943. Recently commissioned, he

had flown three ops since he and his crew had joined the Australian squadron seven weeks earlier.

Scampton's station commander was 31 year old Group Captain J. N. H. 'Charlie' Whitworth DSO DFC who was born in Buenos Aires, and he would work closely with Gibson. 'He would always give a few words of encouragement and wish us well', recalls 22 year old Pilot Officer Edmund Basil 'Chan' Chandler, a recently commissioned rear-gunner in 49 Squadron at Fiskerton who had completed 38 ops on Hampdens in 1941. Chan had earned his nickname because his first gunnery leader did not want any 'bloody Basils here' and because he had a grin like Charlie Chan. He had been involved in several crash-landings and one Channel ditching, on which he and the crew were adrift for eight perilous days. Walking back to Coningsby from Woodhall Spa one August night in 1942, Wing Commander Guy Gibson knocked him down with his car and broke the rear-gunner's leg in four places. (On another occasion, when Gibson had been stopped by a police motorcyclist for driving his small Wholesale Ten Saloon at 93 mph and asked if he knew why he had stopped him, Gibson had replied, 'Was I really going that fast officer? My mind must have been miles away.')[3] Instead of getting a bed at Coningsby, Chandler finished up in RAF Hospital Rauceby for seven months. The 'break' may have saved Chandler's life. Three operations later and after rehabilitation at Loughborough, Chandler returned to ops in March 1943. In April, during a hectic period flying three raids in five days, including a long trip in full moonlight to the Skoda armament works in Pilsen on the 16th, Chandler was told to go to Scampton to see Gibson. After hanging about all day without getting to see him Chandler returned to Fiskerton and told his CO that as far as he was concerned '617 could get lost'.[4]

Many of the crews who arrived at Scampton aerodrome on 30 March had completed fewer than 10 operations and some, as previously noted, had not yet flown one. Dudley Heal, Ken Brown's navigator, had flown seven. Steve Oancia the bomb-aimer mentioned the fact that he 'did not recall volunteering for this transfer'. Basil Feneron had also protested. In Flight Lieutenant Dave J. Shannon DFC RAAF's crew in 106 Squadron only the navigator had agreed to go with his skipper to Scampton after they were posted to the Pathfinders. Shannon was a 21 year old from South Australia who did not look 'any more than sixteen, so he was growing a large moustache to look older'. He had joined the RAFVR in 1940 and trained in England before serving under Gibson on 106 Squadron, completing 36 operations. Flight Sergeant Len J. Sumpter, who became Shannon's bomb-aimer, was a former Grenadier guardsman. 'Tougher than a prize fighter' he had completed 13 operations since volunteering for air crew. From Gibson's old squadron too came Flight Lieutenant John Vere 'Hoppy' Hopgood DFC* and Flight Sergeant Lewis J. Burpee DFM RCAF, 25, from Ottawa, Ontario who had a pregnant wife waiting at home.[5] Hopgood, 21, who came from Seaford in Sussex, has been described as 'English, fair and good looking except for a long front tooth that stuck out at an angle'. It was he who had taken Gibson up to familiarize him with the Lancaster.

Of the 133 men who would crew the Lancasters on the secret operation, only 20 of them were decorated. Gibson selected many of these including McCarthy, Hopgood, Burpee and Shannon, personally. He chose Squadron Leader Henry Melvin 'Dinghy' Young DFC* who came from 57 Squadron at Scampton, as his 'A' Flight Commander. Young, whose father was a solicitor and a second lieutenant in the Queen's Royal West Surrey Regiment and his mother, Fannie Forrester Young, formerly Rowan, an American from a socially prominent Los Angeles family, was born in Belgravia, London on 20 May 1915. Educated in England and in California and Connecticut, he attended Trinity College, Oxford where he studied law and was an Oxford rowing Blue. The first of his ditchings, which earned him his nickname, was in a Whitley in October 1940, when he spent 22 hours in a dinghy in the Atlantic before being rescued, and the second was in November following a raid on Turin. In May 1941 he was awarded the DFC for his service with 102 Squadron and a bar followed in September 1942 when he completed a tour with 104 Squadron.[6] The following summer he married his 33 year old American fiancée.[7] Young has been described as, 'a large, calm man' and 'a very efficient organizer'. 'His favourite trick was to swallow a pint of beer without drawing breath.' By mid 1943 he had completed 65 ops.

From 57 Squadron also, came (reluctantly) Pilot Officer Geoff Rice, a 23 year old Mancunian, Sergeant Lovell, and Flight Lieutenant Bill Astell DFC born in Derbyshire in 1920 and who had joined the RAFVR in 1939.[8] The 'B' Flight Commander was 21 year old Squadron Leader Henry Eric Maudslay DFC who came from 50 Squadron. Originally from the Cotswold village of Broadway in Worcestershire, he was an accomplished middle-distance runner and former Captain of Boats at Eton. He was well-liked and was considered a 'real gentleman' and 'quiet, kind, purposeful – nothing was too much trouble'.[9]

Gibson rang 1654 Heavy Conversion Unit to speak to 'Mick' Martin. He had met the Australian with a 'wild glint in his eyes and a monstrous moustache that ended raggedly out by his ears' at Buckingham Palace when Gibson received his DSO and Martin the first of his DFCs. Harold Brownlow Morgan Martin, born at Edgecliff, New South Wales on 27 February 1918 had been pronounced unfit to fly because of asthma but he worked his passage to England, where he joined the RAF in 1940. Martin was commissioned in 1941. He then served with 455 Squadron RAAF, was transferred to 50 Squadron, with whom he flew a further 23 operations and was then taken off operational flying and awarded the DFC. He was probably the RAF's greatest exponent of low-level bombing. Martin arrived at Scampton on Wednesday 31 March.

At Skellingthorpe, another Australian pilot in 50 Squadron and the crew of *N-Nan* were told that they were being posted to Scampton. Twenty year old Pilot Officer Les Knight DSO RAAF was a trainee accountant from a small outback town. His crew was composed of a rich mix of RAF and Dominion airmen. Sergeant Ray Grayston, a Surrey-born apprentice engineer when he was called up in December 1939, was the flight engineer. He says:

'The two gunners, Sergeant Frederick "Doc" Sutherland and Sergeant Harry O'Brien were Canadians. The wireless operator, Flight Sergeant Bob Kellow was another Australian. Flying Officers Harold Hobday, navigator and Edward "Johnny" Johnson, bomb-aimer, were English. I had serviced Lancasters before volunteering to join 50 Squadron as a flight engineer in 1942. When the other lads found out, they told me I must be crazy. We were losing about 50 aircraft a night at that time. You certainly felt a bit jelly-like in the legs for the first few ops, but once you got over that, you would have volunteered to go every night. It was amazing really; you just got hyped up on it. As you saw the target area ahead, glowing on fire and with all the flak flying up, you wondered how the hell you were going to get through it. That's when you began to think, "My God …" Over the Ruhr in particular, they put up a box barrage, just firing the guns, endlessly, endlessly, hoping to hit something. At first you'd imagine that it would be impossible to fly through this tenor and get out the other side. But when you did, it gave you exhilaration on the back end of the journey. So you thought, well, I want to keep doing that. And at the start of the next op, you never once considered that you were going to die. No, you never reckoned on that. I think that for most people, who flew on operations, the excitement became a sort of drug. I rode high-speed motorbikes before I joined the RAF and it was thrilling. Flying ops was that sort of atmosphere. You never knew when you could be shot, so it was wise to have somebody to take over in an emergency. Even though I was the flight engineer Les would let me fly the plane to get used to the controls. I did quite a few hours flying. Les Knight was remarkably quiet. He didn't smoke or drink, didn't go out with women, couldn't drive a car or even ride a bike. But he could fly a Lancaster! He was a brilliant pilot, even in the worst predicaments. I never heard him issue a harsh word, apart from telling us to shut up because we were all talking at the same time on the radiotelegraphy. As a crew, we were close but we didn't live in each other's pockets. On the ground we didn't socialize at all.'

'Then came the morning' recalls Dudley Heal, 'when we were all called to the Briefing Room. Our new CO, Wing Commander Gibson DSO* DFC* called us to order to tell us that the squadron had been formed to attack a particular target, the identity of which could not be revealed to anyone until briefing for the operation took place. Security would be at maximum and anyone caught talking about the squadron outside Scampton would be severely disciplined. We would be training for an unidentified period by night and at low level. With that we were dismissed.

'During the next six weeks there were few days when we were not flying. At first it was just low level, say 200 feet above the ground. As time wore on more and more flying was over water, the sea, rivers, or canals by day and then gradually by night. Tinted screens were affixed to the Perspex around the cockpit in the day-time to simulate night flying. We practised flying over Derwent Water and attacking the dam with a newly designed bombsight that looked just like a dam, strangely enough. Of course, we all laughed at the idea that we might be going to attack a dam – we all knew that *Tirpitz* was the target. Spotlights were fitted to the underside of the aircraft, which converged to a point on the water when the aircraft was at the required height. [617 Squadron flew a series of low-level training flights all over Britain where they practised over lakes like the Derwent near Sheffield and the reservoirs at Uppingham (Eyebrook) near Corby and Abberton near Colchester and Bala Lake in Wales.] All this time 57 Squadron were steadily plugging over Germany at night and no doubt suffering the same percentage of casualties as the rest of Bomber Command. I don't think they thought much of 617 (as we now were). While we were doing all this low-level flying, one incident comes to mind. We were flying along a canal and Steve called out, "Bridge ahead". Ken, of course, could see it and there was some

discussion as to the size and height of it, ending with Ken saying, "Let's find out", whereupon he put the nose down and flew under it! I still remember those feelings as we were momentarily enclosed on four sides. I did *not* enter that in my log.'

Ray Grayston continues.

'You'd never get a licence to fly that low anywhere in any air force under any conditions. It was forbidden. Locals on the ground who had us flying at rooftop over their homes obviously hated it, but we thoroughly enjoyed it. Gibson was a straight talking, no bullshit sort of bloke. He wouldn't ask you to do anything he had not first done himself. Because we had been flying so intensively we were scruffy, with un-pressed suits and tarnished buttons and when the CO saw us, all hell was let loose. He read us the riot act and told us to parade for a punishment march. Gibson told him, "In that case, I'll be leading them". That shut him up! Gibson made it clear we were there to do a job, not to play silly buggers. But the other two squadrons on the base took an intense dislike to us because we were allowed to violate all the rules of flying. [Up until the day of the operation crews were kept in the dark about its real purpose. But their imaginations raced when Barnes Wallis' bouncing bombs were delivered to Scampton]. Rather than spheres, the mines were cylindrical and were made to spin in reverse before being dropped, so that they would skim over the tops of torpedo booms. They were massive great things that made us wonder how the hell we were supposed to fly with them. We knew the operation was something out of the ordinary, but there was no mention of dams or bouncing bombs. The only test run, using dummy concrete mines, took place off Reculver, Kent with mixed results. The Lanc didn't like the thing hanging underneath it, stuck right out in the slipstream. It interfered too much with the aerodynamics. So on our run with a dummy mine, we thought we were flying at 30 to 50 feet but were actually below that and the splash badly damaged our machine. The tail-plane and back end looked like a sardine can where the water had hit it.[10] It was so simple you could make it with a pencil and a piece of string, but it worked a treat.'

'On 13 May,' recalls Dudley Heal, 'the first of the bombs for our operation arrived. It looked like an outside garden roller and would be slung beneath the aircraft, the bomb doors having been removed and replaced by special fittings. Security at Scampton reached a high point over the next 48 hours. There was no chance of a trip into Lincoln. In the early after-noon of 15 May the Tannoy came to life: "All pilots, navigators and bomb-aimers of 617 Squadron report to

The motif on Lancaster B.I W4118/ZN-Y *Admiral Prune*, which joined 106 Squadron on 6 August 1942 at Syerston, in early November 1942. Wing Commander Gibson, the squadron CO, or his 'B' Flight commander, Squadron Leader John Wooldridge, used *Admiral Prune* often. The smiling face in the cockpit is that of Officer Jimmy Cooper. The white bomb symbol generally indicated a daylight raid. Because the Squadron often dropped sea mines on '*Gardening*' operations and time naval officers were attached to the unit, several of the aircraft including *Admiral Airgoosk*, *Admiral Chattanooga* and *Admiral Foo Banc 5* displayed Admiral-ed nicknames. *Admiral Prune* and Sergeant D. L. Thompson RCAF and crew were lost while outbound on the Turin raid of 4/5 February 1943. Outbound both ngines failed and '*Admiral Prune*' crashed on a hill at Valsonne (Rhône), 30km NW of Lyon. Thompson and three of his crew survived and were taken prisoner. other crew were killed.

) Pilot Officer A. S. Jess the Canadian wireless operator in Squadron Leader Burnett's crew in 44 (Rhodesia) Squadron carrying two pigeon boxes.

Lancaster B.I R5852 OL-Y of 83 Squadron, which previously was EM-R in 44 (Rhodesia) Squadron. This aircraft was transferred to 1654 HCU (Heavy Conversion Unit) at Wigsley and it crashed on 9 September 1942.

Rod-cleaning the front machine guns of Lancaster B.I R5666/KM-F in 44 (Rhodesia) Squadron. Another member of the ground crew is cleaning the cockpit win. Warrant Officer Frank Stott and crew usually flew this Lancaster. They completed their tour, but R5666 failed to return from Nienburg while being flown by Fly. Officer R. R. Michell and crew on 17/18 December 1942. Michell and four of his crew survived to be taken prisoner. Two men were KIA. (*IWM*)

On the afternoon of 17 October 1942 Wing Commander Leonard C. Slee DFC of 49 Squadron led a force of ninety-four Lancasters to the Schneider armaments factory at Le Creusot on the eastern side of the Massif Central, 200 miles southeast of Paris. On 20/21 June 1943 Group Captain Leonard Slee DSO DFC was the Master Bomber for Operation *Bellicose* when fifty-six Lancasters and four Pathfinders of 97 Squadron made a precision attack on the Zeppelin works at Friedrichshafen.

he first unit to operate the 1,650hp l Hercules VI engined Lancaster II 61 Squadron, which had one flight ped with this variant from October 942 to March 1943. The first fully tional squadron was 115, who flew Mark II from March 1943 to April The Mark II was later powered by Hercules Mark XVI, which gave a similar speed to the Melin engined Lancasters.

Chapter 2: The Battle of the Ruhr

Seven men in a crew at Waddington wait for transport to take them to their Lancaster.

A Lancaster illuminated [fires and pyrotechnics du the raid on Hamburg on 30/31 January 1943. (*IWM*

(*Left*) The crew of a Lancaster at dispersal.

(*Right*) Aircrew members of 61 Squadron at Syerston in early 1943 pose for the press (note the censored white area behind) in front of a Lancaster with the name '*Doris*' and thirty-five bombs painted below the cockpit. 61 Squadron operated Lancasters from April 1942 first from Woolfox Lodge, then Syerston (May 1942 to November 1943), Skellingthorpe and Coningsby and from April 1944, Skellingthorpe again and flew more operations (376) with the aircraft than any other Lancaster squadron in Bomber Command. (*via Derek Smith*)

Leutnant Hans Krause, Technical Officer (TO) of I./NJG 3 who on 29/30 March 1943 shot down Lancaster III ED469 EA-A of 49 Squadron flown by Flying Officer George F. Mabee RCAF (26) for his third confirmed victory. ED469 crashed in flames at Eilvese near Wunstorf killing six of the crew. Tail gunner Sergeant G. A. Jones survived, although very seriously wounded and he was repatriated in 1944. (*Hans Krause*)

Back from another trip, torches lodged in flying boots, a 57 Squadron crew converse with ground personnel at Scampton. Shoulder flashes show two of the airmen to be Canadian and another a New Zealander, illustrating the r of nationalities commonplace with Bomber Command crews. Lancaster B.I W4201 DX-F was the 57 CO's persona aircraft, in which Wing Commander 'Freddie' Campbell Hopcroft led his Squadron's first Lancaster operation on 12/13 October 1942 to Wismar. W4201 was eventually written off in a crash-landing at Scampton after being badly up by a night fighter on 13/14 March 1943. (*IWM*)

Bristol Hercules air-coooled radial engined Lancaster II DS604 QR-W of 61 Squadron which was lost with Sergeant A. B. Thomas and crew of 115 Squadron on operation to Frankfurt on 10/11 April 1943. All the crew were killed.

Sixty Lancasters/Mosquitoes involved in an experimental *Oboe* pathfinder attack over cloud-shrouded Essen on 13/14 January 1943, four bombers failed to return. Two of these were from 106 Squadron, whose aircraft appear to have been intercepted by freelancing *Wilde Sau* FW 190s. Another of the squadron's Lancasters had a lucky escape thanks to the action taken by pilot Sergeant P. N. Reed. Soon after leaving the target the bomber was suddenly raked from tail to nose by cannon and machine-gun fire from a FW 190. The fighter made a second attack, scoring several strikes on the Lancaster. Rear gunner Sergeant G. A. V. Twinn was severely wounded and the mid-upper gunner Sergeant J. B. Hood killed by the enemy fire. Reed brought his crippled aircraft, R5700 ZN-G in for a crash-landing at the USAAF base at Hardwick. Repaired, the Lancaster B.I was issued to 9 Squadron, with whom it was lost in the Hanover raid of 22/23 September 1943. Flight Sergeant E. J. Crabtree RAAF and his crew were all killed. (*IWM*)

A famous RAAF pioneer partnership of the air was [repre]sented by two nephews of the [late] Air Commodore Sir Charles Kingsford Smith, the great [Au]stralian flying pioneer and the late C. P. T. Ulm, Kingsford [Sm]ith's navigator in many an air [exploi]t. One of 'Smith's' nephews, [Wing] Commander Rollo Kingsford [Smith,] DSO DFC pilot, of Sydney, [comm]anded 463 Squadron RAAF [f]rom November 1943 to June 1944. Flying Officer Peter [King]sford Smith DFC of Sydney, [(left),] who faces the camera in this [pi]cture, reached Britain in May 1941 and carried out many [bomb]ing operations before he was [ta]ken prisoner on 20 February [194]3. (A third brother, Squadron [L]eader J. W. Kingsford Smith, [who] had been in the RAAF since [1936.)] Pilot Officer John Anthony [C. T.] Ulm (right), twenty-three of [Sydn]ey, only son of C. P. T. Ulm [beca]me a PoW on 6 March 1945. [He] and Peter Kingsford Smith, [by] then a flight lieutenant, were [repatriat]ed in the last days of the war.

(Left) Oberleutnant Lothar Linke, IV./NJG 1 at Leeuwarden in 1943. Linke flew over 100 operational sorties and shot down twenty-seven *Abschüsse* (victories). He KIA on 13/14 May 1943 after shooting down two Lancasters and was posthumously awarded the *Ritterkreuz* on 19 September 1943. *(via Ab Jansen)*

(Right) Wing Commander Guy Gibson DSO★ DFC★ (centre), CO of 106 Squadron 14 from March 1942 to March 1943 with his two flight commanders, Squadro Leader John Searby (left) and Squadron Leader Peter Ward-Hunt DFC (right) at Syerston. Gibson, having completed two bomber tours and one night fighter tou left to form 617 Squadron and Searby took over command of 106. On 7/8 August 1943 Group Captain John Searby, of 83 Squadron, acted as Master Bomber for bombing at Turin, a role he repeated on the raid on Peenemünde ten nights later. Behind is Gibson's Lancaster III ED593 ZN-Y 'Admiral Prune II' which survive least seventy-two ops and finished the war as a ground instruction airframe *(IWM)*

On the night of 13/14 May 1943 on the raid on Bochum, Wing Commander R. V. McIntyre, CO of 100 Squadron at RAF Waltham near Grimsby, and crew in Lancaster III HW-D ED710 were hit by flak near Cologne. McIntyre nursed the bomber back across the North Sea to East Anglia as Flight Sergeant J. D. W. Re RAAF the WOp remained at his station despite being severely wounded in the stomach and thigh to give a running commentary on their position in the event that had to ditch in the North Sea. The Lancaster almost made it to RAF Coltishall, near Norwich, but crash-landed at 0430 hours in a field near the fighter station. O 4 June 1943 McIntyre was awarded the DFC and Renno the DFM for their skill and courage. *(via Mick Jennings)*

Chapter 3: *Chastise*

Lancaster III ED817 of 617 Squadron, which was used to carry out drop tests of the 9,150lb *Upkeep* mine at Reculver before the weapon was finally cleared for use.

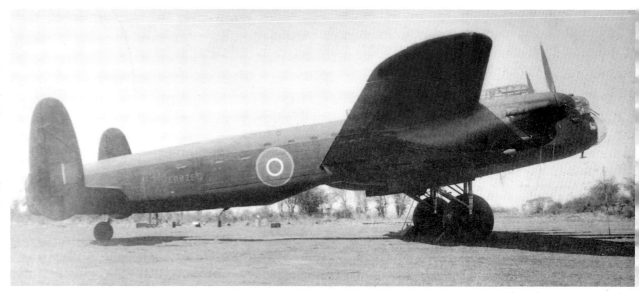

ancaster III ED825 of 617 Squadron which was used at A&AEE Boscombe Down for handling trials of the fully d bomber. This is the Lancaster that ht Lieutenant Joe McCarthy used on e Dam's raid after his original aircraft t unserviceable and he made ten runs t the Sorpe before returning safely to ampton. ED825 was lost with Flying r G. H. Weedon RCAF and crew on 10 December 1943. All were killed.

Guy Gibson's Lancaster III ED932/AJ-G showing the *Upkeep* mine mounted between the pair of side-swing callipers and the belt drive to the weapon. The belt drive was attached to the hydraulic motor in the forward end of the bomb bay by which means the mine was back-spun before release. The mine was filled with a high explosive called Torpex and fitted with a hydrostatic fuse.

Flight Lieutenant David J. H. Maltby DFC and Wing Commander Guy Gibson at Scampton shortly after the Dam's raid for which Maltby received the DSO.

Flight Lieutenant Joseph Charles 'Big Joe' McCart[...] DFC RCAF, a burly twenty-three-year-old, six-foo[...] three-inch Irish-American from New York City. H[...] awarded the DSO for his part in the Dam's raid.

Flight Lieutenant Joe McCarthy's crew (AJ-T). L–R: Sergeant G. L. Johnson, bomb aimer; Pilot Officer D. A. MacLean, navigator; Sergeant R. Batson, front gunner; Flight Lieutenant Joe McCarthy; Sergeant W. G. Radcliffe, engineer; and Sergeant L. Eaton, wireless operator. Missing from this photo is Flying Officer D. Rodger, the rear gunner.

Chapter 4: *Bellicose* and Beyond

(*Left*) *Hauptmann* Herbert Lütje, *Staffelkapitän* 8./NJG 1 inspecting one of his six victims he shot down on the night of 13/14 May 1943. Lancaster B.I W4305 KM-G of 44 Squadron crashed between Bevergen and Hörstel on either side of the Dortmund-Ems Canal. Sergeant J. G. Olding RCAF, pilot, survived but his six crew died. Lancaster III ED667 DX-W of 57 Squadron crashed at Albergen. Pilot Officer J. B. M. Haye, pilot, evaded. Four crew were PoW and two KIA. *Oberstleutnant* Herbert Lütje survived the war scoring a total of forty-seven night and three day victories and he was awarded the *Ritterkreuz with Eichenlaub*. (*Dr Schmidt-Barbo*)

(*Right*) *Leutnant* Heinz Grimm of IV./NJG 1 who shot down Lancaster III ED707 DX-F *Frederick II*, which was lost with Flying Officer E. K. Chilvers RAAF crew on 23/24 May 1943. Grimm died on 13 October 1943 from wounds sustained over Bremen from his own flak defences. He was awarded the *Ritterkreuz* posthumously on 5 February 1944 for his twenty-six night kills and one B-17. (*Ab A. Jansen*)

Lancaster II DS624 KO-L of 115 Squadron, which Sergeant Ken Jolly brought back from Cologne on 29 June 1943 minus the rear gunner and his turret. A bomb from an aircraft flying above was responsible for the damage. This aircraft, which also served with 514 and 426 Squadrons, crashed on 24 December 1943.

German personnel examing the sad remains of a downed Lancaster and its crew.

(*Left*) *Oberleutnant* Dietrich Schmidt, *Staffelkapitän*, 8./NJG 1 who was decorated with the *Ritterkreuz* on 30 July 1944 after his 32nd victory. He ended the war with 40 night *Abschüsse*. Apart from one Mosquito claim on 13/14 January 1944 all his other victories were against *Viermots* (four-engined heavies). During 1944 he claimed three Lancasters in one night on 22/23 April (his 19th–21st kills); three more Lancasters on 3/4 May (23rd–25th) and three more Lancasters on 22/23 May. By the end of the war he had risen to *Hauptmann*, flown 171 operational sorties and claimed forty RAF aircraft at night, thirty-nine of which were *Viermots*. (*Dr Schmidt-Barbo*)

(*Right*) Alec Cranswick DSO DFC was a modest Englishman who flew four operational bomber tours – two as a pathfinder but was killed aged twenty-four on his 107th sortie. Volunteering for the RAF in 1939, Cranswick joined his first operational unit in June 1940 and completed twenty-nine operations with 214 Squadron flying Wellingtons. He later volunteered for duties in the Middle East where he was posted to 148 Squadron and also spent a short spell ferrying aircraft in West Africa. He returned to England in April 1942 as a flight lieutenant DFC and was posted to 419 (Moose) Squadron RCAF. But he flew only five sorties before volunteering for the Pathfinders, joining 35 (PFF) Squadron at Graveley. He flew thirty sorties (his 96th overall) before being rested for six months at PFF headquarters, but returned to 35 (PFF) Squadron in April 1944 for a fourth tour. On the night of 4/5 July Squadron Leader Cranswick's crew was acting as deputy master bomber when at 8,000 feet their Lancaster was hit by flak within seconds of releasing its TIs over the rail marshalling yards at Villeneuve St Georges. Severely damaged, it was not long before the main spar snapped and the aircraft disintegrated in flames before crashing to earth. Only Flight Sergeant W. R. Horner the wireless operator survived.

the briefing-room immediately." The great moment had arrived and we were to spend the next four or five hours learning all about the Ruhr dams, listening to Wing Commander Gibson and to Barnes Wallis, inventor of the bomb we would use. We studied models of the dams as well as the route we were to follow. Every known concentration of anti-aircraft fire would be noted as well as every possible landmark. No effort was spared to equip us for this op. We were dismissed, with the injunction that we were to tell nobody, not even our crew-mates, what the targets were. Preparations continued on 16th and then all the aircrew were called for briefing. We learned that we would form part of the third, reserve wave to take off, would set course for the Möhne Dam but be ready to receive fresh orders en route.

Gibson ended his briefing by saying: 'Well chaps if you don't do it tonight you will be going back tomorrow night to finish it off.'

Ray Grayston continues:

'On Sunday 16 May I had breakfast and saw the officers go off to their briefing. We had been quarantined for six weeks, having no contact with civilians, no access to telephones and being unable to write letters. I'd been married for less than a year, but I couldn't tell my wife what I was up to. So speculation was rife. Some of us thought the targets were submarine and torpedo boat pens. It was a great surprise when we found out where we were going. [The 19 Lancasters were to fly across the North Sea at 150 feet, then across occupied Holland at 100 feet and into Germany at 'nought feet'.] We had to hug the ground so the Germans couldn't vector us with their radar otherwise they would have picked us off like flies.'

A little after 09.00 Gibson 'hatless and hurrying with a red file marked "Most Secret" under his arm, crashed into Flight Lieutenant Harry Humphries, the adjutant's office, with instructions for a flying programme. Harry's first thought was that Gibson meant another training sortie. He said, "No – that is yes to the rest of the station". Seeing Humphries' bemused look Gibson added, "We are going to war at last but I don't want the world to know about it so do not mention the words Battle Order. Just make out a night flying programme." Humphries arranged buses to take the crews out to the waiting Lancasters, checked the estimated return times to ensure that meals were prepared and made himself available to collect cash, wills and letters to next-of-kin. He had "a hell of a job" persuading the WAAF Mess sergeant to give the crews eggs and bacon. They were entitled to it because they were on an operation. The

trouble was that because of the secrecy the instructions didn't carry the words "Battle Order". I argued and cajoled but was getting nowhere until I eventually told her that the flying programme was a bit different to usual. "Why didn't you say so in the first place" she said.'[11]

At Syerston Gibson had rescued Humphries from the drudgery of a committee or adjustment officer responsible for cataloguing and collecting the personal effects of aircrew missing in action. Having been briefed about what his job as 617 Squadron Adjutant would entail, Gibson had cryptically remarked: 'This squadron will either make history or it will be completely wiped out.' From their first encounter Harry Humphries came to see Gibson as a born leader. 'He had enormous willpower and strength of character and was one of those rare men who are completely without fear. He never thought anything about what might happen to him. And to be a leader you have to be a bit cocky, or at least have that inner self-belief and that's what he had. The aircrews loved him. They would go anywhere with him. When he took a briefing they hung on his every word and when it came to flying he knew what he was talking about. But it's fair to say that he didn't have much time for non-flying officers. I was lucky. I always got on well with him but he could be very forthright and he didn't stand fools gladly. During the practice sorties, he fined crews who'd flown too low and come back with leaves and branches in their props. Gibson and men such as McCarthy, Munro, Martin, Shannon, Ken Brown and Bill Townsend were a "special breed". They behaved as though they were fearless. I don't know how they did it. I know I certainly couldn't have done what they were doing.'

At about 15.00 on that balmy, sunny Sunday afternoon, the teleprinters at Scampton chattered out the orders from Group: 'Code name for 5 Group Operation Order B.976 is *Chastise* . . . Zero Hour: 22.48.'

Evening came and Harry Humphries, still none the wiser about the nature of the operation, found the officers' Mess invaded by high-ranking officers and 'serious looking civilians' and so retired to his office. 'Then at last the activity commenced in earnest. The aircrews began to turn up, on bicycles, in battered little cars and on foot. I began to check. Yes, all the buses were ready. The flying rations were OK. The coffee was available and, in the distance, the Lancasters stood silent, ominous looking, waiting to be unleashed at the enemy.' Walking among them Humphries found some lying on the grass surrounded by Mae Wests, parachute harnesses and other items of equipment. He found Maudslay deep in conversation with his crew while

'Dinghy' Young was tidying his room. Another pilot was sprawled in a chair reading a magazine. Before take-off the crews went through a variety of rituals. Several played cards, rolled dice or dozed; many wrote letters home and Doug Webb, Townsend's front gunner took a bath, 'determined to die clean'. Gibson arrived by car and was seen smiling as he chatted to the men he was about to lead into action. 'If he was worried' wrote Harry Humphries 'he certainly didn't show it.' Shortly before the buses arrived I asked him if there were any last tasks to be done. He said, 'I don't think there is anything at the moment' before correcting himself. 'Yes there is. Plenty of beer in the mess when we return. We'll be having a party ... I hope.' Not long after Humphries watched as the Lancasters began lumbering towards their take-off points. They reminded him of ducks, waddling down the runway before launching themselves skywards. After that there was nothing to do but to wait and hope and pray. I went to the mess where I got talking with a WAAF Intelligence Officer who was attached to the squadron. She said something like "isn't it so exciting? No squadron's ever done anything like this" to which I had to admit that I still had no idea what the target was!'[12]

As the crews went out to their waiting Lancasters, Basil Feneron, Brown's flight engineer, pretended to lift the *Upkeep* bomb attached to the underside of the Lancaster. Warrant Officer Abram A. Garshowitz RCAF, Astell's Canadian wireless operator, chalked on their *Upkeep*, 'Never has so much been expected of so few'. Superstitious as ever, David Maltby carried his old oil and grease stained 'fore and aft' hat to the aircraft. Mick Martin as usual carried his small toy koala bear. As a former Boy Scout, Gibson always wore their badge on his right wrist as a lucky charm. He was in a little pain from gout in his feet, probably brought on by the build up to the operation during which he would wear the *Luftwaffe* fighter pilot's inflatable life-jacket he had acquired early in the war over the top of his sleeveless shirt. The German life preserver was less bulky than the RAF issue Mae West. A good omen was that Gibson's Lancaster was coded 'AJ-G', which matched his father's initials and whose birthday it was on this momentous day. Three years earlier, almost to the day, Guy Gibson's Hampden had hit a balloon cable on a raid on Hamburg. 'Hoppy' Hopgood reportedly said to Shannon just before take off, 'I think this is going to be a tough one and I don't think I'm coming back, Dave.' Hopgood is also reported to have said to Gibson in the time honoured service tradition, 'Hey Gibbo. If you don't come back, can I have your egg tomorrow?' Gibson's young wife Eve had once asked her husband if he was frightened of dying. He had thought for a moment before saying calmly, 'no not really. All my friends are somewhere up there waiting for me. When the time comes I shall be quite pleased to see them.' On another occasion driving back to their hotel in Wales on a beautiful evening with the sun just disappearing behind Snowdon, Gibson pulled to the side of the road, turned to Eve and said very seriously, 'Eve, if anything should happen to me, I want you to promise me two things. First you will have a bloody good party and second, you will marry again as soon as possible ... I would hate to think of you alone.'[13]

Joe McCarthy, commander of the second wave of five Lancasters assigned to attack the Sorpe dam, climbed into *Q-Queenie*. A bouncing bomb attack would be ineffective against this target because an earthen wall surrounded the dam's concrete core so McCarthy's crew would have to make a conventional bomb drop. However, *Q-Queenie* was found to be unserviceable. They rushed over to a spare aircraft, *T-Tommy*, only to find the card giving them precise compass deviations vital for accurately flying the carefully charted route was not in the cockpit. The chances of flying the Lancaster at low level (between 75 and 120-feet) through the myriad of flak emplacements and around night fighter bases, which lay between them and their target, were zero without it. Joe McCarthy climbed down from the cockpit for the second time that evening and with his Irish temper near to boiling point, headed for the hangar where he ran into Flight Sergeant G. E. 'Chiefy' Powell, 617's Senior NCO. After a very short, expletive-filled, one-sided conversation, Powell took off on the double to the squadron's instrument section. Unsure of what exactly he was looking for, he managed somehow to locate the route card! McCarthy finally got airborne 20 minutes behind his section.

The Lancasters took off in three waves. The first nine aircraft were to target the Möhne and then carry on to the Eder dam followed by other targets as directed by wireless from 5 Group Headquarters. The second wave of five was to act as a diversionary force and to attack the Sorpe and the final five were detailed as back-up aircraft with alternative targets at Achwelm, Ennerpe and Dieml dams if they were not needed in the main attacks. The first wave would fly in three sections of three aircraft about 10 minutes apart. After crossing the north-west coast of the Wash about five miles north-east of Boston, their route was across Norfolk past East Dereham and Wymondham near Norwich to Bungay in Suffolk and on to Southwold before heading out across the North Sea to Holland and on to the Möhne. The second wave would fly a different route to confuse enemy defences, to the Sorpe dam. This route was slightly further, via the Friesian Islands, so the second wave actually took off first. The third wave of five Lancasters was to set off later and act as a mobile reserve to be used against such dams as were still unbroken. Flight Sergeant Ken Brown's crew were in one of the last five Lancasters (*F-Freddie*) as Dudley Heal recalls:

'Soon after 21.00 hours we watched the first wave of nine aircraft take off in formations of three. This was most unusual for bombers. They lumbered over the grass (Scampton had no runways) with their bombs slung beneath the aircraft, and gathered speed slowly to clear the perimeter fence with little to spare. We silently wished them "God-speed". The second wave had taken off a little earlier as they would follow a different route, rather longer, to distract the defences. We now had something like two hours to wait. I think most of us wrote a letter, just in case, collected our equipment and went down to dispersal to get organized in the aircraft and to chat to our ground crew. They had spent so many hours making sure that all was done that could be done to ensure that everything would work perfectly. We expressed our appreciation for their efforts. It was twenty past midnight when we, in our turn, lumbered across the airfield and climbed slowly into the air, as did the other members of the third wave. We set course according to the expected wind and headed for the coast. We would be in touch with base and had code words with which to signal to base the result of any attack we made. We flew as low as possible over the North Sea, 100 feet and less, to avoid attracting the attention of the enemy radar. At the Dutch coast we were a little off track so I made some adjustments. Steve kept me informed of any landmarks and I realized after a while that we had this tendency to drift off to starboard, so from then on I added or subtracted five degrees whenever the planned route called for a change of course. I was lucky that I had three pairs of eyes up front to report anything of interest to me – and other matters such as the loss of one Lancaster over Holland and another near the notorious Hamm marshalling yards. I was glad that we also had two pairs of eyes, which could see behind, should fighters appear. Our mid-upper gunner incidentally, was off sick and Dave Allatson, from a reserve crew, took his place. Both he and Grant, the rear-gunner, used their guns to good effect during this "op".'

'*N for Nan* took off at 21.59 into a clear sky,' continues Ray Grayston. 'There was no chit-chat. When you're bombed up and you're going out on a raid you're on the alert from the time you take-off until you get back, if you get back. On this mission, the height we were flying at made us even more watchful. We were all on the lookout the whole time for churches, pylons, hills, and tall trees. It was hair-raising stuff. We were flying in threes and were only half a wingspan apart. We couldn't use the radio, so we had to keep in sight of each other to be able to communicate by lights.[14] There was a lot of flak; though most of it went into the sky above where the Germans expected us to be. We also lost one out of our three on the way in. *B for Baker* piloted by Bill Astell DFC was on our starboard side one minute and the next moment he'd gone. Just like that, gone. I believe he flew into an obstruction. Now that's how close you were to sudden death. Whatever the hell he hit ripped the mine off his machine and killed them all.'[15]

The remaining Lancasters swung up the Rhine and arrived over the Ruhr and the first target, the Möhne dam. As Gibson flew over a hill he saw the lake and then the dam itself. In the moonlight it looked 'squat and heavy and unconquerable ... grey and solid as though it were part of the countryside itself and just as unmoveable. We'd never practised anything like it.'

Forty-seven year old auxiliary policeman Wilhelm Strotkamp was on duty guarding the 6,000-kilowatt powerhouse below the Möhne dam. Towards midnight, while doing his rounds, he heard air-raid sirens in the distance. At first he took little notice, as air-raid warnings were not uncommon in the Ruhr in 1943. Then he realized that something was wrong; the RAF did not normally venture over the Ruhr on nights with a full moon but there was one tonight and the water in the lake was at its highest. Fear showed in the eyes of Wilhelm Strotkamp and his fear was soon confirmed when he heard the Lancasters' engines, not droning past overhead, but swarming around the distant end of the lake; and one was getting nearer. He finished his round of the powerhouse as fast as he could, opened the entrance to the turbine room and shouted a warning to the engineer on duty. At that moment the gun on one of the towers opened fire and Strotkamp ran for cover in a cavity in the dam's wall. Then the guns on both towers began non-stop firing. The noise of aircraft engines was now very loud and one thundered right over him, just missing the dam's parapet so that the whole valley appeared to vibrate to the roar of its engines. It was Gibson's Lancaster. A huge explosion tore at Strotkamp's lungs and masses of water spilled over the top of the dam. Drenched to the skin, he began to run as he had never run before until he reached the north side of the valley, hundreds of yards away.

He stopped breathless behind a tree half way up the slope and turned to gaze as though hypnotized at the enormous dam wall. The dam was still intact.[16]

Ray Grayston continues: 'When we saw the location, we thought it was near impossible. The Germans were so certain no aircraft could attack it that they had not defended it with anti-aircraft batteries, which was the good news. The bad news was that the dam wall was at the head of a narrow, crooked reservoir in a steep, wooded valley with a sharp hill at either end and a peninsula jutting out in the middle. We would have to fly over a castle 1,000 feet above the reservoir, drop down like a stone, fly above the water at no more than 60 feet, hop over the peninsula, drop down again and release our mine. Then climb like fury to miss the hill at the far end.'

Gibson went in and sent his mine bouncing three times towards the concrete wall but it sank and exploded sending up a column of water. When the lake settled he saw that the dam had not been breached. The Upkeep mine had probably stopped and sunk just short of the dam, possibly having hit and broken the anti-torpedo nets thus clearing the way for the following mines. Flight Lieutenant Mick Martin DFC RAAF in *P-Popsie* watched the whole process. 'The Wing Commander's load was placed just right and a spout of water went up 300 feet into the air.'

The next two Lancasters missed. Brilliantly-coloured flak from guns in the sluice towers and lower dam wall hit *M-Mother* flown by Flight Lieutenant 'Hoppy' Hopgood.[17] Tracers hit both port engines, the loss of the inner engine cutting off hydraulic power to the rear turret. 'Feather Number 2' ordered Hopgood. In the rear turret Pilot Officer Tony Burcher DFM RAAF who was from New South Wales, could hear the navigator telling Hopgood to come down lower and lower. Suddenly there was a whump and sparks and flames streamed past the Australian's turret. 'Christ, we're on fire,' shouted the flight engineer. One shell exploded in the cockpit and over the intercom the crew heard Sergeant Charles Brennan the flight engineer gasp, 'Bloody Hell!' He had been hit in the face and blood was streaming from the wound. Hopgood shouted grimly to his engineer, 'don't worry, hold your hand-kerchief against it.' Then Hopgood checked the crew one by one; there was no reply from his front gunner, Pilot Officer George H. F. G. Gregory DFM. 'He must have bought it,' he thought. Flight Sergeant Jim Fraser DFM RCAF, the bomb-aimer, released the mine a fraction of a second too late. Bouncing across the lake it leaped over the low parapet and exploded with a vivid yellow flash on the roof of the powerhouse on the other side of the dam.

Hopgood clung grimly to the controls, well aware that he could not gain more height for the crew to bale out. He banked the doomed Lancaster round to the right, away from the valley and said to his crew, 'For Christ's sake get out'.

Fraser immediately grasped his parachute and pulled the escape hatch open. Realizing that he had little chance of survival if he baled out normally, he pulled the D-ring and when his parachute unfolded, he grabbed the silk under his arm and left the aircraft head first. The parachute opened fully just at the moment Fraser hit the ground near Ostonnen and walked away with-out a scratch and, as he was leaving the field, he was arrested by a local policeman and taken away into captivity.

Burcher desperately tried to swing his turret to the fore and aft position but the hydraulics were powered by a pump on the port inner engine, now a mass of flames. The turret could not be actuated hydraulically. 'I'm trapped!' Burcher thought. Then he cranked his disabled turret round by hand before scrambling into the rear of the aircraft to retrieve his parachute but what use was a 'chute at nought feet? Just as he was putting his parachute on he saw Sergeant John Minchin, the 27 year old wireless operator from Bedford, struggling to clamber over the notorious main spar. Minchin, who had already signalled the other aircraft that they were badly hit by firing a red Very flare, managed to get the rear hatch open. Minchin's face was contorted with pain, his right leg shot away. Burcher could have baled out and left him but he grabbed Minchin's parachute, fastened it on the dying man and shoved him out of the rear door pulling his ripcord as he went but could see no chute opening. Burcher then pulled his own D-ring and plugged his intercom into the socket next to the rear hatch and gasped, 'Rear-gunner baling out now!' He just managed to hear Hopgood scream, 'For Christ's sake, get out of here' before he was blown out with the billowing white silk in his arms as the Lancaster exploded. The Australian was found lying in a field, alive, but with a badly injured back after he hit the tail fin. Minchin did not survive the descent and Hopgood and the three other crew were killed when the Lancaster exploded and crashed about three miles beyond a village near the dam where it burst into flames and glowed fiercely throughout the rest of the attack. Almost all the crews saw the crash and there was a long silence on the radiotelephone, which had been freely used before.

Next it was the turn of the Australian with the 'wild glint in his eyes and a monstrous moustache that ended raggedly out by his ears'. Mick Martin recalled: 'There was still no sign of a breach. I went in and we caused a huge explosion up against the dam.' But still the dam held. The mine had probably hit the water slightly off level and thus did not bounce straight and it had veered off to the left and exploded near the southern shore of the lake. Gibson flew just ahead of Martin and to his right to distract the German defences and told his own gunners to fire back. *P-Popsie* was hit but not badly damaged. The fourth and fifth hits on the dam by Dinghy Young and David Maltby finally breached the dam at 00.56 hours. Martin, who flew alongside Young to draw some of the flak, adds: 'The dam at last broke. I saw the first jet very clear in the moonlight. I should say that the breach was about fifty yards wide.'[18]

Gibson, who was now flying on the far side of the dam to distract the gunners, recalled: 'Nearly all the flak had now stopped and the other boys came down from the hills to have a closer look to see what had been done. There was no doubt about it at all. The Möhne dam had been breached and the gunners on top of the dam, except for one man, had all run for their lives towards the safety of solid ground. This remaining gunner was a brave man but one of the boys quickly extinguished his flak with a burst of well-aimed tracer. Now all was quiet, except for the roar of the water, which steamed and hissed its way from its 150 feet head. Then we began to shout and scream and act like madmen over the R/T, for this was a tremendous sight, a sight, which probably no man will ever see again. Quickly I told Hutch to tap out the message, "Nigger" to my station and when this was handed to the Air Officer Commanding there was (I heard afterwards) great excitement in the operations room. The scientist jumped up and danced around the room.

'Then I looked again at the dam and at the water, while all around me the boys were doing the same. It was the most amazing sight. The whole valley was beginning to fill with fog from the steam of the gushing water. Down in the foggy valley we saw cars speeding along the roads in front of this great wave of water, which was chasing them and going faster than they could ever hope to go. I saw their headlights burning and I saw water overtake them, wave by wave and then the colour of the headlights underneath the water changing from light blue to green, from green to dark purple, until there was no longer anything except the water bouncing down in great waves. The floods raced on, carrying with them as they went – viaducts, railways, bridges and everything that stood in their path. Three

miles beyond the dam the remains of Hoppy's aircraft were still burning gently, a dull red glow on the ground. Hoppy had been avenged.'[19]

Gibson, Maudslay, Shannon and Knight flew on to the Dam Busters' next target, the Eder Dam, the largest masonry dam in Germany at 1,310 feet wide, 138 feet high, 119 feet thick at the base and 20 feet thick at the top. The Eder Dam was not defended by guns but, as Shannon said, 'The Eder was a bugger of a job' lying in very difficult terrain along a valley and very hard to find. Shannon only found the dam after Gibson fired a Very light over it. Gibson called Astell but there was no reply and then ordered Shannon to make his attack in *L-Love*. Shannon tried three times to get a 'spot on' approach but was never satisfied. To get out of the valley after crossing the dam wall he had to put on full throttle and make a steep climbing turn to avoid a vast rock face. He described his exit with a 9,000lb bomb revolving at 500 rpm as 'bloody hairy'. Then Gibson told him to take a 'breather' and *Z for Zebra* piloted by Squadron Leader Henry E. Maudslay DFC went in. He made two runs without releasing his mine and then Shannon made two more unsuccessful attempts before launching his weapon. Ray Grayston recalls:

'It was way off centre. Then Maudslay made his run and it was a disaster. His mine bounced over the dam wall and exploded in the valley below. Gibson called him up to ask him if he was all right and all he said was, "I think so" and those were the last words we heard from him. We think he flew on for a while before crashing or being shot down.[20] So then it was us; the last of the main wave of nine aircraft. I suppose we were lucky really. We did one dummy run and got it pretty well right. So we circled and came in again at about 800 feet. As flight engineer, I was responsible for the air speed. I'd tumbled to the fact that if I chopped my engines right back and let them idle then she would glide down to 60 feet. That's what I did – with my fingers crossed that they'd open up again. At 60 feet I slammed the throttles forward and they did. The machine took a few moments to level off and seconds later we released the mine. Immediately afterwards we went into a blistering climb, with engines hammering up through the emergency gauge to get enough power to get out the other end. As we banked, we looked back and, by God, we'd been spot on, absolutely spot on. A huge column of water had been thrown up to about 1,000 feet. We had hit bang in the middle of the dam and had blown a hole straight through it. The bottom came out, then the top fell away and that was it. There was great excitement among the crew about our success. We were all on a high for a few minutes.

Gibson described the breach, 'as if a gigantic hand had pushed a hole through cardboard'. Banking below him, Les Knight reported a 'torrent of water causing a tidal wave almost 30 feet high'. The crew of *N-Nan* watched in awe as car headlights in the path of the water turned from bright white to murky green to nothing. Melvin Young's nickname 'Dinghy' was transmitted back to 5 Group Headquarters to be received with yet more celebration.

The Lancasters flown by Flight Sergeant Ken Brown and Flight Lieutenant Joe McCarthy headed for the 226 feet high Sorpe dam. Dudley Heal says:

'Some time before we were due to reach the Möhne dam, 'Hewie' reported that both it and the Eder had been breached and we were to aim for the Sorpe. We changed course, much encouraged by this news. Barnes Wallis' bomb was designed to be released by an aircraft heading over water towards a dam, the bomb then bouncing over water (like a pebble skimmed over the sea from the shore), hitting the dam and sinking to 20 feet, when it was set to explode. It had been realized quite late in the day that this was effective if the dam was built of concrete but no good for an earth dam, as the Sorpe was. Our instructions, therefore, were to fly over and along the line of the dam at 60 feet, releasing the bomb as near the centre of the dam as we could.'

Arriving over the valley, McCarthy initiated a diving attack on the dam nestled at the bottom of two steep hills. Coming over the top of one hill, using full flaps to keep the speed of his 30-ton Lancaster under control, McCarthy dived down the slope toward the 765-yard long dam. To escape he had to apply full power to his four Packard-built Rolls-Royce Merlins and climb at a steep angle up the side of the second hill. And if that wasn't difficult enough, a thick mist was filling the valley as he arrived. The blinding moonlight turned the mist into a writhing phosphorescent pall, which made it extremely difficult to judge the bomber's height above the lake. On the third attempt to locate the target, McCarthy almost flew *T-Tommy* into the water. It was not until the tenth run that bomb-aimer, Sergeant George 'Johnny' Johnson, was satisfied and released the bomb from a height of just 90 feet. The weapon exploded squarely on top of the parapet, damaging and crumbling for more than 50-yards the crown of the earthen wall.

Shortly thereafter Flight Sergeant Ken Brown attacked the dam. His trip was quite eventful. Even before he reached the Sorpe his gunners shot up three trains en route. They were fired on by flak and hit in the fuselage but suffered no serious damage to the aircraft. Dudley Heal recalls:

'We found the Sorpe dam with no trouble and could see it quite clearly at the northern end of the Sorpe River. The ground rose steeply on each side, heavily wooded, with a church steeple on our line of approach, all, except the river and dam swathed in mist. The only good point appeared to be that there were no defences. After two or three abortive runs, Ken decided to try the Wigsley "gambit" of dropping flares along the approach route. We could see that the top of the dam was already damaged.[21] Eventually avoiding the steeple, dropping the bomb at 60 feet and pulling up sharply over the wooded hill we saw our bomb go off, causing an enormous water spout and an extension of the damage already done.[22] After a good look at it we set course for base, Hewie transmitting "Goner", indicating that we had attacked but not breached the dam. Our homeward track took us near the Möhne dam and we stared in awe at the breach through which the Möhne river was rushing down the valley. After that the journey back was uneventful until we approached the Dutch coast and could see the sea ahead. Then, without warning we were caught and held by searchlights and blasted by gunfire. Even in my curtained compartment I was blinded by those searchlights so how Ken and Basil coped I shall never know, Ken even put the nose down although we were already flying as low as seemed possible and we flew on. Then we were over the sea and I could see shells whizzing over our heads and hitting the water. The searchlights lost their effect and Ken handed over the controls to Basil, while he and I examined the holes in the fuselage. The starboard side of the aircraft at just above head height was riddled. I think there is little doubt that had we remained at the same height, or even attempted to climb, it would have been disastrous. (We learned later that Squadron Leader Young had gone down earlier at this same spot.)[23] Back at Scampton we were the last aircraft but one to touch down. Flight Sergeant Townsend landed about half-an-hour later, having attacked the Ennerpe Dam but, like us, failed to breach it.'[24]

The 'last resort' targets, the Lister (Schweim) and Dieml dams were not attacked. However, the damage inflicted in the first two attacks proved the operation's success. The surge of water from the Möhne and Eder dams knocked out power stations and damaged factories and cut water, gas and electricity supplies. As many as 1,300 civilians, including about 500 Ukrainian women slave labourers died. Eight Lancasters were lost, 53 men were killed and three were captured.

A member of the Hitler Youth found Tony Burcher, who had been blown out of his burning Lancaster over the Möhne dam. The Australian rear-gunner was taken to a police station and locked up in a cell. Lying on a hard wooden bed in agony from his broken back, his immediate problem was to slake his thirst. He called the Obergefreiter guarding his cell door and shouted, 'I want a drink of water!'

The Obergefreiter grunted, 'You want wasser?'

Burcher groaned, 'Yes, wasser – please'.

The Obergefreiter left, only to return with his Feldwebel who looked at the dishevelled and badly injured figure. He went out and returned with a Hauptmann. 'So, you want a drink of water, do you? You English [sic] bastard. Thanks to you and your comrades, there is no drinking water any more!'

A broad grin creased Burcher's face. So the others had done it after all.[25]

Ray Grayston. 'Gibson called up and said simply, "OK fellas, that's your job done. No hanging about, you know. Make your way home." That was easier said than done, of course, because the Germans had woken up to what we'd done and they were out to get us. And they did get a few.'[26]

At Scampton Harry Humphries heard on the radio *G-George*, Gibson's aircraft, asking permission to land. Among the first aircrew the adjutant saw was an excited David Maltby. He called it a 'terrific show, absolutely terrific. Never seen anything like it in my life.' Then quite bluntly, 'Hoppy's bought it. Shot down over the target and I am afraid that we have lost several others too. Some didn't even get there and I am sure Dinghy Young got into trouble and maybe Henry Maudslay' he told Humphries. 'We pranged it though, Adj; Oh boy did we prang it! Water, water everywhere. "Gibby" was everywhere. How the hell the Jerry gunners missed him I don't know …' More crews arrived back and a celebratory party was getting under way in the Mess as Humphries made his way to the control tower. There the grim reality sank in. 'I looked at the blackboard and thought, "Bloody hell", eight aircraft missing with all their crews'. Of course I'd experienced losses before but not on this scale. To think that 53 men, some of whom you'd been with in the Mess only a few hours before, were gone was a blow. When I saw Gibson in the Mess he said, 'It's a bad show Humph, but I think it's probably been worthwhile – or at least I hope so.' Humphries felt like a 'wet dishcloth. It affected me deeply. It was draining and depressing. But you had to get on with it. People would want to know about their loved ones. I just collapsed like a pricked balloon but at the same time made sure that the first milestone in the history of 617 Squadron was duly recorded.'[27]

The results of the operation were radioed to 5 Group Operations Room at Grantham where Air Chief Marshal Arthur 'Bomber' Harris, Barnes Wallis and others were waiting for news. On hearing the code word, Wallis, who until then had been morose, punched the air with both fists. Harris turned to him and said: 'Wallis, I didn't believe a word you said when you first came to see me. But now you could sell me a pink elephant!' The euphoria became more muted when news of the losses came in. Of the 133 men who flew on the raid, 56 failed to return.

N-Nan did make it back, though not without incident. Ray Grayston says:

'We were picked up by searchlights and machine guns and it was so bad that we thought, "This is it". We were so low that the searchlights were beaming straight into the cockpit and blinding Les, who couldn't see a thing. But luckily our Brownings were loaded with 100 per cent tracer bullets, and when "Doc" Sutherland opened up from the front turret, it was like two streams of liquid lightning. Then Harry O'Brien in the rear turret opened up with four Brownings. With all these streams of lightning flying at them, the Germans panicked and ran away from their guns. So we got away with it. If they had stood by their guns, we'd have been shot down for sure. We landed back at Scampton at 04.20 in the morning and went straight into debriefing. All the nobs and senior officers, as well as Barnes Wallis, were there waiting to talk to the pilots, but they didn't have much to say to us. The senior officers didn't mix with the fry. We got egg and chips in our Mess, with rum and coffee. But all we really wanted to do was get into our sacks and go to sleep for a few hours. We had been in the air for almost six-and-a-half hours. The senior officers celebrated for weeks as they visited various messes around the country. Les Knight acted as taxi pilot most of the time because he didn't drink.'

Dudley Heal adds:

'The importance with which the powers-that-be regarded this operation is demonstrated by the fact that Air Chief Marshal Harris, Head of Bomber Command, attended the debriefing of the returning crews, as did Barnes Wallis and the Station Commander, Group Captain Whitworth. I don't think any of us went to bed that night. We were all given a week's leave now and it was during that week that IT happened. Halfway through the week I was sitting at the tea table with my parents and my brother, Les, (my other brother, Don, being at sea) when the doorbell rang. Being nearest, I got up and answered it. It was a telegram for me from Scampton. Back in the living room I held it up and said, "I hope that isn't a recall from leave." I opened it, everybody watching me apprehensively and read it aloud – it said, "Heartiest congratulations on award of the Distinguished Flying Medal. Wingco." We were all speechless. Then my father, who was Secretary of the British Legion Club in Gosport, said, "We're all going down to the Club tonight" – which we did. Back at Scampton after the leave I found that Steve had also received the DFM while Ken had been awarded the CGM (Conspicuous Gallantry Medal). Basically, awards had been given to pilots, navigators and bomb-aimers who had reached and attacked their targets accurately, whether or not they had been breached. Where other members of the crews, gunners for example, had distinguished themselves in some way they could also have been decorated. The matter of rank was always a problem in this connection. Commissioned pilots had received the DSO, a most prestigious decoration, as Ken knew. Non-commissioned pilots received the CGM, which few people had heard of at the time – similarly, if I had been commissioned I would have received the DFC. I think Ken was, as a Canadian, miffed about this class distinction although he did realize that he had received one of the rarest "gongs" of all. For my part I could not have been more thrilled if I had been awarded the Victoria Cross.

'The raid received maximum publicity. Scampton was honoured by a visit from Their Majesties the King and Queen and the decorations were presented by the Queen, (the King being in Africa), at a Special Investiture, 22/6/43 – to quote from RAF records.'

In the message he sent to the crews, congratulating them on their brilliant work, Air Chief Marshal Harris said: 'Please convey to all concerned my warmest congratulations on the brilliantly successful execution of last night's operations. To the air-crews I would say that their keenness and thoroughness in training and their skill and determination in pressing home their attacks will forever be an inspiration to the Royal Air Force. In this memorable operation they have won a major victory in the Battle of the Ruhr, the effects of which will last until the Boche is swept away in the flood of final disaster.'

Congratulations came from the War Cabinet. They were addressed to Sir Arthur Harris by the Secretary of State for Air, who wrote: 'The War Cabinet has instructed me to convey to you and to all who shared in the preparation and execution [of] Sunday night's operations – particularly to Wing Commander Gibson and his squadron – their congratulations on the great success achieved. This attack, pressed home in the face strong resistance, is a testimony alike to the tactical resource and energy of those who planned it, to the

gallantry and determination of the aircrews and to the excellence British design and workmanship. The War Cabinet has noted with satisfaction the damage done to German war power.'

It was, as Wallis said, 'the most amazing feat the RAF ever had or ever could perform'. The massive Möhne, Eder and Sorpe dams served the industrial Ruhr Basin and more than a dozen hydroelectric power plants relied on their waters. So did foundries, steel works, chemical plants and other factories fuelling Germany's war effort. Winston Churchill had authorized the operation and he used it as a coup to seek greater support from the USA. At the time, most of President Roosevelt's advisers were committed to targeting Japan first. The 'Dam Busters' proved that the war in Europe was being prosecuted dramatically well. Two days after the operation, Churchill was given a standing ovation at the *Trident* Conference with Roosevelt in Washington. Gibson, who already had two DSOs and two DFCs was awarded the VC for leading the 'Dam Busters' and many of the officers got DFCs and DSOs.[28] Ray Grayston adds: 'The officers got their invitations to Buckingham Palace. We thought we'd get something sooner or later, but it never happened.'

'That over', continues Dudley Heal, '617 settled down to work again – not, as most of us expected, to the hammering of German cities and industries but to specialized targets which needed accurate bombing by a small force. In August 617 moved to Coningsby, nearby, where there were hard runways which Scampton lacked. Late in August it was noted that massive concrete structures were springing up in Northern France. They were, of course, sites for the launching of V-1 and V-2 weapons, which would require accurate bombing with the biggest possible bombs. They would be 617 targets for the foreseeable future. 617, meanwhile, had moved again, this time to Woodhall Spa, near Coningsby, where we would be the only squadron. Accommodation was temporary at first and the nearby Petwood Hotel, taken over by the RAF, was our billet. In the hurly-hurly of removal we found beds where we could and the first night I shared a room with members of another crew, the captain being Flight Lieutenant [T. V. 'Tom'] O'Shaughnessy. The next day [20 January 1944] they went off for some low level flying and bombing practice, ending up by flying into a rise in the ground off the beach. That night I shared a room with six empty beds.[29]

'It was in February 1944 that Ken began to have problems with his hearing and was occasionally unable to make out what was being said over the intercom. He reported to the MO, as a result of which, Ken was grounded for the time being for medical reports. We were given the choice of flying with another pilot or of being 'rested'. This was difficult off the cuff. We had not yet completed the required 30 ops but we had been with 617 for nearly a year, not forgetting our time with 44 Squadron and with Coastal Command, altogether 16 months under operational conditions. Added to this was the reluctance to change pilots – I said I would prefer to be rested. The other members of the crew felt as I did. It was not long before our postings came through, mine being to Bruntingthorpe, near Rugby. I said "Au Revoir" to the other members of the crew rather than "goodbye". The normal rest period was six months. It was now February 1944, and the war seemed likely to continue indefinitely.

'At Bruntingthorpe I would be teaching *Gee* to would-be navigators under classroom conditions. This left the evenings free, an unusual luxury, and after a while I began to spend some of those evenings, with two or three fellow teachers, cycling to a village called, I swear, Willoughby Waterless, where we would play darts in the only pub, making friends with the locals. Occasionally we would cycle back to camp with a bag containing half a dozen eggs slung over the handlebars. These, with our names pencilled on them were handed in to the Officers' Mess kitchen and eventually served up for our breakfast. I was now a Flying Officer, playing darts instead of helping the war effort. When I was approached by one of the pilots at Bruntingthorpe later in 1944 and asked if I would go back on 'ops' with him I did not hesitate for long. I had to smile when he said he would be joining a special squadron. The new squadron was 214 in 100 Group (Radio Counter-Measures). I agreed to join Flight Lieutenant "Johnny" Wynne DFC and soon we had a complete crew of ten and joined 214 Squadron early in 1945.'

Twenty-two veterans of the Dams raid were killed on ops. Guy Gibson was sent to America as an air attaché but he begged the Air Ministry to allow him to return to operations. At Woodhall Spa Gibson persuaded the CO of 627 Squadron to let him fly a Mosquito, against his better judgement, for the operation to Rheydt on the night of 19/20 September 1944 when he was to act as controller for the raid. It would appear that Gibson did not exactly endear himself to some of 627 Squadron's members but then 617 Squadron has always engendered fierce rivalries. Squadron Leader Frank W. Boyle DFC★ RAAF, a 627 Squadron navigator, encountered Gibson a few times at Woodhall. He reported that, 'he seemed a lost soul, particularly on the last occasion when he dropped in at the Mess. He was upset by the award of Cheshire's VC (and I would understand that after his own VC for the Dam Busters raid), but he reckoned too forcibly and bluntly that, on the basis of Cheshire's citation, he would get a bar to his VC.' Fellow 627 Squadron navigator Wallace 'Johnno' Gaunt DFC recalled that, 'Guy Gibson was a brave man and did a good job leading the Dam Busters but he came back from the USA too full of his own importance. He walked into our mess one night and everybody was talking, playing liar-dice, drinking, etc., so he called out, "Don't you know who I am?" He got very annoyed, as he had expected everyone to stand up and cheer him. In the end he was de-bagged and put outside. A week or so later he did not return.'[30]

While returning over Walcheren after the op to Rheydt, both engines of Gibson's Mosquito cut (according to Anton de Bruyn, a night watchman at the local sugar factory in Steenbergen, who witnessed the incident) and the aircraft crashed, killing him and his navigator 23 year old Squadron Leader James Brown Warwick DFC, an Irishman and veteran of two tours. Steenbergen is a small rural town in the southern Dutch province of North Brabant.

On the Van der Riet farm in the West Graaf Hendrik Polder, the family was asleep. It was about midnight when they all awoke, startled by a terrible noise, followed by a dreadful bang. Leaping from their beds, they rushed to a window overlooking the fields in front of the farm, from which direction the noise seemed to have come and some way off they could see a reddish glow and a tongue of flame. It was difficult to estimate the distance due to a layer of ground fog over the pasture. They assumed that it had been a bomb and after gazing for a while, recovering from the shock and seeing the flames die down, they returned to bed. Next morning Mr Van der Riet went out to start his daily work. He crossed to a shed to collect his tools and to his horror he found a human body slumped against the wall. Upon closer inspection he could see that it was in fact just a limbless trunk with the head hanging loosely. Utterly shocked, he rushed back to inform his wife and sons of his discovery and they too were filled with horror. Van der Riet decided to notify the Chief of Police of Steenbergen, Mr Van der Kassteele who, in turn informed the German Ortskommandant who immediately ordered the farm and crash site sealed off. After a lengthy search two Dutch Auxiliary policemen, Tiny Van Mechelen and Chris Stoffelen and another helper, eventually found two legs and two arms and realized that a second flyer had been in the aircraft when they came across part of a third foot. As the limbs were being placed in a basket, Tiny Van Mechelen noticed a gold ring on one of the fingers. To prevent the Germans from taking it, he tried to remove it but the hand was too swollen, so with his penknife he sliced off the finger and removed the ring, which he slipped into his pocket. Upon returning to the field, they found a piece of skull, a severed hand and a leather portfolio. Upon closer examination of the ring later, they could clearly see the name 'Warwick'. J. B. Warwick and 'an unknown soldier' were buried in Steenbergen cemetery. In February 1945 the name of Guy Gibson was added to the wooden cross and in the spring of that year the inscription was altered to 'Wing Commander Guy Gibson VC DSO DFC and 156612 Squadron Leader J. B. Warwick DFC 19-9-44'.[31]

The most likely theory for the accident is that the fuel transfer cocks were not operated in the correct sequence and the engines ran out of fuel.[32]

Notes

1. Sergeant Austin Williams, the original front gunner, was sent to the Air Crew Refresher Course in Brighton for disciplinary reasons and when he returned at the end of May he was assigned to the crew of Pilot Officer William G. Divall who did not fly the Dams raid because of sickness among the crew. (Divall's crew and one other pulled out at the last minute which made selection for the Dams raid easier as there were only 19 serviceable Lancaster specials and 19 crews able to fly). Williams was KIA on 15/16 September 1943 along with the rest of Divall's crew on the Dortmund-Ems Canal raid. *The Dambuster Who Cracked the Dam: The Story of Melvin 'Dinghy' Young* by Arthur G. Thorning (Pen & Sword, 2008)

2. *Flying For Freedom: Life and Death in Bomber Command* by Tony Redding (Cerebus 2005).

3. *We Will Remember Them: Guy Gibson and the Dam Busters* by Jan van den Driesschen with Eve Gibson (Erskine Press 2004).

4. On 13 May it was back to Pilsen for another try at the Skoda works and during the evening, three days later, two vics of 617 Squadron Lancasters went over at low level. When he got back to the Mess Chandler was told that Scampton had been phoning up for him as Dinghy Young's gunner had gone sick. See *Tail Gunner: 98 Raids in World War II* by Chan Chandler DFC*, USSR Medal of Valour (Airlife 1999).

5. Burpee received his commission shortly after joining 617.

6. Thorning, op. cit.

7. Priscilla Lawson, a graduate of Brearley School, New York and Bryn Mawr College. Thorning, op. cit.

8. By 24 April the number of crews was reduced to 21 and Lovell's returned to 57 Squadron and were replaced by that of Sergeant William G. Divall, 21, from Thornton Heath, Surrey. Flight Sergeant Lanchester and crew had opted to leave 617 Squadron, as Guy Gibson wanted to replace the navigator. *The Dambusters* by John Sweetman, David Coward and Gary Johnstone (Time Warner 2003)

9. Thorning, op. cit.

10. To achieve the right altitude, two Aldis lamps fitted to the fuselage were played on to the water until they met in a figure of eight at precisely 60 feet. Judging the distance from the target proved equally simple, by making use of the twin towers, which flanked both the Möhne and Eder dams. A triangular wooden 'sight' was made with a peephole at the apex and nails at the other two ends. The bomb-aimer would peer through the peephole and when the nails lined up with the towers, release his mine.

11. *Living With Heroes: The Dam Busters* by Harry Humphries (The Erskine Press, 2003)

12. ibid.

13. Van den Driesschen and Gibson, op. cit.

14. Pilot Officer Geoff Rice flew so low that his Lancaster hit the sea before crossing the enemy coast and he lost its bomb. Rice aborted and flew back on two engines. *W-William* flown by Flight Lieutenant Les Munro RNZAF was damaged by flak over Vlieland on the Dutch coast and was also forced to abort. Harry Humphries, op. cit. said, 'first back was Les Munro. His intercom had been shot up. He arrived back with his bomb still aboard to the consternation of his ground crew. Then came Geoff Rice. After that someone had the bright idea of tuning in the radio to pick up the returning aircraft.'

15. Astell's navigator seems to have mistaken their position near Roosendaal. Astell changed track to a southern direction but after a while returned to his original course. This manoeuvre caused them to fall half a mile behind Young and Maltby. They were never seen again. See van den Driesschen and Gibson, op. cit. Astell's Lancaster was fired on by flak guns at Dorsten and was probably hit by shells after delaying when the others turned at a pinpoint. Two lines of tracer came up and Astell's gunners returned fire but *B-Baker* hit high-tension cables and crashed in flames near Marbeck, 3 miles SSE of Borken, Germany. There were no survivors.

16. Van den Driesschen and Gibson, op. cit.

17. There were six 20mm guns positioned on the Möhne dam, two of which were put out of action by bomb blast. One gun on the dam wall and the three near Günne continued throughout the remainder of the attack, putting up sporadic resistance against other aircraft even after the dam had been breached. A week later 23 year old Unteroffizier Karl Schütte who commanded the flak detachment and who helped man the 20mm gun on the North Tower, was decorated with the Iron Cross (Second Class). During the fourth attack, the North Tower gun failed after a premature explosion in the barrel. Helmuth Euler recalled that: 'We bashed away with all our strength trying to clear the jam with a hammer and a metal spike but it was no good. When it came to the fifth attack we did what we'd so often done in training – let loose with our carbines. There was just one flak gun on the road still firing at the aircraft – now they had it all their own way. There was a muffled explosion and when the spray had cleared a bit I had a quick look over the parapet down at the dam wall and shouted, "The wall's had it". The gunners didn't want to believe it at first but the breach got visibly bigger.' See *The Dams Raid Through the Lens* by Helmuth Euler (*After the Battle*, 2001), *Barnes Wallis' Bombs: Tallboy, Dambuster & Grand Slam* by Stephen Flower (Tempus, 2002) and *Dambuster – A Life of Guy Gibson VC* by Susan Ottaway (Pen & Sword, 1994).

18. When Maltby attacked he saw the small breach in the centre made by Young's Lancaster and noticed that there was crumbling along the crown so he turned slightly to port but remained straight and level, and their mine was released. It bounced four times and struck the wall and, according to the quote in the *Daily Mail*, 18 May 1943, 'sent up water and mud to a height of 1,000 feet. The spout of water was silhouetted against the moon. It rose with tremendous speed and then gently fell back. You could see the shock wave at the base of the jet.' Six minutes after Maltby's attack, the breach was confirmed. In the end Young's breach in the centre and Maltby's to the left were joined together by the force of the escaping water to make a single breach 76 metres wide. See *Breaking The Dams: The Story of Dambuster David Maltby & His Crew* by Charles Foster (Pen & Sword, 2008)
19. *Enemy Coast Ahead* by Wing Commander Guy Gibson VC DSO* DFC*.
20. He did. Badly damaged over the Möhne by the detonation of his own *Upkeep* weapon, Maudslay crashed near the German border between the Dutch village of Netterden and the German hamlet, Klein Netterden, 1-miles east of Emmerich, Germany. There were no survivors.
21. Brown made eight runs on the Sorpe but he was still not happy about dropping his mine. On the ninth he dropped incendiaries on the banks of the lake to try to identify the Sorpe dam through the swirling mist. On the eleventh run they saw the dam and Brown's mine was released. The mine exploded on impact, as it was dropped while flying across the dam and not dropped towards it in the planned method, without it bouncing off the surface of the water. The explosion caused a crumbling of 300 feet the crest of the dam wall.
22. The Germans, unsure of the dam's integrity, were forced to drain off over 50 per cent of the reservoir's capacity until the structure could be inspected and repaired.
23. Young's Lancaster was hit by flak at Castricum-aan-Zee, Holland and crashed into the sea with the loss of all the crew.
24. Townsend was ordered to attack the Ennerpe Dam on the Schelme River. He made three runs on the dam before his bomb-aimer, Sergeant Charles Franklin DFM, was satisfied. Their bomb was released, bounced once, and exploded 30 seconds after release. On leaving the target much opposition was encountered but, by great determination on his part, plus the navigational skill of Pilot Officer Cecil Howard from Western Australia, *O-Orange* made it safely back, landing at 06.15. Most of the latter part of the homeward trip was flown in broad daylight.
25. Van den Driesschen and Gibson, op. cit.
26. Pilot Officer W. H. T. Ottley's Lancaster was hit by flak near Hamm as they started to change their route when told to proceed to the Lister dam. Ablaze and with the outer port engine dead, Sergeant Fred Tees, the rear-gunner with 21 operations to his credit, heard Ottley say apologetically, 'Sorry boys. I'm afraid we've bought it.' Their Lancaster crashed just outside the town of Heesen, north-east of Dortmund and blew up. The impact separated the tail of the aircraft from the fuselage and threw Tees out of his rear turret. Severely burned and barely conscious he was found by a local farmer who took him to a flak battery nearby. In hospital doctors found several shell splinters in his back. He was later incarcerated in Stalag Luft V near the Lithuanian border. See van den Driesschen and Gibson, op. cit. The Lancasters piloted by Byers, Burpee

and Barlow, who hit high-tension cables on the outward flight at Haldern, 2½-miles ENE of Rees, were also lost. Barlow's *Upkeep* mine did not explode and next morning, assuming that it was a 'fuel tank' the Mayor of Haldern posed proudly beside the enormous weapon. He nearly passed out when told that the 'fuel tank' was in fact a heavy bomb! Two political prisoners were then forced to defuse the ignition, whereupon the mine was transported to Berlin for examination by German experts. Van den Driesschen and Gibson, op. cit. Pilot Officer V. W. Byers must have realized that he was off track when crossing Texel in the Frisian Islands, not Vlieland as was briefed. While climbing to get a coastal pinpoint, his Lancaster was hit by flak and the aircraft disappeared into the Waddenzee. Only Flight Sergeant James McDowell RCAF, the rear-gunner, was washed ashore and the Germans in Harlingen later buried him. Pilot Officer L. J. Burpee also climbed briefly after crossing the Dutch coast, to find a landmark and was hit almost at once by flak defending Gilze-Rijen airfield. Out of control the Lancaster crashed onto a barracks block on the airfield and exploded.
27. Humphries, op. cit.
28. Brown was awarded the CGM. Joe McCarthy, David Maltby, Mick Martin, Dave Shannon and Les Knight were awarded the DSO.
29. O'Shaughnessy could not find his gunners so he took off from Scampton at 19.30 hours without them in ED 918 AJ-F (the Lancaster flown on the Dam Buster's raid by Flight Sergeant Brown). He crashed 35 minutes later on the beach at Snettisham in Norfolk when he hit the sea, diving from 600 to 60 feet using spotlights to gauge the height of the dive. O'Shaughnessy and Flying Officer A. D. Holding were killed. The W/Op and the bomb-aimer were badly injured.
30. See *At First Sight; A Factual and anecdotal account of No.627 Squadron RAF,* researched and compiled by Alan B. Webb, 1991.
31. Van den Driesschen and Gibson, op. cit.
32. Many crews in 627 Squadron at the time have an opinion about why Gibson crashed. John Watt, a 627 Squadron Mosquito navigator, says, 'Between the two seats and to the rear of the pilot's there was a box on which was mounted two fuel transfer cocks (FTCs). Normally the two outer petrol tanks were run dry before the engine fuel supply was switched to the main tanks for the rest of the flight. When each outer tank was nearly empty a red warning light would come on and the appropriate FTC had to be operated immediately. Being tucked away behind his seat, it was not easy for the pilot to move these FTCs so the job was done by the navigator, who had to grope for the levers in the dark while hampered by a bulky flying suit, Mae West lifejacket, parachute harness and oxygen mask. I remember that we were pointing east at around 20,000 feet somewhere in the region of Lübeck – a very unfriendly area in 1944(!) when Johnny informed me that the port outer tank was nearly dry. When the red warning light came on I fumbled for the lever and turned it over to the main tank. Shortly afterwards the starboard light came on and that engine supply was similarly transferred to the main tank. Unfortunately the starboard light did not go out, but the port warning light appeared again. Both engines then decided that they could not operate efficiently without petrol and gave up trying! After pushing the nose down to gain airspeed to avoid falling out of the sky, Johnny's language made me realize that I had switched the starboard engine back on to the empty outer

tank while the port engine quietly ran out of essential fuel. Having very smartly returned the two FTCs to the correct setting we were fortunate to have the engines pick up again without the possible problem of an airlock in the fuel system.'

It was the opinion of many in 627 Squadron at the time that this is precisely what happened to Guy Gibson and his navigator, but unfortunately they were not quite so experienced on Mosquitoes. See Webb, op. cit.

Chapter 4

Bellicose and Beyond

Everybody said how much easier the 'Eyetie' trips would be after the Ruhr but of course we had to negotiate the Swiss Alps in each direction. Whilst passing through the Alps the Swiss, no doubt wishing to make a point of their neutrality, opened up with their AA fire, which although far from accurate was strange since it came down toward us instead of upwards! Visibility was good and the Alps was an awesome sight.

Warrant Officer Eddie Wheeler

Raids on Ruhr targets continued with Dortmund, the fourth heavy Bomber Command raid of May 1943, on the night of the 23rd/24th. Of 829 aircraft dispatched, 38 bombers failed to return. More than 2,000 tons of bombs, the biggest bomb load ever dropped anywhere in a single night, fell on the luckless city and the great weight fell in less than an hour between 01.00 and 02.00. Bombers all but jockeyed one another for position on the bombing run. Sergeant Ray Foster, rear-gunner in a Lancaster, was startled to see the starboard wing of another Lancaster flash by in front of his own tail-plane. The tip of one bomber's wing passed between the trailing edge of another bomber's main-plane and the leading edge of its tail-plane. 'I could have shaken hands with the bomb-aimer in the other Lancaster,' said Foster. Flight Lieutenant H. C. Lee of Felixstowe, piloting another Lancaster, made his attack late in the raid. But before then he had circled round the target for nearly an hour, awaiting his 'turn'. He was startled just as much as Sergeant Foster: 'As I made my attack a Stirling came streaking out only fifty feet above us and we were bumped by its slip-stream. By this time it was difficult to believe that it was a real town below; the place was so covered with fires and smoke.' The next morning came more accolades and another promise from the Commander-in-Chief, addressed to all crews in Bomber Command: 'In 1939 Goering promised that not a single enemy bomb would reach the Ruhr. Congratulations on having delivered the first 100,000 tons on Germany to refute him. The next 100,000, if he waits for them, will be even bigger and better bombs, delivered more accurately and in much shorter time.'

On the night of the 25/26 May 759 bombers were dispatched to bomb Düsseldorf. Twenty-seven bombers[1] were lost – 21 of which, were victims of night fighters. The raid was a failure due to the difficulty of marking in bad weather. By contrast, the raid on Wuppertal three nights later was the outstanding success of the Battle of the Ruhr. A large fire area developed in the narrow streets at the old centre of the extended, oblong shaped town, which had a population of almost 360,000. Wuppertal had been formed in 1920 by the union of the adjacent towns of Elberfeld and Barmen in the Upper Wupper Valley. The Barmen half of the town was the target for the 719 aircraft dispatched on that Saturday night which was moonless and 292 of them were Lancasters. Sixty-two aircraft turned back early but the remainder, aided by blind-marking systems, devastated about 1,000 acres of Barmen's built up area. Nearly 4,000 dwellings were destroyed, and 71 industrial and 1,800 domestic buildings were seriously damaged. Thirty-three bombers, seven of them Lancasters, were lost.[2]

Early in June Sergeant (later Warrant Officer) Ronald J. Clark and his all NCO crew were posted to 100 Squadron at RAF Waltham (Grimsby) having 'crewed up' in the time-honoured fashion at 1656 HCU (Heavy Conversion Unit) at Lindholme. Jim Siddell, the navigator, was a strong-minded Yorkshireman and the only married man in the crew. Harold 'Ben' Bennett, the flight engineer, was a Lancastrian from Preston and a Halton 'brat' who had joined the crew at Lindholme. Lishman 'Lish' Y. Easby, the wireless operator was from the North Riding and a former civil servant. Les

'Trigger' R. Simpson, a Londoner, was the 29 year old mid-upper gunner. His fellow Londoner was Doug Wheeler, the bomb-aimer. W. G. 'Geoff' Green from King's Lynn was the rear-gunner. The crew were allocated *A-Apple* in which to make six or seven training flights and once they realized that EE139 which, in early July, became *R-Roger,* was theirs a more personal name would have to be thought of. For the present they had other things to think about. The Battle of the Ruhr was in full flow and when the crew's names were posted at the bottom of the battle order for the first time on 11 June, the 'target for tonight' for them and 782 other crews was the heavily defended city of Düsseldorf. They safely negotiated 'Happy Valley's' flak and fighter defences between Cologne and Düsseldorf and bombed the rail yards and factories, returning shaken but un-injured to Waltham. That night the Squadron lost two aircraft and 13 men died with one surviving to become a POW.[3] During the month nine crews were lost, one third of the squadron strength. By mid-June only two crews survived from those that had reformed 100 Squadron at Waltham just a few months earlier. The chances of Ron Clark's crew surviving a tour of 30 operations did not appear likely. They discussed an identity for *R-Roger.* Inspiration was found from the film *Phantom of the Opera,* which was then showing in cinemas. Ron Clark felt that the grand operatic Teutonic sagas of the British and the Germans performed nightly over the Fatherland should have been accompanied by the music of Siegfried. Sergeant Harold 'Ben' Bennett, the flight engineer suggested painting a ghoulish hooded skeleton figure casting bombs out of the night sky. The ex-Halton apprentice might have been influenced by feelings of revenge from his time as a ground engineer in Fighter Command when he had suffered frequent bomb attacks. The name *Phantom of the Ruhr* and the skeletal figure were adopted, though afterwards Ron Clark felt that 'something a little less ghoulish would have been more appropriate'. In front of the *Phantom* motif was the mustard-coloured circular gas detection patch, which appeared on aircraft of No. 1 Group Bomber Command.

On 12/13 June the German defences destroyed 14 Lancasters and 10 Halifaxes from the 503 aircraft raid-ing Bochum. *A-Apple*'s second op resulted in the Lanc being hit by flak over the target, which caused damage to the rear turret but again Clark's crew returned safely.[4] Two nights later, on 14/15 June, the crew was forced to abort the operation to Oberhausen after 2 hours 38 minutes when the R/T failed. They jettisoned their bombs over the North Sea and the sortie was not counted. The target was cloud-covered but once again the *Oboe* sky

marking was accurate. Seventeen Lancasters, from the 197 dispatched, failed to return.[5] *Minnie the Moocher*[6] in 15 Squadron at Wickenby was attacked 30 miles from the target by three or four night fighters as Sergeant A. H. Moores, the pilot who was from Bromley in Kent, recalls:

'Sergeant J. D. Cushing my bomb-aimer, whose home was at Ealing, told me that there were two Junkers 88s below. The next thing I heard was the rear-gunner open up with a four-second burst. I think it was then that he was hit, because I heard nothing more and the intercom was cut off. Sergeant Norcliffe the wireless operator, a Halifax man, thought that we were on fire and in looking for the flames knocked off his oxygen tube. He was so dazed that he said to me, "Me, you, the pilot of this aircraft?" We all believed that there must be a fire owing to the overpowering reek of cordite – actually it came from an enemy shell – and I was expecting our 4,000-pound bomb to go off at any moment. But I was determined not to jettison the bomb after the distance we had flown. So we carried on to the target and when our full load had gone down I heaved a sigh of relief I was amazed to find that the aircraft could still fly true and level. I turned for home. We hit the coast right where we wanted to. When our badly damaged Lancaster touched down at base we found that the rear-gunner had been killed by a cannon-shell. It had smashed one side of the rear-turret. There were holes as big as coconuts in the fuselage and both starboard propellers had been hit. Luckily they had continued to function.'

Fourteen Lancasters were lost from a force of 212 heavies that raided Cologne on 16/17 June.[7] One of the 202 Lancasters which took part was flown by Wing Commander Peter Johnson, commanding 49 Squadron at Fiskerton. As a single-satellite station, Fiskerton did not warrant a group captain as station commander, so Johnson was also station commander. His rear-gunner was Pilot Officer 'Chan' Chandler, who had recently missed a date with certain death had he flown the Dams raid. Cologne was Chandler's 54th operation of the war and it was part of a spell in 'Happy Valley' follow-ing a visit to Dortmund and two to Düsseldorf with Johnson as his pilot. They had carried a maximum load of incendiaries to Dortmund and it was 'a sea of flame' when they left. Large areas were devastated, 2,000 buildings were destroyed and the Hoesch steelworks was put out of action. The 25 May raid on Düsseldorf was not so successful. There was heavy cloud over the target and the Germans had dummy markers and fires. The raid on 11 June had been more successful with 130 acres destroyed in the centre of the city and 140,000 people bombed out. It was another 'sea of flame' when they left. Johnson's Lancaster was hit and all the Perspex was shot out of the front. Johnson 'nearly froze to death' on the way home. On the Cologne trip the target was cloud-covered and marked by 16 heavy bombers of the Pathfinder Force (PFF) using H_2S. Chan Chandler recalls the operation in vivid detail:[8]

'One of the perks of being a tail end Charlie and flying backwards was the marvellous sunsets. Flying to the east the cabin crew were flying into the dark, but in the back, taking off at dusk or even an hour or two after dark, as we went up into the sky so the horizon extended and one could see a second sunset. In Lancs we flew much higher than Hampdens and from the air the colours were often indescribably beautiful. As we climbed eastwards the sunset would slowly fade to be replaced by a purple line with black darkness below and light above. It gave the most eerie sensation; it felt as if you were going to fly clear over the edge of the world like a lost soul flying out into space, never to return ...

"Five miles to target, skipper."

"I see it, seems as though they've got a good fire going."

"Well, maybe we'll stoke it up a bit."

'Obviously we were arriving well into the raid – at the start the streets would be outlined by incendiaries, showing the grid pattern of the town as if all the street lamps were on; then as the high explosives began to shatter the buildings, the fires would take hold, grow and coalesce into one gigantic fire.

"Turn on to target, steer 010."

"Roger, turning – steering 010."

'Up front they could see the blazing town laid out before them and the markers going down on the aiming point. In the tail I was still relentlessly searching the darkness, turret and guns maintaining their never-ending right, up, down, left, up, down. Now we were over the town, covered by a pall of smoke from the bombs and fires through which glowed the fires and the flashes from the bombs. The whole town seemed to be one obscene boiling mass beneath us. Left, right, left. The search now concentrated on the darkness above for the least trace of a flash of light that could be a fighter bearing down out of the darkness on to us, his prey, silhouetted by the fires below. Still, he wasn't likely to follow us down with all this flak about. We were flying through a cloud of black and brown smoke puffs.

"Bomb doors open."

'I felt the altitude alter and the pilot's correction as the big doors came down into the slipstream. Men, women, children, babies, cats, dogs, rats, mice; nothing would live down there. All would be literally boiled alive and then incinerated, the ashes covered by the falling buildings.

"Bombs gone" – the gentle thump as the bomb doors closed.

"Right – let's get the hell out of it." The skipper put the nose down to crack on some speed.

"Carry on steering 010 for about twenty minutes to turning point, skip."

"Roger, steering 010."

'Not far to the right of us a kite suddenly exploded into a ball of flame in mid-air.

"Some poor bastard's just bought it – looks like a night fighter – keep your eyes peeled, Chan."

"Wilco, skip."

"Turning point in one minute on to 355. Next turn approximately forty-five minutes."

"Roger."

"Corkscrew starboard – GO GO GO!"

'The giant Lanc lurched and dived, turned and climbed.

"OK skip, I think we've lost him – Ju 88 just hurtling past. Back on to 355."

'The minutes tick away, each bringing us a little closer to the coast and safety.

"Turning point in one minute – Turn port on to 290"

"Wilco, steering 290"

"Enemy coast ahead about five miles"

"Thanks bomb-aimer, let me know when we cross"

"Wilco -Crossing enemy coast – now"

"Thank you."

'Everyone breathes a sigh of relief as the comparative safety of the North Sea is reached. Still we have all four engines going – should be a doddle unless there are any intruders about.

'Down at the "lonely end" I unclasp my oxygen mask and light a cigarette, the smoke rasping on my dry throat. I pick up my Thermos and have a mouthful of cold coffee and curse at the taste. I relax a bit and enjoy my cigarette, but still with one hand directing the turret in its endless search up, down, right, left, up, down. Too many have been chopped thinking they were safe once they had crossed the enemy coast on the way home, only to find the fighters had chased them anything up to thirty miles out to sea.

'"Coast coming up" – another great sigh of relief all over the kite. Whatever happens now, we are home.

'At last we reach the drome, get in the circuit, and eventually it is our turn to land.

'"Wheels down." Everyone holds their breath. Are they going to? You can feel the part sound, part vibration as the undercart comes down; the sound and shiver of vibration runs down the kite as one side locks in. Two or three heart-stopping seconds later, clunk! and the other side locks in.

'Into the funnel – runway lights ahead – she goes down. The screech as the tyres touch the tarmac hits your ears, then the deceleration as the brakes come on. The tail drum and the tail wheel hammers and yammers until she slows down to taxiing speed. Round the peri-track to dispersal and brakes on, engines off for the first time in eight or nine hours.

'Those four bloody Merlins have shut up. You'd have been in a poor bloody funny state without 'em wouldn't you? Stop bitching and get out of there. Too tired – I'll sleep here. Oh fuck – there's bloody debriefing isn't there? Almost too tired to open the turret doors. Crawl across the spar into the fuselage; legs won't work, have to crawl to the door and stick my feet out backwards. Jimmy the W/Op guides them on to the ladder and helps me down and then gives Mike a hand. A flight van rolls up. We all fall into it and it takes us off to debriefing. One more for the log-book – how many more will we manage, I wonder?'

His next op was on 20/21 June as mid-upper gunner flying with Flight Lieutenant Tommy Taylor. Code-named Operation *Bellicose,* 56 Lancaster bomber crews and four Pathfinders of 97 Squadron were briefed to make a precision attack on the Zeppelin works at Friedrichshafen on the shores of Lake Constance (the Bodensee) near the Swiss border. Zeppelins were no longer being built or housed at the factory, bombed by Royal Naval Air Service Avro 504s in November 1914, but was now turning out *Würzburg* radar, which was used to locate RAF bombers approaching the night fighter zones on the continent. There was also a factory nearby making diesel engines for U-boats. Due to the target's distance from England it would have been extremely dangerous to try a daylight raid and because of the short nights in the summer it would not have been possible to attack and return under the cover of darkness. It was therefore decided to fly on to Allied bases at Blida and Maison Blanche in North Africa to confuse the German night fighter defences in France then, after rearming and refuelling, to attack Spezia on the return trip. It thus became the first 'shuttle trip'. 'As the natives of those parts had rather nasty habits, which included collecting essential bits of one's anatomy' recalls Chan Chandler, 'the Air Ministry thoughtfully provided us with pieces of folded cardboard printed in both English and Arabic to entice them away from their usual practices with the promise of baksheesh, so long as they returned their aircrew 'virgo intacta'. The Air Ministry had obviously taken great trouble to prepare these 'goolie chits', as the aircrew called them, but had either overlooked, or at any rate forgotten, to tell us that none of these blighters could read!'[9]

At Syerston, a pre-war permanent station on the Fosse Way with two Lancaster squadrons, 61 and 106, the bombers began taking off at around 21.45 hours. Pilot Officer Ward Parsons RCAF from Cayuga in QR-L and four other Lancasters of 61 Squadron headed south over East Anglia at the start of a five-hour flight across France and southern Germany to the target area. By this time the Canadian's crew had 25 ops under their belts and they were considered by the 'sprog' crews to be 'Gen Men' and one of the most experienced crews on the Squadron. Being posted to 61 Squadron suited Sergeant 'Nobby' Clark, Parsons' WOp/AG, fine because the main feature of the squadron badge was the Lincoln Imp and, as he was from Thorney and went to school in Lincoln, it had seemed a good omen. So far the omens had been good and as a result of their experience, Parsons' crew, with four other seasoned crews, had been temporarily taken off ops to carry out a series of flying exercises prior to taking part in the special operation.[10]

The raid was also the first to employ a master bomber, Group Captain Leonard Slee DSO DFC to control the main force in the target area sending instruction by radiotelephone over the target. This was introduced following Guy Gibson's successful use of VHF on the Dams' raid a month earlier. The Channel was crossed at maximum height and gradually the Lancasters came down to between 2,000–3,000 feet and then higher again when they crossed the Rhine. Aboard Slee's aircraft was Major Johnny Mullock MC the 5 Group flak liaison officer who had flown with Guy Gibson to Italy and who had participated in raids over the Ruhr to observe the German defences first hand.[11] Mullock was to recall:

'Approaching the French coast at 19,000 feet we encountered heavy cloud and electric storms up to 24,000 feet. We therefore decided to come down below the front and lost height to 5,000 feet. We were suddenly engaged by the defences of Caen or the outer defences of Le Havre – owing to technical difficulties with navigation instruments we were uncertain of our exact position. Four 4-gun heavy flak positions engaged us for about four minutes. During the time we altered course by about 30 degrees every eight seconds, alternatively losing and gaining height by 1,000 feet. The flak bursts were mainly 300–500 feet behind and about the same distance above us. It was noticed that the rate of fire of the guns was extremely high! We flew on below cloud at 2,500–3,000 feet across France and encountered no further opposition.

'About 45 minutes from the target area by which time we had increased our height to 6,000 feet, we had to feather our port inner engine, which had been emitting sparks. And so we continued on three engines until we sighted Lake Constance. As the port inner engine is essential for the Mk.XIV bombsight it was unfeathered and allowed to windmill but shortly after, the engine caught fire. We were unable to feather it or extinguish the fire, which grew in intensity. We jettisoned our bombs and the order to prepare to abandon the aircraft was given, first diving across the lake into Switzerland and subsequently turning the aircraft towards Germany. We were about to bale out, expecting the petrol tanks to explode, when the engine seized up and the fire went out. By this time we were at 4,000 feet but were able to maintain height.'

Slee meanwhile, had handed over control to his deputy, Wing Commander Cosme L. Gomm DSO DFC of 467 Squadron flying *Y-Yankee*. The weather at the target was clear, with Lake Constance and surrounding area bathed in bright moonlight, which enabled the Pathfinders to place their markers very close to the target. Circling Friedrichshafen the crews awaited instructions from the deputy leader. Both attacking elements had been briefed to bomb visually from a height of between 5,000–10,000 feet. There were approximately 16–20 heavy flak guns and 18–20 light flak guns and about 25 searchlights, all within a radius of about six to eight miles of the target. They were more active than expected so Gomm ordered the bombers to climb to the safer height of 15,000 feet before attacking. The first wave of bombers dropped their bombs on the Target Indicators laid down by the Pathfinders and the second wave was briefed to make a time and distance run from a prominent point on the shore of the lake to the estimated position of the factory. Aboard Ward Parson's Lancaster, Sergeant Frank Poole, the bomb-aimer from Weston-super-Mare, got his bombs away on the target. Stronger winds at the higher altitudes caused problems but around 10 per cent of the bombs hit the relatively small target. After the Lancasters had completed their bombing runs they flew south over the French Alps and Mediterranean to North Africa for a landing at either Maison Blanche or Blida airfields. Slee's Lancaster stayed over Lake Constance for 13 minutes and the crew had an excellent view of the attack, as Major Mullock recalls:

'Several aircraft were coned but not for any length of time. Leaving the target area, we continued to fly over the Alps. By skirting the peaks we eventually crossed, gradually gaining height to above about 14,000 feet. The 600-mile flight over the Mediterranean was slow, as we were limited to 140 mph to prevent overheating. Eventually we sighted the Algerian coast and landed safely at Maison Blanche at 07.52 hours, after a flight of ten hours and thirteen minutes.'

Chan Chandler adds:

'On arrival the force circled, waiting for the markers to be dropped by the PFF. Inevitably, some over flew Swiss air space. The Swiss had all their lights on, which was a very pleasant sight, but of course had to demonstrate their neutrality by firing at us. However, we noticed that their flak was bursting well below us. Story has it that some wag flashed down on the Aldis lamp, "You are firing very low" and the Swiss flashed back, "Thank you, we know".

'Soon after the start of the raid the target was obscured by smoke from the bomb blasts. The third special feature of this raid now came into operation. The PFF were called in to drop flares along the shore-line of the lake so that the bombers could identify a prominent landmark. Then, knowing the distance and the bearing from the landmark to the target, they could make a timed run and drop their bombs in the right place. As the target was heavily defended all the aircraft remained circling to distract the flak from those on the bombing run, and then, on instruction from the master bomber, all headed for Maison Blanche near Algiers. Luckily we got to the landing strip without going down in the desert, so we did not have to put the "goolie chits" to the test. However, I have since wondered how many aircrew's bits it took before word filtered back to the caravans that these bits of card could be worth money.'[12]

Before leaving Syerston crews had been briefed that weather conditions at the Algerian airfields in the early morning would not present any problems. 'However' recalls Nobby Clark, 'when we arrived over Maison Blanche at about 1,200 feet we could only get fleeting glimpses of the runway as banks of low mist drifted across the airfield. There were already a number of aircraft in the circuit and pilots were continually calling the tower for permission to land, as fuel was getting short after ten hours in the air. Instead of calling each aircraft down in turn, all we got back from the American controller was, "Ship on the approach now, come on in, the runway's right below you". This confusion resulted in everyone attempting to get down at the same time. Even after landing the danger from collision was not over. As we slowed down at the end of the runway, Danny Towse our rear-gunner from

Kilham, Bridlington, shouted over the intercom, "For God's sake Skip get off the ******* runway quick, there's another kite coming up fast behind", or words to that effect! Maison Blanche was a primitive desert airstrip and while there we all lived under canvas. However to ease the boredom we did managed to squeeze in a visit to the city of Algiers. Quite a change from our usual night out in Newark.'[13]

The new bombing procedures tried during Operation *Bellicose* were deemed successful. In addition, when reconnaissance photographs were examined they showed that 10 per cent of the bombs hit the target factory and many of the near misses destroyed other industrial premises. By flying on to North Africa after the raid the bomber force confused the German night fighters that were waiting for them to return directly to England. As a result there were no Lancaster losses during either part of this operation. On 23 June 52 of the Lancasters that had bombed Friedrichshafen were bombed up and the aircrews were briefed to attack the oil depot at the northern Italian port of La Spezia. After completing the operation the crews were instructed to return to their home bases in England. Eight of the aircraft that bombed Friedrichshafen remained in North Africa for maintenance. Sergeant Nobby Clark continues:

'We took off in QR-L at 20.05 hours and after a one and a half hour flight over the Mediterranean we arrived off the Italian coast just south of the target area. In the distance the skipper saw a target indicator cascading down over the target and quickly turned on our bombing run. Our debrief entry in the Squadron log for this attack records the following: "Pilot Officer Parsons saw one green marker and after identifying the bay visually, bombed 500 yards north of an oil fire from 11,250 feet at 2133 hours. Once clear of the target area we headed northwest over the Maritime Alps and five hours later, after an uneventful flight over France, landed safely back at RAF Syerston at 0437 hours."

'My crew's last two ops were both to Gelsenkirchen, the first on 25 June and the second on 9 July. The latter was my 30th and last sortie of my operational tour and was destined to end in tragic circumstances. Shortly after we had bombed the target, we ran into heavy flak and the only fragment of shrapnel that penetrated the fuselage hit our navigator, Sergeant Bob Dyson and he died shortly afterwards. We headed west for home and by using radio aids and a bit of rough navigation by the second bomb-aimer, whom we had on board for his introduction to ops, our skipper got us safely back to RAF Manston in Kent. We returned to our base at Syerston on 11 July. Two days later the Squadron Commander informed us that it had been decided our tour of operations had been completed and we would shortly be posted as Instructors for training new aircrew.'[14]

In England meanwhile, the Lancaster crews had been kept busy during a week of sustained operations. They had only one day of rest then two nights in succession to the Ruhr area, Krefeld to the west of the Rhine on 21/22 June[15] and the twin towns of Mülheim and Oberhausen near Düsseldorf on 22/23 June.[16] On 25/26 June when 473 bombers attacked Gelsenkirchen and Bochum, 31 aircraft including 13 Lancasters were lost. Sergeant J. S. 'Johnny' Johnston was the flight engineer in *Z-Zebra*[17] in 103 Squadron at RAF Elsham Wolds flown by Flight Sergeant Alan E. Egan RAAF, which was shot down at Bechtrup north of Lüdinghausen.

'Somebody shouted, "There's a yellow marker". Course we all looked away. Next minute I saw this great big wing above my head (as flight engineer I was standing up). We were hit just like as if it was a three-ton truck. *BANG!* We held together for a minute. Then she screamed right across the port wing, hit the propellers and we went out of control. Both engines burst into flames. I got thrown to the floor and banged my head. I got up, or tried to. I could see Alan trying to get her straight. Then she dipped her nose and I went straight down into the nose with all the junk that was on the floor and landed on top of the bomb-aimer. All of a sudden, the nose broke off. I just saw it start to crack. The bomb-aimer and I fell out. I was surrounded by bits of cowlings and pieces of metal all floating around me. I thought I was going up instead of the bits of metal going down. All the planes were coming in like little mosquitoes – line upon line of them. A yellow light from the fires that were just starting lighted up Gelsenkirchen. It was like a watery sunset. Bombs were going down like big golden darts in the yellow light. It was horrifying.

'I was captured and told to climb into the back of a truck. Up I got and in the darkness I could just see some boxes. I put my hand out and felt a flying boot. I thought, 'Gee, that's all right, I want a pair of flying boots'. I put it on and felt around for the other one. All of a sudden I realized that they were soaking wet. I felt horrible because I thought it was blood. Then it hit me. I was sitting on top of coffins. I counted them. There were five on the top layer and six on the bottom. Afterwards I found out that four of them were members of my crew and seven of others.[18]

'At the first stop on the train to my POW camp with two Luftwaffe guards there was a Red Cross train just opposite and I saw little children with bandages round their eyes and their hands on one another's shoulders. A nurse in front and one behind were leading them to the train. This was the first time that I realized what war was really like. It was easy when you were dropping bombs up there. I turned to one of my guards, a good German and asked, "*Where's this?*" He said, "*Mülheim*" (which was still smouldering from a raid the previous Tuesday). I kept silent. I had been on that one too.'[19]

Cologne was subjected to three consecutive heavy raids in late June and early July. Warrant Officer Eddie Wheeler, WOp/AG in 97 Squadron, recalls the raid on 28/29 June when 608 heavies were dispatched:

'After six days we resumed marking operations, this time against poor old Cologne again. We were allocated another *N for Nan*. With no cloud and excellent visibility we bombed from 20,000 feet releasing our markers and 10,000-lb bomb load, which resulted in a huge explosion. Landing at 03.40 hours we decided on another thrash to Cambridge that evening. I had now completed my fiftieth operational sortie, which was as good a reason as any to celebrate.'[20]

A follow-up raid on Cologne by 653 bombers including 293 Lancasters went ahead on 3/4 July when single-engined *Wilde Sau* (Wild Boar) fighter pilots of the *Nachtjagd Versuchs Kommando* (Night Fighting Experimental Command) were employed for the first time. The freelancing single-engined night fighting tactics were hastily introduced under the command of *Ritterkreuzträger* Oberst Hans-Joachim 'Hajo' Herrmann. The former bomber pilot reasoned that his fighter pilots could identify bombers over a German city using the light of the massed searchlights and Pathfinder flares and the flames of the burning target below. Then they could shoot them down. *Geschwader Herrmann* was equipped with Fw 190s and Bf 109s thrown into the fray in *Wilde Sau* operations, a primitive form of night fighting in which the pilots tried to intercept and destroy the bombers in the glare of fires burning below and with the aid of searchlight beams played on the cloud base, forming a *Mattscheibe* or 'ground glass screen' against which the bombers showed up in silhouette. The first *Wilde Sau* operation over Cologne on 3/4 July met with instant success and 12 of the 30 aircraft that were lost were claimed shot down over the target by the freelancing single-engined night fighters.[21]

There were other losses too. That night 26 Lancasters of 460 Squadron RAAF were drawn up at Binbrook, Lincolnshire, for the attack on Cologne. The aircrews and most of the ground crews were at their evening meal when, suddenly, at 18.00 hours, an alarm came. Through an electrical short circuit the entire bomb load of one Lancaster had been released and had fallen to the ground, where the incendiary part of the load was burning fiercely beneath the aircraft. Up went the 4lb incendiary clusters with the 500lb HEs roasting in the centre of the inferno. Two shocked maintenance crewmembers inside the bomber at the time leapt out and tried to roll the 4,000lb bomb away from the mass of burning incendiaries. They saw it was hopeless and ran for safety. They had covered 400 yards when the 4,000lb cookie and the 500lb bombs exploded, scattering the incendiaries among other aircraft. The two airmen were blown to the ground, but escaped with shock. Then the Lancaster next to the first burst into flames and two minutes later its load, which included another 4,000lb bomb and three 1,000lb bombs, exploded, wrecking the bomber, throwing still more incendiaries among the aircraft and setting fire to starter trolleys.

With several airmen, Wing Commander C. E. Martin DFC the squadron CO manned the station fire tender and extinguished as many of the incendiary bombs as possible. Then someone saw smoke pouring from another bomber a little distance away. Martin climbed inside the aircraft with Flight Sergeant A. E. Kan of Victoria, the latter still shell-shocked from the original explosion and they tried to fight the flames with hand extinguishers. When the flames were partly under control another airman climbed into the bomber and disconnected the electrical leads to prevent more bombs from being dropped to the ground. By this time the fire was intense enough to cause the magnesium contents of the fuselage construction to flare up. Almost suffocated, the men had to leap out. Martin climbed on top of the burning, fully loaded bomber and stood there directing the operations until the flames were out. In the meantime the armament officer had checked the delay mechanism of the 1,000lb bombs scattered by the explosions, and other airmen and members of the RAF Regiment attached to the station put out the remaining incendiaries. The flight commanders posted guards around the dangerous bombs still lying around the fragment-strewn field. In half an hour the danger was past, and the ground crews began getting as many aircraft as possible ready for the night's operation. In spite of damaged runways and shrapnel-torn bombers, 17 aircraft roared off the patched-up airfield that night, and all returned safely some hours later after a successful attack on Cologne.[22]

On 8/9 July when Cologne was raided again, seven out of 282 Lancasters were lost.[23] The next main force raid was directed to Gelsenkirchen on 9/10 July when seven Halifaxes and five Lancasters went missing from a force of 418 aircraft. At this time 101 Squadron was the only one of its kind to combine *Airborne Cigar* (*ABC*) electronic countermeasure duties[24] with regular bombing operations, which meant that the squadron flew on almost every major bombing raid until the end of the war. Consequently, 101 Squadron lost 113 Lancasters on 308 raids, plus another 33 destroyed in crashes in the UK. Flight Lieutenant William Alexander 'Scrym' Scrymgeour-Wedderburn's crew was the only one to survive a tour on 101 during 1943. Sergeant Les King, W/Op in the crew, recalls one particularly memorable sortie in *N-Nan*, the crew's 15th, on the night of 12/13 July when 295 Lancasters were dispatched on an 11 hour round trip to Turin, a distance of 1,350 miles there and back:

'It was our first experience to Italy and we experienced very severe weather over the Alpine range. The electrical storms in the Mont Blanc area caused problems like flying blind hoping our altitude was sufficient to clear the highest peaks and St Elmo's Fire was noticeable on the propeller tips and astrodome and when I wound in our trailing aerial it was like a Catherine Wheel firework. We developed engine trouble in an inboard engine when the magneto supercharger failed so we had to feather the propeller but we proceeded to the target and bombed accordingly at the required height of 16,000 feet. The problem now was knowing we would be unable to climb over the Alps but in an emergency we could follow our briefing instructions and proceed to Blida in North Africa. Sergeant Robert Craddock our rear-gunner became concerned, as he was due to become father and his wife certainly would be distraught if we went missing even if later we returned safely. Bill Wedderburn made a decision to get back to base by asking Flight Sergeant Roy Sidwell, the navigator, for a course to fly westwards over southern France, skirting the Pyrenees and reaching the Bay of Biscay to go down to sea level. (Being July daylight would be early so we would be sitting ducks on a more direct route home across France). Eventually we skirted Brittany and reached the coastline of Cornwall. I had made more than one attempt to contact base to notify them of our situation but our signal was too weak at sea level. (I found out later that Gibraltar received my signal and being a powerful station had passed on my attempted message). We thought we would land at St Eval in Cornwall and refuel but our skipper consulted the flight engineer regarding fuel remaining and decided to make base at Ludford Magna. After being airborne 11¼ hours we landed with only enough fuel remaining for five more minutes when all three engines would have cut out.'[25]

Warrant Officer Eddie Wheeler the Wop/AG on *N-Nan* in 97 Squadron adds:

'Everybody said how much easier the "Eyetie" trips would be after the Ruhr but of course we had to negotiate the Swiss Alps in each direction. Whilst passing through the Alps the Swiss, no doubt wishing to make a point of their neutrality, opened up with their AA fire, which although far from accurate was strange since it came down toward us instead of upwards! Visibility was good and the Alps were an awesome sight. Over Turin we came down to 13,000 feet as the flak was haphazard and didn't present the problems we had come to be used to over Germany. With no cloud and clear visibility the target was defined and we took our time to ensure accuracy of bombing. Bomb-aimer Peter Burbridge's words were, "Piece of cake"! Thirteen Lancasters including one flown by South African Wing Commander John Dering Nettleton VC, CO of 44 (Rhodesia) Squadron were lost.[26] An unidentified night fighter shot Nettleton's aircraft down over the Channel on the return. Safely back at RAF Waltham an ice-cream cornet representing a raid on an Italian target was painted underneath Ron Clark's cockpit window alongside the yellow bombs and one red bomb, which signified a trip to the "Big City". Ron and his crew would be responsible for two of the four cornets on *Phantom of the Ruhr*'s bomb log.

An area bombing raid on Aachen on 13/14 July resulted in bombs being released by 374 aircraft, mainly Halifaxes, which devastated large parts of the city, reducing almost 3,000 individual buildings, containing almost 17,000 flats/apartments to rubble and killing or injuring over 1,000 people for the loss of 20 aircraft.[27] Aachen reported that that raid was a *Terrorangriff* of the most severe scale . . .'

Two nights later 617 Squadron carried out its first operation since the Dam's raid in May. Guy Gibson had been told that he had done enough operations and was not allowed to fly again. Squadron Leader George Holden DSO DFC* MID had taken command of the 'Dam Busters' in July. Holden, who as CO of 102 Squadron, had flown Halifaxes on raids over the Alps to Italy, has been described as, 'slight and youthful with fair wavy hair but a brusque manner. Before the war he had worn a bowler and carried a rolled umbrella but was a very tough young man. He had felt very sick once but kept flying on ops, for over a week till he nearly collapsed after landing one night and went to the doctor who said he thought he'd had pleurisy but seemed to be nearly all right now.' It had been decided to keep the Dam Busters in being as an 'old lags' squadron (Harris' affectionate and respectful name for experienced men who only wanted to fly ops) and to use it for independent precision raids on small targets. These would be carried out using the Stabilizing Automatic Bomb Sight (SABS), which had been invented at Farnborough in 1941 and incorporated a bulky gyro. In perfect conditions SABS could aim a bomb very accurately but a bomber using it had to run perfectly straight and level up to the target for 10 miles. Harris said this would result in too many bomber losses but the argument was that SABS could be used economically by a small force operating at a fraction under 20,000 feet over a well marked target. At 5 Group the Air Officer Commanding (AOC), Air Vice-Marshal The Honourable Sir Ralph A. Cochrane KBE CB AFC intended that 617 be trained to use SABS and deliver Barnes Wallis' new 10-ton bombs coming off the drawing board.[28]

In the meantime the targets on the night of 15/16 July were two power and transformer stations in northern Italy. The intention was to disrupt the supply of electricity to the railways carrying German troops and supplies to the battle front in Sicily using 12 Lancasters of 617 Squadron and a dozen more from 5 Group. Because of the distance which was beyond the round trip range of the Lancaster, landfall would be made at Blida airfield, 30 miles from Algiers in North Africa. Six of the Dam Busters were led by Holden to Aquata Scrivia near Genoa and the other six to San Pola d'Enza near Bologna were led by Dams' veteran Squadron Leader David J. H. Maltby DSO DFC. The raids were not successful. No flares or markers were carried and the targets were partially hidden by haze. Maltby reported that he had bombed on target and had seen blue flashes. However one bomb and some of the incendiaries 'hung up' but they had successfully dropped these on the Genoa-Spezia railway line.[29] There was little opposition and two Lancasters of the supporting force were lost.

The 9 Squadron Lancaster flown by Flying Officer M. R. Head RNZAF had taken off from Bardney at 22.15 hours. There was a full moon and visibility was fairly good throughout the flight. After crossing the French coast the New Zealander flew low on a moderate weaving course. Over France a large number of AI radar indications were received, some of them lasting for several minutes. Frequent *Monica* indications were also received during a large part of the flight. At first Head took corkscrew action on receiving the indications but, as this had no apparent effect and no other aircraft were sighted, he came to the conclusion

that the instrument was unserviceable. They flew on to the rendezvous point at the southern end of Lake Garda where R/T communication was established with the leader of the formation. A further five minutes were spent awaiting the arrival of another aircraft but this failed to turn up so the remaining five set course together for the target. Crews had been briefed to make a time and distance run from the southern tip of Lake Garda to a point on the main line west of Reggio where it ran parallel to the main road.

Head's crew were unable to make an accurate first run and turned to make a second attempt: A few seconds later the New Zealander glanced ahead and saw another Lancaster approximately on the same level, at 1,800 feet. The other aircraft was a Lancaster of 50 Squadron piloted by Flight Lieutenant C. H. J. Hunt, which had taken off from Skellingthorpe. It was only about 100 yards off when first seen and there appeared to be no time to avoid a collision by making a turn. Head therefore pulled the control column hard back in the hope that he would pass over the other Lancaster. Hunt apparently sighted Head's Lancaster at the same time and began to turn to port, but almost immediately a collision occurred. As far as Head could judge the starboard wing tip of the other Lancaster hit his port wing about midway along. He believed that the top of the fuselage of the other aircraft struck the underside of the fuselage, possibly its mid-upper turret. His own mid-upper gunner reported a large hole in the fuselage but did not specify its exact position and he also heard someone say that there was a lot of blood near Sergeant E. W. Edwards, the navigator's position. Hunt's Lancaster was seen to crash and burst into flames near Traversetolo 20 kilometres from Parma. There were no survivors. Head at once noticed that the spinner of his port inner propeller had come off and he immediately feathered this engine. The trimming controls of both the rudder elevators were unserviceable and in order to fly straight and level it was necessary to keep the control column pressed right forward and the rudder hard over to starboard. After a short interval he noticed that the port outer engine was only revolving slowly and that the temperature had dropped right down. He feathered this engine also. The rear-gunner reported that he was jammed in his turret and Head therefore decided that he would have to make a crash-landing. He tried to jettison the bomb load but the bomb doors would not open. The bomb-aimer therefore went aft and released them manually. Most of the load fell clear through the hole made by collision, but the bombs could not be released. Meanwhile Edwards had also gone aft and had managed to free the rear-gunner. The decision was taken to try to reach the coast and ditch but the Lancaster continued to lose height and eventually Head ordered the crew to bale out. They all left the aircraft safely except for Edwards, whose parachute caught on the aircraft and he was killed when the Lancaster crashed at Mirandola (Bologna) 30 kilometres from Modena. The other members of the crew were taken prisoner.[30]

All the Dam Busters landed safely at Blida. Les Munro's Lancaster was damaged by shrapnel from his own bomb casing, damage was caused to the bomb-aimer's panel and his starboard tyre burst, although he managed to land safely. After landing Flight Lieutenant Joe McCarthy DSO DFC threw his parachute down disgustedly and said, 'If we'd only carried flares we could've seen what we were doing.'

In North Africa bad weather grounded the Lancasters for 10 days and they finally flew home on Saturday, 24 July via Leghorn (Livorno) where bombs were dropped through the persistent haze into the harbour below. The bombing was uneventful, carried out on a time-and-distance run from Corsica. Back at Scampton the crews unloaded the Lancasters. In spite of everything they could hardly regard it as a fruitless trip, as they struggled to the Mess with crates of figs, dates and oranges, bottles of red wine and Benedictine. Flight Lieutenant Mick Martin DSO DFC jumped out of *P-Popsie* wearing a fez!

The Battle of the Ruhr was fought over 99 nights and 55 days – 5/6 March–23/24 July 1943 – and 24,355 heavy bomber sorties were flown.[31] At the start of the Battle of the Ruhr Bomber Harris had been able to call upon almost 600 heavies for main force operations and at the pinnacle of the battle, near the end of May, more than 800 aircraft took part. Innovations such as Pathfinders to find and mark targets with their TIs and wizardry such as *Oboe,* which enabled crews to find them, were instrumental in the mounting levels of death and destruction. Little it seemed could be done to assuage the bomber losses which, by the end of the campaign, had reached high proportions. During the Battle of the Ruhr Sergeant James W. Boynton was a 'tail end Charlie' or rear-gunner with 156 Squadron. He flew a Pathfinder tour of ops with Flight Lieutenant R. E. Young and crew from RAF Warboys near Huntingdon. For 10 of those operations they flew in *N-Nan.*[32]

'At Warboys,' recalls Boynton,[33] 'it was usually about 11 o'clock in the morning that word got around the station that ops were on for the following night. Aircrew looked for their names on the Ops Battle Order that was posted in the Squadron office. Some names appeared on the list despite having been on ops the previous night and not landing back at base until six or seven that morning. These crews had to be awakened by the billet orderlies at mid-day in order for them to prepare for the coming operation. After a mid-day lunch, our crew would meet in the aircrew locker room, draw our chutes and then board the crew bus, which took us out to our aircraft's dispersal. Once the ground crew had completed the aircraft's daily inspections and dealt with any problems reported from the previous operation, we took her up on a night flying test (NFT). This usually lasted about an hour and consisted of each crewmember checking over all his operational equipment and making sure everything was working correctly.

'The skipper would fly out over the north Norfolk coast to the coastal inlet called the Wash. After checking the area for shipping, we would drop a flame float target into the sea and fire off a few hundred rounds to make sure the eight Browning .303 machine guns were working properly. It also provided good gunnery practice. After returning to base and taxiing the aircraft to its dispersal, the petrol bowser would arrive and the ground crew would begin to fill the aircraft's petrol tanks and the armourers set about loading the correct Target Indicators (TIs) and bomb load aboard the aircraft for the coming operation. If we had had a rough week doing a few ops on the trot, the Medical Officer (MO) would issue us with wakey-wakey pills to keep us awake and alert during the long flight. However, we never took them until the very last moment because sometimes the op was scrubbed just before take-off due to dodgy weather en route, which meant another sleepless night if we had taken a pill too early.

'During the early months of 1943, operational briefings were usually held at 16.00 hours. The actual take-off times depended upon the distance to the target, weather and the rise and setting of the moon. After specialist briefings all the aircrews came together in the Squadron briefing room. At the far end of the room a large map of Western Europe was displayed, with thick red tapes, the route to and from the target. When everyone was settled, the Station Commander arrived and various officers gave us the gen on the night's operation. The Flying Control officer gave us times of take-off in aircraft order. Next the Intelligence Officer described the route out and home, the time to open the attack with our marker flares and where they were to be placed in the target area. Sometimes we would be briefed to drop markers en route to keep the main force on the correct path away from heavy flak. Bitter experience had shown that anyone wandering off track 15 or 20 miles would almost certainly become a sitting duck for both fighters and flak. The Squadron Commander then briefed us on where the most flak and fighters were likely to be encountered, lastly the Met man would give us his weather forecast en route, over the target and for our return in the early hours. Unfortunately he usually got it wrong somewhere along the way, resulting in some of the experienced crews taking the Mickey out of him by shouting out "Was your seaweed wet or dry today?" such banter helped to relieved the tension. All the pilots and navigators would set their watches on the time check, the Station Commander would wish us luck and the briefing was over. This was followed by a pre-op meal and then we would all try and relax until about an hour and half before take-off when the whole crew would meet up again in the locker room. There we collected all our flying gear including our chutes, Mae West, helmets, flying boots, silk under gloves and gauntlets. In addition, because of the intense cold experienced in Lancaster rear turrets, gunners were issued with special electrically heated clothing, which included an overall, gloves and slippers that fitted inside flying boots. All of which offered some welcome comfort and protection against the extremely low temperatures encountered above 10,000 feet. However, on hot summer nights I never got fully dressed in my flying gear until the aircraft had climbed to a cooler altitude. If I had dressed up in my full flying kit on the ground my perspiration would have frozen on me once airborne. After kitting out we went by crew bus out to the aircraft, which was by then bombed up, and ready to go.

'On take-off there was always a small crowd of officers, WAAFs and airmen to wave us off. While on the take-off run I always turned the rear turret facing the port beam with the turret back doors open just in case of a ground loop crash. In many such accidents the rear-gunner often came off the best as the aircraft's main beam area took most of the impact. At around 6,000 feet I left the turret, got fully dressed and then climbed back in to settle down to concentrate on the task ahead. Later, when I started to feel cold I'd plug my electrically heated suit into the aircraft's power supply. We had climbed to our operational height of 20,000 feet by the time we reached the coast and, sometimes on a clear starlit night, I would watch the Norfolk shoreline rapidly fade into the distance and wonder if we would ever see it again. Over the North Sea our skipper always flew straight and level until the bomb-aimer sighted the enemy coast. After that it was weaving all the way to the target. In our opinion to fly straight and level over enemy territory was just plain suicide for a slow heavily laden bomber. At our first crew meeting, the skipper said he believed the only way to survive a tour of forty Pathfinder operations was to have a well disciplined and highly trained crew and a big slice of all the luck going. After completing a few operations we realized that we would encounter more heavy flak areas the deeper we penetrated German air space. So the procedure we adopted to counter the predicted flak batteries, was to fly in an irregular pattern by descending 500–600 feet and then climbing slowly back and also weaving from left to right of the set course. The whole crew, apart from the navigator, were on fighter and friendly aircraft collision watch. The gun turrets on our aircraft never stopped moving from side to side for the duration of the operation. This constant movement and scanning the sky made our aircraft a hard target for both German night fighters and ground defences.

'Once over enemy territory many aircraft would be seen going down in flames on the way to the target. Those I actually saw crash on the ground I reported to the navigator giving him their approximate position, he then plotted them on his chart. On some deep penetration operations over Germany I saw a dozen or more aircraft go down behind and many more burning on the ground. One of the most hated anti-bomber defences employed by the Germans was parachute flares dropped by high flying Ju 88 night fighters. These flares would burst just below the bomber stream and illuminate the whole area thus presenting many bombers as silhouetted targets for the night fighters waiting above. These flares burned so brightly that it was like driving down a well-lit road at night and temporarily blinded anyone who was close by. In such circumstances there was nothing the skipper could do apart from weave more violently than usual and try to fly out of range. The same applied when we got ourselves coned in searchlights. Most large city targets, such as Berlin had a radar-controlled master beam, which was blue in colour. If it locked onto an aircraft, another ten to fifteen searchlight beams quickly latched onto the victim who became a sitting duck for the heavy flak batteries. Experienced bomber crews found the only way to escape the master beam was to dive away from the expected flak barrage coming up from below. The last 20 miles to the target had to be flown straight and level in order to make sure target indicators and bombs were placed accurately on the target aiming point. This was a really dodgy period and we were lucky if something or other did not hit us. Many aircraft were lost at this point, some in collisions and others hit by bombs from above. Stirling and Halifax bombers could only reach about 17,000 feet so they got the lot, the small flak as well as the heavy, plus more attention from the night fighters. Whilst over the target area, I would often see the fighters attacking bombers silhouetted against the fires on the ground. However, once away from the brightly-lit area, identifying a fighter was not easy against a black sky. The German night fighter always had the advantage over the bombers and a very few were shot down by bomber crews.

'It was always a great relief when the bomb-aimer said, "Bombs gone". The aircraft would rear up and wobble as the weight of the bombs left the aircraft, then we knew all we had to do was go home but that could be nearly as bad as getting there. The route home would be more or less straight apart from trying to avoid any known well-defended areas. On some nights if conditions were right the skipper would climb to 27,000 feet then put the nose down and really belt for home. The only snag being that by flying so high the temperature outside was sometimes as low as 60 below freezing. This froze the anti-freeze in the pipes that fired the guns in the rear turret making them useless until they thawed out at a lower altitude. However, the mid-upper guns were electrically fired so were not affected. Once we had crossed the enemy coast and were well out over the North Sea the skipper would bring us down to 10,000 feet, below oxygen-using height. Everything would then start to warm up and we could relax a little more. Tommy Evans the bomb-aimer would come to the rear turret and bring me a flask of coffee and although smoking was banned while flying, many of us broke that rule. After all the operational stress we had suffered over the past few hours, that mug of coffee and a Woodbine went down really well. I personally always carried a good supply of baccy and a well-filled petrol lighter, just in case we were shot down and managed to get on the run for a while. On odd occasions a message would come from base that Bandits (enemy fighters) were suspected of being in the area. That meant no relaxation until we were actually back over base. We would then be given a height at which to circle the airfield and a landing number. When our turn came Air Traffic Control radioed permission to land and once down the skipper taxied the aircraft around the perimeter track to our dispersal and we were welcomed back by our ground crew before being picked up by the crew bus and taken to the locker room.

'After handing in our flying gear we then went along to the debriefing room were a WAAF officer served us with a mug of coffee well laced with rum and the Padre would hand sandwiches around. Then we would sit around a table with an intelligence officer and debriefing would begin. "Did you have any difficulty finding the target? At what time were the TIs placed on the aiming point? How heavy was the flak? Did you encounter any fighters? Did you see any aircraft shot down? How far from the target could the fires be seen?" and many such questions until he had all the information we could give. Next we collected our personal belongings, including a brown envelope containing our wills and last letters home. These had been deposited and locked away in the Squadron office, for safe keeping before take-off. After that we went to the Mess for an aircrew breakfast, before seeking out our billet in a state of utter exhaustion. Hopefully we could get a good morning's sleep before being called once again to go to war.'

When, during the long summer heat wave on 24 July 1943, bomber crews learned that in a few hours time they would be striking Hamburg's port area on the wide Elbe River; no one was unduly troubled. The city was amongst the most heavily defended in the Reich but it did not present too many difficulties in that most of the flight was over the sea and therefore crews would escape the attentions of the flak that was experienced during overland trips to places like the Ruhr. Their greatest salvation though had already come eight days earlier at a meeting of the War Cabinet when Mr Churchill had finally authorized the use of 'Window'. Although devised in 1942, a decision had been taken not to use 'Window' for fear that the *Luftwaffe* would retaliate by using it in a new *Blitz* on Britain. 'Window' was strips of black paper with aluminium foil stuck to one side and cut to a length (30cm by 1.5cm), equivalent to half the wavelength of the *Würzburg* ground and *Lichtenstein* airborne interception radar. When dropped by aircraft in bundles of 1,000 at a time at one-minute intervals, 'Window' reflected the radar waves and 'snowed' the tubes, which made a city like Hamburg, protected by 54 heavy flak and 22 searchlight batteries, virtually defenceless. The aim of Operation *Gomorrah*, as it was codenamed, was to destroy Hamburg and reduce the city as completely as possible to ashes.

Notes

1. 3.6 per cent of the force dispatched.
2. A complete account of the raid on Wuppertal on 29/30 May 1943 can be found in *Battle Over the Reich* by Alfred Price (Ian Allan Ltd, 1973)
3. The Pathfinder marking plan for the 11/12 June raid on Düsseldorf went extremely well until an *Oboe* Mosquito inadvertently released its load of TIs 14 miles north-east of the

city, which caused part of the main force to drop their bombs on open country. Even so, in the city itself damage was extensive and 130 acres were claimed destroyed. Forty-three aircraft failed to return, 29 of which were shot down by *Nachtjäger*. Five of the losses (4 Halifaxes and Lancaster DS647 of 115 Squadron near Kiel) can probably be attributed to to Major Werner Streib *Gruppenkommandeur* of I./NJG 1 who, with Unteroffizier Helmut Fischer as his *Funker*, was flying the first fully operational test sortie in a He 219A-0R2 *Uhu*. The night's victories took his score to 54. Streib exhausted all his amunition and approached Venlo with fuel running low and several instruments u/s. On approach his canopy misted over and he was forced to fly on instruments. Streib lowered the electrically-operated flaps to the landing position and then lowered the undercarriage. The flaps did not lock down and they returned to the normal position. The He 219 hit the runway and disentegrated but remarkably, Streib and Fischer escaped almost uninjured. In June *Nachtjagd* claimed a record 223 victories.

4. *Nachtjagd* was credited with 27 confirmed kills, 21 *Abschüsse* being credited to NJG 1. Hauptmann Egmont Prinz zur Lippe Weissenfeld III./NJG 1 *Kommandeur* destroyed two Halifaxes. Oberleutnant Geiger claimed Lancaster III ED584 of 49 Squadron at Luttenberg near Raalte with the loss of Sergeant J. Hutchison and his crew.

5. Seven Lancasters were shot down by I./NJG 1 during the Oberhausen raid of 14/15 June when the *Himmelbett Nachtjagd* claimed 13 main force aircraft destroyed.

6. Aircraft lettered 'M' were usually known as *M-Mike* or *M-Mother*. This Lancaster got its name from Cab Calloway's popular slow blues song, of the same name.

7. Three Lancasters, ED840 of 156 Squadron, ED553 of 100 Squadron and ED785 of 49 Squadron, were shot down by Unteroffizier Rudolf Frank of 2./NJG 3 to take his score to 12 kills.

8. *Tail Gunner: 98 Raids in World War II* by Chan Chandler DFC* USSR Medal of Valour (Airlife 1999).

9. ibid.

10. *Thundering Through the Clear Air: No. 61 (Lincoln Imp) Squadron At War* by Derek Brammer (Tucann Books, 1997).

11. Mullock had flown with Slee to Berlin on 28 March 1943, as Chan Chandler was to recall: '. . . He wanted to see some flak. We found some for him – or rather it found us. We lost an engine and got a tank holed, plus a u/s compass. So Slee had quite an exciting last trip with 49, but we were to meet up with him again over Switzerland.' (Chandler, op. cit.)

12. ibid.

13. Brammer, op.cit.

14. ibid.

15. When over 700 bombers – 262 of them Lancasters – attacked Krefeld on the night of 21/22 June the raid took place in good visibility and the Pathfinders carried out an almost perfect marking operation. Ground-markers dropped by the dozen *Oboe* Mosquitoes were well backed up by the Pathfinder heavies and 619 aircraft were reckoned to have bombed these markers, dropping more than 2,300 tons of bombs. More than three-quarters of the bombers achieved bombing photographs within three miles of the centre of the city. A large fire ensued, took hold and burned out of control for several hours and 47 per cent of the built up area was laid waste. About 72,000 people lost their homes; the largest figure so far in the war. *The*

Bomber Command War Diaries by Martin Middlebrook and Chris Everitt.

16. Wuppertal was the target for 630 aircraft on 24/25 June when Elberfeld, the other half of the town, unharmed on 29/30 May, was bombed. On 21/22 June 705 aircraft including 262 Lancasters took part and 44 aircraft, nine of them Lancasters, failed to return. The night following, 557 aircraft went to Mülheim where the Pathfinders had to mark the target through a thin layer of stratus cloud. The marking proved very accurate and large fires raged throughout the city destroying over 1,100 houses and damaging over 12,600 dwellings. The post-war British Bombing Survey Unit estimated that this single raid destroyed 64 per cent of the town of Mülheim. The raid cost 35 bombers or 6.3 per cent of the force. (Middlebrook and Everitt, op. cit.). Oberleutnant Gerhard Raht of 4./NJG 3 claimed Lancaster III ED595 of 7 Squadron E of Rilland, Zeeland. Wing Commander R. G. Barrell DSO DFC* KIA when his parachute failed to deploy after he baled out. Hauptmann Werner Hoffmann, *Staffelkapitän* 4./NJG 5 destroyed a Lancaster (probably ED858 of 156 Squadron at Erkelenz) and a Wellington at Dessel/Antwerp.

17. Lancaster I ED528 PM-Z.

18. Egan and the air bomber Flight Sergeant W. Miller RAAF survived and they too became POWs. Flight Sergeant S. B. Elliott RAAF, navigator; Sergeant J. Brown, W/Op; Sergeant H. A. Horrell, mid-upper-gunner and Sergeant C. A. Britton were KIA.

19. ED528 was shot down at Bechtrup north of Lüdinghausen. Sixteen of the bombers lost on the Wuppertal raid were shot down by the NJG 1 including three Lancasters of 100, 101 and 103 Squadrons by Oberfeldwebel Karl-Heinz Scherfling. Oberleutnant August Geiger of III./NJG 1 achieved a triple victory in 43 minutes downing a Stirling, a Halifax and a Lancaster, possibly ED831 of 9 Squadron into the Ijsselmeer off Edam. Bomber Command lost 275 bombers shot down in June 1943.

20. The target turned out to be cloud-covered so sky-marking system was used. This was seven minutes late in starting and proceeded only intermittently. Despite all of this, the main force of nearly 600 bombers devastated Cologne in the most destructive raid on the city in the entire war. Thousands of buildings were destroyed, over 4,300 people were killed and about 10,000 inhabitants were injured while 230,000 people were forced to leave their damaged dwellings. Twenty-five bombers failed to return. Eight were claimed destroyed by I./NJG 1 and 12 by II./NJG 1 over eastern Belgium. Leutnant Heinz-Wolfgang Schnaufer of the *Gruppen Stab* destroyed Lancaster LM323 of 97 Squadron and two Halifaxes. A follow up raid took place on 3/4 July when 653 bombers aimed their bombs at industrial targets on the east bank of the Rhine. Pathfinder ground marking by the Mosquito *Oboe* aircraft and the backers-up was accurate and much devastation was caused.

21. The *Wilde Saus* had to share these victories with the local flak defences, who also claimed 12 successes. Twenty-one crews of II./NJG 1 at St Trond returned with claims for 14 *Abschüsse*. During July 1943-early March 1944 *Wilde Sau Geschwader* claimed 330 bombers destroyed at night. Of the record 290 *Nachtjagd* victories achieved in August 1943 only 48 were by the traditional *Himmelbett* method while the remaining 80 per cent were credited to the *Wilde Sau* units and to twin-engined crews operating in *Wilde Sau* fashion. *Nachtjagd* lost 61 aircraft

in action that same month. Mainly they were flown by green and inexperienced crews.

22. Among subsequent awards was a DSO for Wing Commander Martin. He had been awarded the DFC in February 1942 after taking part in 30 bombing raids. These raids included a solo attack on Berlin in 1941 when, on the outward journey, he failed to receive a general recall signal, penetrated alone into the centre of the city, bombed, and successfully landed in thick fog on his return to England.

23. Despite being hampered by thick layers of cloud, 24 II./NJG 1 crews in the *Himmelbett* boxes in eastern Belgium destroyed three Lancasters and claimed another seven *Feindberührungen* (encounters with the enemy).

24. *Airborne Cigar (ABC)* was a device consisting of six scanning receivers and three transmitters designed to cover the VHF band of the standard German R/T sets and to jam 30–33 MHz (*Ottokar*) and later 38–42 MHz (*Benito.* R/T and Beam). *ABC* emitted a warbling note, which German crewmen christened *Dudelsack* or bagpipes. The British successive transmission of 6–8 jamming tones on the *Nachtjagd* R/T frequencies sounded like a child's cheap music box and it was very nerve-wracking to German night fighter ears. *Seelenbohrer* or 'soul borer' was the night fighter's nickname of the British use of 'Tinsel', whereby a German-speaking crew member blotted out German R/T transmissions with engine noise. 'Tinsel' sounded like a very unpleasant drilling noise.

25. Scrymgeour-Wedderburn and his crew flew two tours before the end of the war.

26. Nettleton had been awarded the Victoria Cross for his leadership on the low level daylight raid on the *Maschinenfabrik Augsburg-Nürnberg Aktiengesellschaft* (MAN) diesel engine factory at Augsburg on 17 April 1942.

27. NJG 1 and NJG 4 were credited with 18 kills. Lancaster II DS690 of 115 Squadron flown by Squadron Leader The Hon. R. A. G. Baird, the son of Viscount and Viscountess Stonehaven, was shot down by Hauptmann August Geiger, temporarily of I./NJG 4 and it crashed at La Cornette. Baird and five of his crew were KIA. Sergeant J. E. C. Odendaal, a southern Rhodesian, survived and was taken prisoner.

28. Born on 24 February 1895, the third son of Baron Cochrane of Cults in Fifeshire, Cochrane was educated at the Royal Naval Colleges at Osborne and Dartmouth before entering the Royal Navy in 1912, transferring to the RAF in 1918. He became the first Chief of the Air Staff of the Royal New Zealand Air Force in 1936. In 1942 Cochrane became AOC 3 Group Bomber Command and with the sacking by Air Chief Marshal Harris of AVM Alec Coryton in February 1943, he assumed command of 5 Group. Cochrane had been a flight commander on 45 Squadron commanded by Harris in Mesopotamia in 1922–24 when the unit flew Vickers Vernons and Victorias on troop carrying duties. (Cochrane retired from the RAF as Vice-Chief of the Air Staff in 1952 and died in 1977 aged 82.)

29. *Breaking The Dams: The Story of Dambuster David Maltby & His Crew* by Charles Foster (Pen & Sword, 2008)

30. Eighteen Lancasters of 5 Group attempted raids on two more transformer stations in northern Italy on 16/17 July. Seven aircraft bombed the Cislago station accurately but the second target was not located and an alternative target was bombed instead. One Lancaster was lost.

31. The main Battle of the Ruhr lasted for four months during which 43 major raids were carried out. Two thirds of these were against the Ruhr and the rest were to other areas including Stettin on the Baltic, Munich in Bavaria, Pilsen in Czechoslovakia and Turin in Italy. Approximately 57,034 tons of bombs were dropped at a cost of 1,038 aircraft (4.3 per cent).

32. In early August the Squadron started to receive aircraft fitted with H_2S and so *Nan* was transferred to 61 Squadron after surviving 25 hazardous Pathfinder operations. Little did the crew know that *Nan* was a lucky aircraft and would go on to complete a further 105 ops over the following year.

33. Brammer, op. cit.

Chapter 5

Hamburg and *Hydra* Come Hell or High Water

It is so densely built that one fire alone would be enough to destroy the whole city ... fires everywhere, with countless incendiary bombs of an entirely new type. Thousands of fires ... will unite in one huge blaze over the whole area. High explosives don't work, but we can do it with incendiaries; What will their firemen be able to do once it's really burning?

Albert Speer describing Hitler at a dinner in the Reich Chancellery in 1940 imagining the total destruction of the capital of the British Empire.

Operation *Gomorrah*, the first of four raids on Hamburg, a city of nearly 2 million people, began on the night of 24/25 July. Bundles of 'Window' were carried in the 791 aircraft[1] that set out across the North Sea loaded with high capacity bombs and incendiaries. By blowing off roofs and shattering windows and doors, the blast bombs would create the powerful draught needed to spread the fires from countless incendiaries to devastate an area about 10 times the area of the City of London. Since Hamburg was far beyond the range of *Oboe*, 74 of the aircraft were equipped with H_2S. These were to help the Pathfinders mark and keep the city marked, the plan being that 20 H_2S aircraft would open the attack by releasing yellow TIs and strings of flares solely on their radar. These would be followed by eight visual markers, which were to identify the target in the glow of the flares and put down red TIs. Finally, the 53 backers-up positioned throughout the bomber stream were to aim their green TIs at the red TIs just beyond the centre of the green TIs to alleviate 'creep back'. The bombers of the main force were to bomb the reds if they were visible, or failing that, the centre of the greens. They were to ignore the yellow TIs.

In the first 15 minutes of the raid the green TIs followed each other accurately into the area around the aiming point. Led by the H_2S PFF aircraft, 728 bombers rained down 2,284 tons of HE and incendiaries in 50 minutes on the dockyards and city districts. However, less than half of the force bombed within three

miles of the centre of Hamburg and there was a marked 'creep back', which continued until the end of the attack, by which time a six mile long carpet of burning incendiaries extended back from the aiming point. Hamburg was such a large city that it made little difference in the final outcome. Severe damage was caused to the central and north-western districts, particularly in Altona, Euimsbüttel and Hohenluft. The roof of the Rathaus was set afire and the Nikolaikirche, the Central Police Station and the long distance telephone exchange in the wealthy district of Rotherbaum were among other known city landmarks to be hit. Four 'blockbuster' blast bombs, 16 other HE bombs and many incendiaries destroyed the famous Hagenbeck Zoo where 140 animals were killed or they had to be shot.[2] In one of the 97 Squadron Lancasters that took off from Bourn at 22.00 hours with 8,000lb of bombs plus target indicators, sat Warrant Officer Eddie Wheeler, the WOp/AG. He noted that there was very little cloud but hazy visibility. At 17,000 feet they ran into the inevitable heavy flak and released their load at 01.05 hours. Two minutes later there was the most violent explosion near the aiming point followed by a glow lasting for 40 seconds. Later all the squadron crews at debriefing confirmed this. 'Window's' effect was noticeable because searchlights wandered all over the sky and the flak was haphazard. The German fighter pilots and their *Bordfunkers* too were blind.'

Many large fires and a pall of smoke were visible as they turned away for the journey back across the dreaded North Sea. Six hours after take off they touched down at Bourn at 04.00. Wheeler thought 'that's another satisfactory night's work over'. Only 12 bombers,[3] just 1.5 per cent of the force, were lost. Without 'Window' losses could well have amounted to around the 6 per cent mark, which had characterized previous raids on this target. 'Window' neutralized the *Würzburg* GCI and GL radars and short range AI, and completely destroyed the basis of GCI interception. Controlled anti-aircraft fire was almost completely disrupted at night and fixed box barrages only remained possible. The new British tactics also combined the use of PFF, the massed bomber stream and new target finding equipment (H_2S). This combination resulted in total chaos to the German night fighter defence system, which was unable to obtain a true picture of the air situation or control the night fighters in the air.

In an attempt to achieve a 'good raid' on a major target while 'Window' remained effective, over 700 bombers were dispatched to bomb Essen on the night of 25/26 July. Included in the force were 294 Lancasters. Severe damage was caused to the industrial areas in the eastern parts of the city. The Krupps Works suffered its most damaging raid of the war and 51 other industrial buildings were damaged with another 83 heavily damaged.[4]

In the next raid on Hamburg, early in the morning of 27 July, 787 aircraft including 353 Lancasters, dropped 550–600 bomb loads of high explosive and incendiary bombs on the densely populated residential area east of the Elbe. This area comprised the districts of Hammerbrook, Hamm-Nord and Hamm-Süd, Billwerder Ausschlag and parts of St Georg, Eilbek, Barmbek and Wandshek. A now familiar sequence of events occurred. First all the doors and windows were torn from their frames and smashed by high explosive bombs and then lightweight incendiary mixtures ignited the attic floors of the buildings. At the same time firebombs weighing up to 15 kilograms fell into the lower storeys. Within a few minutes huge fires were burning all over the target area, which covered 20 square kilometres, and they merged so rapidly that only a quarter of an hour after the first bombs had dropped the whole airspace was a sea of flames as far as the eye could see. Five minutes later a firestorm of an intensity that no one would ever before have thought possible arose.[5] The fire, now rising 2,000 metres into the sky, snatched oxygen to itself so violently that the air currents reached hurricane force resonating like mighty organs with all their stops pulled out at once. The fire

burned like this for three hours. At its height the storm lifted gables and roofs from buildings, flung rafters and entire advertising hoardings through the air, tore trees from the ground and drove human beings before it like living torches. Behind collapsing façades the flames shot up as high as houses, rolled like a tidal wave through the streets at a speed of over 150kph, spun across open squares, in strange rhythms like rolling cylinders of fire. The water in some of the canals was ablaze. The glass in the tramcar windows melted; stocks of sugar boiled in the bakery cellars. Those who had fled from their air-raid shelters sank, with grotesque contortions, in the thick bubbles thrown up by the melting asphalt. No one knows for certain how many lost their lives that night, or how many went mad before they died. When day broke, the summer dawn could not penetrate the leaden gloom above the city. The smoke had risen to a height of 8,000 metres, where it spread like a vast, anvil-shaped cumulo-nimbus cloud. A wavering heat, which the bomber pilots said they had felt through the sides of their planes, continued to rise from the smoking, glowing mounds of stone. Residential districts with a street length of 200 kilometres in all were utterly destroyed. Horribly disfigured corpses lay everywhere. Bluish little phosphorus flames still flickered around many of them; others had been roasted brown or purple and reduced to a third of their normal size. They lay doubled up in pools of their own melted fat, which had sometimes already congealed. In the next few days, the central death zone was declared a no-go area. When punishment labour gangs and camp inmates could begin clearing it in August, after the rubble had cooled down, they found people still sitting at tables or up against walls where they had been overcome by monoxide gas. Elsewhere, clumps of flesh and bone or whole heaps of bodies had cooked in the water gushing from bursting boilers. Other victims had been so badly charred and reduced to ashes by the heat, which had risen to 1,000 degrees or more, that the remains of families consisting of several people could be carried away in a single laundry basket.[6]

Over four nights 3,000 bombers dropped 10,000 tons of HE and incendiary bombs to totally devastate half of Hamburg and kill an estimated 42,000 of its inhabitants.[7] After the fourth raid on 2/3 August by 740 aircraft, 900,000 inhabitants had lost their homes and had fled the city. The exodus of severely confused survivors, some clad only in pyjamas, started going 'no one knew where' until 1¼ million refugees were dispersed all over the Reich, as far as its outer borders. On 20 August Friedrich Reck saw a group of 40 to 50 such refugees trying to force their way into a train at a station in Upper Bavaria. As they did so a cardboard suitcase 'fell on the platform, burst open and spilled its contents. Toys, a manicure case, singed underwear and last of all, the roasted corpse of a child, shrunk like a mummy, which its half-deranged mother has been carrying about with her, the relic of a past that was still intact a few days ago.' An American bomber navigator, who flew a US 8th Air Force daylight mission after the RAF raids on Hamburg noted that every section of the huge city was on fire. An ugly pall of smoke was blowing to the south-west. 'It looked the way that one might imagine Hell to be.' Paralyzed by 'Window' *Nachtjagd* and the *Flakwaffe* were unable to offer any significant resistance. Albert Speer, Minister of War Production, warned Hitler that Germany would have to surrender after another six of these bombing raids.

Since Hamburg and the introduction of 'Window', casualty figures had got significantly lower[8] and in August when Johnny Moss, and his crew of *J-Johnny* in 49 Squadron, returned from leave, their spirits were high. Len Bradfield, the bomb-aimer recalled that when they first began flying ops in March 1943, losses were averaging 5 per cent a night but the crew believed that they were special and that they would survive. 'We were sorry other crews didn't make it back' he recalls, 'but we accepted that this was the way things were. We didn't think it could happen to us. We were an above average crew and expected to go to Pathfinders after our tour. It came as a sharp jolt when the crew we had trained with failed to return from the raid on Mannheim on 9/10 August. Next day, however, was beautiful. The NFT[9] went well. When we saw the fuel and bomb loading we decided it would be a longish operation. After the flying supper we went to briefing. The target was Nürnburg [Nuremberg] with the MAN diesel factory at Fürth being the aiming point. As it was in southern Germany the route was over lightly defended territory as much as possible. Climbing to a height of 21,000ft on track, we crossed the enemy coast at Le Treport and then flew on over France, directly to Nürnburg. "Window" was dropped at intervals on entering German airspace north of Trier. There was about 8/10ths cloud with tops at 14,000ft, which meant we would be silhouetted from above by the bright moonlight. We knew we were in trouble and we generally weaved to give a maximum sky search. All of a sudden, near Wolfstein (south of Bad Kreuznach and NNW of Mannheim, where we could see the glow from our bombing the night before) a night fighter attacked us.

Terry Woods, the mid-upper gunner, spotted the incoming attack and shouted, "Bandit 5 o'clock high!"

'I abandoned scrabbling about on the floor dropping "window" and stood at my guns (being 6 feet 1 inch I could work the turret better standing than sitting). Cannon and tracer fire hit our port wing and port outer engine, setting both on fire. Terry returned fire, followed by Ronnie Musson in the rear turret before he was put out of action because of the loss of the port outer, which produced hydraulic power for his turret. As our attacker broke away over the nose I got in a burst of 30 rounds from the front guns. Johnny started taking violent evasive action to blow out the fire. Sammy Small, the WOp/AG, was standing in the astrodome co-ordinating the defences as we had practised. Almost at once Ron Musson, the rear-gunner called out a second attack. It began at 6 o'clock level, dead aft. All hell was let loose. Shells were exploding "crunk", "crunk", "crunk" against the armoured doors and the 4,000lb cookie in the bomb bay. There was a smell of cordite and fire broke out in the bomb bay and main-plane. I dropped down to the bomb-aimer's compartment and could see the fire raging. I told Johnny and he gave the order to jettison. I did. The attack was still in progress. The night fighter was holding off at 600 yards, blazing away. He didn't close. The fire persisted and Johnny gave the order to bale out – "Abracadabra, Jump, Jump!"

'From beginning to end it had lasted perhaps 1–2 seconds but it seemed like slow motion. The order was acknowledged, except for the rear-gunner. I got my parachute on and pulled up, twisted and dropped the front escape hatch in order to bale out. Ernie Roden, flight engineer and David Jones, navigator were coming down the bomb-aimer's bay. I dived out and fell clear and delayed opening my chute until I was below the cloud. I could still see red and yellow tracer flying by. It is possible that Ernie and David were hit when they baled out. As I broke cloud I could see several small fires, which reinforces the idea that the *B-Baker* exploded. On the ground I chucked my lucky woolly gollywog away. It was nothing personal (I had carried him on all my 18 ops) but I thought it had failed me. He hadn't because later, when I was captured, when I asked about my crew I was told, *Fünf Tot* (five dead). Johnny Moss was the only other survivor, probably blown clear when the Lancaster exploded. A *Luftwaffe* NCO told me three 4-engined bombers had been brought down in a 10-km circle by his unit. At *Dulag Luft* interrogation centre I thought about the attack and concluded that a professional, a real "tradesman" had shot us down.'[10]

Since early August Bomber Command flew five raids on Italian targets with Genoa, Milan and Turin being bombed by the 4-engined heavies. Milan was subjected to a series of three attacks within the space of a few days. On Sunday, 15 August, 199 Lancasters were bombed up for the fourth in the series of raids on the city. Bombing was claimed as, 'particularly concentrated'. Seven Lancasters were lost; some running into accurate flak around Chartres but mostly the victims fell to night fighters. One of them was *Y-Yankee* flown by Wing Commander Cosme Gomm DSO DFC, which was shot down over Normandy by a night fighter. The Lancaster exploded near the village of Beaumont scattering debris over two square miles. The only the survivor was 20 year old Sergeant James Lee, the flight engineer and youngest crewmember on board who, badly burned, had the luck to parachute down onto a hayrick and was taken prisoner. When the Lancasters of 467 Squadron RAAF landed back at Bottesford and entered debriefing, the news was broken to a distraught Section Officer Paula Fisher, a WAAF in the Intelligence Section who had formed a relationship with the highly regarded pilot.[11]

On the night of 16/17 August, as a handful of Lancasters joined other aircraft in another raid on Turin, some Lancasters carried out one of the most dangerous minelaying missions of the war when they blocked the Stettin ship canal, the vital waterway supplying the Russian front. One force of bombers was detailed to attack the port of Stettin while the other force, which was to be detached from the main bomber stream at the last minute, went down to a few hundred feet to lay their mines. Flak ships and batteries defended the canal throughout its entire length of more than 30 miles, and on the night of the attack every gun was in action during the 20 minute operation. Guard ships and motor craft patrolling the canal fired almost every type of AA weapon at the Lancasters flying close above them. But the bombers kept on their steady course up the channel, reached Stettin and laid their mines as hundreds of high explosive and incendiary bombs rained down on the port from the other force. It was an intricate as well as a dangerous operation. To make sure of putting the mines into so small an area an application of Pathfinder technique was used. Three Lancasters went even lower than the main force to lay floating flares in the target area, while others, flying higher, dropped more flares to light up the whole canal. These flares, and searchlights constantly sweeping the water, made the night as bright as day.

Squadron Leader H. B. Locke DFC RAAF flew No. 3 of the marking Lancasters, with four other Australians in the crew. He was detailed to place a precision marker at the northern entrance to the channel, and to drop mines as far north in the channel as possible. He identified the channel before the flares went down by doing a preliminary run. The horizontal beams of searchlights ringed the bay and the flak ships lining the channel came to life as he made his run-in, putting both markers and mines in exactly the allotted area. A flak ship mounting cannon, machine guns and searchlights engaged his aircraft a second after Locke's mines went down. He put his bomber into an evading dive while his gunners blazed away at the enemy positions, and pulled out at water level. By then both gun turrets and all the hydraulic system of the aircraft were useless. There was a bad petrol leak but through superb calculations by the navigator, Squadron Leader H. Makepeace, Locke found a gap on the coast and by flying below trees, was able to dodge the searchlights of successive defensive positions. Despite the lack of almost all navigational aids, dead reckoning by the navigator brought the Lancaster back to England, where Locke made a successful landing at base. He was awarded the DSO.

By early August 'Pluto' Wilson's crew had completed 24 operational sorties and the crew were known as one of the old sweats on 467 Squadron RAAF. Together with other experienced crews, they were taken off routine bombing trips and became engaged in special low level time and distance bombing practice over the Wainfleet bombing range near Skegness. 'At first we thought it strange that it was the most experienced crews who were degraded in this way' recalls, Charles Cawthorne.[12] 'But as the results were being scrutinized by senior staff from Group Headquarters, headed by the AOC, Air Vice-Marshal Cochrane, we soon realized that there was some hidden purpose behind this special training. A few days later the AOC visited Bottesford and told the selected aircrews that they must do better and reduce the number of bombing errors. At this stage we had no idea what was going on but there were rumours circulating around the camp that we might be going to attack the German dams again or maybe the Dortmund-Ems Canal. On 17 August all speculation ended when we were detailed to attend the pre-operation briefing and it immediately became apparent that something very special had been planned. Security around the operations block was unusually severe with RAF Police in far greater numbers than usual.

'There was a great buzz of speculation amongst the crews as we entered the large briefing room. The assembled crews were brought to attention as the station's senior officers entered the room accompanied by a very senior officer from Group Headquarters. The curtain over the map of western Europe was pulled back to reveal red route marker tapes leading to a small target called Peenemünde on the German Baltic coast sited between Rostock and Stettin. I wondered what all the fuss was about because we had never heard of this little place called Peenemünde and the Squadron had attacked both Rostock and Stettin quite recently. The briefing was opened with a statement from the visiting officer from Group. He said, "Peenemünde is a German military research establishment whose scientists are working on new Radio Detection Finding (RDF) equipment as a countermeasure against our night bombers and therefore is a very important target that has to be destroyed at all costs. That is why the operation has been planned to take place in full moon flying conditions and must be carried out at low level. It is imperative that this target is destroyed and I must warn you that if you are unsuccessful tonight, then the Squadron will have to return tomorrow night and on successive nights until complete destruction is achieved." (It was only later when the V-2 rockets started to fall on London in September 1944, that we in Bomber Command and the general public learned the true purpose of this raid i.e. the destruction of the secret V-2 rocket research and production facility.) The Squadron Commander then said it was to be a precision attack on three main target areas. The first and second waves would attack on Pathfinder TIs but 5 Group squadrons were to bomb last in the third wave and would use the new time-and-distance bombing method as the target would probably be obscured by smoke from the first and second wave attacks.[13]

'The objective for the third wave aircraft was the Experimental Works which consisted of over 70 small buildings. (This complex contained vital development data and equipment and the accommodation block, which housed the V-2 Project Director, General Dornberger and his Deputy, Werner von Braun. We did not learn this until much later.) The crews were then informed that a master bomber, Group Captain John Searby of 83 Pathfinder Squadron would control all phases of the raid by circling the target area. If necessary he would give instructions over the VHF radio to the Pathfinders should the TIs need re-positioning or to stop main force creep-back develop-ing. As we listened to the briefing it became clear that this operation was a formidable task but we were deter-mined to succeed as none of us fancied our chances of survival if we had to return again the next night.

'At 21.30 hours our Aussie skipper turned our heavily laden Lanc onto the main runway and once the aircraft was lined up he slowly opened the throttles while I watched the needles swing round in the boost and rev gauges. At the same time my left hand followed the skipper's right as he pushed forward the throttle levers. As the aircraft gained speed the navigator called out the indicated air speed (IAS) over the intercom. With full rudder control and all four engines pulling, the skipper called for me to take over the throttle levers and push them through the gate for maximum power. Moments later with gauges showing 3,000-rpm +14lb/sq.in boost, the aircraft reached a speed of 100 knots IAS and took off into a cloudless summer evening sky. With a positive rate of climb established the skipper called for the undercarriage to be raised and engines set to a climbing power of 2,850-rpm with +9lb/sq.in boost. This was quickly followed by a series of flap adjustments and once the airframe was clean, our Lancaster *F-Freddie* climbed away at 155 knots to join the third wave of the bomber stream off the north Lincolnshire coast. To see scores of heavy bombers assembling in bright moonlight over the North Sea was quite an exhilarating experience. Usually we carried out ops on dark moon-less nights and the only indication other aircraft were around was when we ran through prop wash turbulence or occasionally we saw the red glow from aircraft engine exhausts.

'At 23.35 hours we crossed the Danish coast twelve miles north of the island of Sylt and from our operational height of 18,000 feet I could clearly see small villages and farm houses in the brightly lit countryside. Forty minutes later we were flying over the Baltic and the moonlight presented an eerie picture as numerous islands were clearly outlined against the sea. At this juncture we were flying south-east at 8,000 feet some twenty miles off shore, midway between Rostock and Stettin. In the nose of the aircraft our Aussie bomb-aimer, Swill Campbell, was busy map reading and called over the intercom that we were approaching the headland of Arkona on the north-eastern tip of the island of Rugen. We were now only 40 miles from the target and the skipper turned south to follow the coastline that led directly to Peenemünde. Approaching the target we could see the raid ahead progressing as the first and second wave aircraft bombed the red and green TIs laid down by the Pathfinders. From our position at the rear of the bomber stream there appeared to be little enemy opposition with only moderate light flak and few searchlights. Over our VHF radio set we heard the calm voice of Group Captain Searby assuring the third wave crews the raid was pro-gressing in a satisfactory way and to standby for further orders.

'A few minutes later at 00.42 hours the master bomber ordered the Lancasters of 5 Group to commence their timed bombing runs from the designated starting point at the southern tip of the island. At this point during every bombing raid, aircraft became particularly vulnerable to flak or night fighter attack and on this occasion the seven mile bombing run seemed endless as we frantically searched the crowded sky for the enemy and to avoid a collision with a friendly aircraft. At last, our bomb-aimer announced "Bombs gone" and the aircraft wobbled as it was relieved of its heavy load. The skipper held the same course until the aiming point photograph had been taken and then much to the relief of everyone on board mined back over the sea to start our journey home. As we left the immediate target area, we felt elated that our outward flight had been uneventful and we had made a successful bombing run. But as we commenced our return journey we became aware of increased enemy activity in our vicinity as burning aircraft began to fall out of the sky at an alarming rate. It seemed as if a huge armada of enemy night fighters, who were taking full advantage of the bright moonlight conditions, was attacking the third wave of the bomber stream. (Later, we found out that the German night fighters had been successfully lured away from the Peenemünde area by a diversionary raid on Berlin. However, once the German fighter controllers realized that this was not the main target, the night fighters were ordered to pursue the bombers over Peenemünde.)

'The skipper called over the intercom for everyone to be extra vigilant but without warning we felt our aircraft judder, as it was riddled with both machine gun and 20mm cannon fire. Standing beside the pilot, I clearly recall seeing tracer bullet trails looping high over our port wing and hearing the terrifying noise of the enemy's ammunition hitting our aircraft. George Oliver, our mid-upper gunner, made an immediate response to the attack and our rugged Australian skipper put the aircraft into a violent dive to port in the hope of escaping further attention from the fighter. However, after losing several thousand feet of altitude he announced he was having great difficulty in getting the aircraft out of the dive. Without further ado I leaned over to assist by grasping the control column with both hands and together we pulled it back until the aircraft responded and we were flying straight and level again. On recovery, I checked the engine gauges and fuel control panel and looking aft saw what looked like the whole of the rear fuselage on fire with thick black acrid smoke billowing forward. Out of the smoke climbing over the main spar came George the mid-upper gunner

and David the wireless operator soon joined him. Both had their chutes clipped on ready to jump out of the front emergency exit. I reported the fire to the skipper and expected him to give the order to abandon aircraft, but to my amazement he coolly said, "Well go and put the bloody thing out then". If it had not been for those cool calculated words, we would have all finished our ops tour there and then.

'Armed with fire extinguishers, George and I went aft over the main spar to tackle the blaze and there David quickly joined us. We found the ammunition lines to the rear turret ablaze with one round setting fire to the next with alarming speed. The fuselage was full of thick smoke which made our progress difficult and soon it was realized the dead man's handle, a device for rotating the rear turret in the event of hydraulic failure, had received a direct hit. The turret's hydraulic oil supply had been sprayed around the floor not only adding fuel to the fire but also making it difficult to stand in our rubber flying boots. When all extinguishers had been emptied, we resorted to smothering the blaze with our gloved hands and eventually we succeeded in putting the fire out.

'It was then that we realized the rear-gunner, Paddy Barry, was wounded and trapped in his turret. With the aid of the aircraft axe, George, the mid-upper gunner managed to open the back doors of the rear turret and I assisted in manoeuvring Paddy over the tail-plane and up to the rest bed near the main spar. Despite Paddy's precarious state, we had to leave him and return to our crew positions to report on the fire damage sustained from the night fighter attack and take stock of the battle that was taking place all around us in the bomber stream. From the flight engineer's panel I calculated that we were losing a considerable amount of fuel and after reporting this to the skipper and navigator it was decided we would divert to an airfield in neutral Sweden. At this juncture Swill, the bomb-aimer, and I were told by the skipper to make Paddy as comfortable as possible. By the light of a masked torch, we realized he had sustained a serious injury to his left foot from an exploding cannon shell. I attempted to inject morphine to ease his pain but could not get through his protective clothing. In desperation, I started to cut away his flying boot, which was torn and saturated with blood. In the semi-darkness of the fuselage it was difficult to see any detail and what I thought to be a large piece of boot was in fact a piece of skin which I immediately replaced and bound the wound with a shell bandage. I then returned to my seat in the cockpit and after rechecking the fuel gauges I realized the self-sealing fuel tanks had been effective and the loss of fuel had been stemmed.

Following a hurried crew conference, it was decided we had sufficient fuel to attempt the return journey over the North Sea to England.

'The skipper then announced he was still having trouble controlling the aircraft which continuously wanted to climb and it was necessary for him to stand on the rudder pedals and wedge his back against the seat with fully extended arms to prevent the aircraft climbing. In an endeavour to relieve the physical effort of the situation the skipper and I removed our Mae West's and after inflating them jammed them both between the control column and the pilot's seat. We did not realize that the problem was caused by the loss of our elevator trim tabs, which had been shot away during the night fighter attack. By the time we crossed the enemy coast the skipper was completely exhausted and it became necessary for me to fly the aircraft over the relatively safe area of the North Sea. With great difficulty we changed seats and, by the grace of God, nothing untoward happened during the sea crossing. Approaching the Lincolnshire coast the skipper took over again and David Booth, the wireless operator, called our base for a priority landing due to our seriously wounded gunner and the precarious state of the aircraft. Bottesford responded to our request and the skipper ordered all crewmembers to their crash positions for an emergency landing. I had to remain in my normal crew position to assist the skipper with the handling of the aircraft. On final approach, I was fully prepared to select full flap, which was the normal procedure. But the skipper quickly reminded me that only a couple of weeks before an Aussie pilot on the Squadron called Tillotson had suffered a complete fracture of the rear fuselage on his aircraft following full flap selection after suffering serious battle damage to the rear fuselage. His aircraft's tail fell off with disastrous results. I didn't require any further warning and my hand kept a respectful distance away from the flap lever. In the early morning light after nearly seven hours in the air we glided over the threshold of the runway and touched down at 04.20 hours. With engines spluttering we taxied off the runway and came to a stop on the grass, where we were immediately attended by the fire and ambulance staff who carefully extricated Paddy, our injured gunner. It was now quite light and on evacuating the aircraft through the rear door, I was amazed to see the extent of the damage we had sustained. Internally the skin of the rear fuselage was charred and black from the intense fire and shafts of light pointed to where machine gun bullets and cannon shells had entered and exited the aircraft. Externally, the wings, rear fuselage, tail plane and both rudders were all severely perforated by machine gun and cannon fire. Overall *F-Freddie* was in an appalling state, but miraculously all four engines were undamaged and had functioned perfectly throughout the flight to bring us home.'[14]

Initial reports that morning indicated that the raid had been a complete success, achieved through the element of surprise and the sheer audacity of operating under a full moon and clear skies. Ground controllers were fooled into thinking the bombers were headed for Stettin and a further 'spoof' by Mosquitoes aiming for Berlin drew more fighters away from the Peenemünde force. Out of the total of 606 aircraft assigned, 44 bombers and one Mosquito were lost in the wild mêlée over the target and 32 suffered damage. Two night fighter crews flying Bf 110s fitted with a new and deadly weapons system called *Schräge Musik* destroyed six of the bombers.[15] In the daylight reconnaissance 12 hours after the attack, photographs revealed 27 buildings in the northern manufacturing area destroyed and 40 huts in the living and sleeping quarters completely flattened. The foreign labour camp to the south suffered worst of all. The whole target area was covered in craters. It was inconceivable that the site could ever operate again and at least we had gained valuable time against V-1 and V-2 attacks on London and our impending second front assault forces. This raid probably gave crews their most satisfaction against all other targets attacked.

Within days of this episode, 'Pluto' Wilson's crew and others in Bomber Command were on operations again. On 22/23 August the target for 462 aircraft, 257 of them Lancasters, was the I.G. Farben factory at Leverkusen. The night following Berlin was the target for 710 aircraft, including 335 Lancasters, when Bomber Command suffered its greatest loss of aircraft in one night in the war so far. Seventeen Mosquitoes were used to mark various points on the route to the capital to help keep the main force on the correct track. A master bomber, Wing Commander J. E. 'Johnny' Fauquier the CO of 405 Squadron RCAF, was used. For Warrant Officer Eddie Wheeler, WOp/AG in 97 Squadron at Bourn in Cambridgeshire, it was his first trip to the 'big one':

'It meant a long trip over heavily defended enemy territory and the Berlin defences were savage in the protection of the great city which, the *Nazis* had sworn would never be subjected to air bombardment. What a long way I had come since those dark days in 1940 when there appeared to be no salvation from the gloom and here we were attacking the German capital in strength and talking more and more of an invasion of Europe. This was to be my 57th operation; could I survive to see that 60th operation? It did seem to be inviting the inevitable with each further raid. So many crews had not even reached double figures and with so many more aircraft involved, losses mounted so that the likelihood of aircrews surviving twelve raids was still minimal. For this trip, we had an additional crewmember – a Flight Sergeant Penny who came as second pilot for the experience. Apart from the heavy flak and searchlight activity, the flight was uneventful, far less frightening than any trip to the Ruhr and after bombing from 18,000 feet we were back at base in six hours 35 minutes.'

The raid was only partially successful. The Pathfinders were not able to identify the city centre by H_2S and they marked an area in the southern outskirts of the capital. The main force arrived late and approached from the wrong direction so that most of the 1,700 tons of bombs that were dropped in the space of 50 minutes fell in open country with 25 villages reporting bombs falling on them. Even so, over 2,600 individual buildings in Berlin were destroyed or seriously damaged and two residential areas well south of the city centre were badly hit with a large loss of life, many of whom had not taken shelter when the bombs began falling. Thirty-one bombers fell victim to fighters in the target area with another seven crashing on the way home as a result of fighter attacks over Berlin. The gunner of a 103 Squadron Lancaster claimed that six Bf 109 *Wilde Sau* fighters that approached in pairs attacked them. The badly riddled bomber made it back to Elsham Wolds but 62 aircraft were lost. The Halifax squadrons came off worse, losing 25 of their number while 20 Lancasters and 17 Stirlings were also lost.[16] A Ju 88 night fighter attacked an hour's flying time from the target a Lancaster of 207 Squadron flown by Pilot Officer J. McIntosh, a veteran of the earlier Berlin raids. The rear-gunner, Sergeant R. Middleton from Leeds and the Junkers' gunner exchanged fire. A red glow appeared in the cockpit of the enemy night fighter and it disappeared below but the starboard fuel tank of the Lancaster, then more than half full, had taken hits and was set on fire. McIntosh jettisoned the bombs and turned for home. Three times he dived in an effort to blow the flames out but each time the flames spurted when the bomber levelled out. Luckily all four engines were still working and McIntosh gave them full throttle to cut time to the coast. The flight engineer unsuccessfully hacked at the fuselage to try to make a hole to get an extinguisher into the flames. As the coast of England came into view the port inner engine stopped and an emergency landing was made at the first airfield they saw. With the port wing framework red-hot the Lancaster landed and the station fire fighting personnel soon had the fire out. Another five minutes flying and the metal would have been completely burned through.

Group Captain Hughie Edwards VC DSO DFC, the first Australian air VC, who had taken command of RAF Binbrook on 18 February 1943, flew with the Australian heavies from his station, which took part in the big attack on Berlin. Twenty year old Pilot Officer Roberts C. Dunstan, the Australian one-legged air gunner, was in the rear turret of Edward's aircraft. Dunstan was already an 'old soldier'. When he was 17 he had joined the Australian Imperial Forces, as an engineer, advancing his age a little to enlist. He went into battle with the 6th Division and, on 15 January 1941, he was hit in the right knee by a shell fragment. His right leg was amputated after five operations and he was sent back to Australia, reaching Melbourne the day Russia entered the war against Germany. After seven months in hospital he was discharged with an artificial leg. He returned to school – a returned soldier at 19 – and prepared to take a course in law at the university. Then he began to think about flying, and urged the authorities to let him join the RAAF despite his disability. He was accepted in June 1942. He went to England as a sergeant on 18 November 1942 and at the end of May 1943 joined 460 Squadron. His first operation was an attack on Düsseldorf on 11 June and he finished his tour with an attack on the same target on 3 November. He used to take his crutches with him in the air and when he had to go aft would crawl there on one leg. Dunstan was commissioned in August 1943. During an attack on Kassel in the following October, a fighter attacked his aircraft and a shell smashed through Dunstan's turret and tore his sleeve. The turret itself was so badly damaged that the crew had to cut away the wreckage before they could get Dunstan out. At the end of his tour he won the DSO, the only Australian air gunner to win this award. He was a gunnery instructor when the war ended.[17]

Nine thousand Australians flew on Bomber Command operations, along with 20,000 Canadians and 3,000 New Zealanders who took part in the 'Empire Air Training Scheme'. Flight Sergeant Mick Christensen's crew in 460 Squadron RAAF at Binbrook was fairly typical of those in Bomber Command. Pilot Officer R. H. 'Chad' Chadwick recalls:

'Although we were in a Royal Australian Air Force squadron, the pilot was the only Australian in the crew. I was the only officer and the remainder, all sergeants. The skipper was a tall, strongly built Australian, with very much the look of a Viking and a natural leader. This made no difference. We seven were firm friends with tremendous mutual trust and respect and rank or position had no part in our approach to the job. This was highly desirable, of course, in the making of an efficient bomber crew. As an officer, I felt lucky to have one or two privileges that the others did not get and to make up for this I tried to do a few extra chores around the aircraft, before or after a trip. We all felt ourselves lucky to be on this particular squadron as we found that Australians were a wonderful race with whom to go to war. They had little time for anyone who pulled rank or position and basic discipline was good, but it was a discipline coming from natural leaders with a team keen to get on with the job. As RAF chaps found; an Aussie could call a man "a Pommy bastard" and make it sound an absolute term of endearment! On the other hand, any officer who started to put on airs and graces – very few did – merited the derogatory description "He's gone Pommy".'

Dominion airmen were among the most stalwart and direct members of the whole bunch. 'It was forbidden to have brothers in the same squadron' recalled one Lancaster flight sergeant gunner at Spilsby 'but the Aussies always found ways of ignoring the rules. We had two pairs of New Zealand brothers on our strength. We'd just returned from a raid one day and I was walking behind an Aussie when the CO came across and put his hand on his shoulder. "I'm sorry Dave," he said, "but your brother's plane has bought it. There are witnesses who saw it explode in the air. I'm afraid that there were no survivors."

"That's all right Sir," Dave said. "I'll have his egg and bacon." '[18]

On the night of 27/28 August, 674 heavy bombers were sent to attack Nuremberg. Warrant Officer Eddie Wheeler recalls:

'We were back with another 7,000lbs of "goodies" that were placed on workshops and marshalling yards with the aid of H_2S. On the return searchlights coned us and the heavy flak suddenly stopped, indicating that fighter activity could be expected. Jacky in the mid-upper turret spotted a fighter attacking from the starboard quarter and gave Johnny instructions to "corkscrew" and he and Geoff in the rear turret gave a burst of fire which made *N for Nan* shudder and the smell of cordite in the cabin was pungent. I was sitting at my radio listening to the Group broadcast and as I looked up I saw that there was a clean hole through the crystal monitor about 18 inches above and to the right of my head. A cannon shell had pierced it and gone straight out through the front of the aircraft. I was rigid, not daring to move an inch. The contact was brief and

the fighter sheered off – much to our relief. One of the crews, captained by Flight Lieutenant C. B. Robertson, did not return from this operation.'[19]

On 30/31 August 660 heavies targeted the cities of Mönchengladbach and Rheydt. Approximately half of the built-up area in each town was destroyed for the loss of 25 aircraft, 22 of which were shot down by the by *Zahme Sau*. The very next night 622 bombers assembled in a giant stream and headed for the 'Big City' once more.

Warrant Officer Eddie Wheeler, WOp/AG in 97 Squadron, recalls: 'Our hearts dropped again when we saw that the target was Berlin again. It seemed that the targets were becoming so much harder these days and I gained the impression that time was running out for me and the odds were increasing. I was becoming more nervous than ever before and was looking forward to finishing my tour of ops. Although we had a satisfactory trip we were upset to hear that Wing Commander Burns had been shot down. It was established subsequently that all except two of the crew had been taken prisoner of war.[20] The raids on Berlin were becoming monotonous when we found ourselves in flight again on 3 September against the "Big City". The seven and a half-hour return trip was carried out without too much trouble. There was no moon; no cloud and good visibility and our bombs released from 19,000 feet were seen to burst in a built up area. The flak as usual was intense and accurate but we escaped damage. From the frequency of raids on the Capital City, it was only too evident that the "Battle of Berlin" had started in earnest and we were repaying ten-fold the attacks on London in 1940/41. All our crews returned from this operation, one having to return early after two hours when Sergeant Miller's mid-upper gunner Sergeant Williams was rendered unconscious at 20,000 feet after his electrically heated suit and oxygen supply failed.'

On this night the radio-listening world went by proxy to Berlin with *F-Freddie* of 207 Squadron navigated by Warrant Officer H. F. Connely DFM RAAF from Brisbane, who was on his 50th sortie. The crew took Wynford Vaughan-Thomas, a BBC Home Service commentator, and an engineer, Mr. Reginald Pidsley, with them. Scottie, the flight engineer, was a cinema projectionist in Glasgow before the war. Sparky was bomb-aimer and the mid-upper gunner was in advertising while the rear-gunner was a Sussex farmer. On the first of the thousand raids, to Cologne, in May 1942 a Lancaster navigated by Connely took the only record of the great attack. He and his fellow airmen had remained over the city for 50 minutes, cruising around at about 4,000 feet getting photographs of the great fires. Vaughan-Thomas had to manage with a minimum of facts. They flew over the North Sea with the white breakers on the coastline below them. Nearing Germany with an audible tremor in his voice he said, 'Now, right before us lies darkness and Germany'. Later after describing the crew, the skipper remaining anonymous, he said, 'We are now well out over the sea and looking out all the time towards the enemy coast'. He spoke of 'a wall of searchlights, in hundreds, in cones and behind that wall is a pool of fiercer light, glowing red and green and blue and over that pool myriads of flares hanging in the sky. That's the city itself . . . Its going to be quite soundless, the roar of our aircraft is drowning everything else. We are running straight into the most gigantic display of soundless fireworks in the world and here we go to drop our bombs on Berlin.'

During the run-up to Berlin, the recording disc froze so hard that the release of the bomb broke it. In the broadcast the air bomber's recorded voice was heard saying, 'bombs away,' then counting . . . 'three, four, five, six' after a few seconds' gap. In that tiny interval Pidsley had slipped the broken disc off and put another on.

A *Naxos*-equipped Bf 109 night fighter of II./JG 300 came in just after the bomb doors opened, but the mid-upper and rear-gunners had shot it down almost before the rest of the crew were aware of its presence. The wireless operator called: 'He's down; he's down!' and Connely, rising from his navigator's table, looked back and saw the Messerschmitt float down the sky, a burning mass. The encounter had no effect on the bombing run, and the crew brought back a target photograph showing the Siemens works. Most of the bombing by over 300 Lancasters fell short and the part of the bombing, which did reach the capital's built-up area fell in residential parts of Charlottenburg and Moabit and in the industrial area called Siemensstadt. 'Not too much nattering,' the skipper told them. 'By God that looks like a bloody good show,' said one of the crew. 'Best I've ever seen,' added another. And then after some time, a third voice, rather quieter, speaking with something like awe; 'Look at that fire! Oh boy!' Connely sang 'Annie Laurie' on the way back (as listeners to the famous broadcast heard) 'because he felt so happy'. He did not know he was being recorded.

A total of 22 Lancasters were lost, including two aircraft in 106 Squadron. While the bomb doors of Squadron Leader D. W. S. Howroyd's Lancaster were still open, a Bf 110 attacked without warning from directly astern. There was one definite hit by a cannon shell and the rear-gunner reported that he was severely wounded. Although the pilot carried out the appropriate combat manoeuvres during this and subsequent attacks, three further shells hits were experienced. All of the turrets were damaged; the fuselage hit at the forend of the bomb bays and near the IFF position and the bomb-aimer fatally wounded. Nevertheless, the mid-upper gunner continued to reply effectively to the attacks and his claim to have destroyed the fighter was corroborated by the wireless operator in the astro hatch. As the intercom was severed during the combat the pilot was only aware that the attacks had suddenly ceased. Howroyd continues:

'I had my course already set on the DR compass and flew it for some way. In actual fact, this course was probably 060 degrees, as I did not realize that my DR compass was out of action. We were then at about 10,000 feet so I started to climb and tried to find out the state of my crew The bomb-aimer, Flying Officer T. W. A. Saxby was either dead or dying. The mid-upper gunner had passed out, owing to damaged oxygen supply and I was under the impression that he was dead. I knew that the rear-gunner, Sergeant L. G. A. McKenzie was badly injured. There was no intercom, or call lights and as we were by that time flying at over 20,000 feet it was difficult to make contact by word of mouth. After about half-an-hour, when I had time to check my DR compass against the P4, I found that the former was out of action and remained stationary on changing course. Then, steering by P4 compass and Sperry gyro, we presently made landfall on the south-east coast of Sweden. At the time we did not recognize it and subsequently mistook Lake Vattern for the Kattegat – we were by then up to 27,000 feet, having no means of defence other than height. Our course was 255 degrees until we obtained a fix 70 miles west of Denmark and changed course to 260 degrees. We then knew we had to ditch but hoped to get within 80 miles of the English coast. All this time the wireless operator was trying to get fixes. The flight engineer was acting as my runner and helping the navigator with the wounded. The former had previously said that he was all right but we found out later that he too was wounded. I discovered that my straps had been shot away and the flight engineer managed to fix me up some makeshift ones from oxygen extension tubes. At 04.50 hours he went aft, after I had given him three minutes warning of ditching. That was five hours after leaving Berlin.

'Ditching the aircraft presented no troubles, although only 10 degrees of flap could be obtained . . . I went back and got the pigeon, wireless and other equipment, which might be of use. As soon as it was light and a rather large predatory looking bird had left the area, I launched the pigeon. McKenzie went into a coma and died at about 06.00 hours. At about 09.00 hours I was keeping watch while the crew were asleep and saw two specks on the horizon, which came straight towards us at about 500 feet. They resolved into Hudsons, who dropped smoke-floats and circled us. Emergency rations were dropped and at about 11.00 hours an airborne lifeboat was dropped. At 16.00 hours two Naval Motor Launches appeared and we were taken aboard.'[21]

A 460 Squadron Lancaster piloted by Flying Officer F. H. Randall RAAF was another of the aircraft that failed to return. The flight was uneventful until the approach for bombing the target was made at a height of about 19,000 feet when one or two searchlights held the Lancaster. The Australian pilot immediately put the aircraft into a turn and dive, attaining a speed of about 300 mph IAS, but the Lancaster was soon afterwards coned and fired on by heavy flak. Hits by fragments were registered several times during this time. When the aircraft was coned Randall turned on all the cabin lights and found that this was of great assistance in seeing his instruments. He then made an approximate bombing run on the flares and ordered the bomb-aimer to jettison the bombs. As the searchlights appeared to be thinnest to the north it was decided to leave the target area that way, continuous weaving and a gentle dive were carried out as evasive action against predicted flak as the aircraft was still coned.

After diving to about 14,000 feet, the Lancaster was in such a position that the searchlights were pointing nearly vertically; suddenly the flak stopped and fighters came in to attack. It is believed that there were three fighters – two Ju 88s and a Bf 109. The first attack came from dead astern and level, but although the tracer passed close to the Lancaster, Randall believes that no hits were made on it. The second attack came from about 45 degrees on the port quarter and slightly above and in this attack the port engine was hit and set on fire. Randall cut off the petrol and feathered the propeller and the flight engineer operated the fire extinguisher with the result that the fire went out shortly afterwards. Randall was about to trim the aircraft for three-engined flying after feathering the port outer propeller but found that this was not necessary. There must, therefore, have been some unusual drag on the starboard side and Randall thinks that the starboard undercarriage must have dropped, since the warning light showed red about five minutes later. In addition it was not possible to close the bomb doors.

There were several more attacks and at one stage there were probably two fighters attacking simultaneously from the port and starboard quarters, as there were two streams of tracers intersecting in front of the aircraft. During the second or third attack the mid-upper turret was hit and badly damaged so that it was useless. The gunner whose microphone had been blown off his face, got out of his turret and went aft to the rear turret where he found that the rear-gunner had got out of his turret as his guns were unserviceable due to the barrels being buckled by cannon fire.

Finally, the starboard engine was hit and set on fire and the searchlights then doused and the fighters broke off their attack. The drill, as was used for the port outer engine, extinguished the fire. The mid-upper gunner told Randall later that at this time there was a fire above ... the bomb doors and a considerable quantity of smoke in the fuselage. After feathering the two outer engines, the inboard engines were running at 2850 +9 but it was not possible to maintain height and the control of the aircraft was poor. Randall tried to trim the aircraft but was unable to do so and the aircraft continued diving rapidly. Shortly after telling the crew to stand by to abandon the aircraft, Randall noticed a sudden torrent of wind blowing up from the nose and going out through his Perspex canopy, which had been damaged ... The aircraft, which was at about 7,000 feet, was still losing height and Randall told the flight engineer to get 3000 +2 on the two remaining engines. However, as even then the aircraft continued to lose height, the flight engineer pulled the cut-out when they were down to 5,000 feet and got 3000 +14 from the engines. Randall's idea was to get as far away from the target as possible before it was necessary to bale out.

The port centre and starboard inner petrol tanks were badly holed in the engagement because, on leaving the target, there were only 600 gallons left whereas on arrival there had been 1,200 gallons. After pulling the cut-out, the loss of height was checked and, after jettisoning the bomb carriers, it was possible to climb slowly to 6,000 feet. When it became apparent that the aircraft might be able to remain airborne for some little time it was decided to set course for Sweden ... It was necessary to fly at an IAS of 105–110 mph to maintain height and to keep straight full port aileron and full weight on port rudder applied. The elevator control was forcing the control column back, so that considerable force was required to push it forward and keep the aircraft level, as the trimmer was useless. Moreover, the aircraft kept shuddering.[22] The crew though that they were over Sweden and three of them baled out but they were in fact over Denmark and two landed safely and were taken prisoner. Flight Sergeant N. J. Conway RAAF was killed. By the time the rest of the crew were able to evacuate the aircraft they were being fired at by Swedish AA fire and the Lancaster crashed at Laröd near Helsingborg.[23]

On 5/6 September a force of 605 aircraft, 299 of them Lancasters, was dispatched to bomb the eastern side of Mannheim and then into Ludwigshafen on the western bank of the Rhine. Sergeant Leslie Cromarty of 61 Squadron, manned the rear turret of the Lancaster flown by Flying Officer Bernard C. Fitch this night:

'This was our first operation with the main force and it was a complete disaster from beginning to end. We were so excited when we heard we were flying that night and playing around in our dormitory Johnny Kershaw the WOp/AG swung a broom round his head and hit Harold Pronger, our mid-upper gunner in the eye. He had to go to the MO, who dressed it and advised him not to fly. There was no way that Harold was going to miss the trip. Then the WOp/AG left some of his notes in the Ops room and we had to wait on the tarmac for the WAAF driver to go and fetch them. Next, Flying Officer 'Ginger' Lyons accidentally opened his 'chute and we had another wait while someone brought another. By this time we were half an hour late taking off. We learned later that we should not have taken off so late but Flying Control thought we were a training flight and not part of the main force.

'We flew without incident until we were still some distance from the enemy coast. To my surprise I saw an aircraft approaching from the starboard quarter high. I identified it as a Fw 190. It came in very fast and we began corkscrewing. The Fw opened fire and I thought he had put his lights on. Then I realized it was his cannon. I opened fire at 200 yards with a long burst. Suddenly the Focke-Wulf reared up and began climbing. He was almost out of sight when he seemed to hang on his nose for a few seconds and then the nose slowly began to drop and he began diving. His speed built up and I thought he was attacking again. I could not fire because he was still out of range. I had to wait until he pulled out of his dive and attacked again. Instead, the Focke-Wulf continued to dive, gathering speed all the time. I lost sight of him for a while. Then I saw a flash and a great white ring on the sea. There was no smoke or fire, just a white ring growing bigger. I did not feel elated or pleased. I realized that I had just killed someone. I switched off my intercom and had a bit of a weep.

'Our aircraft was damaged in the attack and we had trouble with the starboard outer engine so we headed back. Big sparks flew past my turret and when I leaned forward I could see the engine beginning to burn. We crossed the English coast and tried to feather the engine. The Skipper called "Mayday" and we got an immediate response when there was a bright flash from the engine and the Skipper ordered us to bale out. I had the choice of either leaving via my turret doors, or climbing out to the rear exit. I chose the latter in case anyone needed help. When I reached the rear door the mid-upper gunner was already there and the navigator, Flying Officer Jennings, was coming down the fuselage. I sat on the step and he signalled me to go. I tucked my head into my knees and rolled out, just missing the tail. I landed in a field full of cows and went to a house for assistance but the only occupant was a woman. From an upstairs window she told me that her 'phone was disconnected. I walked to the road and flagged down a van. It was a RAF vehicle and the officer took me to the Police Station at Newark, which was only a couple of miles away. I contacted base and learned that my Skipper had successfully landed the aircraft by himself. I was the first to report in and return. The others arrived unhurt some hours later. We were given a 48-hour pass. So-called "Survivors" Leave.'[24]

Over 400 aircraft, 257 of them Lancasters, attacked Munich the following night. The Pathfinders discovered that the city was mostly covered by cloud and neither their ground markers nor their sky-markers were very effective. Most of the main force crews could do little else than bomb on a timed run from Lake Ammersee 21 miles south-west of the target. All got their bombs away during a 30 minute bombing period but the bombing was mostly scattered over the southern and western parts of Munich. Nineteen bombers including three Lancasters were lost. One Lancaster pilot on 100 Squadron passed out at 23,500 feet from lack of oxygen and the bomber plunged down. The navigator and flight engineer wrestled for control in the up-ended Lancaster and succeeded in pulling it out at 18,000 feet. At this lower altitude the pilot recovered and took over control. It was then that the bomb-aimer was found to be missing and it was not known whether he baled out or was thrown out. After landing at Waltham it was found that, in the terrific strain of the pull out, cowlings had been wrenched from the outer engines, the astrodome cracked, a canopy panel was missing and the aileron fabric had torn but the structure had held.

It was exactly four months after the famous Ruhr Dam's raid when, on the night of 15/16 September, 617 Squadron, which had moved to Coningsby with its tarmac runway on 30 August, was tasked to carry out a raid on the banks of the Dortmund-Ems Canal at

Ladbergen near Greven, just south of the junction with the Mittelland Canal. Here there was a raised section where aqueducts carry the canal over a river. This time the delayed-fuse mines were the new 12,000lb light-case bomb (not the 12,000lb *Tallboy* earthquake bomb developed later), which had been made in three sections bolted together with a six-finned tail unit on the end. It was so big that it needed special bomb trolleys to move it from the store and it took 35 minutes to be winched into the bomb bay of each Lancaster. The first attempt the night before by eight Lancasters, had been aborted.[25] Squadron Leader David J. H. Maltby DSO DFC and crew, all of whom had flown on the Dam's raid, were lost on the way home eight miles north-east of Cromer when their Lancaster cart wheeled into the North Sea.[26] With little sleep, eight of the crews were ordered back into the air the very next night to try again with the 12,000lb light-case bombs. Ray Grayston, the recently commissioned flight engineer on *N-Nan* captained by Pilot Officer Les Knight DSO RAAF, says, 'We didn't think it was a very good idea and we were right'. The attack on the Dortmund-Ems Canal on 15/16 September was led by Squadron Leader George Holden DSO DFC* MID in *S-Sugar*. That morning the new CO had broken the news of Maltby's death to his wife Nina, who lived near the airfield with their two month old son. 'Too stunned to cry she had told the CO that it was not unexpected. He had been waking up in the night lately shouting something about the bomb not coming off.'[27]

S-Sugar's crew included Flying Officer 'Spam' Spafford as bomb-aimer and three other men who had flown with Gibson in the attack on the Möhne dam.[28] Among the other Dam Busters, Flight Lieutenant Mick Martin DSO DFC, who had returned from leave and had demanded to take Maltby's place, piloted *P-Popsie* the No. 2 Lancaster in the first formation. Flight Lieutenant Dave Shannon DSO DFC, who was due to marry his fiancée, Ann Fowler, a dark, slim Section Officer in the WAAF at Scampton, in a week and was supposed to have left for London to make the arrangements, piloted *L-Love,* No. 2 in the second formation. Maltby was to have been his best man. For the flight to Ladbergen Les Knight and *N-Nan* were No. 3 in the first formation. A fourth Dam Buster crew was captained by Flying Officer Geoff Rice who had aborted the famous raid after hitting the sea on the outward flight, ripping off the *Upkeep* mine and tearing a hole in the bomb bay, flying back on two engines.

In the control tower at Coningsby Joe McCarthy, now a squadron leader with a DSO for the Dam's raid and a bar to his DFC added at the beginning of his third

tour, watched as the eight Lancasters took off and headed east for the Dortmund-Ems Canal at around midnight. Outwardly McCarthy had a personality that matched his physique. His colourful American expletives were freely lavished on all who crossed his path. This was in marked contrast to the more austere profanity of the British pilots. Also watching was a 'languid' WAAF who said, as the Lancasters merged with the darkness, 'My God, I only hope they get there tonight! The trouble the AOC's gone to over this ...' McCarthy turned on her and snarled, 'The hell with you and all the AOCs. What about the seven lives in every kite!' The building vibrated as the door slammed behind him.[29] Near the end of the war, Joe McCarthy adapted to the British way, being seen with a pipe, a walking stick and a dog on a lead. 'If I'm going to be an officer and a gentleman, I'm going to have a crack at looking the part,' he said.

A wall of heavy fog lay along the frontier of Germany and Belgium as the aircraft flew in at rooftop level. It had moved in from the east 'without warning, almost without precedent'. Grayston said:

'The new CO took us across the Dutch coast and over an industrial area with no shortage of anti-aircraft batteries. Bang, bang, bang and all of his fuel tanks were hit. There was a mile of burning fuel flying out behind him and we were panicking to get out of the way before his mine went off. We just made it clear of him as he dropped out of the sky.'

S-Sugar half-turned, dived and rolled to earth. It exploded on the ground in successive bursts as the oil tanks, then the bombs, exploded. Some of the experts said later that Flight Lieutenant Ralf A. P. Allsebrook DSO DFC, the deputy controller, should have called off the operation when the fog had moved in but they pressed on. Allsebrook, an alumnus of Trinity College, Oxford[30] is believed to have bombed eventually but where his bomb went is not known. They never found the wreckage of his Lancaster either. Flight Lieutenant Harold S. Wilson, 28 years old, who came from Tottenham in north London, was heard briefly over the R/T saying something about going in to attack. The 12,000lb bomb was still aboard when his Lancaster hit the ground about 200 yards beyond the canal and it made a crater 200 feet across.[31] Pilot Officer William Divall was heard briefly over the R/T but that was the last anyone ever heard from him. Wilson and Divall had been prevented from flying the Dam's raid in May because of sickness in their crews.

Mick Martin took charge, with Knight's Lancaster on his starboard side and another on the port. The formation turned to avoid an airfield whose flare path could be seen below and eventually the three bombers went around north of Rheims. Martin believed that Knight's Lancaster must have been hit at this stage, because suddenly he found himself with only one accompanying Lancaster. A few minutes later, Knight's calm voice was heard on the radiotelephone: 'I have lost two engines. May I have permission to jettison sir?' At this time Knight must have been only about 50 feet above the ground, in an aircraft faltering to its fate with only two engines functioning and nearly six tons of high explosive on board. It was an example of iron discipline that he should pause to ask permission to drop his bomb.

Martin replied: 'OK, jettison. Good luck!' and he heard the leader of the other formation, invisible in the darkness echo his 'Good luck!' Three or four minute's later Knight's voice was heard again: 'I have successfully jettisoned and am endeavouring to return to base.' The other pilots came in on the radiotelephone with their individual 'good luck' calls. From high above, from one of the escorting Mosquitoes, came too, the good wishes of Flight Lieutenant Charles Scherf, later to become an outstanding intruder pilot. That was the last the bomber men heard of Knight. Ray Grayston recalled:

'At the target area, there was fog and we couldn't even see the ground. We circled at low level and saw a couple of guys fly into the deck. Then we did too. We clipped the top of a wood, had two engines ripped off and had part of a tree sticking out of the starboard wing. We knew we weren't going to last long. Les Knight tried to get us back up to a height where we had a chance of survival if we jumped. He got it to 1,500 feet and ordered us to bale out. But the aircraft was keeling over and Les needed me to help him struggle with the controls. Everyone grabbed their parachutes and dived out ... and that left just Les and me. He had his leg stretched out rigid on the rudder bar and he couldn't move because if he let go, the machine was going to just fall over. So Les said, "OK, I'll do what I can. Away you go." I jumped out at about 800 feet and the chute opened. The Lanc flew straight into a tree, caught fire and Les was killed.'[32]

The bomber men began looking for the target. Martin was then eight to ten miles north of it. Shannon was, at that stage, three or four miles from it, also searching. Martin spent 84 minutes and Shannon 45 minutes in the fog at low level over this heavily defended area in search of their target, and both bombed at last after they had carefully identified it. The only surviving aircraft at this stage were the Lancasters piloted by Martin, Shannon and Flying Officer Geoff Rice, who

tried for an hour to find the canal. Martin spent an hour and a half plunging at 150 feet in the fog around the canal trying to find a good enough sight on the few spots where the high earth bank was vulnerable. Finally, on the 13th run Flight Lieutenant R. C. 'Bob' Hay DFC* his South Australian bomb-aimer and the Squadron Bombing Leader since 617 Squadron's formation, got a glimpse of water in the swirling fog and they at last dropped the bomb. A little later they hurtled back across the canal and saw the water boiling where the bomb had exploded, a few feet from the bank, just a few feet too far, because the bank was still there. It was 70 minutes before Shannon got a quick sight of the high banks of the canal. He wheeled the Lancaster along the water and his bomb-aimer called, 'Bomb Gone!' There was an 11 second delay on the fuse so they only dimly saw the explosion.[33] These three alone returned to Scampton.[34]

Mick Martin was made up to squadron leader and given temporary command of the Squadron. When asked if he thought that the Dam Busters needed a rest to 'fill up' with new crews and train them, he said, 'No. Let's do another one right away and get the taste out of our mouths.' Martin got his way and the night following the Dortmund-Ems debacle, eight Lancasters of 617 Squadron and four from 619 Squadron set out to bomb the Anthéor viaduct near Cannes on the coastal railway line leading to Italy. Another 340 aircraft, including 43 Lancasters, were to attack the important railway yards at Modane in a steep valley on the French Alpine border on the main rail route to Italy, but the marking of the target was not successful and the bombing was not accurate. The visit to the French Riviera did not go well either. The Lancaster crews found the viaduct in the moonlight without trouble 15 miles west of Cannes and saw the 90-foot stone arches curving back across the beach at the foot of a ravine. The plan was to dive to 300 feet and drop 1,000lb bombs with delayed fuses into the stone but the bombs missed by inches, the bombs going through the arches and exploding on the ground. The Dam Busters would later return to the viaduct with even bigger bombs but this first raid simply alerted the Germans to the vulnerability of the structure and soon after the flak batteries moved in. One Lancaster of 619 Squadron was lost when it came down in the sea off Portugal while trying to reach Gibraltar. The Dam Busters now began retraining as a specialist high-altitude bombing squadron to drop bombs on suitable enemy targets. Crews believed, wrongly as it turned out, that their immediate target might be the *Tirpitz,* which was not bombed by 617 until almost exactly a year later.

On 23/24 September Ron Clark and the crew of *Phantom of the Ruhr* came closest to disaster on their last trip, when 627 bombers set out to destroy the northern part of Mannheim. They took off in the *Phantom* with the first wave arriving over the target on time. The weather was clear with the glow of the Rhine clearly visible. Commencing the bombing run at 21,000 feet the *Phantom* was immediately caught by the master searchlight and quickly coned by up to 80 more. Clark put the bomber into a steep dive but the searchlights stayed with them and a flak shell hit the aircraft. One shell damaged the starboard elevator. Another shell, which went through the bomb bay and out through the top of the fuselage without exploding, narrowly missed 'Lish' Easby at his wireless. The shell severed the starboard aileron control causing the aircraft to go out of control. With the control column jammed hard over Clark and 'Ben' Bennett struggled to regain control as they plummeted earthwards. Sergeant Geoff Green was immobilized in his rear turret by the G-forces imposed by the gyrating aircraft and blinded by searchlights. He joked later that at least he had enough light to finish his crossword puzzle and when Lish yelled, 'corkscrew' from the astrodome, the rear-gunner thought it was drinks all round at last!

Clark and Bennett finally succeeded in recovering the aircraft at 13,000 feet but, still held in searchlights, were attacked by a night fighter from astern, damaging the port wing trailing edge and flap. Another shell hit the starboard tail plane. Having just regained control, Clark could see streams of tracer flashing in front of him and knew that despite limited control and considerable damage to his aircraft he had no choice but to throw *Phantom* into another steep dive. He successfully avoided the fighter and recovered the aircraft again, this time at only 4,000 feet but was still followed by the searchlights that now appeared to be almost horizontal in their pursuit of the aircraft. The crew managed to clear the target area and jettison their bombs, but *Phantom* was vibrating violently with the port wing and the tail plane 'flapping up and down'. Despite operating under the most extreme conditions Ben Bennett determined that the severe vibration was due to the starboard aileron trim tab still being connected. Armed with a penknife he delved into the control pedestal and somehow found the right trimming wires, cut them and the vibration stopped. Clark flew the crippled bomber home and landed at Waltham without flaps and only partial aileron control. For their actions that night, saving their aircraft and crew, Ron Clark and Ben Bennett received the DFC and DFM respectively. In the hangar the tail fin from a 30lb incendiary bomb was found in the air intake of one of the engines, indicating that bombs from above had also hit the aircraft. Severe damage was found to the tail and rudder and at least 300 shrapnel holes counted in the aircraft. *Phantom* had survived but it would be out of commission until early November.[35]

Bomber Command continued the offensive against German cities with four raids on Hanover in September--October. On 27/28 September Hanover was the target for 678 aircraft although of these only 612 dropped their bombs, but scattered them in open country. RAF crews were not yet expert with the new H_2S navigational radar, which showed up an expanse of water very well but the Steinhuder Scc, a large lake, which was used as a way point, had been almost completely covered with boards and nets. Millions of strips of 'Window' were dropped but losses were high.[36] On 29/30 September 352 aircraft raided Bochum, losing nine bombers. A Lancaster of 83 Squadron flown by Flying Officer C. P. McDonald RCAF had taken off from Wyton at a little after 18.20 that evening when it went into a dive from which recovery took the combined efforts of the pilot, with his feet on the instrument panel, and the navigator and flight engineer. The Lancaster was still nose heavy so it was headed for home. Once back over England in the area of Swaffham in Norfolk McDonald ordered the crew to bale out. To keep the Lancaster steady for his own exit he jammed a bag between the control column and the instrument panel. The bomber then flew on an approximately straight course for 80 miles before striking the ground. Most of this crew had been interned in Sweden after raiding Stettin in April 1943.[37]

When a bombing force of 294 Lancasters set out for Munich on the night of 2/3 October[38] Warrant Officer Eddie Wheeler DFC WOp/AG in 97 Squadron had no prior knowledge that this would be his crew's final operation together.

'Perhaps it was just as well as we might have been even more nervous in our anxiety to survive. As it was the trip was largely uneventful except that we coaxed Hitch, our navigator to leave his seat and take up position in the astrodome to see what was going on over the target area. His remarks over the intercom brought smiles to our faces when he said, "Christ! Does this sort of thing go on every night?" Seeing the mass of fires in the target area he considered it was "sheer bloody murder". Ginger too was on this raid and he was to be involved in five further operations against Berlin. Our crew was stood down for a few days after this until Johnny called us together and said, "Well lads, do we want to go on, or for some of us at least, shall we call it a day?" For Johnny, Hitch, Jackie Blair and myself, we had done our quota and would ask to be relieved of further operational duty. Bill (flight engineer), Peter (air bomber) and Geoff (rear-gunner) had no option but to continue. Peter anxiously cleaned his pipe, Bill kept shuffling his feet and Geoff nervously fingered his lanyard whilst the rest of us tried to reach a decision. If we old-stagers decided to finish, then Bill, Peter and Geoff would be assigned to a new crew to finish their first tour. Whilst they were hopeful that the crew would not split up, they recognized that we had done our fair share of ops over a long period and in similar circumstances they would say, "enough is enough". Johnny posed the question to us again and there seemed a reluctance to reply. Finally, I said that the last half dozen trips had been a nightmare for me and I had been getting progressively more nervous, so I was going to call it a day. Hitch said he agreed with me and so it was decided to tell the CO, Wing Commander Alabaster, we had made up our minds. Naturally, the other three lads were disappointed but they thanked us for the happy times we had enjoyed at Bourn and we wished them all the luck that was going.'

After several frustrating delays converting from the Halifax, 408 Squadron RCAF became operational with Lancasters on the night of 7/8 October when the target was Stuttgart. Some 343 Lancasters were dispatched, with a further 16 Lancasters carrying out a diversionary raid without loss on the Zeppelin factory at Friedrichshafen. Sixteen of the aircraft in the new Canadian Lancaster Squadron took off from Linton-on-Ouse and 14 returned. One of 408 Squadron's Lancasters flown by Flight Sergeant J. D. Harvey RCAF got into difficulties over Hutton-le-Hole, Yorkshire, 18 miles east of Thirsk and had to be abandoned by the crew. The Lancaster crashed at Manor Farm, Spaunton, where a 51 year old farmer, George Strickland, was killed when the 4,000lb cookie exploded. Altogether, four Lancasters were lost this night when the German night fighter controller was confused by the Mosquito diversion on Munich and only a few night fighters intercepted the main force attack.[39]

New arrivals on 61 Squadron at RAF Syerston in October 1943 included Sergeant C. J. 'Jeff' Gray and his crew who had very little idea of what lay ahead. They were full of youthful exuberance and confident that they came with a good report from their instructors at the Operational Conversion Unit. Why else would they have cut short the final cross country stages and packed them off to a squadron? Gray recalled:[40]

'Our new Commanding Officer seemed unimpressed with us. Shortage of Lancaster aircraft at the OCU might be nearer the mark for your early arrival was his comment, followed by the statement that he would not allow us to commence flying operations until we had made good our shortfall in flying time in Lancasters. However, he would find us an easy target with which to start our operational tour. This promise, was not, as it turned out, a simple one to discharge in the winter of 1943 while serving in a front line squadron of Bomber Command. A few days later a distressing experience awaited us. The whole station was ordered on parade to witness some poor wretch being stripped of his flight engineer's brevet, his sergeant's stripes and finally the brass buttons on his jacket. It seems he had had enough and decided to go home. He made no attempt to run away, he simply went home. The Military Police brought him back to be disgraced in front of comrades. Suddenly a drum started to beat and the sergeant was read a charge of desertion. Throughout this display of cruel humiliation the drum kept beating, then the bareheaded prisoner was marched quickly off the parade ground under escort to start his punishment.[41] If we had been under any illusions as to the realities of the course on which we were now embarked, we were thus shortly disabused.'

As Jeff Gray and his crew waited for an 'easy' target there were plenty of difficult and dangerous ones on the battle order throughout October such as Bremen, Hanover, Leipzig and Kassel, although Berlin was noticeably absent since the costly raids in August. Had they felt obliged, the old sweats would have told them that there was no such thing as an 'easy' target. The operation to Hanover on the night of 18/19 October saw 360 Lancasters set out and 18 lost. Over the target a Lancaster of 166 Squadron flown by Warrant Officer J. F. Thomas steadied up for the run-in, with the bomb doors already open. For minutes there was a fusillade of flak and the mid-upper gunner, Sergeant A. V. Collins, was wounded. After a lull a twin-engined night fighter closed in, firing short bursts, which set the port inner engine on fire and started a fire in the fuselage. Collins, with pieces of flak embedded in his back, stamped the flames in the fuselage out, although this meant leaving his oxygen supply post. Thomas managed to elude the night fighter in a series of evasive moves but over the French coast, at a lower height, the Lancaster was a target for light flak and the bomber was hit again. Over the English coast the port outer engine stopped but Thomas managed to land safely at Kirmington on two engines. (On 2 November Thomas was awarded the DFC and Collins the DFM for their actions on the Hanover raid. Thomas and his crew were shot down on 26/27 November when five of them survived to be taken prisoner and two, including Collins, who tried to assist the rear-gunner, were killed.)

Another Lancaster returned from Hanover on one engine when Wing Commander P. Burnett DFC the CO of 9 Squadron and his veteran crew landed the badly shot up bomber at Bardney after a tussle with a Ju 88 night fighter when nearing home. Sixty cannon shells hit the Lancaster, the majority of which passed straight through but several hit the trimming controls, the airscrew pitch controls and the hydraulic control pipes. Only one engine remained steady, the revolutions of which could not be altered owing to control damage. Of the other three engines, two stopped altogether and the propeller of the third raced like a Catherine Wheel, shedding sparks. Burnett nursed the stricken Lancaster to Bardney, but landing was prevented when another Lancaster crashed on the main runway and only a subsidiary runway, across wind, was available. The undercarriage responded to the emergency system and a landing was effected without mishap. Within four days the Lancaster was reported serviceable, but three new engines and two new turrets had to be installed as well as the replacement of piping and minor components.

One of the Lancasters that failed to return from Hanover was *Z-Zebra* of 207 Squadron, which was piloted by Flight Sergeant Geoff Taylor RAAF and his crew, who had taken off from Spilsby at 17.16 hours. Hauptmann Friedrich Karl Müller, a *Wilde Sau* pilot of Stab JG 300, an ex-bomber pilot and pre-war Lufthansa captain, intercepted them. Müller who was nicknamed Felix or *Nasen* (nose, on account of his aristocratic proboscis) shot *Z-Zebra* down near Reinerbeck for his 19th victory. Taylor describes the loss of his aircraft:

'As the dark horizon of Germany rapidly climbs higher round you, and *Z-Zebra* drops bumping into low cloud, rage grips you again this time at the thought of six men, six friends they are, riding with you and waiting for you to do something, hoping for the act of wizardry that will pull the rabbit out of the fire. Or is it the hat? You can't think which. There's Billy, married, by a few months. You never did meet his wife. Don; due to be married in a fortnight. Joe, long since married and content. The rest of the boys, like yourself, with light-hearted dates for tomorrow night. A bloody fine skipper you turned out to be. Thoughts like these loom rapidly into your consciousness to vanish as quickly, pursued by wishful-thinking calculations of fuel and range. Like a stab in the back, the starboard inner engine suddenly screams and spews flame. Don reaches for the feathering and fire buttons. He might just as well have sat back and sung the Lord's Prayer. Faithfully he plays out the little game he was taught but, in the language of the times, you have had it. Aching with the sheer muscular effort of holding up the plunging port wing, you feel the elevators tighten as the nose goes down with a lurch. Too tired to think, you hear your voice giving the queer little order they taught you one drowsy summer day at the operational training unit in pastoral Oxfordshire; the absurd jingle you had never really thought you would ever use: "Abracadabra, jump, jump. Abracadabra, jump, jump".'[42]

One pilot who refused to jump and would not be pushed was Warrant Officer J. White of 630 Squadron stationed at East Kirkby. His Lancaster came under attack from a night fighter on the night of 20/21 October when the target for 358 Lancasters was Leipzig. The main force bombing was very scattered, the weather was later described as 'appalling' and sixteen aircraft were lost. White's rear-gunner was mortally wounded in the night fighter attack, which also caused crippling damage to the aircraft. With the hydraulics shot through White commenced his attack and then limped home to land at an unfamiliar airfield. When asked if he wanted an emergency landing, when circling with a flaming engine, he replied that a few more minutes waiting for clearance would not matter, as he had already been alight for hours! When he did land he stayed with the fire crew until the flames were extinguished. White was awarded the DFM on 31 December for bringing his badly damaged Lancaster home from Leipzig. He and his crew were shot down on the Berlin raid on 24/25 March 1944 and White died at the controls of his bomber while his crew all baled out and were taken prisoner.

Death was part of the scene and men felt a sense of sorrow when a certain crew had not returned. When, on 22/23 October, 569 aircraft, 322 of them Lancasters, attacked Kassel, 43 aircraft were lost. Eighteen of these were Lancasters. The disruption caused and the destruction in the city was on a grand scale with over 4,300 dwellings, containing almost 28,000 people, destroyed and over 6,700 more damaged. Upwards of 120,000 Germans had to leave their homes. By the end of November the number of dead recovered from Kassel was almost 5,600 people of which, more than 1,800 were unidentifiable. Amid the carnage on the ground one Lancaster returned with a rear-gunner dead in his turret having been killed by fire from the mid-upper turret of another as he traversed his turret to follow the course of a night fighter. This singularly distressing incident could have been avoided if the interrupter gear in the MUG turret had not been destroyed by enemy action.

At Syerston meanwhile, Jeff Gray and his crew still awaited the 'easy' target that had been promised but then from Bomber Command Headquarters came the call for maximum effort from all bomber stations and Gray's crew found themselves briefed, with the others, for Berlin. 'So much for the CO's easy target', Gray remembers. 'As we waited inside the aircraft for the time to start engines, I noticed with growing anxiety, the gathering fog shrouding the dispersal. On this still unfamiliar airfield, my first concern had to be finding the way out of the dispersal to the main runway. Then, much to my relief a white Very light went up from the control tower signifying recall. The operation was scrubbed. We handed back the flying rations including the much prized chocolate bar. It was then that I noticed we were the only ones to do so, one small lesson learnt. We returned to our programme of cross-country flights. There was one consolation in all this. Syerston was only a few miles from Nottingham, famed throughout the RAF for its pretty girls, the fairest of the fair. Between the training flights and the 'promised' easy target, hopefully there would be other delights. Finally, Geoff Ward, my navigator and I were rostered separately for our supernumerary flights. It was the custom to treat the navigator and pilot of sprog crews to a trip with an experienced crew. The target was Düsseldorf, the date 3 November.[43] My experienced crew were about mid-tour. To my surprise they spent a lot of time weaving about. This seemed particularly hazardous in the dark within a stream of bombers although I had heard there were those who favoured such a technique. As we approached the target the weaving continued. I could only guess that the defenders had resorted to a box barrage, each anti-aircraft shell bursting to leave a puff of black smoke, which hung suspended in the night sky, the gaps between growing ever smaller. They showed up clearly in the glow of incendiary fires from below. At any moment I expected the pilot to straighten up in preparation for the bombing run but no, with the bomb-aimer complaining, the weaving continued. Then, more extraordinary still, we broke away, turning left across the bomber stream, then back the way we had come for a second approach. I must say I was most impressed by the cool and steely behaviour of the whole crew throughout this manoeuvre although I could not quite suppress the thought that it might have been better if they had got it right the first rime round. Geoff Ward, being a somewhat phlegmatic Yorkshireman, found nothing remarkable to report from his trip. But one member of 61 Squadron most certainly did.'[44]

Acting Flight Lieutenant William 'Bill' Reid RAFVR and his crew of *O-Oboe* of 61 Squadron crossed the North Sea without incident. Reid, the son of a Scottish blacksmith and not quite 22 years old was on his 10th op. He had enlisted for training as aircrew in 1941 and trained as a pilot in the United States. Reid had been posted to 61 Squadron at Syerston near Nottingham on 6 September 1943. As they crossed the Dutch coast Reid's windscreen was suddenly shattered by fire from a twin-engined night fighter. Flight Sergeant Frank Emerson[45] in the rear turret was unable to open fire immediately because his hands were frozen owing to a failure in the heating circuit, and he could not operate his microphone for the same reason. The rear turret was badly damaged; the communications system and the compasses were put out of action, and the elevator trimming tabs of the Lancaster were damaged. The bomber became difficult to control. Emerson was unaware of the damage that the night fighter had caused to the rest of the aircraft, but it had registered hits in the cockpit area of *O-Oboe*, leaving Reid nursing wounds to the head, shoulders and hands. He said later: 'I just saw a blinding flash and felt as if my head had been blown off. My shoulder was a bit stiff and it felt as if someone had hit me with a hammer. Blood was pouring down my face and I could feel the taste of it in my mouth. It soon froze up because of the intense cold.'

Reid asked, 'Everybody OK?' Miraculously, the rest of the crew were unscathed and, on receiving answers, he said, 'Resuming course.' He didn't say he was hit, but 'the wind was lashing through the broken windscreen and pieces of the Perspex had cut my face'. Despite his wounds and damage to the aircraft, Reid was determined to carry on to Düsseldorf. 'There were other bombers behind us and if we had turned we might have been a danger to them,' he said. Flight Sergeant L. G. 'Les' Rolton the bomb-aimer added later: 'We gave all the oxygen to the pilot, who was navigating by the stars.' Soon afterwards, however, *O-Oboe* was pounced on again, this time by a Fw 190 *Wilde Sau*. The Lancaster was raked from nose to tail with cannon fire. Emerson put up a brave resistance, returning fire with his only serviceable machine gun but the damaged state of his turret made accurate aiming impossible. Flight Sergeant Cyril Baldwin climbed out of his mid-upper turret, which had been hit, to see for himself the extent of the damage to the aircraft. He found 22 year old WOp/AG Flight Sergeant J. J. Mann, a Liverpudlian, lying full length over the body of Pilot Officer John Jeffreys RAAF, Reid's 30 year old navigator from Perth, Western Australia, who was dead with a bullet through his skull. The oxygen system aboard the aircraft had been put out of action. Baldwin helped the badly wounded wireless operator into his seat and put an oxygen tube from a portable supply into his mouth. Reid had also been hit once again. Though wounded in the forearm, Flight Sergeant Jim W. 'Taffy' Norris, flight engineer, supplied him with oxygen from another portable supply and Reid was able to carry on.

En route the bombers encountered heavy flak with searchlights over Holland and night fighters shot down six bombers. A total of 525 aircraft reached Düsseldorf, where the anti-aircraft guns opened up with a vengeance, reaching 15–16,000 feet, occasionally aimed at aircraft held by searchlight cones above this level. Eighty night fighters were reported over the city, as many as 55 of these being twin-engined. The fighters damaged 14 returning bombers while three enemy fighters were claimed destroyed. The 'heavies' opened their attack with three red TIs dropped in salvo by an *Oboe* Mosquito. The serviceability of *Oboe* on this night was very poor with the result that only five bundles of sky-markers and three of TIs were dropped. Seventy-two main force aircraft carried H_2S for navigational purposes and 55 reached the target with their sets in order. There was little cloud and, in the light of a half moon, an accurate ground-marking attack was delivered. Decoy fires at Macherscheid, five miles from Düsseldorf, were started but the main force dropped their HE on the aiming point in the extreme north-east of the city but, with the usual undershooting, the RAF attack spread rapidly south-south-westwards. Most of the 2,000 tons of bombs dropped fell within the built-up area.[46]

Bill Reid flew the course to and from the target by the Pole Star and the moon. He was growing weak from loss of blood, and the emergency oxygen supply had given out. With the windscreen shattered, the cold was intense, and he occasionally lapsed into semi-consciousness. Rolton recalled: 'The Lancaster went into a dive and I saw the engineer pull the pilot off the stick and level the aircraft. That was the first I knew of anyone being wounded. I went back and helped the engineer to control the aircraft. The pilot several times regained consciousness. As one of the elevators had been shot away, the aircraft tended to go into a dive and both of us had to hold the stick.' Bill Reid confirms:

'Considering that I was in the pilot's seat with my left foot jammed on the rudder because of the effect of the elevator damage and having my hands clasped in front of the stick to hold it back – because of the fact that it acted nose heavy – I did have some effect on the plane's reaction. Les Rolton helped by pushing back on the stick from in front and sighting a beacon flashing,

signifying land and asking for the wireless operator's 'flimsy' so that we could find out where we were.'

Norris and Rolton braved heavy anti-aircraft fire over the Dutch coast and, clinging to the stick all the way across the North Sea, kept the Lancaster in the air. Bill Reid continues: 'I do remember Jim shaking me and pointing to the fuel gauges and then downwards, meaning that it was time we landed as we were running out of fuel. I also saw the searchlights to the north of us, for which I headed and it was en route to them that the layout of Shipdham airfield[47] in Norfolk appeared below us.' Reid resumed control, and made ready to land. Ground mist partially obscured the runway lights and Reid was also much troubled by blood from his head wound getting into his eyes. With the hydraulics shot out, he had no brakes for landing, and the legs of the damaged undercarriage collapsed when the load came on, but he got *O-Oboe* down safely. The Lancaster skidded to a halt on its belly as ambulances and crash wagons raced over to the unexpected arrival to help get everybody out of the plane. Reid was given a blood transfusion and spent four days at the Norfolk & Norwich Hospital, before being transferred to a military hospital. It was while convalescing that he was told he had been awarded the Victoria Cross.[48]

Jeff Gray adds: 'During this era, the senior officers of 61 Squadron were much given to the press on regardless, stiff upper lip school of thought. So much so, that the Squadron records at the Public Records Office make no mention of Jock's VC, only a pencil entry added years later draws attention to his courage and determination. After recovering from his injuries Jock was poached by 617 Squadron (The Dam Busters) where his Scottish tenacity was appreciated.'[49]

Sergeant Gray and his crew spent a week at Syerston until their CO's long awaited easy trip finally came on the night of 10/11 November, when 61 Squadron were part of a force briefed to bomb the entrance to the railway tunnel at Modane in the French Alps, through which ran the main rail link into Italy. Gray recalls:

'As a Sprog crew we didn't have a regular aircraft of our own so we had been given QR-M *Mickey the Moocher* for this operation.[50] After getting the green light from the control caravan we turned onto the main runway. As we moved forward I felt at last we were an operational crew. Unfortunately my inexperience almost caused a disastrous ground loop. I wasn't used to the slow acceleration of a fully loaded Lancaster and I opened up the engines too soon before I had full rudder control. Slowly, but inexorably, we began to swing to port. It was decision time. I slammed the throttles shut and we ground to a halt. The crew was a little shaken up but otherwise OK so I decided the best thing to do was to try again. We quickly turned left off the runway, over the grass and passed very close to the control tower and rejoined the queue of aircraft for a second attempt. With McCulloch my flight engineer complaining about the engine coolant temperature going off the clock, we took another green light from the caravan and this time, making no mistakes, we lumbered off into the night. The weather over France was perfect and, by following the railway track, the undefended target was easy to find. However the Pathfinder marking was slightly beyond the target but because of the usual raid creepback, 200 Lancaster crews brought back photographs to show that their bombs fell within one mile of the aiming point. This raid resulted in the railway yard and tunnel being severely damaged, thus preventing war materials getting through to the German army in Italy. Ron Jones our bomb-aimer said our run up to the target was perfect and he felt our bombing result would be good. After such an almost disastrous start to the operation everyone wanted to prove our worth to the Squadron CO. As it turned out Ron was right and a week later Air Vice-Marshal Cochrane sent us his congratulations along with an aiming point photograph. We decided to keep quiet about our bombing success at Modane when talking to our peers and if ever I inclined to immodesty, my crew quickly reminded me of the row of ashen faces on the control tower balcony as our Lancaster hurtled passed.

Meanwhile, on 3 November Bomber Harris had picked up the cudgel aimed at Berlin again, noting Churchill saying that, 'We can wreck Berlin from end to end if the USAAF will come in on it. It will cost us 400–500 aircraft. It will cost Germany the war.' A fortnight later raids on Berlin were resumed, the first of 16 such attacks known as the 'Third Battle of Berlin', going ahead on the night of the 18/19 November when an all-Lancaster force, 440 strong, was sent to pound the German capital. The 'Big City' was covered with a blanket of 10/10ths cloud and both marking and bombing were carried out blindly. Six special Lancasters carried the new H$_2$S Mark III navigational device, which worked on a wavelength of 3cm instead of 10cm, and only one set broke down. Fighters were not very active and there was no evidence that they achieved any success, as only nine Lancasters were lost but a further 90 aircraft were damaged by flak.

On the night of the 22nd/23rd 764 aircraft, 469 of them Lancasters, returned to the *Reich* capital when, because of the dry weather conditions, several 'firestorm' areas were reported and a smoke cloud rose to 19,000 feet. The following night 383 aircraft, mostly Lancasters, bombed the German capital again. The city was cloud covered again and the Pathfinders carried out sky marking though many crews simply aimed their bombs through the cloud at the glow of 11 major fires still burning from the night before. These two raids cost Bomber Command 46 aircraft; all except 15 of them were Lancasters.

The night of the 26/27th was the fourth and last of the great November attacks on the Big City and another 'maximum effort'. At Elsham Wolds 103 Squadron managed 30 Lancasters on the battle order. At Wyton preparations were severely hampered when a Lancaster of 83 Squadron blew up just before 17.00 while an armourer crew were working on it. An electrical failure caused the photoflash to explode and the fuel tanks and bombs exploded. One of Flight Lieutenant H. R. Hyde's crew died and two others who were injured, died a few hours later. Corporal M. W. McDowell a WAAF and four airmen were killed on the ground. Some 376 Lancasters and seven Mosquitoes delivered the attack from a cloudless sky. However, primary blind-markers were scattered short of the target and all but one of the secondary markers had become u/s. The raid itself went well because the German controllers thought that the bombers were heading for Frankfurt and only realized late on that the target was in fact Berlin. The weather was clear over the capital where flak was the main danger and the Pathfinders marked an area about seven miles north-west of the city centre. Thirty-eight war industry factories were destroyed and many more damaged while houses, public buildings and the Berlin Zoo, like the Hagenbeck in Hamburg before it, suffered under the weight of the bombs. Incendiary bombs and canisters of phosphorus set fire to 15 of the zoo buildings. The antelope house and the enclosure for the beasts of prey, the administration building and the director's villa were entirely destroyed, while the monkey house and the quarantine building, the main restaurant and the elephants' Indian temple were left in ruins or badly damaged. A third of the animals died. There were still 2,000 left, although many had been evacuated. Deer and monkeys escaped, birds flew away through the broken glass roofs. There were rumours that lions on the loose were prowling around the nearby Kaiser Wilhelm Memorial Church, but they lay charred and suffocated in their cages. The ornamental three-storey aquarium building and the 30 metre crocodile hall were also destroyed, along with the artificial jungle. The great reptiles, writhing in pain, lay beneath chunks of concrete, earth, broken glass, fallen palms and tree trunks, in water a foot deep, or crawled down the visitors' staircase, while the firelight of the dying city of Berlin shone red through a gate, knocked off its hinges in the background. Over the next few days the elephants who had perished in the ruins of their sleeping quarters had to be cut up where they lay by men crawling around inside the rib-cages of the huge pachyderms and burrowing through mountains of entrails. The crocodile tails, cooked in large pans, tasted like fat chicken. Bear hams and bear sausage were regarded as delicacies.[51]

The scattered condition of the bomber stream over the Big City meant that the Lancasters became easy pickings for the night fighters off track on the return flight and 28 Lancasters were lost. Flak was intense and nine of the losses occurred over Berlin, two of these to fighters. Nine aircraft were shot down on the outbound route, 40 were damaged by flak and 11 damaged by fighters. There were three collisions. Fourteen Lancasters crashed on their return to England and were wrecked beyond repair. The airfields were congested and Flight Lieutenant W. E. D. Bell of 619 Squadron could not obtain permission to land at Woodhall Spa although his fuel was dangerously low. When down to the last few gallons he ordered his crew to bale out, pointed the Lancaster out to sea and abandoned the bomber over the Humber Estuary. All the crew landed safely and the Lancaster was found next morning on the Four Holme Sands. A badly shot up Lancaster of 166 Squadron at Kirmington flown by Flight Sergeant Fennell put down safely at an airfield in the south of England with several wounded on board. En route to the target the Lancaster was intercepted by a fighter over Belgium. The Canadian rear-gunner was wounded in the groin and Sergeant C. Cushing, the mid-upper gunner, was hit above the eye by flying metal when a cannon shell exploded against his turret. The Lancaster's starboard propellers were holed and the navigational instruments, including the compass, were damaged. Fennell decided to drop his bombs on a target of opportunity, a German airfield, and return home steering westward by the North Star. But no sooner had the aircraft risen with the release of the bombs than a Fw 190 *Wilde Sau* attacked and fired from behind. A cannon shell exploded between the flight engineer and the navigator. As the cockpit filled with smoke, the nose suddenly dropped and the Lancaster dived. Fennell ordered the crew to bale out. Wrestling with the controls at 350-mph IAS he believed that the aircraft was doomed. Knowing some of his crew members to be wounded he remained at his post, miraculously regained control and cancelled the order to abandon. Fennell then found that both Flight Sergeant D. B. Harvey, his Australian wireless operator, and

Sergeant J. Smythe, the Irish navigator, had head wounds. The rear-gunner, in spite of his painful wound, kept up instructions to Fennell to 'corkscrew', as the Fw 190 continued making persistent attacks on the battered Lancaster. Locating their position without instruments proved difficult and Fennell came down warily to 3,000 feet, where the crew sighted the lights of an airfield. Descending further to 2,000 feet to try to effect recognition, they were met with intensive fire from light flak. They struck out towards the west and came down thankfully at an airfield in the south of England.[52]

During November and December seven big raids were made on Berlin. Meanwhile, the whole of 61 Squadron moved from Syerston to its new home at RAF Skellingthorpe. Jeff Gray's crew packed their few possessions, waved goodbye to Nottingham and climbed aboard Lancaster QR-*G-George* for the short hop across to Skellingthorpe. '"Never mind", they said, "in Lincoln there are lots of pubs with lots of beer and the girls are just as pretty as the lace making girls of Nottingham". All of which was probably true, but they forgot to mention that Lincoln was surrounded by at least ten other bomber stations and swamped by young men in blue. Soon the long dark winter nights came upon us, the moon faded and Berlin, "The Big City", awaited our coming.'[53]

Notes

1. Three hundred and forty-seven Lancasters, 246 Halifaxes, 125 Stirlings and 73 Wellingtons.
2. The definitive account of the Hamburg raids is contained in *The Battle of Hamburg: Allied Bomber Forces Against A German City in 1943* by Martin Middlebrook (Penguin, 1980).
3. Four Halifaxes, four Lancasters, three Stirlings and a Wellington.
4. Twenty-six bombers or 3.7 per cent of the force, failed to return of which, 19 were destroyed by night fighters – 15 of these to crews of NJG 1 and NJG 3 manning the *Himmelbett* boxes in Holland and over the Dutch-German border. *Wilde Sau* single-engined night fighters that engaged the bomber stream over the blazing city of Essen claimed the four remaining a/c losses.
5. The firestorm was previously exceeded in history only by the fire at Tokyo following the earthquake of 1923.
6. *On The Natural History of Destruction* by W. G. Sebald.
7. On 27/28 July *Nachtjäger* claimed 16 bombers, including four by single-engined *Wilde Sau*. During the third raid on Hamburg on 29/30 July the *Nachtjagd* was credited with 34 kills, equally divided between single-engined *Wilde Sau* and twin-engined crews that were allowed to leave the confines of their *Himmelbett* boxes for the first time. On 2/3 August the *Nachtjagd* shot down 19 of the 30 bombers that failed to return from Hamburg.
8. During the first six attacks in which 'Window' had been used – two on the Ruhr and four on Hamburg – Bomber Command

flew more than 4,000 sorties. From this total, 124 aircraft, just over 3 per cent of the total, failed to return. On average, British losses during the Hamburg raids were no more than 2.8 per cent, whereas in the previous 12 months, losses had risen from 3.7 to 4.3 per cent.

9. In ED625 *B-Baker* the flight commander's aircraft which was fitted with *Monica* tail warning apparatus.

10. *B-Baker* was one of six Lancasters lost when it was shot down by Major Heinrich Wohlers *Kommandeur* I./NJG 6 flying a Bf 110 who claimed a 'Halifax' at Spessbach, NW of Landstuhl to take his score to 18. (Dave Jones died when he landed in a vineyard and was impaled in the throat. Len Bradfield was incarcerated in POW camp and, in March 1945, he attempted escape during the forced march through Germany. He hid in a sugar beet field for three nights but both his feet were badly frostbitten and his toes had to be removed later by a Polish surgeon). On 10/11 August, 653 heavies caused widespread destruction in Nuremberg. Seven Halifaxes and three Stirlings also failed to return, making a total of 16 aircraft lost overall, or 2.4 per cent. Twelve of the losses are attributed to *Nachtjagd*. I./NJG 6 claimed four victories; Hauptmann Wohlers scoring a triple kill. Oberleutnant Heinz-Wolfgang Schnaufer, StII/NJG 1 claimed a Lancaster at Hahnlein and Oberleutnant H. J. Birkenstock, St.I/NJG 6 a Lancaster near Alsenborn. On 12/13 August 321 Lancasters and 183 Halifaxes visited Milan, while 152 aircraft went to Turin. Milan was considered a successful raid and two Halifaxes and one Lancaster were lost. Turin was hit by 152 aircraft and two bombers failed to return.

11. Paula Fisher was told to 'pull her self together' and subsequently was posted from Bottesford. See *Flying For Freedom: Life and Death in Bomber Command* by Tony Redding (Cerebus 2005).

12. *Thundering Through the Clear Air: No. 61 (Lincoln Imp) Squadron At War* by Derek Brammer (Tucann Books, 1997).

13. Altogether, 596 heavies of Bomber Command were taking part.

14. 'After debriefing, we went for our post-op egg and bacon breakfast. Before retiring to our billets for a well-earned rest we visited sick quarters to see Paddy before he was transferred to the local hospital. He later became one of plastic surgeon Archibald McKindoe's wartime guinea pigs and was ultimately fully restored to health despite a much-damaged ankle. Two days later we were all delighted to hear that our skipper had gained the immediate award of the DFC and George Oliver the mid-upper gunner, who was confirmed as having shot down the attacking Me 109 before vacating his turret, was awarded the Conspicuous Gallantry Medal. All the remaining crew-members received the appropriate DFC or DFM decoration at the end of the tour. Following two raids on Berlin the Squadron Commander awarded our crew Tour Complete status on 9 September 1943. We were in fact the first crew to survive a tour of bombing operations with 467 Squadron RAAF since it was formed at RAF Scampton in November 1942. After an end of tour leave, I was then posted with my skipper to 1668 HCU at RAF Balderton and later carried out staff engineer duties with 1660 HCU at RAF Swinderby. This was followed by ground instructor duties at the Lancaster Holding Unit at RAF Scampton.'

15. *Schräge Musik* ('Jazz', 'slanting' or 'Oblique Music') was invented by an armourer, Paul Mahle of II./NJG 5 and comprised two 20/30mm MG FF MK 108 cannon mounted behind the rear cockpit bulkhead of the Bf 110 and Ju 88 night fighters, arranged to fire forwards and upwards at an angle of between 70 and 80 degrees. These fighters did not need to attack *von unten, hinten* ('underneath, behind'). They could attack from the blind spot underneath the bomber with cannon raked at 15 degrees, fired by the pilot using a *Revi C/12D* reflector sight. *Nachtjagd* also successfully employed *Zahme Sau* (*Tame Boar*) freelance or Pursuit Night Fighting tactics for the first time since switching its twin-engined night fighting crews away from the fixed *Himmelbett* system. Oberst Victor von Lossberg of the *Luftwaffe*'s Staff College in Berlin had developed *Zahme Sau*. It was a method used whereby the ground network, by giving a running commentary, directed its night fighters to where the '*window* concentration was at its most dense. The tactics of *Zahme Sau* took full advantage of the new RAF methods. Night fighters directed by ground control, and the 'Y' navigational control system, were fed into the bomber stream by tracking H_2S transmissions as early as possible, preferably on a reciprocal course. The slipstream of the bombers provided a useful indication that they were there. Night fighters operated for the most part individually but a few enterprising officers led their *Gruppen* personally in close formation into the bomber stream, with telling effect (*Geschlosser Gruppeneinsatz*). Night fighter crews hunted on their own using *SN-2* AI radar whose longer wavelength, unlike early *Lichtenstein* AI, could not be jammed by '*Window*', Naxos 7 (FuG 350) a device which homed onto the H_2S navigation radar and *Flensburg* (FuG 227/1) which homed onto the *Monica* tail warning device widely used on Bomber Command heavies.

16. Lancaster losses were 5.4 per cent compared with a corresponding 8.8 per cent and 12.9 per cent for Halifaxes and Stirlings respectively. *Lancaster-The Story Of A Famous Bomber* by Bruce Robertson (Harleyford Publications Ltd, 1964). The losses were 8.7 per cent of the force dispatched.

17. By the end of the year Edwards had taken up an appointment in Air Command Far East Asia and held the rank of SASO (Senior Air Staff Officer) until the end of 1945. He remained in the post-war RAF and was awarded the OBE in 1947. In 1958 he was promoted to Air Commodore and finally retired from the service in 1963. He returned to Australia, was knighted and in 1974 became Governor of West Australia.

18. *Not Just Another Milk Run; The Mailly-le-Camp Bomber Raid* by Molly Burkett & Geoff Gilbert (Barny Books, 2004). On 57 Squadron in 1943 were the Singer twins – A. M. and P. L. – both pilot officers with DFCs.

19. Twin-engined *Nachtjagd* crews operating in *Zahme Sau* fashion claimed 12 of the 33 bombers shot down. Total claims were 28 kills this night.

20. Wing Commander K. H. Burns DFC lost a hand.

21. Bomber Command Quarterly Review No. 6.

22. Report K56, Bomber Command ORS.

23. The loss of 22 Lancasters was nearly 7.0 per cent of the force. The Berlin raid was only moderately effective. The part of the bombing which did reach the built up area fell in residential areas of Charlottenburg and Moabit and in the industrial area called Siemensstadt. Three heavy bombing raids in 10 days by RAF Bomber Command on Berlin had resulted in the loss of 137 aircraft and great loss of life to Berliners in the Siemensstadt and Mariendorf districts, and also to Lichterfelde. It was but a prelude to the Battle of Berlin, which would open with all ferocity in November. On the 3/4 September raid, 20 out of 316 Lancasters were lost.

…crew load a 'Cookie' into the Lancaster's bomb bay. The 4,000lb bomb never became widely used by Bomber Command partly because only one could be …y Lancaster aircraft and none by Halifaxes.

The crew of Lancaster III ED831 *Y-Yoke* in 9 Squadron board their aircraft at Bardney, Lincolnshire, before taking off for the ten-hour round trip to the Zeppelin works at Friedrichshafen on 20 June 1943, one of the longest they would be expected to make. Skippered by Squadron Leader A. M. Hobbs DFC RNZAF, they are Sergeant L. W. Sanderson, navigator, Sergeant K. Mott, bomb aimer, Sergeant C. P. King, flight engineer, Sergeant E. C. Bishop, WOp, Sergeant W. C. Rowlands, mid upper gunner and Flight Sergeant F. Slater, rear gunner. Six nights later on 25/26 June Hobbs and his crew were one of thirteen Lancaster crews that failed to return from an operation to Gelsenkirchen when *Y-Yoke* was shot down into the Ijsselmeer on the homeward trip by a nightfighter. All the crew in this photo plus Flying Officer J. H. Sams, who was a graduate from Oxford University and who had reported from 1660 HCU that day, perished.

Chapter 5: Hamburg and *Hydra* Come Hell or High Water

Pilot Officer W. H. Eager's crew of Lancaster B.I W4236 QR-K *K-Kit* 61 Squadron at Syerston on 30 July L–R: Flight Lieutenant Hewish, ra operator from Heston; Pilot Office who was from Winnipeg; Sergeant WOp from Pontypridd; Sergeant V rear gunner from Romford; Sergea Petts, navigator from Ripley; Serge Sharrard, mid-upper gunner from Toronto; and Sergeant Lawrence, engineer from Barnsley. On 9/10 A 1943 this Lancaster (and a Halifax shot down on the trip to Mannheir *Leutnant* Norbert Pietrek of II./NJ(Three of Sergeant J. C. Whitley's the Lancaster, which crashed at Marbehan, Luxembourg were KIA

Flight Lieutenant Harold Wilson's crew of 617 Squadron who were KIA on 15/16 September 1943 in the disastrous attempt by 617 Squadron to breach the Dortmund-Ems Canal. In May Wilson's crew had been due to fly the Dams raid but owing to illness they were scrubbed from the battle order at the last minute.

On 16/17 September 1943 eight Lancasters of 617 Squadron and four from 619 Squadron set out to bomb the Anthéor viaduct near Cannes on the coastal railway line leading to Italy. The Lancaster crews found the viaduct in the moonlight without trouble but their bombs missed the target. American bombers finally destroyed the viaduct.

In the daylight reconnaissance twelve hours after the Peenemünde attack on 17/18 August 1943 photographs revealed twenty-seven buildings in the northern manufacturing area destroyed and forty huts in the living and sleeping quarters completely flattened. The foreign labour camp to the south suffered worst of all and 500–600 foreign workers, mostly Polish, were killed. The whole target area was covered in craters. The raid is adjudged to have set back the V-2 experimental programme by at least two months and to have reduced the scale of the eventual rocket attack on Britain. (*Australian National Archives*)

Feldwebel Otto Fries and his *Bordfunker Unteroffizier* Fred Staffa of 5./NJG 1 at St Trond in front of their Bf 110G. On 11 August 1943 they shot down Lancaster III JA716 of 97 Squadron at Hanzinelle, SE of Charleroi at 0257 hours for their first kill. Flight Lieutenant W. I. Covington DFC and his crew baled out and five men were taken prisoner. The skipper and his rear gunner, Sergeant J. McKnight, evaded capture. Freis and Staffa were credited with ten victories at night between August 1943 and April 1944, plus two unconfirmed *Abschüsse* in daylight. Flying the He 219 they added another six victory claims to take their final tally to fourteen confirmed and four unconfirmed *Abschüsse*. (*Otto H. Fries*)

On 3/4 October 1943 Kassel was attacked by 547 aircraft, 204 of them Lancasters. Twenty-four aircraft including four Lancasters were lost and the city's eastern and western suburbs were devastated. Some 569 aircraft, 322 of them Lancasters, returned to the city on the night of 22/23 October and caused widespread destruction. Forty-three aircraft, including eighteen Lancasters, were lost.

Five of the crew of Lancaster III LM360 *O-Oboe* of 61 Squadron, 5 Group at Syerston, near Nottingham, who flew the operation to Düsseldorf on 3/4 November Despite the damage to the aircraft and being badly wounded, Reid and his crew managed to nurse *O-Oboe* back to England where they bellied in at the 44th ● Group Liberator base at Shipdham, Norfolk. Back row, L–R: Flight Sergeant Les Rolton, bomb-aimer; Flight Sergeant Frank Emerson, rear gunner Front row: Sergeant Jim 'Taffy' Norris, flight engineer; Flight Lieutenant Bill Reid, pilot; Flight Sergeant C. Baldwin, gunner. Pilot Officer John Jeffreys RAAF, navigator ❘lled and WOp Flight Sergeant I. J. Mann died the next day from his wounds. (*Bill Reid Collection*)

❜) Bill Reid VC during a visit to an anti aircraft battery. Reid and Les Rolton joined 617 Squadron after recovering from their ordeal. On 31 July 1943 Reid ❑e a PoW and Rolton was killed when their Lancaster was brought down over France by a 1,000lb bomb dropped by an aircraft overhead during the bombing of ❘nds of a railway tunnel at Rilly-La-Montage, which was being used as a flying-bomb store.

Lancaster III LM326 EM-Z '*Z-Zebra*' of 207 Squadron on a local flight over countryside east of Grantham and Barkston Heath airfield. 207 Squadron suffered the highest percentage losses in 5 Group and in Nissen-hut rumour was a 'chop' squadron. LM326/EM-Z lasted four months before failing to return from the Hanover raid of 18/19 October 1943 with Flight Sergeant Geoff Taylor RAAF and crew who were shot down by *Hauptmann* Friedrich Karl 'Nose' Müller, a *Wilde Sau* pilot of *Stab* JG 300. All seven crew were taken prisoner. (*IWM*)

Debriefing a 1660 HCU crew at Swinderby on 23 November 1943 following the raid on Berlin. Twenty-six aircraft, eleven of them Lancasters, were lost. 1660 HCU had been formed from the Conversion Flights of 61, 97 and 106 Squadrons in October 1942. During the bombing offensive twenty-four OTUs (Operational Training Units) and eight HCUs (twelve of them equipped or partly equipped with Lancasters at one time or another) sent crews on operations flown mainly by mixed crews of pupils and instructors. Additionally, there were four Lancaster Finishing Schools.

Station personnel at Fisl look at the night flash photographs displayed a technical site following t 22/23 November Berlin (*IWM*)

Public subscription to the cost of specific items of war equipment was given official encouragement by most combatant nations. The First World War veterans of the Salonika Reunion Association in Britain bought a 4,000lb 'Cookie' for delivery to a German target. It is here seen at Syerston before loading in Lancaster I W4198 QR-H *Hellzapoppin!* of 61 Squadron, which has seventy-one ops on the nose. This aircraft and Pilot Officer A. J. D. Eaves and crew were lost on the aircraft's 75th operation on 26/27 November 1943.

Lancaster II D5723 EQ-B of 408 Squadron, which failed to return with Wing Commander A. C. Mair DFC RCAF and crew from the raid on Berlin on 26/27 November 1943. All the crew were killed.

Hauptmann Peter Spoden was one of the leadi[n]g *Tame Boar* pilots who made his first operation[al] flight in a Bf 110 in the Battle of Hamburg 27/28 July 1943. His first victory came on the [night] of the Peenemünde raid 17/18 August 1943 w[hen] he shot down Lancaster III JA897 of 44 Squa[dron] flown by Sergeant W. J. Drew (KIA with five [of] crew – only Sergeant W. Sparks, bomb aimer, survived). In August 1943 Spoden was hospitalized, his *Bordfunker* survived and his fl[ight] mechanic was killed when they were shot dow[n]. Late in November 1943 he shot down a Lanc[aster]. Spoden finished the war with twenty-four nig[ht] one day victories. He was awarded the *Deutsch[es] Kreuz*. Post war Spoden was a senior *Lufthans[a]* pilot. (*Peter Spoden*)

Wing Commander Ray Hilton DSO DFC★ who returned to command 83 Squadron for his third tour in November 1943. He was killed on the Berlin raid on 23/24 November. Hilton had flown at least sixty-four ops.

Chapter 6: To the Big City

Berlin devastated by bombing.

In the USA on 3 December 1943 radio listeners tuned in to hear their favourite foreign correspondent Edward R. Murrow, head of CBS European Bureau in London, begin his broadcast, *This is London*. Murrow, who had become well known in America for his broadcasts during the *Blitz* when the USA was still neutral, proceeded to regale his listeners with a gripping account of his experience over Berlin in a Lancaster the night before. (*CBS*)

A brilliant pilot of aristocratic descent, *Major* Heinrich Prinz Zu Sayn-Wittgenstein served with distinction, first as a bomber pilot in France, Britain and Russia. In August 1941 he transferred to *Nachtjagd* and rapidly became a legend. In seven months in 1942 he achieved twenty-two victories, receiving the *Ritterkreuz* in October of that year. Over the next twelve months he added forty more victories. Award of the Oak Leaves for fifty-four victories followed at the end of August 1943. On 1/2 January 1944 Wittgenstein shot down Flight Lieutenant Leo B. Patkin RAAF (KIA) and his crew of 467 Squadron RAAF for his 71st *Abschuss*. At the time of his death in combat on 21/22 January 1944 Wittgenstein had eighty-three *Nachtjagd* victories (including twenty-three on the Eastern Front) in 170 sorties. And he had been awarded the *Ritterkreuz with Eichenlaub and Schwerter*.

(*Left*) Maurice Chick and his crew in 83 Squadron beside Lancaster III JA967 *The Saint He Will Be Back*. This aircraft and Flight Lieutenant H. R. Hyde's crew were lost on 29 January 1944 when they were involved in a outbound collision with a 463 Squadron RAAF Lancaster and crashed on the Danish Island of Als. There were no survivors from either crew. Hyde had previously had a miraculous escape when his Lancaster (JA686) exploded at dispersal at Wyton on the night of 26/27 November 1943 after an electrical fault ignited the photo flash. One of his crew died and two others who were injured, died a few hours later. A WAAF and four airmen were killed on the ground.

(*Right*) Servicing Merlin engines on the Lancaster.

...ter VN-M of 50 Squadron at Skellingthorpe in the winter of 1943–44. The squadron was stationed at the Lincolnshire airfield from October 1942 and flew the ...ancaster operations in 5 Group.

...d remains of a Lancaster crew.

W4964 *Still Going Strong!* of 9 Squadron flew 106 ops between April 1943 and October 1944.

Lancaster III LM446/PG-H of 619 Squadron a few days after it was taken on charge at Coningsby on 31 January 1944. This Lancaster was one of five that faile⟨d to⟩ return from the attack by fifty-six Lancasters and eight Mosquitoes of 5 Group on the Gnôme-Rhône aero-engine factory and another factory nearby at Gennev⟨illiers⟩ France on 9/10 May 1944. Seven of Pilot Officer J. M. Aitken RNZAF's crew were killed and one was taken prisoner.

Chapter 7: Berlin or Bust

Pilot Officer Howard Farmiloe, aged twenty-two, of 61 Squadron was one of the most junior commissioned s in the RAF to be awarded the DSO during the war. On the last raid of the battle of Berlin on 24/25 March 1944 Farmiloe flew ME596 H-*Hellzapoppin* back against all the odds. He suffered an engine failure outward nd over the North Sea and on the bomb run the second engine on the same wing failed, but he bombed the target from 18,500 feet before setting a course for home, making an emergency landing at Little Snoring in rfolk at 0215 hours. Farmiloe was awarded an immediate DSO, his bomb-aimer and wireless operator each ived a DFM and Flying Officer S. Halliwell, navigator, a bar to his DFC. ME596 was lost with Pilot Officer cL Taylor RAAF and crew on the raid on Rüsselsheim 12/13 August 1944. Taylor and five of his crew were killed. The other member of the crew was taken prisoner. (*Howard Farmiloe*)

Officer P. Ingleby of 619 Squadron at his navigator's table on 14 February 1944. was killed later in the war.

Lancaster III LM418 of 619 Squadron on 14 February 1944. This aircraft was wrecked a month later on 30/31 March on return from Nuremberg. Sergeant J. Parker took off from Coningsby at 2213 hours and on return, crash-landed at Woodbridge. No one was hurt but the Lancaster was consumed by fire. Parker and his crew were killed on the operation to Kiel on 23/24 July 1944.

Oberleutnant Heinz-Wolfgang Schnaufer, *Staffelkapitän*, 12./NJG 1 at Leeuwarden points out his 47th *Abschuss* – he scored his 45th–47th victories on 15/16 February 1944 during a Bomber Command raid on Berlin when forty-three aircraft were lost. The 47th victory was Lancaster B.I W4272 of 622 Squadron, which he shot down into the Ijsselmeer 1km south of Medemblik at 2333 hours. Flight Lieutenant T. L. Griffiths RAAF and his crew were killed.

(*Hans Bredewold via Ab A. Jansen*)

24. The raids were succesful with severe destruction to both targets. Thirty-four aircraft – 13 Halifaxes, 13 Lancasters and 8 Stirlings (5.6 per cent of the force) – were lost while German losses were four *Wilde Sau* and three twin-engined aircraft. The He 219A-0 flown by Oberleutnant Heinz Strüning, *Staffelkapitän* 3./NJG 1 and his *Bordfunker*, Oberfeldwebel Willi Bleier, was damaged by return fire. A bullet severed the control cable from the fuel tank selector lever and, during the flight back to Venlo, Strüning was unable to switch to Tank 1. The He 219's engines quit one after the other and Strüning and Bleier decided to abandon the aircraft. However, the ejector seats refused to fire and so both men climbed out. Strüning hit the antenna mast and tail surfaces of his *Uhu* and suffered bruised ribs and contusions. Bleier probably also hit the machine and he was found dead the next day with an unopened parachute. Bleier had participated in the destruction of 40 RAF bombers. On 24/25 December 1944 Strüning, *Staffelkapitän* 9./NJG 1 was shot down by a Mosquito. Strüning was killed after he hit the tail unit of his Bf 110G-4 while baling out. His total number of victories was 56 *Nachtjagd Abschüsse* in 250 sorties. He had been decorated with the *Ritterkreuz mit Eichenlaub*.

25. While over the North Sea a weather reconnaissance Mosquito reported that there was fog in the target area and the Lancasters were recalled. (*The Bomber Command War Diaries* by Martin Middlebrook and Chris Everitt). Six Mosquitoes from 418 and 605 Squadrons, which had arrived at Scampton on 5 September, were to have dealt with the searchlights, flak and any fighter opposition along the route or at the target.

26. See *Breaking the Dams: The Story of Dambuster David Maltby & His Crew* by Charles Foster (Pen & Sword, 2008), The body of David Maltby, who was 21 years old, was picked up by an RAF ASR launch of 24 ASR at Gorleston and taken ashore. He was buried later at Wickhambreux near Canterbury in Kent where he had been married.

27. *The Dam Busters* by Paul Brickhill (Evans Bros, London 1951).

28. Flight Lieutenants T. H. 'Terry' Taerum DFC, and R. E. G. Hutchison DFC* and Pilot Officer G. A. Deering DFC.

29. Brickhill, op. cit. The plan for Operation *Garlic*, as it was called, was drawn up in great detail by Air Commodore H. V. Satterly, the Senior Air Staff Officer at 5 Group; the same officer who had drawn up the final orders for the Dam's raid.

30. Born in 1920, he went up to Oxford in 1939 but left in 1940 to join the RAF. *The Dambuster Who Cracked the Dam: The Story of Melvin 'Dinghy' Young* by Arthur G. Thorning (Pen & Sword, 2008).

31. Wilson's crew were due to fly the Dam's raid but owing to illness they were scrubbed from the battle order at the last minute.

32. Ray Grayston roamed the Dutch countryside for a couple of days and was given sanctuary in a village until a search party of German troops sent him on the run again. He was captured and ended the war in the infamous *Stalag Luft III*. 'But being an officer gave me better conditions so I've got Guy Gibson to thank for that. Of the other crewmembers of *N for Nan*, Harry O'Brien was captured, "Doc" Sutherland, Bob Kellow, Harold Hobday and "Johnny" Johnson split up and individually trekked across occupied Europe to Gibraltar. In December 1943 they burst into the Officers' Mess at Woodhall Spa wearing French berets.'

33. Brickhill, op. cit.

34. Mick Martin and Dave Shannon were awarded bars to their DFCs and Rice the DFC. Knight was later 'mentioned in dispatches'. Pilot Officer Rice and his crew, all of whom flew the Dam's raid, were shot down on the operation to the John Cockerill steel works at Liège on 20/21 December 1943. The Lancaster was believed to have been hit by flak at 14,000 feet while returning to Coningsby and the aircraft broke up over Merbes-le-Chateau (Hainaut) 22 km SW of Charleroi. Rice was thrown clear as the Lancaster exploded in mid-air killing the rest of his crew. Despite a broken wrist, Rice managed to evade capture for six months until April 1944 by which time the Belgian Resistance had moved him to Brussels. In January 1944 Martin was awarded a bar to his DSO. On 12/13 February 1944 in an attack by 10 Lancasters of 617 Squadron with 12,000lb blockbusters on the Anthéor Viaduct, when running in to attack at under 200 feet through heavy fire, Martin's Lancaster was hit repeatedly. Bob Hay was killed and the engineer wounded. The bomb release was destroyed and the controls badly damaged. Tammy Simpson and Toby Foxlee's brilliant work with the guns enabled the bomber to get clear of the defences and Martin succeeded in flying the crippled Lanc back through severe electrical storms to Elmas Field at Cagliari in Sardinia, where he made an excellent landing in difficult circumstances. (Foxlee and Simpson were awarded the DFC.) The sides of the valley were very steep and the viaduct was defended by guns which damaged both Martin's and Cheshire's low level aircraft. Martin was awarded a second bar to his DFC in November 1944 after he had completed two tours on heavy bombers and one as a Mosquito Intruder pilot. By the end of the war he was the only Australian airman to have won five British awards in the conflict. He was granted a permanent commission in 1945 and commanded 2nd TAF and RAF Germany from 1967 to 1970, retiring from the RAF in 1974 as Air Marshal Sir Harold Martin KCB DSO* DFC** AFC. He died on 3 November 1988.

35. Ron Clark and his crew flew a further five ops with 100 Squadron before being posted with 'C' Flight to form the nucleus of the new 625 Squadron at Kelstern. They flew one more op before being screened, split up and posted. All of them survived the war with the exception of the navigator, Jim Siddell, who was killed over Holland in a Mosquito in 1944. The *Phantom* was transferred to the newly formed 550 Squadron on 25 November and re-coded BQ *B-Baker*.

36. Thirty-three victories for five a/c lost were claimed by 207 twin-engined *Zahme Sau*. Thirty-eight RAF heavies were lost. Seven victories were credited to III./NJG 1. Hauptmann August Geiger achieved a triple victory destroying two Halifaxes and a Lancaster over the Ijsselmeer.

37. A total of 178 victories were credited to *Nachtjagd* for September. The arm was now in a downwards spiral that was not halted until the end of the year when the *Zahme Sau* force had been fully built up and trained to counter the strategic night bombing offensive effectively.

38. Night fighters shot down eight Lancasters.

39. During October 149 RAF bombers were destroyed by *Nachtjagd*. On the Kassel raid of 3/4 October *Nachtjagd* claimed 17 heavies shot down from a force of 547 aircraft and for nine *Zahme Sau* losses. Hauptmann Rudolf Sigmund, Kommandeur, III./NJG 3, KIA either by flak or by return fire SW of Göttingen. He had 27 victories. On 4/5 October when 406 aircraft attacked Frankfurt for the loss of 11 bombers it is

highly likely that these were due to *Nachtjäger* as the *Zahme* and *Wilde Sau* claimed 12 victories. The raid by 343 Lancasters against Stuttgart on 7/8 October resulted in claims by *Nachtjagd* for only two kills but on the Bremen and Hanover raids of 8/9 October *Nachtjagd* claimed 37 of the 623 bombers. Four large-scale *Zahme Sau* operations were mounted by 1 *Jagdkorps* during October. On the 18/19th when Hanover was raided by 360 Lancasters, 190 twin-engined aircraft claimed 14 victories. On the 20/21st I *JD* scrambled 220 aircraft, which claimed 11 Lancasters destroyed from 358 sent to raid Leipzig for nine own losses. On 22/23 October, while 36 heavies bombed Frankfurt as a diversion, Kassel was subjected to an exceptionally accurate and concentrated raid by 569 Lancasters and Halifaxes, which created a firestorm destroying 63 per cent of all Kassel's living accomodation. The 194 *Zahme Sau* dispatched made 40 kills for the loss of only six fighters. Altogether, the RAF lost 43 aircraft. Hauptmann Manfred Meurer of Stab I./NJG 1 claimed Lancaster W4357 of 61 Squadron that crashed at Bühne-Haarbrück, north of Kassel. Oberleutnant Werner Husemann of 7./NJG 1 got a Lancaster, DS778 of 408 Squadron NW of Minden while Leutnant Otto Fries of 5./NJG 1 destroyed Lancaster EE175 EM-R of 207 Squadron. Squadron Leader McDowell RCAF and his crew KIA. The Lancaster crashed at Nettersheim.

40. Brammer, op. cit.

41. 'Lacking in Moral Fibre', as it was euphemistically called, which next to the unknown was the greatest fear to be found. The layman has the harsher but more accurate word for it – cowardice. LMF was bad for morale and was kept out of the press. LMF cases remained a very low percentage of total numbers of Bomber Command. Throughout the war, 4,059 cases were considered – 746 officers and 3,313 NCOs. The 'charges' against most were dismissed and only 2,726 (389 officers, 2,337 NCOs) were actually classified as LMF; a total less than 0.4 per cent of all the aircrews of Bomber Command. The NCOs' total was higher, because there were more of them than officers.

42. *Piece of Cake* by Geoff Taylor (George Mann, 1956). Taylor, Sergeant's Don J. Duff, A. G. McLeod, C. R. Smith RCAF, A. R. Burton, W. Worthington and Flight Sergeant W. J. McCarthy RAAF were taken prisoner. Müller, who received the *Ritterkreuz* in July 1944, destroyed 29 *Viermots* and a Mosquito in just 52 sorties, making him the most successful *Wilde Sau* pilot of all.

43. After a lapse of almost five months the city was the target of 577 bombers on the night of 3/4 November. AM Sir Arthur Harris was in the midst of a campaign of area bombing German cities at night using Lancasters and Halifaxes, while B-24 Liberators and B-17 Flying Fortresses of the US 8th and 12th Air Forces stoked the fires by day. The Düsseldorf operation included a special force of Lancasters equipped with *G-H*, who were to test this precision device for the first time on a consider-able scale in a raid on the Mannesmann steelworks. Fifty-two Lancasters, including 20 blind-markers and 10 Mosquitoes were detailed to carry out a feint attack on Cologne 10 minutes before the start of the main raid on Düsseldorf. Thirteen *Oboe*-equipped Mosquitoes were detailed to hit Rheinhausen, two more, equipped with *G-H*, went to Dortmund and 23 Stirlings and Lancasters were detailed to lay mines off the Friesians. Weather could affect the overall success or failure of an operation. A belt of layer cloud extended from the Dutch coast to 90 miles west of Düsseldorf. Contrails extended at all heights above 15,000 feet. The wind at 20,000 feet was 25 mph and 28 mph at 28,000 feet.

44. Brammer, op. cit.

45. Emerson had flown a first tour on 61 Squadron in Gordon Oldham's crew.

46. The *G-H* trial attack by 38 Lancaster IIs on the Mannesmann Rohrenwerke was successfully carried out at the same time as the main operation. Fifteen aircraft attacked the steel works according to plan but 126 found their sets unserviceable and bombed the city, five returned early and two were lost. Photographic evidence gathered later showed that the accuracy was such that 50 per cent of their bombs had fallen within half a mile of the works.

47. A US 8th AF 2nd Bomb Division base occupied by B-24 Liberators of the 44th Bomb Group.

48. Mann, wounded by shrapnel, died in hospital on Thursday morning. Taffy Norris, who had shrapnel wounds in the shoulder and left arm, did not reveal that he was wounded until he was getting out of the aircraft. He received the CGM. Joe Emerson was awarded the DFM. Baldwin went on to complete his tour. Reid went back on ops in January 1944, this time with 617 Dam Busters Squadron. With him went Les Rolton. On 31 July during a raid on Rilly La Montagne near Rheims, an RAF bomber put paid to the rest of his tour when an a/c overhead released its bombs and a 1,000 pounder hurtled through Reid's Lancaster. Five crew, including Rolton were killed in action. Reid and his WOp/AG, Flying Officer David Luker were thrown clear when the nose of the plane broke off as it spun down. They spent ten months in *Stalag Luft III* Sagan and *Stalag Luft IV* Bellaria.

49. Brammer, op. cit. Night fighters destroyed all of the 18 heavies that failed to return. Three German fighters were claimed destroyed and 37 were damaged. On the night of 4/5 November the RAF carried out mining of the western Baltic, with a Mosquito spoof towards the Ruhr. German radar picked up 50 to 60 RAF aircraft between Cap Griz Nez and the Westerschelde River at 23,000 to 30,000 feet. Their further course was south-east into the southern Ruhr area. As their speed at first was only about 250 mph they were taken to be four-engined bombers but later, taking headwinds into consideration, the defences identified them as Mosquitoes and several night fighters that were ordered off were recalled. Meanwhile, 30 to 50 aircraft at heights between 3,300 feet and 5,000 feet flying at 200 mph, were picked up by German radar approaching the northern part of west Jutland. Night fighters engaged 16 bombers and shot down four without loss. On 8 November 100 Group (Special Duties, later Bomber Support) was created to consolidate the various squadrons and units using the secret ELINT and RCM in the war against the German night fighter air and defence system. In tandem with this electronic wizardry, 100 Group also accepted 'spoofing' as a large part of its offensive armoury and it also controlled squadrons of Mosquitoes engaged purely on *Intruder* missions over Germany. It would need to hone and refine all of these techniques if it were to be of any value against the German night fighter defences. Early in November about 50 German night fighters were equipped with the improved *SN-2* radar, which was relatively immune to '*Window*' but only 12 night fighters and crews were operational, mainly because of the delay in training suitable operators.

50. EE176's nose had received a Walt Disney cartoon of Mickey Mouse, pulling a bomb-trolley on which sat a bomb.

51. *Mit Faltern begann's – Mein Leben mit Tieren in Breslau, München und Berlin* [*It Began with Butterflies – My Life with Animals in Breslau, Munich and Berlin*] by Katharina Heinroth (Munich, 1979) and *Tiere – Mein Abenteuer. Erlebnisse in Wildnis und Zoo* [*Animals – My Adventure. Experiences in the Wild and at the Zoo*] by Lutz Heck (Vienna, 1952).

52. The raids of 22/23, 23/24 and 26/27 November resulted in the deaths of 4,330 Berliners of whom the bodies of 574 were never recovered. (*The Bomber Command War Diaries* by Martin Middlebrook and Chris Everitt).

53. At the end of his tour of operations, Jeff Gray was awarded the DFM. From 18/19 November 1943 to 24/25 March 1944 Berlin was subjected to 16 major raids, which have gone into history as the Battle of Berlin. During the 18/19 November raid, only nine out of 440 Lancaster were lost. An effective *Zahme Sau* operation was mounted against a second force of 395 aircraft simultaneously raiding Ludwigshafen-on-Rhine, a handful of crews shooting down the majority of the 23 aircraft that failed to return. On 22/23 November an estimated four out of 764 bombers raiding Berlin were lost to the *Nachtjagd*, which largely remained grounded due to adverse weather conditions. The next night, 383 bombers again raided the Big City. Twelve *Zahme Sau* crews shot down 13 of the 20 bombers that were lost. On the night of 25/26 November 262 Halifaxes and Lancasters attacked Frankfurt for the loss of 12 bombers. A raid by 450 bombers on Berlin and 178 on Stuttgart on the night of 26/27 November was met with difficult weather conditions in the target area. Thirty-four bombers failed to return.

Chapter 6

To the Big City

'There's a battle going on, on the starboard beam.'

We couldn't see the aircraft but we could see the jets of red tracer being exchanged. Suddenly there was a burst of yellow flame and Jock remarked, 'That's a fighter going down – note the position.'

The whole thing was interesting but remote. Dave the navigator who was sitting back with his maps charts and compasses said, 'The attack ought to begin in exactly two minutes.'

We were still over the clouds. But suddenly those dirty grey clouds turned white. We were over the outer searchlight defences – the clouds below us were white and we were black. D-Dog seemed like a black bug on a white sheet. The flak began coming up but none of it close. We were still a long way from Berlin. I didn't realize just how far.

Edward R. Murrow head of CBS European Bureau in London.

In the USA on 3 December 1943 radio listeners tuned in to hear their favourite foreign correspondent, Edward R. Murrow, head of CBS European Bureau in London, begin his broadcast: 'This Is London'. Murrow had become well known in America for his broadcasts during the *Blitz* when the USA was still neutral;

'Yesterday afternoon the waiting was over. The weather was right; the target was to be the big city. The crew captains walked into the briefing room, looked at the maps and charts and sat down with their big celluloid pads on their knees. The atmosphere was that of a school and a church. The weatherman gave us the weather. The pilots were reminded that Berlin is Germany's greatest centre of war production. The intelligence officer told us how many heavy and light ack-ack guns, how many searchlights we might expect to encounter. Then Jock the wing commander, explained the system of markings, the kind of flare that would be used by the Pathfinders. He said that concentration was the secret of success in these raids, that as long as the aircraft stayed well bunched, they would protect each other. The captains of aircraft walked out.'

Murrow boarded a Lancaster of 619 Squadron RAAF at Woodhall Spa airfield, one and a half miles from the Victorian spa town. His pilot was Acting Wing Commander William 'Jock' Abercromby DFC* and his crew[1] of *D-Dog* one of 458 aircraft taking part in the raid on the Big City, the fifth heavy attack on Berlin within a fortnight:

'I noticed that the big Canadian with the slow, easy grin had printed "Berlin" at the top of his pad and then embellished it with a scroll. The red headed English boy with the two weeks' old moustache was the last to leave the room. Late in the afternoon we went to the locker-room to draw parachutes, Mae West's and all the rest. As we dressed a couple of the Australians were whistling. Walking out to the bus that was to take us to the aircraft I heard the station loud speakers announcing that that evening all personnel would be able to see a film: *Star Spangled Rhythm*, free!

'We went out and stood around a big, black, four-motored Lancaster, *D-Dog*. A small station wagon delivered a vacuum flask of coffee, chewing gum, an orange and a bit of chocolate for each man. Up in that part of England the air hums and throbs with the sound of aircraft motors all day. But for half an hour before take-off the skies are dead silent and expectant. A lone hawk hovered over the airfield, absolutely still as he faced into the wind. Jack, the tail gunner, said, "It would be nice if *we* could fly like that".

'*D-Dog* eased around the perimeter track to the end of the runway. We sat there for a moment, the green light flashed and we were rolling ten seconds ahead of schedule. The take-off was smooth as silk. The wheels came up and *D-Dog* started the long climb. As we came up through the clouds I looked right and left and counted 14 black Lancasters climbing for the place where men must burn oxygen to live. The sun was going down and its red glow made rivers and lakes of fire on top of the clouds. Down to the southward the clouds piled up to form castles, battlements and whole cities, all tinged with red.

'Soon we were out over the North Sea. Dave, the navigator, asked Jock if he couldn't make a little more speed – we were nearly two minutes late. By this time we were all using oxygen. The talk on the intercom was brief and crisp. Everyone sounded relaxed. For a while the eight of us in our little world in exile moved over the sea. There was a quarter moon on the starboard beam. Jock's quiet voice came through the intercom: "That'll be flak ahead." We were approaching the enemy coast. The flak looked like a cigarette lighter in a dark room – one that won't light. Sparks but no flame. The sparks crackling just about level with the cloud tops. We flew steady and straight, and soon the flak was directly below us.

'*D-Dog* rocked a little from right to left but that wasn't caused by the flak. We were in the slipstream of other Lancasters ahead: and we were over the enemy coast.

'And then a strange thing happened. The aircraft seemed to grow smaller. Jack in the rear turret, Wally, the mid-upper gunner and Titch, the wireless operator all seemed somehow to draw closer to Jock in the cockpit. It was as though each man's shoulder was against the others. The understanding was complete. The intercom came to life and Jock said: "Two aircraft on the port beam."

'Jack in the tail said, "Okay sir; they're Lancs." The whole crew was a unit and wasn't wasting words.

'The cloud below was ten-tenths. The blue green jet of the exhaust licked back along the leading edge and there were other aircraft all around us. The whole great aerial armada was hurtling towards Berlin. We flew so for 20 minutes, when Jock looked up at a vapour trail curling across above us, remarking in a conversational tone that from the look of it he thought there was a fighter up there. Occasionally the angry red of ack-ack burst through the clouds but it was far away and we took only an academic interest. We were flying in the third wave. Jock asked Wally in the mid-upper turret and Jack in the rear turret if they were cold. They said they were all right and thanked him for asking. Even asked how I was and I said, "All right so far". The cloud was beginning to thin out. Up to the north we could see light and the flak began to liven up ahead of it.

'Boz, the bomb-aimer crackled through on the intercom: "There's a battle going on, on the starboard beam." We couldn't see the aircraft but we could see the jets of red tracer being exchanged. Suddenly there was a burst of yellow flame and Jock remarked, "That's a fighter going down – note the position". The whole thing was interesting but remote. Dave the navigator who was sitting back with his maps charts and compasses said, "The attack ought to begin in exactly two minutes". We were still over the clouds. But suddenly those dirty grey clouds turned white. We were over the outer searchlight defences – the clouds below us were white and we were black. *D-Dog* seemed like a black bug on a white sheet. The flak began coming up but none of it close. We were still a long way from Berlin. I didn't realize just how far.

'Jock observed: "There's a kite on fire dead ahead." It was a great golden, slow-moving meteor slanting towards the earth. By this time we were about 30 miles from our target area in Berlin. That 30 miles was the longest flight I have ever made. "Dead on time", Boz the bomb-aimer reported, "Target indicators going down". The same moment the sky ahead was lit up by brilliant yellow flares. Off to starboard another kite went down in flames. The flares were sprouting all over the sky – reds and greens and yellows; and we were flying straight for the centre of the fireworks. *D-Dog* seemed to be standing still, the four propellers thrashing the air. But we didn't seem to be closing in. The cloud had cleared and off to starboard a Lanc was caught by at least 14 searchlight beams. We could see him twist and turn and finally break out. But still the whole thing had a quality of unreality about it. No one seemed to be shooting at us but it was getting lighter all the time. Suddenly a tremendous big blob of yellow light appeared dead ahead, another to the right and another to the left. We were flying straight for them.

'Jack pointed out to me the dummy fires and flares to right and left but we kept going in. Dead ahead there was a whole chain of red flares looking like stoplights. Another Lanc coned on our starboard beam; the lights seemed to be supporting it. Again we could see those little bubbles of coloured lead driving at it from two sides. The German fighters were at him.

'And then, with no warning at all, *D for Dog* was filled with an unhealthy white light; I was standing just behind Jock and could see the seams of the wings. His quiet Scots voice beat into my ears. "Steady, lads – we've been coned." His slender body lifted half out of the seat as he jammed the control column forward and to the left. We were going down.

'Jock was wearing woollen gloves with the fingers cut off. I could see his fingernails turn white as he gripped the wheel. And then I was on my knees, flat on the deck, for he had whipped the *Dog* back into a climbing turn. The knees should have been strong enough to support me but they weren't and the stomach seemed in some danger of letting me down, too. I picked myself up and looked out again. It seemed that one big search-light, instead of being 20,000 feet below, was mounted right on the wingtip.

'*D for Dog* was corkscrewing. As we rolled down on the other side I began to see what was happening to Berlin.

'The clouds were gone and the sticks of incendiaries were yellow and started to flow to the preceding waves making the place look like a badly laid-out city with the street lights on. The small incendiaries were going down like a fistful of white rice thrown on a piece of black velvet. As Jock hauled the *Dog* up again I was thrown to the other side of the cockpit and there below were more incendiaries glowing white and then turning red. The cookies – the four 1,000lb high explosives – were bursting below, like great sunflowers gone mad. And then as we started down, still held in the lights. I remember that the *Dog* still had one of those cookies and a whole basket of incendiaries in his belly and the lights still held us. And I was very frightened.

'While Jock was flinging him about in the air he suddenly flung over the intercom, "Two aircraft on the port beam". I looked astern and saw Wally, the mid-upper gunner, whip his turret round to port and then looked up to see a single-engined fighter slide below us. The other aircraft was one of ours. Finally we were out of the cone, flying level. I looked down and the white fires had turned red; they were beginning to merge and spread. Just like butter does on a hot plate. Jock and Boz, the bomb-aimer, began to discuss the target. The smoke was getting thick down below. Boz said he liked the two green flares on the ground almost dead ahead. He began calling his directions and just then a new bunch of big flares went down on the far side of the sea of flame and flare that seemed to be directly below us. He thought that would be a better aiming point. Jock agreed and we flew on. The bomb doors were open. Boz called his directions: "Five left . . . five left." Then there was a gentle, confident upward thrust under my feet and Boz said, "*Cookie gone*". A few seconds later the incendiaries went and *D-Dog* seemed lighter and easier to handle.

'I thought I could make out the outline of streets below, this time all those patches of white on black had turned, caught us, but didn't hold us. Then through the intercom, "We're still carrying it." And Jock replied, "Is it a big one or ;a little one? I'm not sure – I'll check." More of those yellow flares came down and hung about us. I hadn't seen so much light since the day war began. Finally, the intercom announced that it was only a small container of incendiaries left and Jock remarked, "Well, its hardly worth going back and doing another run-up for that". If there had been a good fat bundle left he would have gone back through that stuff and done it all again.

'I began to breathe and to reflect again – that all men would be brave if only they could leave their stomachs at home, when there was a tremendous whoomp, an unintelligible shout from the tail-gunner . . . *D-Dog* shivered and lost altitude. I looked out the port side and there was a Lancaster that seemed close enough to touch; he had whipped straight under us – missed us by 25–50 feet. No one knew how much.

'The navigator sang out the new course and we were heading for home. Jock was doing what I had heard him tell his pilots to do so often – flying dead on course. He flew straight into a huge green searchlight and as he rammed the throttles home remarked, "We'll have a little trouble getting away from this one". And again *D-Dog* dived, climbed and twisted and was finally free. We flew level then and I looked on the port beam at the target area. There was a red, sullen, obscene glare – the fires seemed to have found each other . . . and we were heading home.

'For a little while it was smooth sailing – we saw more battles and then another plane in flames but no one could tell whether it was ours or theirs. We were still near the target. Dave, the navigator, said "Hold her steady skipper. I want to get an astral sight." And Jock held her steady. And the flak began coming up at us. It seemed to be very close. It was winking off both wings. But the *Dog* was steady. Finally, Dave said, "Okay, skipper, thank you very much" and a great orange blob of flak smacked up straight in front of us. Jock said, "I think they're shooting at us". (I had thought so for some time) and he began to throw *D for Dog* up, around and about again. When we were clear of the barrage I asked him how close the bursts were and he said, "Not very close. When they are really near you can smell 'em." That proved nothing; for I had been holding my breath.

'Jack sang out from the rear turret, said his oxygen was getting low, thought maybe the lead was frozen. Titch, the radio-operator, went scrambling back with a new mask and a bottle of oxygen. Dave, the navigator, said, "We're crossing the coast". My mind went back to the time I had crossed that coast in 1938 in a plane that had taken off from Prague. Just ahead of me sat two refugees from Vienna – an old man and his wife. The co-pilot came back and told them that we were outside German territory. The old man reached out and grasped his wife's hand. The work that was done last night was a massive blow of retribution for all those who have fled from the sound of shots and blows on that stricken continent.

'We began to lose height over the North Sea. We were over England's shore. The land was dark beneath us. Somewhere down there below American boys were probably bombing up Fortresses and Liberators getting ready for the day's work.

'We were over the home field; we called the control tower; and the calm, clear voice of an English girl replied, "Greetings *D-Dog*, you are diverted to *Mulebag*". We swung round, contacted Mulebag, came in on the flare path, touched down very gently, ran along to the end of the runway and turned left and Jock, the finest pilot in Bomber Command, said to the control tower, "*D-Dog* clear of runway".

'When we went in for interrogation, I looked on the board and saw that the big slow smiling Canadian and the red headed English boy with the two week-old-moustache hadn't made it.[2] They were missing. There were four reporters on this operation. Two of them didn't come back – two friends of mine, Norman Stockton, of Australian Associated Newspapers and Lowell Bennett, an American representing International News Service. There is something of a tradition amongst reporters that those who are prevented by circumstances from filing their stories will be covered by their colleagues. This has been my effort to do so. In the aircraft in which I flew, the men who flew and fought it poured into my ears their comments on fighters, flak and flares – in the same tones they would have used in reporting a host of daffodils. I have no doubt that Bennett and Stockton would have given you a better report of last night's activities.[3]

'Berlin was a kind of orchestrated hell – a terrible symphony of light and flame. It isn't a pleasant kind of warfare. The men doing it speak of it as a job. Yesterday afternoon, when the tapes were stretched out on the big map all the way to Berlin and back again, a young pilot with old eyes said to me, "I see we're working again tonight". That's the frame of mind in which the job is being done. The job isn't pleasant – it's terribly tiring – men die in the sky while others are roasted alive in their cellars. Berlin last night wasn't a pretty sight. In about 35 minutes it was hit with about three times the amount of stuff that ever came down on London in a night-long blitz. This is a calculated, remorseless campaign of destruction. Right now the mechanics are probably working on *D-Dog*, getting him ready to fly again.'[4]

On the night of 16/17 December 483 Lancasters and 10 Mosquitoes made yet another night attack on Berlin and five more Mosquitoes dropped decoy fighter flares south of the 'Big City'. Large scale jamming of German radio and radar was carried out by using quotations from Hitler's speeches and very sudden jamming of the *Soldatenrundfunksender* (Forces Broadcasting Station) *Anne Marie* by continuous sound from a strong British jamming station. However, the bombers, who flew directly to the capital across Holland and Northern Germany, were plotted with great accuracy, Mosquito *spoof* attacks on Kassel and Hanover were clearly recognized as such and night fighters were sent to intercept the Lancaster force. Widespread mist and fog at 150–300 feet in the North German plains reduced the overall effectiveness of the fighter defence and 23 aircraft, mostly Bf 110s, had to abandon their sorties prematurely. Even so, German night fighters shot down 20 bombers and *Wilde Sau* fighters and flak destroyed five more.[5] Berlin was cloud-covered but the Pathfinder sky-marking was fairly accurate and most of the bombing was in the city area. On the way home the force returned over Denmark but many of the aircraft encountered very low cloud over England and 29 Lancasters either crashed or were abandoned when their crews baled out. Seven of these were Lancasters of 97 Squadron, which had dispatched 21 aircraft from Bourn and had lost one Lancaster and its crew to enemy action on the raid. Only eight of the squadron's Lancasters landed back safely at Bourn. One bomber crashed a mile to the north-east of Graveley killing all the crew. Another Lancaster piloted by Squadron Leader Ernie Deverill DFC AFC DFM who had flown the infamous Augsburg daylight raid, crashed near Graveley with the loss of the pilot and six of his crew. Two more crashed at Bourn and eight crew men were killed and five were injured. Another Lancaster crashed south of Gransden, while another was abandoned in the vicinity of Wyton and crashed in the sea. A seventh was abandoned near Ely, the Lancaster finally crashing four miles north-west of Orford Ness near Sudbourne in Suffolk. One Lancaster that was hit by incendiaries from another aircraft over Berlin limped back with two engines out of action. A signal was received that the crew were ditching off the coast of Denmark but after a short interval the message was cancelled and the Lancaster crossed the North Sea to land on two engines at Downham Market.

On the night of 20/21 December, 650 bombers including 390 Lancasters raided Frankfurt with the loss of 27 Halifaxes and 14 Lancasters, many falling victim to fighter attacks en route to the target. Flight Sergeant Richard 'Dick' Starkey and his crew in 106 Squadron at Metheringham, were flying their third operation this night. They had joined the squadron in October 1943, flying their first op to Leipzig on the 20th. Their second had been to Berlin at the start of the Battle of Berlin in November. Starkey recalls:

'We took off for Frankfurt in aircraft JB534. My mid-upper gunner had been granted compassionate leave and his replacement was a sergeant whose crew had already completed their first tour and he had to complete his by flying with other crews. We had no trouble on the outward journey and flew at 21,000 feet. The target was covered by a lot of cloud so the ground markers were hidden and I also remember that the Germans had lit a decoy fire south of the city. About ten miles north of the target on our return journey we were fired upon by cannon and machine gun from what we presumed was a night-fighter. The rear-gunner immediately instructed me to corkscrew, as enemy tracer came from the port quarter. I did so and after one complete corkscrew, resumed normal course. I could tell that he had been hit around the port main plane and hoped there would be no flames. However, a further attack followed immediately and the aircraft was hit again. I corkscrewed again but neither gunner saw a fighter so we resumed course. The fighter was never seen and although the rear-gunner attempted to open fire on three occasions, his guns failed to function. When we resumed course it was evident that the aircraft had been extensively damaged, because it started to shudder violently and I had great difficulty controlling it. The vibration transferred to my body as I fought to maintain control. The rear-gunner reported that the port fin tail-plane rudder was extensively damaged and a large part had disappeared. As for the main plane we could not see any damage but we knew there was some.

'Soon after the attack the navigator instructed me to change course, but on applying rudder and aileron, the aircraft began to bank steeply and put her back on an even keel by using automatic pilot – manual controls were ineffective. The shuddering continued and I decided that this was due to damage to the port tail plane. I asked the navigator what the remaining headings would be according to his flight plan and log. He informed me that there would be slight turnings to starboard, which meant that I would not have to apply port rudder. At this particular point we did not know that the aileron was just a skeleton, the covering having

disappeared during the attack. I also decided that if we were to get back to base safely, it would necessitate a right-hand circuit.

'We were lucky that the engines were intact, but the shudderings continued and after approximately two and three-quarter hours we approached base. The wireless operator informed the control tower the condition of the aircraft and that it was essential to make a right hand circuit and also that we must land immediately. Permission was given to circuit to the right at 800 feet and other aircraft were ordered to maintain their height. On our approach down the funnel we began to drift to starboard and I dared not counteract this. I switched the landing light on and touched down on the grass, 50 yards to the right of the flare path.

'When the aircraft was examined next morning and the full extent of the damage was revealed, there was severe damage to the port fin and rudder, more than 50 per cent was missing. The port side of the fuselage had been riddled with bullets, which stopped just before the wireless operator's position. Material covering the port aileron had been ripped off and a cannon shell had exploded on the underside of the port main plane creating a jagged hole approximately one foot in diameter. If the shell had exploded further forward it would have hit the fuel tanks and the aircraft would have "gone up". Repairs had to be carried out on the airfield by workmen from Avro and took approximately six weeks to complete. JB534 was transferred to 'A' Flight after the repairs were completed only to crash near the village of Martin when returning from its first operation [on 16 February 1944], killing all the crew except one.'

On the night of 29/30 December Berlin was again the target for RAF Bomber Command and 712 aircraft, including 457 Lancasters, were dispatched. At the 1 Group aerodrome at Elsham Wolds, Sergeant Ben Frazier, *Yank* Staff Correspondent boarded *V-Victor* of 576 Squadron for the operation to the 'Big City' with Flying Officer Gomer S. 'Taff' Morgan and his crew.[6] Frazier wrote:

'England. A small village lay tucked away in the fold of a valley just below the high, windswept, bleak plateau where a Lancaster bomber station was situated. Housewives were busy in the kitchen preparing food, and the men had left their ploughing to come in for the noon-day meal. In the lichen covered Gothic Church, the minister's wife was arranging decorations, and placing on the altar freshly cut chrysanthemums that had managed to escape the north winds and were still blooming in December. The placidness of the village life was in sharp contrast to the bustling activity at the airfield. It seemed as remote from war as any hamlet could possibly be, although the provident farmers, living so close to an obvious military target had wisely provided themselves with shelter trenches at the edge of each ploughed field. Nevertheless, the name of this quiet, lovely village had spread far. By borrowing it, the bomber station had made it one to strike terror into the heart of the Nazi High Command.

'At the airfield, *V for Victor*'s crew lounged around B Flight's Office waiting to see if operations were on. They kept looking up into the sky as if trying to guess what the weather was going to be like. Some of the men chuckled. "Papa Harris is so set on writing off the Big City that he hardly even notices the weather," one of them said. "The last time, there were kites stooging around all over the place. The met boobed that one."

'It was a strange new language. What the airmen were saying was that the last time out the meteorological men had given a wrong steer on the weather, and the planes had been flying all over looking for the field on the return trip. "Papa" Harris was Air Chief Marshal Harris, chief of Bomber Command.

'*V for Victor*'s captain came back from the operations room with the news that there would be ops. That settled the discussion. You seemed to be aware, without noticing anything in particular, of a kind of tension that gripped the men; like they were pulling in their belts a notch or two to get set for the job ahead.

'And with the news, everybody got busy – the aircrews, the ground crews, the mechanics, the WAAFs, the cooks. The ships already had a basic bomb and fuel load on board, and the additional loads were sent out in ammunition trailers and fuel trucks. The perimeter track lost its usually deserted appearance and looked like a well-travelled highway, with trucks and trailers, buses and bicycles hurrying out to the dispersal points. It was just like the preparation at any bomber base before taking off for enemy territory – but going over the Big City was something different. These men had been there before. They knew what to expect.

'In the equipment room, June, the pint-size WAAF in battledress, was an incongruous note. Over a counter as high as her chin, she flung parachutes, harnesses and Mae Wests. The crew grabbed them and lugged them out to the ships. You kept thinking they ought to be able to get somebody a little bigger for the job she was handling.

'In the briefing room, the met officer gave the weather report and the forecast over enemy territory. There would be considerable cloud over the target. The men grinned. An operations officer gave a talk on the

trip. The route was outlined on a large map of Germany on the front wall. It looked ominously long on the large-scale map. He pointed out where the ground defences were supposed to be strong and where fighter opposition might be expected. He gave the time when the various phases should be over the target. He explained where the "spoof" attacks were to be made and the time. He told the men what kinds of flares and other markers the Pathfinders would drop. There was the usual business of routine instructions, statistics and tactics to be used. The Group Captain gave a pep talk on the progress of the Battle of Berlin. And all the while, that tape marking the route stared you in the face and seemed to grow longer and longer.

'Outside it was hazy and growing more so. But this was nothing new. The men were convinced that the weather was always at its most variable and its dampest and its haziest over their field. What could you expect? Ops would probably be scrubbed after all. Hell of a note.

'In the fading light the planes were silhouetted against the sky. They looked, on the ground, slightly hunched and menacing like hawks. Seeing them there, in the half-light you would never guess how easy and graceful they are in flight. Nor would you realize when you see them soaring off the runway, what an immense load they take up with them. It is only when you see the open bomb bay on the ground, that you get some idea of a Lancaster's destructive power. The open bomb bay seems like a small hangar. The 4,000lb block buster in place looks like a kitten curled up in a large bed. It is a sobering sight.

'In the evening some of the men tried to catch a few winks; most of them just sat around talking. The operational meal followed. It was only a snack, but it was the last solid food any one would get until the fresh egg and bacon breakfast, which has become a ritual for the proper ending of a successful mission.

'As there was still some time to wait before take-off, *V for Victor*'s crew sat around the ground crews' hut near the dispersal point, warming themselves by the stove or chewing the rag with the ground crew. The Wingco came around to make a last minute check-up. The medical officer looked everyone over. The engineer officer checked the engines.

'The minutes crept by until at last the time came to get into the planes. The deep stillness of the night was awakened by the motors revving up; one after another until each one was lost in the general roar. The crews scrambled into the planes and took their places. The great ships were guided out of their dispersal areas by the ground crews who gave a final wave as the Lancs moved off slowly down the perimeter track. They appeared more menacing than ever creeping along in the dark with their motors roaring. One by one they turned onto the runway and noisily vanished into the night.

'From now on, until they would return, the members of *V for Victor*'s crew were a little world in themselves, alone and yet not alone. For all around them were other similar little worlds, hundreds of them with a population of seven, hurtling through space, lightlessly – huge animated ammunition dumps. For its safety, each little world depended utterly and completely on its members – and a large dash of luck.

'There was not much conversation over the intercom. When you're flying without running lights on a definite course, and surrounded by several hundred other bombers, you have not time for any pleasantries. The navigator was busy checking the air speed and any possible drift. Almost everyone else kept a look out for other aircraft, both friend and foe. A friendly aircraft is almost as dangerous as an enemy plane, for if two blockbusters meet in mid-air, the pieces that are left are very small indeed.

'Occasionally the ship jolted from the slipstream of some unseen aircraft ahead, and frequently others overhauled *V for Victor*, passing by to port and starboard, above and below. *V for Victor* gained altitude very easily for maximum ceiling. She was a veteran of over 50 ops and had the DFC painted on her port bow to celebrate the fiftieth, but she had the vitality of a youngster. Blondy [Sergeant J. R. O'Hanlon], the wireless-operator, broke the silence. "Taff, the W/T has gone u/s."

'The wireless is not used except in an emergency such as ditching, but it is nice to know it's there. We went on. Occasionally Taff, the pilot, would call into the intercom, "Bob, [Sergeant C. E. 'Bob' Shilling] are you OK?" There would be a silence for a moment while the rear-gunner fumbled to turn on his intercom, until you wondered if he had frozen back there. Then he'd sing out, "OK, Taff." He and the mid-upper gunner [Sergeant A. Newman] were the only two outside the heated cabin. Inside the cabin it was warm and snug. You didn't even need gloves. Jock [Sergeant J. R. "Jock" Mearns], the navigator, wore no flying gear, just the Air Force battledress.

'Up ahead the Pathfinder boys dropped the first route markers, flak shot up into the air and the men knew that *V for Victor* was approaching the Dutch coast. An enormous burst of flame lit up the night off to port. "Scarecrow to starboard," the mid-upper reported on the intercom. Jerry intended the "scarecrow" to look like a burning plane but it did not take long to see that it was not.[7]

'Jock's Scots accent came over the intercom: "Taff, we're eleven minutes late." "OK, we'll increase speed." The engineer pushed up the throttles. Everything was black again below. Occasionally there was a small burst of flak here and there.

"Plane to starboard below!"

"OK, it's a Lanc."

'As *V for Victor* passed it you could seen the bluish flame from the exhausts lighting the aircraft below in a weird ghostly manner. It was unpleasant to realize that our own exhausts made *V for Victor* just as obvious as the other plane.

'Away off the port bow, a glow became visible. It looked like the moon but it was the first big German searchlight belt, encompassing many cities. The beams were imprisoned under cloud.[8]

"That will be Happy Valley," Jock said. Another route marker appeared ahead.

"Tell me when we're over it," the navigator replied. Shortly the bomb-aimer [Flight Sergeant N. A. "Digger" Lambrell RAAF] said, "We're bang over it now."

"OK, Digger."

"Taff, we're nine minutes late."

'The navigator took a couple of astro sights to get a fix. From this he could determine the wind and the drift of the plane.

'Another searchlight belt showed up to starboard. It was enormous, running for miles and miles. It was all imprisoned under the cloud but it was an evil looking sight just the same.[9] The top of the clouds shone with millions of moving spots, like so many restless glow worms, but the impression was much more sinister – like some kind of luminous octopus. The tentacle-like beams groped about seeking some hole in the cloud, some way of clutching at you as you passed by protected by the darkness. The continuous motion of the searchlights caused a ripple effect on the clouds, giving them an agitated, angry, frustrated appearance. Once in a while one found a rift and shot its light high into the sky. Flak came up sparkling and twinkling through this luminous blanket. *V for Victor* jolted violently from close bursts, but was untouched. It passed another Lanc, which was clearly silhouetted against the floodlit clouds.

'Another leg of the trip was completed. The navigator gave the new course over the intercom and added, "Seven minutes late."

"OK, Jock. Mac, [Pilot Officer E. M. Graham, flight engineer] make it 165."

'*V for Victor* passed plane after plane and occasionally jolted in the slipstream of others. A third searchlight belt showed up and this one was free of cloud. It was a huge wall of light and looked far more impenetrable than a mountain. It seemed inconceivable than any plane could pass through and reach the opposite side. You thanked your lucky stars that this was not the target. To fly out of the protecting darkness into the blaze of light would be a test of courage you would rather not have to face.

'Nevertheless, there were some facing it right now. The flak opened up and the searchlights waved madly about. It was a diversionary attack, the "spoof". You watched in a detached, remote sort of way. It seemed very far away and did not seem to concern you at all. Until suddenly, one beam which had been vertical, slanted down and started to pursue *V for Victor*, and you realized that it did concern you very intimately. The seconds ticked by as the beam overtook the plane. But it passed harmlessly overhead and groped impotently in the darkness beyond.

"Four minutes late," Jock called over the intercom.

'The target itself, the Big City, came into view like a luminous patch dead ahead. It was largely hidden by cloud and showed few searchlights. It seemed so much less formidable than the mountain of light just behind, that it came as a sort of anticlimax. Surely, you felt, this cannot be the Big City, the nerve-centre of Europe's evil genius.

'It was quiet. There was no flak as yet, no flares, and just the handful of searchlights. You tried to imagine what it was like on the ground there. The sirens would be about to sound; the ack-ack batteries would be standing ready, the searchlights already manned. You wondered if the people were in shelters.

'But it was too much of an effort. It was too remote. Your problems were flak, fighters, searchlights and whether you were on the course and on time. What happened below was an entirely different problem, which had nothing to do with you. What happened below might just as well be happening on Mars. *V for Victor*'s own little world simply hovering off this planet and leading a life of its own.

'Ever so slowly *V for Victor* crept up on the target. The two worlds were coming inevitably together. But it still had the quality of unreality. It was like a dream where you were hurrying somewhere and yet cannot move at all. Nevertheless, Victor was passing plane after plane and jolted in somebody's slipstream now and again. The other Lancs looked ominous bearing down on the target, breathing out blue flame as they approached.

'The minute of the attack and still the target was quiet. One more minute ticked by – still quiet. The engineer opened up the throttles to maximum speed and increased the oxygen supply. Still quiet. The whole attack was a minute or two late. Winds, probably. Suddenly the whole city opened up. The flak poured up through the clouds. It came in a myriad of little lights. It poured up in a stream of red, as if shaken from a hose. It would be impossible to miss such a brilliantly marked objective. Bright flashes started going off under the clouds. That would be the cookies from the planes ahead. *V for Victor* started the bombing run. The bomb-aimer called the course now.

"Left, left ... Steady now ... Right a bit ... Steady ... steady ... Cookie gone!" *V for Victor* shot upward slightly. "Steady ... Incendiaries gone ..." *V for Victor* surged again ever so slightly.

"Stand-by, Taff," it was the voice of Bob, the tail-gunner. "Fighter."

'Instantly the pilot sent *V for Victor* over to starboard and rushed headlong downward. A stream of red tracer whipped out of the dark, past the rear turret, and on past the wing-tip, missing by what seemed inches. A second later the fighter itself shot past after the tracer, a vague dark blur against the night sky.

"Me 109," Bob said calmly.

'*V for Victor* squirmed and corkscrewed over the sky of Berlin. You wondered how it could be possible to avoid all the other planes that were over the city. But the fighter was shaken off and *V for Victor* came back to a normal course again.

'Down below through rifts in the cloud, you could see that Berlin was burning. The bright, white flame of the incendiaries showed up as a carpet of light, always growing. And flash after flash went off as the block-busters fell. The dark, black shapes of many Lancasters could be seen all over the sky, against the brilliant clouds below. They were like small insects crawling over a great glass window. It did not seem possible that these tiny black dots could be the cause of the destruction, which was going on below. The insects crawled to the edge of the light and disappeared into the darkness beyond. They had passed safely through the target, *V for Victor* close behind.

'Shortly the course was set for the return and Berlin was visible for many miles on the port quarter. The attack was over now. It took only fifteen minutes. The ack-ack was silent. There was no flak flashing over the city, but the city was brighter than ever. The clouds were getting a reddish tinge, which showed that the fires had caught hold below.

'And so the capital of Nazism dropped astern, obscuring the rising moon by its flames. The Government which came into power by deliberately setting fire to its chamber of representatives, the Government which first used wholesale bombing, and boasted of it, was now perishing in fires far more devastating than any it ever devised. It was perishing to a fire music never dreamed of by Wagner.

'But it was impossible to connect *V for Victor* with the death struggles of Berlin. There was no time for contemplation.

"Stand-by, Ju 88 starboard – corkscrew," came Bob's voice. Again with lightning speed, the pilot put *V for Victor* over and dived out of the way. The Ju 88's tracers missed us and shot down another Lanc, which had not been so fortunate.

'After that the route home was uneventful. Crossing the North Sea, *V for Victor* went into a gentle incline towards home base, as if by a sort of homing instinct. The searchlights of England sent out a greeting of welcome. For miles alone the coast they stood almost evenly spaced, vertical sentries guarding the island. Then they started waving downwards in the direction of the nearest airfield. No doubt they were helping home a damaged bomber. How different they were from the menacing tentacles over the German cities. *V for Victor* arrived over the home field. The wireless-operator called base over his repaired equipment. He said simply. "*V for Victor*".

'The clear voice of a girl came pleasantly over the intercom, "*V for Victor*, prepare to pancake". The short business-like message in service slang was a wonderful welcome home. *V for Victor* circled the field, losing altitude.

"*V-Victor* in funnels."

"*V-Victor*, pancake," the girl's voice said. *V for Victor* touched down, ran down the flare path, and turned off on the perimeter track.

"*V-Victor* clear of flare path." The ground crew met *V for Victor* and acted as a guide back into the dispersal area.

"How was it?"

"Piece of cake," someone said. The crew got out, collected their gear, the parachutes, Mae Wests, the navigator's bag, the guns, etc, and then, as one man, lit up cigarettes. The pilot walked around the plane looking for any damage. There was one small hole through the aileron but it was too dark to see it then. The bus arrived and the crew clambered in with all the gear and were taken back to the locker room. June was there, and gathered all the stuff over the counter and staggered away, lost from sight under a mound of yellow suits and Mae Wests. Then back to the briefing room where a cup of hot tea with rum in it was waiting. Each captain signed his name on the board as he came

in. Crew by crew, the men went into the Intelligence room, carrying their spiked tea with them. There were packages of cigarettes on the table and everyone chain-smoked, lighting up from the butt of the previous one. The Intelligence Officer asked brief questions and the replies were brief such as "The heavy flak was light and the light flak heavy". It was over in a very few minutes and you went back to the briefing room and bantered over the trip with the other crews. No trouble, any of them, but there were gaps in the list of captains chalked on the board.

"It's like that," the Wingco remarked. "In night flying, you usually get back intact, or you don't get back at all. If you get coned, or a fighter sees you before you see it, then very often you've had it, but if somebody else gets coned then it's that much easier for you."

'You thought of the other Lancaster the Ju 88 got with the same burst that missed *V for Victor*. And you lit another cigarette. The first signs of dawn were coming over the field now and off in the distance, on the bleak, windswept, little knoll, *V for Victor* stood guard over the empty dispersal points from which other men and ships had gone out a short while before. "... If somebody else gets coned then it's that much easier for you."[10]

On New Year's Day 1944 one of the crews on the Order of Battle when Bomber Command went to Berlin with a force of 421 Lancasters was Flying Officer James 'Gil' Bryson's in 550 Squadron. They had joined the squadron on its formation at Waltham, Grimsby, on 25 November 1943, having transferred from 12 Squadron at Wickenby where they had begun operations on 3 September. The crew's last two trips had been to the 'Big City' before they had received two days of rest. On 1 January 27 year old Major Wittgenstein's score stood at 68 victories and he became *Kommodore* of NJG 2. He was soon airborne in his Ju 88C-6 equipped with *SN-2* radar and *Schräge Musik* and looking for his 69th victory. Sergeant Jim Donnan, Bryson's W/Op, recalls the events that followed:

'We were engaged in routine pre-operational checks and testing of our equipment prior to the main briefing, which commenced in a tense atmosphere. When the curtain was drawn aside exposing the operational map, the target was Berlin for the third consecutive time, only this time our route to the 'Big City' was almost directly from the Dutch coast across an area, which was becoming increasingly dangerous because of night fighter activity. Deteriorating weather conditions delayed our take-off for several hours. It was therefore difficult to relax during this period. As New Year's Day was drawing to a close we were preparing for take-off and at 14 minutes past midnight we were airborne and on our way at last. The sky was dark and overcast as we flew through layers of broken cloud, climbing to our operational height, heading east over the North Sea. As we approached the Dutch coast we could see that the anti-aircraft defences were very active and we became alert to the dangers ahead. Flying over Germany, occasional bursts of flak and flashes lit up the thick, unbroken cloud along the route. While searching the night-fighter waveband I was aware of considerable activity by the German control. We found it necessary to keep a sharp look out even though our trip had been uneventful so far. Our navigator Sergeant Thomas "Rocky" Roxby called for a slight change in course for the final leg to Berlin as we reached a position between Hanover and Bremen.

'It was almost immediately afterwards that a series of thuds vibrated through the floor and the aircraft seemed to bank away to starboard. I leapt up from my seat to the astrodome where I could see the starboard engines were on fire. As I switched over from radio to intercom, I saw that a fire had started under the navigator's table on the floor just behind the pilot. It was soon burning fiercely. The pilot gave the order to abandon the aircraft. I clipped on my parachute and as I moved forward it was found that the front escape hatch would not open. The engineer joined the bomb-aimer in trying to release it. As I stood behind the navigator waiting to exit, the rear-gunner said that he was having trouble with the rear turret. I then signalled that I would go to the rear exit. The navigator was standing beside the pilot ready to exit as I scrambled over the main spar and along the fuselage to the rear door, losing my shoes on the way. When I got there, the mid-upper gunner was ready to leave and the rear-gunner was out of his turret and preparing to come forward. I then jettisoned the rear door as the flames from the starboard wing streamed past, licking the tail plane. Grasping the release handle on my parachute I prepared to jump but I must have lost consciousness, as I have no recollection of what happened next or how I left the plane. When I regained consciousness, my parachute was already open and I was floating in pitch darkness, very cold and my feet were freezing. I seemed to be a long time coming down but as I descended through the clouds, dark shadows appeared and I landed on soft ground in an open space. Gathering up my parachute, I dashed over to a clump of trees, where I sat on the ground shivering and wondering how I could avoid capture.'[11]

One Australian pilot who had a 'ringside' view for ten weeks of the terrifying attacks on Berlin, was Flight Lieutenant Roland King DFC a pilot on 83 Squadron. He took off from Wyton at 16.11 hours on the night of 20/21 January when 769 aircraft, 495 of them Lancasters, raided the 'Big City' again.[12] King had bombed Berlin 10 times, as well as many other important targets, before his 11th and last air visit to the Reich capital. That night his Lancaster arrived over the target without incident, but after bombing something went wrong. The control stick suddenly went dead in his hand and the rudders failed. He found, too, that he had lost his helmet and intercommunication gear and that the aircraft was full of smoke. During the next few seconds King tried to check on his crew's condition, but he could see only two of them. One seemed to be curled up on the inside of the roof, apparently held there by the forces acting on the falling bomber. King released his harness and immediately he, too, was shot upwards. He hit the root then fell back into his seat again. He seized the stick once more and tried to pull the bomber out, but it was useless. This all took place within a few seconds. King believes he lost consciousness; the next thing he remembers is falling through the air, his parachute unopened. He pulled the ripcord, and it spread out above him. He was descending immediately above the target, and the attack was at the height of its fury. Bombs were raining down all around him, and the sky was alight with massed searchlights and bursting flak. The noise then was terrific. He pulled the shroud of his parachute in an attempt to drift outside the city and believes that he did actually drift some little way to the south-west of Berlin, for he came down in a ploughed field. Soon after he landed he heard the Berlin 'all clear'. He freed himself of his parachute, and then, by the light of incendiary bombs burning in a hole nearby, searched for his cigarette case, but could not get at the lighter. His right arm seemed fixed across his body and quite useless. His left hand was smashed, and he was wounded in the head.

It was dark and raining. King wandered round trying to discover where he was. He kept falling into bomb craters, and after half an hour or so he could hear dogs barking. Thinking they might be searching for him, he climbed several fences, then came to a road and set out along it, fighting the urge to sleep, and looking for a haystack to hide and rest in. But a dense plantation of small fir trees blocked his path, and finally he fell exhausted against the trees and tried to sleep. He was in great pain and soon, realizing it was a bad place in which to stay, he moved on again and reached a wide autobahn. It seemed to run to the south-west of Berlin and King followed it. After three and half-hours' walking he heard a motor engine approaching and knew that because of his injuries he would have to give himself up. He kept walking, and soon the vehicle stopped behind him with its light shining on him. It was a motor cycle and sidecar carrying two *Wehrmacht* men. They jumped down, put King in the sidecar, and set out for the burning city, which he could see glowing ahead. The journey was an unforgettable ordeal for the injured man. He was taken first to an army barracks and closely questioned about the type of aircraft he had been flying, but refused to answer. Then he lost consciousness for a time. When he came to he was sent off with two more soldiers on a motor cycle, who were to take him to hospital. The cycle took King through many areas of the burning city while the German soldiers tried to get him into one hospital after another. Three hospitals refused him admittance, for air raid casualties were coming in simultaneously.

The road along which they drove first into the city was walled along the left side by solid flame. The streets were full of people in night attire and every few yards hose pipes crossed the road with wooden ramps protecting them from traffic, most of which seemed to be going in the opposite direction. At one point, they were stopped by a car containing German officers, who got out and asked some questions but let the cycle pass on. King was at last admitted to the Hermann Goering Luftwaffe hospital. He was taken into a room, where he found two RAF men. He remembers sitting on the bed while the Germans cut off his clothes, then no more. He woke up on the operating table. He was two and a half months in the Hermann Goering hospital. His elbow had been severely injured, and he had five operations on it. He had two blood transfusions, both given by one of the RAF men. RAF air attacks occurred almost every night. The patients were hurried down to the air raid shelters in the cellars and there they would listen to the 10 or 15 minute broadcasts of the approach of the bombers. Every time there was an attack the hospital windows were blown out. When the heavies were not over the capital the Mosquitoes 'stoked the fires' in the capital.[13]

On 21/22 January RAF Bomber Command suffered its first major defeat since the big raids on Berlin the previous summer, when 648 aircraft, 421 of them Lancasters, attacked Magdeburg in Prussia, near Berlin and night fighter defences destroyed no less than 57 bombers. In less than 40 minutes Major Wittgenstein, *Kommodore* of NJG 2 flying a Ju 88C-6 on a *Zahme Sau* sortie shot down three Lancasters and two Halifaxes in the vicinity of Magdeburg. It all began when Feldwebel Ostheimer, his radar operator, picked up a 'blip' on his SN-2 screen. It was a Lancaster. He opened fire and flames came from the port wing of the bomber, which spun down and was seen to crash. Bombers were so thick in the stream that Ostheimer picked up no fewer than six 'blips' at once. They made contact with a second Lancaster, which received a short burst of cannon fire before diving away vertically on fire. Ostheimer felt heavy detonations – probably its bomb-load as the Lancaster crashed. Ten minutes later Wittgenstein fired a long burst of fire into yet a third Lancaster, probably the one flown by Flight Lieutenant Leo B. Patkin RAAF of 467 Squadron, which Wittgenstein set on fire with a single burst. The bomber flew on for a few moments before plunging down and crashing in flames at Altmerdingsen, near Burgdorf. The aircraft exploded so violently on impact that roofs and windows of nearby houses were shattered and the crater caused was approximately 25 yards in diameter. Immediately afterwards Ostheimer picked out another bomber, probably a Halifax, and this too went down after only one firing pass. After starting a small fire in another Lancaster, which the crew managed to extinguish, Wittgenstein moved in for the kill. He was about to press the trigger to fire a second burst into the Lancaster when the fuselage and port wing of the Ju 88 was riddled with enemy fire, probably from below. The Junkers went into a dive, whereupon Wittgenstein jettisoned the cabin roof and ordered his crew to bale out immediately, which they did successfully. Early next morning the body of Prinz Wittgenstein was discovered close to the crash site at Lübars. On baling out, his head had probably struck the tail plane, rendering him unconscious and unable to pull the ripcord.[14]

The next main force raid after Magdeburg was Berlin on 27/28 January when 515 Lancasters and 15 Mosquitoes set out from England. Enemy night fighters were committed to action earlier than usual, some being sent out 75 miles over the North Sea from the Dutch coast. Even though about half the night fighters were lured away from the main thrust by feints and diversions, they still managed to shoot down 33 Lancasters. Twenty-two year old Flying Officer Leonard 'Dusty' Miller of 15 Squadron piloted one of the Lancasters on the raid. Len had been born in East Ham in London's East End. He was an engineer apprentice in the London docks where 'they were bombed to pieces'. He considered himself a 'born survivor'. One day in East Ham he and his friend were standing on a street corner when a 2,000lb parachute bomb came down and blew them right across the road. It also blew about four houses down. They went straight away to help dig the people out. Above the trees was another bomb that was swinging on its cords above their heads. Miller remembered going out on a lifeboat to go across to Dunkirk. He got as afar as Gravesend and the Navy stopped them, as they were too young to go! The Company that he worked for wanted them all back to get on with the work! Miller had always wanted to fly. Following a period at 1651 Conversion Unit at Waterbeach, where the crew converted to Stirlings, Sergeant Miller and his crew had been posted to 15 Squadron at Mildenhall on 19 October 1943. They flew three operations on Stirlings before the squadron converted to Avro Lancasters during December. When he first saw the Lancaster Miller 'drooled'. 'It was *the* machine, four engines and it was terrific in handling with all the weight it could carry. It was beautiful to fly. As much as Spitfires are admired, so is the Lancaster. It was a perfect design. The power that surged through the machine was terrific. Such an easy aircraft to fly; it was wonderful.'

On 14 December Len was commissioned pilot officer and life was good at Mildenhall. A 1934 MG he had purchased in 1939 was kept topped up with regular 'donations' of petrol that he 'pinched' from fuel bowsers that were used to refuel the aircraft. There was a drain cock on the tanker and he would crawl underneath with a Jerry can and fill it up. Being quite fit he had no trouble carrying it and no one ever asked. Whenever the opportunity presented itself he and some of his crew would pile into the MG and go to London. If they had nowhere to sleep they would go to his house in East Ham. He made them all swear not to say that they were on operations because his mother used to worry 'like hell!' Miller and his crew furnished their shared quarters with furniture stolen from the squadron leader's offices and they supplemented their rationed coal by raids on the coal dump. Miller led his crew with camouflage nets over their heads to the coal dump with kit bags. Had they been caught they would probably have been looking at seven days in the guard house or a severe reprimand, but as Miller said, 'When you stuck your necks out as far as we did, who gave a damn?'

They certainly stuck their necks out over Berlin, which was cloud covered, and sky marking had to be used. On the bomb run a shell came through into the cockpit of Miller's Lanc and hit his flight engineer, Sergeant Alf Pybus, in the head. The crew only assumed that he might have been wounded, so they wrapped him in Irvin jackets and blankets, the only warm clothing that they had, rolled him up and put the portable oxygen cylinder on him to help him breathe. It was a very stressful time and the crew did not know if Pybus was mortally wounded or just badly wounded. Miller reasoned therefore that the best thing was to get back home with him as quickly as possible. 'He died beside me on the floor' says Miller. 'He had been a very close friend and we had plans to do things together after the war.'[15]

On the night of 28/29 January, 677 aircraft, 432 of them Lancasters, were dispatched to Berlin for the second night running. Part of the German night fighter force was fooled into taking off too soon by the diversion and spoof forces[16] and they headed in the wrong direction, away from the bomber stream, which approached the Big City from over Northern Denmark. This route proved too distant for some of the other German night fighters. Flight Sergeant Les Bartlett, bomb-aimer in Pilot Officer Michael Beetham's crew in 50 Squadron, at Skellingthorpe, recalls:[17]

'The first opposition we met was crossing the enemy coast not far from Flensburg. Searchlights were more active than usual, showing us through a few very large breaks in the clouds, but the Pathfinders were on top form and put down our route markers very accurately, which enabled us to keep out of the most hazardous areas.'

Bartlett's pilot has been described as a 'compact, precise man who would later earn a fierce reputation as a young squadron commander'.[18] In the summer of 1940 Michael Beetham had spent the school holidays at Hillsea Barracks on the hills overlooking Portsmouth with his father, a veteran of the First World War but too old to fight in the Second. Beetham expected to join the army but watching the Battle of Britain dog fights overhead made him realize that he did not want to follow in his father's footsteps. He wanted to be a fighter pilot in the RAF instead. Beetham joined the RAF in 1941 but by then the service needed bomber pilots and in the winter of 1943 he had been posted to 50 Squadron at Skellingthorpe to fly Lancasters.

Bartlett continues:.

'We were in the fifth wave and as we approached Berlin I could see that the attack was in full swing. With the target in my sight I could see numerous large fires and one particularly vivid explosion, which seemed to light up the whole of Berlin with a vivid orange flash for about ten seconds. At the critical moment I called for bomb doors open and then released our bombs bang on target. Just as I was taking my usual checks to ensure that no bombs had hung up we saw a night fighter attacking a Lancaster ahead of us. I jumped straight into the front turret and started blazing away. It did a slow turn to port and then spiralled down to earth. From then on we saw absolutely nothing but occasional short bursts of flak, but no searchlights and no fighters at all.'

Even so, the *Jägerleitoffizier* was still able to concentrate his fighters over the target area where most of the 26 Halifaxes and 20 Lancasters that failed to return were shot down. The cloud over Berlin was broken and some ground marking was possible but bombing was scattered. The western and southern districts were attacked and about 180,000 people were bombed out but 77 other places outside the capital were also hit.

On 30/31 January Berlin was heavily attacked for the third time in four nights, this time by a force of 534 aircraft, which included 440 Lancasters. There were no preliminary diversions and the German night fighters were able to follow the bomber stream until well into the return flight. All bar one of the 33 bombers that failed to return were Lancasters and twin-engined *Zahme Sau* downed all of these. The raid itself took place in complete cloud cover and bombing was scattered once more. Heavy damage was caused to the Big City but 79 towns and villages outside the capital reported falling bombs, most of these exploding in open countryside.

It was clear that new British tactics and new countermeasures would be necessary before a resumption of raids deep into Germany.[19]

For two weeks the moon and weather conditions prevented further main force attacks on Berlin and defensive *Nachtjagd* operations over the *Reich* during February began relatively quietly, no *First Jagdkorps* claims being submitted before the night of the 15/16th when 561 Lancaster crews were deployed as part of a raid by 891 aircraft on Berlin. It was the first time that more than 500 Lancasters had been dispatched thus far in the war and the total quantity of bombs dropped, 2,642 tons, was also a record. Berlin was covered by cloud for most of the raid and heavy bombing fell on the centre and south-western districts but many parts of the surrounding countryside again reported bombs falling. Forty-three bombers – 26 of them Lancasters – were lost.[20] A Conspicuous Gallantry Medal, one of the last made to an Australian for an attack on Berlin, was awarded to Flight Sergeant Geoffrey Charles Chapman Smith, an air gunner on 7 (PFF) Squadron at Oakington. That night Smith, who was born at Marrickville, Sydney on 3 February 1919, flew as rear-gunner in the Lancaster flown by Sergeant Ken Doyle, a Londoner, which took off about 17.00 hours. While with 625 Squadron in late 1943 Smith had shot down a Ju 88 on his first operation over Berlin on 2 December. Now, 30 miles from the 'Big City' trouble began. Smith was searching the port beam when, from the corner of his eye, he saw three white lights. He swung his guns, saw a green

light, and realized that it was an enemy fighter with its identification lamps on. Smith gave the warning and Doyle dived the Lancaster to port as four lines of tracer streamed from the wings of the fighter, now close enough to identify as a Bf 110. Smith poured 150 rounds into the fighter, there was a mighty flash and it blew up. Four more lines of tracer appeared; a Fw 190 was coming in from behind. The Lancaster dived and lost the enemy, but a cannon shell had hit Smith's right ankle and exploded. He was in great pain, his turret was unserviceable and his parachute bag was on fire. Other shells had plastered the Lancaster from its tail along its fuselage up to the mid-upper turret. Doyle called his crew to check for casualties. There was no answer from Sergeant Clarke, the mid-upper turret gunner and the pilot sent the wireless operator back to see what had happened. Clarke was on the floor without his oxygen mask, almost unconscious. His turret had been hit. Though wounded and his left leg fractured by a cannon shell, he had tried to beat out the flames of burning oil from a burst pipe, using his helmet before lack of oxygen had overcome him. Sergeant Don Green the wireless operator jammed an oxygen tube in the mid-upper gunner's mouth just in time to save him and then he climbed into the mid-upper turret to watch for fighters. Doyle called Smith on the intercom and told him he was sending help. But the Australian refused to be moved and he continued to work the guns by hand. Sergeant Window, the navigator who was from County Durham, dealt with the burning parachute.

They were still heading for Berlin but when only 15 miles from the target they found that they could not open the bomb doors and they reluctantly decided to turn back. Crossing a flak belt the Lancaster was hit again. A lump of shrapnel hit the throttle box by Doyle's feet and severed the controls to the port engines. In the meantime Sergeant Syd Richardson, the flight engineer, managed to reach the forward hydraulic jacks on the bomb doors via the bomb bay inspection hatch. He dismantled the connections on the hydraulic system in order to release the pressure to allow the doors to open when they jettisoned the bombs on top of them. Over the sea they tried it and all the bombs except one of the 500-pounders fell through and away. Smith's oxygen mask had frozen and he had taken it off and was breathing the dangerous rarefied air. Over the sea the crew chopped the bombs away, then came aft to free Smith. His turret door had frozen in and this, too, had to be chopped away by Sergeant Alf Astle. Still conscious, Smith tried to pull himself out, but could not free his right leg, which was shattered and twisted around the ammunition belt and controls. The turret was drenched in blood. It took an hour to free him. They gave him morphine and laid him on the floor of the fuselage. Doyle prepared for a belly-landing, in case the tyres had been shot up, but he found the bomb doors would not close and decided to alight on the damaged undercarriage. The bomb-aimer and wireless operator lay on each side of Smith to protect him in case of a crash, but Doyle made a good landing at Woodbridge and there the fuselage was hacked away and Smith and the wounded mid-upper gunner were carried out. Smith's leg was amputated above the knee next morning at the RAF Hospital, Ely.

'If it hadn't been for the skipper, we'd never have got back at all,'' he said later.[21]

This raid on the Big City was really the culmination of the Battle of Berlin. Only one more heavy raid took place on the German capital in this period and that was not for more than a month, although Berliners would be bombed many times by small forces of Mosquitoes. With the planned Allied invasion of Normandy looming on the horizon, Harris knew that his forces would soon be diverted for other duties. The Battle of Berlin was supposed to produce 'a state of devastation in which surrender is inevitable' and since the end of November 1943 Harris had dispatched 34 major assaults on Germany, 16 of them against the 'Big City', yet still no German surrender was in sight.

Berlin must have seemed a 'busted flush'.

Notes

1. Abercromby, who was born in Inverness-shire, had been promoted to squadron leader on 19 November.
2. Flying Officer J. F. Bowyer RCAF, and two of his crew of Lancaster III JA847 PG-C, were killed, the aircraft crashed into the Tegel, a heavily wooded area near Berlin. Four of the crew survived and were taken prisoner. Pilot Officer J. F. Ward and five of his crew were killed after Lancaster III EE170 PG-N was hit by flak north of Magdeburg and burst into flames. As the crew prepared to bale out, the Lancaster exploded. Sergeant G. W. Cross regained consciousness at 5,000 feet and landed safely, albeit with several broken ribs.
3. Murrow's account of the 2/3 December raid, which cost 40 bombers, 37 of them Lancasters, appeared in the morning edition of the *Daily Express* under the banner headline, '*Berlin – Orchestrated Hell of Light and Flame*'. Fifty-three aircraft were damaged by flak. The Bomber Command ORS Report (No. 481) said: 'Unexpected winds en route blew many aircraft off track and nullified the Pathfinders' efforts to make DR runs from Rathenow. Consequently there were gaps in the cloud covering the city; most of the bombing was scattered over a wide area of open country to the south. At the beginning of the attack, heavy flak was fired in a loose barrage up to 22,000 feet around the marker flares, and was predicted at seen targets

through gaps in the cloud. Searchlights were active in great numbers and took every opportunity the weather offered for illuminating the bombers. After the raid had been in progress half an hour and soon after the appearance of fighter flares the ceiling of the barrage was lowered and the flak decreased, although individual aircraft were heavily engaged when coned. The running commentary began plotting the bombers from the neighbourhood of the Zuider Zee and announced that Berlin was the main objective at 19.47 hours, 19 minutes before zero hour. Many illuminated targets were provided for the fighters over the capital.' *Zahme Sau* crews claimed 40 kills, 7 pilots of 2 *Wilde Sau Gruppen* (I. and II./JG 302) claiming another eight *Viermots* shot down over Berlin. At least 32 bombers went down in the main air battle that was concentrated in the target area. It was a one-sided battle; only three *Nachtjäger* were lost in return fire. 460 Squadron RAAF at Binbrook lost five of its 25 Lancasters on this raid, including two carrying press correspondents. Captain J. M. B. Greig of the Free Norwegian Army, representing the *Daily Mail*, who flew with Flying Officer A. R. Mitchell RAAF and crew of Lancaster III LM316 AR-H2, died, as did all the crew. The Lancaster crashed at Döberitz. A night fighter attacked Lancaster I W4881 AR-K, which exploded killing Pilot Officer J. H. J. English RAAF, a native of New South Wales, and three crew, and 40 year old Australian, Norman Stockton of the *Sydney Sun*. Three crew survived to be taken prisoner. Stockton is buried in the Berlin War Cemetery. Flight Lieutenant I. D. Bolton of 50 Squadron from Skellingthorpe, flying Lancaster I DV325 VN-B, was shot down by a night fighter and crashed in the target area. Two crew died. Lowell L. Bennett, a 24 year old war correspondent employed by the *Daily Express*, and Bolton and four of his crew survived and were made POW. Bennett escaped from captivity and managed to file his story at one point but he was later recaptured and held prisoner until the end of the war. Walter King, an Australian war correspondent, returned safely.
4. Wing Commander Abercromby and his crew of Lancaster III ND354 OL-A of 83 Squadron, 8 [Pathfinder Force] Group was one of 28 aircraft lost from a force of 421 Lancasters sent to bomb Berlin on the night of 1/2 January 1944. Sergeant L. H. Lewis, flight engineer, was the only survivor. Murrow continued to report on the war from Europe and North Africa throughout the Second World War. A heavy smoker, he died on 22 April 1965 aged 57.
5. Oberleutnant Heinz-Wolfgang Schnaufer, *Staffelkapitän*, 12./NJG I shot down four Lancasters over Friesland Province to take his total to 40 victories. Lancaster II D5831 QO-N of 432 'Leaside' Squadron RCAF, was intercepted at 19,700 feet by Schnaufer who shot it down for his fourth kill of the night and his 40th *Abschuss* overall. The Lancaster careered over Leeuwarden trailing a sheet of flames and completely disintegrated on impact at Wytgaard followed by the explosion of the bomb load. Flying Officer W. Charles Fischer, the American skipper, and five of his crew were killed. Only three German aircraft were lost. During the 20/21 December raid I./NJG 6 destroyed 10 Lancasters and Halifaxes. They included triple victories by Feldwebel Günther Bahr and Oberleutnant Martin 'Tino' Becker who downed Lancaster DV234 of 50 Squadron at Bodenrode/Bad Nauheim and two Halifaxes in just six minutes. III./NJG 11 claimed four victories on the night of 16/17 December and a Lancaster over Frankfurt by Oberleutnant Hans-Heinz Augenstein on the 23/24th.

6. This famous Lancaster III had originally served on 103 Squadron, as had Morgan (576 was formed from 'C' Flight of 103 Squadron on 25 November) and the Berlin op would be ED888's 58th sortie.
7. It was only after the war that it was discovered that the Germans did not use an explosive device to simulate an exploding bomber. What the men saw, in fact, was a fully loaded bomber exploding, having either been hit by flak or night fighter attack.
8. A *spoof* raid was in progress.
9. Leipzig, where the bomber stream appeared to be heading before turning north-east for Berlin.
10. In all, 20 aircraft (11 Lancasters and nine Halifaxes) failed to return. A long approach route from the south, passing south of the Ruhr and then within 20 miles of Leipzig, together with Mosquito diversions at Düsseldorf, Leipzig and Magdeburg, caused the German controller great difficulties and there were few fighters over Berlin. Bad weather on the outward route also kept down the number of German fighters finding the bomber stream. One hundred and eighty-two people were killed; more than 600 were injured and over 10,000 were bombed out. Despite atrocious winter weather *Nachtjagd* claimed 169 victories during the final month of 1943 against 28 lost.
11. Jim Donnan remained at large for the next 24 hours but when he asked some German civilians for some food and drink he was taken into custody. Lancaster DV189 crashed between Holtrup and Schweringen and blew up with its full bomb load, including a cookie, in a deafening explosion. Bryson and Roxby had been trapped in the cockpit and were killed in the crash. They were interred at Hassel and at Hoya, later re-buried in Hanover War Cemetery. Flight Sergeant Paul Evans, the bomb-aimer and Sergeant Don Fadden, flight engineer had a very lucky escape. They were also in the nose section when the aircraft suddenly dived, pinning them down with the centrifugal forces. They were released when an explosion blew off the front of the nose section, enabling them to escape by parachute just before the bomber crashed. The Lancaster's starboard wing and the incendiary bombs in the front of the bomb bay were set on fire by a surprise *Schräge Musik* attack. Most probably Bryson's Lancaster was one of the six shot down in quick succession by Major Heinrich Prinz zu Sayn-Wittgenstein, his 69–74th victories. DV189 was probably Wittgenstein's third kill of the night. Most of the losses were Pathfinders flying at the front of the bomber stream. Twenty-eight bombers failed to return, 21 of which were destroyed by *Zahme Sau*; two *Gruppen* of JG 302 that operated over the target claimed another four *Viermot* kills, two of which were later officially confirmed to the single-engined claimants.
12. On 2/3 January, 383 Lancasters went to Berlin again and 27 bombers were shot down, mainly over the target. On 5/6 January, 358 bombers raided Stettin with the loss of 16 heavies. On 14/15 January when 498 bombers hit Brunswick, 38 bombers failed to return.
13. On 20/21 January, 35 bombers were shot down by the German defences, which operated the *Zahme Sau* tactics to excellent advantage and who seemed to have rendered 'window' counter-productive. King sailed from Marseilles on the *Letitia* under the prisoner exchange scheme on 23 January 1945, a year almost to the day after he had come down over Berlin. The *Letitia* docked at Liverpool on 2 February, where King was met by RAAF medical and POW officials and taken to the RAF Hospital at Weeton. Next day an Australian Red Cross woman auxiliary drove him to his wife's home in Liverpool, where he met his son, born while he was a prisoner. *Royal Australian Air Force Overseas* (Eyre & Spottiswoode London, 1946).
14. Wittgenstein's 83rd victory (one more than Lent) elevated him to the position of highest scoring night fighter pilot ever. After his death, only Oberst Helmut Lent and Major Heinz-Wolfgang Schnaufer were to overtake him with a higher score. Another leading *Experten*, Hauptmann Manfred Meurer, *Kommandeur* I/NJG 1 was also killed this night. *Eichenlaubträger* Meurer and his *Funker*, *Ritterkreuzträger* Oberfeldwebel Gerhard Scheibe in a He 219A-0 'Owl' were hit by debris from their 2nd victim – a Lancaster – east of Magdeburg and they crashed to their deaths. In less than two years Meurer had claimed 65 *Nachtabschüsse* (night victories) in 130 sorties.
15. The following month, Len Miller was awarded a Distinguished Flying Cross and, on 1 March, he was promoted to flight lieutenant.
16. Five hours before the main force operation, 63 Stirlings and four PFF Halifaxes laid mines in Kiel Bay and six Mosquitoes bombed the German capital four hours before the main attack. Eighteen Mosquitoes bombed three night fighter airfields in Holland. Four Mosquitoes flew a diversionary raid to Hanover and six more Mosquitoes flew *Serrate* patrols at the same time as the main raid.
17. Diary entry. See *The Lancaster Story* by Peter Jacobs (Cassell, 2002).
18. See *Vulcan 607* by Rowland White (Bantam, 2006. Corgi, 2007).
19. The month ended with the *Nachtjagd* scoring an all-time monthly record of 308 Bomber Command aircraft shot down. *I Jagdkorps* claimed at least 223 victories (including 114 during the three Berlin raids 29 January-1 February) but lost 55 aircraft and crews during January 1944. Losses had reduced the front line strength to 179 operational aircraft and crews by 31 January.
20. *Nachtjagd* claimed 39 victories, mainly over the *Reich* capital for the loss of 11 night fighters. Oberleutnant Helmuth Schulte, Technical Officer of II./NJG 5, destroyed three *Viermots* in the greater Berlin area for his 5th-7th confirmed kills. Schulte was awarded the *Ritterkreuz* for 25 victories on 17 April 1945.
21. Green, who suffered from frostbite having lost his gloves while tending to Geoff Smith, Ken Doyle and Alf Astle were all lost in September 1944 on their last operation over Calais. See *Royal Australian Air Force Overseas* (Eyre & Spottiswoode, London, 1946) and *In Action With the Enemy* by Alan W. Cooper (William Kimber, 1986).

Chapter 7

Berlin or Bust

The first Lancaster was given the 'Green Light' from the mobile watchtower and we watched as it slowly climbed away. The remainder all slowly moved around the perimeter track towards the runway and then it was their turn for destination Berlin! The smoke from the engines and the smell of burning high-octane fuel eddied across the airfield. Sixty tons of explosives and incendiaries were to be dropped and the sight of 17 Lancasters, each under full throttles roaring away into the evening sky was an awesome spectacle. Ground crews and a number of other well wishers watched us away before returning to while away the long hours before our return. The smoke and smell slowly thinned and drifted away over the silent airfield and we were on our way to our first bombing operation with the squadron. We were airborne at 18.45 hours. This was to be the order of things for some time to come.

WOp/AG Sergeant Roland A. 'Ginger' Hammersley

Eighteen year old Pilot Officer Maurice Stoneman, flight engineer, and his skipper, Johnny Ludford, walked towards *D-Dog* at East Kirkby airfield, halfway between Spilsby and Coningsby. As usual the two crewmen in 57 Squadron, which shared their Lincolnshire home with 630 Squadron, then went through what had become a normal routine for them. It had become such a regular part of their training practice that they could literally do things with their eyes shut. Blindfolded, they would identify each control switch and button and still blindfolded they would practise other routines such as closing down an engine and feathering the airscrew. On operations this had paid dividends on more than one occasion, no more so than on the night of the Leipzig raid on 19/20 February, when 816 bombers attacked Leipzig and 294 twin-engined and single-engined fighters were sent against the bomber stream. A Ju 88 night fighter attacked *D-Dog*. 'Our mid-upper – Frank Fox', recalls Stoneham, 'saw him at the last minute and shouted, "Dive starboard GO". We did just that. As I was standing up with my seat retracted I was thrown to the side but managed to recover by grabbing the small "Window" handle. We were however, hit in the starboard engine and also lost three inches of a propeller blade. This caused great vibration but unfortunately I was looking at the engine at the time of impact and the flash of the impact temporarily

blinded me. The skipper ordered me to "Feather starboard inner". I did and the "blindfold practice" paid off. I also pressed the fire extinguisher button. I was still unable to see properly but was beginning to recover my eyesight and vision. The fire was put out but the feathering mechanism was damaged and the propeller had to "windmill". This was a good thing as the engine drove the mid-upper turret hydraulics and one of the two generators. We also lost certain hydraulics and collected a large gash on the starboard side just above the main wing, which at 20,000 feet and in that temperature was more than uncomfortable. We went into a dive and lost 10,000 feet and only managed to pull out of it by the skipper and me with our feet on the instrument panel and hauling like hell on the stick. We got back to East Kirkby with difficulty. During 30 ops I only had to feather an engine once through malfunction and during many a ten hour trip the engines did not miss a beat. You just have to love the Merlin and also the rugged build of the Lancaster.'[1]

On 20 February, the Americans launched 'Big Week'. Bomber Command and the USAAF dropped 19,000 tons of bombs on the *Reich* in a true round the clock offensive but losses were high with 224 American and 157 British bombers failing to return in just one week of sustained operations. An attack on Stuttgart on

20/21 February, by 598 bombers, was outstandingly successful. This was due mainly to the North Sea sweep and a diversionary feint towards Munich, which successfully drew the German fighters up two hours before the main force flew inland. Nine bombers only were lost – all of them shot down by night fighters. At East Kirkby the Lancaster piloted by Pilot Officer E. J. Murray, who was about to fly his first operation, swung on take off, bumped across the Stickney Road causing the undercarriage to collapse and then the 4,000lb cookie exploded. Everyone except the rear-gunner, Sergeant W. Davies, was killed. At Fiskerton a Lancaster of 49 Squadron suffered a burst tyre on take-off. It slewed completely around and the undercarriage crumpled and collapsed. The crew were rescued uninjured before the bomb load went up in two explosions which killed six men on the ground and shattered glass over a wide area, including the towns of Boston and Skegness. Four Lancasters and a Halifax crashed in England on their return from Stuttgart. A Lancaster of 100 Squadron failed to return to Waltham near Grimsby after a German night fighter rammed it. When still 200 miles from the nearest friendly coast a violent shock rocked the airframe and the Lancaster lurched and went down out of control. The pilot ordered the crew to stand by to bale out but at 4,000 feet control was regained. When checking the crew the wireless operator found the mid-upper gunner wounded in his turret, which had been crushed and the rear-gunner was jammed in his turret but not badly hurt. The pilot carried on to Ford and landed safely. On close inspection, pieces of fighter were found embedded in the top of the fuselage. It appeared that the night fighter had cut across their line of flight, turning in fast from port while the mid-upper gunner was rotating to starboard so that there was no warning. It had bent the starboard fin and rudder outwards, carried the aerials away and torn a hole six feet long in the wing as well as crushing the turret.[2]

For Bomber Command the first half of March was relatively quiet. Two raids were made against Stuttgart, the first on the opening night of the month when thick cloud made it difficult for the enemy night fighters to enter the bomber stream. Just three Lancasters and a Halifax were lost from over 550 aircraft that were dispatched. A second raid was made on Stuttgart on 15/16 March, this time by over 860 aircraft, which dropped 3,000 tons of bombs in an hour. This time the night fighters shot down 37 aircraft, all except 10 of them Lancasters. One of the crews that survived was piloted by 48 year old Air Commodore A. M. Wray DSO MC DFC* AFC. This highly decorated veteran of the 1914–18 war took a 'sprog' crew to Stuttgart in ND456, which was subsequently written off two months later when it hit a barn on take-off from Woodbridge. Another of the 'sprog' crews at this time was one captained by Frank Hercules 'Herks' Dengate from Tamworth, New South Wales, a 22 year old Australian pilot on 15 Squadron who had trained on Wellingtons and the Stirling. The crew, who arrived at Mildenhall in December 1943, had come together in the usual manner, as Dengate recalls:

'Crewing up had no basis at all, you just picked. You had to try and pick a navigator you thought was a reliable sort of a bloke. Then you'd finish up probably getting a wireless operator or bomb-aimer. You certainly didn't have any chance of looking over their record to see whether they were reasonable sort of blokes or what they were. The navigator got airsick and he coped with it, but it got worse when he got into the Wellington and he was sitting at the table in the little enclosure. This made him sick every time. He still did his job. We even did a trip to France in a Wellington and he was quite satisfactory but it was the first trip we did into enemy territory. The medical people decided that as he got airsick all the time he shouldn't fly. He eventually went into the *Oboe* marking system. His replacement was Flying Officer Art Cantrell, a Canadian and an ex-district inspector of schools; an excellent fellow and very skilful. The crew decided that the sergeant wireless operator, a Scotsman, would have to be replaced as he was always drunk and we could never get him sober to go in the aeroplane. (That fellow was later transferred to 622 Squadron. It took him 18 months to complete a tour and he'd go with anyone that didn't have a wireless operator. Eventually he was awarded the DFM [Distinguished Flying Medal]). The new wireless operator was Frank Watson.

'We now had a better navigator and a better wireless operator than we would have had after we had the changes. [Frank Watson's wife Brenda a WAAF, who was the daughter of the landlord of the 'Jude's Ferry' at West Row, was called the 'Chop Blonde' because everyone who went out with her got the chop. Frank must have broken the spell.] He was a very nice chap and he had been a 'whisky traveller', selling drinks around the countryside. Whisky was his leading sale and eventually that's what killed him, because both he and his wife used to partake of greater quantities. There wasn't an engineer on the Wellington but when we went on to Stirling training at 1651 HCU at Wratting Common, Sergeant Bobby Kitchin joined us as the flight engineer. (After Wratting Common we went to 3 LFS [Lancaster Finishing School] at Feltwell.) The rear-gunner, Sergeant Doug Davis, was very quiet but a very good gunner. He was always awake and sharp. Sergeant Fred Coney was the mid-upper gunner. Once again, very wide awake and keen. Flying Officer Joe Ell, our Canadian bomb-aimer, was a wonderful, reliable fellow. Joe always did an excellent job. He never missed.

'We continued training on the Lancaster until our first operation, to Stuttgart, after I had flown my second dickie trip with another crew to experience the flak and terror of a raid. On all my trips I carried my small Webley 6.35mm automatic pistol in the large pocket of my battle dress in the event of me having to bale out and try to escape. I purchased the gun, which was manufactured in 1909, in London in December 1943. Stuttgart wasn't a good 'prang'. 'We were only just over the water after leaving Britain when an aeroplane suddenly appeared underneath us. We were so close that we could see his instrument panel. At 18,000 feet it was heavy cloud and stormy and we were struggling to keep the aeroplane in the air because it was heavy with ice. We didn't have any de-icing of any kind at all. The only solution was to go down to about 15,000 feet to warmer air, get rid of it and climb again. Many didn't do that. They stayed up there and the icing would increase until it got to a stage that the aeroplane crashed. We lost a terrific number of aeroplanes that night, simply because of the icing. Our next two trips were to Frankfurt when over the target we encountered a Fw 190 followed by a direct hit by flak. On return to base we found 40 countable holes.'[3]

At East Kirkby, Pilot Officer Ron Walker's crew in 57 Squadron waited to fly their first operation since arriving at the Lincolnshire airfield on 17 March. They had crewed up in the time-honoured fashion, as Sergeant Roland A. 'Ginger' Hammersley the 5 feet 4½ inch WOP/AG from King's Langley, who had met his future wife, Nan Webber serving with the WAAF at Barford St. John, recalls:

'By this time I believe that Ron could have flown a Lancaster blindfolded. At 16 OTU Upper Heyford the pilots had sought out the different crewmembers they wished to have in their crew. I well remember the Sergeant I crewed up with coming into our dormitory and asking for a 'sober wireless operator' and found myself being pushed to the front of the crowd of W/Ops and hearing someone say, "This is the one you should have". Sergeant Ron Walker was physically a well-built strong man. Later in conversation I was to learn that since leaving school he had managed his father's farm in Sussex. We talked for a while and I told him that I

did drink a beer or two! Also that I had had some considerable experience wireless operating before my aircrew training commenced and was not shy of using a wireless set. We decided that we would give it a try and fly together and see how we worked out. My luck was in, he was a natural pilot and a quick learner. Later in our flying career, his physical strength saved our lives, or at least saved us from having to land in enemy territory with a wounded crewmember and a damaged aircraft. Flying Officer Ken Bly, a Canadian Air Bomber, a navigator and rear turret air gunner we called 'Jock', joined us. Just before moving on to the conversion from two to four engined aircraft we were joined by Pilot Officer Tom Quayle, the mid-upper gunner and a new navigator, Flying Officer Bertram 'Mack' MacKinnon was accepted by the crew and we by him. Tom Quayle fell and broke an ankle at Aircrew Battle School at Scampton. We were given the choice of another gunner or wait Tom's recovery. We chose the latter and spent all December 1943 at Scampton and a very poor Christmas before moving to 1660 HCU at Swinderby midway between Newark and Lincoln in January 1944. Sergeant Esmond Chung, flight engineer and a new rear-gunner, Sergeant William "Bill" Carver, a former member of the RAF Regiment, joined us. He was in good company as Tom Quayle had also transferred from the Regiment for flying duties and had dropped a rank on doing so. They made a good team and Bill fitted in well with the rest of us.'

Bomber Command's Battle of Berlin was halted on 24/25 March when the 'Big City' was visited for the last time by 811 aircraft and the offensive was switched to attacks on German communications and defences in preparation for the Normandy invasion. 'Ginger' Hammersley recalls:

'The 24th March was a memorable day. On arrival at the Flight Office we found our names on the battle order for the night's operations. The aircraft we were to fly was *T-Tommy*. We set off on bicycles that had been issued to each one of us, to look the aircraft over and check the equipment. The ground crew responsible for the maintenance of *T-Tommy* were a fine bunch and gave us as much information as was possible about it as we went through the checking procedure. The bomb load was one 4,000lb, 48 × 30lb and 600 × 41b. Later we were fully briefed both as individual crewmembers and then all crews together. We soon learned that the target was Berlin – the 'Big City'. At the briefing we were told at what time there would be signals broadcast from Bomber Command; when we would receive weather reports; where the searchlight belt and anti-aircraft guns were known to be and also the positions of known German night fighter units and airfields en route. The Station Met Officer gave a weather report, the indications being that the weather conditions were not too good and we would be meeting quite strong winds at 18,000–20,000 feet. We were issued with amphetamine (wakey-wakey) tablets, these were taken just prior to take-off and would keep the crews wide-awake and on a 'high' for the duration of the flight. If the operation was cancelled, it meant a sleepless night which, for the most of the crews, meant that a wild night of drinking would take place in both the Officers' and Sergeants' mess until the effects of the drug wore off and sleep could take over.

'It was customary for a meal to be prepared for the crews before we flew. We were then issued with a flask of tea or coffee, with chocolate, sandwiches and an apple; armed with a 0.38 revolver and parachute. Codes and Very pistol with cartridges which, when fired, would give the coded colours of the day. We were even given what were understood to be those in use by the German forces that day. After emptying my pockets and locking my personal items into my cage type locker, I joined the crew in the crew bus with WAAF Connie Mills at the wheel. Connie often drove the bus that collected the crews from near the control tower. We were then taken out to *T-Tommy*. We had another look around the aircraft with the ground crew and about an hour before we were due to take-off we settled into our places to await the take-off order. When the first part of the take-off procedure commenced, we were lined up on the airfield perimeter with 17 other Lancasters from the squadron. All crews would by now have taken their amphetamines and would be wide awake.

'The first Lancaster was given the 'Green Light' from the mobile watchtower and we watched as it slowly climbed away. The remainder all slowly moved around the perimeter track towards the runway and then it was their turn for destination Berlin! The smoke from the engines and the smell of burning high-octane fuel eddied across the airfield. Sixty tons of explosives and incendiaries were to be dropped by 57 Squadron and the sight of 17 Lancasters each under full throttle roaring away into the evening sky was an awesome spectacle. Sergeants Frank Beasley and Leslie Wakerell with their ground crews and a number of other well-wishers, watched us away before returning to while away the long hours before our return. The smoke and smell slowly thinned and drifted away over the silent airfield and we were on our way to our first bombing operation with the squadron. We were airborne at 18.45 hours. This was to be the order of things for some time to come.'

At Coningsby, on the edge of the Lincolnshire fens about 15 miles south of Lincoln, at precisely 19.09 hours Pilot Officer Howard 'Tommy' Farmiloe revved *Hellzapoppin*'s powerful Merlin engines at the end of the main runway. He released the brakes and shortly afterwards took-off into a dark, but clear starlit sky. In the airfield circuit they could clearly see Tattershall Castle, of Norman origin but all that remained was the keep, a fine rare medieval brick tower with stone mullion windows and corbelling. The tower's red warning lights coupled with the silver ribbon of the River Witham was a useful navigation aid on night sorties and a very welcome sight to many a bomber crew. After clearing the circuit, the crew settled down in their positions as the Lancaster turned north-east over the small fishing port of Boston and the 242 foot high church 'stump' to join the bomber stream over the North Sea on the first outward leg of the route to Berlin. This was the crew's seventh trip to the 'Big City' and the third time they had flown the favoured northerly route over Denmark. The return route however was potentially a dangerous one. First of all over the north German plain, south of Hanover, then squeeze between flak batteries to the north of the dreaded Happy Valley. With 800 other main force aircraft *Hellzapoppin* headed north-east over the North Sea. Two hours later the Lancaster crossed the coast of Denmark just north of the island of Sylt, only a couple of miles off track, thanks mainly to the skill of our experienced second tour navigator, Pilot Officer Stan Halliwell. At the crew briefing they had been told to expect strong north-westerly winds up to 60 mph at 20,000 feet. The reality was nearer 125 mph when they made our turn south-east for Berlin and yet Sergeant Eddie Davidson, the WOp/AG was still getting a lower wind velocity forecast from Group. It was a ludicrous situation. Due to the high tail wind we were at our final turning point over the Baltic south of Denmark early and found ourselves in the first wave of the bomber stream. Apart from that everything seemed to be going very well.'

At Skellingthorpe, Pilot Officer Michael Beetham's crew in 50 Squadron took-off and set course over the North Sea for a point off the German coast. Flight Sergeant Les Bartlett, the bomb-aimer, recalls:[4]

'This was where our first problems started. The winds were so variable so instead of passing the northern tip of Sylt we went bang into it and had to fly up the island's west coast and then around the top. Chaps were off course all over Flensburg. The next leg took us across Denmark and then down the Baltic coast. Many chaps then got into trouble with the defences of Kiel, Lübeck and Rostock; I saw at least four go down in a very short space of time. We had a near squeak at Rostock as the wind blew us into their defences and we were coned by about four searchlights but after a few violent manoeuvres we managed to shake them off before the flak got into range; they were very tense moments for us. With a strong wind behind us we were soon approaching Berlin. Luckily, over the target a thin layer of stratus cloud had formed which made it difficult for the searchlights to pick us up, so we had little trouble during the bombing run. Shortly after however, things started to get hot as the enemy fighters were waiting for us. Although we saw fighters we were lucky that none attacked us as we dodged the flak and kept out of the defences of Leipzig, Brunswick, Osnabrück and Hanover. Along this leg we saw several combats with kite after kite going down in flames.'

For Pilot Officer 'Dick' Starkey and his crew in 106 Squadron, this Berlin raid was their 20th trip. Starkey, who was commissioned two hours before taking off for Berlin, recounts:

'The outward route was over the North Sea to Denmark then south-east over the Baltic Sea crossing the German coast and continuing south-east before turning south through the target. The trip was one of the worst we encountered because of the strong winds. On the way out over the North Sea the navigator, Sergeant Colin Roberts, was finding winds with speeds far in excess of those in his Flight Plan and coming from a more northerly direction than predicted at briefing. We were "wind-finders" this night and the navigator advised me that the wind speed was approaching 100 mph and should he broadcast his findings back to Bomber Command? I said if he was satisfied with his calculations he must transmit them to England. (A number of aircraft were detailed as wind-finders on every raid. When the navigator had calculated the actual wind speed and velocity they were transmitted back where an average wind speed was calculated from those sent back by aircraft and then relayed to the Bomber Force to use on their journey.) I ordered my navigator to work from his own calculations and ignore the wind speeds being sent back to us because they were far too low. By the time the Danish coast was crossed we were many miles south of track as a result of the high wind speed from the north. (At that time nobody had heard of the Jet Stream. Bomber Command met this phenomenon on this night.) The force was scattered over a very wide front as we approached Berlin well before zero hour. Some captains ordered their navigators to work to the winds broadcast from

England and found them hopelessly off track. Others navigated on their own findings and were reaching points well in advance of ETA but they were not as far off as the others were. We arrived over the target early and I decided to risk going round the city on the eastern side, by which time the PFF markers would be going down and start our bombing run.

'The activity in the sky over the city was awesome and frightening, as were all raids on Berlin. The sky was full of sparkling flashes as anti-aircraft shells from 1,200 guns, the equivalent of an ammunition dump, burst in a box barrage every two minutes. I estimated that anyone getting through that would be very lucky indeed, especially as the aircraft had to be flown straight and level with bomb doors open during the bombing run and take photographs after dropping the bombs. There were also hundreds of searchlights, making two cones over the city, which the bombers had to try and evade. The fighters no longer waited outside the perimeter of the target where they were in little danger from their own flak because we were now severely damaging their cities. They flew amongst us in this area of death ignoring their own safety, meeting the anti-aircraft fire in order to get amongst us and many a bomber was shot down when most vulnerable with bomb doors open. When we were on our bombing run with two other Lancasters whose bomb-aimers had chosen the same markers as my bomb-aimer, Sergeant Wally Paris, a twin-engined fighter flew past our nose with cannon and machine guns firing at one of the Lancasters. There were tracers flying all over the sky as my gunners, Sergeants Jock Jameson, mid-upper and Sergeant Joe Ellick, rear-gunner and the others in the third aircraft joined the targeted Lancaster to return the fire. However, the stricken Lancaster turned over on its back and went down in flames. We did not see anyone escape because we were concentrating on the bombing run.

'The Luftwaffe were now using single-engined fighters in the battle, generally over the target and as I took a quick glance down at the fires I saw twelve of them circling up line astern towards the bombers whose bellies were red from the reflection of the flames below. The searchlight cones held two bombers like moths round a candle; the pilots were tossing their aircraft all over the sky but they were held like stage artists in a spotlight. The next move was from the fighters who came in and inflicted the *coup de grâce*, the bombers plunging down in flames before exploding and cascading in balls of fire to splash among the inferno below. A pilot had to take whatever action he could to get across the target area. One practice was to fly near a coned aircraft and hope the action against it would help him get across. This wasn't always possible because although the brightness was less intense they could be seen. When a raid was at its peak with 800 aircraft bombing in a 20-minute period, the illuminations had to be seen to be believed. The target indicators – red and green chandeliers, 200 feet in length – cascaded down with a shimmering brightness, flak was bursting, filling every part of the sky with twinkling bursts and, as you flew towards them, there was no escape. You thought you would never get through it. Many years afterwards I read that a bomb-aimer who flew on the raid was so awed by the experience that he just repeated, "Jesus Skipper, look at that flak, just look at it, we'll never get through it, just look at it". That summed it up perfectly.

'After bombing the target I gained height to 25,000 feet and with relief at surviving the anti aircraft, searchlights and night fighter defences but we had another fight on our hands before we reached England. The strong head winds and night fighters had not finished with us. It soon became apparent that our ground speed was very slow and we did not appear to be making much progress. As we crawled our way west to the next change of course, which was to take us north-west between Hanover and Osnabrück, the navigator was continuously amending his air plot to try and keep us on course but we were being blown south of our intended track. It soon became apparent that the conditions were getting worse and because of the effect of the wind on navigation found ourselves further west than the point where we should have turned north-west to fly between Hanover and Osnabrück. Instead we amended our course to fly between Osnabrück and the Ruhr making sure we kept well clear of the latter area.

'We had seen many aircraft shot down since we left Berlin, proof that the force was well scattered and aircraft were being picked off. As we looked towards the Ruhr we saw many more that had wandered over that area shot down, so they had flown into the two heaviest defended areas in Germany – Berlin and the Ruhr – in one night. I was concentrating our efforts to get to the coast without further trouble when a radar-controlled searchlight was suddenly switched on just below the aircraft. (These searchlights had a blue-white beam and more often than not hit the aircraft at the first attempt.) The searchlight knew they were near us because the beam started creeping up in front of the aircraft. I put more power on and raised the nose to maintain our position above the beam but it still continued creeping towards us. I was just on the point of putting the nose down and diving through it when it was switched off. Talk about a dry mouth. If the searchlight had found us it would have been joined by others and, as was the customary practice, a night fighter in the vicinity would have attacked us as we were caught in the beam.

'Our last turning point was near the Dutch border. Although our ground speed was very slow the intensity of the defences had slackened off and for the first time in the raid, fighter activity had ceased. Maybe they had landed to refuel because we were approaching their airfields in Holland. We did not have any further trouble and eventually reached the North Sea coast. I pushed down the nose of the aircraft and did a very fast descent to 2,000 feet to the relief of the crew who were thankful to have the raid almost behind them. The wireless operator, Sergeant George Walker received a signal ordering us to divert to Wing, an OTU near Luton. It was a dark night and normally as you approached the coast you saw the odd searchlight. But we did not see one light. I was surprised when the navigator told me that according to his calculations we had already crossed the coast and gave me a course to Wing. We were by then well inland with navigation lights on flying at 2,000 feet but could not see a thing. Suddenly a searchlight switched on to us followed by two more. They could not have been practising because they could see the lights of our aircraft. I cursed as they held us, thinking back to the hundreds we had evaded over Germany only to be caught in the beams of a searchlight battery in England. I was told afterwards that a crew of ATS girls operated the lights. We eventually landed at Wing after a flight of seven and a half hours on the last big raid to Berlin.'

On board *T-Tommy* in 57 Squadron meanwhile, 'Ginger' Hammersley decoded the weather reports as they came in. 'It became apparent from "Mack's" findings that they were not as he expected them. We were faced with greater wind speeds than those indicated in the signals being sent to us from Command, so we used our own. We were late arriving over the target and we could see there were great fires as the run in towards the target commenced. Having bombed successfully we headed back towards home, only to be told that we would have to land at the fighter airfield at RAF Coltishall in Norfolk. The time we spent flying was seven hours, 30 minutes. We were debriefed and fed, then shown to our sleeping quarters. We made the 35 minutes flight back to East Kirkby the following afternoon, leaving at 15.00 hours by which time the fog that had prevented our landing the previous night had cleared. Of the 17 Lancasters from the squadron that flew this operation, one made an early return and two others failed to return. We made our reports at the squadron office before heading for our huts to await the evening meal.'

At Skellingthorpe, there was no sign of Pilot Officer Michael Beetham's crew but all was well, as Flight Sergeant Les Bartlett, recalls:

'Luckily, we got through and back home although we had to divert to another base. In the debrief we found out that it had been a bad night although our squadron had suffered no losses.'[5]

At Coningsby there was no sign of *Hellzapoppin* and Tommy Farmiloe's crew either. Sergeant Eddie Davidson recalls the events that had unfolded after nearing the target:

'As we approached the German coast between Lübeck and Rostock, bomb-aimer Ken Vowe reported heavy flak and searchlights ahead. Shortly afterwards the gunners reported a burst of air to air tracer very close on the port side and shortly afterwards saw an aircraft explode and fall away in a number of burning fireballs. It was always a sickening sight to see one of our own aircraft go down. Soon afterwards the visual *Monica* equipment[6] pinpointed an enemy night fighter only 500 feet away at 2 o'clock. Both gunners shouted almost together over the intercom, "I can see the bastard" followed by Ray Noble, the rear-gunner, shouting over the intercom, "Dive to port skipper". All six Brownings of the rear and mid-upper turrets started firing as the skipper dived at the start of the corkscrew manoeuvre, which was so sharp and steep that after hitting my head on the roof, I ended up on the floor with all my signals books scattered around me. My stomach was in my mouth as the corkscrew seemed to go on forever, then the skipper pulled sharply out of the dive and flew straight and level while Ray Noble and "Wally" Patchett, the mid-upper gunner, scanned the sky. It had worked; the enemy fighter had lost us.

'After getting a new course from the navigator, Stan Halliwell, the skipper started to climb, hoping to get back to 20,000 feet. After picking up and sorting out my papers I realized it was time to listen out for the half hourly Met Report from Group, which again gave no indication of the true wind velocity. About half an hour later I saw another blip on the *Monica* screen indicating an aircraft about 600 yards away at 11 o'clock and as I opened my mouth to yell a warning, Ray Noble shouted, "Enemy at 11 o'clock, corkscrew starboard go". This time I stayed in my seat having fastened my belt and heard the gunners opening up but I could still see the blip on the *Monica* screen following us down on the port side and I instructed the skipper "Corkscrew port". We could feel the kite shudder as the skipper tried to level out and George Jerry, the flight engineer screamed, "For Christ sake Tommy, take it easy or you

will tear the bloody wings off". The violent corkscrew manoeuvre worked, for we lost the fighter and as we tried to gain height Ken the bomb-aimer said, "I can see a glow right in front of us; it must be Berlin". Sure enough, as we climbed we could see the glow spreading and there was a sigh of relief when the skipper said, "We're early but I'm going in". The high winds had scattered the main force and some aircraft bombed Berlin half an hour before the Pathfinders marked the target area. It was time to listen out again for the half hourly reports from Group. With all the excitement I had missed the last two reports, so as usual I disconnected myself from the intercom and listened out on the W/T for the wind speed broadcast. Reading the message I could see they still were not reporting the actual wind speeds! Switching the set off I suddenly became aware of a high-pitched whine coming from one of the engines. In a panic, I switched back into the intercom system and heard the flight engineer saying the revs on the port outer had increased to 3,800 rpm and the skipper telling him to shut down the engine and feather the prop. "The runaway prop," says Farmiloe, "created a fearsome noise and sent ice splinters against the fuselage. I tried to feather it but without success and it was not long before there were indications of fire. I tried diving, etc, but nothing, including the fire extinguisher, solved the problem and the fire continued on and off all the way. Worse, the port inner also gave problems and had to be feathered, this time fortunately successfully. Flying just above stalling speed and rapidly losing height, I managed to keep the plane under control and continue towards Berlin."'

Eddie Davidson was standing in the astrodome on fighter watch when he saw flames pouring out of the faulty engine and thick smoke trailing back over the wing and tail. 'We were ordered to prepare to abandon aircraft. With both port engines dead we were in a desperate situation. The port outer was still burning with its un-feathered prop windmilling, thereby making the aircraft very difficult to control even with full rudder trim and full opposite rudder. By now we were approaching the illuminated target area and still on course for the aiming point. Shouting over the whine from the port inner the skipper ordered "Stand by, let's go in and drop the load and get out of the target area as quickly as possible, then we will bale out". Without a word Ken Vowe got back into his position in the nose of the aircraft. Ahead, red and green target indicators could be seen going down punctually at 22.30 hours and in the glow of the following bomb flashes on the ground and enemy searchlights I could see hundreds of black flak clouds exploding against the illuminated background. This indicated only too clearly the fierce flak barrage put up by the defenders against our attacking aircraft. With all these distractions going on around him I could hardly believe I was hearing Ken's seemingly unconcerned, quiet but distinctive Yorkshire accent begin his patter to the skipper "Left, left, no right, left again, steady!"

'In the meantime molten metal and flames still poured out of the port outer and incredibly, the enemy's searchlights, fighters and flak batteries ignored us. Still losing height we continued our bombing run and at 22.35 hours, with a green target indicator in the bomb-sight, Ken dropped our bomb load on the burning city below. Not waiting for a target point photograph to be taken, the skipper quickly closed the bomb bay doors and turned away onto a westerly course of 208 degrees, which led to position 'E' on the return route. Then started the debate over the intercom, should we bale out so close to the target area or try to get as far away as possible. Of course we really had no choice, if Tommy ordered us to "Bale out" we would have to go. I for one did not fancy baling out and was delighted when he decided to keep going as far as possible. We were now down to 13,000 feet. By keeping the aircraft's indicated air speed (IAS) at 140 mph, just above stalling speed, the skipper found the fire and whine of the port outer was at a minimum but the physical effort of controlling the aircraft was taking its toll on him. At this point, Ken came out of the bomb-aimer's position and wrapped his arms round the rudder bars and braced himself, thus taking some of the strain off the skipper's legs. In the meantime the flight engineer tried to trim the aircraft by draining petrol from the port tanks into the two starboard wing tanks.

'Despite everyone's efforts we continued losing height and at 9,000 feet we decided to jettison as much equipment as possible. Opening the starboard rear door I started by chucking out the flame floats, rest bed and even the Elsan toilet. As I passed the D.C. power accumulator I glanced at the dial and saw it was indicating zero. Not believing it I tested my radio receiver. It was almost dead and even the interference mush was faint. I called the skipper to tell him the bad news that our electrical power was almost gone and I couldn't use the wireless transmitter. Only the generator on the starboard inner engine was working, the port outer, because of the fire, was dead. We decided to switch off everything electrical apart from essential equipment so that with luck we might build up enough power in the accumulator to send out an SOS. The two gunners were ordered to leave their turrets. If they tried to rotate them the accumulators would be completely

drained. After much argument they agreed to dismantle their guns and with my help the six Brownings were thrown out along with all the ammunition. This left us feeling naked and defenceless. Unbelievably we had not been attacked by night fighters or been caught by flak and searchlights. We had the feeling that "somebody was looking after us". The navigation *Gee* box, identification friend or foe set (IFF), oxygen bottles and anything else I could lay my hands on was thrown out. The mid-upper and rear-gunner, with nothing else to do, sat near me with their backs against the main spar and learned the secret of the wireless operator's crew position in Lancaster aircraft. Being near the main hot air duct it was the warmest place on board. With the *Gee* box gone and the radio direction finding (RDF) compass unserviceable the bomb-aimer obtained a visual fix of a river east of the Zuider Zee and a course alteration was made. In order to confirm this position the skipper asked me if I could try to get a radio fix. Switching on, I tuned to the emergency frequency and sent out an SOS. At 01.20 hours I logged a third class fix and a request for details, in code, of our situation. Nine minutes later Group Air Traffic Control gave me a first class fix and a further request for information. Halfway through my reply the power went, but this fix showed we were heading south down the Belgian coast. We were now down to 4,000 feet and still losing height so the skipper decided to set a westerly course for the Norfolk coast and he ordered the crew to prepare for ditching. Donning our life jackets we prayed we would not have to ditch in the cold North Sea.'

'We were struggling to hold 4,000 feet', recalls Tommy Farmiloe 'and we were slowly losing height. Once over the coast the order to "prepare to jump" was changed to "prepare to ditch". We got shot at by coastal flak ships (actually a British convoy proceeding up the North Sea) but managed to survive. Then my wireless operator got a home bearing in response to his Mayday call. As we neared the East Coast (lucky it was not the South Coast, as we would not have got over the cliffs!) a single searchlight came on and pointed us in the direction of Little Snoring, a long runway emergency aerodrome.'

'After what seemed like an eternity' continues Eddie Davidson 'we crossed the coast near Cromer at about 500 feet. The skipper then used his VHF R/T set to send out a Mayday call and received the reply, "Give details". In the circumstances, Tommy's reply was quite polite. "Just look up and you will see the problem for yourself. We are on fire". There was a pause and then a voice said, "Follow the searchlights". Immediately on our port side a searchlight came on making an "O" on the clouds and then it came down to lay a beam along the ground. As we reached the end of its light, another searchlight came on and pointed us forward. This happened three times until the runway lights of an airfield came on and we were told, "Circle at 400 feet". The skipper replied, "For God's sake I am at 150 feet now. I'm coming straight in". In preparation for a possible crash landing the navigator joined the two gunners and myself as we sat facing the rear with our backs against the main spar. Ken, the bomb-aimer, refused to leave his position holding the rudder bars and the flight engineer also refused to move. They both very bravely stayed to help the skipper land the aircraft. The undercarriage was then lowered [using the emergency air bottle] but nobody knew if it was locked and would stay down or if the brakes would work. With tremendous effort the skipper got us down in one piece in spite of the runway lights being switched off half way down the landing run.'

'With the port outer still burning and no services', continues Tommy Farmiloe, 'we were unable to signal our approach but struggled in with no flaps at 140 mph. We reached the centre of the runway but to my horror, instead of slowing down, we went faster and faster, eventually going off the end of the runway into complete darkness. We shut off everything that could be shut off and rolled through hedges and across several fields until we hit wet ground. The plane stopped and tipped up on its nose with the tail straight up in the air. We got out FAST, ran away and sat in a group laughing ourselves silly! My crew said that it was the only *good* landing I ever made, but I like to think that there was at least one other! Then we set off to follow the wheel tracks back to the Little Snoring field and control tower. It was still pitch dark. The control staff were amazed, as we had not been noticed! All I cared about was getting all my crew home safely and that we did!'[7]

Eddie Davidson continues:

'The engine fire at last went out and it was only when we climbed out on to the fuselage we saw the nose of the aircraft was embedded in a water-filled ditch. "Just my luck," said Tommy, "to fall off here and drown in some rotten ditch". Someone quickly answered "Not you skipper, you could walk on water tonight". As we waited by the side of the aircraft we were puzzled why no fire engine or any other emergency vehicle had followed us to investigate our predicament. So I climbed back into the aircraft through the cockpit escape hatch to get the Very pistol and cartridges. After climbing out again I stood on the wing and started firing off some red distress flares. It was the first time I had ever had the opportunity to use the Very pistol and I enjoyed it.

About half an hour later a wagon drove up and we were taken to flying control where we found out we had landed at RAF Little Snoring, a Mosquito base near Fakenham. Later the skipper and navigator were driven away to the officers' mess while the rest of us were taken to a very cold and empty dormitory hut for what was left of the night. In the morning after inspecting the damage to *Hellzapoppin* we waited for our Squadron to send an aircraft over to collect us. Shortly after lunch *O-Orange* arrived and we returned to Coningsby. Later we learned that the exceptionally strong winds experienced during the operation had scattered the main force and many aircraft flew south of the intended return route over the strongly defended Ruhr area with disastrous results.'

While considerable damage had been inflicted on the German capital, the cost paid by Bomber Command was high. Ferocious German defences, aided by the un-forecast winds that scattered the bomber stream, claimed a staggering total of 44 Lancasters and 28 Halifaxes. Night fighters in the target area shot 14 of these bombers down[8] and it was believed that about 50 aircraft were brought down by flak. The BBC announcer calmly announced towards the end of the news bulletin that, 'Seventy-three of our aircraft are missing'. 'Missing' seemed to lessen the blow for civilians listening at home and to RAF morale. No one ever said they had died. In RAF circles they had 'got the chop', 'bought it' or had 'gone for a Burton'. The life expectancy of a wartime pilot was 40 hours and that did not do a lot for the confidence but almost everyone got on with the job. One never thought that one day he could be the one who did not return. It always happened to someone else. That the loss of 73 aircraft was 8.9 per cent of the force was not for public consumption and 'Missing' did not include additional losses in men and machines caused by aircraft that crashed in England like *Hellzapoppin* or those that returned with dead and wounded on board. One Lancaster returned with two seriously injured gunners after a reported fight with a Focke-Wulf *Kondor* and the wireless operator, Sergeant K. T. C. Williams, had to direct the pilot, Flight Lieutenant R. W. Picton, from the astrodome. A Lancaster of 57 Squadron landed at East Kirkby having been very badly damaged by an encounter with a Fw 190 *Wilde Sau*. The turrets were put out of action, there was a five-foot diameter hole in the main plane and flaps were shot away and the tanks holed. Both rudders were shattered, the instruments smashed and the intercom system disrupted; yet the bomber made it home. The pilot had extreme difficulty in maintaining control and had to land without flaps and instruments. He touched down at 160 mph and the Lancaster swung off the runway and collided with another aircraft. Apart from the rear-gunner, who had been killed in action, the crew were remarkably uninjured but this was another Lancaster that had to be written off.

The heavies of Bomber Command were destined never to return to the dreaded 'Big City'. The night of the last Berlin raid went down in Bomber Command folklore, as 'the night of the strong winds'.

The morning of the 26th found Pilot Officer Ron Walker's crew at East Kirkby on the battle order again as 'Ginger' Hammersley recalls:

'Again a thorough check was made of the aircraft and its equipment. Later there was the full briefing on similar lines to that for the Berlin operation. The target was to be Essen and our bomb load was one 4,000lb, 85 × 30lb and 1,500 × 4lb bombs. Twelve crews were briefed for the operation. My own crew took off at 19.24 hours, bombing the target in spite of a heavy barrage by anti-aircraft guns. It was 00.55 hours when we landed back at base. Results of the attack were not observed due to prevailing cloud conditions and some crews did not see the target indicators. All our colleagues arrived safely after making their attack and we suffered no losses. At debriefing the coffee and rum were served to us while we waited for our turn. There were two days off from flying which gave us the chance to take stock of what we had so far achieved and I made my first visit to Boston, transport being supplied by our own M/T section.

'When the two local pubs, the 'Red Lion' in East Kirkby and the 'Red Lion' at Revesby had beer available, and we were not flying, the lads would go along and spend an enjoyable evening drinking and singing. Sometimes the 'Red Lion' at Revesby would run out of glasses and we drank out of jam jars. I am sure we enjoyed our beer more when we were drinking from jam jars than when we had normal beer glasses. These evenings relaxed the tension and for a while we could forget the war and our flying missions. During the period between the attack on Aachen and Juvisy, I was able to get away from the airfield into Boston, transport being provided from the motor transport section. There was a late night pick-up point at Boston Stump, if I missed my transport home then it was a long walk to East Kirkby. I enjoyed myself, even though I still only had a vague idea about how to dance. Girls accepted that of others like me, and myself. The walk sobered me up.'

On the night of 26/27 March, Frank Dengate's crew at Mildenhall did their first trip to the Ruhr when the target for 811 aircraft, 577 of them Lancasters, was Essen. Adverse winds had delayed the opening of the attack on the crew's first op to Stuttgart 12 nights earlier and at Essen the city was covered by cloud although the *Oboe* Mosquitoes marked the target well and this was a successful attack. Only nine aircraft, six of them Lancasters, were lost. Dengate's crew returned safely to Mildenhall and waited for their next op, wherever it might be. By now the crew had settled down to the operational routine, as Frank Dengate recalls:

'Between raids we did training with our own fighters on mock attacks and also formation flying and cross-country. Also, we did practice bombing, mainly in daylight, as all our raids on Germany at this time were at night. Mildenhall was an old base so we had comfortable quarters and very nice brick buildings with mess halls and bars. As long as you weren't listed you were free. We would know by about 10 o'clock whether we were operating or we had to go and test our aeroplane. The ground crew were waiting to test to make sure that everything was satisfactory so you'd be ready for the next day. We had a very close relationship with our ground crew. They were wonderful chaps. They waved us off and they waited for us to return. Between the period when we landed to the time we were ready to do our next test, which would probably be a day and a half, quite often they'd work flat out, day and night to get it done. They were very important and we were so dependent on them that we got very close to them. Quite often they didn't sleep at all during busy operating periods [and] we'd have to take another aeroplane because they hadn't finished the inspection. Our individual aircraft was *K-King* and my second name is Hercules so we put *Hercules K-King* on it. We'd do a test flight in the morning, before the next trip the following night. We'd test everything ready for the next run. You could never be sure whether they'd found all the problems that were involved.

'Unless it was a special trip of some kind we went to the briefing straight after lunch. It might have alternatives, in which case you went to your briefing earlier. The different members of the crew had already completed their briefing. The navigator set up his route. The wireless operator would be getting useful information from the wireless mob. The gunners would be checking their information about fighters and so forth. Then you all come together into the main briefing. It told you the targets, whether you were backup crew or third across the target or something like that. The Met gave details of what they presumed the weather was going to be like. They'd never be sure, but they had a fair idea. It could change very easily;

especially when we went to a place like Friedrichshafen when 3½ hours was the time to the target. We did a lot of trips to the Ruhr. Industry and the people that operated the machinery were in the same category. Blood flowed fast if it was the Ruhr because it was a terrible area. The flak concentration was terrific. If we were on backup, then we'd be first into the target for the attack, which was better than being last. The risk of fighters was the same the whole way though. In most cases the planners would try to keep us away from flak areas on our route so that you didn't get a lot of flak other than when you crossed the coast. The target area was the risky part. You held your breath until the bombs were gone because we had to wait until the flash would turn up and indicated where the bombs fell and we could clear out and get cracking on the way home.

'The briefing lasted about an hour and the navigators had to be there early because they had a lot of work to do. Sometimes the radio fellow was there with him to get his information. We depended on the navigator to tell us what speed, height, direction and so forth were required. If I varied our speed, it upset the navigator. It was very exciting being told the target and everyone took a big sigh of relief. We were on edge from the time we got all the information till the time that we got back. The station CO wished us goodbye. After the briefing we went straight over to our aeroplane, normally in a small van driven by one of the WAAFs, with all our parachutes and gear. Once in the aircraft we checked that everything was correct, that the switches for the bombs were all OK and that the radio was operating satisfactorily. Then we waited for start up time. The crew would be checking their equipment. The gunners would be setting themselves down; putting their electric plugs in and making sure their heating was working. The engineer, who was sitting beside me, would be checking all these gauges and making sure we had the correct amount of fuel and that the temperatures and everything was right. I would start up when we were about due for take-off. Then I lined up on the taxi track, came round to the take-off point and got a green light that told me that we were the next and away we'd go. There was always tension on take-off. You had a terrific load to lift off the runway. Everyone was holding their breath and hoping that nothing went wrong until we were in the air. The aeroplane was very heavy with fuel and bombs, which varied according to the distance we were going. At full power the loading on the aircraft was horrific and it probably took the full length of the runway to get the wheels off the ground. I'd whip the wheels up as soon as possible to get maximum speed. This was the dangerous point, because if you crashed with the load you had on, you would finish. This happened sometimes. Testing the aeroplane beforehand was the big thing that made it satisfactory. The Lancaster behaved very well under fully loaded conditions really but if one of your motors lost power for some reason or other, that was enough. You were in need of full power and full speed to get that load off the ground. So everyone was tensed up until they saw the trees clearing under them.

'We flew straight off and up to a point on the coast and across the sea. We couldn't climb much higher than 20,000 feet with a bomb load. We'd try and get to 20 because this was a reasonable height to get away from as much of the flak as possible. Some got brave and dropped down to 12,000 feet over the target but it didn't help because we were in a mass of aeroplanes. If you got out of that stream, the radar got you straight away and the fighters would be vectored onto you so the great advantage was to stay in the stream. We were routed over the lightest covered flak points but it was usually a pretty heavy flak run along the enemy coast. You soon knew when you were passing over enemy territory. Inside the aircraft there was plenty of noise but not much vibration. The Lancaster was quite comfortable. The only talking was to make sure the gunners were awake and checking every now and again that everyone was satisfied and awake in their positions. You quite often got air bumps from the aircraft ahead. Sometimes you didn't even have an indication of whether you were on the right track or in a stream. You simply paid attention to the navigator and timing. We were supposed to go over the target within a ten-minute period, so we had to be fairly accurate on our timing so that a mass of aeroplanes went over at the same time. The bomb-aimer was normally preparing himself for the bombing run. The flight engineer was pretty busy all the time on the instruments, monitoring the petrol consumption, checking temperatures and the oil and calculating what you've got to get to the target and home again. The wireless operator was listening out the whole time for any coded emergency signals from home to warn of a change of route or overcast conditions.

'Approaching the target, everyone tensed up and hoped that the bomb-aimer would get his job done quickly. Flak passed you all the time. All you saw was the spot where it went off and then it came slowly and then "*pssht*" past. You hoped it didn't stop on you. Big explosions in the air were pretty frightening. It was a bit of a shock to a young fellow, and mostly young fellows we were. There'd be terrific flak. In the middle of all this there should be some Target Indicators dropping. If there wasn't it was up to you to find the aiming point.

Over the intercom the bomb-aimer would be saying, "Left, left, steady" and, "right, right, steady". If there was wind you would drift to one side. Then the bomb-aimer pressed his button, which automatically dropped the photoflash. The flash meant he'd taken his photograph of the aiming point and he'd tell me to clear out. A straight and steady approach was the final breathtaking section of the trip. You're in the middle of all the flak and other aeroplanes and you're moving your aeroplane about to get on the same track as everybody else so you're likely to collide with other aeroplanes in the process. It was certainly a great relief when you felt the aeroplane leap and you knew the bombs had gone. We had a set point to turn on, probably 45 degrees first and then another 45 so that you didn't make a quick turn away. Then we'd get onto our home run route. That's when we had to be very careful because the fighters, who normally didn't attack over the flak infested target, wanted to get into our track so that they could shoot us down. You turned your aeroplane continually to check they were not underneath. If the gunners spotted a fighter aircraft they had to straight away tell you, "Aircraft starboard go". You would dive straight away towards that side, whether left or right, so that they could not fire their guns at you. They didn't have to manoeuvre at all except to get under the aeroplane. If you weren't seen they just pulled the trigger and blew your tanks to pieces. They might get the bombs at the same time. These were not normally live until after they left the aeroplane when the spinners on the front activated the bomb. If there was a fire onboard the aircraft everyone would grab the nearest extinguisher and try to extinguish it and the engineer would decide whether to evacuate or not. The rear-gunner would simply swing his rear turret right round and fall out backwards. He had to put his parachute on first though. The mid-upper gunner and all the other crew would have to go down and out through the bottom. The pilot would stay in his seat as long as possible to hold the aeroplane level. He was last in the queue. If there was an explosion everyone got out where they could. As long as it wasn't fire in the petrol tanks, there was a reasonable amount of time to get out.

'As far as searchlights were concerned it was a matter of diving and increasing speed, getting away from the lights if it were possible. They were pretty good, particularly if a mass of them came on together. Then we were blinded by the power of light. We would have to dive and get down, increase speed and get away. As soon as the light got us, then all the flak was concentrated on the one aeroplane.

'On the way home we had to watch that we weren't too relaxed because enemy fighters could be following us, even over Britain, to shoot us down around the home aerodrome. If we had engines out we had priority to land. Otherwise we just took our turn. If we got a red light, we had to go round again. We normally had plenty of fuel to spare unless there'd been a loss of fuel. We would report this and get priority to land if necessary. If we lost an engine, that got landing priority too. It was a big relief to be home. The ground crew would be there to welcome us and always carried out a very careful inspection because we didn't know what flak we'd collected on the way. It could have gone through a cable and left it hanging. We went straight over to debriefing and took our turn. We'd get a ration of rum if we wanted it and we'd pour it into Joe Ell our bomb-aimer. He got really high on the rum. The briefing officers asked if we'd had flak on the way across, whether we'd had any attacks, what our calculated point of the bombing was and whether we reckoned that we were at an aiming point or not. If we were on backup they wanted to know how the master bomber was, whether we got the right instructions and if you saw any aircraft shot down. Quite often there'd be plenty of them, but we wouldn't know who they were. We were pretty weary by this time but they were quite quick in getting us through. Then we went and had a meal and off to bed. We'd be absolutely "plonked" out by this time.'

Notes

1. The Leipzig raid cost 82 Lancasters and Halifaxes and one Mosquito; the worst casualties so far. The majority were destroyed by *Zahme Sau* (four aircraft were destroyed in collisions). Feldwebel Rudolf Frank of 3./NJG 3 destroyed five Lancasters to take his score to 34 kills. Oberleutnant Martin 'Tino' Becker, *Staffelkapitän*, 2./NJG 6 aided by his *Bordfunker* Unteroffizier Karl-Ludwig Johanssen claimed two Halifaxes and two Lancasters to take his score to 10 victories. Becker's *Gruppe*, I./NJG 6 claimed eight victories. *Nachtjagd* lost just 17 fighters.
2. Two further effective *Zahme Sau* operations were directed against Bomber Command raids before February was out. On the 24/25th 209 *1 Jagdkorps Zahme Sau* crews destroyed 31 Lancasters and Halifaxes of a 734 strong force raiding Schweinfurt (Bomber Command lost 33 aircraft). I./NJG 6 claimed a Lancaster and a Halifax destroyed but NJG 6 lost five Bf 110s and four crewmen in air combat. Oberfeldwebel Fritz Schellwat of 6./NJG 1 downed a Lancaster SE of Saverne for his 17th victory and Hauptmann Eckart-Wilhelm 'Hugo' von Bonin, *Ritterkreuzträger* and *Kommandeur* of II./NJG 1 destroyed two *Viermots* for his 28th-29th kills. One of his victims was Lancaster JB721 of 156 Squadron with the loss of five crew. Three 156 Squadron aircraft failed to return from Schweinfurt. The next night 165 twin-engined *Zahme Sau* claimed 19 heavies

during the raid on Augsburg. Four other bombers were lost in collisions and three were probably lost to flak. Total *Nachtjagd* claims for February were 183 bombers destroyed.

3. Frankfurt was raided on the night of 18/19 March by 846 aircraft, including 620 Lancasters. For the loss of six twin-engined night fighters (including two of I./NJG 6) the German defences claimed 22 heavies, 11 of which were attributed to the *Zahme Sau* of I *Jagdkorps*. Five crews of I. and II./NJG 6 destroyed four Halifaxes and a Lancaster. The same city was subjected to another devastating raid by 816 aircraft on 22/23 March, from which 26 Lancasters and seven Halifaxes failed to return. Frankfurt all but ceased to exist. Almost 1,400 people perished in these two raids and 175,000 inhabitants were bombed out. I *Jagdkorps* crews claimed 38 heavies destroyed. Six of these (four Halifaxes and two Lancasters) went to Oberleutnant Martin 'Tino' Becker, *Staffelkapitän*, 2./NJG 6 and Unteroffizier Karl-Ludwig Johanssen, his *Funker*, during a *Zahme Sau* sortie from Finthen aerodrome. Four victory claims were credited to I./NJG 2, three of which, were destroyed by Oberleutnant Heinz Rökker.

4. Diary entry. See *The Lancaster Story* by Peter Jacobs (Cassell, 2002).

5. ibid.

6. *Monica* was a radar warning transmitter with a tail mounted aerial and had a range of between 1,000 feet and up to 2–4 miles.

7. 'It was a "team effort" like so many. As a result, I think that I was the youngest pilot officer to be awarded a DSO. My navigator got a bar to his DFC and my bomb-aimer and wireless operator each got DFMs. Nobody goes for medals – you just want to do the job and get home! I never saw the field again in daylight until years later when Tom Cushing kindly invited my wife and I over. When he drove us along the old runway in his Land Rover it was immediately apparent as to why we accelerated instead of slowing down. The field was like an inverted saucer and once we had reached the middle it was all downhill!'

8. Feldwebel Rudolf Frank of 3./NJG 3 claimed three aircraft, including Lancaster ME640 of 460 Squadron RAAF at Teglingen and ND657 of 630 Squadron at Altharen. Oberleutnant Heinz Rökker, *Staffelkapitän* 1./NJG 2 destroyed two Lancasters and a Halifax. Oberleutnant Martin 'Tino' Becker of 2./NJG 6 claimed a Lancaster at Wörlitz/Passau. Rökker claimed another Lancaster near Mönchengladbach on 26/27 March when a 705-strong force went to Essen. Nine Lancasters and Halifaxes failed to return, most probably all being shot down by twin-engined *Zahme Sau*.

Chapter 8

'There's a War on Tonight'

Usually the members of two crews shared a Nissen hut. We've been there and seen the adjutant come along and collect all the stuff out of their lockers and you knew that crew hadn't made it. Within a day or so, a new crew came in and they'd ask, 'What's it like?' We'd say, 'Oh, bloody awful. It's terrible.' You put the fear of God into them. We were a rotten lot in that respect. It was just devil may care. On low flying exercises if we saw people on farms working on a haystack we made a point of just shooting over the top and pulling the nose up quickly so that the slipstream from the four fans blew the straw all over the poor buggers! The times we were reported for this! The CO just told us not to blow anymore haystacks down. May as well talk to a brick wall.

Bomb Aimer, Sergeant Derek 'Pat' Patfield

Powerful winds from the north that carried the four-engined heavies south at every stage of their flight to Berlin on the night of the 24/25 March affected hardened old soaks and 'Gen Men' and the 'sprog' crews alike. Low lying Fenland and dykes were no barrier to chill winds and rain that came sweeping in from the North Sea to make life on the far flung airfields in Lincolnshire quite unbearable for the men of all nations who had come to fight in Bomber Command. Primitive wartime facilities cloaked in wintertime fog threatened to dampen the resolve of resolute Aussies and Kiwis who had left their Antipodean sunshine and, equally, those from Canada's prairies, occupied Poland and the cities, towns and villages all over Britain. At the beginning of 1944 the ramshackle base at Skellingthorpe was shared between 50 Squadron and 61 Squadron. But as both were building up their operational strength, it was not long before an acute accommodation problem arose and the 'Lincoln Imps' had forsaken 'Skelly' to move to Coningsby on a three month detachment. Coningsby, at least, offered more in the way of home comforts. But for young 'green' aircrew arrivals like Norfolk-born Sergeant 'Pat' Patfield and others, most of whom were in their late teens or early twenties, it was still a shock to the system after their training in Canada. The young bomb-aimer had learned bombing and gunnery at Lethbridge, Alberta. And he had attended Air Observation classes at Malton, Ontario,

before returning to England with ice skates bought in Moncton, a petrol cigarette lighter, given as a Christmas present by a family in New Brunswick, and many photos including the snows near Niagara Falls. Further training had continued at places from Newquay in Cornwall to near the Welsh border at Hereford and quite a number of airfields around the Midlands and Lincolnshire before the seven crew members concluded their training at the Lancaster Finishing School at Syerston near Nottingham. Like debutantes they 'came out' to join the ranks of the Lincoln Imps.

With the exception of Tommy Thomas, the navigator from 'somewhere in London', who had crewed up with them only a week or so before, they had trained together for a number of months previously. Two of the crew really were returning home after their travails. Pilot Officer Desmond 'Denny' Freeman their 21 year old RAFVR pilot was from Gainsborough. On 29 December 1940 Denny Freeman's father, Luther Henry Freeman, had died on service with the 11th Lindsey (Gainsborough) Battalion, Home Guard aged 42. Sergeant Leslie 'Jimmy' Chapman, the wireless operator hailed from Melton Washway near Spalding. Eva and Ernest Chapman's only son had gone to the Saracen's Head School in Whaplode before going to work on the land and there he could have stayed because his work in food production was so important that he was not conscripted. But the 20 year old had insisted on joining up. Frank Devonshire, the flight engineer, was from Birmingham. Bill Smith, the rear-gunner, was from somewhere near St Helens, Lancashire. On ops Bill would talk about women until they got to the enemy coast and then even he shut up. 'Old Bill' was a real 'rough diamond'. His only interest in life was meeting girls and going out with them. He always said he had a hell of a job to convince girls he was christened Bill Smith! After the war he said he was going to be a gigolo and get paid to keep women happy! As Pat Patfield said, 'He was just the bloke for a rear-gunner'. Arthur 'Dep' Sherriff was the mid-upper gunner and oldest member of the crew at 34 years of age.

The crew had flown their first op to Frankfurt on 18/19 March and the second had followed on 26/27th, to Essen. 'The experience of being told that "There's a war on tonight and you're on the list",' recalled Sergeant 'Pat' Patfield, 'was received with a certain amount of foreboding, in spite of the fact that during training we had been anxious to get on with the real thing. Word would go round operations were on. The standard phrasing was, "There's a war on tonight". You went into the Ops Room and there'd be a list of the crews on the big Ops board, but it wouldn't say the target. That was usually about lunchtime. Just after lunch you went out to the aircraft and checked all the equipment – which you did everyday even if you weren't on ops. The ground crews would be working on them anyway and we'd just take it up for a short air test.'

Though short in stature Derek Patfield had a lot of nerve and courage. During his boyhood he had dived from the rigging of a moored sailing vessel into a river, which was quite a feat for a boy of his age. He always had an eye for a pretty girl. Though Lincoln had a castle and a cathedral, he and his friends were not interested in them. They were only interested in meeting the girls at the 'Saracen's Head'. Since enlisting in the RAF in 1942 Derek's mischievous sense of fun, which he had demonstrated during civilian air-raid duty, had not deserted him either. The Norfolk 'dumpling' was now the perfect little Lincolnshire 'imp'.

'Usually the members of two crews shared a Nissen hut. We've been there and seen the adjutant come along and collect all the stuff out of their lockers and you knew that crew hadn't made it. Within a day or so, a new crew came in and they'd ask, "What's it like?" We'd say, "Oh, bloody awful. It's terrible." You put the fear of God into them. We were a rotten lot in that respect. It was just devil may care. On low flying exercises if we saw people on farms working on a haystack we made a point of just shooting over the top

and pulling the nose up quickly so that the slipstream from the four fans blew the straw all over the poor buggers! The times we were reported for this! The CO just told us not to blow any more haystacks down. May as well talk to a brick wall.

'When operations were on, pilots, navigators and bomb-aimers reported to the various sections for the individual briefings. We'd be told the bomb load, but not what the target was. We always had a flying meal of eggs and bacon. The flight engineer told you the fuel load and by that you'd pretty well know if it was going to be a long trip. If you had a heavy bomb load and medium fuel load, chances were it was going to be a short trip. Then we went in for the main briefing all together. We'd be briefed on the different coloured Target Indicators and bombs and which ones to bomb. The actual bomb load was explained, what we were carrying and the terminal velocity of the bombs (the speed of the bombs going down). Terminal velocity, height of the target from sea level, forecast wind speed and direction and the speed of the aircraft all had to be set on the bombsight. Then we would be told the target and issued with our target maps before going over any salient points, land marks en route and what to look for on the target. Then it was a question of going back to the crew room to check personal equipment. If you were lucky you got an Irving jacket but it was mainly a canvas type flying suit with two or three jumpers underneath. Our girlfriends gave us all lucky charms. I had a tin badge and a stocking, which I would wrap around the bombsight. I didn't go bananas if I hadn't got it with me. We wore a Mae West and a parachute harness but the parachute was stowed in a little cubby-hole in the side of the fuselage. In an emergency you had to clamber out of position and hook the parachute on to the harness before you dived out. The advantage of my position was that I actually knelt on the escape hatch so I could pull the rubber pads back and get out – hopefully. You'd be lucky if you had time to do that.

'When you drew your parachute from the parachute section you also drew your escape kit with little silk maps of the area you were operating, wakey-wakey tablets, fishing line, unnamed packets of cigarettes and currency. If you came down over Europe and fell into the hands of the escape committees they could forge all the documents for you, but they couldn't get photographs. We had photographs taken on the squadron and sewn into our flying suit so, we already had the pictures for them. Flying rations consisted of a packet of boiled sweets and a flask of coffee or tea. My biggest faux pas was when I was throwing 'Window' out of the chute. I'd go to get my sweets and find that I'd thrown them down the hatch as well! Some rotten Jerry had my sweets.

'We'd all come together and wait for the crew buses to take us out to the aircraft about an hour before take-off. Most crews peed on the tail wheel for good luck. Damn silly things we did! Then we piled into the aircraft and made ourselves comfortable. On some of the daylights in the summertime it was terribly hot in the aircraft, which had been sitting out in the sun. We had no fans and all this flying gear on, which we needed because we'd freeze up higher. We sat there swearing our eyeballs out, waiting to take-off. Then the green flare would go up and No. 1 aircraft would taxi out and the others all followed. It was an Air Ministry directive that bomb-aimers should not be in the nose on take-off or landing but I'm afraid I disobeyed this order. I could hardly move for bundles of 'Window' stacked in the nose. By the time you got all your maps sorted out you didn't want to move just for a few minutes, then fight your way back down again. You knew damn well that if you didn't take off and it crashed you were going to be killed anyway. Whether you were a few yards back didn't make any difference. The take-off was the worst part. On board were 2,000 gallons of high-octane petrol, eight tons of high explosive bombs, 1½ million candlepower magnesium flares and high-pressure oxygen bottles. If the aircraft didn't get off the ground there'd be quite a big bang so, you always breathed a sigh of relief once you got in the air!

'We didn't take the wakey-wakey pills until we were on the way. It was the sensible thing to do. Some blokes took them as soon as they got in the aircraft at the dispersal but you might be on the dispersal for half an hour or more before you took-off. Sometimes, especially if the weather clamped in, the op was scrubbed. Some crews had already taken the wakey-wakey pills, so they couldn't sleep when we went back to the billet. The pills would give you a bit of a headache but we put that down to tiredness and stress.

'When we left the English coast, going out, it was the bomb-aimer's job to select and fuse all the bombs on the panel. It usually brought a corny remark from someone, as I passed my message, "All bombs fused and selected" to the navigator to enter in his log.

"What do you mean, '*foosed*'?"

Apparently my Norfolk dialect didn't lend itself kindly to the word "fused" and it sounded like "foosed". I was usually referred to as a "Swede" or a "Dumplin".

'Over 10,000 feet we went on oxygen. On a lot of flights, when we were flying high, the moisture from our breath froze in our oxygen masks. We had to keep squeezing our oxygen mask and the corrugated pipe that came down to break the ice. It wasn't a very nice smell but we had to be on oxygen all the time over 10,000 feet. Our oxygen masks had a microphone on the end, so it was quite a lot of weight hanging down. We didn't have steel helmets and flak vests like the Americans; just a leather helmet and canvas flying suit.

'Usually the pilot was strict on intercom silence. We kept quiet unless we had something to report. It would be quiet and all of a sudden I'd say, "Bomb-aimer to navigator, we're just crossing the coast". He would acknowledge it and it would go quiet again.

'We had as many as four or five maps, on which we marked out the route and turning points. These had to be checked with the bombing leader and each one of us to make sure they were accurate. We had a target map as well. We had to 'Window' at a certain rate depending on our point on the route. If an area of radar-controlled searchlights and guns were coming up, I'd just chuck bundles out as quickly as possible. They were brown paper parcels done up with string. I had to pull the string off and then I'd have all the individual bundles of 'Window'. Each individual bundle had a piece of brown paper wrapped round with an elastic band or piece of string to pull off and then I shoved it down the chute beside me. Before long you were just mixed up with paper, string and 'Window'. That got a bit tiresome.

'You could not see much at night. If we had to come down and make a forced landing I couldn't see if it was a wood or a field or houses below. It was awful being unable to see what was happening. We even lost some chaps who went to investigate flak damage to the aircraft and went straight out a hole in the fuselage. I definitely preferred daylights. You could see what was happening and we had a fighter escort on some of them.

'It was quite interesting to see aerial combats at night. I could see tracer the bombers fired. It was a different colour to fighter tracer. To demoralize the bomber crews, the Germans fired up shells containing Very lights, oil and explosives so, when the shell exploded, it mimicked an aircraft blowing up. They did demoralize us, especially when they were right near. We were told about these shells, but that was all eyewash. They were really aircraft exploding.

'I was in my compartment all the time, unless there was a lot of fighter activity. Then I'd get up in the front turret. There was no bottom to it. It was open. There was a little platform to kneel on when bombing. You stood on that and you were in the front turret. There wasn't a lot of room. I was always glad I was small. Quite honestly I failed to see how you were going to get out in an emergency. I was kneeling on the emergency hatch, surrounded by parcels of 'Window'. If you had to get out quickly, you had to chuck all the bundles of 'Window' out of the way and pull back the rubber pads and then you'd have a job finding the hatch release handle. The rear-gunner used to say he was lucky. He saw what he'd been through. At the front you saw all you were going into. I'd identify the target by the surrounding area. You had to be quick to identify flying bomb sites, to get your bombs down in time. They were not self-evident like a big factory or marshalling yard because they were well camouflaged. You just went by your maps and photographs, but we all did our own navigation and bomb run.

'I was given the job of leading the squadron on a daylight to St Leu. That was quite a responsibility. I looked for some fields, one of which was marked with what was almost a Cross of Lorraine. Being the lead aircraft on a daylight I thought, "Where the hell are those fields?" Was I relieved when I saw the river! Then I saw the fields. There were all sorts of underground works there as well. The river was a wonderful landmark. When travelling at 200 mph you had to keep your eyes open to see the target far enough ahead to line the aircraft up and get it in your bombsight. We even passed V-1s on the way on one or two daylights and I saw some V-2 rockets going up – they went pretty fast.

'The bomb release point could be one to four miles to the target – depending on our height. I had to release the different bombs in a certain order to keep the aircraft stable and the different sized bombs had a different time in the air. They had to be arranged so they went down at a similar point. I had selector switches and a sweep arm went round, made contact and each contact released a bomb. Lots of things affected hitting the target. I had to set the height of the target above sea level on the bombsight. That came from our maps. If that was wrong the bombs' angle of flight would be wrong and the bombs wouldn't hit the target. I had to take drift and speed and direction into account as well. The winds were given to us at briefing, but we had to check it on the bombsight. Even at night I'd check. It is surprising what you could see at night. Headlands, marshalling yards and railway lines shone if there was a bit of a moon. There was a compass on the bombsight so I could give the navigator a bearing on any pin point and he could check his navigation. He'd start re-navigating on any pin point I gave him. I'd set drift on the bombsight so that the graticule was at an angle. Then I'd bring the aircraft round so the graticule lined up to the target. The aircraft went slightly sideways to allow for drift.

'It didn't do to worry about the people in the towns and cities. As far as we were concerned it was a target

and we were interested in pasting the German war machine. That was all we were interested in. At 20,000 feet you were only concerned with hitting the target. I'd think about what we were told when we graduated: you had the station personnel, ground crew and six other blokes all working getting you over the target, with one thing in mind – to drop the bombs on that target. That's the way I thought about it and I always made sure I had got the Aiming Point. That's why I'd have a clear conscience, knowing I got the AP in the graticule of the bombsight and everything was in order when I released the bombs.

'Getting back to base it was often misty. The 'dromes were so close together there was the risk of collision, in the circuit, with other aircraft. We were all circling and fatigued and it might be ten minutes before we landed. If you were firing off reds because you'd got injured on board, or damage to the aircraft, you got priority. As soon as we landed we had to open the bomb doors. At dispersal the bomb-aimer would look in the bomb bay to make sure you'd got the fuse links hanging down from each lug. That meant the bombs had gone down live. If you didn't fuse the bomb, or the solenoid froze up, the arming links wouldn't be caught by the solenoid and held in the aircraft pulling away from the fuse of the bomb. If the arming links weren't in the bomb bay they'd gone down attached to the fuse and that bomb went down safe. The arming links prevented the detonator going down to detonate the bomb. The chances were, even though you were dropping from thousands of feet, that the bomb wouldn't explode but just make a dirty great hole in the ground.

'The squadron buses would come out to pick us up. First we'd hand in our parachutes and parachute harness, our escape kit and any special maps we had. Then we went to debriefing and had a cup of tea and a cigarette. "What was it like? What was the opposition like? What was the condition of the target?" The morning after the operation the bombing photographs were on the board in the Ops Room. Everybody ploughed in to see how they'd got on.

'You hoped you'd finish the tour, but basically all the time, nobody really thought that they would. You'd wake some mornings and see empty beds of crews that had gone and then you saw them scrubbed off the operations board. It was peculiar really. You just accepted the fact you'd be bloody lucky if you got through and the chances were you wouldn't. It was a peculiar world. At night all the might of the *Luftwaffe* and *Wehrmacht* was against you, trying to kill you. Then, a few hours later – perhaps that evening if you weren't on ops – you'd be in Lincoln going out with the girls, or in the pub among normal people. You jumped from war to peace, peace to war, within a few hours and so it went on week after week.'

One of the perks of Bomber Command aircrew was a break from operations every six weeks with six days off and a rail warrant home. At Coningsby on 30 March, Pilot Officer E. A. 'Ted' Stone, the regular skipper of *N-Nan*, was about to go on leave to his home in Bridgewater, Somerset. Just before he and his crew left camp Ted was called into the CO's office where Wing Commander R. N. Stidolph asked him to delay their crew leave for 24 hours and fly a maximum effort operation later that night. In return Stidolph promised that upon their return to Coningsby the following morning, he would have a Sprog crew fly Ted to the nearest airfield to his home. Stone agreed though he and everyone else at aircrew level for that matter did not know what the maximum effort was.

At Metheringham Pilot Officer Dick Starkey and his crew in 106 Squadron were nearing the end of their tour of 30 operations. They had been scheduled to take part in a raid on Brunswick on the night of 29 March. However, four crews were on the last 10 trips of their tours and it looked as though they would complete their tour at about the same time, so it was decided to stagger the remaining trips. Starkey's crew were therefore told to stand down for the Brunswick raid but this operation was then cancelled because the Met forecast was not good. On 30 March Starkey's Flight Commander told him that his crew would be stood down. Starkey recalls:

'I informed the lads of the order but as one man they said that as we had been a stand down crew for a cancelled operation one of the other crews should do so for the raid and they asked me to see the Flight Commander again. Although I had to decide whether or not to let the order stand, I agreed that we should be put on the Battle Order and gave my views to the Flight Commander. At first he said the order would not be reversed but after some thought he changed his decision.'

That afternoon at crew briefings on the Bomber Command airfields throughout the north-east and Midlands they learned what their destination for the maximum effort was. Many probably expected another raid on the 'Big City' or even Schweinfurt, Leipzig or several other German cities, but it was Nuremberg. Apart from attacks by a few Mosquitoes, this 'most German of German cities', as Hitler called it, and the scene of his infamous National Socialist Party rallies before the war, had not been heavily bombed for seven months. Perhaps a raid on the birthplace of *Nazism*

would go some way to proving that 'a state of devastation' would make surrender 'inevitable'.

The attack on Nuremberg by 572 Lancasters and 214 Halifaxes and nine Mosquitoes, was planned for what would normally have been the middle of the stand down period for the main force, when a near full moon would be visible. And their lords and masters had opted for a 'straight in, straight out' route, with none of the jinks and deviations that might cause the night fighter controllers to make the wrong decisions about their destination. An indirect route with four shorter legs was suggested by Air Vice Marshal Don Bennett but the forthright Australian AOC of 8 (PFF) Group was the single dissenting voice. The plan was countenanced by the AOCs of the three Lancaster Groups – Air Marshal Sir Ralph A. Cochrane KBE CB AFC commanding 5 Group, by Air Vice Marshal E. A. B. Rice, the South African commander of 1 Group, and Air Vice Marshal R. Harrison of 3 Group, a Yorkshireman. Then, under protest, approval was finally given by Air Vice Marshal C. Roderick Carr of 4 Group, a New Zealander, and Air Vice Marshal C. M. 'Black Mike' McEwen of 6 Group, RCAF, both of whose Halifaxes were more vulnerable than the faster and more reliable Lancs.[1] After the turning point over Belgium crews would fly a long outward leg of 265 miles through a well-defended part of Germany, past known fighter beacons *Ida*, south of the Ruhr, *Otto* near Cologne and *Heinz* close to the Ruhr. But a strong tail wind was expected, which would speed the bombers along the 'long leg' in just 62 minutes' flying time. Reports were that there would be high cloud on the outward route and that the target area would be clear for ground-marked bombing.

At Metheringham some of Pilot Officer Dick Starkey's crew, with only three weeks to go to the end of their tour, were not alone among the many hundreds of assembled bomber crews who began to have reservations. Many, not least among the old sweats and 'gen men', were filled with a sense of foreboding.

At Dunholme Lodge Flying Officer John Chatterton DFC of 44 Squadron, whose crew had flown 22 ops and after some early mistakes and a great deal of luck, had developed into a competent unit, able to rely totally on each other, had a feeling of unease. It was not helped by the fact that he was flying the Squadron's spare Lancaster, *E-Easy*, instead of his beloved *Y-Yorker*, which was having an engine changed after 'collecting some heavy metal' over Berlin six nights previously:

'For the last five months we had spent night after night clawing our way through varying densities of cloud to attack the major cities of Germany, including eight to the 'Big City' itself. Despite the constant anxiety of icing and flak, this damp cloak of darkness was just what we burglars needed to enable us to creep in and creep out again, without being apprehended by the vigilant night fighters. Every now and then we realized that we were hitting civilians when bombing German targets and we tried to shut this out of our minds. We felt much better when we went on to marshalling yards; we felt that we were fighting like the Eighth Army or the Battle of Britain boys. It was good clean fighting.

'Some time ago, with our accumulated experience and Jack's navigational skill, we had been made the Squadron's 'wind-finder' and PFF supporter.[2] I relished this job of wind-finder. It meant that we took off alone about half an hour before the rest of the Squadron came queuing up along the perimeter track, with radiators and tempers overheating. We then flew along in a relatively uncluttered sky to join the first wave of the Pathfinders in order to give them support against the searching German radar by thickening the shower of "Window".'

At this time a third of Bomber Command's airmen were from the Commonwealth. At Waddington Squadron Leader Arthur William Doubleday DFC RAAF, a farmer from Wagga, New South Wales and now the 'B' Flight Commander in 467 Squadron RAAF, warned his crew: 'Look boys it's on for young and old tonight. Just keep your eyes on the sky.'[3] Warrant Officer Jim McNab, a Scot among the Australians in 467 Squadron adds, 'Five of our crew were Aussies and they were a lot more outspoken than we were. Because it was bright moonlight they questioned the wisdom of the operation in no uncertain manner. But the briefing officer said it was all OK. He said that a reconnaissance Mosquito had reported that there was plenty of cloud and the only hole in the cloud was over Nuremberg. This satisfied everyone. The morale was really terrific as it always was and this was our 26th operation.'

It was only after the crews had been briefed that information from a reconnaissance Mosquito indicating that the route would be clear of cloud but that the target would probably be covered, was withheld. The raid would go ahead as planned.

One of the 18 crews in 57 Squadron at East Kirkby who were briefed for the raid was Pilot Officer Ron Walker's. His bomb-aimer, Sergeant 'Ginger' Hammersley noted that they were in the first wave after the Pathfinders and 'like the flight to Berlin, it looked as if we were set for a long trip'.

At Coningsby 61 Squadron assembled 14 Lancasters. *N-Nan*'s pilot, Flying Officer E. A. 'Ted' Stone was by now probably regretting that he not gone on leave after all. *V-Victor,* flown by Pilot Officer J. A. Haste, an Australian from Maylands, South Australia, was a Lancaster veteran although the crew were flying only their eighth operation. Another Australian, Pilot Officer J. A. Forrest, was at the controls of *Mickey the Moocher.* Pilot Officer Donald Paul was flying *R-Robert.* Flying Officer Bernard C. Fitch and his crew of *Royal Pontoon* were regarded as the 'Gen Men' or 'Old Sweats' of the Squadron, as Sergeant Leslie Cromarty DFM the rear-gunner, recalls:

'Our squadron had taken a battering. We were on the Berlin raid less than a week before, when Bomber Command lost over 70 aircraft and so we only had about a dozen crews left this night. We were the most experienced crew. Next came Squadron Leader E. H. Moss DFC [an Oxford University graduate who had been a school master, in *P-Peter,* whose crew were on their 20th operation]. We had an outstanding navigator, Sid Jennings, and also the best aircraft in the Squadron. *Royal Pontoon* was a Canadian-built Lanc with Rolls-Royce Packard engines with paddle-bladed props. It could climb much higher than most other Lancasters. We never did find out just how high it could go because at 30,000ft the contrails would begin and we would drop below that height for obvious reasons. We were flying as "wind-finders" as usual.'

Q-Queenie was piloted once again by Pilot Officer Denny Freeman whose crew were flying their third op. His bomb-aimer Sergeant 'Pat' Patfield, recalled:

'The usual business of briefing over, we were soon clambering aboard *Queenie* out at her dispersal point at the edge of the airfield, though just prior to which we had all gazed up into the open bomb bay to have a good look at the bombs hanging there. We had seen them or similar ones before but they always fascinated us just the same. And so in we climbed and were soon making ourselves as comfortable as the cramped crew positions permitted. As we plugged in our intercom we ceased our somewhat idle chatter about girls and got down to the serious job of checking equipment, controls, guns and radio etc. and waited somewhat nervously for the four engines to burst into life. We didn't have long to wait before we were rumbling round the perimeter track towards the end of the runway, accompanied by other Lancs of our squadron which, in the rapidly fading daylight, gave the appearance of large, dark birds of prey. On to the runway, engines revving hard. A green light from the caravan. Brakes off. We were away.

'As usual, I sat in the nose of the aircraft on take-off (rules are made to be broken) and got settled down with maps spread out, parachute stowed near – very near, the numerous fairly heavy and bulky brown covered parcels of 'Window' stacked all around me. In a few seconds, which were only broken by the orders of the pilot and acknowledgment of the flight engineer, with engines straining to get the over-laden aircraft into the air, the jolting ceased and, with the engineer's "Undercarriage Up", we knew we were really on the way. With a remark from one crew member, "And to think I had a bloody date in Boston tonight", we settled ourselves to our allotted tasks, en route to Nuremberg. We did not know it then of course, but this was to be the last time that we flew together.

'Gaining height, we flew off to the rendezvous where we could see the dim shapes of other Lancs turning on to course. Taking up our position, we joined in the gaggle for we didn't fly in formation. Indeed it would have been extremely dangerous to attempt to do so. We headed for a point on the south-east coast of England on the first leg of the flight plan. Looking down through the Perspex blister in the nose, the ground, what could be seen of it, looked strangely quiet and I often wondered how many people stopped and peered skyward as the drone of the bombers disturbed the peace of the evening sky. I know I had, many times during training, wondering whether I would join them one day. Where were they going and how did they feel? Well, now I was here and the main thought in our minds was not whether we would get back OK – you just didn't think of that – but what it'll be like at the target. Hope we could find it and then let's get back to that egg and bacon and bed.

'There wasn't much chatter over the intercom, just the odd remark or two, which usually concerned the opposite sex. The flight engineer took his instrument readings, the navigator was busily working intently at his small table, working out the next course for the pilot, the wireless operator getting his set lined up, and listening for messages and the numerous other things a wireless operator did. The two gunners, who always seemed so remote from the rest of the crew, were busy swinging their turrets around and peering into the darkness for anything, which shouldn't be there. The pilot as ever, was intent on his instruments and usually oblivious to what was happening elsewhere. Having put the correct settings on the bombsight computer, I was now gazing downwards in the hope of picking up some recognizable landmark which, after checking with a map, would be passed to the navigator as a "pinpoint" to check against his calculated position. Map reading was the bomb-aimer's primary job, next to actual bombing and even at night it was surprising how many geographical landmarks could be seen. The hardest part was reading maps, as in the nose no lighting was permitted and the only source of light was from a "blacked-out" flashlight with a few tiny pinpricks to allow a very small percentage of light to pass through. At last the Suffolk coast appeared and crossing it we really felt we were on our way. The usual instruction from the pilot to both gunners, "OK gunners, keep your eyes skinned"!'

At Metheringham the procedure was the same. Dick Starkey recalls:

'We took off and climbed on course over the Norfolk coast towards Belgium. The moon was bright and almost full, making near daylight conditions. At our cruising height of 21,000 feet the air temperature was very low and the bomber stream began making condensation trails as we flew en route, over Belgium towards the long leg which ran from south of the Ruhr east to a turning point north-west of Nuremberg. It was this long leg that crews were apprehensive about because it ran for over 200 miles. Flying conditions over Germany were ideal for fighter aircraft against slow bombers who had inferior armament and the sky was absolutely clear with a near full moon and four-engined bombers making condensation trails which could be seen for miles. The fighters began their attack and from the number of tracers being fired, it appeared there were combats everywhere; I saw around 30 aircraft go down in a short period and, as we continued to the target, the ground became covered with burning aircraft.'

Flying Officer John Chatterton was about to make a routine intercom check on the crew when suddenly, the mid-upper-gunner, Bill Campion 'an eighteen-year-old Canadian of an excitable nature, but possessing the sharpest eyes on the Squadron, bless him' came on. 'Hey, Skip! Are the engines OK? There seems to be smoke coming from them!' The rear-gunner, a phlegmatic Glaswegian and the perfect foil to the eager Canadian, said, 'Wheesht yer bletherin' Champ – they're contrails!'

'Contrails! How did he know? We had never made them before, although we had often admired the pretty patterns left by the USAAF on their daylight raids 10,000 feet above us. Everyone craned their necks to look behind them through side blisters and astrodome but without much success. Then Ken nudged my right arm and pointed down, where a thousand feet below another Lanc was leaving four long white fingers, which were twisted into a cloudy rope by the slipstream – a perfect invitation to the night fighters. I decided to climb out of the layer of humidity, but *Easy* was very reluctant and Ken had to put the revs up to 2,750, the throttles being already fully open. However, by now we had used about a third of our seven and a half tons of fuel, so with much mushing she was able to heave herself up another few hundred feet, as the clutching fingers of fog snapped on and off a few times and finally disappeared. While Ken was synchronizing his propellers again I called the nav. "Pilot to navigator, how much longer on this leg, Jack?" As usual, his calculations were right up to date and he immediately replied, "I've just got a fix on Giessen. We are about two thirds of the way along, about twenty minutes if you can manage to stay on course." I grinned to myself, which was a mistake as the slight wrinkling of the oxygen mask allowed some icy condensation to trickle down my chin – after all it was minus thirty-five outside and the cockpit heating of *Easy* was on a par with the rest of her. The wry smile was a tribute to all navigators. Sitting there behind their curtains, at a vibrating plotting table where just hanging on to pencils and protractors was a work of art, precise mathematicians, who couldn't really understand why ham-handed pilots were not able to hold a course to one degree. Our crews appreciated that we had got one of the best.

'Using *Gee* until it was jammed at the Dutch coast and H$_2$S, Jack worked swiftly to calculate winds, which were then transmitted back to Group by the W/Op, Jock Michie, who had to risk breaking the radio silence that all bombers observed. At Group the winds from all sources were averaged out and re-transmitted back to the bomber stream in the half hourly "group broadcast". The wind-finders complained that Group were far too conservative and always played safe with the averages. Jack was still disgruntled about the last Berlin raid when he had found winds of well over one hundred knots due to freak weather conditions (since known as "jet stream"). Group would not accept them, which badly upset the planned time over the target. The intercom crackled again: "Nav to pilot. Group has done it again, Johnny. They are still using the forecast winds, which will put everybody north of track."

'Unwelcome proof of this came from both gunners who had been reporting unusually large numbers of "scarecrow flares", mostly off to the port quarter and quite a way behind. "Scarecrow flares" had been first mentioned at briefing some weeks earlier with the explanation that the Germans were sending this impressive firework up to 20,000 feet to look like exploding aircraft and lower our morale. We hardened

cynics were pretty sure that they *were* exploding aircraft, but knowing nothing of the night fighters using upward-firing tracer-less cannon we could not understand why there were not the usual exchange of tracer in the normal "curve of pursuit". What the gunners were reporting were the deaths of over fifty bombers. This was the night that the German controllers got their calculations right and ignored a spoof attack in north Germany, deciding that the bomber stream would use a favourite flak gap just south of Cologne to penetrate into the hinterland and maybe turn left to Leipzig or Berlin. Me 110 and Ju 88 squadrons had been pulled in from the north and south to orbit fighter beacons *Ida* and *Otto* near Bonn and Frankfurt. They could hardly believe it when they found the bomber stream flying en masse between the two beacons and into their waiting arms, like the gentlemen guns in a partridge shoot waiting for the coveys to sweep over them. The resulting slaughter was much the same.'

Squadron Leader Arthur William Doubleday adds:
'They started to fall within ten minutes of crossing the coast and from then to the target the air was not only of good visibility but seemed to be bright. The moon was really shining brightly although it wasn't a full moon.'[4]

As they flew over the North Sea Warrant Officer Jim McNab was not alone when he realized that the meteorological forecast was wrong. There was no cloud: 'One of our chaps said we were for it and he was right. Nuremberg was the only place covered by cloud. I could see Lancasters being shot down by anti-aircraft guns and fighters. It was so light that I could clearly read the squadron letters and identification numbers on the Lancasters flying next to us.'

Pilot Officer Starkey of 106 Squadron continues:
'We continuously operated the "banking search" looking for enemy aircraft coming up from below. This was achieved by turning steeply to port for 15 degrees to see if fighters were preparing to attack and then banking to return to the original course. Our *Fishpond* aircraft detector failed to work on the Nuremberg raid. [The bombers were attacked just before they reached the Belgian border and the attacks lasted for the next hour.] We had been flying the long leg for many miles. When we were in a position 60 miles north-west of Nuremberg our luck changed. A fighter attacked with tracer and cannon fire, which hit the port main-plane and outer engine, flashed past outside the Perspex covering of the cockpit and between my legs. I remember praying we would not go up in flames. However, within

three or four seconds the port outer engine and mainplane were alight. It was always the one you didn't see that shot you down as in our case and if *Monica* had been available we would have been aware of the fighters' approach.

'There was only one action to take; I gave the order to abandon aircraft. The engineer, Sergeant Johnnie Harris feathered the port engine as he helped me with the controls because we were going down at a very fast rate and the next few seconds I remember vividly. The bomb-aimer, Sergeant Wally Paris, acknowledged my order to bale out and said he was leaving the aircraft. The navigator, Sergeant Colin Roberts, came to the cockpit to escape through the front hatch. The rear-gunner, Sergeant Joe Ellick also acknowledged the order but said he could not get out of his turret (this was because the port outer engine powered the turret; the alternative way was to turn the turret by hand controls in order to fall out backwards). There was no reply from the mid-upper gunner, Sergeant Jock Jameson and the wireless operator, Sergeant Jock Walker. I assumed they must have been killed by the burst of fire, which ran along the side of the aircraft. Johnnie Harris handed me a parachute from one of two in the rack at his side. I managed to connect one of the hooks on the chute to the harness I was wearing (we did not wear seat type chutes), at the same time trying to control a blazing aircraft, which was diving at well over 300 mph. I gave up all hope of survival and waited for the impact; a terrifying experience. That is the last thing I remember because the aircraft exploded with a full bomb load (we had no time to jettison) and 1,500 gallons of high octane fuel, which must have ignited and caused the explosion. As I lost consciousness I did have a feeling of being lifted out of the cockpit and must have been propelled through the Perspex canopy. When the petrol tanks exploded in the port wing outside my window a fireball must have been created in the aircraft, which would incinerate anything in its path and I must have been just ahead of it as I was blown from the aircraft. Many years later I was told an unopened parachute was found next to the body of the flight engineer who had landed in a wood six kilometres from the wreckage of the aircraft. We were only two feet apart in the cockpit when the aircraft went up and Johnnie Harris must have been blown out like me but I was lucky my parachute had opened, probably by the force of the explosion.

'When I regained consciousness and realized what had happened my first thought was, "where am I?" Then I heard the sound of aircraft engines as the main force passed overhead and I was suspended somewhere over Germany. I expected to feel the parachute supports in front of my face but could not find them. I thought I was coming down without a parachute! I desperately groped around and located the one hook attachment and hung on. This attachment was well above my head; evidently the part of the parachute that once it opens rises to a position over your head. I wasn't aware of this. By this time I did not know how quickly I was descending. I was coming down without flying boots. As I looked up I saw the canopy of the parachute quite clearly in the bright moonlight. It was riddled in parts with a number of burnt small holes, some of them half an inch in diameter. It was terrifying because I was afraid that my descent might be too fast for a safe landing. Although the moon was bright I could not see the ground but there were several fires burning, which I took to be from our aircraft. The fires did not help me to judge my altitude because I did not know the size of them. I also had facial injuries and a nosebleed. These must have occurred when I was blown out of the aircraft.[5]

'As my thoughts dwelt on landing, I hit the ground with an almighty wallop and rolled backwards down a small hill. When I reached the bottom I regained my wind and could see hills silhouetted against the night sky. My neck and back were very painful and when I attempted to stand, my right leg collapsed. It was out of line just above the ankle and I knew it was broken. I must have then lost consciousness again and when I came to the moon was low in the sky behind the hills. I could not walk and waited for someone to arrive. I soon heard shouting in German and realized I had left Metheringham a few hours before where everyone spoke English and here I was for the first time listening to a German voice. I saw a torch about 200 yards away so I shouted back and the torch came towards me. A number of people arrived and the torch was shone in my face. I could make out both young and elderly men; one of the younger men started shouting and was about to hit me in the face with a rifle when he was stopped by one of the elderly men. One or two of them went off to search the wreckage and the others wrapped me in the parachute, placed me on a stretcher and carried me to a horse-drawn cart, which took me to a small village called Königsberg about 1,000 metres away.'

Flight Lieutenant Tim Woodman who, with his navigator-radar operator, Pat Kemmis, were in a Mosquito night fighter of 169 Squadron supporting the operation noted: 'Instead of the bomber stream being five miles wide it was more like fifty. Some had already been shot down and before I reached to the far side of the stream they were being shot down on my left. Masses of

'Window' were being tossed out of the bombers, which also jammed our radar. We tried three times but each time came up below a bomber, the rear-gunner spotting us the third time, his tracer coming uncomfortably close whilst his pilot did a corkscrew. It was hopeless. We were doing more harm than good. Ahead the bombers were being shot down one after another, some going all the way down in flames, some blowing up in the air, the rest blowing up as they hit the ground. I counted forty-four shot down on this leg to Nuremberg. What was happening behind I could only guess . . . I was inwardly raging at the incompetence of the top brass at Bomber Command.'

The 14 Lancasters of 61 Squadron were experiencing varied fortune. Near Cologne *R-Robert* flown by Donald Paul passed night fighter-beacon *Ida* and was attacked by a Ju 88 night fighter. Over the next 15 minutes vigorous corkscrewing by the pilot and good work by the gunners managed to stave off two further attacks. Flight Sergeant R. A. F. Griffin, the navigator, saw a stream of tracer bullets, probably from the mid-upper turret, going straight into the Ju 88's belly but with no apparent effect. They had heard that the Junkers had armour plating and their .303 bullets could not damage them. During the defensive manoeuvres the Lancaster had lost altitude and suffered severe damage to two engines and Paul had to shut them both down. Still losing height and down to 10,000 feet, the skipper had no alternative but to jettison his bombs and turn for home. Later, after throwing everything moveable out of the aircraft in order to maintain height and flying speed over the North Sea, Paul managed to land safely at Manston on the Kent coast. The 'Gen Men' of Squadron Leader Moss's crew were killed when Hauptmann Fritz Rudusch of 6./NJG 6, flying a Bf 110 night fighter, shot down their Lancaster near Rimbach, north-west of Fulda. Major Rudolf Schoenert of NJGr.10 flying a Ju 88 fitted with *Naxos* aircraft location equipment, which homed in on H_2S signals, detected *V-Victor*, flown by Pilot Officer Haste. Schoenert's crew followed the Australian's aircraft for over half an hour picking up intermittent H_2S signals and finally, when he saw the Lancaster heading for home at 20,000 feet he positioned his night fighter under the bomber and fired shells from his *Schräge Musik* weapon into *V-Victor*'s right wing tanks. The aircraft caught fire and crashed near Namur in Belgium. There were no survivors.

Leslie Cromarty aboard *Royal Pontoon* continues:

'As we flew south of Cologne at about 26,000ft, Len Whitehead the mid-upper gunner, and I, began reporting aircraft going down. Sid Jennings got a bit fed up with logging them after a while and told us that as there were so many they must be "scarecrows". As we began approaching the target area a Lancaster flew close alongside us. It was upside down and blazing like a comet. I asked Sid to come and look at this "scarecrow". We tried to turn away from it but it seemed to follow us. Then it slowly dipped and exploded. As we approached Nuremberg we were horrified to see the great spread of the target area. Most aircraft were turning and bombing too soon. We saw the last of the PFF aircraft going down with TIs pouring out of it. We continued turning on to the target but by the time we arrived all the markers had gone out. We began to circle. Sandy Lyons, the bomb-aimer, thought he saw either a railway station or yard and so we bombed that and left the target area. We continued to log aircraft going down as we flew along the "Long Leg".'

Meanwhile, *Q-Queenie* had crossed the enemy coast and was heading for the *Otto* night fighter beacon near Frankfurt. It was not long before searchlights probed the darkness and then the crew realized the absence of flak, which meant mainly one thing; night fighters. 'Pat' Patfield immediately started undoing the brown paper parcels of 'Window' and began shoving the small bundles through the small chute in the side of the fuselage to disrupt enemy radar defences. 'It wasn't long before maps, brown paper, string and myself began to get mixed up' he recalls. 'The blessed chute wasn't large enough to push the brown paper out as well! For the next half-hour or so very little happened and then there was an exchange of machine-gun fire to our port. Only a short exchange, but suddenly from that direction we saw a glow in the sky, small at first but soon becoming larger, until we could plainly make out the outline of a Lanc, burning fiercely. It continued flying steadily for a while and then turned and went down in a shallow dive. "Lanc gone down to port!" I yelled to the navigator, whose job it was to log such incidents. This was our first experience of real air-to-air combat and with a remark from the pilot, something like "Bugger me! Did you see that? Keep a lookout gunners". I know we all felt that funny feeling in the pit of our stomachs reserved for such occasions. It wasn't long before we saw more exchanges of gunfire. There we were, droning along feeling very much on our own one minute and the next being rudely awakened to the fact that this was definitely not the case and we were the hunted!

'Suddenly the whole sky before and above us was lit by what appeared to be huge fireworks. Fighter flares! We had heard all about these during training. They were the things most feared by bomber crews and here they were. Hanging in the sky like giant magnesium chandeliers, they were being dropped by German planes flying above the bomber stream in lanes three or four abreast and stretching out far in front of us. We then fully realized that we were far from being alone! Other bombers could be clearly seen on either side and ahead of us and it made us feel as naked as the day we were born, exposed to everything! Very soon combats could be seen taking place all over the sky. Sometimes there followed a ruddy glow lasting only a few seconds and ending in a terrific explosion. At others, like the first encounter we had seen, the bomber would burn steadily and begin to lose height. These were the lucky ones, or so we thought, as they were having enough time to bale out. We did in fact see two or three parachutes floating down from time to time. "Two going down to port and one to starboard" I passed this information back to the navigator for logging. I always admired the navigator in his tiny compartment, not being able to see what was going on but hearing it all over his intercom. In the midst of this, he was working calmly on such things as courses and wind speeds with his charts and pro-tractors etc., while such a commotion was going on outside. Sometimes, 20,000 feet below, a large, solitary explosion marking the end of a plane and perhaps its crew, could be seen as it hit the ground. Other explosions frequently occurred on the ground also, an exploding "stick" of bombs, which had been released from a bomber in distress. Although unavoidable in most cases, these should not have been released until the bomber had turned away from the stream as the incendiaries burning on the ground made the bombers stand out clearly to any fighter as they flew over. The battle raged fiercer, encounters all around, explosions and fires and at one time we counted 13 aircraft going down all at once.

'"Gunners, can you see any fighters?" the pilot kept asking. To which the usual reply was, "Not near enough to have a go at". I kept standing up in the front gun turret to man the front guns just above my head, but I did not see anything to have a go at.

'Scared? Of course I was, with a horrible sinking feeling in the pit of my stomach, would I see my 21st birthday next week? I wondered, surely we must be attacked!

'Without warning, over the intercom, we heard the gunners firing like mad and a yell from Bill, the rear-gunner, "Look out, skipper, three of 'em coming in!" At the same time there was a terrific explosion. Things whizzed around and there was a sickly smell of smoke and cordite. I was almost thrown on my back as the

aircraft tilted at a crazy angle and the nose went down. My first impressions were of small flames all around me and my face all wet and sticky. Blood, I thought but I seemed to be in one piece and felt no pain. This sticky mess turned out to be hydraulic oil from the gun turret, as a considerable part of it had disappeared and the severed pipes had spewed out their contents over me!

'We were still diving steeply when the pilot yelled, "I've got her under control but we're in a mess!" The gunners were swearing and I heard three voices saying rather feebly, "I've been hit skipper". It was Frank Devonshire, the flight engineer, Tommy the navigator and Jimmy the wireless op.

'In the nose I had already pulled aside the rubber cushioning on which I knelt, exposing the emergency hatch in readiness to make a quick exit. But the order didn't come, which was just as well, as I discovered afterwards that the hatch had been chewed up quite a bit and was wedged fast! Needless to say I had already hooked on my parachute! "Come up here as soon as you can Pat," yelled the pilot. I told him I had a bit of a fire amongst the brown paper strewn around me – the wrappings from the parcels of "Window" – but fortunately I managed to put the fires out, mainly by sitting on them! Then I clambered up into the main cabin. Frank was half-standing, half-kneeling and beat-ing furiously at a glow by his instrument panel; Tommy was slumped over the remains of his chart table and Jimmy Chapman, the wireless operator, was sitting by his set with blood streaming down his face. With some relief I saw Denny Freeman at the controls and noticed the shattered windscreen in front of him. "We can still fly", he said, "We've lost a lot of height. I'm turning north and then making for home. Keep a lookout gunners. The engines are still going but one's spitting."

'Eventually we got the fires out. They were only in the cabin and fortunately they were small. "Pat, we're over Germany so better get rid of the bombs. If we're going down we don't want to take them with us," said Denny. So clambering back into the nose I pressed the bomb "tit". I suppose Denny had opened the bomb doors! Down they went but as the indicator lamp didn't work in the release switches I couldn't tell if they had all gone. I clambered back down the fuselage, still with parachute on and lifted up the small inspection covers over the release hooks of each bomb position. One had hung up. It was the 4,000-pounder! Probing through the small opening with a short hooked length of wire the Air Ministry supplied for the purpose, I at last managed to release the "cookie".

'The next concern was for the injured. Jimmy helped me with the navigator. What we took to be a cannon shell had torn a huge hole in his chart table, taking a lot of his hand with it. We tied up his arm as best we could and got him to the "rest bed", half way down the fuselage. We then discovered that the escape hatch in the roof immediately above the rest bed was missing and an icy blast was coming through, though we didn't give it more thought at the time. We plugged in his oxygen and intercom, gave him a shot of morphia from the first aid kit, and went back to Frank. Jimmy insisted that he wasn't badly hurt but he didn't look too good so we decided he had better sit down by his radio to take it easy. He did but he started fiddling with the set and set about getting a "fix" to define our position.

'When I got to Frank, he was about "all in" and sitting on the fuselage floor. His right arm looked a mess. His flying suit around the elbow was badly torn and sticky with blood. My knowledge of first aid being limited to cut fingers, I was horrified to see bits of torn flesh and bone sticking out and was rather at a loss what to do. So I tore his sleeve open more and tied a thick bandage near the shoulder as a makeshift tourniquet. I gave him a shot of morphia and tied his arm up in a sling – all this in almost total darkness – then sat him down on the floor behind the pilot.'

E-Easy's crew in 44 Squadron were, according to John Chatterton, 'the lucky ones at the front end, having managed to slip through the deadly gap before the wolves gathered. We had ploughed on towards turning point "C" where we made a right-handed turn almost due south towards Nuremberg 76 miles away. Normally, a steep turn like this would have thrown off many fighters, but conditions this night so favoured them that they were able to follow round the corner and shoot down another 30 bombers. In the perfect conditions it was easy to follow the bomber stream and the aces among them managed to shoot down six or seven apiece[6] before they had to break off and refuel. At the target Scotty, the bomb-aimer, came into his own. He increased his "Windowing" rate to the maximum number of bundles per minute and about halfway through the 20-minute run to the target he handed the job over to Ken with obvious relief, and took up a prone position by the bombsight. But now another adverse factor was bedevilling the raid. The Met men, who had promised us high cloud to hide in on the long leg, had also predicted that Nuremberg would be clear of cloud for the attack. The marking force of Pathfinders were, therefore, stocked up with near-ground bursting TIs, which couldn't be seen through cloud and so when they opened the attack five minutes before zero hour these fell useless and unseen. Some of the markers carried a few "sky-markers", a parachute flare released above cloud so that the bomb-aimers could direct their bombs through a theoretical spot in the sky resulting in a fall on the target. Unfortunately, to be accurate, the flare release and bombing runs must be downwind and here we had a crosswind of 75 knots, so that when two very lonely red flares appeared dripping yellow blobs, Scotty gave me a stream of "left, lefts" in an attempt to follow them. This was no way to do a bombing run and I consulted the nav, who agreed that the town on his H_2S screen was drifting away to the right. I had to make a quick decision. "Right Jack, we'll drop them 'on the box'! Scotty, abandon bombing run. I'm turning onto 270°M."

'We headed back to Nuremberg and although the centre of towns gave a mushy picture, Jack was able to pick up the river and gave Scotty the "now" to drop the load which fell without trace through the cloud. I felt the exhilarating "twang" under my feet as the straining floor reasserted to normality and *Easy* surged upwards like a tired hunter taking the last fence after a muddy chase. I held the course for 30 seconds for the obligatory photoflash and camera run, both useless tonight, but which one day would earn the crew an aiming point photograph and 48-hour pass. In the middle of a normal raid this always seemed the longest half-minute of my life with searchlights and flak all around and a hideous inferno below. But here at Nuremberg it was quite un-real. A bit of flak about, the odd sky-marker still drifting on a reciprocal underneath and the occasional bump of a slipstream passing at 90 degrees to us. The latter reminded me that it was a bit dicey on a different course to everybody else, so I hastily turned on to 201°M for the 31 miles out of Nuremberg to position "D" where we thankfully took up a westerly heading that would take us home. The gunners reported that the target had livened up a bit after we left, but not very much and, after several minutes, they called our attention to another target away over to our right, which seemed to be cloud free and with a lot of action. Tongue in cheek I asked Jack if he was sure we had bombed Nuremberg and received the expected forceful reply, with added information that the burning town was probably Schweinfurt (we learned later that about one third of the force went there by mistake).'

Flight Sergeant Les Bartlett, bomb-aimer in Pilot Officer Michael Beetham DFC's[7] crew in 50 Squadron, which contributed 19 Lancasters, one of which crashed on take-off at Skellingthorpe, recalls:[8]

'Everything was quiet during the climb to 20,000 feet over the Channel. We crossed the enemy coast and as we drew level with the south of the Ruhr valley things began to happen. Enemy night fighter flares and their familiar red Very signals were all around us and in no time at all combats were taking place with aircraft going down in flames on all sides. So serious was the situation that I remember looking out at the other poor blighters going down and thinking to myself that it must be our turn next; it was just a question of time. We altered course for Nuremberg and I looked down on the starboard beam at the area over which we had just passed. It looked like a battlefield. There were kites burning on the deck all over the place with bombs going off where they had not been jettisoned and incendiaries burning across the whole area – such a picture of aerial disaster I had not seen before and certainly hope never to see again. On the way to the target the winds became changeable and we almost ran into the defences of Schweinfurt but altered course in time. The defences of Nuremberg were nothing to speak of; a modest amount of heavy flak, which did not prevent us doing a normal approach and we were able to see the TIs dropped by the Pathfinders and score direct hits with our 4,000lb "cookie" and our 1,000lb bombs and incendiaries.'

Squadron Leader Neville Sparks DFC AFC, one of the Pathfinders of 83 Squadron, looked on horrified at the shambles over Nuremberg. 'As was the custom, we left England after the stream had gone and, highly laden, we passed them on the way. We were flying at 19,000 feet and the main force were 3,000 feet above us. Contrary to the forecasts there was no layer cloud. The forecast was for the moon to be at about half its full strength. In fact it was about as bright as it could be. The night too was as clear as a bell – no clouds – with fantastic visibility. Anyway, we were catching up with the force on the second leg of the trip – the 250 miles between Charleroi and Fulda – when the slaughter began and we had an incredible view. In the 60 or 90 minutes after midnight we saw sparkles of cannon fire, some distant and some almost directly above us. This was followed by explosions, fires, plunging planes and a scattering of fires on the ground as far as the eye could see. I saw three planes blow up as they collided and one of them, a Pathfinder, blazed like a torch as its flares ignited. My navigator, Doc Watson, marked 57 ticks in his log on the way to Nuremberg. Each tick was a four-engined bomber we had seen shot down by German fighters.'

'On this occasion' says Sergeant Roland Hammersley, 'the Pathfinders were hardly required, as the moon was brilliant and other aircraft were plainly visible nearby. Although our wave received little attention during the attacks we could see the battles taking place around us and there were a considerable number of aircraft being shot down as we flew on deeper into Germany. The Pathfinder aircraft were about five minutes late on target and their marking was rather scattered. However, my crew bombed from 21,000 feet and "Mack" MacKinnon, the flight engineer, informed me later that we had hit our target. The flight home was a long haul south of Stuttgart, north of Strasbourg and Nancy, heading towards the French coast. We crossed the coast near Dieppe and so back to Lincolnshire and base. At debriefing we told of the aircraft that we observed being shot down. One of our own crews, pilot Flight Lieutenant E. W. Tickler CGM was missing.'[9]

'On the way back,' continues Squadron Leader Neville Sparks 'a powerful head wind blew up unpredicted at briefing. We were diverted to Downham Market and I rushed to the CO there who happened to be my cousin "Lofty" Cousins to tell him that we had seen planes fall from the sky like pigeons dipped in lead. Doc Watson showed his log to the CO who immediately got on to the AOC and told him it had been a "killer" raid. We did not know then that it was the worst in the history of the RAF but we were pretty sick about what we had witnessed. There were rumours about a leak but how could you tell what was true? It certainly looked like an ambush from where we were watching. It was the most terrible thing I had ever seen, the more so as it had a certain wild, primitive beauty about it.'

With their eyes peeled, Pilot Officer Michael Beetham's[10] crew were able to successfully get out of the target area which, as Flight Sergeant Les Bartlett[11] says, 'was always a dodgy business' and set course for Skellingthorpe. 'However, the varying winds continued to cause us a dance and we found ourselves approaching Calais instead of being 80 miles further south so we had a slight detour to avoid their defences. Once near the coast it was nose down for home as fast as possible but even then we saw some poor bloke "buy it" over the Channel. Back in debriefing we heard the full story of our squadron's effort: four aircraft lost with another written off on take-off. It was the worst night for our squadron and for Bomber Command.'[12]

Anxious eyes at bases throughout the Midlands and north-east England scanned the horizon for returning Lancasters and Halifaxes. Fourteen bombers reached England only to crash with further loss of life. At Bardney where 16 Lancasters had been dispatched, one was missing[13] and Pilot Officer H. Forrest limped home with a dead mid-upper gunner after being attacked by a night fighter near Beacon *Ida*. The night fighter had sprayed the area between the rear door and the end of the bomb bay and the whole of the fuselage up to the mid-upper turret was in flames. Sergeant B. Pinchin the rear-gunner could see the mid-upper gunner getting down from his turret and he began crawling up to the front of the aircraft. Forrest decided to jettison the bombs and dive to put the flames out. At 13,000 feet the fire finally went out. Forrest stayed with the bomber stream and carried on to the target and back to Bardney where Sergeant B. T. Utting, who was from Fakenham in Norfolk, was removed from the aircraft. He was apparently unmarked but the medical officer found that a small fragment of cannon shell had entered his stomach and cut the small intestine.[14]

E-Easy in 44 Squadron may have 'lacked an aero-dynamic finesse' but the Lancaster lived up to its name and it got back safely to Dunholme Lodge, even if it was not as quickly as John Chatterton would have liked.

'At last over the sea we had put the nose down a fraction to gain speed without caning the engines or spoiling Ken's proud fuel record of over one air mile per gallon. With these tactics and a bit of navigator's log cooking in our beloved *Y-Yorker,* we could normally rely on being the first back. (Our ground crew had a considerable bet on it.) But when, at last, I called for landing instructions I was a bit narked to hear my mate, Australian Roy Manning in *Q-Queenie,* get 'No. 1 to land'. And so to interrogation – just a normal sort of trip – 1,500 miles, seven and a half hours and the Squadron lost two aircraft.'

Of the 17 Lancasters of 106 Squadron that had been dispatched from Metheringham, three failed to return, all probably falling victim to a night fighter. Squadron Leader Doubleday was first back at Waddington and Air Marshal Cochrane called him up to the control tower.

He asked, 'How did it go?'

I said, 'Jerry got a century before lunch today.' He didn't quite – he got 95.

Sixty-four Lancasters and 31 Halifaxes (11.9 per cent of the force dispatched) were lost (and 10 bombers crash-landed in England); the worst Bomber Command loss of the war.[15]

For those on stand down, waiting for news was intolerable. At East Kirkby, Pilot Officer J. 'Cas' Castagnola DSO DFC of 57 Squadron, who had flown the Berlin raids, had a strong feeling at this time, and he was not a suspicious type, that the Germans knew

several operations in advance. 'A number of times when we were at full stretch and most vulnerable we would find the German fighters already there above us, waiting. Specialist raids were never talked about but the main force mass raids were different. It could happen quite simply. Maybe a crew would be stood down from a raid for some reason and they would naturally head for the "local" to celebrate. Someone would say, "You not going today?" And they would answer, unthinking, "No thank God. It's Nuremberg via Fulda and they're welcome to it." No leak was intended but we were only kids. You could certainly hear such a conversation about 5 Group too often for comfort in any one of the three pubs we used in Boston. There was the Red Cow in Market Square; the White Hart in the town centre and, in another pub known as Rose and Twink, the landlord had two lovely daughters.

By the time *Royal Pontoon* began approaching Coningsby they were about half an hour late and the crew thought that they would be worrying about them thinking they were lost. Just north of Paris the crew had seen a number of searchlights round a town. They had all been very quiet up to that point and Les Cromarty thought that the skipper must have thought that they were all dozing off because he dived among the search-lights and Len Whitehead had a ten-minute shoot-out with them. Nevertheless, there was little the mid-upper gunner could say about the Nuremberg raid. It was one that Whitehead and most of the others tried to black out from their minds. 'We were just sitting ducks' is all he would say about the operation though rear-gunner Les Cromarty recalls the landing back at base where another shock awaited him:

'Our call sign was "Starlight" and we used to land on the number system. When we called up we expected to get at least 15 or 16 and be stacked, but instead we got, "Number one, pancake". We just could not believe it and so we called again, but got the same reply. We were in fact the first to land, shortly after an aircraft from 619 Squadron crashed off the end of the runway. One or two more aircraft landed but I think most of the others landed at other airfields.' Word came in that Don Paul had put down at Manston. Only 10 crews in 61 Squadron reported bombing the target. One of them was Ted Stone, who now took up his CO's promised flight home and he headed for Bridgewater a few hours after the debriefing. *Mickey the Moocher* made it back after running into problems returning over the North Sea, having encountered stormy conditions off the north Norfolk coast. The Lancaster was struck by lightning on the front turret causing Pilot Officer

J. A. Forrest to lose control and the aircraft plummeted towards the sea. While in a blinded and shocked state, the Australian pilot ordered the crew to bale out while he tried to pull the aircraft out of the dive. Forrest managed to regain control at 1,000 feet and he immediately countermanded the order to bale out. Unfortunately, it was too late to save the lives of the mid-upper gunner, Flight Sergeant Harold W. Pronger and wireless operator, Sergeant L. Darben, who was from Walthamstow, London. They had already parachuted into the sea and were presumed drowned. This took the number of missing aircrew to 16.[16] The ground crew told Les Cromarty that his friend Harold Pronger, who was from Bundaberg, Queensland and the WOp/ AG, had baled out over the North Sea. Cromarty wanted to go out on a search right away but the ASR section told him that because the water temperature was so low no one could survive for more than an hour. 'I think that the worst thing about those raids was losing one's friends. After a while you just became hardened to it but eventually you just stopped making close friends with anyone outside your own crew.'

There was no sign of the two Lancasters that were overdue.

From the time of being hit, *Q–Queenie*'s crew had forgotten about fighters and the pandemonium. It was just luck that they were not attacked again. All of the able bodied on board were working feverishly to save lives and get *Queenie* home, even if it meant that some of them had to perform tasks they were unaccustomed to, as 'Pat' Patfield recalls:

'The bomb-aimer, being second navigator among other things, the pilot asked me to do what I could about navigating us home. The chart table was a shambles, with torn maps, quite a bit of blood about, no protractors or any other navigation instruments to be seen anywhere. This wasn't a bit like the navigation exercises I'd done during training. And the crew was hoping I would get them home! Fortunately, I had the bit of the chart showing our last position worked out just before being hit. Knowing that we had turned north and roughly taking the ground speed of the aircraft and approximate time since turning, I made a guess at the distance we'd travelled north. Then I measured this from the scale on the chart with my finger! I was able to put a cross on the chart, which looked all right. I made a guess at the drift from the flight plan and passed the course to the pilot. I was still trying to establish our true position when Jimmy passed me a bit of paper with a position written on it. Thank Heaven he had got his set to work and obtained a fix.

I took the scrap of paper and had great difficulty in trying to work out which was longitude and which was latitude. I tried to plot this fix but I didn't succeed.

'The next thing I knew was finding myself under the remains of the chart table and hearing the pilot calling over the R/T, "Mayday! Mayday!" This was the distress call for immediate assistance. I realized then that we must be over England but what a short journey! Only a few minutes before we had been over Germany, or so I thought! Anyway, what was I doing here on the floor and I attempted to get up. "Pat's coming round" I heard Jimmy say as I saw him coming to help me up. Oh my head! It was splitting, or so it seemed! "You passed out", said Jimmy "and you have been out a long time. You started dancing about soon after I gave you a second 'fix' and then flopped out on the floor. I couldn't see any sign of injury but I then saw that your oxygen mask had two fairly big holes in it (shrapnel or bullets, we found out later), so I guessed you'd passed out from lack of oxygen, but we daren't come down too low at the time."

'That was it then. No wonder it had seemed a short journey back! Naturally, when safe to descend where normal breathing was possible, the pilot had done so and I'd eventually come round. What a time to have a sleep!

'The pilot was still calling "Mayday, Mayday". Then came an answer, "Searchlights will home you".

'On my feet now, with nothing worse than a sickly headache, I saw from the cabin windows searchlights wavering from the vertical position almost to the ground, like a giant arm beckoning. Following these we soon saw a cone of three searchlights poised stationary. These marked the 'drome. Shortly, over the R/T the controller called us. "This is Horsham St Faith. Another plane is landing. Do a circuit and land." We almost cried with relief! To me this call made me feel much better. We were over or at least very nearly over, Norwich, my hometown. Horsham St Faith was in the suburbs. I really felt that I was home.

'Again the controller's voice but not with the message we had hoped for. "*Q-Queenie*, runway blocked – proceed to Foulsham aerodrome." Then they gave us a course to fly. We came to the conclusion that the other aircraft landing at Horsham was possibly a crippled bomber from the same raid. Foulsham was only a few minutes' flying time away and we seemed to be flying fairly well so the pilot acknowledged and off we flew. Very shortly we could see another cone of three searchlights and so as we approached we called up Foulsham. Answering us, they told us it was clear to land.

' "Undercarriage going down" said the pilot. "Blast, the indicator isn't working!" (This was the green light on his panel, which lit up when the wheels were locked down.) The warning horn was sounding, which should have stopped if the wheels were properly locked in the down position.) He looked out of his side window at the port wheel. It seemed down OK. "How about the starboard, Pat?" he called. Well, it was down but it didn't seem to be fully down and I told the pilot so. He swung the aircraft about, as much as he dared in an endeavour to make it lock down but it wouldn't.

' "Get ready for crash landing. I'm going down," said the pilot. Jimmy went to the rest bed to hang onto Tommy while I sat down with Frank with my arm around him, behind the pilot's seat. "Here we go, hold tight," yelled the pilot. A sickening lurch as we hit the runway, more bumps, but we seemed to be doing OK. The pilot was holding the plane over onto the port wheel, which was apparently locked down. The starboard wheel was flapping about uselessly. As we lost flying speed the starboard wing began to drop and then the wingtip dug into the ground. This swung us completely round as we grated to a stop. Our fear now was fire!

'Getting up we gathered our wits and made our way down the fuselage to the exit door. The gunners had just opened it when voices outside shouted, "OK, we'll get you out" and, illuminated by the headlights of a jeep and an ambulance, we saw figures clambering in to help us. Fortunately no fire occurred. Poor old *Queenie* had crumpled quite a bit but didn't catch fire thank goodness.

'Little was said as the injured were taken in the ambulance to sick quarters and we who were not injured were taken in a jeep to the crew room, where a number of officers including the CO flocked round us with cigarettes and soon, mugs of hot tea. "Put something in it" said the CO. "I reckon they need it." And out of the blue came a bottle of whisky and they put a very generous amount in our tea! With apologies they told us they'd have to spend a little time interrogating us about the raid before we could go to bed. This over, we were taken to a Nissen hut where beds had been prepared. Sleep? What an effort. I kept being sick in a pail, which I had asked to be left near the bed. My head was going round and round and I felt, as if it would burst. Eventually I slept. When we got up at about midday, on reporting to the CO, we were told we'd be flown back to Coningsby. We went to the sick quarters to see about the injured but we were not allowed to see them. The MO (Medical Officer) told us that Jimmy had quite a lot of small pieces of shrapnel in his back

and just under the scalp. Frank's elbow was badly smashed and he had shrapnel in his side. Tommy's hand was also badly smashed and (I believe) frost-bitten, caused by the icy draught blowing on him from the escape hatch opening. I never saw either of them again.

'We then went to have a look at *Queenie*. There she was, lying out there in the middle of the aerodrome, lying over onto a crumpled wing, her two starboard propellers bent over the engine nacelles. We clambered into her and looked around. What a mess and holes were everywhere. How it was that the engines kept functioning, we'll never know. Those three German fighters had riddled her but she had brought us home though she was now a write-off.'

Later that day the crew of *Q-Queenie* flew back to Coningsby and they were interrogated. All four un-injured members of the crew were given a fortnight's leave commencing the next morning. Denny Freeman was awarded the DFC for bringing the crippled Lanc home safely, while Jimmy Chapman was awarded the CGM for getting his wireless set working again, obtaining fixes, plotting them and helping to navigate after 'Pat' Patfield had passed out.

The crew of *Q-Queenie* never flew all together again. Frank Devonshire was invalided out of the service and 'Tommy' Thomas never flew again either. Flight Sergeant Bill Smith regrettably never had the oppor-tunity to take up his new 'career' as a 'gigolo'. Sadly he was killed in action on the night of 7/8 July during the operation to St-Leu-d'Esserent when the Lancaster he was flying in was hit by flak and exploded in mid air killing the entire crew. He is buried at Marissel French National Cemetery. Flying Officer Denny Freeman and four of his crew were killed in action on 24 September when his Lancaster was hit by flak and crashed into the sea during the operation to attack strong points at Calais. Derek Patfield was not surprised Denny Freeman got killed 'because he was a bit lax in his discipline. They went low over the French coast and shot up some naval installations and they got him. He shouldn't have done it, but he was that type of bloke. He was a good pilot and wouldn't have any talking on the trip unless it was essential.' 'Pat' Patfield did another 30 raids after Nuremberg. Although they were not without incident none would be quite as bad as 30/31 March, which became known as 'the biggest chop night' of the war for Bomber Command.

'Three operations flown', wrote Sergeant Roland Hammersley 'and I had seen the loss of 176 crews from Bomber Command. No good news for the rest of us. We were granted leave and once we had obtained clearance from the squadron office, I was away into Lincoln. I hitched a ride in a lorry and then on to London and Watford by train making the final leg home on a bus. I had already said to the lorry driver that we would most likely find that the Nuremberg night operation would show heavy casualties and when the news was out, my thoughts were confirmed. Dad was on leave and with Mum we visited his favourite pub, "The Oddfellows" in Apsley End. The company was good and cheerful. It was during the evening that I told Dad for the first time that I was serving on a bomber squadron and flying operations. The news was out that there had been considerable casualties on the Nuremberg raid and I told him that I had flown that operation, asking him not to tell Mum. However, he could not keep the news to himself and I found him telling all and sundry in the pub. "My boy was on that raid last night!" The news soon filtered through to Mum and then the tears flowed. I felt sorry that I had said anything, but by then it was too late.'

Notes

1. See *The Nuremberg Raid* by Martin Middlebrook (Penguin, 1973).
2. Lancaster crews were required as 'supporters' for the PFF Lancasters of the 'Flare Force'. This meant arriving at the target at the same time but flying at 2,000 ft below the 'Flare Force' to attract the flak and enable them to carry out a straight and level run. After drawing the flak the 'supporters' then re-crossed the target to drop their bombs.
3. Later Wing Commander Doubleday DSO DFC who commanded 61 Squadron.
4. Night fighting in good visibility was ideal and the weather over Belgium and eastern France was 0/10ths to 4/10ths thin cloud while Holland and the Ruhr were cloudless. At Nuremberg there was 10/10ths cloud at 1,600–12,000 feet but the cloud veiled at 16,000 feet with generally good altitude visibility. Jamming was carried out on a large scale but Mosquito spoof attacks on Cologne, Frankfurt and Kassel were identified for what they were because, to the German defences, they were apparently flying without H₂S. The heavies on the other hand could quite clearly be followed on radar by their H₂S bearings. As the bomber stream was clearly recognized from the start, it was attempted to switch in night fighters as far west as possible. All units of 3 JD were switched in over radio beacon Bonn. 2 JD was brought near via radio beacons Bonn and Osnabrück and switched in by radio beacons Bonn and Frankfurt respectively. 1 JD was brought near via radio beacons Bonn and Harz and switched in by radar station north of Frankfurt, as was 7 JD. Single-engined units from Oldenburg, Rheine and Bonn were directed via radio beacon Frankfurt to radio beacon Nürnberg. Night fighter units from Ludwigslust, Zerbst, Jüterborg and Wiesbaden were led directly to radio beacon Nürnberg. Altogether, 246 twin- and single- engined night fighters were engaged. Despite the British jamming the first interception of the bomber stream in the area south of Bonn was successful. From there on in the bomber stream was hit repeatedly and the majority of the losses occurred in the Giessen-Fulda-Bamberg area. A staggering 82 bombers were lost en route to and near the target.
5. Apart from Starkey, only Sergeant Wally Paris, the bomb-aimer, survived when he was hurtled from the exploding aircraft. Pilot Officer Starkey and his crew were possibly shot down by a Bf 110 flown by Oberleutnant Martin 'Tino' Becker, *Staffelkapitän*, 2./NJG 6 as the 37th aircraft to go down on the Nuremberg raid. Becker and his *Bordfunker* Unteroffizier Karl-Ludwig Johanssen had taken off from Finthen airfield for a *Zahme Sau* mission. (I. and II./NJG 6 operated 19 *Zahme Sau* Bf 110s and four in *Himmelbett* sorties.) They were guided by 3 JD into the bomber stream to the south of radio beacon *Ida* whereupon they intercepted and shot down six bombers between 00.20 and 00.50 hours with their *Schräge Musik* cannons. After returning to base to re-fuel and re-arm, Becker and Johanssen took off on a second sortie and they claimed their seventh kill of the night when they destroyed a Halifax south of Luxembourg. Next day Becker received news that he was awarded the *Ritterkreuz*.
6. Hauptmann Martin Becker, *Staffelkapitän* 2./NJG 6, shot down seven for his 20th to 26th *Abschüsse*, which earned him the *Ritterkreuz*.
7. Beetham's citation for the DFC included a mention of the Augsburg raid on 25/26 February 1944. He and his crew completed their bomb run and turned for home when the flight engineer said that the coolant temperature on one of the port engines had begun to rise alarmingly. Beetham cut the power and feathered the propeller. Flying on three engines they lost height and flew 600 miles over enemy territory alone. Beetham went on to fly a total of 30 operations, 10 of them to Berlin. See *Vulcan 607* by Rowland White (Bantam, 2006. Corgi, 2007).
8. Diary entry. See *The Lancaster Story* by Peter Jacobs (Cassell, 2002).
9. A Bf 110 flown by Oberleutnant Helmuth Schulte of II/NJG 5 shot down Tickler's crew who were on their 15th operation. Four crew were killed. Tickler and two others survived and they were taken prisoner. Only 110 Conspicuous Gallantry Medals (Flying) were awarded in the Second World War. When it was instituted in November 1942 it was to right the anomaly that existed between officers and NCO airmen in that there was no equivalent to the DSO, which was awarded to commissioned officers only. Nothing existed for the non-commissioned airmen between the DFM and the VC.
10. In 1982 during the Falklands War, Air Chief Marshal Sir Michael Beetham GCB CBE DFC AFC was in his fifth year as Chief of the Air Staff and he initiated the plan to use Avro Vulcans in *Black Buck* raids against Port Stanley. He retired with rank of a Marshal of the Royal Air Force.
11. Later in his tour of operations Les Bartlett was commissioned and he was awarded the DFM.
12. Diary entry. See Jacobs, op. cit. In all, 50 Squadron lost three Lancasters missing in action in addition to the one piloted by Flight Sergeant G. C. Bucknell that crashed on take-off. One returned damaged. Fifteen men were killed and seven taken prisoner. All four of 156 Squadron's losses resulted from actions by the German night fighters. A Ju 88 piloted by Oberleutnant Köberich of II/NJG 2 shot down ND476 piloted by Captain F. Johnsen from Bergen, Norway. All eight crew, who were on

their 25th operation, were killed. Oberleutnant Köberich also shot down ND406, flown by Warrant Officer J. A. Murphy. Murphy and five of the crew who were on the 19th operation of their second tour were killed. One man survived and was taken prisoner. A night fighter shot down ND492 flown by Pilot Officer L. Lindley. Lindley survived but all six of his crew died. A night fighter, probably flown by Oberleutnant Martin 'Tino' Becker of I/NJG 6, shot down ND466 flown by Squadron Leader P. R. Goodwin. Four of Goodwin's crew, who were on the 17th operation of their second tour, were killed. Goodwin and the two others were taken prisoner. 514 Squadron had dispatched 19 Lancasters. Four were shot down by night fighters and two crashed, one near Sawbridgeworth, Hertfordshire, and the other at Waterbeach, and one Lancaster was damaged. Twenty men were killed, 10 taken prisoner and six injured in the crashes. Pilot Officer Evan W. Chitty, RAAF, was making his final approach at Waterbeach when his crew heard the control tower in their earphones. 'Who's that bloody fool making a right-hand circuit?' Another pilot was desperate to get down and had cut in. Chitty had no option but to open up his engines and overshoot but at that moment, a flurry of snow caused him to lose sight of the ground. A few seconds later there was a horrible shudder as the wheels were torn off and then the Lancaster, in a nose-down attitude, hit the ground hard. Chitty and four more escaped with various injuries. It was some time before Sergeant J. Shepherd, the mid-upper gunner

could be found and lastly the body of Sergeant A. B. Pattison, the bomb-aimer, lying crushed under a wing. It was never discovered how he had got into this position. See *The Bomber Command War Diaries* by Martin Middlebrook and Chris Everitt. Chitty formed another crew and he and this crew were lost without trace on the operation to Caen on 30 July 1944.

13. W5006 piloted by Flying Officer J. G. R. Ling was shot down by Oberleutnant Martin Drewes, *Staffelkapitän*, 11./NJG 1 with the loss of all except one of the crew, who were on their 25th operation.

14. See Middlebrook, op. cit.

15. The Nuremberg raid took *Nachtjagd*'s; total for March to 269 RAF bombers destroyed. Oberleutnant Martin Drewes, *Staffelkapitän*, 11./NJG 1 claimed three Lancasters. Oberleutnant Witzleb and Oberleutnant Walter Prues of III./NJG 1 each claimed a *Viermot* at 00.12 and 00.31 hours respectively. Oberleutnant Helmuth Schulte of 4./NJG 5 achieved four victories and Feldwebel Rudolf Frank of 3./NJG 3, three. *Nachtjagd* lost just nine Bf 110s and Ju 88s (four of which went down to return fire). Since the start of the Battle of Berlin Bomber Command had lost 1,047 aircraft and another 1,682 returned with severe battle damage.

16. Flight Lieutenant J. A. Forrest and five of his crew were KIA on the night of 24/25 June 1944 on the raid on Prouville. A seventh crew member survived and he was taken prisoner.

Chapter 9

Night Fighter Nights

As I lay there I saw a stream of sparks pass a few feet above the cockpit, from back to front and going up at a slight angle. This caused me some confusion. If the sparks were from a burning engine they were going the wrong way. It was some little time before I realized that the sparks were in fact tracer shells from a fighter that I did not know was attacking us. The illusion that the tracer shells were going upwards was no doubt caused by the fact that our Lancaster was going into an uncontrolled, screaming dive, but because of the slow-motion effect that I was experiencing, I did not appreciate this fact. This whole episode had taken 2 or 3 seconds at most, then the slow-motion effect began to wear off, and I became aware of the screams of the bomb-aimer. Lying in the bomb-aimer's position in the nose of the aircraft, he had caught the full force of the explosion, although this was not immediately apparent.

Sergeant C. H. 'Chick' Chandler, flight engineer

'*Achtung, Achtung!*'
'*Lisa-Marie 7*'-'*Rolf*'-*Marie 6.*
'*Rolf*'-*Lisa-Marie 5*'-'*Marie 4*'-*Rolf*-(more).
'*Rolf*-'*Stop*'-*Marie 2*'
'*A little Lisa*-(same height)-*Lisa-Marie 1*,
'*5-Rolf-Marie 1*'
'*A little Siegfried* (climb)-*Rolf-Marie 1*'
'*Lisa-Lisa*-*Stop*-*Marie 0,8-a little Rolf*'.

Hauptmann Helmut Bergmann listened impatiently but attentively to the long litany of instructions from his *Bordfunker* crouched in the cockpit of their Bf 110G-4 night fighter as they continued their *Helle Nachtjagd* (night chase) across the French countryside. Thirty minutes earlier the 23 year old *Staffelkapitän* had lifted the Messerschmitt with its deadly electronic wizardry and heavy firepower off from the 8./NJG 4 base at Juvincourt and he had then climbed at maximum rate to an operational height of 5,300 metres. Their route was to take them to one of the *Himmelbett Räume* (four poster bed boxes) each one of them a theoretical spot in the sky, in which one to three fighters orbited a radio beacon waiting for bombers to appear. Each box, about 20 miles square, which had names like *Hamster*, *Eisbär* (Polar Bear) and *Tiger* (around Terschelling Island), was a killing-zone in the path of hundreds of incoming prey. All approaches to occupied Europe and Germany were divided into circular and partly overlapping areas, which took full advantage of Bomber Command's tactic in sending bombers singly and on a broad front and not in concentrated streams. The *Himmelbett Räume* and the *Nachtjäger* were orchestrated by *Jägerleitoffiziers* (JLOs or GCI-controllers) in Battle Opera Houses. Though the JLOs were far removed from the actual battles, high tiered rows of *Leuchtspukers* or 'Light Spitter girls' projected information onto a huge screen for them and operators moved the plots on the *Seeburg* plotting tables.

The *Jägerleitoffizier* announced monotonously at regular intervals, 'No *Kuriere* in sight' and Bergmann had to continue orbiting. Bergmann, who had sixteen confirmed night *Abschüsse* (victories) was impatient to add to his score and he probably did not concern himself with the bombers' destinations. The Nuremberg raid had brought, for a brief period, the virtual cessation of heavy attacks and Bomber Command seemed to mainly be focusing on transportation targets and *Luftwaffe* airfields in France and Belgium. Tonight, 10/11 April, 908 aircraft were to attack five marshalling yards, four in France and one in Belgium. Although the *Nachtjagdgeschwader* did not know the actual numbers involved, the night predators were unconcerned, satisfied in the knowledge that there would be scores of ubiquitous black '*Fat Cars*' for them to aim for.

Bergmann was one of many who eagerly awaited the code word from the *Jägerleitoffizier* that would send him scurrying into action in *Krebs* his allotted box. Suddenly, as if by magic, 'Have *Kurier* for you, *Kirchturm* 10 (1,000 metres), course 300°, *Kurier* flying from two to 11'[1] sounded in the earphones of his *Bordfunker*.

Startled but composed, the three-man crew reacted with excitement and enthusiasm. According to the information from the *Jägerleitoffizier* they were only a few kilometres behind a British bomber! The enemy aircraft had been picked up on *Würzburg* ground radar, fixed on the plotting table and transmitted to the Hauptmann and his crew stalking the bomber. As soon as the *Bordfunker* picked up contact on his *Lichtenstein* radar set, he transmitted '*Emil-Emil*' to alert his JLO. But there was no indication yet on the *Lichtenstein*. It was 02.20 hours. They hoped to reach the '*Fat Car*' before it left the range of the *Würzburg* ground radar.

'1,000 metres, 800 metres, 500, 400, 300 metres!' Power off and minimum speed in order not to overtake him, Bergmann had to attack from behind and that at the dangerous rear turret of the *Viermot*!

'There he is!'

Their eyes looked out and focused on a black shape of the Britisher. Small, bluish exhaust flames made it easier to keep the target in sight. Four engines, twin tail, were recorded almost subconsciously. No sudden movement, that might attract their attention. Calm now! Guns armed? Night sight switched on? Everything OK! Now Bergmann could see that it was an Avro Lancaster. He applied a little more power and approached him cautiously. He was exactly behind him at about 100 metres' range. The rear turret was clearly recognizable. His *Bordfunker* kept silent.

'*Pauke! Pauke!*' ('Kettledrums! Kettledrums!')

Bergmann had obtained visual contact of his target. It was a Lancaster, crossing gently from starboard to port. Bergmann's *Bordfunker* immediately transmitted '*Ich beruhe*'. Then they closed in rapidly for the kill. The equipment was checked and the four machine guns and two MG-FF 2cm cannon were loaded and cocked. At the *Bordfunker*'s feet were ammunition drums with 75 rounds each for the pair of deadly cannon. Now the *Lichtenstein* screen was aglow with the green time base and the ground blips, which also showed their altitude.

'250, 200, 150 metres.' A slipstream shook the Messerschmitt. They were close!

At 100 metres Bergmann pressed the gun button on the stick and was startled at the rattle of the cannon. He stayed behind the great night bird firing and observing the projectiles striking the rear turret and the fuselage. Strikes peppered the fuselage and danced along the wing

root. An equally short burst of brightly coloured tracer disappeared into the Lancaster's wing and fuselage. He must have been hit! The Lanc burst into flames. Doomed, it fell away to port in a flaming death dive, impacting in a French field near Vieux Mesnil.

'*Horrido!*' ('Tallyho') exclaimed Bergmann over R/T to ground control to announce his first success of the night.

Bergmann twisted and turned the 110, looking for more '*Fat Cars*'. Ten minutes later the crew found what they were looking for. It was another Lancaster. Another burst and it went down a few kilometres north of Salarnes. '*Horrido!*' South-east of Sailly five minutes later they downed yet another Lancaster. Cries of '*Horrido!*' filled the airwaves once again. Bergmann's fourth victim went down to his guns north-north-west of Achiet-le-Petit. It had been only 23 minutes since the first encounter. Just seven minutes later a fifth Lancaster was destroyed in about as many seconds and fuel from its ruptured tanks ignited and lit up the night sky with a reddish hue. The stricken Lanc impacted at Beauquesne. Four minutes later Bergmann made it six. The downed Lancaster's engines buried themselves deep into the French earth near Vignacourt. North of Guignemicourt their seventh and final victim, all of them Lancasters en route to the marshalling yards at Aulnoye, went down in a screaming death dive. It was now 03.06.

Naxos and *Flensburg* equipment homing onto H_2S equipment and the *Monica* tail-warning device might have identified some, if not all, of Bergmann's victims. Bomber crews were warned about this possibility and they were instructed not to leave sets on too long but the one sided encounter with the night fighter had lasted a devastating 46 minutes, with five victims being dispatched in the first 30 minutes. It may be that the Hauptmann had downed some of them, if not all, or if out of ammunition, he may well have given his *Bordschütze* free range with his two MG-FF 2cm cannon. Changing ammunition drums in a twisting and turning night fighter would have made his task almost impossible but not if the pilot pulled alongside to allow the *Bordschütze* to blaze away. In any event all seven *Viermots* took his score to 23 and counted towards the *Staffelkapitän*'s coveted *Ritterkreuz*.[2]

Altogther the raids on the night of 10/11 April cost Bomber Command 19 aircraft. Greater destruction however, occurred at their targets. At Aulnoye 340 houses were destroyed or damaged in the attack on the marshalling yards and 14 French civilians were killed. At Ghent, where the Merelbeke-Melle railway yards on the main line to Brussels were hit, losses to Belgian civilians was even greater, when bombs flattened over 580 buildings including seven schools, a convent and an orphanage and over 1,000 other buildings were damaged, causing 428 deaths and 309 injured. There was destruction too at Kirmington, where 22 Lancasters of 166 Squadron took off for the raid on Aulnoye. As the fifth Lancaster roared along the runway a few minutes after 23.00 a wing dipped. Careering to one side it lurched from the runway. Strained by the momentum of the heavy bomb load, the undercarriage collapsed and the fuselage ploughed along the ground for a few yards before coming to rest. Pilot Officer D. C. Gibbons' crew, uninjured, jumped out only just in time as it burst into flames. With all four tanks blazing the fire crew, who had raced up in their tender, realized that it was hopeless. Since the crew was safe, they withdrew to await the explosion, which so damaged the runway that it was unserviceable and the remaining 17 of the squadron's aircraft could not take-off.[3]

At East Kirkby Ron Walker's crew, who had just returned from leave, were one of 14 crews in 57 Squadron who bombed the St Pierre-des-Corps railway marshalling yards at Tours in bright moonlight. They had to make two bombing runs over the target before they were certain that they could aim their 13,000lb bomb loads without killing and injuring French civilians in the vicinity. The yards were seriously damaged and there were no reports of any French casualties. Walker's crew were not troubled the following day when they were on the battle order with 10 other crews to fly a night raid on Aachen in *Q-Queenie*, loaded up with 13,200lbs of high explosive. It proved a successful trip in spite of the German defences, who shot down nine Lancasters.[4]

At Coningsby since the beginning of 1944, 617 Squadron, now commanded by Wing Commander Geoffrey Leonard Cheshire DSO** DFC had successfully employed the tactic of marking and destroying small industrial targets at night, using flares dropped by a Lancaster in a shallow dive at low level. Cheshire, who was on his fourth tour, was born in 1917 at Chester and was educated at Stowe and Merton College, Oxford where he was a member of the University Air Squadron between 1937 and the outbreak of war. At 25 he had been the youngest group captain in the RAF and he had dropped back to wing commander so that he could resume bomber operations.[5] Five years earlier he had gained an honours degree in law at Oxford and, at 24, on leave in New York, he had met and married 41 year old Constance Binney, who had been an American

movie star. In England Cheshire liked a suite at the Ritz when on leave, and to bask in The Mayfair cocktail bar.[6] On the night of 8/9 February Cheshire had led a dozen of his Lancasters to bomb the Gnome et Rhône aero-engine factory at Limoges, 200 miles south-west of Paris. The factory was undefended except for two machine guns and Cheshire made three low-level runs in bright moonlight to warn the 300 French girls working the night shift to escape. On the fourth run he dropped a load of 30lb incendiaries from between 50 and 100 feet. Each of the other 11 Lancasters then dropped a 12,000lb bomb with great accuracy. Ten of the bombs hit the factory and an eleventh fell in the river alongside. The AOC, Air Marshal the Hon Ralph Cochrane, was quick to appreciate that if a single aircraft could mark a target accurately for a squadron then it should be possible for a squadron of properly trained crews to mark targets with similar accuracy for the whole Group. The Lancaster was vulnerable to light flak at low level and a more manoeuvrable aircraft was required for the operations Cochrane had in mind. Cheshire was aware of the limitations of the Lancaster and he had already decided the best aircraft for low level marking. He briefed the AOC on his ideas and Cochrane allocated 617 Squadron a Mosquito.

The Dam Busters' first Mosquito sortie was on 5/6 April when the seemingly fearless Cheshire and his chunky little navigator, Flying Officer Pat Kelly, marked an aircraft factory at Toulouse, on his third pass, with two red spot flares from a height of 800–1,000 feet.[7] This led to the meeting at Bomber Command HQ, which resulted in 5 Group – the Independent Air Force, as it was known in Bomber Command – receiving its own PFF force with 8 Group no longer enjoying its hitherto unchallenged monopoly over pathfinder tactics. Nos. 83 and 97 Lancaster Squadrons moved, from their respective Pathfinder bases at Wyton and Bourn, to Coningsby to rejoin 5 Group, as backers-up and 617 Squadron and 627 Mosquito Squadrons were redeployed from Coningsby and Oakington respectively to Woodhall Spa. The two PFF Lancaster squadrons did not like the idea of marking being undertaken by the Mosquitoes. They saw themselves being reduced to 'flare carrying' forces. Mosquito crews stunned into silence by the news that the new task would be 'dangerous' and 'possibly, not altogether effective' were struck by a feeling of 'grim foreboding' that settled on the squadron 'like a patch of low stratus'. It soon became apparent that they were very much the poor relations at Woodhall. While the famous Dambusters 'lorded it' in Petwood House, 627 were relegated to a batch of Nissen huts on the far side of the airfield. Their only amenity, apart from their own Messes, was 'a tiny one-roomed ale house down the road, run by a little old lady – the beloved "Bluebell Inn". The Mosquito crews even had to go to Coningsby for briefing and debriefing. Ground crews were dismayed to find that the mobile canteen now seemed to go round 617 Squadron's dispersal first, which was the rule rather than the exception and that few NAAFI wads were left when their turn came.'[8]

In the station cinema at Coningsby, Cochrane and Cheshire addressed the assembled Lancaster crews of 83 and 97 PFF Squadrons, and Mosquito men of 627 Squadron, as to their new role. Cochrane opened the meeting by saying that 617 Squadron had made a number of successful attacks on important pinpoint targets and it was now intended to repeat these on a wider scale. The Lancaster pathfinder squadrons were to identify the target areas on H_2S and were to lay a carpet of flares over a given target, under which 627 Squadron would locate and mark the precise aiming point. 5 Group Lancaster bombers would then destroy the target. Cheshire, a tall, thin and imposing figure, took the stand in front of the assembled crews who all knew of his legendary reputation in the RAF, and he explained carefully how the low-level marking business was done. What the Lancasters had to do was lay a concentrated carpet of hooded flares, the light from which would be directed downwards onto the target, making it as bright as day. The small force of Mosquitoes would orbit, find the aiming point and then mark it in a shallow dive with 500lb spot-fires. The marker leader would assess the position of the spot-fires in relation to the aiming point and would pass this information to a 'master of ceremonies' in one of the pathfinder Lancasters. The MC would then take over and direct the main force Lancasters in their attack on the target.

A number of the raids that were now taking place were in preparation for the invasion of France by the Allied forces. The invasion required destruction of the French railway system leading to the landing area. The best method of doing this was by employing heavy bombers, but grave doubts existed at the highest level as to the accuracy with which this could be done. Winston Churchill was adamant that French lives must not be lost needlessly and eventually it was agreed that 5 Group should undertake a mass attack on a marshalling yard in the Paris area, to prove the case one way or the other. Juvisy was selected as the target. The marshalling yard was attacked on the night of 18/19 April by 202 Lancasters led by Leonard Cheshire, after the target was marked at each end with red spot-fires by four Mosquitoes of 627 Squadron.[9]

Ron Walker's crew at East Kirkby flew a Lancaster that sometimes was called *Battling Oboe* and, by others *Olive Oyle*. It was now allocated to the crew for their regular use. 'Just about every other crew on the squadron' recalls Ginger Hammersley, 'was to fly this operation; eighteen in all. We were away at 20.55 hours and all went well until we made our attack on the target. The bomb load was thirteen 1,000 pounders, which we dropped from 5,000 feet. (The height from which we bombed varied according to the type of target. The attack on Tours took place from 6,600 feet and on Aachen from 17,200 feet). Then the hydraulics failed and one of the 1,000lb bombs refused to release. So instead of returning to East Kirkby, we set course for RAF Woodbridge, an airfield that had an extra long runway. This we required, as our brakes might not work. The bomb bay was open with the 1,000lb bomb still inside and likely to drop out on landing. So using my radio, I advised base of our predicament and Woodbridge of our pending arrival. The whole crew was involved in a discussion over the intercom, regarding our serious plight. Should we parachute out? Would it be fair to leave Ron and possibly Essie to try a landing? As a crew we all agreed to sit it out and pray the bomb stayed locked in place, for we knew that if it released when the wheels touched down, we would all perish. Ron eased the Lancaster down to effect a gentle landing and the bomb held fast. Our hearts pounded, as we all admitted later. We were instructed to park the aircraft at a point as far away as possible from buildings. We were collected by lorry and taken to the control tower to learn that the whole area had been cleared of personnel just in case there was an almighty explosion if the bomb dropped out of the bomb bay. We heaved a sigh of relief along with the staff on duty. After being debriefed we were given rum, coffee and sandwiches and taken to accommodation, which had been set aside for us for the night. It was 18.05 hours before we were cleared to leave and make the fifty minute trip home to our base. The fortunes of the squadron crews on the Juvisy raid were varied. Of the 18 that took off, two made an early return and brought their bombs home, one crashed near Peterborough, my own crew landed at Woodbridge; this left fourteen to make the journey back to base.'

The bombing was concentrated, the yards were put out of action, few French lives were lost and all but one Lancaster returned safely to base. The railway yards were so badly damaged that they were not brought back into service until 1947.

Ginger Hammersley recalls: 'There was no let up in the flying. The battle order for the 20th showed Ron Walker's crew at East Kirkby listed and they would be using *O-Oboe* with the same weight and type of bombs as dropped at Juvisy. The target, just north of Paris, was the marshalling yards at La Chapelle. At the briefing all crews were instructed not to bomb unless there was a certainty of hitting the target. It was policy not to hit the areas surrounding the marshalling yards as these generally contained buildings occupied by French citizens. I was well fed, well briefed and wide-awake when at 21.45 hours we took off for the second visit to Paris in as many days. There was considerable opposition from enemy anti-aircraft guns as we once again dropped our bombs from low level. This time we made it back to base without any problems. Two of the crews from the squadron were missing. Now those I first met on 24 March were getting thin on the ground.'[10]

The real test of the new tactics had still to be made – against targets in Germany. 5 Group was therefore unleashed against three of these targets in quick succession – Brunswick on 22/23 April;[11] Munich two nights later[12] and Schweinfurt on 26/27 April.[13]

'After a night off, main force operations were resumed on 22/23 April when Düsseldorf, Brunswick and Laon were the targets. With operations on, my name was again on the battle order along with the rest of the crew. *O-Oboe* was loaded with a 2,000lb MC bomb, plus 6,700lbs of incendiaries including a new type, codenamed the 'J' Type Cluster. It was a late take-off so after ensuring that the equipment in the aircraft was in satisfactory order, I retired to my bed for a rest and a well-earned sleep. The target was Brunswick. At the briefing we were given details of the 'J' Type Clusters.[14] The take-off at 23.45 hours was smooth and the flight went without any mishap. Losses from the force that night were light, with just four aircraft failing to return. 57 Squadron was not affected. We made our attack from 20,200 feet. As we headed away, the fires from the target could be seen from a considerable distance; the attack had served its purpose. Two crews from the squadron had made early returns, turning back for base with technical problems. The rest of us, fourteen crews, all bombed the target and then made a safe return home. That I might survive the full tour of 30 operations was becoming a real possibility, my confidence was high. The flight to and from Brunswick took six hours.'[15]

The night's three operations cost 42 aircraft, including 21 Lancasters, 13 of them failing to return from the attack on Düsseldorf. At one of the 15 Squadron dispersals at Mildenhall, ground crew anxiously awaited the return of Pilot Officer Oliver Brooks' Lancaster III, whose crew were on their 17th op. Their trip to Düsseldorf was to prove quite a flight, as Sergeant C. H. 'Chick' Chandler, the flight engineer, recalls:

'It was 01.10 hours on the morning of 23 April when we were hit simultaneously by heavy flak and cannon fire from an Me 109 at the precise moment that our bombs were released on Düsseldorf. I was standing on the right-hand side of the cockpit, as was usual during our bombing run, with my head in the blister to watch for any fighter attack that might occur from the starboard side. The bombs were actually dropping from the aircraft when there was a tremendous explosion. For a brief period of time everything seemed to happen in ultra-slow motion. The explosion knocked me on my back; I was aware of falling on to the floor of the aircraft, but it seemed an age before I actually made contact. I distinctly remember 'bouncing'. Probably lots of flying clothing and Mae West's broke my fall, but under normal circumstances one would not have been aware of "bouncing". As I fell, I "saw" in my mind's eye, very clearly indeed, a telegram boy cycling to my mother's back door. He was whistling very cheerfully and handed her the telegram that informed her of my death. She was very calm and thanked the boy for delivering the message.

'As I lay there I saw a stream of sparks pass a few feet above the cockpit, from back to front and going up at a slight angle. This caused me some confusion. If the sparks were from a burning engine they were going the wrong way. It was some little time before I realized that the sparks were in fact tracer shells from a fighter that I did not know was attacking us. The illusion that the tracer shells were going upwards was no doubt caused by the fact that our Lancaster was going into an uncontrolled, screaming dive, but because of the slow-motion effect that I was experiencing, I did not appreciate this fact. This whole episode had taken 2 or 3 seconds at most, then the slow-motion effect began to wear off, and I became aware of the screams of the bomb-aimer. Lying in the bomb-aimer's position in the nose of the aircraft, he had caught the full force of the explosion, although this was not immediately apparent.

'As the speed of things returned to normal, for some reason I was unable to get to my feet. My assessment of the situation, which was completely wrong, was that a bomb had exploded on leaving the aircraft and that the rear end of the aircraft had been blown off. Therefore, I decided, I should not waste time going to the escape hatch in the nose, but should make my way aft and step out into space, thus saving time fiddling with escape hatches. My frustration was immense, knowing that my very life depended on some quick positive action, but I was unable to get to my feet, let alone clip on my parachute and move quickly to the rear of the aircraft. (It was many years before I realized that, because of the unfortunate position I was in, plus the effect of "G" when a Lancaster goes into an uncontrolled dive from 22,000 feet, I had very effectively been pinned to the floor of the aircraft.)

'Pilot Officer Oliver Brooks regained control at about 14,000 feet, and then I was able to get to my feet and clip on my parachute. Here I had another quite ludicrous experience. Always when flying, my parachute harness was tight, even to the extent of being uncomfortable, and my buckles were all done up (some crew members left the bottom buckles undone for comfort and ease of movement). Having clipped on my parachute the harness felt very loose and generally slack. Knowing that mine was always tight, I put this slackness down to imagination and convinced myself that it was all a nervous reaction. There is no doubt that given the order to "bale out" I would have jumped. What I didn't know, and it wasn't discovered until later, was that a lump of shrapnel, or possibly a cannon shell, had passed through the back of my harness, cutting the straps and leaving them hanging by a few threads. Had I jumped, my 'chute and I would have parted company!

'A few seconds later the aircraft went into another uncontrolled dive and was recovered at about 7,000 feet. Only a very short period of time covered these incidents. The pilot really had his work cut out trying to control a very heavily damaged aircraft and had feathered the port inner engine, which had caught fire. He gave the order to prepare to bale out.

'By now the crew were beginning to sort themselves out. When the aircraft recovered from its first dive, Ron Wilson, the mid-upper gunner, vacated his turret to find that his flying boots and the H2S were on fire. Unfortunately, the three parachutes had been stowed on this piece of equipment and were destroyed. In order to extinguish the fire it was necessary for him to disconnect himself from the intercom, so he was unable to relay this information to the rest of the crew. Baling out was not now an option, and after hasty consultation it was decided to set course for the emergency landing strip at Woodbridge. If we could at least make the coast we might be able to "ditch".

'My task now was to check the aircraft for damage and casualties. My checks started at the front of the aircraft, in the bomb-aimer's compartment. I am afraid to say that my sheltered life had not prepared me for the terrible sight that met my eyes. It was obvious that this area had caught the full blast of the flak, and

Alan Gerrard had suffered the most appalling injuries. At least he would have died almost instantaneously. Suffice to say that I was sick. At this stage I risked using my torch to shine along the bomb bay to make sure that all our bombs were gone. My report simply was that the bomb-aimer had been killed and that all bombs had left the aircraft.

'Next stop was the cockpit. The pilot had really worked wonders in controlling the aircraft and successfully feathering the engine that had been on fire. Then on to the navigator's department; on peering round the blackout screen I saw that Ken Pincott was busy working over his charts, but that Flight Lieutenant John Fabian DFC, the H2S operator (the Squadron navigation leader) appeared to be in shock. However, once I established that there appeared to be no serious damage, I moved on. The wireless operator's position was empty because his task during the bombing run was to go to the rear of the aircraft and ensure that the photo flash left at the same time as the bombs. Next, down to the mid-upper turret, where Ron Wilson had re-occupied his position, albeit only temporarily. (Unknown to me, he had suffered a wound to his ear that, although not too serious, would keep him off flying for a few weeks.) On reaching the next checkpoint I was again totally unprepared for the dreadful sight that confronted me. Our wireless operator, Flight Sergeant L. Barnes, had sustained, in my opinion, fatal chest injuries and had mercifully lost consciousness. It was found later that he had further very serious injuries to his lower body and legs. He died of his wounds before we reached England. From the rear turret I got a "thumbs up" sign from "Whacker" Marr, so I rightly concluded that he was OK.

'As well as having to report the death of our bomb-aimer, and the fatal injuries to the wireless operator, I had to report the complete failure of the hydraulic system. The pilot was already aware of the fact that we had lost our port inner engine through fire, and that our starboard outer was giving only partial power. The bomb doors were stuck in the open position, and the gun turrets had been rendered inoperative because of the hydraulic failure.

'Next I carried out a check on our fuel. From the gauges it looked as though we had not sustained any major damage to any of our main tanks, but I thought it prudent to carry out a visual check on the outside. Any fluid coming from the mainplane would almost certainly have indicated that at least one tank was holed. It was then that I discovered that where our dinghy should have been, there was a gaping hole in the mainplane. The dinghy had been shot away. Our alternative possible escape route through ditching was now also out of the question.

'I sat down to work out how much fuel we had left, and at what rate it was being used. This was not easy given the fact that we had two engines at full bore, one feathered, and one not giving much power but still churning round a propeller that was stuck in coarse pitch. These figures would give me the length of time that we could keep the aircraft flying. When I arrived at the figure and was in the process of double-checking, the navigator asked me what my figures were. I stalled for time, saying that I had not quite finished. I asked him how much time we required. He gave me his figure and I felt a flood of relief as my figures gave us 20 minutes in hand. After a few seconds I told him that we had at least ten minutes and possibly a little more.

'We now had, in effect, two spare crewmen. Only one of our two navigators was needed since the H₂S was destroyed, and the gunners' positions could not be operated because of the hydraulic failure. The many tasks, such as tending the wounded and throwing overboard as much equipment as possible, were left to them. (Fabian took over the navigation while Ken Pincott took the dead wireless operator's position and radioed SOS messages repeatedly to England, but to no avail because the aircraft was too low for the calls to be received.) The rear-gunner remained in his turret. I was able to concentrate on our critical fuel condition. Gradually I became more confident as each check and crosscheck bore out my original figure of 20 minutes to spare.

'It was at this stage, sitting on my toolbox in front of the engineer's panel that I became very aware of the red warning lights indicating the loss of our port inner engine. They appeared to be glowing like beacons (quite wrongly I am sure, but I thought that they could be seen from miles away by any fighter that happened to pass overhead – my remedy was to chew some chewing gum and stick it over the lights). Many thoughts now struck me. We were struggling along on two engines with a third giving only partial power. We had no gun turrets working. We had started our journey at about 7,000 feet and because of the damaged state of the aircraft we could not maintain height. Should we be attacked, any sort of evasive action was out of the question. In our very badly crippled state any violent manoeuvre would have resulted in complete loss of control and certain disaster. We were well within range of even the lightest ack-ack, and our predicament obliged us to make a direct route from Düsseldorf to Woodbridge; there was no question of avoiding heavily defended areas. There was also a distinct possibility that

through miscalculation or mismanagement we could run out of fuel.

'In spite of all this I can remember very little of the actual trip. Certainly enemy searchlights at between 3,000 and 4,000 feet heavily coned us, but for some unaccountable reason we were not engaged. Again, quite without reasonable explanation, I cannot recall being unduly alarmed, possibly because I had by now resigned myself to my fate, or because I was so aware of our critical fuel situation that I had pushed all other problems to one side. There was one "silver lining" to the problems. We had steadily lost height from the moment we had headed towards Woodbridge, in spite of the fact that we had jettisoned all possible equipment, including guns and ammunition. Because our bomb doors were stuck open and there was a gaping great hole in our starboard wing, with other smaller holes all over the aircraft, our engines were using fuel at an alarming rate trying to pull our very unstable aircraft through the air. Just when it seemed that all was lost, the fact that we had used so much fuel and consequently weight, meant that the pilot was able to coax the aircraft from just above the sea to 500 feet on crossing the coast.

'Almost as we reached Woodbridge I was faced with another problem. I had no means of testing the emergency system that should enable the undercarriage to be lowered pneumatically. We would have to wait until the aircraft was actually over the runway on our final approach. There was no way that we could go round again – it would either work or it wouldn't. Since I was the flight engineer, it was my task to attempt to lower the wheels so that instead of sitting in my crash position, I was standing next to the pilot as we came over the end of the runway. The other crew members sat with their backs to the main spar, feet braced against a part of the aircraft in front of them, hands clasped behind their heads. Ron Wilson, instead of taking up the recommended crash position, had opted to stay at the rear of the aircraft and cradle the wireless operator, who, unbeknown to him, had already died.

'As we passed over the threshold lights (the Emergency Landing Strip at Woodbridge was 250 yards wide and 2½ miles long, or about twice as long as a normal runway) I yanked on the toggle that should have lowered the undercarriage. To my horror, there was no response. At this stage the dreadful "slow-motion" effect returned. We were crabbing very slowly from left to right. I saw very clearly every runway light as we passed it. The ground appeared to come very slowly towards me. I thought, "How stupid to have survived the many problems of the past couple of hours only to be catapulted through the windscreen on arriving!" I made a very conscious effort to hang on to the pilot's seat and waited for the crash.

'As we hit the runway I saw very clearly and distinctly the Perspex blister on the starboard side break away and "float" towards the rear of the aircraft. To my utter amazement I found myself still standing as we careered down the runway. By now the slow-motion effect had left me again and I was fully aware that we were careering down the runway at 120 mph on our belly. When the aircraft eventually came to rest I was still standing and clinging to the pilot's seat. Our crash-landing must have been perfect, and my theory is that because the bomb doors were stuck in the open position, they gave a slight cushioning effect and softened the initial impact. Almost before the aircraft had ground to a halt I was through the top escape hatch situated immediately above the flight engineer's position.

'Since I had experienced the "slow-motion" effect on a few occasions, I was in a state of near terror, probably due to an excess of adrenaline, something that most of us were not aware of in those days. I really did feel so relieved that I got to my knees and kissed the ground. Almost immediately someone thrust an incident report into my hand asking details of damage and fuel states, etc. In my intense anger, I am afraid that my remarks were very blunt and would not have been appreciated in the least!'

After these attacks 5 Group turned exclusively to support of the bombing campaign against interdiction targets for Operation *Overlord*. So far as Brunswick and Munich were concerned, considerable damage was done. In the case of Munich, 90 per cent of the bombs fell in the right place, doing more damage in one night than had been achieved by Bomber Command and the 8th Air Force in the preceding four years.

On 23/24 April RAF bombers carried out minelaying in the Baltic. Four Halifaxes and a Stirling failed to return. When, on the night of 24/25 April, 637 aircraft bombed Karlsruhe and 234 Lancasters and 16 Mosquitoes raided Munich, the raid on Munich cost nine Lancasters. Eleven Lancasters and eight Halifaxes from the Karlsruhe raid were lost while two OTU Wellingtons went missing on a diversionary sweep over the North Sea by 165 aircraft.[16]

'We were briefed to fly operations to Munich on 24 April', recalls Sergeant Ginger Hammersley in 57 Squadron, 'along with 15 other crews. The bomb bay was filled with one hundred and thirty-six 36lb incendiaries and six 500lb "J" type clusters. Taking off at 20.50 hours we headed south, crossing the Sussex coast near Selsey Bill. The Dutch coast was identified on the radar (H_2S) and then we headed deep into southern Germany before turning in a north-easterly direction towards Munich. There was a long wait as the target was identified and the markers, bright coloured flares, were dropped. Those carrying out this work were Wing Commander Leonard Cheshire, Squadron Leader Dave Shannon and Flight Lieutenant R. S. Kearns, all from 617 Squadron and flying the Mosquito twin-engined aircraft. Looking down at them from our higher altitude, I wondered at the time, who on earth I was watching fly so close to the ground as just about every gun available to the defence force was firing at them? At 20,000 feet we too were getting our share of intense gunfire, so we decided to fly away from the area on a five minute "dog leg" before joining in the mass of aircraft awaiting the order to "Bomb". When the order came, we made our bombing run and dropped them successfully from 19,700 feet, only to find that there was a hydraulic failure and we were again in trouble. Leaving Munich in a south westerly direction towards Austria and the Swiss border, then crossing the Rhine and heading first south of, then north and then west of Paris, towards the English Channel and the comparative safety of England. (Two German Night Intruder Fighters, shot down a Lancaster returning from a separate raid over the East Coast.) Later I read the official report on the Munich raid. It read. "NJG 6 was operating in the Munich area. The RAF force attacking Munich met very little trouble except from fighters and flak at Munich and in the withdrawal south of Augsburg, in which neighbourhood extension of defences was suggested. It is probable that three aircraft fell through flak over Munich, one to flak when coned in searchlights on the southwest outskirts and three to fighters near Munich, Ülm and Strasbourg, a total of four to flak, three to fighters and two to unknown sources."

'Using the radio I sent a signal to base advising them of our hydraulic problem and that we would be landing at Hartford Bridge not far from Basingstoke. I was becoming quite an expert at signalling base to report our problems! By now the crew was listed as a "Wind-finder", that is, the navigator and crew up front would prepare a weather report. Then it would be my job to code it and transmit it to base, a task we continued to carry out until the end of the tour of operations.'

The following night, the main force was stood down. On 26 April, 21 year old Sergeant Pilot Roy Bradley and his crew were 'fresh into the world' of 106 Squadron at RAF Metheringham in 5 Group. 'With the sublime ignorance and enthusiasm of our kind, we entered into a world of young but established tradition, with the almost routine air of nonchalance and without any preconceived notions of tomorrow. Forenoon of the 26th and Squadron Leader A. O. Murdoch, RNZAF, the Flight Commander, told me that I was to be his co-pilot that night. He suggested that the afternoon might be well spent "in the pit". Come evening and the very air was charged, as only it can be when "there is one ON". Then the corny jokes and the nervous giggles, the haze and the maze of the briefing. So it's Schweinfurt.[17] I'd never heard of it before. Funny that. Couldn't even work up a feeling about the name. It hadn't the ring of Essen and Frankfurt. It wasn't far from Frankfurt though, a couple of loops of the River Main to the eastward. And there are two Frankfurt's. Not that it mattered very much. Next, the studied confusion of getting the gear, the truck to the kite, the gathering dusk and JB601 *V-Victor* in semi-silhouette showing all the majesty of her breed, the centrepiece in this moment of unspoken reverence and devoted activity. I took another look at the outsize rabbit painted on the nose, hindquarter thumping and ears bristling in the defiant "V". I wondered who painted it? It's very well done but in what seemed no time at all, which happily cut down the time for wondering what the hell I was doing here, the engines were humming their harassed hymn of harnessed energy, the wheels were rolling and we were joining the line. We turned onto the runway and, with their given freedom, the engines sped us towards a shadowy horizon. I looked back and down. Could so much have really happened in the past few hours, down there within the scattered confines of what spelt RAF Metheringham? Lying in the wispy band that rests between a darkening earth and a paling sky was the form of Lincoln and its cathedral identity. They said it was a sight permanently etched in the mind of so many of 5 Group.

'We were still climbing. We were heading south. There was a lessening definition of view. The sky was filling up. By the time we were all en route, this was going to be some mighty aerial brick, of metal and men. But it was comforting to know that you were in company.[18] *V-Victor* seemed a nice kite. I wished I had a greater sentiment for it. Maybe if it were my own it would be different. These chaps had had it for some time. (Did somebody really say it was their 13th?) Judging by the bombs painted on her nose *V-Victor* could tell a lot of people's stories.

'It was quite black now. The others were still out there. We were still in company, but it didn't give quite the same feeling of comfort now that I couldn't see

them. Quiet enough. It was not far now from the southeast turn point near Paris. There was a long, long leg coming up then! We were on the long leg. Fair old amount of flak. Funny how it gave the feeling of a lot of little men down there flicking away at outsize cigarette lighters that won't light. No flak now. Uncomfortably close glimpses of exhausts. Hell, there were a few being knocked down. I wondered how many, if any, got out.

'Now us! Now us! No. 4 was on fire. Then 3! Was this it? Then it came: "Jump, jump, jump, jump."[19]

'Chute on ... and blank ... a sightless blank ... is this what it was like to be dead or was it all happening to somebody else? I opened my eyes. The blackness had gone. If I had died, I didn't know about it. But this was the earth I was lying on. And that was a tree above me. The sky beyond was a pale blue. Then the blackness again ... Hell, it was cold! My left leg looked a mess. I felt so stiff and sore all over. I couldn't stand! My flying boots had gone. Not surprising – those suede jobs were a pretty stupid design. Funny thing, it was the first time I'd worn them since early Flying School! This was real earth and that was a real tree all right. Did I come through that? The chute was there, strung out around me. I tore a length for a bandage. Somehow or other I hadn't "bought it". Were any of the others around I wondered? I called out. There was no response. The rising damp air carried my breath into the surrounding solitude. I buried my chute and crawled away, slowly, painfully and cursing the rough foliage, which defied my progress. And then, a grassy corridor; this was easier. It sloped away before me and down to a main road ringing to the crunch of marching feet materializing into a squad of German soldiers, which didn't exactly surprise me. Then they were out of sight. With alternating grunts and yelps I landed at the roadside, crossed on all fours and rolled thankfully into the comfort of a ditch. It was getting a struggle holding off the blackness ... More footsteps ... a man and a girl. No time for ceremony or second thoughts; I raised myself up and asked them to help me get to England and to bring a doctor. Then into the blackness again ...'

The Schweinfurt raid was a failure. The low-level marking was inaccurate and unexpectedly strong head winds delayed the Lancaster marker aircraft and the main force. As a consequence, much of the bombing fell outside the city. German night fighters carried out fierce attacks throughout the period of the raid, which resulted in the loss of 21 Lancasters.[20]

Sergeant John B. Johnson, a mid-upper turret gunner in Pilot Officer G. J. L. Smith's crew in 57 Squadron at

East Kirkby, who flew his first op this night with Flying Officer Walker and crew to Schweinfurt, recalls:

'Pilot Officer Smith was flying with Squadron Leader M. I. Boyle DFC, the "B" Flight Commander's crew, as the "second dickey" for operational experience before taking his own crew on an operation. I did not have time to unpack my kit before meeting my crew and start the preparations for that night. After briefing we went out to the aircraft and went through a routine pre-operation check of equipment. After shutting the engines down we got out of the aircraft and the crew went one way and I made my way towards the next aircraft. It was strange but the other crew did the same thing; they walked one way but the one member walked towards me. As we approached each other I realized that it was my pilot, he took his helmet off and he had a very large red band across his forehead from the helmet that was far too tight for him. I can still see him standing there because within a few hours he was dead. Two aircraft crashed into each other over the target. One man baled out. I am sure that it was my pilot in one of those two aircraft I saw go down.'[21]

At around midnight, 44 year old M. Galais, a factory worker living in simple lodgings in Gourzon, Haute-Marne, which also served as headquarters for his resistance group, had received reports that the German night fighter aerodrome near St Dizier seemed active. Galais, a professional soldier for 25 years, and four years in the underground, pondered the implications of the message from Dr Rény in St Dizier that any wounded Allied airmen must first be brought to him. Overhead was the heavy steady drone of RAF bombers. Galais looked up and his heart went out to the crews. He could feel for them and with them. And one was in trouble! Galais stood rooted, eyes piercing the darkness and ears cocked. In the village of Laneuville-à-Bayard and the surrounding farmhouses many French people held their breath and many hearts were pounding, as the whine of disaster grew closer. There was an explosion, which seemed to break about the listening ears and in the swift eternity, which followed, there came the sickening crunch of metal onto earth from the direction of the canal. Gathering helpers, Galais hurried along the Route Nationale, to the church on the corner and over the bridge. He had already briefed people in the surrounding villages if ever an aircraft was heard to be in difficulty or crashed. They must immediately take to the fields and lanes in search of survivors before local German forces came on the scene and then, if questioned later, they must 'know nothing'. In Flornoy its few dozen inhabitants included two sisters and one

brother in the Geoffrin family. Mariette, the eldest, would proudly send pigeons winging their way to England with laboriously scrawled messages clipped to their legs. Marcelle, the youngest, thrilled to the exciting fear of the moment with all the simplified objectiveness of a teenager, but saddened to tears for torment of the living. Pierre, the gamekeeper, reflected solemnly that there was no time to be lost. If there were survivors, then Pierre would find them. Marcelle demanded that she keep him company. They set out into the night. It was getting light.

V-Victor had crashed between the Marne Canal and Laneuville-à-Bayard. Galais gazed with mixed emotions at the wreckage. The scene was photographed, items of possible interest to the Germans removed, the bodies of seven crew taken to nearby shelter. First arrangements for a fitting burial were already in hand.[22]

Pierre and Marcelle did not feel the cold and their tiredness. As they passed the great Forêt du Val, a German patrol from the direction of St Dizier went by them. As the Geoffrins rounded the bend in the road they heard a voice calling to them from the ditch. It was Roy Bradley.[23]

On 27/28 April the target for 322 Lancasters was Friedrichshafen, deep in southern Germany, on a bright moonlight night in order to achieve better accuracy. The disastrous raid on Nuremberg four weeks earlier, which had been flown in not disimilar conditions, was uppermost in the minds of the crews when they were briefed. At Mildenhall Flight Lieutenant Len 'Dusty' Miller, DSO of 15 Squadron, pilot of Lancaster LL801 was flying his 32nd operation. He could have stopped at 30 ops but Miller had wanted to finish when the rest of his crew finished. The route to the target was carefully planned, the use of diversion and spoof raids confused the German night fighter controllers and the Lancasters arrived over Friedrichshafen without being intercepted. However over the target it was a different story. Thirty-one Bf 110s and three *Luftbeobachter* (air situation observer) Ju 88s were successfully guided into the stream via radio beacon *Christa* and they wreaked havoc. No less than 18 Lancasters were shot down.

About 50 miles short of the target a twin-engined night fighter attacked the Lancaster flown by Warrant Officer R. G. Peter RAAF of 35 Squadron, then at 17,000 feet. The Australian pilot saw the fighter first as it approached rapidly in front, directly ahead and nearly level with the Lancaster. The mid-upper gunner saw it also but he had no opportunity to open fire and Peter 'corkscrewed' immediately. Although no bullets were heard striking the aircraft, hits were evidently sustained in the starboard outer engine, as no power could be obtained from it and flames came from the exhaust. After stopping the engine and feathering the propeller the flames died down at once without the use of the extinguisher. Then the Lancaster proceeded on three engines, bombed the target from 16,000 feet and set course on the homeward route. A few minutes later Peter's Lancaster was attacked again. This time there was no warning. The night was dark and there were no searchlights, flak bursts or other signs of enemy activity. The wireless operator, who was standing in the astro-dome, saw tracer coming from astern and then a fire broke out in the fuselage. No one saw the fighter, which may have been below the gunners' range of vision. The fire spread and soon the fuselage between the mid-upper and rear turrets was well alight. Smoke poured into the pilot's compartment, so that Peter was unable to see his instruments and the Lancaster, still flying with three engines only, went into an uncontrollable spin. Peter ordered the crew to bale out. Sergeant A. S. Brereton, navigator, and Flight Sergeant G. G. Foulkes RAAF, flight engineer, baled out, acting on the captain's instructions. (Brereton was subsequently captured but Foulkes was killed.) Then the air bomber reported that the fire had destroyed both gunners' parachutes and that his own parachute had opened prematurely. The opening of the front escape hatch had, by this time, cleared the smoke from the pilot's compartment and it was now possible to see the flying instruments. But Peter could not push the stick forward and the bomber continued to lose height as it went round in a flat spin. Eventually, when indicated height was 3,000 feet and speed only 100 knots, the stick responded. With the port engines throttled back and full power on the remaining starboard engine, the Lancaster came out of the spin. Lake Constance and the fires at the target were within sight and Peter turned back, resolved to ditch the burning Lancaster on the lake, despite the fact that the front hatch had been jettisoned. A crash landing in such a mountainous region could not be risked and he ordered the crew to their ditching stations. Although there was no moonlight to help him and one engine was unserviceable, Peter made a perfect ditching with very little impact. Water rushed in over him and the rear-gunner had to be assisted out of the aircraft as both he and the mid-upper gunner had sustained injuries from the fire. However, all five crew were in the dinghy within one minute of ditching. After about an hour they reached the Swiss shore of the lake and landed safely on neutral territory. Peter evaded and the other four were interned.[24]

'Dusty' Miller's crew meanwhile, were coming up for their bomb run[25] when they were hit hard by a 'whole hailstorm of cannon fire and bullets from beneath' from the guns of a Bf 110 night fighter flown by Oberleutnant Martin 'Tino' Becker of 2./NJG 6 who later claimed a Halifax near beacon *Christa*. 'It set our petrol tanks on fire', Miller recalled. 'I gave the order to bale out. The flight engineer [Flight Sergeant G. Mead] clipped my chest chute on and the bomb-aimer [Sergeant A. Beazley-Long] put his chute on but he couldn't get the hatch open at first. He said it was stuck but I realized that because we were going down in a heavy dive, the suction was holding it. So I pulled the nose up and he got it free and out he went. The flight engineer sat on the edge of the hatch and was waiting to go. I could see him sitting there so I came up behind him, put my boot on his back and pushed him. Then I thought the other crew hadn't moved, so I went back to the cockpit to see what was happening but they were slumped over in their positions. I assumed very quickly that the cannon fire had hit them because all the intercom and electrics had gone out and they couldn't hear me on the intercom. At that point my earphone controls got whipped up round the control stick and I couldn't get away from it so I ripped it off, breaking the cord, and made my own way down to the hatch and pushed myself out. All the while we were still taking fire from night fighters and the port fuel tanks were on fire. We were at 22,500 feet at the time and my chute must have caught the top of the hatch because when I came round it was flapping on its retaining swaps and I had to pull it down to pull the rip cord. It didn't work, so I was falling, head first and pulling my chute out of its pack, hoping it would open. I remember the moon above revolving as I fell.'

Len Miller must have been blown out of the aircraft when it exploded, killing four of his crew.[26] As he descended he felt for his parachute. It was about three or four feet above his head, having come off the clips on his chest harness, just hanging on the strap harness above his head. He pulled the chute pack down to his chest by the straps and pulled the rip cord. The parachute did not open so he had to rip it open by hand. It must have opened no higher than 1,500 feet because almost as soon as it had, the RAF pilot was on the ground, or more precisely, hanging upside down in a tree with one leg stuck in the harness of his parachute:

'I remember laughing because I was holding the tree so hard not wanting to release the chute or harness in case I fell and broke my neck. So I slid down the tree slowly hanging onto the trunk; it's as black as the ace of spades out in the forest, and I was only about two feet off the ground. When I stood up I did see the other two members of my crew come down, so that was good.' He never saw his two crew again until after the war, as they were taken prisoner. Miller recalls: 'I found a stream nearby and walked down that in case there were dogs about. Then I had a drink and found a big holly bush. I used to play cowboys and Indians as a youngster and we'd chase each other through the bushes. Holly bushes are hollow in the middle and when the leaves fall and dry they are very hard and make a lot of noise. Very useful thing, holly bushes, if you know about them.' Miller was wearing grubby overalls over his flight gear so no one took any notice of the disheveled pilot. His mother had sewn pockets inside the overalls where he kept chocolate, and pepper to use against dogs, and other items. And the overalls also allowed him to blend into the local population more readily than an RAF flight suit because they made him look like a plumber or an electrician. After a short nap in the holly bush and a meal of chocolate and energizing malt tablets, Miller made his way south toward Switzerland. Upon approaching a town, he noticed a German soldier on a bicycle and he waited while the soldier went into a building and put his roguish ways to good use. Miller stole the bicycle and sped off hoping he could find an aerodrome and steal an aircraft and get home. He did not find an aerodrome but he made it all the way to Mulhouse on the Rhine in occupied France, and almost on the Swiss border. He was stopped by a German officer who wanted to know where Grossman's Platz was. Miller did not understand German but he understood Platz and he pointed across the road and said, 'Ja, Ja'. The German officer went and Miller cycled off like mad. Finally, he reached the Swiss border. He recalls:

'It was a terrific barbed wire fence about 9 feet high and about 13 feet wide with sloping banks and patrolling guards. Lucky for me a young tree had grown up through the wire so while a guard went by I lay in the shadow of the tree with my face covered with dirt. As soon as he'd gone, I climbed the tree and stood on one of the posts and dived into the other side and Switzerland.'

A Swiss guard apprehended Miller and he was eventually interned. He was placed in a big hotel with a Swiss officer in charge. The inmates were allowed to take lessons or other educational pursuits. Miller took piano lessons and when the old lady who taught him gave him the bill every week, he added a couple of extra noughts on the end and the bill was sent to the British Embassy who gave money to pay the bills. Miller pocketed the extra and had some saved up for when

he decided to leave the country after the invasion of France. Miller and an Australian named Colin took a train to the French border and hiked through the countryside to avoid border patrols. Colin got terribly blistered feet and he could hardly walk so Miller carried him about 20 miles when they encountered two young boys and he asked them where the French resistance was. They left and later two men with Sten guns arrived and took them to a farmhouse. They looked after them for a couple days and gave them two bicycles which they later used to get to Bourg. During their time with various resistance groups Miller and Colin went on several raids, blowing up railway lines and attacking troops on the tracks. They soon got used to the idea of blowing up trains and found it was 'quite good fun'. After about six months Miller and his friend had to leave. A 75,000 franc reward had been placed on their heads and finally they were flown out in an aircraft that re-supplied the resistance. When he got back to London Miller was given a month's leave to see his family, who had since moved in with his cousin's family because of the bombings in London. He was sent to RAF Warboys where he transitioned onto Mosquitoes and he flew two final operations, both over Berlin and one on Hitler's birthday. 'He was doing a big broadcast when we went over and all the sirens went off and we shot down all the radio stations, so he didn't get his big radio broadcast,' Miller said, with a note of satisfaction.[27]

During May-June Bomber Command was, apart from three major raids against German cities towards the end of May, fully committed to destroying the *Wehrmacht*'s infrastructure in France and bomber losses were relatively light. Operations in support of the D-Day build up continued throughout May. On 1/2 May 120 aircraft, of which 96 were Lancasters, attacked Chambly, the main railway stores and repair depot for the northern French system. About 500 HE bombs fell inside the railway depot area and serious damage was caused to all departments; the depot was completely out of action for 10 days. Over 130 Lancasters attacked the aircraft assembly factory at Blagnac airfield at Toulouse where the Germans were using four large buildings, two pairs at right angles to each other, for the repair and overhaul of tank and aircraft engines, much of the airfield having storage dumps dispersed around it. The aiming point for this raid was at the apex of lines drawn from the sides of the main buildings as they met at right angles. The intelligence briefing was 'light flak in the area' but this turned out to be an understatement. Arriving over the target, flares from the Lancaster Pathfinders burst over the four Mosquito markers as arranged, illuminating the area in almost daylight conditions to enable the Mossies to identify and mark the aiming point. It also made it very easy for the defences to pick out 627 Squadron aircraft going around in circles just above them.[28] One of the markers was hit but the marking was successful and the Lancasters severely damaged the entire factory. Other targets that night included the railway yards at St Ghislain and Malines, while the Société Berliet motor vehicle works at Lyons was attacked by 75 Lancasters including one piloted by Wing Commander J. S. Bennett DFC with a newly arrived 'sprog' crew at North Killingholme for their first 'op'. Forty-six Lancasters bombed the Usine Lictard engineering works outside Tours, which was being used as aircraft repair workshops. This factory had been bombed a few days earlier by the 8th Air Force's B-17s, but photographs had shown that nearly all the bombs had fallen in the surrounding fields. PFF Lancasters of 83 and 97 Squadrons dropped a yellow target indicator 10 miles from Tours, from which the four low-level marker Mosquitoes set course accurately for the target area to drop their spot-fires. Having dropped the yellow TI the Lancasters headed directly to the target – identified it on H₂S and discharged hundreds of illuminating flares above it. Approaching Tours, crews saw 'a great carpet of light' suddenly spread out in front of them. The target was marked accurately and the marker leader then called and told the controller who broadcast to the main force on W/T and VHF to bomb the clump of red spots. This was done and the target was flattened.

On Wednesday 3 May, 346 Lancaster crews, two *Oboe* equipped Mosquitoes and four Pathfinder Mosquitoes of 617 Squadron were briefed for that night's operation. At Elsham Wolds in north Lincolnshire, overlooking the Humber, Jack Spark DFM, wireless operator in Flight Sergeant Fred Browning's crew in 103 Squadron, bemoaned the cold: 'There was nothing between us and Russia and that was where the winds came from. It was a good station. There was a happy atmosphere but we all knew we had a job to do and we did it. The spirit of co-operation and comradeship was terrific. We were called to briefing on the afternoon of 3 May and I think we were all relieved when the covers were taken off the maps and we saw that our target was in France. We had had some horrific operations to Germany. France was considered an easy option; so much so that the powers-that-be had decided that raids to France only merited a third of an operation. We had to make three French raids to one over Germany.'

There was the usual anticipation of the string drawing out the route to the target. It was a short string. Everyone gave a sigh of relief as French targets were supposed to be easy. Then the Intelligence Officer introduced the reality, Mailly-le-Camp, a pre-war French Army tank depot near Epernay east of Paris, about 50 miles south of Rheims. Many had never heard of it before. Crews were told that it was a *Panzer* depot and training centre, reported to house up to 10,000 *Wehrmacht* troops.[29] British Intelligence had received word that the Panzer Division was due to move out the next day so it had to be attacked that night. The penny dropped. It was just another raid but this one really mattered. One rear-gunner on 103 Squadron at Elsham Wolds who was flying his first op was scared. He didn't mind admitting it. He did not know what to expect. There was a feeling of excitement mixed with fear but all other thoughts were pushed to the backs of their minds. Mailly-le-Camp would be Derek Patfield's fifth op. By now 61 Squadron had returned to Skellingthorpe and Patfield, who had been promoted to flight sergeant, had crewed up with Pilot Officer Ron Auckland's crew. Patfield recalls that: 'He was a bit older and he was very good. He was strict as well. I was glad we had a strict pilot, because you had to instil a sense of discipline to work as a team. It was no good just doing what you liked. You had to keep a routine to stick to. We were briefed to "get the target" because there were French people all around it.'

For Pilot Officer G. E. 'Ted' Ball's crew in 49 Squadron at RAF Fiskerton in Lincolnshire, Mailly represented their 16th operation.[30] Sergeant Ronnie H. 'Squiggle' Eeles, the rear-gunner recalls:

'The morning of 3 May was uneventful until we were advised operations were on that evening. I cannot recall whether an NFT was carried out prior to briefing. Briefing details stressed the importance of Mailly-le-Camp and the need to destroy it in company with 1 Group. As a crew, we were apprehensive of the raid arrangements in view of the planned concentration of aircraft over the target in a short space of time, particularly as crews were given bombing heights with only 100 feet variations in altitudes which obviously increased the risk of collision. Our individual bombing height was to be 7,100 feet and the target was to be marked by Wing Commander Leonard Cheshire in a Mosquito. Our bomb load was high explosive bombs only. Flying Officer Martin DFM (AG) was to accompany us. I understood his task was to observe anti-aircraft activity.'

No. 5 Group was the first wave of 163 Lancasters and was to attack the south-east part of the camp while

153 bombers of No. 1 Group made up the second wave. Their target was the north-west section of the camp. Thirty aircraft were to concentrate on an area near the workshops.[31] Wing Commander Leonard Cheshire was the 'marker leader' in one of the four PFF Mosquitoes of 617 Squadron, who were the experts in marking confined and difficult targets that could not be accurately located by purely radar aids. Since 617's Lancasters were not involved in this operation it was not considered necessary to give the Dam Busters' marker crews the usual full main force briefing. They were just given the elements that applied to the actual target area – time of first flare fall, – timing of the first wave of 5 Group aircraft – lull time for the marking of the area allocated to the second wave of 1 Group aircraft.[32] Eight Mosquitoes of 627 Squadron would be at a slightly higher level and were to dive bomb the light flak positions, which were known to be around this depot. The raid was timed to begin at 00.01 hours 'when all good troops should be in bed'.

Sergeant Ronnie 'Squiggle' Eeles continues:

'Our take off time was 21.57 hours with the usual "wave off" by Station personnel at the end of the runway. I had a sense of foreboding that something was different, as I did not have the usual exhilaration when taking off on full power. I thought that something was going to happen and I would not be coming back. What had also struck me as strange was that when I entered my turret at dispersal, for the first time ever the WOp/ AG (Kernahan) had closed the turret doors behind me, as they were difficult to close oneself with full flying clothing due to the restriction space. I had thanked him – the last I was ever to speak to any member of the crew. The flight to the target area was uneventful. At the lower than usual operational height I found my electrically heated suit was unnecessary and I kept switching it on and off to maintain a reasonable temperature.'

It was a beautiful spring night, soft and starlit. Crews could see the shadows of aircraft above them. The Mosquito force arrived over Mailly, five minutes before zero hour as briefed.[33] Although the target was marked accurately Cheshire passed the order to the main force controller, Wing Commander L. C. Deane of 83 Squadron, to send in the main force, who were orbiting at a holding pattern to the north, and bomb. Deane instructed the wireless operator to give the 'start bombing' order but the message was distorted. In some cases the VHF radio frequency was drowned out by an American Armed Forces Network broadcast. Some men thought that the Germans were trying to jam their communications. Only a few Lancaster crews picked up

the garbled message and went in and bombed. So too did a handful of other aircraft flown by experienced captains who realized that delaying dropping their bombs and circling the yellow datum point, that had been laid near the village of Germinon, could be disastrous. Deane knew that the delay in starting bombing by the main force was serious and he tried to send the message by Morse but it failed to transmit. (It was found later that his radio was 30 kilocycles off frequency.) Cheshire also tried to get through but he was unable to do so either. He then tried to abort the raid but this failed. The first wave did not receive instructions and began to orbit the target and the German night fighters moved in and began to shoot down the Lancasters.

'Outside, hell had broken out' recalls Jimmy Graham, a member of the crew of *Q for Queenie* of 576 Squadron. 'German night fighters had arrived in force and were attacking the circling bombers. Lancaster down ... and another ... and another ... two fly into each other and explode in the air and others scatter so that they are not hit by the debris. And still there was no attack order. Stan, the mid-upper gunner, and I kept our eyes open but no fighter attacked us. There were plenty of other targets.'

One rear-gunner recalled: 'We circled and circled for what seemed an eternity without receiving any instructions. During this time the German fighter activity became more intense. There was tracer everywhere and aircraft were going down in flames all around us but still no instructions. One could sense the bombing force getting restless, like a herd ready to stampede. This was emphasized by the remarks made over the air, some of which should have turned the night sky blue. I heard one pilot's voice, "For Christ's sake shut up and give my gunners a chance". When I heard this remark I thought – "God help them if they are being attacked with this lot going on". But always the same stock phrase, "Don't bomb. Wait".' A RAF pilot wrote: 'I switched on for the Main Controller's commentary and was surprised to hear him ordering the main force to wait, as the target had not yet been marked. The air was really blue with a succession of replies from the main force. I had never before heard R/T indiscipline and this was really the measure of the panic and fear that was abroad that night. This was quite enough for me – I had no intention of joining the crowd round those death-trap markers, so we turned east towards the darker sky ... We heard brief snatches of R/T, on one occasion what sounded like an English voice screaming, "For Christ's sake! I am on fire!"'

Jack Spark in Fred Browning's crew heard the screams. It was a sound he would never forget: 'It frightened me half to death. Then this cold, commanding voice broke in.'

A rough Australian voice said, 'If you are going to die, die like a man – quietly.' Spark found it more shocking than the scream.

Browning said, 'To hell with this. It's like moths caught in a candle,' and he flew on and started circling 30 miles away.

Suddenly R/T was broken by a strong Australian voice who declared, for all to hear: 'The hell with this; let's go before we're picked off.'

And go they did. So too did *Q for Queenie*. The pilot lined them up for a clear run in and the bombs were dropped right on target before they made a bee line for home without further incident 'but going like hell'.

One Canadian voice said: 'If this is a third of an op, I'm half way to LMF.'

Another Canadian who asked to come in and bomb was told, 'No do not bomb'. After a few anxious minutes the same distinctive Canadian accent was heard asking again: 'Hello Pathfinder, can we come in and bomb now?' He got the same reply. 'Continue circling'. He said, '**** the RAF, we're coming in'.

A wing commander came up on the R/T, identified himself and said, 'This has got to stop. Cut your R/T and wait for instructions to bomb.' But the frightened voices continued.

'Pull your finger out master bomber; we're dying out here'.

One of the Pathfinders said, 'I've been hit. I've got to go down.' It was said in such a matter of a fact way, as if he was saying that he was going out for a walk.

The deputy controller, Squadron Leader E. N. M. Sparks of 83 Squadron, had been instructed to take over only if the master bomber was shot down or he was given instructions to do so. He was aware that Deane had not been shot down and that his messages somehow were not getting through so Sparks took over and gave the order to bomb. The order was five minutes late but that was an eternity to the waiting crews. 'When the order to bomb was finally given the rush was like the starting gate at the Derby,' recalled one pilot. In 20 minutes 1,500 tons of bombs were dropped but by this time nine Lancasters were crashing in flames. Many of the German soldiers on the ground sheltered in the woods when the first bombs dropped and then returned to the camp thinking that the raid was over. They were not ready for the ferocity of the second wave and many were killed in the open. Some dived into the trenches but many were buried alive as the sides of the trenches

fell in on them or walls collapsed over them. Then the water tower was hit and the flood of water poured into the trenches, drowning some of the men who were trapped there.

Flight Sergeant 'Pat' Patfield in Ron Auckland's crew in 61 Squadron, all of whose 12 Lancasters made safe returns, says: 'It was another balls up. We had to orbit for over fifteen minutes over a yellow TI we dropped and wait for the target to be marked. While we were stooging round the *Luftwaffe* came in and started shooting bombers down, although we flattened Mailly-le-Camp.[34] While we were orbiting they got in the shelters. While we were being shot down, they were taking cover. German night fighters had a whale of a time shooting everyone down.'

Fw 190 *Wilde Sau* fighters working without radar but by searchlight and moonlight and the bombers' 'marker flares' destroyed six bombers.[35]

Flight Sergeant Les H. 'Lizzie' Lissette RNZAF was pilot of a 207 Squadron Lancaster, which was attacked by a Fw 190. The 26 year old pilot's girlfriend had been a nurse on a hospital ship bombed off Crete and was believed lost but 'Lizzie' a tough, powerfully built New Zealander, who had been a teamster with four horses hauling logs out of the mountains near Napier, never spoke much about it. A third attack soon finished off the bomber. Tracer hit the port wing, blowing off the dinghy hatch. The dinghy then commenced to inflate and then shot back over the tailplane like a big hoopla ring. Lissette could see down through the wing to the ground. The port undercarriage was partially down.

Twenty year old Flight Sergeant Ron 'Curly' Emeny the mid-upper gunner, reported a fighter coming in, port quarter down. They were hit again in the bomb bay and a small fire started. Emeny came from Bow and was an apprentice motor cycle engineer in Civvy Street. The crew had become his second family. One thing that he had learned was to get on with all types of people and this was particularly true of the crew on a Lanc. One man had been a gamekeeper and he lived in a tree house he built in the woods at Spilsby between raids, even in the depths of winter. He was a good crew member but he preferred the fresh air.

Sergeant Nick Stockwood the 20 year old flight engineer, an ex boy apprentice, was from Chipping Norton. Sergeant Ron Ellis, the 26 year old rear-gunner from Doncaster, married with a young daughter, had been a boy apprentice engine fitter before the war. Failure of the port outer engine meant that his turret was u/s and the hand rotation was shot away. Before anyone could help him Ellis was hit by another burst of fire: 'I've had it' he said on the intercom. Lissette

The most successful nightfighter crew ever. L–R: *Oberfeldwebel* Wilhelm Gänsler, *bordschütze* (gunner), *Oberleutnant* Heinz-Wolfgang Schnaufer and *Leutnant* Fritz Rumpelhardt, *Bordfunker* (radar operator). By August 1943 Schnaufer's score had reached twenty-three and by mid-December he had scored forty victories. In 1944 he scored sixty-four victories, a feat unequalled by any other night-fighter pilot. In 1945 he scored fifteen victories, including nine in a single twenty-four-hour period on 21 February, to reach a final score of 121. Schnaufer shared 100 victories with Fritz Rumpelhardt, twelve victories with *Leutnant* Baro and eight with Erich Handke. Wilhelm Gänsler shared in ninety-eight of Schnaufer's victories. (*Ab A. Jansen*)

21/22 February 1944 *Oberfeldwebel* Günther Bahr of 1./NJG 6 flying Bf 110 2Z+IH with *Feldwebel* Rehmer as *Bordfunker* and *Unteroffizier* Riediger as *tze* shot down seven Lancasters of the Worms force in quick succession 2034–2050 hours, all on their bombing run to the target with their bomb loads still on. ahr survived the war having scored thirty-five night and two day victories. He was also awarded the *Ritterkreuz*. (*Günther Bahr*)

n 24/25 February 1944 209 *Tame Boars* destroyed thirty-one Lancasters and Halifaxes of a 734 strong force raiding Schweinfurt. *Hauptmann* 'Hugo' Eckart-von Bonin, *Ritterkreuzträger* and *Kommandeur* of II./NJG 1, seen here with his regular *Bordfunker Oberfeldwebel* Johrden destroyed two *Viermots* for his 28th and . His 28th *Abschuss* was Lancaster III JB721 of 156 Squadron flown by Flight Lieutenant J. A. Day DFC, which crashed at Briey, NE of Metz at 2136 hours. one other of the crew were PoW while five men died. Day fractured a leg and he was later repatriated. von Bonin was decorated with the coveted *Ritterkreuz* ruary 1944 and he ended the war with thirty-two victories. Two of his brothers, also serving in the *Luftwaffe*, were killed on the Eastern Front and his father, gislav von Bonin, was captured by the Russians in March 1945 and never seen again. (*Hans Grohmann*)

The 101 Squadron aircraft equipped with ABC were distinguishable by their large masts above the fuselage as here on Lancaster B.I ME590/SR-C. On 26 February 1944 Flight Sergeant R. Dixon piloted the aircraft back from Augsburg, where at 20,000 feet his aircraft was hit by flak, which fractured hydraulic lines and they were attacked by an Me 110, whose fire perforated the elevators before the Lancaster could evade. Dixon crash-landed at home base, Ludford Magna. The crash wrecked part of the FIDO (Fog Investigation and Dispersal Operation) pipe-work in the process. Burning petrol and allied fuels, this apparatus successfully cleared fog from runways and was responsible for the safe landing of many bombers, particularly in the winter of 1944–45 when fifteen airfields were then equipped with FIDO. 101 Squadron's aircraft normally carried a bomb load for the briefed target but were spread throughout the bomber stream. ME590 was repaired, converted from Mk I to Mk III and pensioned off to a Conversion Unit.

(*Left*) Warrant Officer A. F. 'Red' Browne DFM, rear gunner in Flight Lieutenant Ron Walker's crew in 57 Squadron. He is wearing a bright yellow Taylor Su͏ had in-built buoyancy and electrical heating to help prevent gunners from freezing in their uninsulated and unheated turrets.

(*Right*) Pilot Officer Freddie Watts of 630 Squadron at the controls of Lancaster III ND554 LE C *Conquering Cleo* at East Kirkby on 25 March 1944. Watts an͏ crew completed eleven operations from January to March 1944 and after the 30/31 March Nuremberg raid they were asked to go to the Pathfinders but they di͏ want to drop flares so they went to 617 Squadron at Woodhall Spa for Special Duties. They did not want to lose *Conquering Cleo* so they took the aircraft with ͏ and Watts and crew flew four ops in *Conquering Cleo* with 617 Squadron before it was returned to 630 Squadron in mid-June 1944. The crew completed their t͏ 29 October in LM695/N, bombing the battleship *Tirpitz* in Tromsø Fiord with a 14,000lb *Tallboy* on their 37th trip. ND554 and Flying Officer R. B. Knight F͏ and crew were lost without trace on the 8/9 February 1945 raid on Pölitz. (*Dennis Cooper*)

FRANKFURT
K 3178

9 March 1944 846 aircraft including 620 Lancasters set out to bomb Frankfurt. Twenty-two aircraft, ten of them Lancasters, were lost. Four nights later on
March, the city was bombed again, this time by 816 aircraft, 620 of them Lancasters. Thirty-three aircraft were lost, twenty-six of them Lancasters. This raid was
ere than four nights earlier and 948 people were killed and 120,000 bombed out.

On 20/21 December 1943 *Oberleutnant* Martin 'Tino' Becker of *Stab* I./NJG 6 was credited with the destruction of a Lancaster and two Halifax bombers. He scored his first victory on 23/24 September when he destroyed a Lancaster (possibly DV174 of 460 Squadron RAAF) near Speyer during a raid on Mannheim. He would fly in all weathers and in the weeks following he scored a further five *Abschüsse* against RAF *Viermots* before the year was out. On 19/20 February 1944 Becker reached double figures and on the night of 22/23 March he claimed six Lancasters and Halifaxes shot down. On the Nürnburg raid on the night of 30/31 March Becker shot down Lancaster III ND466 of 156 Squadron flown by Flying Officer J. V. Scrivener RCAF (PoW). Four of the crew were killed. Becker ended the war with fifty-eight night kills (all four-engined bombers) and the *Ritterkreuz* and *Eichenlaub*. (*Karl-Ludwig Johanssen*)

On the night of 14/15 March 1944 eighteen Lancasters were lost and 100 Group lost two Mosquitoes and a Fortress III during radio countermeasure duties in support of the Main Force. *Hauptmann* Martin 'Tino' Becker of Stab IV./NJG 6 and his *Funker Unteroffizier* Karl-Ludwig Johanssen (pictured) in a Ju 88G-6 claimed nine of these aircraft, the highest score by a German night-fighter crew in any single night. Becker shot down six Lancasters before expending his last ammunition and Johanssen, manning the twin rear facing machine guns, then destroyed two Lancasters and a Fortress III. Johanssen's three victims counted towards the grand total of his pilot so the B-17 was Becker's 57th official victory. Johanssen is pictured receiving the *Ritterkreuz* two days later. (*Karl-Ludwig Johanssen*)

Flying Officer P. J. Richards is 'chaired' by his crew of *C-Charlie* after finishing his tour on their return to Metheringham from the Frankfurt raid of 22/23 March. (*IWM*)

Flight Lieutenant Frank Dengate DFC RAAF
of 15 Squadron. (*Dengate*)

The crew of *K-King* in 15 Squadron 1944 in front of *E-Easy* at Mildenhall. L–R: Doug Davis, rear gunner; Frank Watson, wireless operator; Frank Dengate RAAF, pilot; Fred Coney, mid-upper gunner; Joe Ell RCAF, bomb aimer; Bobby Kitchin, flight engineer and a replacement navigator. (*Fred Coney*)

Sergeant Derek 'Pat' Patfield, bomb aimer in Denny Freeman's crew in 61 Squadron at Skellingthorpe in spring 1944. (*Patfield*)

Sergeant Leslie 'Jimmy' Chapman, wireless operator in Denny Freeman's in 61 Squadron who was awarded the Conspicuous Gallantry Medal for hi actions on the Nurmenburg raid 30/31 March 1944. (*Patfield*)

Pilot Officer Desmond 'Denny' Freeman RAFVR (21), pilot of *Q-Queenie* of 61 Squadron at Skellingthorpe in spring 1944. Freeman was KIA on 24 September 1944. (*Patfield*)

Sergeant Frank Devonshire the flight engineer, in Denny Freeman's crew. result of the Nurmenburg raid 30/31 March 1944 the crew of *Q-Queenie* n flew as a crew again. Devonshire, badly injured, was invalided out of the s and 'Tommy' Thomas never flew again either. (*Patfield*)

Flight Sergeant Bill Smith the rear gunner in Denny Freeman's crew. Smith was KIA on 8 July 1944. (*Patfield*)

Lancaster B.I R5856 QR-Q
Q-Queenie of 61 Squadron at
Skellingthorpe in spring 1944.
This Lancaster was lost on
8 July 1944 on the operation to
St Leu-d'Esserent. (*'Pat' Patfield*)

Relaxing between ops.
617 Squadron 'Dambuster'
aircrew in the sergeants mess at
Woodhall Spa, Lincolnshire
probably in the spring of 1944.
(*Dennis Cooper*)

A B-17 Flying Fortress crew in the 96th Bomb Group at Snetterton Heath, Norfolk with a Lancaster crew of 622 Squadron at RAF Mildenhall in spring 1944. Note the unpainted 'Window' chute beneath the nose of *F for Freddie*. (*IWM*)

Lancaster III ED731 AS-T *Dante's Daughter* of 166 Sq on which an American pilo completed a tour of operat gets a '65th raid completed symbol from ground crew member LAC F. Turner a Kirmington. This Lancaste began its operational servi 103 Squadron in March 1 was passed to 166 in Septe that year. It completed mo seventy sorties before bein with Flying Officer T. L. RCAF and crew on 24/25 1944 in the last major RA Bomber Command raid of war on Berlin, when seven 'heavies' were lost. Teasda five of his crew were killed survived to be taken priso 'scoreboard' acknowledges awarded to the pilot. The cream symbols are for raid Italian targets. (*IWM*)

Lancaster B.I L7540 seen here in 83 Squadron markings (the letters OL-U freshly painted over the old 44 Squadron codes on which squadron it served from January 1942) awaiting 4,000lb HC bombs. L7540 finished its career with 5 Lancaster Finishing School in 5 Group at Syerston and was SOC in April 1944.

Lancaster B.I LL845 *Lonesome Lola?* of 9 Squadron, which flew ninety-seven ops between March 1944 and August 1945 before going to 15 MU.
Lancaster *I'm Easy* of 9 Squadron.
Lancaster *Cutty Sark II* of 9 Squadron.

Commanders W. L. Brill (right) and A. W. Doubleday, two farmers from Wagga in New South Wales, whose war careers marched almost in step, typifying many famous Australian partnerships. After volunteering for the RAAF they were called up together in 1940 and thereafter their promotions were simultaneous. When they became wing commanders Brill commanded 463 Squadron RAAF and Doubleday 61 Squadron RAF. Each was awarded the DFC and DSO. Brill added a Bar to his DFC later. Both were original members of 460 Squadron RAAF.

Chapter 9: Night Fighter Nights

The *Himmelbett Räume* and the *Nachtjäger* were orchestrated by *Jägerleitoffizier*s (JLOs or GCI-controllers) in 'Battle Opera Houses'.

With the change from close-controlled *Himmelbett* to bro controlled *Wild* and *Tame B* night-fighting in the summe 1943, the night air battles ov Third Reich were directed fr five huge *Divisiongefechtsstän* (Divisional Battle Comman in Holland, France and Ger The central HQ during the of Berlin was the Battle Roo *Luftflotte Reich* in Berlin-Wa (pictured). *Generalmajor* An Nielsen Chief of Staff of *Lu Reich* and the officer in over control (right) and Oberst V Falck, since late 1943 '*Ia Fl* Senior Operations Officer responsible for the deploym operational *Nachtjagd* units keep a close eye on the development of a Bomber Command raid during the Berlin. Note the brightly pa telephone in front of Falck, was his 'Hot line' with Gör (*Falck*)

the JLOs were far removed from the actual battles, high tiered rows of *ukers* or 'Light Spitter girls' projected information onto a hugh screen for d operators moved the plots on the *Seeburg* plotting tables.

This unusual night photograph was taken during a bomber attack on the tank and lorry depot at Mailly-le-Camp, southeast of Rheims on the night of 3/4 May 1944. The photograph shows a Lancaster flying just above the rising mushrooms of smoke. Forty-two Lancasters were lost. (*'Pat' Patfield*)

Pilot Officer R. R. Reed of 61 Squadron did a remarkable job of piloting and was awarded a well-deserved DSO for bringing back Lancaster B.I ME703/UL-S2 from the costly raid on Mailly-le-Camp. Enemy fire shattered the rear turret, killing the gunner and damaging the elevators and rudders along with the oxygen and electrical systems. Because of the electrical failures the radiator flaps were inoperative, causing engine overheating. The rear turret wreckage made control so difficult that Reed had to have help from both the flight engineer and bomb-aimer in order to keep pressure on the control column and rudder pedals. (*IWM*)

Photo-reconnaissance picture
Mailly-le-Camp after the raid
Lancasters and fourteen Mos
of 1 and 5 Groups on the nig
3/4 May 1944. (*via 'Pat' Patfielc*

...r III LM446 PG-H of 619 Squadron, which was one of five Lancasters that failed to return to Dunholme Lodge from the raid on the Gnôme-Rhône ...ine factory and another factory nearby at Gennevilliers, France on 9/10 May 1944. Seven of Pilot Officer J. M. Aitken RNZAF's crew were killed and one was ...soner.

A 61 Squadron Lancaster fitted with the H₂S airborne radar transmitter taxies out for take off at Skellingthorpe and is waved off by WAAFs and RAF men.

Lancaster B.I R5868 *S-Sugar* of
467 Squadron RAAF is prepared for the
99th op on 10 May 1944 when the target
that night was the marshalling yards at
Lille. This famous Lancaster had flown
sixty-eight operations with 83 Squadron
at Scampton and Wyton, as *Q-Queenie*
July 1942-August 1943 before joining
467 Squadron RAAF at Bottesford in
September. *Sugar* returned safely from
the raid on Lille but the Squadron lost
three Lancasters, the heaviest loss it had
suffered.

Pilot Officer (later Squadron Leader)
T. N. Scholefield RAAF and his crew get
kitted up in front of Lancaster B.I R5868
S-Sugar of 467 Squadron RAAF, which
has ninety-nine ops recorded on the nose.
The Göring quotation 'NO ENEMY
PLANE WILL FLY OVER THE REICH
TERRITORY' was added by LAC
Willoughby one of the engine fitters
around the time that *Sugar* had completed
eighty-eight ops. Scholefield, who was
from Cryon, New South Wales and his
crew, flew *Sugar* on four ops, including the
100th on 11/12 May 1944 when the target
was Bourg Leopold in Belgium.

Lancaster B.I R5868 *S-Sugar* of 467 Squadron RAAF after its sortie on 11/12 May 1944 to Bourg Leopold in Belgium. *Sugar* was one of those that had not completed its bombing run when he order 'stop bombing' was given and on withdrawing from the target area was attacked by two Ju 88 nightfighters. *Sugar* was at 16,000 feet when first attacked but was down to 9,000 feet by the time the attacks were over. The 'Cookie' was jettisoned in the North Sea and a return to Waddington was made without further incident. The rear gunner, Flight Sergeant K. E. Stewart of Sydney described the incident in an interview with waiting newspaper reporters. 'They came in alternately attacking first one side and then the other. At times they were firing at us from a range of only 200 yards. The mid-upper gunner and I opened fire and we feel sure that we damaged one. Altogether we were attacked seven times in seven minutes. It was really the grand co-operation between all the crew, which enabled us to get away. "Old Sugar" went beautifully. She is a grand old bus.'

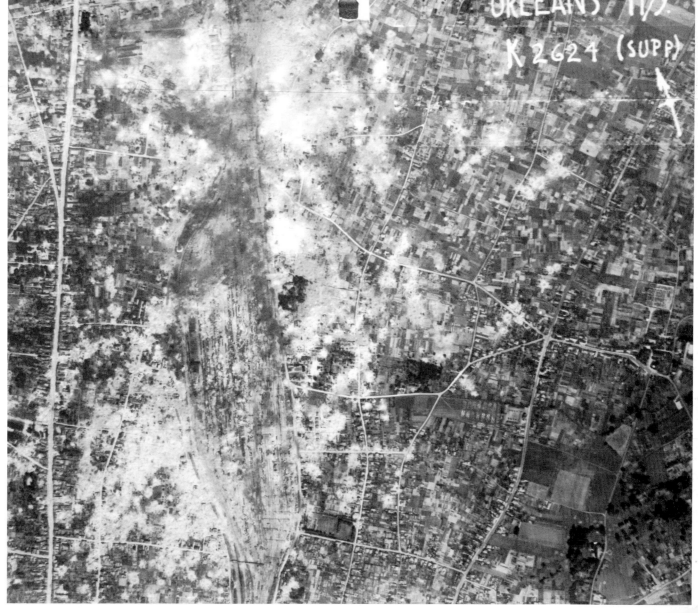

n 19/20 May 1944 118 Lancasters and four Mosquitoes of 1 and 8 Groups carried out a arly accurate attack on ilway yards at Orléans. ancaster was lost. After rther raids by Bomber mand, on 4/5 July 282 Lancasters and five osquitoes of 1, 6 and 8 ps accurately bombed rléans and Villeneuve. rteen Lancasters were lost, eleven from the euve attack and three from the Orléans raid.

(*Left*) A *Tallboy* being hoisted aloft. By the end of the war 854 of these fearsome weapons, which were filled with approximately 5,760lbs of Torpex D high explo had been dropped on a variety of targets ranging from shipping, U-boat and E-boat pens to viaducts, canals and V-weapon sites.

(*Right*) Flying Officer C. Rodgers and crew of Lancaster B.I ME739/LE-D *D-Dog* of 630 Squadron after landing at East Kirkby at 0126 hours on 19 April 1944 Juvisy raid was the first operational sortie for the aircraft. It would serve the squadron well for twelve months, being lost with Flying Officer A. V. Cameron RAA crew on the Leipzig operation of 10/11 April 1945, exactly a year after its delivery to the squadron. Cameron and three of the crew were taken prisoner and two Sergeant J. R. Dicken also baled out but his parachute was on fire and he was killed. (*IWM*)

460 Squadron RAAF was a three-flight squadron with an establishment of thirty aircraft. For virtually the whole time it was equipped with Lancasters and it claimed to have dropped more bombs on the Reich than any other squadron in Bomber Command. The squadron flew more Lancaster sorties than any other squadron, suffering the highest losses in 1 Group. Lancaster B.I W4783 AR-G was from its original complement received in 1942 and after completion of the 90th trip on 20/21 April, when it was flown by Flying Officer J. A. Critchley's crew, (pictured) 1944 the veteran 'Lanc' was presented to the Australian War Museum. Although 460 was an Australian squadron, many air crewmembers were British – in this crew the flight engineer and the two air gunners. A Binbrook C-type hangar can be seen in the background. (*IWM*)

ordered the crew to bale out. Emeny turned his turret round, reached for his parachute, put it on and turned the turret round again to jump for it. Only the parachute was not there when he reached for it. All the lights had gone out and he was crawling through thick, black, choking smoke feeling for it. He was lucky. He put his hand right on it. It had broken loose and was rolling about on the floor. Emeny put the parachute on and made for the rear door. Just before he jumped, he picked up the intercom and told Lissette that he was leaving. Lissette said: 'I thought you'd left already, you curly black headed bastard' but his words did not come easily. Emeny could hear him gasping as he fought to control the Lancaster and keep it steady, long enough for them all to escape. They were probably the last words he spoke. Lissette stayed at the controls until the Lancaster crashed at Chaintreaux in Seine-et-Marne.[36] He was critically injured and he died later in a French hospital. Emeny had to jump through flames. Within seconds of leaving the Lancaster one of the wings broke off and went over his head. Emeny had lost his second family.[37]

Unteroffizier Erich Handke[38] *Bordfunker* describes how his pilot, Hauptmann Martin Drewes *Kommandeur* of III./NJG 1 flying a Bf 110G-4/U1 and one of the few fitted with the upward-firing *Schräge Musik,* also from Laon-Athies, 65 miles away, shot down five Lancasters on what was his 113th operational sortie.

'In the area of Chamäleon (south of Compiègne) we were directed into the bomber stream and, at a height of 2,500–3,000 metres [8,100–9,700 feet], I immediately had contacts on my radar on a reciprocal course but by the time we had turned, they were out of our radar range. We flew on and finally saw the target burning in front of us and this enabled us to get into the bomber stream. I guided my pilot with the *SN-2* onto the nearest bomber and at 600 metres we could see it. The weather was wonderful, almost full moon. The flak was putting a barrage over the target. We decided not to follow the Lancasters over the target for fear of being hit by their bombs. Twenty kilometres [12 miles] to the south we again headed after the bombers, descending all the while, as they had, in the meantime, lost height to 2,300 metres [7,500 feet]. We sat under a Lancaster, which was only at 2,400 metres and shot from underneath into the wing, which burned at once. Almost immediately the bomber went down in flames. It was our 41st *Abschuss.*

'I had already found another target on my screen at 270 degrees, which meant that it was a homebound aircraft. It was flying away to the west at 2,000 metres

[6,500 feet] and at a distance of 500 metres [550 yards] we spotted it; it was another Lancaster. We got 500 metres underneath it and then climbed to within about 70 metres under the cockpit area and we fired this time into the fuselage because we could now be sure there were no bombs there. The Lancaster erupted into a bright fire and it soon crashed, ten minutes after our first victim.

'Then I again caught a machine on my radar while we were already overtaking it. It flew just in front and underneath us. We dived down fast and we spotted it 500 metres [550 yards] to our left and over us. Again we positioned ourselves quite far underneath, pulled up slowly and fired into the middle of it. There was a bright fire and immediately the Lancaster plunged down. It exploded into several parts and crashed eight minutes after our second and just like our 42nd, it came down on the banks of the river Seine near Romilly. This was our 43rd kill.

'Then Schorsch our *Funker* suddenly saw one passing diagonally over us. We immediately banked towards it. As visibility was so splendid we could keep our eyes on it easily. Again we dived down, re-positioned ourselves low underneath, as of course we didn't want to be seen, and slowly pulled up but the Lancaster also climbed, so that only at a height of 3,000 metres [9,700 feet] did we get into effective firing range. We fired a long burst of fire vertically with our *Schräge Musik,* again aiming into the middle of the bomber. The whole tail unit broke off and, engulfed in bright flames, the Lancaster plunged down. It was six minutes after our third *Abschuss.*

'The next one was immediately spotted by Petz, which weaved quite violently whilst climbing all the time. We adapted to its weaving pattern and flew along 500 metres [550 yards] underneath it. After ten minutes, when we had reached a height of 4,300 metres [14,000 feet], Schorsch saw another one closing in from behind but this one flew on a steady course. Then I spotted two more to the right and over us, of which we picked out the aircraft that cruised on most steadily. The others were only 600 metres [660 yards] away when we shot up this one from below, at a distance of 80 metres. At the same instant, it plunged down in flames and my pilot had to pull away sharply. This caused us to lose contact with the others and unfortunately, we didn't succeed in finding them again. All our kills were Lancasters. Our final victim crashed 50 kilometres [32 miles] south-west of Paris near Dreux.'[39]

Squadron Leader Sparks the deputy controller, continues:

'As we left the target my rear-gunner, Warrant Officer 'Tiger' Teague, reported four fighters on our tail. I immediately started a corkscrew, intending to lose height rapidly from 3,000 feet to return as near to ground level as possible and I took a straight line from Mailly towards England. During our second steep bank to the left I saw another fighter directly beneath us, perhaps 1,000 feet below. I pressed on with the corkscrew but this chap somehow put perhaps a dozen cannon shells into my starboard wing fuel tanks. We had no nitrogen suppression and, in a short time, the top skin of the wing had burnt through with a mass of flame. I had seen so many Lancasters with burning wings that I knew my aircraft had at most two minutes before the main spar failed with a consequent uncontrollable spin. I gave the order to bale out in my No. 2 method, which was unofficial but known and practised by my crew. This method was that the crew were to get up and get out without delay and any intercom. This they did and I was sitting there keeping an eye on the burning wing and calling up all crew positions to check that no one was left on board. None was and all lived. As I was calling the last position, the wing folded up and I immediately made a turning dive through the front hatch.'[40]

Sergeant Ronnie H. 'Squiggle' Eeles recalls:

'On arrival at Mailly we were directed to proceed to a point 15 miles away and there orbit a yellow marker. After a few minutes we did not like this at all and the crew were worried, as visibility was clear and good and we knew from experience the danger of hanging around enemy territory any longer than absolutely necessary. We were circling this flare for approximately half an hour and becoming increasingly worried, as it appeared impossible to receive any radio instructions due to an American Forces Network Broadcasting Station blasting away. I remember only too well the tune *Deep In The Heart of Texas* followed by hand clapping and noise like a party going on. Other garbled talk was in the background but drowned by the music. Whilst this noise was taking place I was suddenly aware from my position that several Lancasters were going down in flames; about five aircraft, and the fire in each was along the leading edge of the mainplane. I saw some of these planes impact on the ground with the usual dull red glow after the initial crash. My job was to keep my eyes open for enemy aircraft so I did not dwell for more than fleeting seconds on these shot down planes. At this stage I did not see any night fighter activity nor anti-aircraft fire but with regard to the latter we were still orbiting 15 miles from Mailly.

'At about 00.30 hours my pilot commenced his run in to the target and I could then see several planes burning on the ground. I do not remember hearing any instructions to the pilot from outside sources but obviously he would have obtained clearance to proceed with the bombing. During the bombing run, with the bomb-aimer directing the pilot, there was a sudden huge bang and a blinding pink red flash along the port side of the aircraft, followed immediately by the pilot saying (not shouting), "Christ, put on chutes chaps". Within a second of this the plane was hit again by anti-aircraft fire along the fuselage. There was a sizzling sound in the intercom system and then it went dead. The pink red glow on the port side persisted and I assumed we were on fire.

'I was disconnecting my electrical suit plug and leaving my flying helmet on the seat with intercom and oxygen connected when I now come to a point which has always mystified me and to this day I still think of it at times. I had a vision of my mother's face outside my turret and she said, "Jump son, jump". I was at this stage about to vacate the turret anyway. On leaving my turret and attaching my parachute, I saw the mid-upper gunner (Sergeant "Speedy" Quick) already at the fuselage door. He was using an axe to open the door and this came as no surprise as this door had previously given trouble due to difficulty in opening. Our ground crew had checked it out more than once and said they could find nothing wrong with it. By the time I reached the door Sergeant Quick had left the plane. I could see nothing in the fuselage as it was full of smoke and the plane itself seemed to be out of control.

'I rolled out of the plane in the recommended way to avoid hitting the tailplane but my legs did, in fact, brush along the underside. Fortunately my flying boots remained on. I have no recollection of pulling the parachute's "D" ring although I had it in my grasp as I baled out. I have simply no idea of when it was pulled. Being at a low level the descent did not take long but it was quite a pleasant sensation whilst it lasted. I was unaware of any noise but would have been a distance from Mailly. I came down somewhere in the area of Rheims. On looking down during the descent I thought I was heading towards what I thought was a small lake surrounded entirely by woodland. Suddenly and unexpectedly I landed heavily in what turned out to be a clearing (not water). Although I did not realize it I was actually floating backwards but on hitting the ground my head was protected by the padded collar of my Taylor suit otherwise I would probably have been injured about the head.

'On the ground I could hear bangs, maybe bombs in the distance and shouts and dogs barking in the near vicinity. I freed my parachute harness and discarded my Taylor and inside electric suits. The chute drifted across the open space and came to rest against the nearby trees. I tore off my brevet and sergeants chevrons and placed them in my battle dress pocket. I made no attempt to hide or bury the chute and left the area. I recall at this time a Mosquito flying past very fast and low in the direction of Mailly presumably, probably to take a last look at the target.

'For the remainder of the night I kept walking and at dawn heard voices in a nearby field by a large fire. As I was uncertain if this was a crashed aircraft with military or merely farm workers I gave the area a wide berth. At this time an observation plane approached at low altitude and slow speed, very close to where I was. I hid behind a tree and do not think I was noticed. Walking on, I came to the outskirts of a village and saw German troops and motor cycles and sidecars manned by soldiers. Cautiously approaching the end small cottage in this village, I rushed through the front door. A very elderly Frenchman and his yapping dog were naturally surprised and he tried to push me out, shouting "Allemandes, Allemandes". In view of the noise and perhaps his fear that I was in his cottage, I immediately left and ran out of the village. All I really wanted to know was where I was as I had my silk escape map with me. I next remember coming up towards an isolated large house but remember nothing further. Although I was not injured in any way I must have passed out. I suppose by then it was probably about nine a.m.

'When I came to, I was lying on the ground and I was being kicked about the body. On opening my eyes a German officer was pointing a pistol at my head and I was surrounded by several soldiers. I was walked back I believe to the same village I had left, searched in some presumably Army HQ and then taken to a cell. Whilst there I was told a rear-gunner had been taken out of the turret of a crashed plane and was very badly injured. I asked if I could see him but the request was refused. After two days I was taken to another town where I was placed in a cell with a navigator from 50 Squadron but after a few hours we were separated. Thereafter I was taken under guard to Oberursel Interrogation Centre at *Dulag Luft* near Frankfurt.'[41]

It had been while crossing the English Channel that Flight Lieutenant Tom Bennett, navigator of the 617 Squadron Mosquito flown by Flight Lieutenant Gerry Fawke, realized how bright the moonlight was. An advantage of being in the second wave was that they could see the 'party' starting well ahead of them and the final run in could be made by visually steering towards the action. To Bennett the raid had seemed at first to be 'progressing favourably' and everything had appeared to be 'as normal as one would expect on a raid of this size'. However, he was shocked when he saw that the yellow route markers, placed north of the camp at Germinon to mark the datum point, were visible from 'a long way off'. If they could see them from that distance 'so could the Germans'. They were shocked again when bombs began falling as they tried to mark for the second wave. No one appreciated the chaotic conditions that were developing above.[42] For the first and only time they heard another voice across the ether. 'Well get a move on, mate,' said a calm but firm Australian voice. 'It's getting a bit hot up here.' This was the first indication they had that everything was not going according to plan. Satisfied with a job well done the Mosquito crew readily obeyed their order to 'cut and run' and Bennett set course for the return route. They had seen no aircraft shot down until they were on the first leg away from the target. Then they saw the first 'ghastly' sight of a Lancaster hitting the ground and exploding in flames: 'The fireball illuminated the pall of oily smoke that was always part of such a macabre scene. To our mounting horror and concern, that was not the only casualty. Again and yet again, the tragedy was repeated. I tried to convince myself that it was German night fighters that were being shot down but the funeral pyres were too large for that. When a fifth bomber was cremated beneath us Gerry said, "Not a healthy area for a twin engined aircraft, Ben, let's find another way home." It was pandemonium in the air. Lancasters were jinxing in the sky trying to escape from the Messerschmitts and Junkers. Our gunners were aiming at the enemy but they could only hold the fighters in their sights for a few seconds before they had flown on. We didn't waste time. We were as likely to be shot down by one of our planes. The Mosquito could have been mistaken for a German night fighter. I gave Gerry a rough course for the nearest safe part of the coast and then busied myself in the niceties of tidying up to ensure that we crossed the coast at a reasonably safe spot. I could not exorcise from my mind the glimpse of hell we had seen or the thought of the crews that had been flying the planes that had crashed ... Our worst fears were confirmed later that day – 42 Lancasters missing; 14 from 5 Group and 28 from 1 Group. My first reaction was that 5 Group had stirred the hornet's nest and 1 Group had taken the stings.'[43]

163

It was as they flew over Mailly-le-Camp that the pilot of a Lancaster from Elsham Wolds had a feeling of disaster. Squadron Leader Charles Wearmouth DFC recalls:

'I saw the Lancasters circling over the datum point and I knew they were asking for trouble. It was absolute mayhem. We flew straight on several miles out from Mailly. I waited for the order to go in and bomb but all we could hear, was Glenn Miller and his music – The American Forces Radio. Then we heard the order to go in. The navigator gave us a course that took us straight in over the target. We dropped our bombs and flew straight on and home. We didn't see any German fighters and we weren't attacked but we saw aeroplanes that were. Two Lancasters exploded alongside us; another was diving towards the ground leaving a trail of smoke. Two parachutes emerged before it too exploded. We could see broken aircraft, flames and smoke, so much smoke. It wasn't until we were being debriefed that we realized how disastrous the raid had been.'

At debriefings some crews praised the 'precise' and 'accurate' marking. At Spilsby Squadron Leader Blore-Jones of 207 Squadron added this rider: 'Yellow TI on datum. No orders from Controller. Complete chaos in target area. Controller inefficient and crew discipline bad.' A further comment from 49 Squadron at Fulbeck was: 'Congestion over target to a degree of suicide – 18–25 minutes wait for order to bomb.' At Elsham Wolds Fred Browning's Lancaster was one of the last to return to the station. Jack Spark DFM recalls: 'Although our ground crew were pleased to see us there was a subdued air in the camp'. Mailly-le-Camp at least changed the policy that raids over France only counted for a third of a op; from now on they counted as a full operation. It meant that Spark and his fellow crew had finished their tour. The rear-gunner on 103 Squadron, who was just starting his tour and had not known what to expect, made it back to Elsham Wolds also. He hardly had the strength to climb out of the Lancaster when it landed. He was absolutely exhausted. He had not done anything to make him feel so tired but he supposed that reaction had set in. He and the rest of the crew looked around the Lancaster. It had been knocked about and it would need to be patched up before it flew again. All of them were subdued as they went to the debriefing. They took their coffee to the debriefing table. The coffee had a lot of rum in it. The rear-gunner did not like rum. 'What the hell' he thought. 'We had got home and I was alive. It tasted good.'[44]

The Lancaster piloted by Pilot Officer R. R. Reed DSO of 576 Squadron returning to Elsham Wolds needed assistance and he radioed ahead. That sounded ominous to men in charge of the runway in the big, heavy, four-wheeled caravan, with its glass dome on top. They scrambled into the glass house where they watched the Lancasters leaving at 30 second intervals and returning hours later, many of them badly shot up, some on three engines and demanding priority. The fire engines and ambulances were lined up and then they heard the throb of the engines as the Lancasters approached. Everything else was forgotten in the excitement of landing. Shocked at the state of some of them, one stayed in the mind of a flying control officer for the rest of his days. Those in the tower saw Reed's ailing Lancaster first and recognized the throes of a dying aircraft, tail down with the two propellers on the port side standing immobile. There was a gaping hole where the H_2S should have been and there was something heavy and bulky hanging behind the tail wheel. There was no finesse in getting down. The Lancaster came straight in, down wind, fast and low over the hedge and, as it hit the runway, the rear turret parted from what was left of the tail structure and bounced in a rolling arc towards those watching on the perimeter track. Sergeant A. A. H. Hodson was killed. Crash tenders and ambulances were already racing across the grass towards the Lancaster, veering towards it as its undercarriage collapsed and its wings and propellers gouged the ground. The Lancaster twisted, slid and stopped. The radio operator had been mortally wounded in the fighter attack that had crippled the aircraft. The mid-upper gunner had jumped down from his turret to care for his wounded colleague and had dropped straight through the hole where the H_2S had been. His chest type parachute was still in its stowage.[45]

Squadron Leader Charles Wearmouth DFC concludes:

'I always reckoned that we were the luckiest crew in the squadron. We flew 34 operations and only had trouble on two of them, Essen and Mailly-le-Camp. We lost an engine before we reached Essen and another over the target when a German night fighter attacked us All I could think about was getting the crew home. The rest of the bomber crews had left us behind and we had the skies to ourselves but the Lancaster flew steadily on. As we approached the English coast two Mosquitoes flew out and accompanied us in. We landed at West Malling in Kent. The CO phoned Elsham Wolds to say we were safe and he was told to send us home by rail so we were given travel warrants and taken down to the station. We were in full flying kit; boots, helmets, parachutes, the lot and not a soul took any notice of us. We got to King's Cross and a lady porter came over and said, "I'll give you a hand with your luggage" and she picked up a parachute by its handle and immediately the parachute was fully open and towing the porter down the platform.'[46]

On 6/7 May 149 aircraft attacked railway installations at Mantes-La-Jolie, a suburb of Gassicourt, for the loss of two Lancasters and one Halifax. Lancasters and Mosquitoes also raided Sable-sur-Sarthe and 52 Lancasters attacked an ammunition dump at Aubigne Racan for the loss of one bomber, which was piloted by Flight Lieutenant J. M. Shearer RNZAF and an NCO crew with Air Commodore Ronald Ivelaw-Chapman, the Elsham Wolds Station Commander, aboard. The New Zealander pilot and five of his crew were killed. One man evaded capture and Ivelaw-Chapman, who had only just taken up his position after a staff job, in which he had access to details of the coming invasion, survived and he was taken prisoner. His importance was never realized and the Air Commodore, the highest-ranking officer to be lost on an operation in a Lancaster, was treated in the usual manner.[47]

On 7/8 May 471 sorties were flown against five targets in France for the loss of 12 aircraft. After the attack by 53 Lancasters and eight Mosquitoes of 5 Group on the airfield at Tours, in which one Lancaster and one Mosquito were lost, Ron Watkins' crew in 57 Squadron were attacked by a night fighter while on the bomb run. 'Ginger' Hammersley, who was on his 14th operation of his tour, recalls:

'Ken Bly had warned of horizontal tracer on our starboard side and Bill Carver, of a fighter attacking someone on the port quarter. Whilst Bill kept an eye on this action from the rear turret, Tom Quayle was searching above and to the rear from his turret on top of the Lancaster. Things happened quickly, Tom called, "Fighter, Fighter, Corkscrew port – Go!" Ron needed no second telling and we went down to port in the first move of the corkscrew and the remaining bombs sprayed out from the bomb bay in all directions. I could hear Tom's and Bill's guns firing and then the crash of cannon shells and bullets from the fighter hitting our aircraft. Pulling out of the initial dive, I heard Bill call, "Are you all right up front?" Ron hastened to reassure him. In the meantime Tom had seen a fighter about 400 yards astern and just above us, identified it as a Ju 88 and opened fire simultaneously as the Ju 88. Bill quickly joined in. We were doing 250 mph on the first dive, yet the Ju 88 passed us in a vertical dive. We hoped that his dive terminated on the ground and not before. Ron completed two cycles of the corkscrew, Ken yelled to keep weaving, but Ron decided to turn onto a course 323 degrees true. Already deep into France there was no desire to go any deeper. On turning onto our course and clearing the defences, Bill was heard to call, "Skipper, I've had it". I immediately left my wireless set and went back to the rear turret, letting Bill know I was with him on arrival. He was in a sad state. Face, arms and legs were simply streaming with blood. I helped him out of the turret and with some difficulty, managed to get him along the fuselage to the rest bed. Ken had clipped on his parachute in case we had to abandon the aircraft and, on hearing the news of Bill, he came back to help me for a few minutes. He then checked the rear turret, only to find it was too badly damaged to be used. We were without any defence for the rear end! Ken rejoined me at the rest bed and we set about caring for Bill.

'Meanwhile Esmond Chung had completed an engine check and discovered the port outer engine had no oil pressure and had to be switched off and the propeller feathered. This put the power for the *Gee* navigation equipment out of action. To counter-balance the loss of the engine, Ron began to wind the rudder trim, only to find that it went round and round and did little more, so he had to jam the rudder over to starboard. Esmond went down into the nose and hung onto the rudder bar to ease the strain off Ron. Really, a rope was needed but that had to wait a while, whilst Bill's wounds were dressed. It was necessary to cut away clothing from his arms and legs. There were several nasty wounds bleeding profusely in both legs. These Ken and I covered with wound dressing pads and applied a tourniquet for a short while to each leg. His face wounds were bleeding and Ken slapped a wound dressing straight onto his face. I had to remind him it was necessary to uncover his nose, as it would help Bill to breath that much better. Having dealt with Bill's wounds, I now found the rope that was required up front and thus Ron and Esmond were able to have some of the strain of holding a straight course removed. Mack MacKinnon told us that we were about 50 miles from the French coast. This also reminded us of the briefing before the operation when we were told of the heavy coastal defences, in particular the light anti-aircraft batteries.

'After injecting pain-killing drugs into Bill's arms, I acted as another pair of eyes from the astrodome. By now Ron had decided to take the aircraft down as close to the ground as possible and we literally hedge-hopped across France with the three engines giving us 180 mph. Ron's skill as a pilot now came to the fore. It was agreed that we should get up to 10,000 feet to cross the French coast to avoid the light flak guns. We were nearly too late. As we commenced the climb, one battery opened fire at us. Ron immediately put the Lancaster into a dive straight at the guns. I watched in amazement from the astrodome, as the coloured tracer fire came flashing by my head and to each side of the aircraft. Later I discovered that we had been hit along the length of the bomb bay doors in that incident. We pulled up out of the dive and were away into the darkness as the gunfire stopped. We crossed the coast at 10,000 feet as intended, avoiding the Channel Islands. Bill was feeling the strain, being semi-conscious much of the time. He was not plugged into the intercom at this stage. In one of his brighter moments, he indicated that he wished to talk, so he was switched into the circuit.

'After clearing the Channel Islands, Tom said that there was another aircraft approaching, which he identified as a fighter. Ron was asked to turn a little to starboard and Tom opened fire with the four guns in his turret, it was a long burst, Ron then put the aircraft into a corkscrew. The night fighter appeared not to appreciate our gunfire and dived away to port and was not seen again.

'We passed over St Alban's Head and commenced to send out a "May Day" distress call. Hurn answered faintly but did not switch on its approach and runway lights. However, ahead there was another aerodrome, Tarrant Rushton, which did "light up", so we went in there. Other aircraft preparing to land were instructed to wait until we were down, Ron made a good landing on three engines and called for an ambulance. This pulled alongside us as we came to a stop near the control tower. Bill was helped from the rest bed, out of the aircraft and into the ambulance by several willing hands. He went off to Station Sick Quarters, whilst the rest of us were taken off for debriefing and breakfast. After breakfast we made our way to sick quarters only to find that Bill had already been taken to the Military Hospital in Shaftesbury. We all admired his fortitude and courage in the somewhat harassing circumstances. The flying time had been 4 hours 15 minutes. Later, when looking at the aircraft, it was in a mess. The rear turret was sheeted over and the signs of battle damage were all too obvious.'[48]

On 8/9 May the largest operation of the night was an attack by 123 aircraft on rail yards at Haine-St-Pierre, which cost six Halifaxes and three Lancasters.[49] One of the bombers that failed to return was a 405 'Vancouver' Squadron RCAF Lancaster flown by Flight Lieutenant Chase. Flight Lieutenant Tim Woodman and Pat Kemmis of 169 Squadron, supporting the operation, could clearly see the bombers, as many as 10 at a time but no sign of German night fighters. He and Kemmis

'sniffed around' for 109s and 190s over the target area but they saw none. Woodman then saw three Halifaxes 'weaving like dingbats' up at 6,000 feet. Below the leading bomber he and Kemmis could see a twin-engined aircraft climbing up to attack. It was a Bf 110 of I./NJG 4, flown by Leutnant Wolfgang Martstaller and his radar-operator/air gunner, who had taken off from Florennes at 03.00 hours. They had just shot down Chase's Lancaster and were after another victim. In a letter to his parents on 12 May, Martstaller wrote: 'The sky was fully lit, so we could easily see the Tommy. We saw at least 10 bombers. However, we could only concentrate on one aircraft. When I was near him and fired (and my burst of fire bloody well blinded me!) the *Schwinehund* fired off a flare with a signal pistol, so that an enemy night fighter could post us).'

Martstaller, however, was unable to pick off another of the bombers because he was attacked immediately by Woodman and Kemmis. The Mosquito pilot fired a two-second-burst and Martstaller dived into the darkness, Kemmis following him on *Serrate*. Martstaller soared up in a steep climb and Woodman fired from 800 yards. This time he opted out and took the Mosquito on a chase across the French countryside at treetop height. Though they could not see him as he flew away from the moon, they easily followed him on *Serrate*. Martstaller went into a steep dive to almost zero feet ('at night!') but still he could not escape from the Mosquito's attention. The German made the mistake of flying towards the moon and Woodman saw the moonlight glint off his wings. He fired and got some strikes on his fuselage and wings as he flew across a wide open space, which looked like an aerodrome. Martstaller went into a steep turn and, firing 50 yards ahead of him to allow for deflection, Woodman hit him again. White smoke poured from the 110's port engine and, closing to 150 yards, Woodman gave him another two seconds burst and hit him again. Martstaller was fortunate to spot a field in which to belly land. He and his *Bordfunker* were slightly injured from shrapnel. Next day they discovered that a large explosion they had seen two miles away was 'their' *Viermot* 'with seven crew-members burned to death'. Martstaller ended his letter, '*We were so happy!*'[50]

Further raids were made on 9/10 May on coastal batteries in France and on 10/11 May rail targets were bombed. On the night of 11/12 May, 429 bombers of the main force made attacks on Bourg-Leopold, Hasselt and Louvain in Belgium. The target for 190 Lancasters and eight Mosquitoes of 5 Group was a former Belgian *Gendarmerie* barracks at Leopoldsburg (Flemish)/Bourg-

Leopold (French), which was being used to accommodate 10,000 *SS* Panzer troops who awaited the Allied invasion forces. The weather was bad with low cloud and poor visibility and a serious error was made with the broadcast winds. As a result, the aircraft were late over the target area and consequently flare-dropping was scattered and provided no adequate illumination. An *Oboe* Mosquito flown by Flight Lieutenants Burt and Curtis, of 109 Squadron, dropped a yellow marker. The Mosquito marking force of 627 Squadron arrived late over the target with the result that the *Oboe* proximity marker was seen by only one of the marking aircraft and it, unfortunately, seemed to burn out very quickly. Flare dropping was scattered and did not provide adequate illumination of the target. Haze and up to 3/10ths cloud conditions hampered the marking of the target. The 'marking leader' then asked the 'master bomber' (Squadron Leader Mitchell of 83 Squadron), if he could drop 'red spot fires' as a guide for the flare force. The master bomber agreed and 'RSFs' went down at 00.24 hours in the estimated vicinity of the target. Unfortunately, the 'main force' started to bomb this red spot fire immediately it went down and half of the main force bombed this. The result of this was the five Mosquitoes of 627 Squadron returned to Oakington with their bombs and were unable to mark the target. Immediately Mitchell ordered '*stop bombing*', as he realized it was impossible to identify the target but VHF was very poor, particularly on Channel 'B' and the Germans had jammed Channel 'A'. Only half the main force received the 'stop bombing' instruction and 94 Lancasters bombed the target. At 00.34 hours a wireless message, 'Return to base' was sent out to all crews.

One of the aircraft that failed to return on 11/12 May was a Lancaster of 166 Squadron flown by Pilot Officer Geoffrey J. R. Clark, which was probably shot down by Oberleutnant Gottfried Hanneck of 6./NJG 1 for his first victory.[51] 'In the early morning of 11 May my crew and I were detached from Deelen to Düsseldorf. In the evening we came to immediate readiness at around 18.00 hours and one hour later, I was ordered to fly to Melsbroek near Brussels and 'towards the enemy' as I was told. I touched down at Melsbroek at 20.42 hours and came to immediate readiness again. Our patience was really tested as only just before 23.00 hours our night fighter *Jägerleitoffiziers* reported aircraft flying in. After having been ordered to scramble at 23.20 hours, we flew in the direction of the Ruhr area in the hope of intercepting the *Viermots* during their outward flight. And we succeeded; we caught one on our *SN-2*! My radar operator gave me courses to steer to get a visual

on the target. However, before we caught a first sight of our target, a steam of tracer appeared before me, which smashed into a *Viermot*, putting it on fire and it plunged down out of control. All of a sudden, the night sky was turned into daylight by the burning bomber and I had to break off and 'hide' into the darkness some distance away, fearing that the massed firepower of other *Viermots* would 'fry' me!

'In the meantime, I had arrived over the edge of the flak zone, so I turned away and started searching for a new target in the withdrawal route of the British. We were successful in our search, as we flew several tracks to the west and north-west. Thus, we got a new contact on the *SN-2,* a four-engined aircraft that tried to get home and away at high speed, whilst slightly losing height. This time, no 'colleague' was chasing the same target. I slowly got closer, until I could make it out with my bare eyes. Approaching at the same altitude (13,000 feet) I gradually lost some height and positioned myself 100 to 150 metres beneath my target. It now hung over us, as large as a barn door. I put my sights on the fuselage and with the *Schräge Musik*. I fired through the whole length of it, by slowly pushing my aircraft down and away from the bomber. We watched how many hits registered in the whole fuselage; our target dived down steeply and crashed onto the ground in the area of the mouth of the River Scheldt. We saw how it exploded on impact, with a huge detonation and a sheet of flames. Time of our *Abschuss* was 00.48 hours. Fifty minutes later we touched down on our aerodrome at Deelen, it was a good landing and we were unhurt. Later on, our weapons mechanics established that I had used ample ammunition. This was quite understandable, as I was only a novice who wanted to make sure of the kill. During my later *Abschüsse* I was more economical![52]

George Vantilt, a 15 year old Beverlo boy, recalls:
'The raid of 12 May had brought the terror of war again to the doorstep of the people of Beverlo. Eighty-four people were killed and many more were wounded. One lady died one year after the raid. She lost her whole family and could not get over her grief. Low flying aircraft woke us up that night. We lived in the Korspelstraat No.3. We had no air-raid shelter. Together with my parents and sister we ran to the neighbours who had a shelter in the garden. Once inside, the first bombs were falling very close. We were thinking that they bombed the coal mine at Beringen.[53] We all prayed. The constant change of air pressure hurt our ears. I can assure you it was hell on earth! The family escaped unhurt and our house, too, was lucky. As we came out of the shelter, fires were all around. Most of the people

had small farms and even now when I smell burnt hay I think of that terrible night in May. The day after the raid we all went to the village. The road called Zuidstraat was hit the most. It was totally destroyed. The dead cows in the fields spread a terrible smell. The people were shocked and in one house a complete family was killed. Everybody in the village lost a relative or friend that night. The next Sunday after the raid we went to church as usual. After the service, my friend and I went to the crash site of a Lancaster, which had exploded in mid-air during the raid. The place where one of the crewmembers had died could still be seen as a print in the cornfield. Parts of the aircraft were scattered over one kilometre.'[54]

On the night of 19/20 May Bomber Command resumed operations with raids by 900 aircraft on five separate rail targets in France, two French coastal gun positions at Le Clipon and Merville and a radar station at Mont Couple. At Le Mans 112 Lancasters and four Mosquitoes attacked rail yards and caused serious damage. Three Lancasters, including two 7 Squadron aircraft, one carrying the CO and master bomber, Wing Commander John Fraser Barron DSO* DFC DFM a New Zealander from Dunedin, and the other his deputy, Squadron Leader J. M. Dennis DSO DFC, were lost in a collision over the target. Crew reported hearing Barron, who was 23 years old, and was flying his 79th operation, talking to another Lancaster crew before the night lit up with a huge explosion.[55] The railway yards at Orléans were bombed accurately by 118 Lancasters and four Mosquitoes without loss but a similar force found that their target at Amiens was cloud-covered and the master bomber ordered the attack to stop after 37 Lancasters had got their bombs away. The most difficult sorties of the entire night[56] were flown by 113 Lancasters and four Mosquitoes of 5 Group, who attempted to bomb the railway installations in the centre of Tours where a previous raid by 5 Group had destroyed the St Pierre-des-Corps yards on the outskirts of the town. Both the marking and the bombing force were ordered to carry out their tasks with particular care and to be prepared to wait until the master bomber was satisfied that the surrounding housing areas were not hit. Pilot Officer Ron Auckland of 61 Squadron flew one of the Lancasters that took part. His bomb-aimer, 'Pat' Patfield, who was on his sixth op, recalled that it was another 'funny do'.

'I settled down in the nose of the aircraft with my maps and prepared for what we anticipated would be a fairly short trip of about 4½ hours. Not flying over Germany we were not unduly worried. The outward flight, apart from a fair amount of flak, was fairly uneventful. Some distance from Tours we could see the area illuminated by the marker flares and I got ready for the bombing run. By now the flak was more intense. I tried to ignore it as much as possible, concentrating on getting the target aligned in the bombsight graticule by giving the usual instruction to the pilot. "Left-left-right-steady"-etc. Just as I was about to give the order, "Open bomb doors" there was a hell of a crash and a shout from the pilot and the aircraft vibrated like a mad thing. Obviously, I thought that we had been hit by flak. The aircraft went up on one wing. "We're OK – Pat, can you bomb?" called the skipper. I said, "Yeah." The bombsight graticule was vibrating badly but things seemed to be OK. We had, by now, turned slightly off target but I took an average and let the bombs go. Normally, when the Lanc crossed the target you would release the bombs as the aiming point reached the cross wire. As we left the target area, the skipper said: "Right Pat, you'd better come up here quick, we've been hit by another Lancaster."

'After I'd closed the bomb bay doors, I went up. In spite of the poor light I could see that there was about 10 feet of the port wing slashed open, the port outer prop was bent back over the wing and the port inner sounded like a bag of nails. The Perspex top of the cabin just above the pilot's head was also broken. He told us that the aircraft, which had hit us, was flying in almost the opposite direction and had just skimmed over us. Only another foot or so lower and there would have been an awful big bang and "curtains" for the lot of us. With the vibration now minimized by nature of the dead engine, we carried on, and headed for home. After a while the port inner engine gave trouble and the prop had to be feathered. This meant continuing on the two starboard engines only. We were getting pretty low as we approached the south coast of England so it was decided to make an emergency landing at Tangmere airfield in Sussex. We were all relieved in making a safe landing. The next day, leaving our somewhat bent Lanc on the airfield after collecting our charts and equipment, we were flown back to Skellingthorpe. How true it was, I cannot vouch, but apparently the aircraft which hit us had made a dummy run over the target, turned around to make another run up and had crossed the bomber stream. The aircraft was later being identified by the damage to its underside caused by the collision. For bringing his damaged aircraft safely back, Ron Auckland was awarded a well-deserved DFC. I was to do a further 14 operational flights (before joining another crew for the remainder of my tour of 33 ops) with Ron. Incidentally, on this flight, our target photograph showed that we had hit the marshalling yards OK!'

Bomber Command directed its might against German targets once again on 21/22 May when 532 aircraft raided Duisburg. Twenty-nine Lancasters were lost, *Zahme Sau* crews claiming 26 bombers shot down, most of them over the southern provinces of the Netherlands.[57] The next night, 22/23 May, Dortmund was severely hit by 361 Lancasters and 14 Mosquitoes for the loss of 18 Lancasters. A second stream of 225 Lancasters and 10 Mosquitoes that went to Brunswick lost 13 Lancasters. Two nights later Bomber Command's main objectives for 264 Lancasters, 162 Halifaxes and 16 Mosquito bombers were the Westbahn rail station in Aachen and the Rothe Erde marshalling yard east of the town. Aachen was an important focal point for traffic moving from the Ruhr to France.[58] No aircraft were lost on the raids on Eindhoven (where bad weather prevented bombing), the French coast or Antwerp but 25 Lancasters and Halifaxes failed to return from the attacks on Aachen-West, which was well hit, and the Rothe Erde yards, which escaped serious damage.[59]

After a night of minor operations on 26/27 May, the men of Bomber Command steeled themselves again for main force attacks on Bourg-Leopold, the Rothe Erde railway yards at Aachen, a railway junction at Nantes, the airfield at Rennes and coastal batteries on the French coast. Altogether, over 1,100 bombers, mine-layers and Mosquitoes, who visited targets in Germany, were dispatched against 17 separate operations. Bomber crews were cautioned that the target at Bourg-Leopold in the north-east corner of Belgium was a rectangle image of lines dividing it diagonally and Allied prisoners were on the close side and to the left so they were told, 'Don't undershoot'. This time 331 aircraft[60] were to finish the job that had ended in disaster a few nights earlier. A lone Mosquito bomber had already dropped a yellow flare on the target and it was backed up by a Pathfinder Force dropping flares when the bombers arrived. Five *Oboe* Mosquitoes dropped TIs and the third and most accurate salvo fell 320 yards short of the aiming point. The early visual markers were wide to the south but a salvo of 'whites' went down 250 yards south-west of the aiming point. Wing Commander S. P. 'Pat' Daniels of 35 Squadron, the master bomber, saw early bombs fall among the camp buildings and the aiming point soon became obscured by smoke. Daniels reported:

'Our load for the trip to Leopoldsburg was 28 hooded flares, six TIs yellow, five TI yellow and one 4,000lb "cookie". The weather over the target was no cloud and the vertical visibility good. The target was identified visually, aided by a red TI and flares. On approach to the target at 01.59 hours two red TIs were seen on aiming point. I broadcast from 02.01 hours to 02.13 hours. Our own yellow target indicator was dropped on the NW end of the red TI. I instructed the main force to bomb on the yellow target indicators. White TIs were well backing up yellows. I instructed the main force during the last 3 mins to bomb on whites to port and this with one-second overshoot. The main force bombing was good. One large explosion from the centre of target, rising well above ground with minor explosions in the air and this at 02.07 hours.'

Nine Halifaxes and one Lancaster were lost on the Bourg-Leopold raid. In all probability they were all shot down by prowling *Nachtjäger* over Belgium. One Lancaster each was lost attacking the coastal batteries and Nantes and 12 Lancasters failed to return from the raid on Aachen. One of the Lancasters of 166 Squadron that took part in the attack on the Rothe Erde railway yards and was seriously damaged by fighter attack was *Fair Fighter* flown by Flight Sergeant S. G. Coole. Sergeant A. W. Downs the flight engineer recalls:

'We had already done 10 ops in *Fair Fighter* and were half way to the Belgian coast on the way home from Aachen when we were attacked by a Bf 109. The intercom was damaged and smoke filled the cockpit. The skipper motioned that he had lost control of the rudders; the port engine temperature was rising and we were losing power on the others. In the thick smoke the rear of the aircraft seemed to be all right and I went back to take a look. With the W/Op and mid-upper gunner we put the fire out and then found that the rudder control had been shot through and the rear-gunner injured – as well as three of the parachutes having been riddled with incendiary bullets. I made a rough repair to the rudder control and went back up front. The skipper decided to make for Woodbridge. The rudder control gave way again and we had to blow down the undercarriage using the air bottle, as the hydraulics had gone. We also had no flaps. It was a fast touchdown and almost at once the aircraft veered to starboard; the brakes had been damaged so we had to go where the Lancaster wanted to go! On reaching the edge of the runway we hit an incline and the aircraft was momentarily airborne again. A terrific roar and then the aircraft stopped. We had come to rest in a wood and we all clambered out. After breakfast and a rest we took another look at our Lancaster and realized how lucky we had been to survive. That afternoon an aircraft came down from Kirmington to collect us and in due course we had a brand new aircraft, which we named *Fair Fighter's Revenge.'*

Following the raid on Bourg-Leopold Marcel Heselmans, a resistance fighter code-named *Sixtus*, whose brother Leon was also in the resistance, cycled to see the damage to Bourg-Leopold so that he could transmit information to England. According to *Sixtus*, 7,000 German soldiers were killed or missing and 218 German women, who arrived on 26 May to receive nursing training, were also killed. He added that the spirit of the German soldiers at Leopoldsburg was totally destroyed. Many were still absent and hiding in the surrounding woods and had deserted. Civilian casualties were 22 killed. All the buildings 'including the big messes' had been destroyed. The 'Cavalry Camp', which held many Belgian political prisoners survived the attack. The guards had closed the doors and ran away leaving the prisoners locked up unattended. Marcel, together with other members of his team, was taken prisoner a few weeks later and he was shot on 15 July 1944, as he tried to escape when he was transported from the interrogation office to the prison of Hasselt.

An operation to Angers went ahead on the night of 28/29 May when 118 Lancasters and 8 Mosquitoes attacked the railway yards and junction. Frank Dengate recalls:

'We did the usual air test in daylight then attacked Angers – 1,780 gallons of fuel and 10,885lbs of bombs. This was a strange trip. We flew across England at 1,000 feet from Cambridge to Lands End. It was wonderful sight seeing all road traffic stopped below and people waving – the noise of a few hundred Lancasters must have been deafening on the ground. Then out we went to sea and east towards France. As we got closer we climbed to 19,999 feet, the idea being to avoid early radar warning by the Germans. It was a very good prang. No flak. No fighters.'[61]

The long range heavy gun battery at St Martin de Varreville, behind what was to be *Utah* beach, presented a threat to Allied shipping approaching Normandy and also to the troops landing on *Utah* beach. It was decided that 5 Group would attack this precision target, so on the night of 28/29 May, a force of 64 Lancasters, led by a flare force from 83 and 97 Lancaster Pathfinder Squadrons and four Mosquitoes of 627 Squadron, flew to St Martin de Varreville. The flare force identified the gun battery on their H$_2$S sets and laid a carpet of flares over the target. At zero hour minus five minutes, the Mosquitoes roared in at 2,000ft and identified the gun battery visually. They released their red TIs on the battery, creating a box of flares around it. The master bomber now called in the main force, with each aircraft carrying several 1,000lb armour-piercing bombs and the target was obliterated.[62]

On 31 May/1 June, 219 aircraft[63] in another operation in support of the forthcoming invasion, attacked the railway marshalling yards at Trappes in Paris in two waves. The purpose of the operation, carried out in brilliant moonlight, was to disrupt German troop movements and war materials from eastern France, central Germany and the occupied countries. As the bombers approached the target area, flying high above the almost 10/10ths low lying cumulus, the target area was apparently full of night fighters. The master bomber called for assistance but the anguished reply from the deputy master bomber was, 'I bloody can't. I've been hit', whether by one of the numerous bursts of heavy flak in the target area at that time or enemy fighter activity. Several aircraft, including some squadron commanders', were lost. On the whole, enemy fighter activity was considered intense in the target area. Presumed to be a relatively easy target, Trappes apparently lived up to its name and had become an operational aircraft trap. The presence of 14 Bomber Support RCM aircraft and 16 *Serrate* and nine *Intruder* Mosquitoes may have had something to do with the low loss rate as did other operations this night.

Pilot Officer Ron Walker's crew were one of four crews in 57 Squadron at East Kirkby who flew *Gardening* sorties, laying sea mines in the Kattegat, as Sergeant 'Ginger' Hammersley, recalls:

'Before we were briefed, we carried out air to air and air to sea firing from the gun turrets. At the same time all equipment was checked ready for the minelaying operation we would be carrying out that night. The firing and testing took 45 minutes after taking off at 14.40 hours. At briefing there was invariably an officer from the Royal Navy who specialized in minelaying. We were to carry six Mk.VI mines which had to be dropped following a timed flight from a point given at briefing and based on the reading given by the H$_2$S radar equipment. The whole flight would be at low level so as to avoid the enemy radar detection equipment. The target was in the Kattegat, well down this waterway between Denmark and Sweden and not far from Kiel Bay. The altitude for the bombing run right up to dropping the mines was to be at 4,000 feet. We were away at 21.35 hours in fine weather. There was no opposition and all the mines were dropped into place as briefed, after which all the crews returned safely to base. We landed at 05.20 hours, a total of 7 hours 45 minutes flying time. Later the *Wall Newspaper* reported: "A long low-level flight in near daylight conditions by four aircraft of 57 Squadron is worthy of note. These four took off into the fading sun of double summer time at 23.40 hours to fly at 500 feet around the northern tip of Denmark and down the Kattegat to drop their sea mines off Alborg, returning by the same route. The late sunset and early dawn were linked by the midnight sun and for the whole flight it was possible to see clear to the horizon. From two miles out we could see clearly Gothenburg's neutral waterfront ablaze with street and house lights, this was a rare sight after the experience of a blacked out Europe."

'Whilst the four crews that had flown the mine-laying operation were sleeping during the daytime on the 1 June, the squadron was preparing for a night attack on the Saumur railway junction. Fifteen crews took part in the attack and all returned safely to base. On 2 June I was promoted to flight sergeant. Great rejoicing and a couple of beers in the mess bar that night. Ten crews, including my crew, were briefed to destroy the Wireless Telegraphy Station at Ferme-D'Urville on the French coast that night with 4,000lb MC and sixteen 500lb MC bombs per aircraft. Our take-off was at 23.00 hours. It was 3 hours 40 minutes later when we returned from the attack, which had proved successful against light opposition. There were no squadron losses. There were operations on for the 4th but my own crew was stood down and the attack took place by 15 crews from the squadron on enemy gun emplacements at Maisy on the French coast. All returned safely.[64] On the 5th a check was carried out to see how we were faring as a crew and to see if we were all still capable of carrying out our duties to the full. This proved to be satisfactory. We were also on the battle order for an early morning attack on the 6th.'

Almost everyone had known for several weeks that the invasion of France was imminent but only the Chiefs of Staff knew when and where. Wing Commander Rollo Kingsford-Smith RAAF,[65] CO of 463 Squadron, which operated Lancasters at Waddington, recalls:

'In June I heard more and more accounts about the masses of Allied troops, guns and tanks building up in the south of England. It was obvious a very substantial army operation would soon begin but I was too busy with my own war even to think about the Army's activities, let alone find out any more details. On the evening of 5 June the Operation Order coming through on our teleprinter began: "Main force aircraft from 53 Base will attack the enemy gun battery at Pointe du Hoc. Objective to destroy enemy gun positions at 4.50 am on 6 June."'

Allied intelligence had pinpointed 73 fixed coastal gun batteries that could menace the invasion. The gun positions were bombed throughout May, with a heavier than average attack by both day and night three days before D-Day. Now they were to be bombed again during the night of 5 June. Pointe du Hoc, a cliff rising 100 feet high from a very rocky beach, 3.7 miles west of Vierville, where a six-gun battery (thought to be 155mm, with a range of 25,000 yards) could engage ships at sea and fire directly onto *Omaha* and *Utah* beaches.

'In my mind this attack would be about the most important my squadron had ever made' says Kingsford-Smith 'and we were all determined that it would succeed. The location given in the operation order was on the Normandy coast. To me it meant that Allied forces could be landing there immediately after we had finished with the enemy gun battery. I say, "could be landing" because the weather forecast for the English Channel for the 6th was terrible and it seemed quite unsuitable for the small craft that the invasion forces would be using.'

Notes

1. Figures on a clock face, i.e. east to west in the northern part of the night fighting area.
2. The highly prized Knight's Cross was awarded to Bergmann after he destroyed six Lancasters on the night of 3/4 May.
3. *Lancaster-The Story Of A Famous Bomber* by Bruce Robertson (Harleyford Publications Ltd, 1964).
4. Lancaster III ND395 of 83 Squadron was destroyed by the Aachen flak defences. All the other eight losses were due to *Nachtjäger*. One *Viermot* each by Oberleutnant Werner Baake and Feldwebel Rauer (on his 1st combat sortie) of I./NJG 1 at Venlo and Major Heinz-Wolfgang Schnaufer of Stab IV./NJG 1 at St Trond claimed two heavies (Lancaster III ND389 of 83 Squadron west of Turnhout, and Lancaster I LL899 of 49 Squadron near St Leonhard) destroyed. At the end of 1943 Schnaufer's night victories stood at 40, with four Lancasters being shot down on 16/17 December.
5. In October 1944 Group Captain Hugh S. L. 'Cocky' Dundas reached the rank at the age of 24.
6. *The Dam Busters* by Paul Brickhill (Evans Bros, London, 1951).
7. Cheshire used this aircraft on 10/11 April to mark a Signals Depot at St Cyr during a dive from 5,000 to 1,000 feet. These successes led to 617 Squadron receiving four FB.VIs/XVIs for marking purposes.
8. *At First Sight; A Factual and anecdotal account of No. 627 Squadron RAF*, researched and compiled by Alan B. Webb, 1991.
9. Three *Oboe* Mosquitoes of 8 Group also took part in the operation.
10. The target at La Chapelle was marked by three 617 Squadron Mosquitoes. Six Lancasters failed to return from this raid. Main force targets included Cologne and four rail targets in France

and Belgium. Two hundred and forty-seven Lancasters of 5 Group and 22 Mosquitoes were dispatched to the rail target at La Chapelle. Another 175 aircraft attacked Lens, while 196 aircraft attacked rail yards at Ottignies in Belgium. Four Lancasters were lost on the Cologne raid. None of the aircraft attacking Ottignies was lost.

11. The raid was not successful. The initial marking by 617 Squadron Mosquitoes was accurate but many of the main force of Lancasters did not bomb these, partly because of a thin layer of cloud, which hampered visibility, and partly because of faulty communications between the various bomber controllers. Many bombs were dropped in the centre of the city but the remainder of the force bombed reserve H₂S-aimed TIs, which were well to the south. Damage caused was not extensive.

12. When 637 aircraft bombed Karlsruhe and 234 Lancasters and 16 Mosquitoes raided Munich.

13. Sir Arthur Harris had sanctioned the release of the Mosquitoes to 617 Squadron and insisted they could be retained only if Munich was hit heavily. While no award of the Victoria Cross was ever made for a Mosquito sortie, Cheshire's contribution to the success of the Munich operation on 24/25 April, when he led four Mosquitoes of the marking force in 5 Group, was mentioned in his VC citation on 8 September 1944. In part it said, 'Cheshire's cold and calculated acceptance of risks is exemplified by his conduct in an attack on Munich in April 1944. This was an experimental attack to test out the new method of target marking at low level against a heavily defended target situated deep in enemy territory. He was obliged to follow, in bad weather, a direct route, which took him over the defences of Augsburg and thereafter he was continuously under fire. As he reached the target, flares were being released by our high-flying aircraft and he was illuminated from above and below. All guns within range opened fire on him. Diving [from 12,000 to 3,000ft and then flying repeatedly over the city at little more than 700 feet] he dropped his markers with great precision and began to climb away. So blinding were the searchlights that he almost lost control. He then flew over the city at 1,000 feet to assess the accuracy of his work and direct other aircraft. His own was badly hit by shell fragments but he continued to fly over the target area until he was satisfied that he had done all in his power to ensure success ... for a full 12 minutes after leaving the target area he was under withering fire, but he came safely though ... What he did in the Munich operation was typical of the careful planning, brilliant execution and contempt for danger which has established for Wing Commander Cheshire a reputation second to none in Bomber Command'. The crews who took part were: Cheshire and Pat Kelly; Squadron Leader Dave Shannon DSO and Len Sumpter; Flight Lieutenant Terry Kearns and Flight Lieutenant Hone Barclay, and Flight Lieutenant Gerry Fawke and Flight Lieutenant Tom Bennett. The four aircraft flew to Manston on the Kent coast to begin the operation. Shannon dived from 15,000 to 4,000 feet but his markers hung up, while the fourth Mosquito got four spot flares away. Shannon received a bar to his DSO in September 1944 after he had completed many more important operational sorties with 617 Squadron. The most outstanding of these was when he flew as deputy master bomber and deputy leader to Wing Commander Cheshire on the Munich raid.

14. A liquid-filled 30lb incendiary bomb, which was not as effective as was hoped and many failed to explode. Bomber Harris glee-

fully pointed out that the Germans, who recovered these, warmly welcomed them and the petrol content was used as *ersatz* motor spirit for their vehicles.

15. All Groups except 5 Group dispatched almost 600 bombers including 323 Lancasters, to Düsseldorf in what was described as an 'old style heavy attack on a German city'. (*The Bomber Command War Diaries* by Martin Middlebrook and Chris Everitt). Brunswick was visited by 238 Lancasters and 17 Mosquitoes of 5 Group and 10 Lancasters of 1 Group, while 181 from four Groups attacked the railway yards at Laon in two waves.

16. *Nachtjagd* claimed 28–31 kills with Hauptmann Heinz-Wolfgang Schnaufer destroying four *Viermots* for his 53rd–56th victories. Two nights later Schnaufer claimed two more kills (Lancasters of 156 and 408 Squadrons). On six nights, 21–28 April, 1,407 night fighter sorties were dispatched, which resulted in claims for 135 bombers destroyed. During the whole of April 215 victories were claimed by *Nachtjagd* crews.

17. That night, 26/27 April 1,060 aircraft of Bomber Command were to raid Essen, Schweinfurt and Villeneuve-St-Georges, 493 aircraft going to Essen and 217 Halifaxes, Lancasters and Mosquitoes attacking the southern end of the railway yards at Villeneuve-St-Georges.

18. Two hundred and six Lancasters were heading for Schweinfurt, which was to be marked by eleven Mosquitoes of 627 Squadron, which had recently transferred to 5 Group from 8 (PFF) Group.

19. They had been hit by a Bf 110 night fighter flown by 22 year old *Experte* Oberleutnant Heinz-Wolfgang Schnaufer *Ritterkreuztrager* and *Gruppenkommandeur*, IV./NJG1. *V-Victor* was one of the 'Night Ghost of St Trond's' two Lancaster victims that night. During 1944 he achieved 64 victories; a record that was unequalled in the *Nachtjagd*.

20. In all, 30 aircraft (28 per cent) were lost this night. The award of the Victoria Cross was made after the war, on 26 October 1945, to Sergeant (later Warrant Officer) Norman Cyril Jackson RAFVR, a flight engineer in a Lancaster of 106 Squadron, which was shot down near Schweinfurt. A German night fighter hit the Lancaster and a fire started in a fuel tank in the wing near the fuselage. Jackson climbed out of a hatch with a fire extinguisher, with another crew member holding the rigging lines of his chute, which had opened in the aircraft. Jackson lost the fire extinguisher and, as the fire was affecting both him and his parachute rigging, the men in the aircraft let the parachute go. Jackson survived, though with serious burns and a broken ankle received on landing with his partially burnt parachute. The remainder of the crew baled out soon afterwards. Jackson was born in 1919 at Ealing. He was a fitter in civilian life and joined the RAF in October 1939. His first operational tour was with Coastal Command and he joined Bomber Command in 1943. He had completed 30 operations on 106 Squadron up to the time of his capture.

21. He was. Smith was killed when Lancaster I ME679 DX-K of 57 Squadron was involved in a collision with Lancaster I of 44 Rhodesian Squadron piloted by Flying Officer G. W. Oldham DFC who was a Rhodesian who had flown his first tour on 61 Squadron. There was only one survivor from Boyle's crew. All seven of Oldham's crew died. Two I./NJG 6 Bf 110s were lost to flak and return fire but the *Nachtjagd* crews returned with eight *Abschüsse* plus three probables. The Schweinfurt force lost 21 Lancasters, or 9.3 per cent. At Asten near Eindhoven *Ritterkreuzträger* Oberfeldwebel Rudolf Frank of 3./NJG 3, flying a Bf 110G-4 night fighter with *Schräge Musik*

cannon from Vechta claimed his 45th and final *Abschuss* (Lancaster III ND873 of 12 Squadron) before he and his crew were hit by debris from their quarry. Frank and Oberfeldwebels Schierholz and Schneider crashed to their deaths. Frank was posthumously promoted to Leutnant at the end of April on Hitler's birthday. II./NJG 5 and I. and II./NJG 6 dispatched 33 *Zahme Sau* Bf 110s against the stream of 206 Lancasters heading for Schweinfurt.

22. Sergeant D. Clark, Pilot Officer W. F. Collins RAAF; Flight Sergeant S. Evans, Sergeant E. A. Hatch, Sergeant L. A. G. Izod, Squadron Leader Murdoch RNZAF and Sergeant J. E. Rees, were buried in graves near the village.

23. Bradley, who was badly wounded, was taken to St Dizier and to Dr Rény's clinic where he was given the best treatment that his limited supply of drugs and paper bandages would allow. However, the young pilot had lost a lot of blood and further risks to all concerned would serve no purpose so the German controlled hospital at Chaumont was contacted and he was hospitalized. The medical orderly ironically, had once lodged in Lincoln. After two visits from the *Gestapo* Bradley was put on a train under guard for L'Hôpital Beaujon at Clichy in Paris, an imposing building of 11 floors and a huge entrance hall, boasting busts of Hitler and Goering. Bradley shared a room with a young American bomb-aimer, Otto P. Mathis, from Cleveland who seemed in 'bad shape'. On 9 May Bradley 'celebrated' his 22nd birthday and then, with other aircrew, began the train journey to Frankfurt and *Dulag Luft* and finally, POW camp. Bradley's own crew was posted to 619 Squadron at Dunholme Lodge where they received a new pilot, Flying Officer L. A. Hall. On 9 August 1944 in Lancaster I ME866 this crew was involved in a collision with a Lancaster of 50 Squadron over Châttellerault near Poitiers. Only Sergeant Clelland, in Hall's crew, survived and similarly, only one member of the 50 Squadron Lancaster survived.

24. Bomber Command Quarterly Review No. 9.

25. In all 1,234 tons of bombs were dropped on the target thanks in no small part to the marking by the PFF Force. Bomber Command later estimated that 67 per cent of Friedrichshafen's built-up area was devastated and German officials later admitted that this was the most damaging raid on tank production of the war.

26. Sergeants R. Watson and J. G. Eastman and Flight Sergeants A. Matthews and W. Cully. The Lancaster crashed at Schoenau, a small village on the west bank of the Rhine and opposite the little German community of Rheinhausen (Oberhausen). Some 16km west-north-west is the French town of Selestat. Those who were killed are buried in Schoenau churchyard. That same night 15 Squadron lost another Lancaster to a night fighter when Flying Officer S. J. R. Soper RCAF and his crew were killed. In all, the force lost 18 Lancasters. Thirteen confirmed victories plus a probable were credited to a Ju 88 *Luftbeobachter* crew, Austrian-born Hauptmann Leopold 'Poldi' Fellerer of II./NJG 5, and I./NJG 6.

27. After the war he spent two years in the Royal Auxiliary Air Force flying Spitfires. Every year since the war Miller, Beazley-Long and Mead met under the station clock at Charing Cross on the anniversary of their escape and in 1979 they travelled together to visit the graves of the four other crew members at Schoneau. During the late 1980s-early 1990s Len Miller met, and became firm friends with, Martin Becker, the former Luftwaffe officer responsible for the deaths of four of Len's

crew. It was only the exceedingly poor health that both men later suffered and eventually Len's passing, that brought that friendship, and many others, to an end.

28. Webb, op. cit.

29. Mailly actually accommodated a *Panzer* regiment HQ, 3 *Panzer* battalions belonging to regiments on the Eastern Front and elements of two more as well as the permanent training school staff.

30. The crew flew their first operation, an 8 hour 5 minute trip to Schweinfurt in Lancaster ND573 on 24/25 February, followed by 14 further ops 25/26 February (Augsburg)-1/2 May (Toulouse).

31. Five Special Duties Lancasters of 192 Squadron at Binbrook and six Mosquitoes and three ECM Halifaxes of 100 Group also took part.

32. Squadron Leader Tom Bennett DFM.

33. Marking began at 23.58 hours. Zero hour was 00.05. The first two Mosquitoes arrived early at the rendezvous and flew on for 30 miles before returning to the site. Nos. 87 and 93 PFF Squadrons had already dropped flares and these lit up the area so that Cheshire, dropping to 1,500 feet from 3,000 feet, had no problem in locating his two red spot flares on target. Cheshire was not happy with their position and called up Squadron Leader Dave Shannon in the accompanying Mosquito to mark the site that needed to be bombed more accurately, dropping his red spot fires accurately at 00.06 hours. Cheshire told the master bomber to hold the main attack off until he was satisfied. After Shannon had dived down to 600 feet to lay the markers, Cheshire gave the master bomber the go ahead. The green TI dropped by the *Oboe* controlled Mosquito was timed at 23.59 hours and fell 800 metres north of the centre of the target. Shannon's marking was completed seven minutes later. The target was marked on time.

34. Approximately 1,500 tons of bombs were dropped on Mailly and 114 barrack buildings, 47 transport sheds and workshops and some ammunition stores were hit. Two hundred and eighteen Germans were killed or missing and 156 were injured. One hundred and two vehicles, including 37 tanks, were destroyed. Damage to the buildings was German assessed as '80 per cent destroyed, 20 per cent worth repairing'. The only French civilian casualties were 14 people killed when falling aircraft fell on them.

35. All from I./SKG10, a single-engined fighter bomber and fast recce unit. One pilot, Feldwebel Otto Heinrich of the 3rd *Staffel*, claimed three destroyed for his first and only three combat victories. Heinrich was KIA on 22 May.

36. Oberleutnant Richard Delakowitz of 7./NJG 4 destroyed three *Viermots* south-west of Châlons-sur-Marne.

37. Ron Emeny, whose head was badly burned, and Flight Sergeant Jack Pittwood, navigator, who was from Warley near Birmingham, were taken in by the underground who sent them along the lines into Spain and they were flown home from Gibraltar. Emeny was posted to Coningsby, to the Pathfinder Force, but was not allowed to fly over France until the Allies had reached the Rhine. But his burns had not healed as well as he thought and he became a member of Archibald McIndoe's 'Guinea Pig Club' at East Grinstead, remained in the RAF post war and retrained as a wireless operator on Valiants and Vulcans. See *Not Just Another Milk Run; The Mailly-le-Camp Bomber Raid* by Molly Burkett & Geoff Gilbert (Barny Books, 2004). Nick Stockwood and 18 year old Sergeant Phil King, WOp/AG, from Birmingham, who shortly before baling out had said, 'The

whole arse end's on fire', also evaded capture. A week after returning home, Stockwood died of pleurisy. Sergeant Laurie Wesley, the bomb-aimer, who came from West Bromwich, baled out and was captured. He was sent to Buchenwald concentration camp but was released at the end of the war. See *Flying Into Hell* by Mel Rolfe (Grub St, 2001)

38. Handke, born 2 November 1920 in Darmstadt, trained as a *Bordfunker* during 1941–42, crewing up with Feldwebel George Kraft and joining 12./NJG 1 in October 1942. The team rapidly made a name for themselves, scoring 14 kills during the following months. Their partnership came to a violent end on 17/18 August 1943 when Kraft, flying with another *Bordfunker* was shot down by Wing Commander Bob Braham DSO DFC* of 141 Squadron. Kraft's body was washed ashore in Denmark four weeks' later. Handke then joined the crew of Oberleutnant Heinz-Wolfgang Schnaufer with whom he claimed five *Abschüsse*, before briefly flying on sorties with Oberfeldwebel Karl-Heinz Scherfling and contributing to the destruction of two more bombers. Shortly before the end of 1943 Handke had teamed up with Hauptmann Martin Drewes who, at the time, was *Staffelkapitän* 11./NJG 1 and an *Experte* with seven victories and Oberfeldwebel Georg 'Schorsch' Petz, *Bordschütze*. On 1 March 1944 Drewes assumed command of III./NJG 1 and this team went on to score 37 kills in less than 5 months.

39. Drewes' fifth victim (Lancaster EE185 KM-A of 44 Squadron, which crashed at Dreux with the loss of Pilot Officer Allen W. Nolan RAAF and his crew) almost fell on top of the Bf 110 and Drewes had to dive steeply to avoid his flaming victim. The five Lancasters shot down in a 40 minute period took Drewes' score to 34 victories. Hauptmann Helmut Bergmann of 8./NJG 4 destroyed six Lancasters in 30 minutes for his 29th–34th victories. (The *Ritterkreuzträger*'s score stood at 37 when, on the night of 6/7 August, his Bf 110G-4 was shot down in the Avranches-Mortain area by a Mosquito. No trace was found of the crew and it was not until 1956 that Bergmann's badly burnt remains, which had been recovered from a crash site near St James in mid-August 1944, were formally identified. Bergmann, who was probably shot down by a 604 Squadron Mosquito, was buried in the large German military cemetery of Marigny, Manche). Oberleutnant Dietrich Schmidt, *Staffelkapitän*, 8./NJG 1 flying a Bf 110 destroyed three *Viermots* for his 23rd–25th confirmed victories: His 23rd victim crashed near Chavanges, followed by a second Lancaster kill 16 minutes later, near Mailly-le-Camp. His 3rd victory of the night came down near Romilly.

40. Sparks and five others in his crew (two POWs) evaded, after baling out of Lancaster III JB402 OL-R. The French Resistance found Sparks and told him that his rear-gunner had shot down one of the German fighters. Sparks was back with 83 Squadron at Coningsby seven weeks later.

41. 'Arriving in Frankfurt in late evening a bombing raid was in progress and I was taken by my guard into a large air raid shelter. Local inhabitants did not seem concerned although there would be no doubt that I was a shot down flyer. After 12 days in solitary confinement apart from two interrogations, I was passed out to the transit camp. I met Speedy Quick who was attached to the small HQ staff working in the kitchen and distributing clothing and Red Cross food, etc. He had no news of any other members of the crew and we concluded they must have all been killed. I was then moved to *Stalag Luft III*, Sagan, in Silesia (East Compound).' Eeles learned later that of the 346

bombers dispatched to Mailly-le-Camp 42 Lancasters (or 11.6 per cent) were lost (two more were so badly damaged that they had to be written off). Ball's crew, less the two gunners, returned to base in their severely shot up Lancaster even though the aircraft had been further holed in a night fighter attack after the anti-aircraft damage. Pilot Officer Ted Ball was awarded an immediate DFC. On completion of repairs, ND647 was relegated to 1653 CU, where it was lost during fighter affiliation on 8 April 1945. Pilot Officer Ball's crew, with two other Squadron gunners, went on to fly on ops but towards the end of their tour they were shot down, probably by 'friendly fire' from another Lancaster, on 7/8 July 1944 during an attack on a flying bomb storage depot at St Leu d' Esserent (Credeil, France). There were no survivors. Their average age was 22.

42. Flight Lieutenant Terry Kearns flew the fourth 617 Squadron Mosquito.

43. Squadron Leader Tom Bennett DFM writing in Burkett & Gilbert, op. cit. No. 1 Group losses included five out of 17 crews from 460 Squadron RAAF at Binbrook and Nos. 12, 50 and 101 Squadrons each lost four crews. One Mosquito *Intruder* and one RCM Halifax were also shot down.

44. Burkett & Gilbert. op. cit.

45. ibid.

46. ibid.

47. Later ACM Sir Ronald Ivelaw-Chapman GCB KBE DFC AFC. Robertson, op. cit.

48. Pilot Officer Ron Walker was recommended for the immediate award of the DFC and this was made in June.

49. Five French targets were bombed in 452 sorties and 12 aircraft were lost – seven Halifaxes and four Lancasters.

50. Lancaster ND587/D crashed at 03.45 hours at Gallaix (Hainaut) 12km east of Tournai. Martstaller was killed in a crash on St Trond aerodrome in August 1944.

51. Hanneck had entered the *Luftwaffe* in July 1939 and trained as a fighter pilot during the next year. Expecting a posting to an operational unit, he was selected to serve as an instructor instead. Throughout 1942 he served in a liaison unit on the Eastern Front but he became so bored that he volunteered for night fighter pilot training. He had finally been posted to 6./NJG 1 in April 1944 and on 1 May he started flying at Deelen near Arnhem.

52. Geoffrey Clark and three crew KIA when the aircraft crashed at the hamlet of Elkerzee north-east of Haamstede. Three survivors were taken prisoner. After *Nachtjagd*'s successes during the Mailly-le-Camp raid, just a few *Zahme Sau* operations were mounted by *First Jagdkorps* during the remainder of May. On the nights of 11/12 May and 12/13 52 and 65 night fighter crews respectively achieved 12 and 13 victories.

53. Twenty-eight houses were flattened; 40 houses were evacuated and 528 houses damaged.

54. Most probably Lancaster I LL792 of 467 Squadron RAAF flown by Pilot Officer J. F. Ward with Wing Commander J. R. Balmer OBE DFC RAAF and crew, which was making its final bomb run when it was attacked by Oberleutnant Fritz Lau of 4./NJG 1. LL792 exploded with a full bomb load, killing all eight crew. It came down 2km west of Beverlo. Five Lancasters were lost on the raid.

55. John Barron had joined the RNZAF at the age of 19, arriving in England in March 1941. He joined 15 Squadron as a sergeant pilot on Stirlings. After a tour of 42 ops he was rested and became an instructor. Less than four months later he returned

to operations with 7 Squadron and flew a second tour. On 14 February 1943 Barron completed his second tour and he returned to instructing, this time for over a year. On 28 April 1944 he again volunteered to return to operational flying, and was given command of 7 Squadron, now flying Lancasters.

56. All told, seven Lancasters were lost this night. 143 aircraft – 106 Halifaxes, 32 Lancasters and five Mosquitoes accurately bombed railway yards at Boulougne without loss.

57. Over England Feldwebel Johann Trenke and Unteroffizier Beier of 6./KG51 claimed three Lancasters and two Liberators shot down respectively.

58. Another 59 Lancasters and four Mosquitoes were dispatched to Eindhoven to bomb the Philips factory; over 200 bombers were to attack coastal gun positions on the French coast and 44 Lancasters and seven Mosquitoes attacked the Ford Motor factory at Antwerp.

59. Before the bomber stream reached Aachen, the *'Night Ghost of St Trond'*, Oberleutnant Heinz-Wolfgang Schnaufer of St.IV/NJG 1, claimed five Halifaxes destroyed in 14 minutes. He 219 *Uhu* ('Owl') aircraft of I./NJG 1 at Venlo destroyed another seven of the Aachen raiders. II. and III./NJG 6 were guided to the Aachen force via radio beacon *Ida*. Despite strong intruder activity and jamming of the *SN-2* radar, these claimed five Lancasters and Halifaxes destroyed plus one 'probable' *Viermot* for the loss of three Bf 110G-4s.

60. Two hundred and sixty-seven Halifaxes, 56 Lancasters and eight Mosquitoes.

61. Only one aircraft was lost. Flight Sergeant T. R. Teague RNZAF piloted Lancaster I LM108 of 622 Squadron. Five crew were taken prisoner and two evaded capture.

62. On 6 June the 101st Airborne Division landed behind *Utah* beach as planned, but amid a certain amount of confusion.

However, by 06.00 hours Major General Maxwell Taylor had mustered one sixth of his force and with this he captured the exits from *Utah* beach. An element of the 502nd Regiment had orders to overrun the battery and to crush the garrison if necessary, but Captain Frank Lilleyman, the first US soldier to land in Normandy on D-Day, reconnoitered the battery and discovered that it had been bombed and abandoned as a result of the 5 Group attack on 28/29 May. A document captured soon afterwards revealed that the Officer Commanding, *Heer Kust Artillerie Regiment 1261*, reported the bombing attack had begun at 00.15 hours, parachute flares having been dropped first in great numbers. He said that the battery had been hit 'with uncanny accuracy', approximately 100 bombs of the heaviest calibre having been dropped in addition to several hundred smaller ones. Very large bombs had made several direct hits on the gun casement and it had burst open and collapsed. As a result of the destruction caused by the attack he had cleared the remainder of the battery out of the position into three farms in the Mesier area.

63. One hundred and twenty-five Lancasters, 86 Halifaxes and 8 Mosquitoes.

64. On 3/4 June 127 Lancasters and 8 Mosquitoes continued with deception raids on coastal batteries at Calais and Wimereux. On the night of 4/5 June a gun site at Boulogne was to have been the target for 10 Lancasters of 15 Squadron but half an hour before briefing the operation was cancelled. Bad weather affected the night's operations against two of the three coastal batteries in the Pas de Calais and they could only be bombed through cloud.

65. A nephew of Sir Charles Kingsford-Smith MC who, with fellow pilot C. T. P. Ulm and crew. made the first trans-Pacific flight 31 May-9 June 1928 in Fokker F.VIIB/3m *Southern Cross*.

Chapter 10

Dawn of D-Day

When a signal came saying we only had 2½ miles to go our troops put their packs on and got under cover. My crew also got down and I closed the armour plate covers of my cockpit and opened the slots through which I could see all around me. You could hear bursts of machine-gun fire from the shore and the wicked snarl of bullets ricocheting in the sea and over our boats. Some were uncomfortably close. Occasionally a column of water would shoot up near us and then we would hear the sound of the gun that had fired the shell. Then Jerry started lobbing over mortar shells and putting them very close indeed-None of the chaps were laughing and joking then. Suddenly we were up to the outer defences. Engines flat out. The obstacles were built of heavy timber forming tripods, on top of which were Teller mines. It would have been just too bad if we had touched one of these. I felt the craft sticking on underwater obstacles and in a moment we were up against the inner beach defences and could go no further. I gave the order to 'down ramp', our armoured doors were opened and our troops began to disembark. Mortar shells were bursting on the beach, which they had to cross, and among our craft as Jerry had now got our range.

On the sand, just clear of the sea, were the bodies of soldiers who had landed a few minutes before. Many others were in the sea itself; slowly moving back and forth as the waves rushed in and retreated.

I watched our commandos as they slowly walked through the surf and up the beach. Some didn't reach us. They would fall quietly on their faces and lie there in the water. I saw one spin about suddenly and sit down, his face covered in blood.

Some chaps would throw away their packs to drag their fallen comrades ashore. 'I didn't feel scared anymore – just numb as I wondered how much longer it would be before I got my "packet". It's a horrible feeling, the realization that death is about to strike you.'

Newfoundland-born landing craft coxswain Bill Mills from LSI(S) *Prinses Astrid*,
a converted Belgian cross-Channel passenger vessel with a capacity for
507 troops and eight landing craft, which arrived off *Sword* Beach at
05.42 on 6 June with The Highland Light Infantry on board

When Roland 'Ginger' Hammersley went to briefing at East Kirkby in the afternoon of Monday 5 June the only information he and the 57 Squadron crews received was that they would be attacking three enemy 170mm heavy gun positions at La Pernelle on the Cotentin Peninsula. Before the war young Roland had shared their three-bedroom council house, with its fair sized garden in Apsley End, with three brothers and a sister, Gladys. Their father had served in France in the First World War with the Royal Field Artillery. During the late 1930s Walter Alfred Hammersley was in and out of work plying his trade as a carpenter and joiner.

In 1939 he re-mustered, enlisting in the Royal Corps of Military Police. His wife Elizabeth, who somehow had managed to keep the family well fed and clothed during the days prior to war, kept chickens and introduced rabbits to supplement the rations as the war dragged on. Walter, the eldest child, had joined the Royal Artillery and Leslie, who was two years younger than 'Ginger' Hammersley, had joined the Royal Marines. Leslie, who was with the 541 Landing Craft Assault Flotilla aboard HMS *Empire Mace*, had been in Southampton for some time and was involved in moving mail from the dockside around the dock to the many units as they moved into place during the build-up of the invasion forces. The *Empire Mace* had a civilian crew captained by a Captain Smith, who had run a ship through the blockade during the Spanish Civil War. At last the move for embarking on assault craft day was called. The *D-Day* invasion, postponed by 24 hours because of bad weather, finally began with thousands of ships and aircraft setting out for five beach landing areas on the Normandy coast. It was a miserable wet morning as men trundled into Southampton's mean little dockside streets. It seemed that, despite all the secrecy, everyone knew what was going to happen. There seemed to be nothing but Redcaps keeping troops and public apart. The dockside was a mass of organized chaos as vehicles, soft-topped and hard, manoeuvred to board their respective craft.

Leslie's landing craft was at the dockside and during a lull in the work he watched the flow of guns, tanks, lorries and troops with orders being shouted from all sides. Suddenly, amidst all the confusion, orderly as it was, alongside of his landing craft in a line of mobile field guns, came one with his brother, Sergeant Walter Hammersley, directing its movements. Leslie was hanging over the side of an assault craft. The brothers stared at one another with a look of instant recognition. It was only a brief meeting, their first since the summer of 1942. They had only a few moments in which to chat and then Walter was away and being loaded onto a LCT (Landing Craft Tank). Walter and Leslie eventually moved out to their positions in line with what seemed like thousands of other vessels as the weather slowly got worse and they set off for Normandy, Leslie in the *Empire Mace*, Walter in his LCT with its four assault guns chained down. They were to fire onto *Gold* beach over the heads of the 50th Tyne Tees Division in front of them. It was terrifying in its majesty, with the flotsam of war everywhere.

Overhead, massive aerial support was given before dawn to the Normandy landings as over 1,000 aircraft, including 551 Lancasters, bombed coastal batteries at 10 strong points along the fringes of *Gold, Juno* and *Sword* landing beaches. As part of the 'cover' plan, for every bomb dropped west of Le Havre, two were dropped on batteries to the north. Walter and Leslie's brother 'Ginger', in the tiny WOp/AG position in *O-Oboe*, with its equally tiny side window to port, had little time to look out at the invasion fleet as the Lancaster flew over the English Channel towards the Cotentin Peninsula on this momentous day. *O-Oboe*, and 15 other Lancasters in 57 Squadron, had begun taking off from East Kirkby at 01.40 hours with a bomb load of eleven 1,000lb AN-M and four 500lb GP bombs. As the Lancasters were crossing the English Channel the young WOp/AG's *Fishpond* was swamped with blips. It was apparent that there was either a huge flock of birds, thousands of aircraft or a vast fleet on the sea immediately below their Lancaster. Hammersley reported this to Ron Walker, his pilot, and the navigator. Walker banked the aircraft to port and starboard and they could see that the water below was covered in a huge fleet of vessels heading towards the French coast. Thousands of men poured across *Gold* beach where, Leslie Hammersley passed Walter and his gun. As the Royal Marine ran in towards the sandy shore, Walter told him that his unit was shelling the beaches and positions in front and that they were doing a good job too. At La Pernelle the Lancasters got their bombs away at around five minutes before 04.00 but the Cotentin Peninsula was cloud covered and they probably missed their target because at 05.25, guns from two of the batteries fired on Allied minesweepers. It was much the same story at Fontenay, Houlgate, Longues, Grandchamps-Maisy, Merville, Mont Fleury, Ouistreham and St-Martin-de-Varreville before the Lancasters headed for home. The 10 batteries each received on average 500 tons of bombs. After the first landings Leslie Hammersley went back and forth to Southampton taking supplies and troops to *Gold* and *Omaha* beach heads for about six days before being withdrawn for a refit to the landing craft.[1]

Cloud interfered with the bombing all along the invasion coast and most of the Lancasters' bomb loads, including those of about 100 Lancs that were detailed to 'soften up' the Merville battery with 4,000lb bombs, missed their targets completely. One exception was at Pointe du Hoc, as Wing Commander Rollo Kingsford-Smith recalls:

'We took off at about 2am and had a leisurely flight down England to the south coast and across the Channel to the Normandy coast flying between 6–7,000 feet. There was low cloud most of the way but it started to break up as we approached France. I still did not know whether the Allied Forces would land. But about five miles out from the coast, when I could just discern the dark grey surface of the sea beneath in the early twilight, the fleet of invasion barges right below opened their throttles for the dash to the beach. It was too dark for me to see the boats but their increased speed made white wakes and these showed up clearly. I knew it was 'on'. Some of the wakes were all over the place. There must have been a few collisions at that level. Undoubtedly it was the most thrilling and emotional experience for me in all the years of the war. Until that moment Bomber Command had alone been taking the war to the Germans. For all I knew it would continue on and on until my crew and I finally joined the killed-in-action list. A massive army on the continent meant it was not unreasonable to think that the war might finish and I might get to see Grace and Sue (wife and daughter) again. The battery was well marked by the Pathfinders and from a relatively low height, about 6,500 feet. We all took our time, each aircraft dropping 13,000lbs of bombs. The whole Pointe was battered; the battery including its concrete bunkers was destroyed. Even a part of the cliff tumbled into the sea. US soldiers [2nd Ranger Battalion], who, about two hours later (had they been on time they would have seen and heard us), scaled the cliff to attack and silence the guns not knowing of our attack. They reported the shambles of shattered concrete and steel they saw when they reached the top.

'On the first day after the Allied armies had landed, their foothold on French soil was still precarious and they could have been in real trouble had the German armoured divisions been able to get there rapidly. Our squadrons were taken off the long flights into Germany and were kept busy attacking both the German tanks and their rail transport routes in and around the Normandy area. We went back to Normandy to destroy a rail and road junction at Argentan about 50 kms from the beachhead. I was Controller for this raid and as it would have been a vital transport junction for the Germans on the following day, I was determined it would be pulverized with nil or absolute minimum damage to the adjacent village. At the planning conference I agreed to a bombing height of 6,000 feet but we all bombed lower. The target was accurately marked. I held up the attack for about five minutes to avoid confusion with another target under attack a few miles away. There were a few complaints but not many and it was another successful raid. Milling around the target in the dark and held back by their CO, the operational discipline was always excellent but the radio comments (always with no call sign) were typically Australian – pertinent, disrespectful, sometimes rude and usually funny. The raid report given by Squadron Leader Vowels, my most experienced Flight Commander in briefing session on return. "Sortie completed. Cloud base 6,000 feet. Vis good. Cluster of green TIs 01.27 hours. 2 × 1,000lb and 14 × 500lb bombs drop height 5,000 feet. Bomb bursts all around and on TIs – straddling and on road junction. Attack went very well, even though it opened about five minutes late through the Controllers order. Control very good and there was no hitch to original plan. TIs were practically bang on. Max error was about 30 yards. Was fired on by British Navy who ceased fire when colours of the period were

fired." Alec Vowels' comment of being fired on by the British Navy was not unusual around D-Day. The English Channel was full of Allied Naval ships who continued to fire on us as we went across backwards and forwards – fortunately they were not as accurate as the Germans and I was not aware that they did any harm.

'I think I was the last to bomb at Argentan and my approach to the bomb release point was made on a shallow descending dive. Our bombs were always dropped rapidly one after the other and on this occasion they were dropped at about a micro fraction of a second intervals so they fell in a stick right across the target. I was possibly over keen and was too low, so when the first bomb exploded, its blast hit my aircraft with a really severe thump. In a flash I realized that as I was still losing height each successive blast would be harder and heavier. At this late stage being brought down by my own bombs may have showed my determination to press home the attack but it would have been a stupid way of finishing my career. My own report to the intelligence officer at debriefing states: "Sortie completed. Thin layer cloud, base about 6,000 feet. Bombing appeared good and attack successful. Train on fire possibly ammunition train. 4,000 feet. 01.40 hours. 2 × 1,000lb MC, 14 × 500lb GP. Attack delayed 5 mins to avoid any possibility of the force bombing green TI's of the eastern target which were put down late. Markers quite good. Majority of bombs appeared overshoot slightly and were to the west of the road junction – in the rail siding." We landed back at base after a very short return flight – one of the best aspects of fighting so close to base. The self-inflicted damage the ground crew found was a fairly small dent under the tail plane.'[2]

It was almost daylight when 35 Lancasters from RAF Mildenhall attacked gun sites on the French coast north of Caen and west of Le Havre between 05.00 and 05.13 hours, just before the Allied landings. Red and green TIs were dropped by the PFF and spread for about 600 yards along the beach. The reds were believed to be in the right place but the greens were very scattered. 15 Squadron dropped three hundred and five 500-pounders and 622 Squadron, two hundred and eighty-eight 500-pounders. All aircraft returned safely.

Frank Dengate recalls: 'On *D-Day* we operated twice in the one day. Once at dawn and another later on in the day, to Lisieux – a good prang. We did the job. They were only 1,000 yards ahead of our boys and so it was very accurate bombing. Once again the Pathfinders did the job. They dropped TIs where they wanted us to bomb. You can imagine the mess it made to the armour. I'd reckon half of the fellows would be smashed with the shock just from the bombing, even if it didn't destroy the tanks. Imagine sitting in a tank and getting 1,000-lb bombs dropped on top of you. It'd be a bit of a shock I think. It was very successful. Our boys were able to move forward. We didn't know it was *D-Day*. Nobody told us. It was kept a complete secret. Even to those operating. We were just told to bomb the defences along the shores of the D-Day landings. As we came back in the dawn, we could see the terrific mass of shipping going towards the French coast, so we realized it was D-Day.'[3]

One of the last Australian bomber crews out early on the morning of 6 June was a Lancaster crew captained by Flight Lieutenant F. L. Merrill DFC RAAF. To his crew it had been just another sortie in the pre-invasion softening-up when they took off in the small hours to attack a coastal gun battery. They were scheduled to be among the last of the night bombers to bomb that night and thus were among the first to see the invasion begin. They came down below the clouds on the way back, rounded the south-western side of the Cherbourg Peninsula, passed over a then seemingly empty French coast, and set course for home. Nearing Alderney, off the tip of the peninsula, the whole island seemed suddenly to burst into flames as the anti-aircraft defences opened up – unsuccessfully – on the Lancaster ahead. A few minutes later the invasion fleet came into view, filling the scene as far as the eye could reach, as ships of every kind moved across to Normandy.

At East Kirkby 57 Squadron were debriefed and after a brief rest period the crews found that they were again on the battle order with another evening briefing, as with the rest of the RAF, as 'Ginger' Hammersley recalls:

'We were to be thrown into the battle to establish the beach heads on the Normandy coast. Our part was to prevent movement of enemy reinforcements from the rear of their defences through into the battle area. Along with thirteen other crews we were briefed to attack bridges in Caen over which there were enemy troop movements. *O-Oboe* carried eighteen 500lb GP bombs. The flight out to the target was uneventful and we made our attack from 5,000 feet as briefed. Then, without any warning, the aircraft was raked with cannon and machine-gun fire, with a short reply from the rear-gunner. Ron Walker put the Lancaster into a dive to starboard and commenced to corkscrew away from the area. There was no more fire from the enemy aircraft, identified by Flying Officer Crombie from the astro-

dome, as a Ju 88. Ron called all members of the crew to check if all was well. There was no reply from Tom Quayle in the mid-upper gun turret so I went back along the fuselage to see what the problem was, only to find that Tom had been killed in the action. His wounds were such that he must have died instantly. I told Ron of Tom's fate. Ken Bly came back from his place in the nose of the aircraft, not believing what I had said and obviously taken aback by the event. I persuaded him to return to his place in the nose position and with Ron's permission, I advised base of the attack made upon us by the enemy fighter and the death of the gunner. From the inside of the fuselage, it was obvious that we had sustained a lot of damage from the cannon fire from the fighter and care in landing would be required, particularly as the aircraft was not handling too well. The reply from base said that an ambulance would be ready to receive us.

'It was nearly 5am as we circled the airfield and headed down wind when we were given permission to land. Although we made a not too bumpy landing, a tyre burst, the starboard wing broke open and out came the dinghy, which inflated and was dragged along the runway. We headed towards the waiting ambulance and the medical team led by the Station Medical Officer. On entering the aircraft they looked at Tom and quickly confirmed my original diagnosis that he had lost his life when we were hit by the cannon and gunfire from the enemy fighter. Furthermore the Lancaster was in a mess. Both gun turrets were damaged, the bomb bay had been hit, there were many cannon and machine-gun bullet holes in the fuselage and both the port, tail and mainplane were damaged. A sad night indeed. After the debriefing, we met the Medical Officer who prescribed drugs to get us all off to sleep for the day. I slept well into the next day and felt much rested when I awoke. With the rest of the crew, I was stood down from flying for a few days, although the squadron was still active with attacks on the enemy in support of our land forces in Normandy.[4]

Raids on the communication targets continued on the night of 7/8 June when 337 aircraft were dispatched to bomb railway targets at Achères, Juvisy, Massy-Palaiseau and Versailles. At Mildenhall 17 Lancasters of 15 Squadron and eight of 622 Squadron took off to attack the important rail and road junction at Massy-Palaiseau about 14 miles south of Paris. The target was very well marked with red and green TIs and bomb bursts were concentrated amongst them. The railway track could be seen in the light of the explosions. Crews bombed from only 6,000 feet and at this altitude they encountered intense light flak on the leg into the target.

They also met considerable fighter opposition. Seventeen Lancasters and 11 Halifaxes were lost. A Lancaster of 15 Squadron, flown by Flight Lieutenant W. J. Bell DFC, was badly shot up by a Messerschmitt 110 night fighter and his navigator, Sergeant C. W. Kirk, was killed by a cannon shell. Bell crash-landed at Friston airfield near Beachy Head and the aircraft immediately burst into flames but all the crew escaped with minor injuries. Three other 15 Squadron crews including Squadron Leader P. J. Lamason DFC RNZAF, 'A' Flight Commander and his crew of *H-Harry* who had an average of 40 operational sorties between them failed to return. Lamason and one of his crew were taken prisoner while three others evaded and two were killed.[5]

On 8/9 June 483 aircraft attacked rail targets at Alençon, Fougères, Mayenne, Pontabault and Rennes to prevent German reinforcements from the south reaching the Normandy battle area. Three Lancasters and a Mosquito failed to return. That same night the first 12,000lb *Tallboy* bombs, developed by Dr Barnes Wallis, were used when 25 Lancasters of 617 Squadron dropped these fearsome weapons on the a railway tunnel near Saumur to prevent a Panzer unit moving up to the Normandy front by train. The target area was illuminated with flares by four Lancasters of 83 Squadron and marked at low level by three Mosquitoes. The *Tallboys* were dropped with great accuracy and the tunnel was destroyed in a 'miniature earthquake'.

On the night of 10/11 June, 432 aircraft attacked rail targets at Achères, Dreux, Orlèans and Versailles. Frank Dengate's crew were one of those who attacked the Dreux marshalling yards and he reported cloud 'all the way then clear – a good prang'. Fifteen Lancasters, including one from 15 Squadron flown by Flight Lieutenant W. Dobson, an Australian from Geraldton, Western Australia, who had joined the RAF on a short service commission before the war, and three Halifaxes, failed to return. There were no survivors in Dobson's crew. Another of the Lancasters lost on the raid on Dreux was one of 90 Squadron flown by pilot Pilot Officer T. A. Burnett. Most of the crew were flying their first operation. Only Burnett and the mid-upper gunner Sergeant D. A. F. Munday had flown a previous operation. The aircraft left Tuddenham at about 22.45 hours and reached the target area without incident. The night was dark but clear. Just as the Lancaster was making the bombing run, flying at 7,000 feet, it was attacked from ahead by an enemy aircraft, variously described as a Ju 88 and a Fw 190. The W/Op saw the fighter dive under the port wing and the rear-gunner saw it come in on the starboard side. Sergeant W. F. Gallivion the rear-gunner opened fire. The Lancaster

had been hit in the port wing between the engines and No. 2 tank was badly holed, emptying almost immediately. The flight engineer changed to another tank, as No. 2 was in use during the attack. Meanwhile Burnett corkscrewed and the aircraft overshot the target. He turned to make another run and the bombs were dropped at 01.03 hours. The aircraft was then hit by flak either on the port inner engine or between the engine and the fuselage. The engine caught fire and, at the pilot's order, the flight engineer feathered it and cut off the idle cock. Burnett then cut off the master cock. The propeller stopped and the flight engineer pushed the fire extinguisher button. However, the fire did not go out and the engineer reported the whole wing on fire. Burnett then ordered the crew to bale out as the aircraft was falling very rapidly and was very bumpy.

The W/Op detonated the IFF set and took the flimsies giving stations, frequencies etc., putting them with his escape gear. He then put on his parachute and went to the rear exit. The exit was open when he reached it. He plugged in to report he was baling out but got no reply. He then took off his helmet, climbed the step, put his head between his knees and rolled out. He remembered only that he pulled his ripcord but knew nothing of the descent or landing. The bomb-aimer was still in the nose of the aircraft when the order was given to bale out. The escape hatch was covered with bundles of 'window' and in among these his intercom became unplugged so that he did not hear the order to bale out. Meanwhile the navigator and flight engineer put on their parachutes. The flight engineer went forward and saw the bomb-aimer hesitating by the escape hatch. He made signs to the bomb-aimer to bale out; the latter opened and jettisoned the hatch, which jammed for a short time. He then took his parachute, clipped it on and went out feet first, followed by the engineer. The aircraft at this time was falling very fast and although the bomb-aimer stated that he was about five minutes in the air, the engineer landed after 10 to 15 seconds. The aircraft was already burning when it hit the ground at Grandvilliers near Tillieres-Sur-Aure. Burnett and Munday were killed and Sergeant Gallivion baled out and was taken prisoner. Two sergeants and Warrant Officer G. A. Hartwig RAAF descended safely by parachute and evaded capture.[6]

When, in March, Group Captain Hamish Mahaddie had been looking for volunteers for 635 Squadron, a new Pathfinder squadron that was just being formed, he visited 51 Squadron flying Halifaxes at Snaith, and Sergeant Larry Melling, after discussing the possibility with the rest of the crew, had decided to volunteer.

They successfully completed the course at the Pathfinder Navigation Training Unit at Warboys, where were introduced to the Lancaster. After a 45-minute familiarization flight Melling was sent off on his own. The following evening he was given a 25-minute night circuit and again turned loose on his own. There followed mock operations to check the accuracy of his flying and the navigator's performance and to assess the bomb-aimer's accuracy. Finally, they were posted to 'B' Flight, 635 Squadron at Downham Market in Norfolk on 27 May. Melling recalled:

'On arrival at a Pathfinder Squadron new crews were first given a "Support" role until they proved that they were able to meet the stringent requirements of accurate navigation to ensure arriving at the target within plus or minus 30 seconds of the assigned time. The accuracy of the bomb-aimer was also assessed, based on the bombing photos taken automatically when the bombs were dropped. Crews were divided into "visual markers" and "blind markers", the latter relying mainly on H_2S to identify and mark the target. We were assigned as a "blind" crew and, as a result, the bomb-aimer had to do additional training in reading the H_2S screen; he became known as Nav2. On the night of 11/12 June in ND811 (F2-T), we attacked the railway yards at Tours in order to disrupt the transport of German army reinforcements to the front in Normandy.[7] When we arrived at the target the area was covered in solid cloud and we were instructed by the master bomber to descend below cloud for our bombing run. I do not know what the altimeter setting was in the target area but when we dropped our bomb load my altimeter was reading 1,500 feet. Hitchcock, my tail gunner, shot at and extinguished a searchlight and I can still recall seeing the wet cobblestones on the streets of the town! Further operations to disrupt enemy lines of communication to the Normandy area continued during the rest of June, with a couple of trips to attack V-1 launching sites.'

In the small hours of 13 June a Lancaster of 75 Squadron RNZAF, its pilot, Pilot Officer G. McCardle RNZAF, unconscious, was flown from France and put down safely by Warrant Officer Alexander 'Alec' Hurse RAAF. The 24 year old Australian bomb-aimer from Victoria, who had flown 29 ops when they took off to bomb Nantes, had never before been alone at an aircraft's controls. The Lancaster had taken off from Mildenhall in the starlight at about midnight, for the railway centre of Nantes and all was quiet as it flew in over France, coming down from 7,000 to 2,000 feet to get below the cloud to bomb. Then, over the target, after it had bombed, six searchlights picked up the Lancaster. McCardle corkscrewed and during this manoeuvre the Lanc was hit simultaneously three times, twice in the port wing and once in the cockpit. McCardle was wounded in the neck, leg and side. He was just able to say on intercom, "I'm hit; I'm hit – get out!" The navigator, Flying Officer A. H. R. Zillwood RNZAF called Hurse up forward to see the pilot. Hurse found him clutching the stick to his chest, just conscious, but unable to see because of his injuries. The aircraft was going almost vertically up through the cloud and out of the searchlights' glare. Hurse took the control column from the pilot and levelled up while Zillwood got McCardle out of his seat and laid him beside the bed. Hurse had never had any training as a pilot, except that he had had a little dual instruction in a Stirling bomber but there was no one else in the crew who could take the controls and he felt confident he could get the aircraft back to base. He was not so sure he could land it. On the way back the wireless operator received a message to land at a grass airfield about 400 miles from Nantes. There the Lancaster, with Hurse at the controls, arrived at 04.50 hours. White flares were sent up to guide it in. Hurse circled twice while he asked whether anyone wanted to bale out, but everyone said, "No" and Hurse brought the Lancaster down to a "definitely unprofessional" landing. It bounced four times swung to port, and stopped. This achievement by Hurse resulted in the award of a CGM for the temporary pilot and Flying Officer Zillwood was awarded the DFC for his part in the night's ordeal.

On the night of 12/13 June 671 aircraft attacked communication targets, mostly railways in France and a stream of 286 Lancasters and 17 Mosquitoes headed for Gelsenkirchen. Seventeen Halifaxes and six Lancasters failed to return from the communication raids[8] and 17 Lancasters were brought down on the Gelsenkirchen raid by the German defences.[9] Oberleutnant Dieter Schmidt, *Staffelkapitän*, 8./NJG 1 and his crew, Schönfeld and Schlosser, who were all on their 126th operation claimed one of the Gelsenkirchen raiders:[10] Schmidt recalls:

'We took-off from Leeuwarden in Bf 110 G9+AS (Anton Siegfried) and approached the Ruhr for the first time in this period of darkness. We were fairly late. I was flying at full throttle. The attack was already in full swing, mainly explosive bombs. The last bombs were falling as we got close to the target. Where was the departure route? I guessed over to port, across the Zuidersee and therefore continued towards north. I was right. Soon we had them before us. Kurt guided with the *SN-2*. Soon I saw one directly in front. At short range I could clearly make out the eight exhausts – a *Viermot* – distance 500 metres and relatively fast. It was fairly hazy but not bad. I attacked from 100 metres and from behind as usual, between the engines, aiming a little low, pressing the buttons and pulling a little up and there it was. The entire starboard wing was on fire. For a moment I saw clearly the port one with the low-mounted engines brightly lit. It looked like another Lancaster. Then we broke off quickly to port and up. Blazing fiercely he passed below our starboard wing. Pieces were breaking away. Kurt saw two parachutes. Then he went vertically down to crash. The radio beacon *Kurfürst* was 10–20 kilometres to the south-east.'[11]

On 14 June 221 Lancasters and 13 Mosquitoes carried out Bomber Command's first daylight raid since the departure of 2 Group to the Second Tactical Air Force at the end of May 1943, when they attacked German E-boats at Le Havre. Included in the force were 22 Lancasters of 617 Squadron, each loaded with a 12,000lb *Tallboy* bomb. Harris was still reluctant to risk his heavy bombers on daylight operations but Spitfires escorted both waves of the attack and only one Lancaster was lost.

On 15/16 June 224 aircraft attacked railway yards at Lens and Valenciennes. Frank Dengate recalls: 'There was cloud almost to Valenciennes but the target was clear. We bombed on the master bomber's instructions as he checked the target indicators in relation to the true target. We lost five aircraft.'[12]

On 16/17 June, 405 aircraft of Bomber Command began a new campaign aginst V-1 flying-bomb launching sites in the Pas de Calais with raids on four targets accurately marked by *Oboe* Mosquitoes.[13] The following night Frank Dengate's crew went to Montdidier to bomb a rail junction to prevent movement of reinforcements to the invasion front line: 'There was complete cloud cover and the master bomber radioed the code words "Monkey Nuts", which meant "Do not bomb". It was important when bombing over France not to bomb if conditions were not favourable, to avoid stray bombs killing French civilians. So we returned with our bombs, 8,876lbs of them. We saw some flying bombs and hoped that they didn't get as far as London.'[14]

On 18 June a flying bomb struck the Guards Chapel at London's Wellington Barracks, killing 121 people. Next day the decision was taken to give priority to attacking the launch sites as well as the storage depots.

On 21 June 322 aircraft in loose formations and escorted by Spitfires were dispatched in daylight to bomb three flying bomb sites in northern France. 15 Squadron's target was Marquise/Mimoyecques but cloud prevented accurate bombing and so the master bomber gave the code word 'Buttermilk' and the aircraft returned with their bomb loads intact. Cloud forced the abandonment of two of the raids after only 17 aircraft had bombed and at the third target, at St-Martin-l'Hortier, the heavies bombed through 10/10ths cloud. Because of Allied air superiority over France, daylight raids became increasingly common. Unlike the American 8th Air Force, RAF Bomber Command operated in a giant gaggle and not usually in formation, thereby cutting losses to flak. That night, 133 Lancasters and six Mosquitoes headed for the synthetic oil plant at Wesseling, a town nine miles south of Cologne and 123 Lancasters and nine Mosquitoes set out for another synthetic oil plant, at Scholven/Buer. Clear weather conditions were forecast for both target areas, which were to be bombed simultaneously and it was planned to use the low-level marking method but both targets were covered by 10/10ths cloud so at Wesseling H_2S was used and at Scholven/Buer Pathfinder aircraft provided *Oboe*-based sky-marking instead. Eight Lancasters at Scholven/Buer were shot down and the Wesseling force lost 37 aircraft. Three of the Lancaster squadrons were particularly badly hit, with 619 losing six of the sixteen aircraft dispatched and 44 and 49 Squadrons losing the same number each, while at East Kirkby five Lancasters failed to return and a sixth ditched in the North Sea off Great Yarmouth.[15]

Flight Lieutenant Ron Walker DFC and his very experienced crew of 83 (Pathfinder) Squadron had lifted off from Coningsby's long runway in Lincolnshire at 23.18 hours. Their 45th operational flight proved relatively uneventful until they reached Eindhoven when Hauptmann Heinz-Wolfgang Schnaufer, Kommandeur of IV./NJG 1, attacked them. Schnaufer's cannon shells ripped into the Lancaster that was still loaded with bombs and the bomber exploded. It was his 81st confirmed victim. Walker was blown from the bomber and, though unconscious, he miraculously survived with only a bruised leg and back. His crew died in the aircraft. Walker was quickly helped by Dutch Resistance workers and, after a series of adventures and hair-raising escapes evading German troops, he reached the home of a very brave woman, Jacoba Pulskens in Tilburg on 8 July. With two shot down navigators Roy Carter RCAF and Jack Knott RAAF they awaited their next move across the Belgian border to safety but six members of the *Gestapo* burst into the house and in a flurry of shots the three aircrew were killed. Jacoba Pulskens was arrested and after much suffering at the hands of the Germans was put to death in a gas chamber in February 1945.[16]

On 23/24 June 390 heavies and 22 Mosquitoes carried out attacks on four V-1 sites in the Pas de Calais area and 203 Lancasters and four Mosquitoes set out for rail yards at Limoges and Saintes. All four flying bomb sites were hit. Seven Lancasters, including five from 463 and 467 Squadrons at Waddington, were lost on the night's operations. One of the three 463 Squadron Lancasters shot down on the raid on Prouville was piloted by Pilot Officer J. F. Martin RAAF, which was shot down by a night fighter and crashed east of Abbeville. Sergeant T. A. Malcolm RAAF, the bomb-aimer, was the only survivor. He wandered about France for about a month before he was picked up by the *Gestapo*, who took him to a civilian prison near Paris. When the Allies reached Paris, he was taken, with eight other Australians, to the notorious concentration camp at Buchenwald where he saw the shrunken heads and the human skin lampshades. After a few days, Malcolm was transferred to *Stalag Luft III*. Fourteen Lancasters in the Mildenhall squadrons took part in attacks on the V-1 site near L'Hey on the edge of a forest not many miles inland from the French coast. A Lancaster in 622 Squadron flown by Flight Sergeant W. H. Cooke RNZAF was shot down. Cooke and one other member of his crew were killed while five survived to be taken prisoner. Frank Dengate's crew had a lucky escape when a trigger-happy gunner in another aircraft fired at their Lancaster.

Flight Lieutenant R. G. Wharton, rear-gunner in *F for Freddie*, a 7 Squadron, 8 (PFF) Group Lancaster at Oakington, flown by Flight Lieutenant Brian Prow, whose target was at L'Hey, recalls:

'Prow had recently been promoted master bomber in the Pathfinder Force (a highly prized position) the members of which were chosen carefully and had to pass stringent tests before being accepted by D. C. T. Bennett (soon to be AVM Bennett, a legend in the RAF). Our crew had been granted the honour of leading the attack on the L'Hey site and we carried special multi-coloured bombs which, on exploding, marked the target with the chosen colour of the day. The colour was not disclosed to crews until just before take-off in order to ensure that the enemy did not have the opportunity of duplicating the colour before the main attack began or during it. "Jerry" quite frequently did just that, much to our discomfort, for that meant we had to go in once again to re-mark. It also meant that the following bomber force was torn between the choice of two targets; ours and Jerry's and his were always well away from the real target. Brian did not disguise the fact

that he intended this trip to be a success. With all preliminaries duly completed we took-off at 00.30 hours and headed for the target. The outward flight was uneventful. Only sporadic anti-aircraft fire was directed at us as we crossed the French coast and soon we were approaching our target. We found the site very well camouflaged but as we had special equipment, coupled with radar co-ordinates, which gave our navigator pin-point accuracy, we quickly found our marking point and dropped our markers. On this occasion the main force bombers arrived precisely on time and began their bombing. A couple of aircraft passed over our marker when suddenly there was an almighty "Bang" followed by a display of pyrotechnics that was a joy to behold. At least it was to us for that told us that the raid had been successful. The whole scene convinced us that a fuel dump or maybe an ammunition dump had been hit for shell-bursts were taking place hundreds of feet in the air and in all directions.

'The successive explosions were rocking us at 5,000 feet, providing everyone with a grandstand view until Brian's voice came over the intercom, "There is a Lancaster being attacked by a Junkers 88" and he ordered our bomb-aimer in the front turret to open fire on the attacker. After a short burst from his two Brownings everything went quiet and the bomb-aimer reported a stoppage, whereupon Brian manoeuvred the plane to enable the mid-upper turret and me to fire at the attacker. The mid-upper gunner had chosen that moment to visit the Elsan so it was left to me to deal with the situation. The rear turret was fitted with four Brownings, which were capable of firing 1,000 rounds per minute from each gun; a *very* formidable hail of bullets to encounter. Immediately I got the enemy aircraft in my sights I opened fire with a five-second-burst and that was sufficient. I hit the Junkers on the starboard engine. He went down steeply and exploded just before he entered the clouds.

'There was a certain amount of excitement, which I think contributed to a lapse in concentration so necessary to maintain at all times, particularly over enemy territory and we failed to spot another Me 210 positioning for an attack. As he straightened up I called the mid-upper gunner and told him to open fire. Our combined firepower proved too much for him and he broke off the engagement. We learnt later that we had scored hits and he had force-landed in a field near some Resistance fighters who, at the first opportunity, set his plane on fire. We had hardly regained our breath however, when suddenly we were hit. The starboard tailplane received a large hole and the line of fire continued up the fuselage tearing an even larger hole in the mainplane. In fact it shot a petrol tank in the wing clear out; just one gaping hole. As the aircraft broke away to position itself for another attack I recognized it as a Me 210 and it was equipped with the fixed angled firing cannon on the top of the fuselage. The pilot could position himself well under his target and adjust to the direction and speed of its prey, then drift slowly upward and slightly astern to make his attack. This was no time for aircraft recognition and I lost no time opening fire on the attacker. I was lucky for I definitely scored hits. The tracer bullets that I used were obviously hitting him for there were no ricochets and my bullets were not going past him. Soon I had verification for he suddenly dived through the clouds and we observed a brilliant and widespread flash of light from the ground.

'Brian was by now wrestling with the controls, attempting to keep the Lancaster flying and gradually he was able to steer a course for home. "Bloodied but unbowed". A more detailed assessment was made to the extent of the damage. To put it into the words of our flight engineer. "A bloody great hole in the tailplane with attendant damage to the tail-fin, part shrapnel holes in the fuselage all the way from the rear turret to the main wing member and another bloody great hole in the starboard wing that you could drop a bloody piano through. Other than that, I cannot possibly see why we are still flying." I dared not tell him that there was nowhere to rest my feet for there was nothing but a gaping hole when I looked down. Also, my guns were useless for the hydraulics had been shot away. I reckoned that Brian had enough on his mind concentrating on getting home. He asked for a course for Woodbridge, a recognized emergency-landing site and called for silence on the intercom to allow him to nurse our faithful *F for Freddie* home. Lurching, swaying, crabbing but always fighting to reach home we at last crossed the English coastline practically in line for landing at Woodbridge but on asking permission to land we were told to identify ourselves before they would switch the flarepath on. Brian was livid but we had to obey regulations and fire flares, which were the colour of the day, We landed not knowing whether our wheels had locked, and the flight engineer fired all six of the remaining flare cartridges over the airfield. We gently rolled to a stop. A second or two later *F for Freddie* tilted slowly to starboard and the wing settled down on the grass, then slowly the port wing dropped too. I swear I heard a sound very similar to a sigh, as if to say, "Well I managed it lads. I got you home." I manually wound the rear turret to astern, opened the two small doors to evacuate the turret and then I placed

my head in my clasped hands, resting on the sight, relaxed and said a little prayer.'

Flight Sergeant Derek Patfield was relieved to get home too. They had taken off from Skellingthorpe in a thunderstorm for the marshalling yards at Limoges and they had their navigation lights on 'practically all the way to the target', which he recalls, 'was a bit drastic. My position got absolutely soaked because it leaked like a sieve around the front turret. My two guns and the four propellers were all arced in blue static electricity – St Elmo's Fire. The wireless op had to let down the trailing aerial before we came in to land to earth all the static from the aircraft. It was quite a "do" what with all the thunder and lightning. I had never been so cold and wet before in my life.'

On 24 June 321 aircraft, including 200 Halifaxes and 106 Lancasters, attacked three V-1 sites in the clear over the Pas de Calais without loss. Sixteen Lancasters and two Mosquitoes of 617 Squadron bombed the flying-bomb site at Wizernes with their *Tallboy* bombs, the Dam Busters losing one Lancaster. That night 739 aircraft, including 535 Lancasters of all groups, attacked seven V-1 sites. It was a clear, moonlit night and 22 Lancasters were lost, mostly to night fighters. At Prouville the Pathfinder Force was inaccurate and no markers were even seen by most of the 467 Squadron crews. Therefore the controller ordered that the force would orbit until the target was effectively marked. This was in a heavily defended area, with many guns, searchlights and, worst of all, heavy fighter opposition. Very many aircraft were seen falling in flames. The Lancaster flown by Pilot Officer S. Johns was attacked, the crew clearly hearing the cannon fire from the fighter before feeling the impact of shells, which started a fire raging in the rear. Flight Sergeant E. D. Dale, the mid-upper gunner, was trapped by the fire and with his intercom destroyed, assumed that the aircraft could not survive. He baled out but his parachute was 'coned' by searchlights and the German gunners apparently shot at the descending gunner. Johns meanwhile sent his navigator and flight engineer back to fight the flames, which were eventually extinguished and Johns brought the battered Lancaster home. When the aircraft landed it was found that the rear turret had been almost ripped from its housing and Flight Sergeant J. J. Fallon, the gunner, was also missing. His parachute was still in the aircraft and it was concluded that he must have been blown out of the turret by the night fighter attack.[17]

Next day 323 aircraft pounded three more V-1 sites, which were very difficult to hit. Wing Commander Leonard Cheshire, the CO of 617 Squadron, who always tried to increase bombing accuracy, accompanied 17 Lancasters and two Mosquitoes to the Siracourt flying bomb store in a P-51 Mustang, with the purpose of using it as a low level marker aircraft. What is remarkable is that the Mustang had only arrived that same afternoon, courtesy of the US 8th Air Force, and this was Cheshire's first flight in it! His Lancasters scored three direct hits on the concrete store with *Tallboy* bombs and Cheshire landed safely back at Woodhall Spa in the dark.[18]

On 28/29 June 230 bombers hit the railway yards at Blainville and Metz for the loss of 18 Halifaxes and two Lancasters.[19]

Many operations were flown in direct support of the Allied armies. The Lancasters bombed battlefield targets to assist ground forces and mounted attacks on flying bomb sites and depots. In the early hours of 30 June a 75 Squadron Lancaster blew up at Mepal and four other Lancasters, hit by the blast, were also put out of action. Later that day 266 aircraft carried out a raid on a road junction at Villers-Bocage. Tanks of two *Panzer* divisions, the 2nd *SS Das Reich,* which was in Toulouse, and the 9th, were believed to be en route to Normandy and would have to pass through the junction in order to carry out a planned attack on the Allied armies in the battle area. The raid was orchestrated by the master bomber, who ordered the bombing force to drop down to 4,000 feet in order to be sure of seeing the markers in the smoke and dust of the exploding bombs. Frank Dengate, now an acting squadron leader in charge of 'A' Flight in 15 Squadron, flew on the raid and recalled that it was 'a good prang, 10 miles ahead of our troops. We lost one aircraft to flak over the target [a Halifax was also shot down] and also, "Z" of 15 Squadron was involved in a collision over Mildenhall but both aircraft were OK. In all, 1,100 tons of bombs were dropped with great accuracy on the road junction and the planned German attack was called off.'

On 2 July 374 Lancasters and 10 Mosquitoes attacked three flying bomb sites. 15 Squadron went to Apps Beauvoir, a storage base for V-1s, escorted by Spitfires. Frank Dengate recorded that it was 'a good prang – no losses'. For his navigator, Flying Officer Art Cantrell, it was his last trip and he was subsequently posted to the Canadian OTU at Honeybourne. Meanwhile, the land battle in Normandy was hotting up and bombing raids were made on rail targets and flying bomb sites. Frank Dengate returned from a six-day leave. On 12 July he and his crew in *K-King* took part in a daylight operation by 153 Lancasters and six Mosquitoes to the railway yards at Vaires, on the outskirts of Paris, but the target area was covered by cloud. The master bomber sent the code word 'Buttermilk' to abandon the attack after two of the Mosquitoes had marked and 12 of the Lancasters had bombed. Frank Dengate recalls: 'We had to bring our bombs back home again. Flak hit us and wiped out one of our engines. I had to feather it to stop it catching fire. We were going slow back to base and we were on our own. It was a bit risky. Fortunately my wireless operator got up in the astrodome and with his Aldis lamp sent a message to one of the other aircraft in our squadron to send some escorts. Sure enough, a Spitfire came and escorted us home. The German fighters were always ready to have a crack at an individual aeroplane and you didn't have much chance. When we got to Mildenhall I found I had no brakes. The line was cut. I hit the deck and we still had the bomb load on board. I feathered the other outer engine and kept the two inner engines for directing the aircraft for taxiing. I was heading for the hangars so I swung the aeroplane left, jumped the slit trenches and went through a fence into a beautiful wheat field ready for harvest at West Row, where we spun round in a semi circle. We eventually stopped without damage and the ambulance and fire engines and everyone else followed through and made the wheat field one great flat mass. It worked out all right but the farmer was upset and came out shaking his fist!'[20]

On 4 July more 'daylights' were flown when 328 bomber crews – mostly Halifaxes – attacked V-1 flying bomb sites in northern France again. Also, the Lancasters of 5 Group were given a special target, a flying bomb site at St-Leu-d'Esserent in the Pas de Calais, which was to be hit first by 17 Lancasters of 617 Squadron, supported by a Mustang and a Mosquito. One of the 5 Group Lancasters that took part was *Q-Queenie* in 61 Squadron at Skellingthorpe where Flying Officer Harold Watkins' crew were assigned the aircraft for their fifth operation of their tour. Flight Sergeant Edgar Ray, who had trained as an observer in South Africa but, because of a desperate shortage, had become a bomb-aimer, recollected:

'The Station Tannoy would call up crews and inform them of meal and op briefing times. Usually we ate the bacon and egg flying meal before the operation, then bomb-aimers and wireless operators left for specialist briefings. Bomb-aimers went to the Bombing Office that was situated at one end of a small Nissen hut. Our Bombing Leader was Pop Nugent, a second tour Aussie Flight Lieutenant. The other half of the hut was the domain of 61 Squadron's Maps and Charts Queen, a luscious, very well formed WAAF Corporal, who ensured that we all had full topographical map cover for the Continental part of our sortie. In the Bombing Briefing we were given details of the bomb load to be carried, total weight, bomb types, bomb delay times, position of bomb types in the bomb bay and pressure settings for the Mk.XIV bombsight. All this information was recorded on the bomb-aimer's flight gen sheet. After the specialist briefings the crews met up in the main briefing room. As we entered this large Nissen hut, eyes were immediately drawn to a huge map of Western Europe at the far end of the building, with coloured tapes stretching across its surface indicating the route from base to target and back. Some idea of the target was deduced earlier by the crews from the amount fuel and type of bombs that had been loaded aboard the aircraft.

'St-Leu-d'Esserent consisted of an area of large caves tunnelled out some years before the war and used by the French to grow mushrooms. The Germans cleaned up the inside of the caves and used them to store V-1 flying bombs. The aim of the attack was to collapse the roof of the caves, which had been estimated to be about 25 feet thick. A subsidiary aim of the raid was to devastate the road and rail communications running between the caves and the river. At the briefing we were warned that the area was heavily defended by flak units and to keep a sharp lookout for night fighters. This was an all-5 Group bombing operation with a few 8 Group Pathfinders. 9 and 617 Squadrons carried the big 12,000lb *Tallboy* bombs while the rest of the Lancaster force carried about the same weight of bombs made up of 1,000lb and 500lb HEs. Many of the bombs were fitted with six-hour delay pistols.

'After the main briefing we all went to the locker room and emptied our pockets of any items that could be helpful to the enemy in the event of being shot down and captured. Next I changed into my flying kit and tested my flying helmet and oxygen mask on a test rig, drew parachute, Mae West and escape equipment. This contained a silk handkerchief map and currency of the area over which we would fly. (For long night operations over Germany the gunners and bomb-aimer had to wear plenty of clothing to keep warm. The heating never seemed to work properly at these crew stations resulting in sub-zero temperatures. W/Op and navigator wore minimum flying clothing because their station received blasts of excessively hot air. Only the pilot and engineer were lucky enough to work in a moderate temperature zone within the aircraft). After kitting up, all the crews went out to the waiting buses or made their way to the aircraft dispersal on motorcycles, bikes or in their own cars. Upon arrival at the dispersal I would first check the bomb load and sign a receipt

for the bombs. We would enter the aircraft, run up engines, check all essential equipment then shut down. The skipper would then sign the Form 700 signifying that he was satisfied with the serviceability of the aircraft. We then had a tense period of waiting at the dispersal, chatting with ground crew until engine start-up time.

'The dispersal was usually littered with 500lb and 1,000lb general-purpose bombs. These were left around the area, as there was insufficient time to take bomb deliveries to the bomb dump where they should have been fused. The armourers usually prepared the 500- and 1,000-pounders at the dispersals. Specialist bombs like the 4,000lb cookies and 4lb incendiaries were stored at the bomb dump. When these were required for an operation they were loaded onto bomb trolleys and driven to a fusing shed before being taken to the aircraft dispersals. When ops were "on" the station armourers had the dangerous and backbreaking task, bombing up each of the forty aircraft with five tons of bombs. Sometimes if the target was changed it meant removing all the bombs from every aircraft and replacing them with a different type of load before de-fusing and making safe the downloaded bombs at the dispersals. As engine start-up time approached we boarded the aircraft and settled down in our take-off crew positions. Once the engines had been started we soon merged with a line of slow moving aircraft around the perimeter track and joined the queue of Lancs waiting their turn to move forward onto the main runway for take-off. The green go light had been received from the air traffic caravan, the skipper quickly got the aircraft lumbering down the runway and off on the first leg of the route to the target area. One feature of take-off with full fuel tanks was the cones of fuel vapour, which surrounded each prop and trailed well behind each wing. All very pretty but most disconcerting for the mid-upper gunner!

'The bomb-aimer's contribution on the way out to the target varied greatly between night and day sorties. At night, very little could be seen. On the long haul across the North Sea to targets in north Germany all was dark on reaching the enemy coastline. Getting a pin-point visual fix on the enemy coast was a hit and miss affair, resulting in many complaints from the navigator in his curtained-off office. Daylight raids were a totally different experience for the bomber crews and bomb-aimers in particular. I could see everything that was happening ahead. Topographical maps were used continuously and map reading occupied most of my time. Most of the daylight raids were on targets in

France and after crossing the French coast I could track visually all the way to the target area.

'The aiming point at St-Leu-d'Esserent was a limestone hillside overlooking the river Oise. We made our attack at 01.30 hours from 15,000 feet. Throughout the bomb run the German defences threw up heavy flak and after "Bombs gone" we thankfully turned away from the target area. Suddenly, Carson Jack Foy, our rear-gunner, yelled over the intercom. "Fighter! Fighter! Corkscrew port – Go!" Our Skipper dived the aircraft to port at the start of the corkscrew manoeuvre. At the same time we heard Jack's guns chattering away as the fighter dived past and disappeared underneath us. Shortly afterwards came a second attack. Jack called "Corkscrew" and hammered away again with his guns at the incoming fighter. This happened twice more during the next ten minutes and Jack continued firing hundreds of rounds even though three of his four guns overheated and went and out of action.

'Our extensive fighter evasion tactics had taken us gradually south of the target area and, after the final attack, north-west. This threw us off our planned course and even from my bomb-aimer's position I could see nothing of the ground to help with a visual fix. Eventually our navigator Doug Hockin got a good *Gee* fix, despite the jamming from a German radio station on the Eiffel Tower and a course was set for home. We landed back at Skellingthorpe at about 03.30 hours, extremely tired after such a stressful experience. At the debrief Jack Foy reckoned that he hit the night fighter that attacked us and saw it falling away after its fourth attack. He was credited with a probable night fighter victory in his log. Anyway, we were all thankful that Jack had such good night-vision. He saved our lives that night. The next morning our flight armourer inspected all the aircraft's guns. He reported that the rear turret gun barrels were so worn, due to the overheating that they must be replaced before the next sortie. Over the following three weeks we flew another four bombing sorties against various targets in support of the Allied ground forces in France.'

'July started out with a continuation of trips in support of the invasion forces' recalls Sergeant Larry Melling 'and I did my first daylight operation, to Caen, on the 7th. Much has been written about the effectiveness of this raid but I believe that it certainly resulted in saving many lives of the ground forces who had been held up in that area for some considerable time.[21] Two days later we were detailed to attack a V-1 launching site at L'Hey near Paris (when 347 aircraft bombed six launching sites). We made our bombing run at 15,000 feet amid a few black puffs of flak and made a long slow turn to starboard to begin the trip back home to Downham. Just as we completed the turn the aircraft lurched suddenly, the port wing came up and there was a rattling of shrapnel against the fuselage. A glance out of the port cockpit window showed white smoke coming from the port inner, meaning that we were losing coolant but of the port outer there was no sign at all – just the bare firewall with some cables dangling loose. Sergeant J. E. Blyth, the flight engineer, had already started the feathering procedure for the port inner and I immediately shut off the fuel cock to the port outer. Then began the struggle to trim the aircraft to fly on only two starboard engines. Full right rudder trim and full aileron trim were not sufficient to accomplish this; it took full right rudder and a somewhat starboard-wing-down attitude to maintain anything like a semblance of a straight course. I checked that all crew members were unhurt. As we had no way of being certain that we had not sustained any further damage from the shrapnel, the decision was made in concert with my flight engineer to head for Manston, the emergency airfield in Kent, rather than return to Downham Market. The flight to Manston took about an hour.

'Flight Sergeant L. Bell, my bomb-aimer, suggested that he could relieve the pressure on my right leg by using the long bar of the control lock as a lever by putting it in front of the rudder pedal and across, behind the throttle control pedestal. Unfortunately the bar proved to be too short and all that was achieved was a slight bend in it. By placing both feet on the right rudder pedal I was able to relieve the strain to some extent. Thus we flew back to England in a slow descent, crossing the Kent coast at some 5,000 feet. At this time I had a total of some 450 flying hours as a pilot, of which only 45 were on Lancasters, with a grand total of 21 landings! Accordingly, as we approached Manston I informed my crew that I was going to land the aircraft but that if they wanted to bale out I would not hold it against them. They all decided that they would stay with me, which gave me a much-needed boost of confidence. I instructed them to take up their crash positions behind the main spar, with the exception of my flight engineer, who I asked to remain with me to handle flaps until I was committed to the landing.

'When I got down to about 800 feet on the approach I realized that I was lined up on a railway track and the runway itself was about a mile off to port. With only the two starboard engines operating there was no way I was going to attempt a turn to port, so I had no choice but to do a 360 turn to starboard! This resulted in my being correctly lined up but when I gave the order for full flap at some 500 feet on final, my flight engineer had already taken off for his crash position! Blyth later told me that when I had to make the turn around to get lined up with the runway, he was convinced that I wasn't going to make it! We did, however, land quite safely and there was no further damage to the aircraft.[22] During my career I landed many times on three engines but this was the only occasion when I had to land a four-engined aircraft with only two engines operating and two on the same side at that! Speaking with my tail gunner a couple of years ago, he assured me that it was the smoothest landing I had ever made!'

On 12 July a dozen crews in 57 Squadron at East Kirkby were briefed for an attack on the railway junction at Culmont-Chalindrey. 'This was part of the work being undertaken to prevent German reinforcements being moved into the battle area in Normandy via the French railway system' remembers 'Ginger' Hammersley. 'This looked like being a reasonably easy operation. In the bomb bay were eight 1,000lb MC and four 500lb GP bombs. It was 21.45 hours when we lined *R-Robert* up at the take-off point on the runway. There was a wave from the small crowd of airmen and WAAFs who invariably made the effort to be at the take-off point to see us off. Then we set off down the runway lifting off at 110 mph and headed away to rendezvous with the other aircraft in the force that was to make the attack. The route took us close to the Channel Islands. Way up ahead of us, two aircraft were seen to be approaching and they were immediately identified as German night fighters. Ken Bly quickly manned his front gun turret and opened fire at one of the approaching fighters, a Ju 88, which turned over on its side and went down in a dive with smoke coming out of it. The other Ju 88 veered away and did not return when the mid-upper gunner fired his guns at him. Unfortunately, in the mêlée the bombsight was damaged. Our briefing for attacks on French railway marshalling yards was that we had to be able to guarantee to hit the rails and not the surrounding buildings. With a damaged bombsight this could not be guaranteed so once again we headed back towards base, after part of the bomb load had been jettisoned into the English Channel. Four hours after take-off we landed at East Kirkby. Our claim for a Ju 88 was, at first, declared as a "probable" but later, when other crews confirmed seeing it hit the sea, it was changed to a "kill". All the other squadron crews made their attack followed by a safe return, although, nine crews were diverted to other airfields. East Kirkby was unable to allow them to land owing to poor weather conditions. After debriefing and an egg and bacon breakfast, I slept well. After lunch, our crew flew *R-Robert* to test that all was well. The bombsight had been put right and a 20-minute flight was all that we needed to confirm all systems were in good order.

'At East Kirkby at this time 57 Squadron received a visit from an American crew in the 389th Bombardment Group at Hethel near Norwich. Captain Cobb was the crew commander. My own crew acted as their hosts. On the 15th we were flown to Hethel by Captain Cobb in their B-24 Liberator for a short stay with them. The Americans made a great fuss of us and we were wined and dined in a manner quite unlike anything we had experienced on an RAF unit. "Food glorious food!" They were so well fed. I tucked in and made the most of the experience. The American crews were briefed for an operation to be flown on the morning of the 17th and we went along with them. Then, in the early hours of the 17th, we met Captain Cobb and his crew to fly in the "assembly ship", a B-24D decorated in brilliant yellow and green bands painted round the fuselage. We were airborne at 05.45 hours and I enjoyed a most fascinating sight as I watched the Group aircraft being called together into formation by means of coloured "Very Lights" whilst the 389th were forming up. In the distance I could see other Groups assembling and gradually coming closer. Then the time came when the group was ready to head out over the North Sea and Captain Cobb dived the B-24 away to starboard and returned to Hethel where we landed after 2 hours 30 minutes flying. Colonel Robert B. Miller, the CO was there to see us return. It was a most welcome breakfast, at which the noisy conversation was an eye opener. The talk was about the crews; planes; whether or not all the aircraft would return; the damage sustained the previous time the group had flown an operation and so on! I would have welcomed a sleep after breakfast but there was so much talk that it was impossible. After lunch, it was time to say our good-byes, Squadron Leader Wyness arrived with his crew to take us back to East Kirkby and our kind of war, and a much different squadron atmosphere.

'The same evening we were briefed for an attack that was to take place the following morning against German forces in the vicinity of Caen. Seventeen crews were briefed for the attack, which was to take place 2,000 yards in front of the Allied ground forces and aimed at the Monteville steel works where the German forces were strongly entrenched. Mack stood down from flying and Flight Lieutenant J. Simms took his place. This operation would see him complete his tour.

P-Peter was "bombed up" with eleven 1,000lb AN-M59 type bombs and four 500lb AN-M64 type bombs. The total force consisted of over 900 aircraft attacking five different villages in the same area. We took off at 03.37 hours heading for the English Channel and then the French coast. Dawn was breaking and we found ourselves being escorted by a Spitfire, the pilot of which had realized we were off track and nudged us over to starboard and into the main force battle order. It was a wonderful sight, over 1,000 aircraft together at one time. On the ground our forces had been warned to keep their heads down and protect their ears as we flew in and made our attack. Later I learned that Wally, my older brother, was down below watching and guessing, correctly, that I was taking part in helping him and his fellows in their struggle to move forward against a very stubborn enemy. Four hours after take-off we landed at East Kirkby ready for debriefing and a good breakfast, only to learn that we were on the battle order for another attack that night.

'The visit to Hethel followed by the night briefing and preparations for the attack on the steel works, had left me tired and I slept well until called to attend briefing for the night's attack, on the railway yards at Revigny by ten crews. For this flight we had an extra man in the crew, Flying Officer M. Blank, a pilot who had arrived on the squadron a few days earlier with his crew. This would be his first operation. Ken Bly was sick and Flight Lieutenant J. Honniball took his place. It was a mixed bomb load consisting of ten 1,000lb MC with half-hour delay fuses, two 500lb GP with 72 hour delay fuses and two 500lb GP with half-hour delay fuses. Our *O-Orange* was well loaded and we were ready for the fray after we had subjected the aircraft to a thorough check late in the afternoon. We took off at 23.00 hours and all went well until we were about 50 miles from the target when simultaneously we heard the rear-gunner open fire as we were struck by bullets and cannon fire from a German night fighter, of which we had received no warning. I heard Mack who usually was a very placid person, say "What the hell's that?" Ron reacted immediately and commenced evasive action. The enemy gun and cannon fire had set the tail end of the fuselage on fire and we lost a great deal of height, dropping from 19,000 feet to about 12,000 feet before control was regained. A Ju 88 followed us down and as we levelled out he came over the top of our aircraft. "Red" [Flight Sergeant Alan Brown] in his mid-upper gun turret, was alert and watching him and he opened fire and hit the Ju 88 with the full firepower from his guns and the enemy aircraft went down. At this moment, in the organized mêlée, Mack went to the rear

of the aircraft carrying a fire extinguisher. As he went past me, I pulled at his right arm and told him to take his parachute, but he failed to hear me. I followed Mack to the rear turret and helped "Goldie" [Pilot Officer Bill Golding RCAF] out of the turret and along the fuselage to the rest bed. His turret was badly damaged and unserviceable. He had suffered bullet wounds as well as serious burns to his feet and legs. His rubber flying boots had started to melt and I cut them away from his feet and legs so that the full extent of the damage to him could be seen. Whilst this was going on, Mack and Esmond were trying to put out the internal and external lights, all of which had switched on. They were fortunate and most of them were extinguished. The intercom had failed and we were only able to contact each other with written notes. Mack gave Ron a course to fly, as it was essential to return to base as soon as possible. I gave Goldie an injection of pain-killing drugs and dressed his burns with the burn dressing gel from the first aid kit. Once I had made him comfortable. I returned to my post at the wireless set, which was still functioning and with Ron's permission, called up base and gave them details of our predicament, of the need for the Medical Officer and an ambulance to be ready to receive us on arrival. The bombs we carried were jettisoned into the English Channel.

'The fact that the wireless was still working was something of a miracle, all the radar equipment had been put out of action leaving Mack to navigate us home by dead reckoning. The landing was bumpy and, unbeknown to us, one tyre had been damaged and it burst as the wheels touched the runway. Goldie was soon away to the Medical Reception Centre and from there to the Military Hospital at Rauceby where the crew visited him the next day. Goldie had three toes that were severely damaged, removed. That visit was the last time I saw him. As for Blank, he had been well and truly "blooded". One crew made an early return with a hydraulic failure in one of the gun turrets; another crew failed to return and was posted as missing and the remainder successfully completed the attack. Following our landing at base we were debriefed and, knowing of the damage we had sustained, the station and base commanders were at the debriefing. A long discussion took place as to whether or not it should be declared our last operation. I had completed the tour having flown 29 operations. The last operation had seen us land at 03.25 hours after a most exciting but exhausting flight of 4 hours 30 minutes. The tour was completed just two days before my 22nd birthday. The past five months had seen me grow from a young excited Sergeant WOp/AG into a man matured by his experi-

189

ences of the violence of war, with all its suffering, for those in the air and on the ground. The crew was granted leave, but before leaving for our various homes, we had a discussion as to whether or not we should seek to join 617 Squadron. Two of the crew were not too keen, so the idea was abandoned.'[23]

At Mildenhall the crew of *K-King* took part in several more operations in July including, on the 18th, the big attack by 942 aircraft on five fortified villages in the area east of Caen, in support of Operation *Goodwood*, the British Second Army's armoured attack. The *Luftwaffe* was noticeable for its absence and Frank Dengate reported that it was 'a wonderful prang on target indicators. 5,000 tons of steel – I wouldn't have liked to be under that lot'. Four of the targets were marked by *Oboe* and at the fifth target where *Oboe* failed, the master bomber, Squadron Leader E. K. Cresswell and other Pathfinder crews employed visual methods. In all Bomber Command dropped more than 5,000 tons of bombs from 5,000–9,0000 feet for the loss of just five Lancasters and a Halifax, though Frank Dengate recorded that there was 'lots of flak'. The 16th *Luftwaffe* Field Division and the 21st Panzer Division were badly affected by the bombing. By way of a change, on 20/21 July Frank Dengate and his crew were part of a force of 147 Lancasters and 11 Mosquitoes that attacked the oil plant at Homburg. Dengate reported that there were 'plenty of night fighters and medium flak and heavy fighter attacks on the way home'. Twenty Lancasters, including two in 622 Squadron and *L for Love* in 15 Squadron, were lost on the Homburg raid. Nine Lancasters were shot down on the operation to bomb railway yards at Courtrai[24] and seven Halifaxes and one Lancaster failed to return from the strike on the synthetic oil refinery at Bottrop. *Nachtjagd* shot down an estimated 15 aircraft from the Bottrop/Homberg force.[25] One of the *Stab* III./NJG 1 Bf 110G-4 night fighter crews comprised Hauptmann Martin Drewes, Feldwebel Erich Handke, *Bordfunker* and Oberfeld-webel Georg 'Schorsch' Petz, air gunner. After shooting down a Halifax and trying to down another that disappeared into the night, Drewes positioned the Bf 110 under PB174 of 405 'Vancouver' Squadron RCAF, a PFF unit. Flight Lieutenant J. D. Virtue RCAF, 28 years old, from Toronto, Ontario was flying this Lancaster. Erich Handke recalls what happened next:

'Schorsch said we were too close but before I could say anything at 50 metres range Drewes aimed at the port inner engine and close to the fuselage (as I could see by the aerial mast on top of the cabin roof). Then it happened. We must have hit the bomb-load because

the Lancaster disintegrated into a thousand pieces! Our machine was struck several times and we went down steeply out of control. All around us were white flames and a thousand green stars. The Lancaster must have been a Pathfinder. We had no intercom. We were thrown about. Most of the time I was stuck against the cabin roof. We went down perhaps 1,000 metres (the attack had been at 5,800m) when I said to myself, "It is no use. Drewes can never regain control; I must get out." I gave two tugs of the roof jettison lever. (Schorsch had done the same at the rear). The rear cabin roof flew off. I pushed off a little to the rear and was caught at once by the slipstream and pulled upwards. My heel just touched the tail. I was clear of the machine and went down, somersaulting. Suddenly there was no more engine noise and briefly I saw our machine and the burning wreckage of the Lancaster going down.[26] I was angry that we had been torn out of a beautiful stream where we could have shot down so many more.'[27]

Frank Dengate's crew's next operation was a 'daylight' on 22 July in *K-King*, their old aircraft, when 48 Lancasters and 12 Mosquitoes carried out '*Oboe* leader' bombing of four weapons' sites through 10/10ths cloud. 15 Squadron's aircraft were part of the force that tried to knock out the flying bombs and V-2 rockets at Mont-Candon. 'There were only eight aircraft in pair's formation, one behind the other. We formated on two Mosquitoes, which were on a radio beam from England and when they crossed a second beam they dropped their bombs and so did we. I don't know what the results were, as we were over cloud. There was no flak and no fighters and none of our aircraft were missing.' This raid was a first for Sergeant Larry Melling in 635 Squadron also. 'We were assigned to attack a V-1 launching site at Linzeaux but this was a totally different kind of operation. Eight Lancasters were sent in formation with an *Oboe*-equipped Mosquito and the Mosquito captain instructed us when to drop the bombs. Never having flown anything larger than a Harvard in formation, the three-hour flight, keeping station with the other aircraft, was a major effort and I am sure that I also lost at least 10lb in perspiration juggling the controls to stay in position. The raid was apparently a success because the same tactics were repeated five days later. In the meantime, we had completed night raids to Kiel and Stuttgart.'

On 23/24 July, Kiel was the first major raid on a German city for two months and was the target for 519 Lancasters and 100 Halifaxes. The raid caught *Nachtjagd* napping and only four aircraft, all of them Lancasters, were shot down and only one other bomber (a Halifax) was lost on the other bomber raids that same night. The first of three heavy raids on Stuttgart, over a period of five nights, went ahead on the night of 24/25 July when 461 Lancasters and 153 Halifaxes were dispatched to the city which, being situated in a series of narrow valleys, had largely escaped the attentions of Bomber Command. Stuttgart had been the destination for Frank Dengate's crew on their first operation on 15 March. Now he and some of *K-King*'s crew were on their 31st trip. The force encountered heavy icing at 14,000 feet and they had to drop down to get rid of it before climbing back up to 19,000 feet at the target. Many aircraft turned back. Seventeen Lancasters and four Halifaxes were lost but *K-King*'s crew made it back to Mildenhall. Flying Officer Joe Ell had now done 28 trips and Sergeant Fred Coney and Sergeant Doug Davis had completed 29 trips each while Bob Kitchin had also flown 28 trips.[28]

On 25 July 90 or more Lancaster crews in 5 Group were briefed for a daylight raid on St-Cyr airfield and a German Air Force Signals Depot (Philips factory) on the southern outskirts of Paris. Another 93 aircraft including 81 Lancasters of 5 Group were allocated flying bomb sites and the Watten storage site. At Skellingthorpe Harry Watkins' crew names appeared once again on the Battle Order sheet in the Squadron office. *O-Orange* became airborne from Skelly's main runway at 17.30 hours and they soon joined up with other Lancasters to form a loose gaggle of 97 aircraft flying over the English Channel before heading inland for the Paris area. Edgar Ray crawled past flight engineer Fred Jowitt through the hole into the bomb-aimer's compartment in the nose of the Lancaster. 'This area' says Ray, 'was very restricted due to the bulky packages of "Window" stacked inside. The weather was fine with continuous cloud cover at 12,000 feet and once in the target area the raid soon developed into a very concentrated attack with aircraft jockeying for position on their bombing run. At 19.55 hours we commenced our run up to the target aiming point through a barrage of moderate flak. From my position in the nose of the aircraft I could see many Lancasters flying close by, releasing their deadly cargo. Moments later I had the target in my bombsight and pressed the tit to release our load of 11,450lb HEs. Within seconds disaster struck, as I felt our aircraft shudder and then fall away to starboard in an uncontrolled dive. The skipper hauled back on the control column and managed to regain control before calling over the aircraft's intercom for a damage report from all crew positions. Ken Johnson our mid-upper gunner reported

that we had been bombed from above and that a large section of the starboard wing tip was missing. Further investigation revealed that a second bomb had broken off the starboard tail fin and rudder, while a third had removed the whole of the rear turret carrying away Jack Foy our rear-gunner. While the skipper fought to control our severely damaged aircraft, Johnny Ware, the wireless op reported our predicament and 5 Group Flying Control diverted us to RAF Wickenby, eight miles north-east of Lincoln, for an emergency landing. Fortunately we managed to get down without any further mishap. This was our 10th operation and the loss of Jack under such circumstances was a big shock to all of us. From that day on I began to wonder if the rest of us would finish our tour in one piece.'[29]

On 25/26 July 412 Lancasters and 138 Halifaxes returned to Stuttgart and other large forces bombed Wanne-Eickel and flying bomb sites in France.[30] On 26/27 July 178 Lancasters and nine Mosquitoes of 5 Group attacked rail yards at Givors for the loss of four Lancasters and two Mosquitoes.[31] Two nights later, 494 Lancasters and two Mosquitoes hit Stuttgart again. There was a bright moon and German fighters intercepted the bombers over France on the outward flight. Thirty-nine Lancasters were shot down. Eighteen Halifaxes and four Lancasters were lost in a separate raid on Hamburg by 307 aircraft, 106 of them Lancasters, in the first heavy attack on the city since the Battle of Hamburg just a year earlier. It was as if the great fire in the summer of 1943 had not been cataclysmic enough but before the winter set in about half of the evacuees returned to their proud domain, factories reopened and commerce resumed. Some had hope restored by the regeneration among the ruins that autumn of a second flowering of many trees and bushes, particularly chestnuts and lilacs, that had been burned in the summer raids.[32] A summer on and this time round the bombing was not well concentrated. The Germans estimated that only 120 aircraft bombed in the city area, with no recognizable aiming point but this raid, one more in the long series of catastrophes that befell the city, was purely to snuff out the civilian population once more. Though western and harbour areas received the most bombs, a large proportion of the attack fell on areas devastated in 1943. A total of 265 people were killed and more than 17,000 Hamburgers had to flee or were evacuated from their dwellings, many of which were temporary wooden accommodation, garden sheds and basements of ruined homes damaged in this raid or those previously.[33]

It was for his role of 'Primary Blind Marker' over Hamburg this night that Squadron Leader H. F. Slade DFC RAAF of 156 Squadron in 8 (PFF) Group won the immediate award of the DSO. The 'Primary Blind Marker' was another PFF innovation and had the responsibility of making a run over the target and releasing markers entirely by radar methods. The equipment used enabled the navigator to see a 'picture' of the ground when above cloud. All bombing attacks at night above cloud-covered targets were carried out using this method; the marking aircraft dropping sky flares, which the main force used as an aiming point. While running in to attack the target with bomb doors open, Slade's Lancaster was heavily engaged by flak and two-thirds of the port aileron and corresponding wing area almost up to the main spar was shot away. The aircraft went into a spiral and became almost out of control before Slade could regain partial control. Then the bombs were dropped and course set for base. The pilot could see from his cockpit that a large section of the upper wing was projecting vertically upwards and acting as an air brake, making control of the aircraft very difficult. All turns had to be made to starboard by throttling back the starboard engines. Crossing the enemy coast, the aircraft was again heavily fired on by the ground defences. Slade took evasive action and the violent motions of the aircraft broke off the vertical section of the wing, restoring a certain amount of aileron movement and increasing control. When the bomber was crossing the North Sea the undercarriage was lowered, and the stalling speed was found to be 140–145 knots. Slade requested an emergency landing at Woodbridge and made a direct approach, touching down at 140 knots. The port tyre had been holed by flak and, soon after touching down, the port undercarriage, then the starboard undercarriage, collapsed. Although the aircraft was wrecked the crew got out with only a few cuts and bruises.[34]

After these raids the bombers reverted to tactical targets, bombing the V-weapon sites at Thiverny, Bois de Cassan, near Paris, Forêt de Nieppe, Forêt de Mormal and Hazebrouck both by day and by night. On 3 August 1,114 aircraft – 601 of them Lancasters, made bombing attacks on these targets and Trossy St Maxim flying bomb stores in northern France. Six Lancasters were lost on the raid on Trossy St Maxim and one from the Bois de Cassan raid, which received a direct hit from an anti-aircraft shell and blew up. The aircraft and its bomb load erupted in a huge pall of dense black smoke centred by bright reddish orange flames. Several minutes later, when the dense black smoke began to disperse, a vacant space could be observed where the Lancaster had been. During the daylight attack on a suspected V-1 storage depot at Trossy St Maxim on 4 August, Acting Squadron Leader Ian Willoughby Bazalgette DFC RAFVR of 635 Squadron, the 'master bomber' who was on his second tour showed great gallantry. Bazalgette was 26 years old, born in Calgary, Alberta, and was brought up in England where he joined the army in 1940 before transferring to the RAF in 1941. His Lancaster was badly hit by flak just short of the target and both starboard engines were put out of action, the wing and fuselage set on fire and the bomb-aimer seriously wounded. Bazalgette however, pressed on to the target while the crew tried to douse the fire and he dropped his markers. With only one engine still running and the starboard wing a mass of flame the order to bale out was given. The bomb-aimer was incapacitated and the mid-upper gunner had been overcome by fumes and were unable to bale out so Bazalgette put the aircraft down in a field near the French village of Senantes but the Lancaster exploded, killing all three on board. When the surviving crew returned to the UK they told the story and Bazalgette was awarded a posthumous Victoria Cross on 17 August 1945.[35]

August 1944 saw Sergeant Larry Melling and 635 Squadron involved in several support operations, including the 'Falaise Gap' and, among other operations, their first daylight trip to a target in the Ruhr – Homberg.[36] 'The month also saw me having a test exercise as a "blind-marker" with the Squadron Navigation Officer. At this time I had completed 26 operations and was presumably now considered safe enough to be entrusted with the job of actually marking a target for the main force, although some considerable time was to elapse before I was given that job.'

At the beginning of August 1944 squadrons were informed that a decision had been made to commence a 'round the clock' bombing campaign against Berlin. Instead of returning to bases in Britain after bombing Berlin, they were to continue their operational flight eastwards, to land at pre-arranged bases in Russia where the Lancasters and Halifaxes would be refuelled, bombed up and re-armed for the return flight. Meanwhile, the US 8th Air Force would commence their operational daytime flights to Berlin and Russia to land at the bases vacated by the RAF aircrews on their return flight to Berlin and Britain. Arrangements were made but after a few false starts, the operation was scrubbed. Apparently, Stalin himself had cancelled the operation because of supposed difficulties of aircraft recognition between unfamiliar British and American bomber air-

Chapter 10: Dawn of D-Day

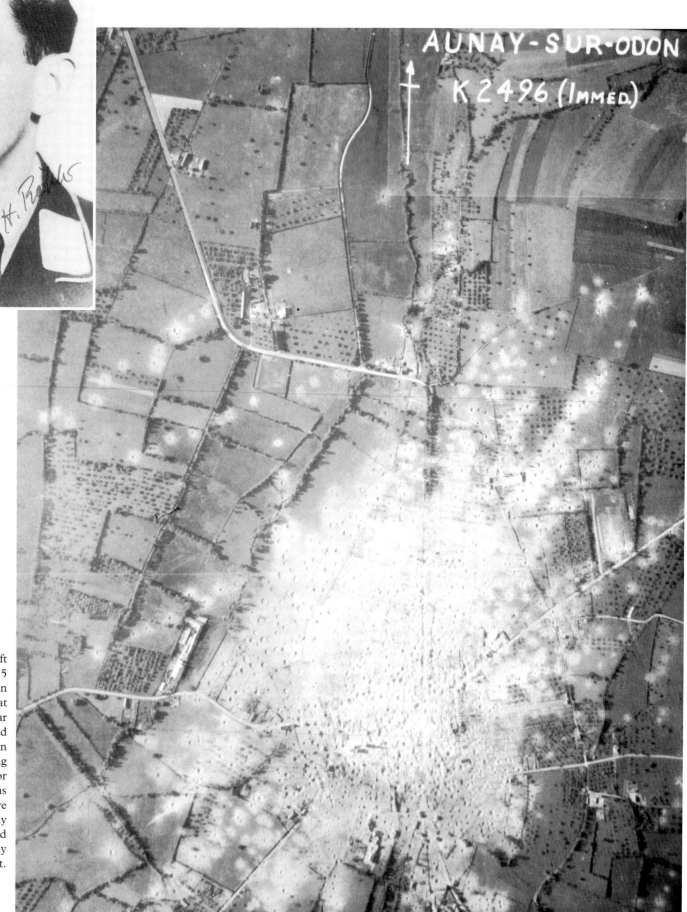

Oberleutnant Heinz Rökker, *Staffelkapitän*, 1./NJG 2. On the night of 22/23 March 1944, flying a Ju 88R-2, he destroyed two Lancasters and a Halifax to take his tally to 17. On the night of 6/7 June 1944 Rökker claimed five Lancasters in the area around Caen. On the night of 7/8 August 1944 Rökker claimed three Lancasters NE of Le Havre for his 38th–40th victories. Rökker survived the war with sixty-three *Nachtjagd* victories (including fifty-five *Viermots* and one Mosquito), plus one in daylight in 161 sorties. He was awarded the *Ritterkreuz with Eichenlaub*. He was the 8th highest scoring *Luftwaffe* night fighter pilot of the war. (*Heinz Rökker*)

AUNAY-SUR-ODON
K 2496 (Immed.)

5 June 1944 337 aircraft
ng 223 Lancasters of 4, 5
Groups attacked German
and vehicle positions at
r-Odon and Évrecy near
hese raids were prepared
xecuted in great haste, in
to an army report giving
of the presence of major
units. The weather was
ar and both targets were
fully bombed. At Aunay
king was shared by 5 and
ups and was particularly
te. No aircraft were lost.

On 27/28 June 1944 214 Lancasters and nine Mosquitoes of 1, 5 and 8 Groups attacked Vaires and Vitry railway yards. The 8 Group raid on the important railway yards at Vaires on the outskirts of Paris was particularly accurate. Four Lancasters were lost – two from each raid. On 12 July 153 Lancasters and six Mosquitoes of 1, 3 and 8 Groups visited the yards again. The target area was covered by cloud and the Master Bomber ordered the attack to be abandoned after two Mosquitoes had marked and twelve Lancasters had bombed.

VAIRES/PARIS M/yd.
Immediate K 2708.

During a daylight bombing of enemy forces at Vi Bocage on 30 June 1944, 75 Squadron Lancaste was hit by flak splinters, one striking flight engine Sergeant P. McDevitt in the knee and causing ex bleeding. The pilot Squadron Leader N. William seeing that McDevitt was losing blood rapidly, e land on one of the Advanced Landing Grounds Normandy beachhead where medical attention c sought. This was the first RAF heavy' to make us of these small strips. This photograph, taken nex shows Williamson presenting bomb-aimer Flying G. Couth with Camembert cheese produced in t to mark his 23rd birthday. Other members of the Flying Officer Watts, navigator, Sergeant J. Russ gunner; Sergeant R. Jones, mid-upper gunner an Sergeant S. Cooke, wireless operator. ND9I7 wa four Lancasters lost during a daylight raid on So 4 November 1944. (*IWM*)

Canadian built Lancaster X KB745 VR-V of 419 'Moose' Squadron RCAF flown by Flying Officer Rokeby photographed over Normandy in the summer of 1944 by 1st Lieutenant Joseph H. Hartshorn DFC, an American pilot on the squadron who flew thirty-four ops. The exhaust gases from the leaded petrol caused the grey streaks on the wing. KB745 and Flying Officer G. R. Duncan RCAF and crew flew into a hillside at Goldscleugh near Rothbury, Scotland setting course for Norway and an attack on the U-Boat pens at Bergen on 4 October 1944. All the crew died.

Lancasters flying above the huge clouds of smoke from fires during the daylight attack on flying bomb sites in the Pas de Calais area on 2 July 1944. Three sites were attacked by 374 Lancasters and ten Mosquitoes of 1, 3 and 8 Groups and though cloud affected all of the raids good concentrations of bombs were thought to have been dropped at all targets. No aircraft were lost.

On 4 July 1944 seventeen Lancasters, one Mosquito and one Mustang of 617 Squadron attacked the flying bomb store in a large cave (formerly used for growing mushrooms) at St-Leu-d'Esserent, north of Paris and bombed the site accurately and without loss. On the night of 4/5 July 231 Lancasters and fifteen Mosquitoes mostly from 5 Group but with some Pathfinder aircraft, continued the attack with 1,000lb bombs in order to cut all communications to the store. The bombing was accurate but thirteen Lancasters were lost when enemy fighters attacked them. On 7/8 July St-Leu-d'Esserent was attacked again, by 208 Lancasters and thirteen Mosquitoes, mainly from 5 Group but with some Pathfinders. The bombing as accurately directed on to the mouths of the tunnels and on to the approach roads, thus blocking access to the flying bombs stored there. Night fighters intercepted the bombers and shot down twenty-nine Lancasters and two Mosquitoes. 106 Squadron from Metheringham, lost five of its sixteen Lancasters on the raid and 630 Squadron from East Kirkby, lost its CO, Wing Commander W. I. Deas, who was flying his 69th operation. Finally, on 5 August 742 aircraft including 257 Lancasters attacked the St-Leu-d'Esserent and Forêt de Nieppe storage sites. (*via 'Pat' Patfield*)

ST. LEU D'ESSERENT

REPORT N.S. 1300

A Royal visit to Mildenhal. 5 July 1944 when crews in 622 Squadrons operated fi station. (*via Fred Coney*)

A low level photograph taken after the attack on the V-2 rocket site under construction at Wizernes in Northern France on 17 July 1944 by sixteen Lancasters of 617 Squadron with a Mosquito and a Mustang as marker aircraft. The 'Dambusters' aimed 12,000lb *Tallboy* earthquake bombs with 11-second delay on the huge concrete dome, 20-feet thick, which lay on the edge of a chalk quarry protecting rocket stores and launching tunnels that led out of the face of the quarry pointing towards London. One *Tallboy* that apparently burst at the side of the dome exploded beneath it, knocking it askew. Another caused part of the chalk cliff to collapse, undermining the dome, with part of the resulting landslide also blocking four tunnel entrances, including the two that were intended for the erected V-2s. Though the construction was not hit, the surrounding area was so badly 'churned up' that it was unapproachable and the bunker jeopardized from underneath. The site was abandoned and the V-2s were pulled back to The Hague in Holland where, in September the Germans began firing them from mobile launchers. (*IWM*)

20/21 July 1944 302 Lancasters and Mosquitoes of 1, 5 and 8 Groups ed the railway yards and a 'triangle' ail junction at Courtrai in Belgium. Both targets were devastated as this shows. Nine Lancasters were lost. (*via 'Pat' Patfield*)

(*Left*) On 23/24 July 1944 100 Halifaxes of 6 Group along with fourteen Lancasters and five Mosquitoes of 8 Group attacked an oil refinery and storage depot a Donges near the mouth of the River Loire. The target was severely damaged and a tanker was hit and capsized. (*via 'Pat' Patfield*)

(*Right*) A Lancaster flying over the oil storage depot of Bec-d'Ambes near Bordeaux on 4 August 1944 when 288 Lancasters of 1, 3 and 8 Groups attacked Bec-d'Ambes and Pauillac in clear conditions and without loss.

Lancaster II LL734/JL-O of 514 Squadron flown by Flying Officer C. B. Sandland on the aircraft's 33rd sortie during the attack on the V-1 site at Les Catellier 27 July 1944. Twelve Lancasters of 514 Squadron dropped eighteen 500-pounders on *Oboe* marking. Five V-1 sites were attacked this day by seventy-one aircra thirty-six of them Lancasters. All targets were cloud-covered and most of the bombing was 'confused and scattered'. LL734 was later transferred to 1668 HCU was wrecked on 23 January 1945.

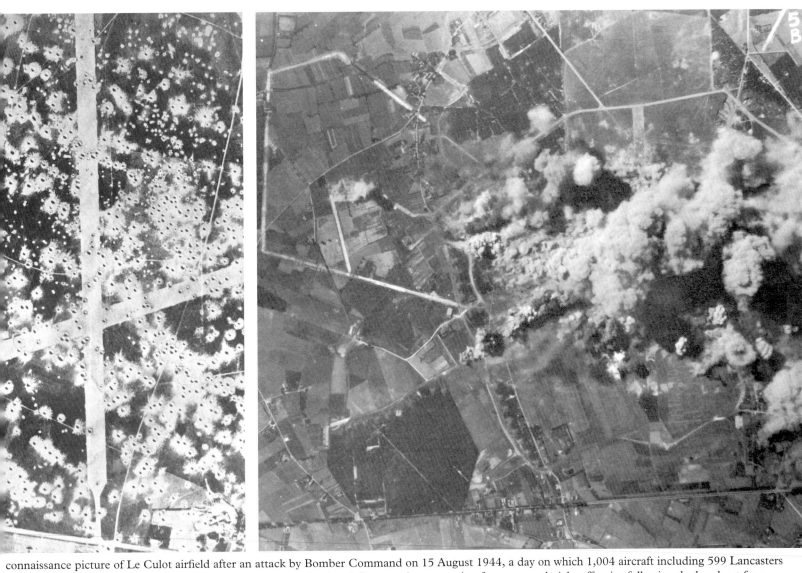

...connaissance picture of Le Culot airfield after an attack by Bomber Command on 15 August 1944, a day on which 1,004 aircraft including 599 Lancasters ...nine German night-fighter airfields in France, Belgium, Holland and Germany in preparation for a renewed night offensive following the breakout from ...dy. Three Lancasters were lost on the raids.

...olkel airfield in Holland on 15 August 1944, the second photo of which is taken from 15,000 feet. Visibilty was perfect as more than 1,000 aircraft attacked ...elds in Holland and Belgium and all raids were considered successful. *(via 'Pat' Patfield)*

...r III ED860 *N-Nan* of 61 Squadron with her air and ground crews. *N-Nan* completed its 100th op on 27/28 June 1944 when Flying Officer B. S. Turner flew ...ft on the operation to the Vitry railway yards.

Chapter 11: 'Round the Clock'

Canadian Flying Officer Jack F. Hamilton, mid-upper gunner in the crew of Lancaster JO-J '*Jumpin' Jive*' of 463 Squadron RAAF. The trip to Königsberg on the night of 29/30 August 1944 was his 21st trip (and longest at almost eleven hours) in a tour of thirty-three trips from 6 June to 17 October 1944. Hamilton had started out as a tail gunner at OTU but as he was six feet tall and too big for the gun turret, he had problems with the gun sights, so he had to switch to the mid-upper position. (*Jack Hamilton*)

Lancaster III ED588 VN-G *G-George* of 50 Squadron, which was lost with Flying Officer A. H. 'Tony' Carver and crew on the operation to Königsberg on 29/30 August 1944. All but one of the crew were killed. This aircraft, which was originally assigned to 97 Squadron in early 1943, completed 128 operational sorties.

KÖNIGSBERG
KNOL (Immitd)
DIST 23 C

on Königsberg on the night of 29/30 August 1944 by 189 Lancasters of 5 Group was one of their most successful attacks of the war. Only 480 tons of bombs carried because of the range of the target but severe damage was caused around the four separate aiming points chosen. This success was achieved despite a e delay in opening the attack because of the presence of low cloud; the bombing force waited patiently, using up precious fuel, until the marker aircraft found the clouds and the Master Bomber, Wing Commander J. Woodroffe, allowed the attack to start. Bomber Command estimated that 41 per cent of all the nd 20 per cent of all the industry in Königsberg were destroyed. There was heavy fighter opposition over the target and fifteen Lancasters were lost.

A *Tallboy* spin-stabilised, deep penetration bomb on its Type H special transporter at Bardney on 9 September 1944. If dropped from the optimum height of 18,000 feet the *Tallboy* took 37 seconds to reach the ground where it impacted at 750mph and penetrated 25 feet into the surface before exploding.

Flying from a temporary Russian base, twenty-eight Lancasters of 9 and 617 Squadrons attacked the battleship *Tirpitz* (indicated by the arrow) in Kaa Fjord, no Norway on 15 September 1944. The smokescreen failed to prevent some accurate bombing and the battleship was hit by one of thirteen Tallboys dropped. This other damage rendered the ship unserviceable for sea action and never went to sea again, being used instead as a floating gun battery. Unfortunately, this was no realised by Allied Intelligence.

...or Joe of 463 Squadron RAAF at ...ington in 1944 with fifty-nine ops ...d by Russian stars. Lancaster III ...1 Uncle Joe, which had a picture ... and operations also denoted by ... flew 115 ops with the squadron. (Jack F. Hamilton)

Lancaster III EE176 QR-M *MICKEY THE MOOCHER* of 61 Squadron at Skellingthorpe in 1944. L–R: Jim Leith, flight engineer; Den Cluett, rear gunner; Pete Smith, bomb aimer; Flying Officer Frank Mouritz RAAF, pilot; Arthur Bass, mid-upper gunner; Laurie Cooper, navigator; Dave Blomfield, WOp. Aircraft lettered 'M' were usually known as *M-Mike* or *M-Mother*. (Frank Mouritz)

RAF ground technicians work to repair the damaged wing of a Halifax at Woodbridge. In the background is Lancaster II LL624/JI-B of 514 Squadron, which after it was badly battle-damaged for the fourth time on 28 September 1944 it was SOC. (*IWM*)

Lancaster III EE139 'B-B
550 Squadron, better kno
PHANTOM OF THE RU
North Killingholme with
Officer Joe C. Hutcheson'
just before its 100th op o
5 September 1944 on a d
raid against Le Havre, Fr
(Note the mustard-colour
circular gas detection pan
appeared on aircraft of 1
Bomber Command and t
ice-cream cones in the fir
rows of the bomb log den
raids on Italian targets in
EE136 began it career in
100 Squadron at Waltham
Grimsby in May 1943 an
least twenty-nine sorties v
unit until in November 19
joined 550 Squadron. Du
11/12 June 1943 to 21 N
1944 *PHANTOM OF TF
RUHR* completed 121 tri
surviving five night-fighte
and returning with severe
scars on five occasions. T
and the ghoulish figure w
creation of Sergeant Har
Bennett, the aircraft's firs
engineer who had been a
engineer in Fighter Comr
the early part of the war.
(*Len Browning*)

y Dortmund-Ems Canal at Ladberg after the 'Tallboy' attack on the night of 23/24 September 1944.

'Window' cascades from Lancaster B.I NG126/SR-B of 101 Squadron piloted by Warrant Officer R. B. Tibbs en route to Duisburg during Operation *Hurricane* on 14/15 October 1944. The *Airborne Cigar* (ABC) aerials are prominent above the fuselage. Few photographs of these special aircraft exist owing to the censor's work, but this still came from a motion film taken by the Bomber Command Film Unit and eliminating the masts was not possible. The aircraft carried special radios and a German-speaking operator and *Luftwaffe* ground and airborne radio transmissions were intercepted and misleading instructions passed on to German fighters. On 14 October 957 RAF heavies dropped 3,574 tons of high explosive and 820 tons of incendiaries and that night 1,005 more bombers dropped 4,040 tons of high explosive and 500 tons of incendiaries on the city. In all 101 Squadron flew 2,477 ABC sorties in the Second World War. (*IWM*)

On 21 October seventy-five Lancasters of 3 Group carried out a daylight attack on a German coastal battery at Flushing on the Dutch Island of Walcheren. Bombing was very accurate and one Lancaster failed to return.

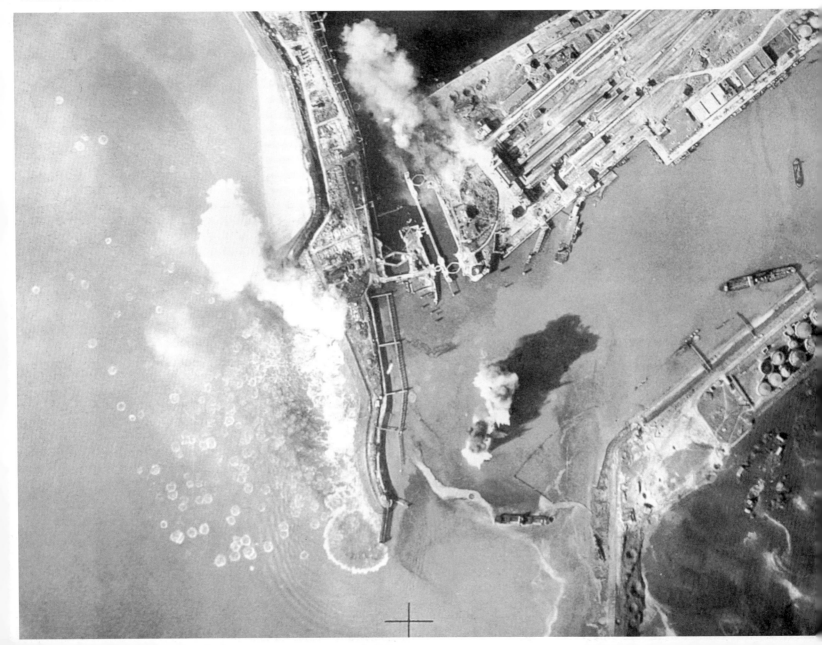

an island. Bomber Command sent many heavy bombs down on the built-up walls of the Dutch Island of Zoutelande (Walcheren) at the mouth of the River On 29 October 1944 358 aircraft – 194 Lancasters, 128 Halifaxes and thirty-six Mosquitoes – of four Groups attacked eleven different German ground in good visibility for the loss of one Lancaster. This picture shows the sea rushing in over part of the fortifications the Germans had established on the island. the bomb craters on the arms of the sea wall on each side of the breach touch one another, so precise and so concentrated was the bombing.

44 (Rhodesia) Squadron took Lancaster III LM625/KM-H *Sky Floosie* on charge in June 1944. The employees of Shabani Mines in Southern Rhodesia contributed £1,255 and this was used for a petrol bowser. On hand for the photograph were twenty-one-year-old Flying Officer Plenderleith who had thirty-four ops to his credit, nineteen-year-old Flight Sergeant Van Niekerk, who had flown twenty-six ops and Corporal Simpson, a fitter; all these men coming from Shabani. *Sky Floosie* has seventy-eight bombing ops on the noise, the bombs in white denoting daylight raids. In mid-1945 LM625 was transferred to 75 Squadron and after a spell with 39 MU was scrapped in October 1945.

Leutnant Horst Rüdiger Blume claimed one victory in 1943 and two more in 1944, a *Viermot* on 12/13 Aug[ust] and a Lancaster on 4/5 November before he was killed in a crash south of Lübbecke during a non-operatio[nal] flight ten days later on 14 November 1944. (*Steve Hall via John Foreman*)

A 4,000lb 'Cookie' and other bombs hurtle down on Gelsenkirchen from 17,000 feet on 6 November 194[4]. 738 aircraft, 324 of them Lancasters, carried out a daylight raid on the town. The aiming point was the N[ordstern] synthetic-oil plant. The attack was not well concentrated but 514 aircraft were able to bomb the approxim[ate] position of the oil plant before smoke obscured the ground and 187 aircraft then bombed the general town. Three Lancasters and two Halifaxes were lost. (*via 'Pat' Patfield*) craft, by Russian aircraft. It is possible that if Stalin had agreed to the original operation codenamed *Thunderclap*, upon Berlin in August 1944, Dresden might possibly have escaped destruction later in the war.

Flight Lieutenant G. A. C. Overgaauw of 207 Squadron, one of several Dutch pilots flying Lancasters in the RAF, left Spilsby on 15 August for a raid on Deelen airfield in his native Holland, with eleven 1,000lb and four 500lb bombs. It was the Amsterdam born Dutchman's 33rd operation. A direct hit on the bomb bay of his Lancaster caused the aircraft to explode in mid-air and crash near Arnhem killing all the crew. On the last day of August, when over 600 aircraft, 418 of them Lancasters, bombed nine V-2 rocket store sites in northern France, six Lancasters were lost. One of them was a 166 Squadron aircraft piloted by Flying Officer E. B. Tutty RAAF, which was shot down bombing Agenville. Tutty and one other member of the crew evaded and two men were killed. The three others including the W/Op, Flying Officer Donald Pleasance, were captured. Pleasance had been issued with a packet of condoms to protect important parts of the wireless set. When he was searched the condoms were discovered by the Germans and one of them said, 'You vil not be needing zeeze now!'[37]

Aircrew became very sensitive to the changing moods of a station, which swung from being easy and light hearted when operations were off, often when the weather was bad, to a palpable tension when the operation was 'on' and the target was known. At Elsham Wolds, high above the flat fenlands of Lincolnshire, bounded by the Humber Estuary and the Weir Dyke to the north, when ops were scrubbed a wave of relaxation spread across a station. Buses or trains were provided to take crews into Scunthorpe or Brigg. Scunthorpe was a grimy steel town, lying in the shadow of vast slag heaps. There were three pubs, the Bluebell, the Oswald and the Crosby. It was generally accepted that aircrew NCOs used the Bluebell. It would not have been out of place in a Western. It had a large, open saloon bar with a sawdust-covered floor and a raised wooden platform in the corner on which a man in bowler hat played nonstop. It only needed busty, silk stockinged girls to complete the illusion but the ladies provided did their best and this made up in humour what it lacked in propriety.[38]

When ops were 'on' the wind that came out of the dark sky to the east filled the windsock in the signal square and lifted the pennant on the runway control van. It chilled the airmen gathered in groups on the perimeter track and ruffled the hair of the WAAFs who huddled in the shelter of the control tower. It also helped the Lancasters of 103 and 576 Squadrons take-off, disappearing towards the dark sea, heavy with their fuel and bomb loads. Those off duty would watch them taxi out. Most had their top hatches open and helmeted figures would be waving at those on the ground. *L-Love* was known for the lavatory paper, which streamed from the open hatches and the cloth caps pulled down over the helmets of the Australian crew. To them the lavatory paper and the cloth caps were as much an essential to their safe return as the efficiency of the crew and the aircraft. One day, with the crews out at their Lancs ready for the off, they were stood down for an hour. WAAFs were told to take refreshments out to them. One of the WAAFs saw them standing round waiting, joking while she poured out the tea. They were calling each other, saying things like, 'The Germans have got it in for you tonight but don't worry, we'll eat your egg and bacon for you.' There was always a fried meal waiting for them when they returned from ops. The WAAF could not stand it. It was not funny and she refused to go out to waiting aircrews again, it upset her that much.[39]

Notes

1. One thousand and twelve RAF aircraft bombed coastal batteries; 110 aircraft of 100 Group carried out extensive bomber-support operations. Two Halifaxes and one Lancaster were lost. Twenty-four *ABC*-equipped Lancasters of 101 Squadron patrolled all known night fighter approaches. (Two Intruders and 1 *ABC* Lancaster were lost.) Fifty-eight aircraft flew diversion operations. Thirty-one Mosquitoes bombed Osnabrück without loss. In all RAF Bomber Command flew 1,211 sorties. Operations *Taxable* and *Glimmer*, both devised by Wing Commander E. I. Dickie, created 'Phantom Fleets' on enemy radar screens. *Taxable* involved 16 Lancasters of 617 Squadron and was a joint RN/RAF operation aimed at making the Germans believe that an invasion force was attacking the French coast between Dieppe and Cap d'Antifer. Attacks on enemy radar installations had all but destroyed their effectiveness, but care had been taken to leave enough operational, to allow the Germans to deceive themselves that their radars were showing an invasion fleet. Twenty-four Lancasters of 101 Squadron and five B-17 Flying Fortresses of 214 Squadron, carrying 82 radio jammers between them, obliterated the German night fighter frequencies for more than five hours. One Lancaster was shot down.
2. 'The final raid of my tour of operations was a few days later on 14 and 15 June when we attacked a German *Panzer* (tank) force concentrated at night, hiding under cover of trees in a wood. With information from the French Resistance we knew exactly where they were. On 17 June my replacement, Wing Commander Donaldson RAAF, arrived and the next day I started my end of tour leave.'

3. On 5/6 June *Luftwaffe* activity was almost non-existent, putting up just 59 fighters to intercept the invasion forces but only two *Nachtjäger* submitted one claim each. Finally, Oberleutnant Helmut Eberspächer, a fighter-bomber pilot of 3./SKG 10 flying a Fw 190G-3 claimed three Lancasters at Isigny and Carentan while Feldwebel Eisele of the same unit claimed another Lancaster at Isigny-Lessay-Vire.

4. On 6/7 June 1,065 RAF bombers dropped 3,488 tons of bombs on rail and road centres on the lines of communication behind the Normandy battle area for the loss of 10 Lancasters and a Halifax.

5. The other two crews were Flying Officer C. D. Woodley RCAF in *A-Apple* and Flight Lieutenant W. E. Palmer in *M-Mother*. There were no survivors from either crew. 622 Squadron lost two Lancasters. Pilot Officer J. E. Hall in *E-Easy* and Flight Lieutenant R. G. Godfrey RAAF in *C-Charlie* both failed to return and there were no survivors from either crew.

6. K report. *Nachtjagd* claimed 21 Lancasters and Halifaxes with Hauptmann Paul Zorner *Gruppenkommandeur* of III./NJG 5 being credited with three Halifaxes and a Lancaster in the Dreux area to take his score to 52. Leutnant Walter Briegleb of 10./NJG 3 was credited with four Lancasters (three in the greater Paris area, his 4th victim crashing 25 km E-S-E of Rouen) to take his score to eight confirmed victories.

7. On 11/12 June 329 aircraft attacked railway targets at Èvreux, Massy-Palaiseau again, Nantes and Tours for the loss of three Lancasters and a Halifax.

8. Pilot Officer Andrew Charles Mynarski RCAF was awarded a posthumous Victoria Cross for his bravery on the Cambrai raid. His Lancaster, of 419 Squadron, was attacked by a night fighter and set on fire and the crew were ordered to abandon the aircraft. Mynarski, who was the mid-upper gunner, was about to jump when he saw that the rear-gunner was trapped in his turret and he went through fierce flames to help. The rear turret was so badly jammed that it could not be freed and the trapped gunner eventually waved Mynarski away. By the time he left the aircraft, Mynarski's clothing and parachute were on fire and he died while being cared for by French civilians soon after he landed. The rear-gunner was fortunate to survive the crash and his report on Mynarski's courage led to the award of the Victoria Cross. Pilot Officer Mynarski was born in Winnipeg and joined the RCAF in 1941 as a WOp/AG. He was posted to England in 1943 and was commissioned in 1944. The 28 year old Canadian is buried in the small cemetery at Meharicourt, east of Amiens.

9. Hauptmann Gerhard Friedrich, *Staffelkapitän,* 1./NJG 6 and Hauptmann Joachim Böhner of St.I./NJG 6 at Deelen both claimed a Lancaster from the Gelsenkirchen force, probably LM158 of 90 Squadron, which crashed 2 km W of Laag Soeren. Friedrich, who was awarded the *Ritterkreuz* on 15 March 1945, was killed in action on 16/17 March when his Ju 88G was hit when it collided with, or was destroyed by, the explosion of a 576 Squadron Lancaster he was attacking. Oberleutnant Lau, Unteroffizier Sarzio and Leutnant Gottfried Hanneck of II./NJG 1 also operating from Deelen, each claimed a *Viermot* destroyed. Oberleutnant Hanneck shot down five Lancasters and Halifaxes in June/July.

10. Lancaster LL678 of 514 Squadron.

11. On 9 August we got confirmation of a crash of a Lancaster near Warminghaven, 30kms east of Arnhem. Further confirmation

12. by the *Reichsluftfahrtministerium* (RLM or *Reich* Air Ministry) followed in February 1945.

13. Six Lancasters were lost on the Lens raid. Another 297 aircraft attacked ammunition and fuel dumps without loss.

14. Another bomber force comprising 321 Halifaxes, Lancasters and Mosquitoes raided the synthetic oil plant at Sterkrade/Holten. No aircraft were lost on the raids in Northern France but 31 RAF aircraft were missing from the operation to Sterkrade/Holten though *Zahme Sau* claimed 37 kills. The route of the bomber stream passed near a German night-fighter beacon at Bocholt just 30 miles ftrom Sterkrade and the *Jägerleitoffizier* (*JLO,* or GCI-controller) had chosen this beacon as the holding point for his night fighters. Twenty-two of the bombers that were missing were Halifaxes.

15. Three hundred and seventeen aircraft attacked railway targets at Aulnoye, Montdidier and St-Martin-l'Hortier. One Lancaster was lost on the Montdidier raid. All targets were covered by cloud and the master bombers at Aulnoye and Montdidier ordered their forces to stop bombing after only seven and 12 aircraft had bombed respectively.

16. The losses, 27.8 per cent of the force, were all shot down by *Zahme Sau*. I./NJG 1 was credited with 16 kills that were claimed by eight *Owl* crews and II./NJG I received credit for six victories.

17. In June 1946 the Germans responsible for the shooting were put on trial in Essen and four were sentenced to death.

18. Two of the squadron's Lancasters and their experienced crews, failed to return. Flight Lieutenant R. R. Cowan's crew had completed 31 trips, plus three 'one-thirds', while Pilot Officer A. A. W. Berryman's crew had completed 16. See *1944 The Air war Over Europe June 1st-30th* by John Foreman. (ARP, 1999)

19. Cheshire would fly his 100th op on 8 July and he was withdrawn from operations.

20. Or 8.7 per cent of the force. Thirteen *Zahme Sau* crews were credited with 21 *Viermot* kills.

21. A primed cookie bomb was on board and the aircraft remained in the field for three days until it was considered safe to work on. PB112 *K-King,* which was repaired, later flew with 195 Squadron and was lost on a day raid on Witten on 12 December 1944.

22. The Canadian 1st and British 2nd Armies were held up by a series of fortified village strongpoints north of the city and the first plan was for Bomber Command to bomb these villages but, because of the proximity of Allied troops and the possibility of bombing error, the bombing area was moved back nearer to Caen, covering a stretch of open ground and the northern edge of the city. The master bomber, Wing Commander S. P. 'Pat' Daniels of 35 Squadron, orchestrated a highly accurate raid and 2,276 tons of bombs were dropped. Only three aircraft were lost of the 447 'heavies' and 20 *Oboe*-equipped Mosquitoes dispatched. By the evening of 8 July the whole of Caen, north of the Orne, was in British hands.

23. ND811 F2-T which, after the two engines were changed, was returned to Downham Market and continued to fly until it was shot down on 4 August at Trossy St Maxim. The pilot, Squadron Leader Ian Bazalgette, was to lose his life and be awarded a posthumous VC.

24. In August Pilot Officer William Henry Golding RCAF and Mack MacKinnon were awarded the DFC and 'Ginger' Hammersley the DFM. In September Ken Bly was awarded the

DFC. Flight Sergeant Alan 'Red' Brown was later awarded the DFM.

24. Two of which were destroyed on their way back by Obstlt Lent, *Kommodore* NJG 3 off Dover for his 106th and 107th victories.

25. In total, 971 sorties were flown on 20/21 July for the loss of 38 aircraft. Eighty-seven heavies bombed V-weapon sites at Ardouval and Wizernes and 302 Lancasters and 15 Mosquitoes bombed rail targets at Courtrai. One hundred and fifty-three heavies and 13 Mosquitoes attacked the synthetic oil refinery at Bottrop and 147 Lancasters and 11 Mosquitoes attacked an oil plant at Homberg. Twenty-one Lancasters and 7 Halifaxes failed to return from the Bottrop/Homberg raid. 75 Squadron RNZAF at Mepal lost seven of its 25 Lancasters.

26. PB174 LQ-P crashed at Tubbergen, north-east of Almelo. Virtue and six crew were killed in action when the aircraft exploded. The Dutch Resistance hid sole survivor, Flight Sergeant M. S. Stoyko RCAF, rear-gunner. Drewes' Bf 110G-4 crashed near the Dutch-German border. Feldwebel Erich Handke's 58th and 59th *Abschussbeteiligungen* earned him the rare award for a *Bordfunker* of the *Ritterkreuz* on 27 July.

27. Handke, Drewes and Petz baled out safely near Twente where their *8th Staffel* was stationed. Oberleutnant Dietrich Schmidt, who had also downed two Lancasters (HK569 of 75 Squadron and LL859 of 622 Squadron, picked them up and he drove them to the nearest hospital. Schorsch, who had a bomb splinter in the left forearm and a flesh wound in the right, had his arms put into plaster casts. Drewes had released his harness straps and he was catapulted out through the cockpit roof which was torn off and left hanging around his neck. He had only managed to lose it with some difficulty and had dislocated his arm in the process but, at a farmhouse shortly after landing, it had snapped into place again when he leaned on a table. On 27 July Hauptmann Martin Drewes received the *Ritterkreuz* for his 48 victories. He added one more kill to his total, on 3/4 March 1945. He was decorated with the Oak Leaves to his *Ritterkreuz* three weeks before the capitulation of *Nazi* Germany.

28. Frank Dengate adds: 'Cantrell, Ell and myself were awarded the Distinguished Flying Cross whereas the other members of our crew got no recognition although they took the same risks. I was asked to stay on as Squadron Leader Flight Command with 15 Squadron but with my crew split up I had had enough for the present. I took 14 days glorious leave and early in August I was posted to 29 OTU. Before returning to Australia I was posted to 467 Squadron RAAF at Waddington and Metheringham, where we trained to go to Okinawa to attack Japan but the Yanks dropped the atomic bomb and consequently probably saved my life and the lives of my crew as well as thousands of others.'

29. Pilot Officer Carson 'Jack' Foy is buried in the local cemetery in Fontenay-le-Fleary in Versailles. His grieving parents in Canada received a heartfelt and moving letter of condolence from Harold Watkins who said that he 'had never found him wanting in courage and the high principles for which [they] were striving'. He ended his letter, 'it is a terribly high price we are having to pay and I have lost many close friends. I only hope to God that when peace does come the ideals, the way of life that we're fighting for, will become a lasting reality ... only this could justify the sacrifices that are being made today. I can't say more.' Dixie Dean, the sergeant in charge of the crew's replacement aircraft, had continuously serviced an aircraft with the code QR-*X X-Ray* since 1939 when the Squadron flew Hampdens. Edgar Ray recalls that LL911 served them well for the rest of our tour but was eventually lost on 8/9 February 1945 while carrying out its 99th operation with the Squadron. *Thundering Through the Clear Air: No. 61 (Lincoln Imp) Squadron At War* by Derek Brammer (Tucann Books, 1997).

30. Eight Lancasters and four Halifaxes were lost on the Stuttgart raid and one Mosquito *Intruder* failed to return.

31. Two of the Lancasters were claimed by Leutnant Otto Huchler of 2./NJG 2 for his first two victories. *Nachtjagd* units intercepted the stream on the outward flight and, aided by the bright moonlight, shot down 39 Lancasters. On 20/21 July II./NJG1 destroyed three *Viermots* (two by Unteroffizier Sarzio, and Lancaster III NE164 of 550 Squadron, which crashed at Ottrott near Strassburg by Oberleutnant Gottfried Hanneck, *Staffelkapitän*, 6./NJG 1.

32. *The Battle of Hamburg: Allied Bomber Forces Against A German City in 1943* by Martin Middlebrook (Penguin, 1980).

33. *The Bomber Command War Diaries* by Martin Middlebrook and Chris Everitt (Midland, 1985).

34. *Royal Australian Air Force Overseas* (Eyre & Spottiswoode, London 1946).

35. Trossy St Maxim, which cost two Lancasters, was thought to be a V-1 storage site but after the war captured German documents revealed that it was a dummy site, as was Bois de Cassan.

36. On 27 August, when 243 aircraft were dispatched in the first Bomber Command daylight raid to be flown since 12 August 1941, when 54 Blenheims of 2 Group attacked the power stations at Cologne for the loss of 10 aircraft.

37. He was incarcerated in *Stalag Luft I*, Barth. Post war Pleasance became a major film star and he appeared as Ernst Stavro Blofeld in the James Bond film, *You Only Live Twice* and as a RAF POW at *Stalag Luft III* in *The Great Escape*. Donald Pleasance OBE died in France on 2 February 1995.

38. Pilot Officer Peter Beechey writing in *Not Just Another Milk Run; The Mailly-le-Camp Bomber Raid* by Molly Burkett & Geoff Gilbert (Barny Books, 2004).

39. Lilly Taylor and Peter Beechey writing in Burkett and Gilbert, op. cit.

Chapter 11

'Round the Clock'

'Time to get up Flight. You're on this morning.

'If there's ever a low point in anybody's life this was it: To be woken at 04.00 hours knowing you were going to war!' Allen crawled out of a warm bed into the frozen Nissen hut. Gathered up towel and soap and shivered miserably in the wintry gap between the hut and the ablutions blocks where he splashed water hurriedly over his face, no time to shave! The desperately early breakfast of bacon and egg and mug of hot sweet tea, preceded briefing, where they had dispensed with the niceties of hiding the target behind a curtain. The red tape, which slithered disconcertingly across the map like a long tail of blood, led from Norfolk to a suburb of the huge German inland river port and industrial city of Duisburg. 'Christ' they said sourly, slumping on to the hard wooden chairs, 'It's bloody Homberg again'.

Allen Clifford, navigator

Flying Officer Jack F. Hamilton went out to Lancaster *Jumpin' Jive* at Waddington dressed, as usual, in heavy, bulky flying clothing, which, to his chagrin, often created a problem regarding urinating. The Canadian mid-upper gunner often had to urinate in his flying clothes during an op and as he says, 'the piss usually ended up in my flying boots where it sometimes froze!' Hamilton's other operational problem was that he was six feet tall and when he had started out as a rear-gunner at OTU he found that he was too big for the gun turret and he had problems with the gun sights. By the time he began his tour in 463 Squadron RAAF on 6 June, an English gunner who was much smaller than he was had taken over the rear turret of *JO-J*. Rear-gunners were in the coldest part of the Lancaster and they had to wear a lot of heavy, bulky flying clothing, some of which was electrically heated. If an air gunner had the misfortune to urinate in an electrically heated part of the suit, it could short it out, freeze and cause frostbite, amputation or death. Hamilton was glad that he would not have to occupy the tail turret for almost 11 hours when *Jumpin' Jive* was one of 189 Lancasters that set out that night, 29/30 August, for Königsberg as another 400 Lancs went to Stettin. It was Hamilton's 21st op and the longest one of his tour to October 1944. It would also be one of the most successful 5 Group attacks of the war.

'We flew across southern Sweden on the way in, which was against international law. After that our course on our starboard side was along the German Baltic coast, sometimes over water and sometimes over the land close to the shore. This is when the German night fighters first attacked. One night fighter flew right over us. I thought that he was attacking us but he overshot and shot down a Lancaster a little below on the port side over the water. Several more Lancasters were shot down from this point all the way to Königsberg. There was also a lot of flak along our route. Just short of Königsberg we were attacked by what I thought at first was a Mosquito but turned out to be a Me 210, which looked very much like a Mosquito. However he overshot us and missed. There appeared to be a lot of Mosquito Pathfinder aircraft over the target and they closely resembled twin-engined German aircraft in the dark of night. We bombed the target (we think) and headed back down the Baltic during which time we could see several Lancasters shot down but we were not attacked and I assume that we again crossed Sweden. About this time we were advised by radio to expect heavy concentrations of night fighters. They hit us over Denmark and a considerable battle ensued at a medium altitude, as we started to descend to the North Sea. Our aircraft was not hit but several Lancasters were shot down at this point and we had to take evasive action to evade the night fighters who appeared to be in great strength. We decided to reduce altitude and increase our speed to the coast but the fighters were still on our tail. We did not fire back so as not to give away our position from our tracer fire. We had some minor damage, which had to be from the fighters as there was little or no flak. Finally, in desperation, we increased speed and dropped down to ground level when about halfway across Denmark to the coast. Just as we crossed the coast at zero level, a flak battery opened up on us and we had to climb up to a few hundred feet to get out of the low flak. After we left the Danish coast we could look back and see the air battle continuing but I did not see any more Lancasters shot down. We made it back safely to our 'drome at Waddington where I received a commission as a pilot officer the day after the raid.'[1]

A further 23 Lancasters were lost in the raid on Stettin, one of which was a 626 Squadron aircraft flown by Flying Officer R. C. Hawkes RCAF. Fourteen miles from the Swedish coast at 13,000 feet and climbing to 18,000 feet two Ju 88s attacked them without warning. *Fishpond* was fitted but was not being monitored. Both fighters opened fire from dead astern with cannon tracer. One of the crew was seriously injured and the hydraulics to both turrets were severed. Only the mid-upper could be rotated manually. A large hole was torn in the starboard wing and fire erupted in both starboard engines. A fire also broke out underneath. The elevator and rudder were holed but still had enough control to corkscrew. Sergeant C. G. Ockwell, the flight engineer, feathered the starboard outer but the inner would not feather. Ten seconds later the fires broke out again and spread to No. 1 petrol tank. Flight Sergeant H. D. C. Allison RCAF, the mid-upper gunner, saw a Ju 88 on a parallel course and fired. It burst into flames and dived down through the cloud. 'We levelled at 9,000 feet and headed for Sweden. The fire was now well spread and there was a danger to the spar and we therefore abandoned aircraft. Everyone baled out safely and the aircraft crashed about one mile from Bastad.'[2]

The operation to Stettin had been Hawkes' 25th operation. Königsberg that same night was Flight Sergeant 'Pat' Patfield's 32nd, and penultimate, op in 61 Squadron. He had flown 14 ops with Ron Auckland's crew and when they had finished their tour he had got on another crew. Auckland had completed many successful sorties including 11 attacks on Berlin. 'Königsberg,' Patfield recalls, 'was a very long trip indeed, almost 350 miles the other side of Berlin. We got hit quite badly over the target by anti-aircraft fire. The engines kept going but the DR compass had been toppled and the other one smashed, so we were on our own. The skipper said, "It'll soon be daylight, we're on our own and we'll be a sitting duck for fighters. The only thing for us to do is hedge hop." We came down and hedge hopped over Denmark. We saw some Germans rushing out to anti-aircraft guns as we just whizzed over. We were hopelessly off course. We just got back by map reading. When we came over the sea the engines started spluttering. "Take up ditching positions." But we got back and when they dipped the tanks they were completely dry. That was the record duration of 12 hours 15 minutes. I don't remember being tired. We were so keyed up we probably didn't feel tired until afterwards.

'I finished my ops with a raid on Brest on 5 September and then I got commissioned. It was rather a non-event, because I didn't realize I'd done the 33 ops. Also I hadn't been with the same crew all the time. I was just told that was "it". No celebration, nothing. I must have felt relief. I hadn't got to go out again. We all knew that it was around 30 trips and just kept going until we were told that was "it". I volunteered for a second tour, but quite a lot of aircrew were coming through so, I wasn't accepted. I'd got a good record of bombing so technically I was okay for a second tour. I stayed with 61 Squadron doing air tests, local flying and familiarization around the area with new aircrews. We'd go to Wainfleet with 9lb practice bombs and watch the new bomb-aimer bomb and watch him map reading etc.

'As a brand new pilot officer I was given a posting in London. At this particular place they had about 10 officers. When we went into lunch in the Mess we all stood by the table and waited for the CO to come in and sit down. Then we all sat down. What shocked me was the CO was a squadron leader, a 'wingless wonder', whereas on the squadron we were hobnobbing with squadron leaders and wing commanders on Christian name terms. It was at the height of the V-2 rocket attacks. I had just left off one day and a V-2 burst in the sky about a mile above us. Debris was everywhere. We dived in the doorways of a building. After only about three weeks I put in a posting to get away. I couldn't stand it coming straight off a squadron.'

During early September German positions around Le Havre were attacked on six separate days. Emden too was bombed on the 6th in the first large raid on this city since June 1942. It was also the last Bomber Command raid of the war on Emden. Only one Lancaster, that of the deputy master bomber, Flight Lieutenant Granville Wilson DSO DFC DFM of 7 Squadron, a 23 year old Northern Irishman, was lost. Wilson's bomber received a direct hit by a flak shell and he was killed instantly, together with his navigator and bomb-aimer, Sergeants

197

D. Jones and E. R. Brunsdon. The five other members of the crew baled out safely. The bombing was accurate and seen to be a mass of flames. Raids in daylight continued against synthetic oil plants at Castrop-Rauxel, Kamen and Gelsenkirchen (Nordstern) by heavily escorted formations of Halifaxes and Lancasters on the 11th and eight bombers including three Lancasters, two of them Pathfinders, were lost to flak. That evening, 226 Lancasters and 14 Mosquitoes set out on the devastating raid on Darmstadt, a city of 120,000 people, but no major war industries to speak of. The role of music in the evolution and collapse of the *Reich* was part of maintaining everyday routines regardless of disaster. Early that same evening the people of Darmstadt huddled in front of brown wooden wireless sets with their illuminated dials bearing the names of the foreign stations like Radio Roma, to listen to some songs from the sensuous Rococo world of Strauss's magical music.[3]

A fierce fire area was created in the centre and in the districts immediately south and east of the centre. The Prince of Hesse stood on the outskirts of his park and looked towards Darmstadt, 15 kilometres away. 'The light grew and grew until the whole of the southern sky was glowing, shot through with red and yellow.' At least 12,300 inhabitants, some of them foreign workers and POWs, were reported killed and 49,200 people were made homeless. Twelve Lancasters were lost. Existence in repulsive and rotting ruins throughout the Fatherland was intolerable and many were reduced to city cave dwellers barely living on 'unappetizing meals concocted from dirty, wrinkled vegetables and dubious scraps of meat'. Mobile cookers, traditionally called *Gulaschkanonen*, provided emergency meals for bombed out air-raid victims. Yet still the German people, cold and hungry, were expected to remain stoic in the face of repeated air raids.

With the Allied armies advancing across France, the Chief of Air Staff once again gained control of Bomber Command, which resumed its area bombing campaign and also mounted a new precision bombing campaign against oil and transportation targets. It was not a happy prospect for new crews but for the old soaks who were nearing the end of the tours, September brought welcome relief, though not for all. In the afternoon of 17 September 760 aircraft, 370 of them Lancasters, dropped more than 3,000 tons of bombs on German positions around Boulogne in preparation for an attack by Allied troops. Precision bombing was necessary because the Allied lines were only 200 yards away. To ensure accuracy the Lancaster flown by Squadron Leader G. R. Gunn MiD RNZAF of 75 Squadron RNZAF

at Mepal came down to 3,000 feet, at which range the flak was intense and accurate. With two engines shot out of action, Gunn was fortunate to make it back across the Channel where he crash-landed at Hawkinge. Gunn died of his injuries four days later. The German garrison meanwhile, had surrendered soon after the bombing attack.

On 24 September listeners tuning in to their wireless sets to hear the news, heard the announcer say that the previous night Lancasters of Bomber Command had carried out a successful attack on the Dortmund-Ems Canal near Ladbergen, just north of Münster. Families held their breath waiting for the usual sting in the tail. It came with the ominous words, 'Fourteen of our aircraft are missing.' Another seven bombers failed to return from the attack on Neuss. Most of the damage to the Dortmund-Ems Canal, whose aiming point was the twin aqueducts over the River Grane where the level of the water was higher than the surrounding land, was caused by two direct hits by 12,000lb *Tallboy* bombs dropped by 617 Squadron at the opening of the raid. The other Lancasters carried 14,000lbs of HE in their bomb bays and 1,500 gallons of petrol to get them to their target. One of them was *K-King* in 61 Squadron, which was flown by Squadron Leader Hugh W. Horsley AFC, a very experienced pilot although most of his crew were on only their fourth operation. His flight engineer was Pilot Officer Charles A. Cawthorne DFM who after flying on 'Pluto' Wilson's crew in 467 Squadron in 1943 was called back in July 1944 to do a second tour of operations and had joined Flight Lieutenant Hugh Horsley's crew at 1661 HCU, RAF Winthorpe near Newark. They first flew together as a crew in a Stirling on 20 July. On 2 September they started their Lancaster training at 5 Lancaster Finishing School, RAF Syerston. Eight days later they were posted to 61 Squadron, Horsley was promoted to squadron leader and immediately took command of one of the flights. On 17 September they flew their first operational sortie against the French port of Boulogne in *Mickey the Moocher*. It was the veteran aircraft's 107th operation. Little did Cawthorne know that his second tour of operations was destined to end over Holland after just two weeks.[4]

K-King joined the bomber stream heading for the Dutch coast at 20,000 feet and 20 minutes later, in the Eindhoven area, Sergeant H. W. Jennings, the mid-upper gunner, spotted a twin-engined night fighter approaching for an attack. It was a Bf 110 piloted by Leutnant Otto Teschner of IV./NJG 1. Jennings shouted over the intercom, 'Skipper, corkscrew, port. Go!' Horsley obediently dived the Lancaster to the left and down but the night fighter was too dogged for them. On the fifth corkscrew the 110 scored hits on the centre of the fuselage and port wing, killing Jennings and the wireless operator, Flight Sergeant G. Twyneham. The bombs were jettisoned and Horsley tried to make for home with the two port engines shut down but they were losing height alarmingly fast and he had to order the crew to bale out. The navigator and bomb-aimer were soon captured and taken prisoner but Horsley, Charles Cawthorne and Sergeant Reg Hoskisson, rear-gunner, got clean away after landing and evaded capture. After many adventures all three eventually returned to Skellingthorpe to resume operations.

On 27 September Harry Watkins' crew at Skellingthorpe completed their 30th and final 'op'. The bomb-aimer, Flight Sergeant Edgar Ray, felt lucky to have been able to complete the tour, 'before the winter months set in.

'Like most of the primitive wartime stations, "Skelly" was a little short of comfort. The Nissen hut accommodation was abysmal. When it rained, water flowed in through the door at one end of the hut and out by the door at the other end. Our flight engineer, Fred Jowitt, would blame the puddles on his fictitious horse, which he kept in the hut. Needless to say, the horse received many heavy beatings for the mess. The beds were iron-framed and seemed minuscule to anyone who wasn't a midget. We didn't have any lockers, only one shelf and two hooks for all our belongings and washing in cold water was the norm in the ablutions. The cinema fiction of "Let's have a party tonight boys" just didn't exist during my period with the Squadron. An occasional night out with the crew in Lincoln, Newark or Nottingham was all we could manage. Even then we ran the risk of being awakened, half sober at 03.00 hours for a dawn take-off. If flying was scrubbed for the whole of No. 5 Group, then the two-coach train that ran between Lincoln and Nottingham would be already overflowing with Australians from RAF Waddington and other types before it reached our local station at the small village of North Hykeham. The return journey was usually aboard the early morning milk train with the last few miles from Lincoln railway station to camp being on foot.

'Because of the intense operational flying schedule we had little chance of getting to know anyone else on the Squadron, apart from a working relationship with our ground crew. They had great pride in their aircraft and worked long hours to keep it serviceable for operations. We were privileged to fly their aeroplane and woe-be-tide anyone in the aircrew who left a dirty aircraft after returning from operations. Flak damage, blood, etc, were acceptable, but sandwich papers, "Window" wrappings and any other piece of rubbish left in the aircraft soon brought down the wrath of the ACH/Airframes on the guilty party, no matter what his rank.

'Flying on ops was not all activity by any means. On many of the deep penetration sorties, long periods of anxious quiet were experienced, with *George* the automatic pilot engaged. Sometimes lights would be seen on the ground or stars would be reflected on the bomb-aimer's clear vision panel and as these appeared to move with the oscillations of the aircraft, it was tempting to interpret them as engine exhaust flames from a night fighter. From the bomb-aimer's position in the nose of the aircraft I had a 180-degree view of all the enemy activity en route. Despite the bomber stream being carefully routed between the known heavy flak defences, there was often someone off track flying over these areas. This soon brought a searchlight and flak reaction from below, resulting in the sight of aircraft falling away on fire and leaving burning wrecks on the ground to became a route guide to the rest of the main force. During most of this time the bomb-aimer had little to do apart from keeping a sharp lookout for other aircraft and stuffing out bundles of "Window" at the correct time and place to confuse the ground radar, controlling the night fighters and predicted flak batteries.

'The Lancaster crew's biggest blind spot was directly below the aircraft. To combat this a small Perspex bubble was installed in the nose compartment. This bubble had an open rear end and was just large enough to accommodate the bomb-aimer's head. By contorting himself the bomb-aimer could scan the area beneath the aircraft to check against night fighters with upward firing 20-mm cannon. Sometimes the German fighter defences would detect the bomber stream early and release strings of parachute flares in a corridor approaching the target. Fighters would then sit up above waiting for a likely target to attack. The worst conditions were when searchlights illuminated a cloud sheet below the attacking force. This gave a perfect backdrop for high-flying night fighters as dozens of bombers were silhouetted against the cloud. On one raid our skipper remarked that it was a particularly spectacular display and for once Doug Hockin, the navigator, got out of his seat, put his light off and poked his head out from behind his black out curtain. He took one look and disappeared back into his chair muttering "Never again".

'Half an hour from the target ETA, the wireless operator switched on the very high frequency (VHF) radio and we listened out for any instructions from the raid's master bomber. Nearing a target area things hotted up. Pathfinder marker flares and red and green target indicators (TIs) would be seen ahead. As the target was approached I would select the appropriate switches on the bombing panel, wind up the "Mickey Mouse" release timer, and ensure that the aiming point photo camera (and its heater cloak) was switched on. I rechecked the Mk.XIV bombsight computer settings and looked out over the target area for the correct TI display. The bombing run was the time when crews were most vulnerable to defensive predicted flak batteries. Weaving was out as far as we were concerned. Not only did weaving increase the risk of collision, it also took longer to pass across the target area than flying straight and level. When the correct TIs were identified, the skipper would lower his seat and fly on instruments as this gave a much steadier bombing platform. As we approached the aiming point I gave him the following instructions and he would take immediate action while repeating the instruction over the intercom.

"Bomb doors open."

"Master Switch On." (Pilot operated switch for bomb release).

"Bombs Fused and Selected."

"Left, left, right, steady."

'When the aiming point came into the cross wires (actually cross lights) on the sighting head, the bomb release tit was pressed and the aircraft wobbled as bombs fell off in sequence.

"Bombs Gone."

"Photo Taken." (lights flashed after timed run).

"Bomb Doors closed."

"Let's get the hell out of here!"

'After clearing the target area and turning onto our return course, things became quieter and I would check the bomb bay for hang-ups. This was done by shining the Aldis lamp through a small door in the bomb-aimer's compartment into the bomb bay. Hang ups occurred because the suspension loops on the top of some of the bombs were so roughly made that the bombs did not readily slip from the bomb cradle hooks in the bomb bay. If there were any, releasing the bomb was a fiddling task. I had to use a long hooked piece of wire to manually operate the release catch on the offending bomb station through small access panels on the aircraft floor.

'After the intense activity around the target area, the long drag home seemed to go on forever. While the tension was lower, we still had to remain vigilant all the way back home. On two occasions when nearing our base at Skellingthorpe we received the warning code word "BOGRAT" over the R/T. This meant that German intruders were suspected around our base area. The Bograt procedure for aircraft from each base was to fly on a designated heading, usually north-westwards until recalled for landing. The air traffic control procedures for landing the returning bombers from operations was very slick at Skellingthorpe. Typically, one aircraft would be turning off at the far end of the runway, a second turning off halfway down, a third just gliding over the runway threshold while a fourth would be on final approach.

'At the end of my tour, I was commissioned and moved across the road into the officers' Nissen huts. These were exactly the same as the NCOs but only had eight beds instead of fourteen. We did have an occasional Batwoman come in and clean the floor and tidy the beds. Most newly commissioned personnel found getting kitted-out with an officers No. 1 uniform a protracted affair. One could buy an officer's forage cap and a Pilot Officer rank shoulder braid for your battle-dress very quickly, so this is what we wore around the station and in the officers' mess while we waited for our new No. 1 uniforms to appear. However, when going off station during this waiting period, I would wear my trusted flight sergeant kit, and eat in the Sergeants' mess before leaving camp for a night out with the boys.'

During October-December 1944 15 out of 20 raids on the Ruhr were in daylight. Even in broad daylight, Bomber Command was able to operate in relative safety. Sergeant Larry Melling in 635 Squadron at Downham Market recalls: 'October started with a raid on the 4th to the German naval base at Bergen in Norway, an 8-hour trip that commenced just before dawn and was carried out in clear weather conditions over the whole route. We flew up the east coast of England and Scotland, then crossed the North Sea at 50 feet or less to sneak under the radar. We climbed to 18,000 feet just before the Norwegian coast and descended again immediately after the bombing run. Flying a Lancaster at low level like that was an unusual thrill. The following night[5] we were detailed to attack Saarbrücken, taking off just before sunset. On returning to base I was a little apprehensive about landing in the dark, as my last flight had been some six weeks earlier. I was, therefore, really on my toes for the approach and touchdown, which was just as well because immediately after touchdown the aircraft swung to starboard and off the runway. Subsequent investigation showed that the starboard tyre had been punctured by flak shrapnel and was completely flat.'

On 6 October when 320 aircraft, including 46 Lancasters, attacked the synthetic oil plants at Sterkrade and Schloven/Buer, just two Lancasters and seven Halifaxes were lost. A 635 Squadron Lancaster at Downham Market, flown by Flight Lieutenant George A. Thorne, came home with part of the tail shot away over Gelsenkirchen and only two functioning engines. A SOS signal had been sent out to report a ditching position but the two faithful Merlins kept the aircraft airborne and Thorne decided to put down at Woodbridge by Sutton Heath, a frequently used 'port in the storm' in Suffolk for aircraft in trouble. The pilot crossed the coast at 500 feet and the aircraft began losing height. Then a third engine packed up, causing the Lancaster to yaw. Near Ipswich the Lancaster hit H/T cables, which ripped the tail unit off. Within six miles of Woodbridge, Thorne realized that he would not quite make it. Shutting down the last engine to glide in evenly, he came down in a gentle dive towards a field at Shottisham to make a belly-landing in a stubble field 200 yards short of Bussock House. The Lancaster burst into flames and all except the wireless operator 26 year old Sergeant J. D. Crabtree from Rochdale got clear. Someone dragged the pilot out and he regained consciousness lying on a hayrick. By his side was a tray of tea with a spotless white tray cloth and silverware brought out by the lady of the house!

The memory of attacking Bremen on the night of 6/7 October when Bomber Command also visited Dortmund,[6] would be forever imprinted on the mind of Bill Burke, a 20 year old, six-feet tall non-commissioned navigator on 207 Squadron, operating from Spilsby in Lincolnshire. When he had turned 18 in 1942, Burke had had no hesitation in applying to join the RAF. He did not fancy the Navy, as the thought of being perpetually seasick did not appeal to him at all. His father's stories of the fighting conditions at Passchendaele and on the Somme set him against the army. So if he had to go into a service he thought that the RAF would be best and he would 'emulate the knights of the air from the First World War'. He had been flying on operations continually since August 1944. It had been an exciting tour, full of experiences. On the Bremen raid his Lancaster was 'coned' by searchlights and hit by anti-aircraft fire which, amongst other things, cut the oil pipelines to the rear turret rendering the turret virtually inoperable. Then, almost immediately, the rear and mid-upper gunners began screaming that a Ju 88 night fighter was commencing a stern attack. 'We were all but defenceless,' Burke recalled 'and I sat there waiting for a hail of machine gun and cannon fire to

come streaming down the fuselage putting paid to my life. But no – the fates were kind. Suddenly we flew into dense cloud and were lost to the night fighter.

'As a consequence of such experiences I was a shade "flak happy". In other words the strains and stresses of going into battle 30 times and seeing so many comrades in the Squadron fail to return from raids had affected my nerves. For example, my hands had a typical "Bomber Command Twitch", which sometimes called for an effort to light a cigarette. In these circumstances one might well think that by the end of my tour I would have been more than happy at the prospect of a safe posting possibly to an instructor's job in Training Command. But far from it – I liked the life on an operational squadron and wanted to stay there. My 21st birthday was five months away and at that age one can crave excitement. Danger, like drugs, can become habit forming and one wants a regular "injection" of danger and the enormous elation, which one experiences when the danger is past and one is still unharmed. It was also a glamorous life. The contract was that you flew the RAF's aeroplanes with the statistical likelihood that you would be killed, wounded or taken prisoner. In return the RAF paid you well, gave you a great deal of freedom and time off with leave every six weeks and extended to you a variety of privileges which few enjoyed in wartime Britain. These included such things as aircrew meals of bacon and eggs, special sweet rations, petrol for use in private cars and sheets to sleep in. If you weren't required for flying you could do more or less what you liked; large numbers of air crew in "Bomber Counties" such as Lincolnshire largely spent their spare time in pubs and dance halls, getting "stoned" and chasing the ladies. Cities such as Nottingham were an air crew paradise and the "White Hart" in Lincoln was like a 5 Group "Headquarters". To turn one's back on this sort of *Boys Own Paper* life and the conscious pride that goes with being a member of an acknowledged corps d'elite was unthinkable to me at the time. So I decided to volunteer for an immediate second tour of operations. It was an utterly foolish and foolhardy decision, akin to applying for and then signing one's own death warrant, but one doesn't think that way at twenty. One then has a supreme confidence and a belief that it will be the other guy who doesn't come through safely. However, I did decide that although I wanted to continue fighting, I "wanted out" of Bomber Command. Instead I decided that I would like to fly in Beaufighters in Scotland on anti-shipping strikes. I thought that would be exciting and also that it would be satisfying in the sense that one would know whether or not one had been successful. Either a boat was there or it was sunk. Unfortunately my application for a switch to Beaufighters was turned down out of hand. I say "unfortunately" but, in fact, it might be more appropriate to use the word "fortunately" as I later discovered that there was a very high "chop rate" amongst air crew attacking enemy shipping guarded by flak ships. At the same time as my transfer application was rejected I was told that if I did want to continue operational flying I could be fixed up with a navigator's job on 627 Squadron of Pathfinder Force, based at Woodhall Spa. If I accepted the offer I could have a commission and so a deal was done.'[7]

On 14 October, in Operation *Hurricane*, Duisburg received a pounding when just over 1,000 Lancasters, Halifaxes and Mosquitoes, escorted by RAF fighters, raided the city. Another 1,251 American bombers, escorted by 749 fighters, hit targets in the Cologne area. According to the directive issued to Sir Arthur Harris, *Hurricane*'s purpose was, 'to demonstrate to the enemy in Germany generally the overwhelming superiority of the Allied Air Forces in this theatre ... the intention is to apply within the shortest practical period the maximum effort of the RAF Bomber Command and the US 8th Bomber Command against objectives in the densely populated Ruhr.' Nearly 9,000 tons of bombs were dropped on Duisburg in less than 48 hours. In the daylight hours 957 RAF heavies dropped 3,574 tons of high explosive and 820 tons of incendiaries for the loss of 13 Lancasters and a Halifax to flak. American casualties were just five bombers and one fighter. That night, which was fine and cloudless, 1,005 RAF heavies attacked Duisburg for the second time in 24 hours in two waves and dropped 4,040 tons of high explosive and 500 tons of incendiaries, losing five Lancasters and two Halifaxes. One of the five Lancasters that was lost fell victim to Leutnant Arnold Döring, an experienced 27 year old fighter pilot of 7./NJG 2 at Volkel aerodrome in Holland flying the Ju 88G-6. It was his 20th aerial victory.[8]

Despite the enormous effort involved in Operation *Hurricane* that same night RAF Bomber Command was even able to dispatch 233 Lancasters and seven Mosquitoes of 5 Group to bomb Brunswick. Flying Officer Frank Mouritz RAAF, one of the Lancaster pilots who flew on the raid, was flying only his fifth operation since joining 61 Squadron at Skellingthorpe from 5 LFS Syerston nearby. He had carried out his first operation on 27/28 September, a 6½-hour trip to Kaiserslautern flying with another crew with no duties except to gain experience. The trip was uneventful and the young Australian was amazed at the sheer brilliance of searchlights and explosions of bombs, flak and photoflashes at the target. Even the biggest firework display he had ever seen was nothing compared with this. During the next 10 days or so Mouritz and his crew carried out their first two operations, a daylight to Wilhelmshaven on 5 October, and another daylight to Bremen on 6 October. They were then allocated a permanent Lancaster, *Mickey the Moocher*, by now a veteran of 119 trips.

'It was quite something to have our own plane,' Mouritz recalls. 'Another milestone in our air force career. The ground crew was very proud of their plane and the number of trips completed. This showed good maintenance and a lot of luck. We hoped that the luck had not all been used up as it was usually considered that to survive a tour required about 70 per cent luck and 30 per cent skill. By this time *Mickey* was nearly worn out. The four engines were close to the hours for a complete change, the controls were sloppy and she had dozens of patches on wings and fuselage. She took a lot of runway to get off the ground with a full load of fuel and bombs. We were the new crew given the oldest Lanc on the squadron but we were proud of her. She took us on our first trip on 11 October, a daylight one to the Dutch coast, with a fighter escort to bomb sea walls (dykes) in an attempt to flood German artillery batteries that were holding up the advance of the British ground forces. The raid was not successful although we bombed from low level. At this stage I could sense through *Mickey* the feelings of all the crews that had survived over 100 trips in this special aircraft, passing on their experience and good luck for a successful tour; a sort of feeling of comradeship and well-being which is hard to describe. *Mickey* was something to look up to, a guiding star.

'The 7½-hour night flight to Brunswick was an area attack with cookies and incendiaries. This was also a milestone as 15 October was my 21st birthday and we had our first fighter combat. Nearing the target area the mid-upper gunner spotted a fighter approaching from the port quarter above. It then appeared to sideslip into position behind them, he ordered the pilot to corkscrew as he opened fire, while also giving the rear-gunner the fighter's position and who, upon seeing it too, also opened fire. The fighter dived quickly away; the mid-upper gunner giving it a final burst as it disappeared out of range.[9] Our next trip, on 19/20 October, was another night area bombing one, 7 hours to Nürnburg with 263 Lancs and seven Mosquitoes, with a large amount of casualties and damage inflicted. We were beginning to get a little confident now with our navigator keeping us on time and track and hence in the middle of the stream and our bomb-aimer directing the bombing run with precision, and we were obtaining good target photos. Our next trip was another daylight one to the Dutch coast to attack the same batteries as before, also unsuccessful.'

That same night another 565 Lancasters and 18 Mosquitoes in two forces 4½ hours apart went to Stuttgart as Sergeant Larry Melling in 635 Squadron recalls: 'We were given our first official task as "blind-marker" when we were "blind illuminators" to mark the Stuttgart railway yards for the visual crews. From here on in we acted as "blind-markers" on almost all occasions.' Not many bombs fell on the yards, the most serious damage being caused to the central and eastern districts of Stuttgart and in some of the suburban towns.[10]

On 23 October, when 112 Lancasters bombed the Flushing battery positions at Walcheren, a Lancaster of 619 Squadron, flown by Squadron Leader Purnell, touched down at RAF Woodbridge after the bomber was hit by flak over Walcheren and a fire started in the bomb bay. Purnell ordered the crew to bale out but only four left the aircraft and were scattered over two countries. By the time the coast of England was reached the navigator and flight engineer baled out safely and were found shocked and burnt.[11]

On the night of 23/24 October Bomber Command dispatched 1,055 aircraft[12] to Essen to bomb the Krupps works. This was the heaviest raid on the already devastated German city so far in the war and the number of aircraft was also the greatest to any target since the war began. Altogether the force carried 4,538 tons of bombs including five hundred and nine 4,000-pounders. More than 90 per cent of the tonnage carried was high explosive because intelligence estimated that most of Essen's housing and buildings had been destroyed in fire raids in 1943. Just eight aircraft, five of them Lancasters, were lost. October had signalled a great decrease in the effectiveness of *Nachtjagd* opposition to the night bomber. This was a combined result of the Allied advance into the continent and the technical and tactical countermeasures employed. The German warning and inland plotting systems were thrown into confusion. Low-level and high-level *Intruder* played no small part by causing the enemy to plot hostile aircraft over very wide areas, as well as forcing him to broadcast frequent warnings of the presence of hostile aircraft to his own fighters.[13]

Bomber Command's last major raid on Düsseldorf took place on 2/3 November when 561 Lancasters, 400 Halifaxes and 31 Mosquitoes visited the city. More than 5,000 houses were destroyed or badly damaged in the northern half of the city, plus seven industrial premises were destroyed and 18 seriously damaged.[14] The next major night raid was on 4/5 November when Bochum and the Dortmund-Ems Canal were the objectives for the main force. Some 749 aircraft attacked the centre of Bochum and more than 4,000 buildings were left in ruins or seriously damaged. Three Lancasters from the 174 dispatched by 5 Group, failed to return from the raid on the Dortmund-Ems Canal and 23 Halifaxes and five Lancasters were missing from the raid on Bochum.[15] On 6/7 November, when 235 Lancasters and seven Mosquitoes of 5 Group again attempted to cut the Mittelland Canal at Gravenhorst, crews were confronted with a cold front of exceptional violence and ice quickly froze on windscreens. Flying Officer Frank Mouritz RAAF of 61 Squadron said goodbye to an old friend when he flew *Mickey the Moocher* on her last operation. The marking force had difficulty in finding the target due to low cloud and the bombers were told to bomb at low level. Mouritz had to select full flap and wheels down to enable him to lose height in time and he was one of only 31 Lancasters that bombed before the master bomber abandoned the raid due to low cloud.[16]

Forty-eight Mosquitoes dispatched to Gelsenkirchen on a 'spoof' raid to draw German night fighters away from the Mittelland attack, and a 3 Group raid on Koblenz, had better luck. The Gelsenkirchen raid began as planned, five minutes ahead of the two other attacks, at 19.25 hours. The city was still burning as a result of that afternoon's raid by 738 RAF heavies. Ten Lancasters failed to return from the Mittelland debacle. Three of these were shot down west of the Rhine in just 16 minutes by Leutnant Otto Fries and his *Bordfunker* Feldwebel Alfred Staffa of 2./NJG 1, flying a He 219.[17] Of 128 Lancasters of 3 Group that raided Koblenz, two failed to return.

On 8 November 136 Lancasters of 3 Group were assembled on their airfields to bomb the Rheinpreussen synthetic oil refinery at Meerbeck on the west bank of the Rhine at Homberg. They would be using G-H, a kind of *Oboe* blind bombing device in reverse, operated by aircraft carrying a transmitter and receiver, which measured distances from two ground stations. G-H had proved its accuracy on the raid on Düsseldorf on 3/4 November,[18] but a bomber now needed seven minutes instead of four, for a straight and steady run up to the target. This was a lot to ask of any crew, particularly in daylight. Australian Flying Officer Les Hough captained one of the crews at Methwold, in 218 (Gold Coast) Squadron, who would be taking part. 'Hough', recalls Flight Sergeant Allen Clifford, navigator, whose job it was to release the bombs, 'had cheerfully vacated his newspaper editor's chair in Adelaide, for a chance of kicking Hitler's arse. He was a hard-bitten forthright journalist who loved his beer and he had the distinction of being thrown out of the snotty "University Arms" in Cambridge for being rowdy. He was a typical iconoclastic Aussie who wouldn't be messed about and had to be treated with kid gloves by senior officers. He was also a charming fellow and a brilliant pilot.' Hough's crew were the usual eclectic mix of Commonwealth aircrew. Clifford came from Darlington. Sergeant Harry Burnside the W/Op came from Nottingham and, like the rest of the crew, he drank, smoked and chased girls. Flying Officer John Barron, a Londoner, had a polished upper-class "pommie" accent, which irritated the Skipper but did not impair their working relationship. Warrant Officer Jack Tales, engineer, a dour Yorkshireman, had needed no persuasion to start a tour after his wife was killed in an air raid on Sheffield. Sergeant "Geordie" Lawson, mid-upper gunner, came from Hetton-le-Hole, Sunderland. His accent was so broad that Clifford was often the only one who could understand what he was saying. Les Hough frequently said, "For Chrissake Geordie, take it slowly. What the bloody hell did he say Chiefie?" This was all right on training flights but on ops it was potentially catastrophic and his aircraft recognition was "fairly marginal". Rear-gunner Sergeant Stan Lee from Bristol was diffident but extremely capable, with a West Country accent almost as impenetrable as Lawson's.

"Time to get up Flight. You're on this morning."

'If there's ever a low point in anybody's life this was it: To be woken at 04.00 hours knowing you were going to war!' Allen Clifford crawled out of a warm bed into the frozen Nissen hut, gathered up towel and soap and shivered miserably in the wintry gap between the hut and the ablutions blocks where he splashed water hurriedly over his face; no time to shave! The desperately early breakfast of bacon and egg and mug of hot sweet tea, preceded briefing, where they had dispensed with the niceties of hiding the target behind a curtain. The red tape, which slithered disconcertingly across the map like a long tail of blood, led from Norfolk to a suburb of the huge German inland river port and industrial city of Duisburg.

'Christ', they said sourly, slumping on to the hard wooden chairs, 'It's bloody Homberg again'.

The decision had been taken that autumn, not before time, to break Hitler by laying waste to his oil plants. Without oil, the Third Reich should fall apart. Lancasters and Halifaxes and Mosquitoes, of 6 and 8 (PFF) Groups respectively, had attacked the synthetic

oil refinery on 25 October, reeling against the blistering flak as the Germans sought to defend their dwindling supplies of fuel. The refinery was covered by cloud, and bombing was scattered in the early stages but later became more concentrated on the sky-markers. No aircraft were lost but the results of the raid were unknown so on 1 November 226 Lancasters and two Mosquitoes of 5 Group, with 14 Mosquitoes of 8 Group, again attempted to attack the plant. Again the marking was scattered and only 159 of the Lancasters attempted to bomb. Despite these two raids against Homberg, its refinery was still pumping out fuel for the German war machine.

The crew was taken by bus to dispersal, climbed into Lanc HA-C and started preliminary checks. Allen Clifford handed Hough a small sheet of paper. On it he had written a complete synopsis of the Homberg trip so that the skipper had all the information on courses, heights, speeds, times and turning points to get them to target and back home in case the navigator was killed or injured. It was Allen's 21st sortie. They were told they would fly out through clear skies and into a bank of cloud over eastern France, Germany and the Rhine. It turned out to be the reverse. They climbed slowly to 18,000 feet over Ely to pick up their slave aircraft. Meanwhile other aircraft from the squadron were picking up their slave aircraft at different locations. Over France they flew straight into heavy cloud. In dense cloud their acolyte aircraft spilt away so there was no danger of colliding. The tail wind was much higher than predicted, a fearsome 170 knots, so they were going in ahead of time. They broke cloud into clear sunshine, just short of the Rhine. Our aircraft, which were supposed to be formatting on them, were well scattered, but gradually pulled towards them. They were the first wave in and Clifford could see others coming behind, so instead of approaching in neat formations, they were in a bit of a gaggle and had to formate fairly hurriedly. With the possible exception of the steel town of Solingen, the flak was worse over Homberg than anywhere they had been. Coming off target at Solingen they were attacked by a Me 163, the Komet rocket plane, that hurtled like a dart up between their mainplane and the tail and disappeared.

Nearing Homberg they were at 18,000ft so their gunners were aiming on radar traces. All the bombers behind were obscured by 'Window'. Hough's aircraft, the first in, did not have 'Window' cover. One minute the sky was clear, the next, as they approached target, it was full of bursting shells, what the chaps called 10/10ths flak. They had seen many bombers shot down, mainly over target; some hit by their own bombs, and collisions, especially at night. A cookie once fell between their starboard wing and the tail plane, tumbling end over like a grotesque pillar-box, no more than five feet away. If it had struck the Lancaster the bomb would not have exploded, but it would have broken the aircraft in half. They had twice been hit by fighters. Clifford adds: 'By November 1944 the Luftwaffe was not exactly a spent force because they had more fighters than earlier in the war, but didn't have any very good pilots. In a fight you needed experience!'

The bomb doors were open on the long approach to the target when they were hit by a savage burst of flak. A fearsome clatter was followed by smoke swirling into the fuselage. The smoke was soon sucked out by the slipstream, revealing a four-foot-square hole by the back door in the side and floor. There was a pained gasp from Stan Lee, the shocked rear-gunner: 'Ugh! I've been hit.' He looked for blood and was relieved to find none. A lump of shrapnel had hammered on the outside of the tail turret, jarring his shoulder before falling harmlessly away. More seriously, the starboard inner engine was alight and defying Jack Tales' frantic efforts to feather it. Jack Tales, the engineer, began pumping fuel from tanks near the fire across to those in the port wing. The pilot was trying to ignore the worrying damage to his aircraft and complete a smooth run over the target. They were early but there was no question of them going round again. The Lanc jumped violently as the cookie and 2,000-pounders fell away. A moment later the starboard outer packed up. Allen Clifford was in a torment as flames licked over the starboard wing. They knew that the British Forces were not much further to the west. They only needed to keep airborne for a few minutes; bale out and they'd be home and dry. That was their intention as they turned out of the target, but they were now clawing their way against a powerful wind and doing only about 80 mph ground speed, the wing burning fiercely and beginning to flop. Then the Skipper roared, 'Go! Everybody out'.

Jack Tales found the pilot's parachute and clipped it on Hough before heading for the escape hatch. The bomb-aimer had already gone. Allen thinking aghast: 'God this is a final thing to do.' His only training for baling out had been learning a forward roll on a gym mat. He glanced at the stream of flames and knew what had to be done. He exchanged waves with the grim-faced pilot, still at the controls and steeled himself to drop headfirst out of the hatch. He was dragged out like a leaf by the slipstream, which whipped his helmet away. As he fell on his back another figure rolled out of the aircraft. They were still up in the flak and no one

had ever thought to explain the usefulness of getting quickly away from the bursting shells. As a stunned Clifford pulled the ripcord, 300 feet below the blazing Lanc, the starboard wing fell off. His parachute opened with a bang. He watched the remains of the aircraft fall past and explode on the ground. It was bitingly cold and Clifford looked up to see 'our chaps going home'. Theirs was the only Lancaster lost on this raid. Suddenly all was quiet. Clifford heard the swishing of the wind and it seemed a very long way to the ground.

The door to the rear turret was jammed and Stan Lee was forced to use a handle to open it. He went through and remembered nothing until he was floating serenely at the end of his parachute. Lee recalls:

'The Germans were shooting at me as I descended and I saw a crowd running towards one of our chaps who had just landed. I learned later that it was the engineer. I landed in telegraph wires, which saved my life. A dozen men and women, shouting and bawling, eventually dragged me to the ground. One middle-aged woman was screaming, egging on the men who were beating me. A man from the *Volkstrum* carrying a rifle, who took me to a large building where I met Allen Clifford, rescued me.'

Jack Tales had landed in a field, shed his parachute and was wondering which way to go when he was surrounded and viciously attacked by the Germans. He was handed over to three men who had arrived on a motor cycle combination. They included two *SS* men, Schoester and Opretza, who dragged Tales on to the bike in the direction of Moers, but they turned into a lane and rattled past the farm of Johannes Quernhorst. Shortly after, he heard two shots and ran out to find the airman still alive. He reported the shooting to the police, returned to find Jack Tales dead – a desolate man who had recently admitted there was nothing to live for. Burnside and Lawson were also dead after hesitating near the rear door. The tough brash pilot Les Hough stayed resolutely at the controls to give his crewmates time to leave but ran out of time.

Allen Clifford realized that he was being blown over Duisburg and at less that 3,000 feet he heard the alarming *phhht, phhht, phhht* of rifle and machine-gun bullets, zipping past. He recalls:

'You don't realize until you're near the ground how fast you are going and I shot past a big town clock as all-clear sirens were wailing. My flying boots hit the heavy pantiled roof of an old three-storey house and I went straight through up to my waist and was jammed, unable to move. I saw a dozen men from the *Volkstrum* in the garden shooting at me with rifles; bullets hitting the roof all round me. Anyone who can't hit a bloke at that range couldn't be much of a shot, but they weren't going to miss forever. I undid my parachute harness, wriggled like mad and fell about eight feet into the attic on to a board floor. I hurt my left leg and lay there winded, covered in blood from scratches and abrasions. A trapdoor flew open; a group of men poured in and grabbed me. Somebody shouted what was obviously: "Where's your gun?" (We were issued with Browning automatics but I couldn't see any of us shooting our way out of Germany, so I never took it! I later learned that if I had been carrying a gun I would have been shot out of hand!) I was dragged from the attic and tossed down the stairs, luckily not breaking anything. I was flung through the door on to the pavement. People were everywhere. They dived on me, kicking, hitting, savaging, and I tried to protect my face with my arms.'

A single shot rang out and the men were pulled off. A large *Luftwaffe* Feldwebel yanked Clifford to his feet and steered him to a motorcycle combination. He put him into the sidecar and drove off one-handed pointing the pistol at him. He stopped in a quiet street and told him in English that he would be all right provided he avoided the SS. Clifford was left at a police station, put into a cell and joined shortly afterwards by a dishevelled and shocked Stan Lee. That afternoon armed soldiers paraded them through Duisburg. People shouted, '*Terrorflieger*' and threw stones at them. They were marched through badly damaged property and put up against a factory wall. A line of soldiers stood with rifles against their shoulders. Stan said in a horrified voice, 'They're going to shoot us'. Clifford felt protective of Stan and said, 'For God's sake don't let them see you're frightened' and he pulled himself together, although they were in a depressing situation. The Feldwebel barked an order and as the two terrified airmen waited for the bullets, a fat old woman appeared, shrieking, placing herself fearlessly between the airmen and their execution squad. Stan Lee said, 'She ran in front of Allen and I, screaming what sounded like "Propaganda! Propaganda!" at the soldiers. They shouted back at her but she stood her ground and saved our lives.'[19]

Lancasters at last put the *Tirpitz* out of action in Tromsö Fjord, Norway, on 12 November. It was the third attack made on the 45,000-ton battleship by Bomber Command with 12,000lb bombs, but this was the first time the attackers were able to see the ship properly. In the first attack in September, when the *Tirpitz* was in Kaa Fjord, the Germans put up a smokescreen so rapidly that only one or two of the first aircrews to arrive could see the ship. One 12,000-pounder hit and seriously damaged it then, but the hit was

too far forward to be conclusive, although the ship must have been useless as a fighting unit for at least six months.[20] When the *Tirpitz* moved westward for repairs in a German dockyard and to avoid the Russian advance into Norway, it was attacked once more on 29 October but again the bomber crews could obtain only an oblique view of her through cloud. On Sunday morning, 12 November, the weather was clear and there was no smokescreen. The *Tirpitz* was first sighted when the attacking force of 30 Lancasters of 9 and 617 Squadrons, led by 26 year old Welsh Wing Commander J. B. 'Willy' Tait DSO*** DFC*, was about 20 miles away. She was a black shape clearly seen against the clear waters of the fjord, surrounded by the snow-covered hills, which were glowing pink in the low Arctic sun. A plume of smoke rose slowly from the big ship's funnel. When the force was about 10 miles away the peaceful scene changed suddenly; the ship opened fire with her main armament and billows of orange-brown smoke, shot through by the flashes of the guns, hid her for a moment, and then drifted away. One 12,000-pounder apparently hit the *Tirpitz* amidships, another in the bows and a third towards the stern, and there were also two very near misses which must themselves have done serious underwater damage.

Probably the last of the Lancaster crews to see the *Tirpitz* after the attack were the tour expired crew of a 463 Squadron RAAF movie-Lancaster, captained by Flight Lieutenant Bruce A. Buckham DFC RAAF. This crew, plus two BCFU cameramen and Guy Byams of the BBC, and W. E. West of the Press Association had flown on the first raid. Now the crew of six Australians and one Englishman and two BCFU cameramen saw the first wave go in and drop their bombs, getting some near misses and the direct hit amidships. After this only the forward guns continued firing. Then the second wave went in and the Australians saw hits on the stem, amidships and finally on the bows. All the ship's guns stopped firing, but the ground defences were still throwing up a screen of light and heavy flak. Heavy black smoke hung over the vessel as the movie-Lancaster went down and circled it close in. Suddenly the crew saw a great explosion and then a sheet of flame and the *Tirpitz* began to heel over in a cloud of smoke. When the Lancaster made a final close circuit of the ship, with the cameras still turning over, she was lying on her side, half submerged, with her red hull gleaming in the sunlight.[21]

The bombing offensive against German cities and oil targets continued unabated with raids in November on Homberg, Wanne-Eickel, Harburg, Hamburg and

Dortmund among others. The aiming point for the raid on Harburg by a force of 237 Lancasters was the Rheanania-Ossag oil refinery. Officially part of Hamburg, Harburg was really a quite different community, being separated from the main part of Hamburg by five miles of docks, waterways and Hamburg's industrial suburb of Wilhelmsburg.[22] Seven Lancasters were shot down and 119 people were killed and over 5,000 bombed out. When the population of this German city emerged from their air-raid shelters and were out in the streets again they saw flames leaping into the black sky on the horizon above the harbour. Harald Hollenstein, son of a German mother and a Swiss father, who spent his childhood in Hamburg, still drowsy, abruptly woken from sleep for the second time, watched the play of colours, 'fascinated; the red and yellow of the flames mingling against the background of the dark night sky and then separating again'. Even later he never saw such a 'clean, brilliant yellow, such a bright red, such a radiant orange'. Hollenstein stood in the street for minutes on end watching this 'symphony of slowly changing colours'. He never again saw such deep, bright colours 'not in any painter's work'.[23]

On 21 November, the synthetic oil plant at Homberg was attacked by 160 Lancasters with the loss of three aircraft, all of which were from 514 Squadron. Flying Officer J. H. Tolley flew one of those that did not make it back to Waterbeach. On the run-up to the target the aircraft was 50 yards to the port quarter of the leader and slightly below. There was considerable flak, presumed predicted, during the run-up. Normally, an aircraft in this position releases its bombs as soon as it sees the leader do so. Consequently, they opened up the bomb doors as soon as the leader did and the air bomber was waiting with his hand on the bomb release. Just as the formation neared the release point Tolley and the air bomber saw that the leader was jettisoning his bombs all together. They could see no reason why the leader was not bombing normally and the air bomber prepared to release his bombs. Just as he did so there was a blinding flash below the leader, as though one of his bombs had exploded. The Perspex in the air bomber's compartment, the pilots cockpit, and the mid-upper turret were shattered and the fuselage was scarred on the starboard side with small holes. The faces of both the pilot and air bomber were pitted with minute cuts. Both were temporarily blinded by the flash, and by blood streaming over their eyes.

Tolley lost control of the aircraft and, while he groped for the controls with the wind lashing his face, the aircraft lost 3,000 feet. His intercom had become unserviceable and as he could not reach the emergency signal light, he waved the crew forward with his hand, indicating that they should bale out. While they were putting on their 'chutes, however, Tolley regained control and signalled the crew to wait. He could see better now and he managed to rejoin the bomber stream, though the aircraft was at 15,000 feet and well below the others. The engineer had previously tried, without success, to plug the pilot's intercom into a different socket, but the pilot was now able to do so himself, and called up the rest of the crew.

All the crew replied, except the rear-gunner, Sergeant W. H. Ellis, so Tolley told the wireless operator to go back and investigate. The wireless operator opened the bulkhead doors and saw through the inspection panels that the bomb doors were open and he could see the ground below; air was rushing through the fuselage with the force of gale. The wireless operator reported this to Tolley, who ordered the mid-upper gunner to go instead. The mid-upper gunner, who had already left his turret when it was smashed, managed to reach the rear of the fuselage, where he found the rear hatch was open and on opening the rear bulkhead doors discovered that Ellis had gone. His parachute was missing. Ellis must have baled out within a few miles of the target.

The Lancaster was now flying normally and on track. Suddenly the starboard inner engine burst into flames, apparently due to an oil leak. Tolley feathered the engine, the Graviner was used and the fire put out. A few minutes later the starboard outer engine revs began to fluctuate and dense white fumes poured out of it, suggesting a coolant leak. This engine was also successfully shut down and the propeller feathered. The wireless operator sent a distress message back to Waterbeach, although he did not think that the message would be received as the aerials were badly damaged. Tolley had now formated on another Lancaster and the wireless operator also signalled to this aircraft with the Aldis lamp. The Lancaster had flown for 20 minutes since the flash occurred when the port-outer revs began to fluctuate and the engine finally burst into flames. Fire drill was again carried out correctly and with success. The intercom then failed completely. Thereafter, all Tolley's instructions had to either be given by gesticulation or written down on paper.

The aircraft, now flying on one engine and unable to maintain height, entered a belt of cloud at 12,000 feet. Below this cloud the weather was bad with poor visibility. Tolley brought the aircraft down to 2,000 feet and, at this height, passed over an airfield near Antwerp. It was impossible to turn the aircraft and land there, so he flew on and, seeing three suitable adjacent fields ahead, he decided to land. Tolley had managed to get the flaps down about 10 degrees, and he made a perfect belly landing. The aircraft came to rest after travelling about 50 yards over soft mud. No one in the crew was even bruised. The position of landing was Doorn, south of Antwerp, behind the Allied lines.[24]

The Mittlelland Canal was attacked again on 21/22 November and this time the canal banks were successfully breached near Gravenhorst. Fifty-nine barges were left stranded on one short section alone and the water drained off over a 30 mile stretch. Near Ladbergen the Lancasters, some of them flying as low as 4,000 feet, also breached the Dortmund-Ems Canal in the only branch of the aqueduct which had been repaired since the last raid. The water once again drained out of the waterway.

Over 70 Lancasters joined over 170 Halifaxes in a raid on the oil refinery at Castrop-Rauxel and 18 more were part of the attack on Sterkrade synthetic oil refinery while over 270 Lancasters attacked the local railway yards at Aschaffeburg on this night of high activity. At Aschaffeburg about 500 houses were destroyed and 1,500 seriously damaged. Many old buildings were struck, including the local castle, the Johannisburg, which was hit by five HE bombs and had a 4,000lb 'Blockbuster' burst nearby. Two Lancasters were lost on this devastating raid and two Lancasters failed to return from the raid on the Mittlelland Canal.[25]

Then, on the night of 26/27 November, 270 Lancasters and eight Mosquitoes of 5 Group went to Munich. Before the main briefing at Fulbeck, Sergeant 'Ricky' Dyson, rear-gunner in the crew of Flying Officer Desmond 'Ned' Kelly RAAF in 189 Squadron, was officially introduced to Flight Sergeant Doug Presland's crew, as he would be flying in *Q-Queenie,* as a replacement for the rear-gunner who was sick. Dyson had joined up in 1935 because he was very unsettled at home. His mother was more or less on her deathbed and it was the time of the depression. His father had a piano business in Windsor but the wireless was coming in and the piano trade was very badly affected. Lord Trenchard's expansion of the RAF was greatly advertised in the local press and Dyson saw that the RAF offered an exciting career to young people with imagination and a flair to do daring things. It was an ideal way to travel. He trained as an air-gunner during 1944 and had flown ops on 9, 106 and 44 Squadrons before being posted to 189 Squadron that October. He recalls:

'I knew Presland's crew by sight, having mixed socially in the Sergeants' Mess, so this helped enormously and I found them to be a great bunch of lads. It was moon-

light when we reached the dispersal area but by the time we took off at 23.35 hours the weather had closed in and within a few seconds we entered a thick layer of low cloud. As the aircraft climbed the flight engineer called out the air speed (90–95 mph) to the pilot and it seemed to remain at that speed while we made a climbing turn. After reaching about 1,000 feet for some reason we lost height and "sank". I looked out of the turret and saw trees and hedges whipping past at about 100 feet and was about to warn the pilot when we hit a hill, 500 feet above sea level. We had been airborne just 11 minutes. There was a terrific dull thud, then a crunching and screeching sound as the aircraft hurtled and tore its way along the ground, shuddering from nose to tail as it went. There was a series of loud bangs and thuds as the aircraft broke its back, followed by a blinding flash and a huge explosion. Then silence. Whether I was "knocked out" I cannot remember but I do remember still sitting in the rear turret with a piece of fuselage burning fiercely behind me. The turret with this piece of fuselage attached had been thrown about 50 yards clear of the main wreckage but the doors had jammed and it was getting hotter by the second. I managed to free myself of the yellow Taylor flying suit I'd been wearing. With the aid of the axe on the turret wall I chipped away at the heavy duty Perspex of the Clear Vision Panel in front of me. With great difficulty I managed to squeeze sideways and I went head-first through the opening over what remained of the four Browning machine guns. I fell to the ground, landed on my back and scrambled to my feet. I ran petrified into the darkness ahead and only stopped when I came to a hedge to look back. The whole field seemed to be alight with burning debris. Seeing the flames I realized with horror that somewhere in that inferno was the rest of the crew! I shouted something and raced towards the main part of the wreckage. As I got nearer I could hear screams. Screams of people being burnt alive. Eventually I found some of the lads and tried to help and comfort them until the rescue services arrived. Doug Presland was semi-conscious, in great pain and calling for help. Half in and half out of the burning cockpit trapped by both legs, he was in great danger of being roasted by the terrific heat. Somehow I managed to free him and pull him to safety. The mid-upper gunner, Flight Sergeant Fender was also trapped. He was unconscious when I found him in his turret, his back and legs jammed hard against the twisted metal and his head embedded in the electrical junction box in the roof. In my shocked condition I tried in vain to release him. Later he was cut free from the wreckage, alive but with terrible injuries. Like me he had been thrown clear still in his turret. I went to help somebody else whose clothing was alight. Incendiaries had landed on his stomach. I put my hands down to extinguish the flames but felt my hands disappearing into his stomach. When I pulled them out they were wet with boiling blood. He was already dead from other injuries. Only days later did I realize how lucky I had been to survive a similar experience without serious injury.

'By the time the rescue services arrived, the field in which we had crashed, between Saltby and Croxton Kerrial resembled an inferno. The aircraft was fully laden with fuel and a mixed load of HE and incendiary bombs and wreckage was spread over a large area. The heat was terrific as the fuel tanks, bombs, oxygen bottles and ammunition from the gun turrets exploded, causing flaming debris to be flung high into the air and many pieces landing on the dead and injured. There was great danger as fragmented bomb cases and exploding ammunition whistled through the air in all directions. This scene, with the pungent and awful smell of burning flesh, burnt cordite and petrol and the pall of acrid smoke is one that I have never been able to obliterate from my mind.

'The three of us who survived were taken in an ambulance to an American base hospital a few miles away. Doug showed great courage. Although in great pain from his very serious injuries and burns to his face, hands and parts of his body, he managed to crack jokes, especially about the welfare of his moustache! His first concern was the fate of other members of his crew. Doug later had to have a leg amputated. After a long time in hospital and discharge from the RAF he became a schoolmaster and later a headmaster in Essex. Flight Sergeant Fender had to undergo numerous operations and he had a metal plate fitted in his head. After about two years in hospital he married his nurse. Having had excellent treatment for the few injuries I had sustained (mainly shock and minor burns to hands and face) I was discharged from hospital within two weeks and sent home on leave. Three weeks later I returned to Fulbeck and to 189 Squadron and resumed flying duties with Ned Kelly and crew. During the days and weeks which followed, the squadron was actively engaged on operations, both by day in support of our forces in France and by night against targets deep into Germany.'[26]

After this latest major raid on Munich, tens of thousands were camping out around the Maximilianplatz. On the nearby main road an endless stream of refugees was moving; frail old women with bundles containing their last possessions carried on sticks over their backs. Poor homeless people with burnt clothing, their eyes reflecting the horror of the firestorm, the explosions blowing everything to bits, burial in the rubble or the ignominy of suffocating in a cellar.[27]

The following night over 340 Lancasters attacked Freiburg, which was not an industrial town and had not been bombed before by the RAF. It was chosen because it was a minor railway centre and because many German troops were believed to be based there which could hinder the American and French advance in the Vosges only 35 miles to the west. In just 25 minutes 1,900 tons of bombs reigned down on Freiburg, destroying 2,000 houses and causing over 7,000 casualties. The railway yards were not hit and one Lancaster was lost. Over 290 bombers, including 102 Lancasters, also bombed Neuss, and 145 Lancasters revisited the town on 28/29 November. Halifaxes and Lancasters also bombed Essen. Then, on the 29th, over 290 Lancasters attacked Dortmund but bad weather reduced the effectiveness of the marking and the bombing was scattered. Minor raids by up to 60 Lancasters each were carried out against Bottrop and Osterfeld before Duisburg was attacked on the last night of November by over 570 aircraft. The target area was completely cloud covered but much fresh damage was still caused. On the night of 2/3 December a large force of bombers, including 87 Lancasters, carried out a devastating raid on Hagen.

During the first few weeks of December Lancasters carried out several daylight raids. One was made on the Hansa Benzol plant at Dortmund and another was on the small town of Heimbach in the Eifel region in support of American ground forces. By now American troops were only a few miles away and preparing to cross the River Roer. The Germans were about to release water to flood areas through which American troops were planning to advance so the destruction of the Urft dam (also referred to as the Heimbach dam), a large reservoir dam at the head of the valley in which ran the River Roer, was called for. The attack, on 4 December, by 27 Lancasters and three Mosquitoes of 8 (PFF) Group, included *J-Johnny* in 582 Squadron at Little Staughton flown by Flight Lieutenant Art Green. Sergeant Bill Hough, the wireless operator on the crew, recalls:

'We arrived at briefing and on checking the crew list we saw that the Gunnery Leader, Squadron Leader F. G. Grillage, was a replacement for 'Mac' McKeon, the mid-upper gunner who had shot himself through the hand two days earlier. McKeon decided to clean his pistol and in the process put the muzzle into the palm of his hand and pulled the trigger. I do not think he was playing Russian roulette but there was one up the spout and it went clean through his palm, ricocheted off the floor and out through the wall of the hut. The target was 15 to 20 miles inside Germany from its border with Belgium and only 25 miles or so ahead of the front line at the time. This was to be very much a 582 show with 16 of our aircraft marking, including the master bomber, Squadron Leader Mingard and his deputy, Lieutenant Edwin Swales SAAF.[28] There was to be additional marking by 109 Squadron. The met forecast was not too good with some thundershowers in the area and 5–6/10ths' cloud cover.

'We were first off at 08.05 hours carrying TIs and some bombs. The route took us across the French coast at Dunkirk with about 160 miles to run from there, mostly over Belgium and an ETA over the target at 09.45 hours. No need to worry about flak now as most of this formerly occupied territory had been retaken by the Allies. We were now flying above almost 10/10ths cloud but the horizontal visibility was good. Other aircraft were in sight and we seemed to be on the starboard edge of the stream. Tension heightened as we skirted Brussels with about 80 miles and 30 minutes to run. We were not quite sure where the front line was and it tended to be rather fluid anyway. With 40 miles to run, it happened. Warrant Officer Johnny Campbell, the rear-gunner, burst in on the intercom: "Unidentified aircraft starboard quarter, level (14,000 feet). Range, three miles." I fancied myself at aircraft recognition and immediately stood up under the astrodome. The aircraft was closing very quickly and I identified it almost immediately as an Me 262. Before I could regain my seat Johnny again burst in: "Another enemy aircraft dead astern – up, corkscrew starb . . ."'

'His words were lost in an almighty clatter and bang, the second aircraft firing its four 30mm cannon from a range of about 500 yards, the rear-gunner firing back and hits being registered on our port wing and engines. We had fallen victim to some very clever tactics using a decoy. The first aircraft went underneath us and the second over the top at a tremendous speed (this was our first encounter with a jet of any kind and their speed of over 500 mph certainly showed up against the Lanc's 170 or so). Black smoke, presumably from the fuel tanks, poured from the wing and the port outer was quickly enveloped in flames. Fire extinguishers were operated up front and we went into a shallow dive but the fire only seemed to intensify, although the aircraft was still being held steady. Art obviously realized he would not be able to hold her much longer and the order came, "Abandon aircraft – abandon aircraft".'

'Time was obviously short, so the two gunners and myself were told to use the rear exit. One moves pretty quickly in these circumstances and I grabbed the parachute pack and made my way to the rear exit. As I passed the mid-upper gunner I gave him a bang on the legs with my hand in case he had not got the message. Johnny Campbell had the turret centred and was just climbing out as I reached the exit. He indicated that I should go first and while I clipped on my 'chute, he opened the exit door and immediately there was a tremendous roar from the slipstream air. As I stood in the doorway preparing to dive out, my 'chute suddenly burst open and the canopy deployed outside the aircraft, billowing above the fuselage with the lines bearing on the rear edge of the door. I seemed to be snagged against the fuselage side unable to move. I do not know to this day what happened. I can only conjecture that either the 'chute handle caught on something, or the force of the slipstream somehow sucked on the pack and pulled out the 'chute. Anyhow, at this time no one was theorizing and Johnny Campbell quickly sized up the situation, got hold of me bodily and with some assistance from the billowing canopy, pushed me out of the door. Once free I was pulled by the 'chute *over* the top of the tailplane, banging my head on the top of the exit as I went out and hitting an ankle on the front edge of the tailplane, then between the fins, free of the aircraft. My first sensation was a feeling of peace and quiet after the last hectic three or four minutes, for that is all it was. Peace after the roar of the engines and the howling slipstream. But I quickly realized that I had another problem. My harness had not been as tight as it should have been. (I think it was a common practice to slacken them off a little while sitting for hours) and instead of being tight up in the crotch, it had slipped along the right leg towards the knee so that I was in imminent danger of parting company from the 'chute. I therefore held on grimly to the lines with both hands and began to enjoy the ride down. *J-Johnny* had disappeared from sight but one Me 262 did pass close enough to be recognized.

'As I neared the ground, still hanging on tightly, I could see that I was going to land in a field on the outskirts of a village and I could see people making towards the area. I did not make a copy-book landing due to the loose harness and a fairly strong breeze but I was OK and the villagers soon grabbed my 'chute and held on to me. After fifteen minutes or so two Yanks, for we were in the American sector, appeared in a jeep and took me off to hospital nearby. I learned later that I had landed at Juprelle near Tongres and the hospital was at Hasselt.

'I was kept in hospital for about four days and spent a further night at an American phi base in a nearby chateau. I was not aware at the time of the fate of the rest of the crew, nor was I aware that I had been posted missing and my family informed. On 9 December I was again taken in a jeep to Brussels airport where I was able to hitch a lift in an RAF Dakota calling first at Northolt, then finally to Down Ampney. From Down Ampney I made my own way towards base, by train, arriving in the square at St. Neots late in the afternoon. I still had on the clothes and flying boots, but not my helmet and parachute harness, that I had set out in six days earlier. A telephone call to Little Staughton secured me transport and I finally arrived back at base somewhat behind schedule. That was the longest op I did, No. 13. Possibly we achieved a double first in this trip; the first aircraft of Bomber Command to be shot down by an Me 262 and the first airman to bale out safely over the tailplane of a Lancaster.[29] Our flight had terminated at 09.25 hours. The master bomber was unable to locate the target, although both he and the deputy went down to 4,000 feet, so the raid was abandoned at 09.51 hours.'[30]

A night of truly massive proportions occurred on 17/18 December when 1,310 aircraft bombed Ülm, Munich, Duisburg, Hanau, Münster and Hallendorf. At Ülm 317 Lancasters dropped 1,449 tons of bombs during the 25-minute raid and one square kilometre of the city was completely engulfed by fire. Eight Halifaxes were shot down on the Duisburg raid and six Lancasters were lost on the raids on Ülm and Munich. Four of the Lancasters failed to return from the attack on the old centre of Munich and at railway targets. One was a 467 Squadron aircraft flown by Flying Officer T. E. Evans RAAF, which was abandoned on the way back over France in the vicinity of Châlons-Sur-Marne. Hanging head first, Evans' flying boot caught in the forward escape hatch of the spiralling Lancaster and he pulled the ripcord of his parachute in a final, desperate effort to get clear and was dragged out to safety. So violent was the tug that three panels of silk were ripped from the parachute, but it held sufficiently to carry him. Evans had pushed on to Munich although one engine was failing and the rear turret had become unserviceable soon after leaving England. The bomber barely cleared the Alps, but reached the target, and the bombing run was begun. Suddenly came further trouble. The starboard fin and rudder were almost entirely torn away by flak, 12 feet of the starboard mainplane was ripped from the failing engine which cut out completely, and the bomber went into a spin, completing an orbit in the midst of the rest of the bomber stream. The navigator, Flying Officer D. K. Robson RAAF said later that Evans regained control by sheer strength at 7,000 feet and ordered parachutes on. Evans was struggling hard at the controls and the whole aircraft was vibrating horribly. The Lancaster had been flying two hours away from Munich and was down to 3,000 feet when it became completely uncontrollable, and again went into a spiral dive. Evans ordered 'abandon aircraft', but the bomber was down to 1,500 feet when the captain himself jumped, got caught, and was dragged to safety by his chute. The bomber followed the parachuting crew down and almost hit them in its passage. It struck the ground with a great explosion when the crew were still about 200 feet up. Evans was slightly injured in the leg as the result of his ordeal, but no one else was hurt. The crew were assisted by the French and were soon back with their squadron in Britain. Evans was awarded a DFC two months later.[31]

Attempts were always being made to improve bombing accuracy and one such scheme that December was the 'Formation Daylight'. The idea was for an *Oboe* equipped aircraft to act as lead aircraft for a small force of Light Night Striker Mosquitoes, each carrying 4,000-pounders to attack small, vital targets in daylight, thus achieving, it was hoped, great precision. Two 582 Squadron Lancaster B.VIs, specially adapted for the leadership role, were at first allocated. The Lancaster VI was good for 28,000 feet but its cruising speed was incompatible with the Mosquito IX or XVI. It was to carry an extra *Oboe* pilot and navigator of 109 (Mosquito) Squadron to fly the specialized bombing run. This arrangement was not popular with the *Oboe* Mossie crews. One of these was Flight Lieutenant Bob Jordan and Ronnie Plunkett of 105 Squadron at Bourn, who were asked to operate the *Oboe* on the operation, on 23 December, an attack on the Cologne/Gremburg railway marshalling yards to disrupt enemy reinforcements for the Battle of the Bulge. Twenty-seven Lancasters and three Mosquitoes would make the raid. Jordan and Plunkett were to lead the second formation of 10, while Squadron Leader Robert A. M. Palmer DFC* of 109 Squadron and his crew, would lead the first formation in an *Oboe*-equipped Lancaster, borrowed from 582 Squadron. Palmer, who was 24 years old and had been promoted to squadron leader at age 23, had completed 110 sorties at this time, having been on bombing operations since January 1941. At Graveley Jordan and Plunkett were detailed to fly on Lancaster PB272 *X for X-Ray* of 35 Squadron, flown by Flying Officer E. J. Rigby and his usual crew. Jordan and Plunkett were to take over the aircraft 60 miles out from the target to operate the *Oboe*. *X for X-Ray* was airborne at 10.38 with eleven 1,000lb MC on the racks. Their outward run was normal except that two Lancs touched wings and went down. When the two Mosquito men took over, their aircraft came under predicted heavy flak and caught fire, which the crew were able to extinguish. Since they were not 'on the beam' they did not get a release signal and had to jettison the bomb load from 17,000 feet. 'We had a clear view of Squadron Leader Palmer leading the first formation just ahead' recalls Plunkett, 'and his aircraft came under intense AA fire. Smoke billowed from the Lanc and I wondered why he did not bale out there and then, because there seemed to be no hope for them. A German fighter then attacked them but they carried on and completed their bombing run. The Lanc then went over on the port side and went down. I cannot think what, other than sheer determination, kept him on the bombing run. He carried out his duty in textbook fashion. After this we went down to 6,000 feet and Rigby did a good job getting us all back to Manston.' In April 1945 the award of a posthumous Victoria Cross was made to Squadron Leader Robert Anthony Maurice Palmer.

On seeing the release of Palmer's bomb load, Edwin Swales SAAF of 582 Squadron, who was flying his 33rd operation, dropped his bomb load and then turned off the target. He was immediately attacked by five enemy fighters who carried out five successive attacks on the Lancaster. Swales' gunners fought back furiously and claimed one of the German fighters destroyed and two more damaged. Swales was subsequently awarded a DFC for his coolness under fire.

On 26 December the weather at last improved and allowed Bomber Command to intervene in the Ardennes battle and almost 300 bombers, 146 of them Lancasters, were dispatched to bomb German troop positions near St. Vith. Two Halifaxes were lost and a Lancaster, hit by three bursts of flak 10 minutes flying time from the Belgian lines, was set on fire. The crew, with the exception of the rear-gunner who was killed, fought the fire for 65 minutes using all the extinguishers and even the contents of the thermos flasks as well as parachutes, to damp down the flames. The heat buckled the whole of the rear fuselage and the rear and mid-upper turrets were burnt out. Exploding ammunition had further damaged the aircraft and control was difficult but it held together for an emergency landing behind the Allied lines in France.

More 'daylights' took place on 28 December, to Cologne-Gremberg again, and to Koblenz the follow-

ing day. That same night the rail yards at Troisdorf and synthetic oil plants at Scholven-Buer were attacked for the loss of a total of four Lancasters. During bombing up for the raids at Waterbeach, a Lancaster of 514 Squadron exploded, killing nine and injuring four people, completely wrecking a second Lancaster and damaging two others.

Christmas and the New Year came and went with von Rundstedt's abortive counteroffensive still underway. Hope faded for an end to the European war in 1944 and the question, 'How early in 1945 can it be finished?' became linked urgently with thoughts of homes not seen by many for three, four or five Christmases. It was a question that still appeared no nearer an answer as the ice began to form again in northern Europe, as the winter winds began to scour the airfields of Britain once again. As winter moved over Europe in 1944–45, crews faced temperatures of 50 to 60 degrees below freezing point, electric storms and fogs. Even alcohol-filled compasses froze on some attacks. As soon as ice on mainplanes thawed a little, large pieces flew off and drummed along the fuselage like enemy fire. Sometimes air and ground crews had to dig their aircraft out of the snow on the day before an operation and then clear the runways of up to two feet of snow. Squadron Leader D. Sullivan DFC and his crew in 463 Squadron RAAF found conditions over a target in the Ruhr so bad that it was impossible to bomb. Carrying out instructions, Sullivan returned to base with the full bomb load. The weather was bad there, and they were diverted to another field. At the strange field Sullivan found he could not adjust his altimeter for the prevailing barometric pressure. Stormy conditions on the return journey had affected the radio equipment. Torrential rain made the night intensely dark, but the landing lights were just visible and Sullivan decided to land. On the approach, without the altimeter to assist, and with rain streaming down the windscreen, the Lancaster hit the tops of some trees. Only superb coolness on Sullivan's part brought it to rest safely, though the only casualty was a rabbit, caught up in the landing, which was found dead in the bomb-aimer's compartment.

It certainly seemed that 1945 would be the last year of a war that the long-suffering Britons had endured for the last past five years. The *Luftwaffe* was powerless to stop the inexorable advance westwards but despite the declining effectiveness of *Nachtjagd* during late 1944, an all-time record of 2,216 aircraft destroyed was claimed that year. Losses in air combat, in ground attacks and in accidents rose steeply and 114 German aircraft had been destroyed during November-December. At the beginning of 1945 there was one last attempt to try to halt the Allies. Since 20 December many *Jagd Gruppen* had been transferred to airfields in the west for Operation *Bodenplatte,* when approximately 850 *Luftwaffe* fighters took off at 07.45 hours on Sunday morning, 1 January, to attack 27 airfields in northern France, Belgium and southern Holland. The four-hour operation succeeded in destroying about 100 Allied aircraft but it cost the *Luftwaffe* 300 aircraft, most of which were shot down by Allied anti-aircraft guns deployed primarily against the V-1s and by 'friendly' flak.[32] The heavies carried out no night bombing operations on 3/4 January but, on the night of the 4/5th, 347 Lancasters and seven Mosquitoes controversially attacked Royan at the mouth of the River Gironde. Upwards of 800 French civilians were killed. Four Lancasters were lost and two more collided behind the Allied lines in France and crashed. The number of aircraft lost in mid-air collisions is not known but it is generally accepted that the numbers were few. Sergeant David Fellowes, a rear-gunner on 460 Squadron RAAF during 1944–45 recalls:

'The morning of 7 January started much the same as many others. The last minute scramble to complete one's ablutions, into battle-dress and a quick dash to the Sergeants' Mess for the last remains of breakfast. Then to the anti-room for a look at the previous day's papers and with the crew complete, a gentle walk to the hangers and B Flight office. Our skipper Art Whitmarsh followed us in. Soon, amid the noise and smokey atmosphere the telephone rang. An Aussie voice yelled, "Quiet!" The noise stopped and Bob Henderson, our Flight Commander, replaced the phone. "OK it's on". We all knew what he meant. We had heard it all before. Last night the crew had been to Hanau, a successful operation with all our aircraft returning safely. Crews dispersed to their individual sections leaving the pilots with the Flight Commander. Ken de la Mare, the mid-upper gunner and I departed for the Gunnery Section in the same hanger and carried out the routine daily inspection of our .303 Browning machine guns. A quick pull through with 4 by 2, check the return springs, read the latest Orders and sign the book. A walk to our dispersal where we were met by Sergeant Spud Murphy with his team of fitters and armourers who were responsible for our aircraft. Spud, with his black curly hair, always had a wide grin is more like an Irish gipsy than a real Aussie digger.

'The turret covers had already been removed and with the help of the armourers the guns were fitted, the systems checked, spare light bulbs, fuses and finally what little Perspex we had was given a quick polish. Most of the Perspex had been removed, which was more draughty and a lot colder but it improved night vision and made less work. As a last job, I fitted the celluloid caps over the flash eliminators. I then replaced the turret cover, met up with the other crew members and hot footed it back to the Mess. As we entered the foyer there for all to see was the 'Battle Order'; a list of names, aircraft, main briefing time etc. but there without mistake under 'B' Flight was our aircraft; *O-Oboe* ND968/G. Flying Meal, 15.30 hours. Briefing 16.15 hours. Back to our married quarters No. 13 where Sergeant Art Sheppard, the flight engineer and I shared a small room upstairs. Soon a fire was burning in the grate. The kettle was on and a quick brew up, feet up and relaxation for soon the game would be on again and one more operation less to do. A call at 15.00, flying sweaters on and we walked to the mess. We went into the servery with its large trays of fried eggs, streaky bacon, baked beans and fried bread, plenty of bread and margarine all to be washed down with hot tea or coffee. Somebody dropped his plate and a mighty roar went up, then quietness for a few seconds before the low murmurings returned but not for long as it was time to leave. We put our greatcoats on and joined the growing crowd on its way to the Briefing Room.

'In a few minutes we saw the Corporal SP outside the double doors which we passed through. Past the rows of tables and chairs, the low stage with black curtains closed to the front, we took our seats in line with the Skipper and navigator sitting in the aisle seats. The room was thick with cigarette smoke and noise, for the room was almost full. Eighteen crews were operating tonight; 126 men. The Intelligence Officer, Flight Commander and specialist officers took their place on the platform either side of the curtains. Loud and clear came the call, "Atten-shun". Everybody stood. It was quiet and down the aisle walked the Station Commander, Group Captain Keith Parsons and Squadron Commander Mike Cowan. A curt "Good evening Gentlemen" was followed by a mass murmured reply and followed by "Be seated," as the Intelligence Officer drew the curtains apart and the target was revealed – MUNICH.

'A large groan went up. For all to see the thin red tape stretched from Binbrook southwards to Reading then altered course to Beachy Head, over the Channel southeast towards a point north of Mulhouse where the track turned north-east and headed towards Stuttgart. Just before Stuttgart a right turn onto a south-easterly heading, passing Ulm on our port side on to Memmingen and then a left turn heading directly for Munich. This was to be the second attack on Munich this night. 5 Group squadrons were to attack with an H hour of 20.30. Us in 1 Group at H hour 22.30. The briefing went on. We could expect moderate to heavy flak with fighter activity. The target marking would be *Parramatta*[33] with emergency sky marking. Finally the Met-man. A small cheer went up as he told us "10/10ths cumulus from France to the target area with tops to 8,500 feet with a frontal belt lying south-east of Paris with winds at 18,000 feet of 27–30 knots and tops to 8–10,000 feet near the target". There would be no moon during the operation and there was the likelihood of snow on return with possible diversions. Thus, the briefing came to an end. The Squadron Commander wished us well. The Station Commander wished he were going. Everybody stood as the hierarchy left.

'The crews dispersed to the changing rooms where they emptied their pockets. Then into flying overalls, long socks, flying boots, gloves, helmet, check the oxygen mask, collect parachute and harness (oh yes sign for it). I then put on my Mae West and harness and collected the escape kit, which was placed in the inner battle-dress pocket. Then it was out into the cold night. The crew bus soon arrived and with other crews with aircraft in adjacent dispersals, we were soon there. We were met by Spud Murphy. He told us all was well and the aircraft serviceable.

'We climbed aboard, stowed our chutes and carried out the necessary pre-flight checks. I stuck wakey-wakey tablets onto a strut with a piece of chewing gum. With time to spare the crew gathered at the small ground crew shelter for a last cigarette. Art Whitmarsh signed the Form 700 and most of us went for a quick "leak". Then, with harness fastened, it was into the aeroplane. While Art Sheppard; Flight Sergeant D. Collett, navigator, Flight Sergeant P. Turnbull, bomb-aimer, and Flight Sergeant J. Wilson, wireless operator, went forward I clambered over the Elsan, turned onto my back and slid over the tail spar. Legs down and you were there. I checked to see if my chute was secure, removed the cotton reel from the oxygen economizer, closed the doors, plugged in the intercom and connected the oxygen tube to my mask tube. I fastened the seat belt, opened the breach covers and armed the four Brownings, making sure they were all cocked and Fire/Safe to Safe. This was followed by a call to the Skipper, "Rear Gunner ready, turret serviceable". "OK" came the reply and one heard the others reporting. At last it was time to start the engines.

'Now it was time to check the turret's operation, full rotation, guns elevated and depressed. I switched the gunsight to "dim", checked the radar systems and reported all systems serviceable. One could hear the power increased to the engines. We moved forward, then almost stopped as the brakes were checked. A quick thumbs up to the ground crew as we taxied out of the dispersal and onto the perimeter and joined the queue of Lancasters. We slowly went past the hanger and Control Tower, downhill past the bomb dump and then to the end of Runway 22. In turn we moved onto the runway, where I did my final checks. We got a steady green from the runway controller, the engines roared, the brakes were released and the take-off run started. The mighty Merlins gave full power, the tail came up and I was airborne. The tail swung a little and was corrected. I heard the engineer call, "Full power, temperatures and pressures normal" and we were airborne at 18.47.

'The flaps and undercarriage came in and the Skipper called for 2,650 +9 and *Oboe* climbed away with a 4,000lb cookie and incendiaries. We turned onto course for the rendezvous at Reading. As we climbed to our first height the guns were set to "Fire" and I started the gunners' methodical search pattern, reporting other aircraft that may put us at risk. Occasionally the whole aeroplane shuddered from the turbulence made by other Lancasters joining the bomber stream. Eventually we reached our flight level and the navigator gave the Skipper a time for Reading and a new course to steer. At the appointed time we turned onto the new course and started to climb to our next flight level, carrying on to the next turning point at Beachy Head. So far, so good and soon we altered course again, crossing the Channel to the French coast and the long leg towards Mulhouse. Paris was passed well to the south of us. A shower of red sparks flew past my turret but this was no cause for alarm as it was the engineer clearing the engines. So on we droned, soon to run into the front with its associated cloud as forecast by the Met-man. The thought of flying in cloud in daytime was bad enough but at night in a bomber stream was not at all pleasant. The turbulence, sometimes in the tops then in the clear seeing the stars in the dark sky above, there were times when you couldn't see the wing tips, the dampness but we keep going. Sticking to the briefing we flew on toward the high ground of the Vogeses that rises up to more than 4,600 feet and close to the German border. The weather worsened with more frequent turbulence. A voice on the intercom suggested that we should climb above the weather. There was unanimous agreement and after a second or two the Skipper called for climbing power. I felt the mighty bomber climb through the murky skies and in a few minutes we were in and out of the tops, seeing the stars in the dark sky and the dim shapes of other Lancasters who had climbed earlier. Then "CHRIST" came a shout over the head phones together with a crash and the tearing of metal. *Oboe* rocked. "We've been hit" said another voice. "Did you see that other Lanc? It's falling away." Our port wing dropped and *Oboe* fell back into the clouds in a spin. Art Whitmarsh was fighting with all his strength to regain control and after what seemed an eternity we were straight and level. The Skipper called for bomb doors open and Jock jettisoned the bombs "Safe". The clouds lightened with a flash; our bombs or the other Lanc, who knew?

'Our four engines were still running, the Skipper still struggling to maintain control as he told us that the ailerons were jammed. He called for a head count and serviceability check. The Skipper decided that we must return if possible. The wireless operator was instructed to advise Binbrook on W/T. The IFF was switched to "ON" and a gentle turn was started for a course to the emergency airfield at Manston. The engine power was increased and slowly we started to climb to clear the cloud and the front, also to reduce the risk of icing. Eventually we reached 20,000 feet and were able to see and estimate the extent of the damage. The trailing edge of the starboard wing was well chewed up, the aileron and wing tip missing, Ken in his mid-upper turret reported that the floor and starboard side of the fuselage were missing as was the H_2S assembly for about ten feet. Ken was assisted out of his turret by using the escape rope and the help of the wireless operator to the relative comfort and safety of the flight deck.

'The tail end of the aircraft was swinging with lots of vibration. It was impossible for me in the tail to come forward. I was given the option of baling out but I preferred to stay and stick with each other. Besides, we were still subject to enemy fighters. The Skipper reduced the power and this helped reduce the vibration, so we flew on but with a lower speed. Not a lot was said. The Skipper had his hands full maintaining our crippled machine. Eventually the Channel came up, with a descent to Manston which could be seen. The Skipper decided to make a flapless landing. The undercarriage was lowered. Thank Goodness they both extended as indicated by the two green lights and with a long flat approach a safe landing was made at 00.49 hours. We taxied slowly behind a "Follow Me" ATC truck and parked the aeroplane. The engines were closed down. It was so quiet. Slowly we emerged from the exits, me from the door, the rest of the crew via the front escape hatch down the ladder. We looked at the damage. I suppose we said a silent "Thank You". Then it was

into the transport for a debriefing in Air Traffic Control. The night's events were recalled, then a phone call to Binbrook to confirm that we were safe. A meal was soon provided and then we had a long sleep.

'It snowed during the night but next morning we inspected the aeroplane. It was not a pretty sight. The way she held together was a tribute to Avros. The starboard side of the fuselage from the trailing edge almost to the entrance door was missing, as was the floor from the bomb bay, three feet of wing tip and the trailing edge were all mangled and chewed up by the other Lancaster's propellers with little left of the aileron. A phone call from Binbrook instructed me to remove parts of our radar system as we operated with "Village Inn"[34] and "Z" equipment and to bring these back with me. However, due to bad weather at Binbrook and snow at Manston an aircraft was unable to come for us and whilst having a snowball fight outside Air Traffic Control we were told to clear off and get the train. We were given money, railway warrants and transport to Ramsgate but what a scruffy dishevelled crew we looked There was not a razor between us, so into a barber's shop we went where we were given shaves by ladies running their husbands' business. Now feeling more human, after a well earned drink we had a crew photograph taken, then we boarded the train to London. But it was no wonder we were stopped by the RAF Service Police. We wore no hats and were in flying boots, Mae West's etc. but their attitude was soon put to right by good Australian phraseology. A few hours later we were back at Grimsby with transport to take us back to camp for another debriefing. Our next flight was a short cross country and then the "Game" was on again.'[35]

On the night of 5/6 January when 664 aircraft bombed Hanover, 23 Halifaxes and eight Lancasters failed to return. The majority were shot down by an effective *Zahme Sau* operation.[36] The 35 Squadron Lancaster piloted by Flight Lieutenant Phil Bryant returned, missing one crewmember. In the opinion of the crew, Bryant was an extremely good skipper as well as being an excellent pilot. The crew that night consisted largely of 'odd bods' but they soon gelled into a good working unit under Bryant's able leadership. Their trip was uneventful up to the target, which they reached on time and marked with fair precision. After dropping their bombs they headed for home and Bryant engaged in some fairly active weaving to avoid any predicted flak or fighters that might be around. They soon cleared the target area and settled down on course for Graveley. Phil Bryant announced, 'I am going to call each crew member in turn to check that everyone is OK. Please answer when you're called.' They were all called from nose to tail by their crew stations and all answered, 'OK Skipper' until he came to the mid-upper gunner, an Australian Flying Officer named H. E. D. 'Bob' Figgis. No answer. He called three or four times. Still no reply. Finally, after checking the rear-gunner, Bryant asked the wireless operator to go back and check the mid-upper turret, assuming that Figgis had a faulty intercom or that it had become unplugged. It was quite a shock, therefore, when, a few minutes later the wireless op called: 'Hello skipper, wireless op here. There's nobody in the mid-upper turret and the rear door is open.' An amazing display of crew discipline followed. There was no speculation, no discussion. Phil Bryant merely said, 'Right. Rear-gunner, please keep an extra good lookout and wireless op please cover the mid-upper position from the astrodome.' Not another word was said on the subject until they entered the Graveley circuit and were about to land. Then at last somebody said, 'I wonder what happened to old Bob Figgis.' Later some discussion took place at debriefing and all who knew him well agreed that Bob was an extremely steady and reliable type and the last person anyone would expect to lose his nerve or do anything silly. So it remained an unsolved mystery and was soon forgotten.[37]

On 6/7 January over 600 aircraft set out to bomb two important German rail junctions at Hanau and Neuss. Many of the bombs dropped by 468 Halifaxes and Lancasters at Hanau, and 147 Lancasters at Neuss, missed the targets and fell in surrounding districts. Hanau was reported to be '40 per cent destroyed' while in Neuss, over 1,700 houses, 19 industrial premises and 20 public buildings were destroyed or seriously damaged.[38] The following night Bomber Command returned to area bombing with the final major raid on Munich by 645 Lancasters led by nine Mosquitoes. The raid was claimed as successful with the central and some industrial areas being severely damaged. Eleven Lancasters were lost and four more crashed in France. There followed separate raids on Krefeld and the U-boat pens at Bergen and two raids on the rail yards at Saarbrücken, one in daylight on the 13th and again that night. A second bomber force raided the oil plant at Pölitz, near Stettin. This was, for Flying Officer Frank Mouritz RAAF, pilot of Lancaster III *M-Mike* of 61 Squadron the night that he and his crew nearly 'bought it':

'It was our 20th operation. We were an experienced crew (but not too experienced to be over-confident) and we were to attack, for the second time, a synthetic oil refinery at Pölitz, near Stettin on the Baltic coast in northern Germany. This was our maximum range on this route and we carried full fuel tanks of 2,154 gallons and 12,000lb of 500 and 1,000lb High Explosive bombs – some with delay fuses. The route out was over the North Sea to Denmark, across the Kattegat to southern Sweden, then turning south across the Baltic to the north German coast. The return route was to be similar. Denmark, being occupied, was heavily defended by German armed forces, Sweden however, although neutral, shot up quite a lot of light flak but never in our direction so it was relatively safe to fly across their territory. The attack, purely a 5 Group operation, was planned as a blind attack through cloud but it was changed to a visual one, as the target was clear. Although we carried out our usual fighter search there was no real danger till we neared the target after crossing the Baltic. We bombed on time through very heavy flak and numerous searchlights, as the refinery was very heavily defended. After bombing we set course for home over the Baltic, on the briefed route over Sweden, and then over Denmark. This meant that the *Luftwaffe* had little trouble working out the probable times and position that the returning bombers would cross Denmark. No doubt the Nazis had agents in Sweden that radioed their passing to Germany.

'The skill of the navigator and bomb-aimer in map reading kept us on track as there was little cloud cover and the coast lines were fairly visible. On nearing Denmark we went into maximum banking searches at every 1 or 2 minutes, and saw several flashes of gunfire from aerial combats. We were about 15–20 minutes on the route home after crossing the western Danish coast and I was easing up on the banking searches thinking that a couple more would be sufficient, when the silence of the intercom was broken by the mid-upper gunner. "Twin engined aircraft underneath". He did not say which side down but as he could not see straight down it must have been on the starboard side. My reaction, which luckily must have been the correct one, was to put the Lancaster into a violent diving turn to starboard and called out "going down starboard". The wing had just started to drop when we heard explosions and saw flashes under the starboard wing between the inboard engine and the fuselage. Possibly five or six shells, probably 30mm, hit us and as we dived I heard our guns firing. One of the gunners called out excitedly "we've got him and he is heading for a cloud bank below on fire".

'In retrospect, we assumed that the mid-upper gunner had sighted him before he was in his best position and our violent diving turn had spoilt his aim. He had to break away to avoid a collision and as we were nearly on our side the two gunners were able to rake him with our six Browning machine guns across his top. As I straightened out the Lanc I found that our emergency signal lights at each crew station had come on and we were lit up and in full view if the fighters were hunting in pairs. I called out to the wireless operator to get to the fuse panel and pull out the appropriate fuses. Dave's reply in his slow Queensland drawl was "Hell, I'm just taking a broadcast". The calmness in Dave's voice reduced the panic that was beginning to appear in the crew. This all took place in a few seconds. The problem of the lights was solved by the rear-gunner smashing his light with his cocking toggle, short circuiting the bulb and blowing the fuse. By this time, of course we had all lost our night vision.

'I levelled the plane and returned to our course and started to take stock of our damage – from the front we could not see any fires – by calling each member of the crew in turn from back to front, asking for a report on themselves and their equipment. No one had been wounded and all the equipment, except the flight engineer's, was functioning. He reported that we had lost some power on the starboard inboard engine, and that he was possibly losing fuel from the starboard inboard tank. The Lancaster has three tanks in each wing, all interconnected and it was the rule to draw them all down together so that no tank held maximum fuel, as this could be lost if punctured. The air space above the fuel in the tank was filled with inert nitrogen gas to help prevent fires. Jim Leith, the flight engineer, immediately started to run down the holed tank by feeding the fuel from it to all engines. We also adjusted the controls to bring the bad engine up to the others and carefully watched the gauges. The navigator had a problem with his protractor and calculator etc. as they were tangled due to the violent manoeuvre we had carried out. He had them all tied to a centre point with pieces of string but they took some sorting out. We had just settled down and began to analyze the combat when the rear-gunner reported an object going past his turret followed by another one. The flight engineer managed to have a look at the damaged wing with his torch and reported that the dinghy cover was missing and so was the dinghy. We assumed that was what the rear-gunner had reported. The navigator, F/E and myself had a discussion on the distance to base, fuel consumption and remaining fuel. Having lost our dinghy, a ditching in the North Sea was out of the question. The other alternative was to return to Denmark and bale out. However we worked out that if we flew at our most economical airspeed and height we could make the English coast with a small margin to

spare. I did think about putting out a mayday call but left it for the time being as we still had 3½ engines and probably enough fuel.

'We discussed the combat and concluded that the fighter plane, a Junkers 88, had probably been following us on his radar for some time, waiting until we stopped the banking searches and that the decision to bank to starboard was the correct one. If we had turned to port he could have followed us down and used his front guns as well. Many years later when reading the accounts of the night fighters, I learnt that their preferred aiming point, when attacking from below, was between the inboard engine and the fuselage. This was possibly to give the crew a chance and also that a loaded Lanc has bombs stretching along underneath the centre section of the fuselage and a strike on the fuse of a bomb would blow up both aircraft. So we headed for home at the most economical speed with the rear-gunner keeping a lookout for any more pieces of wing flying past the turret. Nothing further happened and I was tempted to try to lower the undercarriage, to test it, soon after we crossed the coast but decided to leave it until we entered the circuit in our normal manner. On arriving at base I lowered the undercarriage, which made the right sort of noises and vibrations and the indicator light came on so I completed the approach. As soon as we touched the runway I knew that something was wrong. The aircraft tried to drop the starboard wing and I managed to hold it up with full aileron till we lost speed. Then it dropped down; something dragged on that side. We left the bitumen and slewed around in an ever-decreasing circle till we ended up, luckily almost in our own dispersal point. The starboard tyre had been shot to pieces. An inspection of *M-Mike* next morning showed that most of the underneath starboard wing plates were missing or holed. There were some holes in the lower section of the fuselage but no major structural damage. The loss of power had been due to some ignition leads being cut. Repairs were carried out at our aerodrome but the Lanc was out of action for nearly six weeks. The Ju 88 was later confirmed as damaged, as another crew had seen the combat and the Junkers going down into cloud, on fire. He may have ended up in the North Sea. When we analysed the action we realized that the sighting by the mid-upper gunner had saved us, and that on future operations extra banking searches would have to be carried out on the return journey and at irregular intervals.

'I was very pleased with the overall crew reaction with little or no panic. We realized that constant surveillance and not allowing ourselves to relax on the way home would be necessary for survival on the remaining operations. This had been our longest trip, 10 hours 30 minutes airborne. Photo reconnaissance stated that the plant was reduced to a shambles. However, we attacked it again in three weeks time and the production of oil ceased, proving to be a great setback to the German war effort.'[39]

Somewhere on a distant airfield stood a neglected 1934 Standard 10 motor car, much used, even ill-used, in the past but nobody cared. The three men from the aircrew that drove it had gone missing together with four additional crewmembers of Lancaster 'Y' PB842, on an operation to an oil plant at Pölitz, near Stettin, on 13/14 January 1945.

A few weeks before, in December 1944, Flight Sergeant Frederick Woodger Roots, air-gunner, Brian Curran, his Australian pilot and Bob Wilson, the Scottish navigator, had visited the Roots in Cockfosters, London and had acquired the car. Mr Roots, a news-paperman on the *Daily Mail,* spent a lot of time helping them patch it. They froze as they grovelled beneath it, tracing broken circuits and tightening loose controls, for garage staff were short. In RAF parlance, there was no 'joy' in the battery, no 'joy' in the self-starter Eventually they drove it off on the way back to more bombing operations with 619 Squadron from Strubby, Lincolnshire, a 5 Group station near Alford, not far from Skegness and Mablethorpe.

Twenty-one year old Fred Roots was formerly on the staff of the Press Association, Fleet Street and had joined the RAF in 1942. He spent his period of training in Canada and the Bahamas, passing his Elementary Flying Training School final air and ground examinations for pilot on 29 September 1942. He was then posted to 38 EFTS at Estevan where he soloed on an Anson II and continued flying Ansons until 3 January 1943, when he was taken off the course; it was thought that he would not make a service pilot in the required time. Roots then underwent gunnery training in Canada, eventually receiving his air-gunner brevet. Coastal Command training in Nassau in the Bahamas followed and he was allotted to a crew that flew Mitchells and Liberators. However, the crew was disbanded and they returned to the United Kingdom to be retrained on Wellingtons, Stirlings and Lancasters for 5 Group Bomber Command.

Roots' crew started bombing operations early in October 1944. All went well until 13/14 January 1945. One morning soon after, the Roots received a telegram. It did not 'stun' – it was less merciful. It admitted them to a vast community that mourned in every country or grimly and bleakly fought for hope. Their air-gunner son was reported missing on a bombing trip over Germany. Friends and neighbours are very kind at such times. Some came bravely in to help; others just as kindly stayed away. Two pressed whisky into their hands. 'Give her a drop tonight,' they said. 'It'll help a bit.' The RAF was kind too. The wing commander wrote in practical, encouraging terms, stressing the sound experience of the crew, the qualities of the pilot.

Their grey sojourn was mercifully brief. On the third day came another wire: 'Safe but interned'. The speed of it shook them. How the neighbourhood leapt with them! Even the telephone girls, whom they never saw, rejoiced as the calls sped in and out. The butcher and the baker, the parson and the milk girl heard the news. Everyone called. Someone brought more whisky. 'For a toast to your boy and his pals – and all the others too.' (The giver's son-in-law was home with her, with his legs shot off).

Friday the 13th had begun like most other nights on operations for Fred and the rest of his crew, as he recalls:

'We set off in the usual way from Strubby, having gone through the usual preliminaries, including brief-ing, inspection of our aircraft, guns and turrets, etc. and of course our special egg, chips and bacon meal as always. We climbed into *Y-Yoke* PB842 and settled down into our respective positions in the aircraft. As always I was in the rear turret, with its four Browning .303 machine guns. Our usual bomb-aimer, Sergeant Charlie Lockton, was sick and Flight Sergeant M. P. Quigley took his place. He and Sergeant Johnny Haigh, the wireless operator and Sergeant David Drew, the flight engineer, all came from Huddersfield. The mid-upper gunner, Flight Sergeant E. A. M. 'Abdullah' Blakeley, completed the crew.

'As usual, the commanding officer, padre and many of the station personnel were facing the runway to wave us off with the "thumbs up" sign as we took off. We were routed over Sweden and the flight was com-paratively quiet with only the occasional anti-aircraft activity. Over Sweden the Swedish anti-aircraft gunners opened up, to comply with international requirements from a neutral country. However, the aiming was intentionally 'friendly' and we had no need to take evasive action. Closer to the target was a quite well defended area because of the oil refineries at Pölitz and the number of warships with anti-aircraft guns and the flak became more intense. However, we flew safely on until we reached our bombing run to the target. I was obviously keeping an alert lookout for enemy night fighters. It was during the last few minutes of our run-in that I saw the Me 410 night fighter. Because he was sufficiently distant and flying a parallel course to us, I knew at that time that there could be no immediate danger and it was better that the bombing run continued so that we could get rid of our bombs. However, immediately I saw the Me 410 turn towards us – the pilot had to turn his aircraft towards us in order to sight his guns – I opened fire with my four guns at the same time, giving the order to Brian to corkscrew to port – the evasive action devised by Bomber Command. The Me 410 continued to close in until he was within point blank range and I continued to shoot. Just before the German night fighter came in, our bomb-aimer had released the bombs on to the target. I imagine the enemy pilot had been waiting to see the bombs released, knowing of the danger to himself if they were to explode!

'By this time I imagine that the Me 410 must have been extensively damaged, for he fell away from us and the fight came to an end. I claimed the enemy aircraft to be damaged, as I did not actually see it fall to the ground. David, our flight engineer, later my brother-in-law, claimed that he definitely saw the Me 410 fall away to earth. Just before this we felt a judder in the aircraft and a few minutes later our engineer noted that the fuel indicator for the port inner tank registered empty. A shell from the enemy fighter's cannon had entered the tank, causing a hole and the fuel to leak out. The miracle was that it did not burst into fire. By this time we had left the target area and were starting our return journey home again across Sweden.

'Discussion then took place on the intercom and estimates were made as to how much fuel we had left and how far we could reach. The progress of the Allies in France was, by now, well advanced and we wondered whether we could fly back, away from the main stream of bombers and alone across enemy territory, in the hope of reaching Allied lines and baling out. It was doubtful whether we would even reach our own lines; it was also more likely that our lone aircraft would be attacked and shot out of the sky. The only reasonable alternative was to make for Sweden and either bale out or land the aircraft. The machine was flying well so it was decided to make for Rinkaby satellite airfield of the Swedish Air Force.

'As we approached the airfield we shot off emergency cartridges from our Very pistol. The airfield, apparently, was not equipped with night flying equipment, so all available cars and lorries were driven on to the runway and we landed by their lights, finishing very close to the boundary fence. We destroyed all our secret radar equipment and one of the lorries with armed guards led

us to the administrative buildings. We were interrogated very briefly and, of course, revealed only our names, ranks and numbers. We were then fed and entertained with beer in the officers' mess. We had a very friendly evening with the officers and were supplied with sleeping accommodation. Next day we were taken for a walk, under armed guard, along one of the snow-covered country roads and were put on the train at the local station. We travelled to Stockholm and on to the office of the Air Attaché at the British Embassy. We were told not to make any attempt to escape, as the Air Attaché would do his very best to get us home. There was nowhere to escape to and the attaché's office would be much speedier. We were then put on a train and transported to Falun for another brief interrogation and a medical examination. I believe arrangements were made for us to cable home so that we could reassure our families that all was well. We were taken by army coach to our "internment camp" (Internezingsager IV Korsnas) where we were to spend our internment. Here the proprietress and her staff gave us a warm welcome. The cook, a plump motherly lady, described herself, in what little English she knew, as our "Swedish mother". They all became our good friends. Our internment camp was a small hotel and we were waited on with good food and comfortable surroundings.

'During my stay at Korsnas there were thirteen British internees. We were the only crew who had been able to land our aircraft; the others had parachuted out, one member being badly burned, while another was the only survivor of his crew. We had nothing to do but enjoy ourselves. It was an enforced holiday. We were allowed into the village and into the town of Falun and were advanced some of our pay by the Swedish Army and the Air Attaché's office in Stockholm. We were taught to ski by an instructor from the Swedish Army and we met local people, who were very friendly. Our stay was all too short, however. The Air Attaché, true to his word, made arrangements for our pilot, navigator, mid-upper gunner and myself to be flown home on 27 February 1945, as special envoys aboard a Dakota of BEA. Senior officials debriefed us at the Air Ministry on our return to London.'

In Cockfosters, north London, Mr and Mrs Roots awaited the return of their son. The post office had looked up the Roots's telephone number to get the telegram from Stockholm to them more swiftly. The girl who dictated the telegram said, 'Is it the good news we thought?' and they heard her call to other girls – 'It is – it is!'

At the Air Ministry a pleasant WAAF Corporal said, 'I wish we had thousands more cases as happy as this.'

They made them feel comfortable and easy in little rooms with deep chairs. They sent an officer with a file of signals. Yes, there were ways to write, wire and send parcels. So who cared about an old, battered treasure of a car standing idle on an airfield? The Roots could only wish that other parents might have the same comforting news. But how did it happen that days after all this the airfield chaplain sent a long, hand-written letter of consolation, encouragement and hope in their grief and anxiety? Did no one tell the padre anything but the bad news?

By the beginning of 1945 few German cities had escaped heavy bombing. Those who tried to escape the constant bombing and the moraines of rubble, which reached up to the first floors of their houses, fled from the devastated cities and were now living in caves in the countryside. The white faces of the underground cavern dwellers looked like 'the faces of fish coming up to the surface to snatch a breath of air'.[40] Those who existed among the debris of the devastated cities refused to give in to the effect of the catastrophes insidiously creeping up on them and some tried to maintain a social life as if nothing had happened. In one German city a woman cleaned the windows of a building 'that stood alone and undamaged in the middle of the desert of ruins'. Onlookers thought she was a madwoman and they felt the same when they saw children tidying and raking a front garden.[41] Trams would stop in the middle of nowhere and people would emerge suddenly 'as if they had sprung from the grey scree'. In suburbs that had not suffered at all Germans were sitting out on their balconies drinking coffee. 'It was like watching a film; it was downright impossible', said one diarist. 'Over Germany destruction thickens' wrote another observer, adding that 'rats had grown fat on corpses housed in the rubble of our cities.' After the destruction of Halberstadt Frau Schrader, who was employed at a local cinema, got to work with a shovel commandeered from the air-raid wardens immediately after the bombs fell, hoping 'to clear the rubble away before the two o'clock matinee'. Down in the cellar, where she found various cooked body parts, she tidied up by dumping them in the washhouse boiler for the time being. Twenty years earlier Fritz Lang's 1924 film *Kriemhilds Rache* ['Kriemhild's Revenge'] in which a nation's entire armed forces move forward almost deliberately into the jaws of destruction, finally going up in flames in a stupendous pyromaniacal spectacle, was shown in cinemas in Germany. It clearly anticipated the rhetoric of the Thousand Year *Reich*'s 'final battle'.

Lying in bed at night in their home at Moulton Washway in Lincolnshire, Louie Chapman and her mother Eva listened in the darkness to the sounds of Lancaster bombers taking off for another raid deep into Germany. Louie said to herself 'That's my brother going over'. 'Jimmy' Chapman was 23, two years older than Louie was. She knew him as an ordinary land worker who had never even gone to grammar school but she was understandably proud of her wireless operator-air gunner brother. The *London Gazette* for 9 May 1944 announced that he had been awarded the CGM for his actions on the 30/31 March raid on Nuremberg. It went on to mention that Chapman had been wounded in the back, neck and head but bravely remained at his post obtaining fixes, which were of inestimable value in establishing the aircraft's position at various stages of the return flight. After recovering from his wounds Jimmy Chapman had returned to operations with 61 Squadron at Skellingthorpe where he flew ops alongside 35 year old Flight Sergeant Arthur Sherriff, the crew's air-gunner who had been awarded the DFM for his actions on the same raid. By the start of 1945 the two brothers-in-arms had survived some of the most dangerous operations of the war. 'Surely' thought Louie, 'the war could not go on for much longer and then Leslie hopefully, would be back home for keeps'.

At Skellingthorpe on 1 February both the men were on the Battle Order for the 5 Group raid on Siegen, which was to be visited by 271 Lancasters and 11 Mosquitoes. Leslie Chapman and Arthur Sherriff saw that they were flying with Squadron Leader Hugh Horsley AFC who had baled out over Holland on 24 September and had spent months on the run evading the Germans before the area was liberated by the advancing Allied armies. Sergeant Reg Hoskisson, who had been Horsley's rear-gunner on that raid, had also evaded capture and he now took the same position on board NF912. Sherriff was a replacement for the mid-upper gunner on the crew who was sick. At around 15.15 hours Skellingthorpe reverberated to the sounds of scores of Rolls-Royce Merlins revving up as one by one the Lancasters of 50 and 61 Squadrons began taking-off. As usual a large number of personnel from both squadrons were standing by the flying control caravan at the end of the runway to cheer the crews off. At 15.42 hours Horsley taxied their Lancaster onto the runway, received a green light from the flying control caravan and he turned onto the runway. He opened up the four Merlins and NF912 soon gathered speed, lifting off in a steady climb. When it reached 500 feet some of the onlookers noticed that the propeller on the port outer engine had been feathered. Feathering of the props on the three remaining engines quickly followed! The Lancaster came down in a slow diving turn heading back over the airfield. As it rapidly lost height Horsley just managed to skim over *P Peter,* which was still on its dispersal pan, before making what seemed like a perfect wheels-up landing in the overshoot area at the end of the main runway. It had all happened in less than a minute.

Shortly afterwards the underside of the Lancaster collapsed under the weight of 1,500 gallons of petrol and 13,000lbs of bombs as it skidded along the runway.[42] Within seconds the 4,000lb cookie detonated and, in turn, set off the rest of the bomb load in a blinding flash followed by a loud explosion, which resonated around the airfield. Some of the watching ground staff started to run towards the crash site to see if they could help the crew. When they got there they found a huge crater. The Lancaster had broken up into small pieces of distorted metal scattered over a large area, except for the engines and the rear turret, which was lying on its side a short distance away. The station emergency services arrived at the appalling scene of carnage and destruction to find, to their amazement, that Reg Hoskisson was still alive! As the fireman carefully extracted him from the wreckage, his first concern was for the rest of his crew. He was then taken to hospital suffering from severe shock and a piece of shrapnel embedded in his back. Horsley, Arthur Sherriff and Jimmy Chapman, and the other three men on board perished.

There was one other casualty that resulted from the crash. Jimmy Chapman's grieving mother Eva died the following year.

The early months of 1945 saw a tremendous increase in Bomber Command's operations, both in tempo and number, 40 raids being mounted in February alone.[43]

On 2/3 February Bomber Command mounted raids on Mannheim, Wanne Eickel, Wiesbaden and Karlsruhe by 1,200 aircraft, about 250 being ordered to raid Karlsruhe. Due to adverse weather conditions and extensive *Luftwaffe* night fighter activity near and over the targets, operations were only partially successful. Twenty-one aircraft failed to return, including 11 from the Karlsruhe force and another 13 crashed in liberated French territory.[44] It was a bad night for 189 Squadron, with four aircraft failing to return to Fulbeck, as air gunner Sergeant Ricky Dyson who, on the night of 26/27 November 1944, had suffered such a tragic flying accident, recalls:

'My last memories of Ned Kelly and the boys were at briefing and at the dispersal area before take-off. As fate was to ordain, Frank Cowlishaw, our mid-upper gunner was on the sick list and Frank Fox was destined to fly in his place (the fortunes of war?). We were timed to take-off about 20.00 hours and arrive over the target at 23.20 hours so we had quite a long night ahead of us. We were all in high spirits, laughing and joking with other aircrew and among ourselves. We all must have had our own form of anxiety before a raid – the tenseness and butterflies in the tummy were common to us all I think. Once inside the aeroplane however, this nauseating excitement disappeared, as one became occupied with one's tasks and checks etc. It was a cold February night. It wasn't a bad night as far as visibility was concerned. I made sure that my guns were in the upright position, which they had to be after two accidents earlier on where, in the excitement, the gunners had inadvertently fired their guns and caused havoc on the ground! We had a good take-off. I remember seeing the party on the flare path. As you went down the runway, one bit of fear came and I was very grateful when I heard the air speed being called out, which was just above stalling speed. Over Reading there was a rendezvous, where all the bombers came into one stream. As part of the stream, there was safety in numbers and you felt quite comfortable. France was occupied by friendly forces so it wasn't until you reached Germany that you were over enemy territory. You were then conscious of the flak and possibility of fighters and so you were very much alert and you'd already tested your guns over the Channel to make sure all were firing OK and that your gun sight was in good working order. Then it was just a matter of keeping a cool head and searching and keeping in touch with your mid-upper gunner.

'The outward leg was uneventful. I tested my guns over the Channel as usual and received confirmation from Frank Fox that he too had done the same (chat over the intercom was kept to a minimum and was mostly of a technical nature). The weather was cold and clear when we joined the main bomber stream but over France we did encounter icing-up conditions and an electrical storm, with cloud formations thickening from above. When we reached Germany we were flying at 17,000 to 18,000 feet. To our dismay on reaching Karlsruhe we encountered solid cloud beneath us at about 16,000 feet obscuring the target. To make matters worse we became "sandwiched" since the cloud above had thinned considerably, allowing the moon to shine through. These conditions certainly assisted the enemy night fighters and greatly added to the difficulties of the bomber force.

'We were on time as we neared the target area but owing to the weather conditions we had to bomb on the coloured sky markers, which together with chandelier flares glowed through the cloud. These had been dropped by the Pathfinder Force giving a diffused illumination to the whole target area. Whether we dropped our bombs or not I wasn't sure because there was a blinding flash and a terrific explosion and what happened just before was a bit of a blur! The whole of my body seemed to be propelled upwards and yet at the same time my head and neck felt as though they were being forced down below my shoulders and into my stomach. Then I must have passed out! The next thing I remembered was somersaulting earthwards in mid-air. I had been blown out by the force of the explosion with my rear turret being blown to pieces around me! (Yet another miracle it seemed!) My six friends and companions all died in that tragic moment in time as Lancaster PB840/K plunged earthwards in a ball of flame. I doubt whether the exact cause of the explosion will ever be known. We either fell victim to an enemy night fighter, or, as I believe, we may have collided with another Lancaster, which could have been taking avoiding action away from fighters or searchlights. This was not uncommon and was rated a calculated risk as the bomber stream narrowed at varying heights to converge on the Aiming Points. Tragically, whatever the cause the terrible result remains the same.

'To return to my sudden and dramatic departure from the rear turret. The realization that I was still alive came as a great relief but, as I recovered my senses, I was also aware, with a feeling of deep anxiety, all was not yet over, since I was still somersaulting and falling towards the ground! In a fearful panic I reached for my parachute pack, which thankfully was still there and dangling behind me (it was a seat type pack that was a normal issue to pilots and also to rear-gunners). I felt for the D-ring release on my harness and pulled until the ring and wire attachment came free in my hand. I prayed that the pack itself was not burnt or damaged in some way and for an awful moment I thought that it wasn't going to open! Then I felt a terrific jerk. I looked up and with great relief saw the huge canopy filling with air. My brain was by now quite clear and I was soon in an upright position with my hands grasping the parachute guide lines with which I was able to steer. The full horror of what had happened now came over me, as I saw what appeared to be a huge box-like inferno falling like a stone in the dark part of the sky. I could see bits and pieces falling from it, burning and aflame as they fell. With horror I realized that I was witnessing the death of some, if not all of my friends with whom I had

been joking a few hours before. Their average age was only 22 years and, like so many, were so young to die during those terrible years of war.

'As the exploding and flaming mass disappeared into the cloud below, the despair for my friends turned to thoughts of my own self-preservation, as I realized I was being blown back to the target area. I quickly pulled on the chute guide lines, praying I would be able to avoid being caught in the many searchlights with their beams weaving menacingly about the sky. However, I was soon out of range and gazed, fascinated, at the sight below and to my left. Karlsruhe it seemed was alight from stem to stern. It was like looking down on a carpet of gold with the chandelier flares suspended above, illuminating rivers of red from bursting incendiaries. The green sky markers winked intermittently with yellow and black smoke billowing skywards. Streams of multi-coloured tracer shells were bursting from the anti-aircraft guns and there was a series of explosions as sticks of high explosive bombs burst, sending red and yellow flames high into the air. It was an awesome spectacle of great beauty, which I had seen many times before from the rear turret of a Lancaster bomber on its return leg to England.

'Whilst watching this terrible and beautiful scene, my attention was drawn to my feet. They were freezing cold! I looked down to discover I had neither boots nor socks (they had, I think, been sucked off by the blast as *K-King* exploded). Thoughts now crowded in on me and with apprehension I wondered whether I had any injuries? Was my face burnt? Were my legs and feet OK? I felt and tasted blood but as I felt around my eyes, nose, ears etc. all seemed OK. I entered broken cloud and was more conscious of my rate of descent and the exhilarating sensation, as I swayed and floated at the end of a parachute. Through the gap in the cloud I glimpsed woods and snow-covered fields and the target area was now a diffused red glow. I pulled on the parachute guide lines and steered myself away from the woods and prayed that when the time came I would make a safe landing. I could faintly see what I thought to be a cluster of buildings and steered to avoid them also. I was just beginning to enjoy myself when I realized that the fields were getting a lot closer. Then suddenly, without warning, the ground seemed to rush up to meet me and I landed with a bump in a snow covered field. Directly my feet touched the ground, I tried to relax, allowing my legs and body to go limp as I rolled over. I was dragged a short distance across the field as the parachute canopy collapsed. On recovering my breath, I remembered the release button on my harness. I banged it hard and the harness fell away. I had landed safely with no bones broken!

'As quickly as I could I gathered up the parachute canopy and stumbled to a wooded spinney nearby. After tearing up some of the silk to bind my feet, which were bruised and freezing from the cold, I buried the remainder beneath a pile of leaves and then tried to take stock of the situation. My wrist watch was missing but I estimated the time to be about 01.00 hours. I felt scared, cold and miserable, very much alone and I wondered again about the fate of the rest of the crew. I thanked God for my own survival. My only injuries were slight burns to my hands and face, a few cuts and bruises, very cold feet and scorched hair. As I realized how lucky I had been I became aware that the yellow flying suit I was wearing was conspicuous so reluctantly, I took it off and hid it beneath another pile of leaves. I thought about escaping and checking I still had my escape pack containing a compass, silk map, chocolate and foreign money etc., I wondered how far I was from the French border. Without my flying suit I was feeling the cold and became increasingly concerned regarding the state of my feet and the danger of frost-bite. I thought that the best thing was to go in search of some boots or socks while it was still dark. Rightly or wrongly, I left the comparative shelter of the wooded spinney, with the hope of finding some in a barn or a shed. However, by this time I must have been suffering from delayed shock. I wandered across a field, ankle and sometimes knee deep in mud, hearing dogs barking and whistles blowing in the distance. I guessed they were search parties out looking for survivors. I must have wandered about for some time, as it was beginning to get light when I came across a shed in a farm-yard. While I was searching for footwear I so urgently needed, the door burst open and I was confronted by a uniformed German soldier. And so it was; with his rifle and bayonet pointed at me, I reluctantly became his prisoner.'[45]

On 7/8 February main force targets included strong German defence positions at Goch and Kleve, which had to be smashed before an attack by the British XXX Corps across the German frontier near the Reichswald. The Dortmund-Ems Canal was also targeted and Mosquito bombers carried out raids on Magdeburg, Mainz and five other targets. On 8/9 February Bomber Command returned to attacks on synthetic oil plants when Pölitz was bombed by 475 Lancasters and seven Mosquitoes. Twelve Lancasters failed to return and a 625 Squadron Lancaster returned to Kelstern with part of a Halifax tailplane wrapped around its own tail, following a collision over the Danish coast on the return.[46] Wanne-Eickel and Krefeld were also attacked. There followed a series of minor operations involving Mosquito bombers mainly while the main force was grounded, 9-12/13 February.

Bomber Command though was merely building up for an operation that has since gone down in history as one of the most controversial bombing raids of the war.

Notes

1. 5 Group lost 15 Lancasters on the Königsberg raid. Bomber Command estimated that 41 per cent of all housing and 20 per cent of all the industry in Königsberg was destroyed. At Stettin 1,569 houses and 32 industrial premises were destroyed and 565 houses and 23 industrial premises were damaged. Over 1,000 people were killed and 1,034 people injured.
2. Bomber Command ORS 'K' Report. The raid was successful, the Lancasters hitting parts of the port, which had escaped damage in previous attacks.
3. Klaus Schmidt, *Die Brandnacht* in *On The Natural History of Destruction* by W. G. Sebald.
4. *Thundering Through the Clear Air: No. 61 (Lincoln Imp) Squadron At War* by Derek Brammer (Tucann Books, 1997).
5. 5/6 October, when 531 Lancasters and 20 Mosquitoes were dispatched.
6. The attack by 246 Lancasters on Bremen was the last of 32 major raids on this city during the war and five Lancasters were lost. Five hundred and twenty-three aircraft, 247 of them Lancasters, attacked Dortmund. Five aircraft, including two Lancasters were lost.
7. *At First Sight; A Factual and anecdotal account of No.627 Squadron RAF.* Researched and compiled by Alan B. Webb, 1991. Sergeant (later Pilot Officer) Bill Burke flew his last operation in the early hours of 4 January 1945 on the Germans holding out in Royan, which was marked by 627 Squadron. As he remembered it, 'the beleaguered garrison had irritated the local populace by venturing out to rustle cattle. If that was so, then a visit by 5 Group's 200–250 bombers was a heavy price to pay for their fillet steak!'
8. In summer 1943 Döring had completed 348 operational sorties as a bomber pilot in KG 53 and KG 55, seeing action during the Battles of France and Britain. In the Russian campaign he destroyed 10 aircraft in the air (including three 4-engined TB-3 bombers over Stalingrad one night) flying a He 111 fitted with extra machine guns. He claimed a further eight aircraft destroyed as a *Wilde Sau* pilot in JG 300 and three more night victories in NJG 2 and NJG 3.
9. One Lancaster failed to return from Brunswick.
10. Six Lancasters failed to return, five of which, were shot down by *Zahme Sau Nachtjäger*. Larry Melling was awarded the DFC on 27 March and he was commissioned on 1 November. He flew his 61st and final op on 25 April 1945. His navigator, bomb-aimer and W/Op were also awarded the DFC and his two gunners and flight engineer, the DFM.
11. *Lancaster-The Story Of A Famous Bomber* by Bruce Robertson (Harleyford Publications Ltd, 1964).
12. Five hundred and sixty-one Lancasters, 463 Halifaxes and 31 Mosquitoes.

13. On 7/8 October, in riposte to the enemy R/T communications used in its *Zahme Sau* operations, Lancasters of 101 Squadron, fitted with *Airborne Cigar* (*ABC*) carried out jamming of the enemy R/T frequencies. These Lancasters also carried a specially trained German-speaking operator. This night the order '*All butterflies go home*' was broadcast on the German night fighter frequency, resulting in many German night fighter pilots returning to their airfields. The most outstanding '*Window*' success of the month was perhaps on 14/15th when 1,013 heavies went to Duisburg and 200 to Brunswick. It was anticipated that the Duisburg raid, by low approach, radar silence and shallow penetration, would get through with little trouble but that the Brunswick force might be strongly opposed. A '*Window*' Force was therefore routed to break off from the Brunswick route and strike at Mannheim. This had success beyond all expectations, for the Brunswick attack was almost ignored because the Mannheim area was anticipated as the main target. Just one bomber from the Brunswick force was lost: Lancaster ME595 of 61 Squadron was shot down by flak at Rieseberg, 6 km NW of Köningsbuttel; there were no claims by *Nachtjäger*. October also saw the introduction of *Dina*; the jammer used against FuG 220 *Lichtenstein SN-2*. *Dina* was installed in the *Jostle*-fitted Fortresses of 214 Squadron. This was frequently used in the '*Window*' force, as were *Jostle*, H₂S and *Carpet*, thereby more effectively giving the simulation of a bombing force. A further realistic effect, also born in October, was created through the cooperation of *PFF*, which, on several occasions *Oboe*-marked and bombed the *Spoof* target. (The '*Window*' Force itself had not yet arrived at the bomb-carrying stage.) The noise of *Oboe*, which had until that time always preceded real attacks only, was thought to give still more confusion to the German controller.

14. Eleven Halifaxes and eight Lancasters failed to return, four of these aircraft crashing behind Allied lines in France and Belgium.

15. Most of the night's bomber losses were due to *Nachtjagd* fighters. Hauptmann Heinz Rökker of I./NJG 2 was credited with two Lancasters and two Halifaxes and Hauptmann Hans-Heinz Augenstein of IV./NJG 1, three Lancasters. Oberleutnant Erich Jung of 6./NJG 2 claimed two Lancasters shot down north of Essen.

16. Mouritz and his crew were later allocated a new QR-M. He recalled: 'What a difference it was to fly. When doing our first air test with no bombs and limited fuel, I opened the throttle on take-off and we were flung back in our seats. She behaved like a sports car. We had now completed 12 trips and flew the new *Mickey* (although no art was ever painted on the nose) to the end of our tour except for a few weeks in January and February when she was being repaired after getting shot up and having a dicey landing.'

17. Fries and his *Bordfunker* Feldwebel Fred Staffa had become a very experienced night fighting team. They were credited with 10 confirmed night kills August 1943-April 1944, plus two unconfirmed *Abschüsse* in daylight, a B-17 on 17 August and a P-47 on 14 October 1943. On 9 July 1944 they had been posted to 2./NJG 1 at Venlo airfield.

18. When 115 Squadron in 4 Group and 38 Lancaster IIs in 6 Group RCAF carried the device. Of the 38 Lancaster IIs, 15 attacked according to plan, 16 having equipment failures. More than half the bombs dropped by G-H landed within half a mile of the aiming point.

19. The soldiers meekly shouldered arms and the prisoners were moved back down the street silently giving thanks to the one civilian in the vengeful city who had shown them mercy. Allen Clifford recalls a small cold dark room where he spent 10 days solitary confinement at the *Dulag Luft* Interrogation Centre near Frankfurt. Some men he met later had rooms with a little high window that let in light, but Clifford's was windowless, and just high enough to stand up in, but not long enough to lie down. He had to sit on a bare stone floor, getting disorientated because he could not see or feel anything. Clifford had no bed, no blanket; nothing except a tiny electric element heater screwed to the wall. He got down on the ground and squinted up at the red wire when it was occasionally switched on to make sure he was not blind. Once when he was to be interrogated the door of his cell was opened at the same time as the one opposite. Standing there blinking was a gunner, a taciturn New Zealand farmer called Parky Parkinson. Allen had been crewed up with him on Hampdens in Canada. He had time only to exclaim, 'Bugger me' before they were taken in opposite directions. Clifford did not see him again. He and Stan Lee ended up at *Stalag IIIA* at Luckenwalde near Potsdam.

20. On 11 September 38 Lancasters of 9 and 617 Squadrons, accompanied by a PR.XVI Mosquito to provide up-to-date target information and weather reports, flew to their forward base at Yagodnik on an island in the Dvina River near Archangel, in northern Russia. One Lancaster returned en route and six others fell victim to bad weather and crash-landed in the Soviet Union. On 15 September the attack, by 28 Lancasters, 20 of which were carrying *Tallboys* and 6 or 7 others, twelve 500lb 'Johnny Walker' oscillating mines, went ahead and considerable damage was caused to the battleship. Two days later, returning to Lossiemouth, one of the Lancasters crashed in Norway with the loss of all 11 men on board. Subsequent PR revealed that although badly damaged, the *Tirpitz* was still afloat (albeit beyond practical repair, although this was not known at the time). On 17 October a detachment of four PR Mosquitoes of 540 Squadron was dispatched to Dyce to keep watch on *Tirpitz*. Information from the Norwegian resistance stated that the ship had left Kaa Fjord on its way south for Tromsö Fjord, where it was to be used as a heavy artillery battery. On 29 October 37 Lancasters (18 Lancasters each from 9 and 617 Squadrons plus the photographic aircraft from 463 Squadron) took off from Lossiemouth and attacked the *Tirpitz* in Tromsö Fjord. Some 32 Lancasters dropped *Tallboy* bombs on estimated position of the capital ship (30 seconds before the attack a bank of cloud came in to cover the ship). Though no direct hits were achieved a *Tallboy* near-miss by the stern caused considerable damage, distorting the propeller shaft and rudder, which flooded the bilges over a 100 foot length of the ship's port side. The damage meant that the *Tirpitz* was no longer able to steam under her own power. One of 617 Squadron's Lancasters, which was damaged by flak, crash-landed in Sweden and the crew was later returned to Britain. By the time that the attack was over, various decoded *Ultra* code-cipher intercepts revealed that the *Tirpitz* was no longer seaworthy but the War Cabinet decided that the battleship must be sunk.

21. *Royal Australian Air Force Overseas* (Eyre & Spottiswoode, London, 1946). At least two *Tallboys* hit the ship, which capsized to remain bottom upwards. The crew of the *Tirpitz* had been reduced from a complement of 2,000 to about 1,600,

Chapter 11 (*cont.*): 'Round the Clock'

On 16 November 1944 in support of a US Army offensive, 1,880 RAF Bomber Command 'heavies' attacked the supposedly fortified towns of Duren, Julich and Heinsburg ahead of the advance.

Lancaster B.I PD228 G1-A of 622 Squadron, flown by Squadron Leader R. G. Allen and crew 8,500 feet over Heinsburg on 16 November 1944. (*IWM*)

(*Left*) *Leutnant* Gustav Mohr a *Wild Boar* Bf 109 pilot claimed five night *Abschüsse* serving with 2./NJG 1 from 1 September to December 1944. Whilst shootin[g] his 5th victim (a Lancaster on 12/13 December 1944) he was injured by return fire and was forced to bale out of his Bf 109G-6, which effectively ended his ca[reer] the *Nachtjagd*. (*Steve Hall via John Foreman*).

(*Right*) Lancaster III ND521 UL-L[2] of 576 Squadron after a starboard undercarriage collapse on 18 November 1944. The aircraft was soon repaired and con[tinued] operations with 57 Squadron.

Ground crew installing a propeller unit on SE-L of 431 'Iroquois' Squadron at Croft. Halifaxes were replaced by Canadian-built Lancasters on the squadron [on] 10 October 1944.

Flying Officer Bob Purves (left) usual pilot of P4-V
Vicious Virgin/Baby, 'B' Flight, 153 Squadron,
Squadron Leader McLaughlin and Wing Commander
F. S. Powley DFC AFC, the CO. Powley was a
Canadian from Kelowna in British Columbia who had
joined the pre-war regular air force on a short service
commision in 1936. On the night of 4/5 April 1945 he
and Squadron Leader Gee's usual crew of RA544
P4-U perished on a mine laying sortie in the Kattegat.
Powley and Flight Lieutenant A. J. Winder's crew
were each victims of *Major* Werner Husemann a
thirty-two *Abschüsse* ace of I./NJG 3.

The Mittelland Canal after a raid by 138 Lancasters
on 21/22 November 1944, which completely
demolished the aqueduct over the River Glane and
breached the embankments on both sides and left
30 miles of canal, dry. On 1/2 January 1945 152
Lancasters and five Mosquitoes of 5 Group carried
out an accurate attack on the Gravenhorst section of
the canal. Half a mile of banks were pitted with bomb
craters and some parts were breached. No aircraft
were lost.

The ground crew of Lancaster III ND458 '*Able Mabel*' of 100 Squadron who had serviced the aircraft since arrival on the squadron congratulate Canadian pilot Flight Lieutenant John 'Jack' D. Playford DFC RCAF who flew the aircraft on twenty-six ops including its 100th on 1 February 1945. Sergeant W. Hearn, who was from West Wickham, shakes hands with Playford while Corporal R. T. Withey, from Henley and LACs J. E. Robinson, from Solihull, J. Hales, Tottenham, and J. Cowls, Penzance, look on. *Able Mabel* which has 119 ops on the bomb log was destined to complete 134 ops, the 127th and last operational raid being 25 April to Berchtesgaden, an *Exodus* trip on 27 April and six *Manna* sorties. ND644 HW-N '*N-Nan*' completed 112 sorties on the squadron before it was lost on 16/17 March 1945.

Flight Sergeant Jimmy Chapman CGM of 61 Squadron who was killed when his Lancaster crashed on take off from Skellingthorpe on 1 February 1945. (*Derek Patfield*)

Flight Sergeant Arthur 'Dep' Sherriff DFM (35) air gunner, of 61 Squadron who was killed when his Lancaster crashed on take off from Skellingthorpe on 1 February 1945.

Chapter 12: All Clap Hands for the Walking Dead

Lancaster B.I RF160 QR-E pictured here with Flying Officer Ray Lushey and crew was delivered to 61 Squadron at Skellingthorpe in March 1945.

Wing Commander David M. Balme DSO DFC who took command of 227 Squadron in March 1945. Balme had flown a tour with 207 Squadron whom he joined as a Flying Officer in March 1943, reaching the rank of Squadron Leader ten months later. After the war he became a professor.

(*Left*) Lancaster B.I PD336 WP-P of 90 Squadron, blows up after taking a direct hit at 23,000 feet over Wesel on 19 February 1945 killing the CO, Wing Com. P. F. Dunham DFC, Flying Officer T. Metcalfe RCAF, Flying Officer H. F. J. Carlton, Sergeant L. A. Page, Sergeant J. E. Bozeat, Pilot Officer F. A. Creswell Sergeant J. E. Bennett. PD336 came down in the Rhine near Xanten and the bodies of the crew were recovered at nearby Bislicker. Dunham had only recently command of 90 Squadron following the death on 2/3 February of Wing Commander W. G. Bannister who died when his Lancaster I HK610 was involved in a collision with PD336 which was flown by Flying officer C. W. R. Harries, 33 minutes after take off from Tuddenham at the start of the operation to Wiesbaden Bannister was a pre-war athlete who had represented Great Britain in the 1936 Olympic Games in Berlin. HK610 crashed at Hengrave near Bury St Edmunds.

(*Right*) Wing Commander W. A. 'Bill' Forbes, CO of 463 Squadron RAAF from June 1944 until his death in action on 21/22 February 1945 when he and his c were one of nine Lancasters that failed to return from the operation to the Mittelland Canal. Forbes and two of his crew were killed and five were taken prisone other Lancasters crashed in France and Holland.

Flight Sergeant F. Wadge DFM and his crew of *J-Jig* in 100 Squadron who returned from Stuttgart on 20/21 February 1945 with about six feet of the port wing sliced off after a collision with a German night fighter. Four nights later, on 24/25 February on the operation to Schweinfurt, everyone in this photo except the wounded member of the crew, were killed. Wadge took off from Waltham (Grimsby) in Lancaster III ND593 HW-B at 1830 hours but at 211 hours they returned overhead their base due to the pilot being taken ill. They were advised to jettison part of their fuel load but at 2145 hours a radio message indicated that they were in trouble and an order to jettison the bombs was transmitted to the crew. Wadge turned the Lancaster out to sea and disappaeared without trace.

dwebel Helmut Bunje, *Flugzeugführer*, 4./NJG 6 who shot down three Lancasters on the night of 23/24 February 1945 on the Pforzheim raid. Bunje survived
nd he scored twelve *Abschüsse* in 4./NJG 6. *(Helmut Bunje)*

ancaster B.I NG358 LS-H of 15 Squadron in 1945. The two yellow bars on the fins show that this aircraft is a *G-H* leader and the bulge beneath the fuelage
ns the scanner for the H_2S airborne radar transmitter. The clover shaped marking in front of the mid-upper turret is a gas detection panel designed to change
the presence of toxic gas. *(IWM)*

Cologne under attack on 2 March 1945 when two raids were mounted against the city, the first by 703 aircraft including 376 Lancasters and the second by 155 Lancasters of 3 Group. In the second raid however, only fifteen Lancasters bombed because the G-H station in England was not functioning correctly. The main raid was highly destructive with the Pathfinders marking in clear weather conditions. Between 11 May 1940 and 31 May 1942 RAF heavy bombers attacked Cologne on no less than 144 occasions. The 2 March 1945 raid was the last on Cologne, which was captured by American troops four days later. Only the blackened 13th century Gothic cathedral (its towers were not built until the 19th century) is recognizable. *(via 'Pat' Patfield)*

Lancaster III PA995/BQ:V *The Vulture Strikes* was the third Lancaster of 550 Squadron to complete 100 raids, reaching the century on 5/6 March 1945 with Flying Officer George Blackler DFC and crew. Blackler finished his own tour on this night when the target was Chemnitz. All those in the squadron associated with this aircraft posed for a commemorative picture although the bomb log only has ninety-eight bombs. Included are the CO, Wing Commander J. C. MacWatters DFC, two WAAFs, the padre and the inevitable dog mascot. George Blackler, who flew Victor on twenty-seven ops, is in the cockpit. *The Vulture Strikes* was one of three squadron Lancasters that failed to return from the next operation, when Flying Officer C. J. Jones RCAF and crew were lost on the operation to Dessau on 7/8 March. Jones and two fellow Canadian crewmen died. (*IWM*)

On 14 March 1945 thirty-two Lanc and one Mosquito of 5 Group with *Oboe* Mosquitoes of 8 Group attack Bielefeld and Arnsberg railway viad Germany. Twenty-eight Lancasters dropped 12,000lb 'Tallboy' bombs 617 Squadron Lancaster of Squadr Leader C. C. Calder dropped the fi 22,000lb 'Grand Slam' bomb, at B The Arnsberg viaduct, 9 Squadron' was later found to be undamaged b misses at Bielefeld created an earth effect which caused 100 yards of th viaduct to collapse, as this photo by Lockheed F-5 Lightning of the US Force shows.

Officer Les Sutton and his crew of Lancaster *K-King* of 514 Squadron at Waterbeach. L–R: John Britain, Alf McBurrugh, engineer; WOp; Bob Tores, rear Les Sutton, pilot; Shorty Evers, mid-upper gunner; Joe Speare, bomb aimer; Ray Hilchey, navigator. (*Les Sutton*)

Officer Les Sutton and crew of 514 Squadron perched on top of Lancaster *K-King* at Waterbeach. L–R: Shorty Evers, mid-upper gunner; Alf McBurrugh, ; Ray Hilchey, navigator; Joe Speare, bomb aimer; Bob Tores, rear gunner; John Britain, WOp; Les Sutton, pilot. (*Les Sutton*)

On 21 March 1945 the Arbergen railway bridge over the River Weser was attacked by twenty Lancasters of 617 Squadron who dropped 'Ten Ton Bombs' on the structure and damaged two piers of the bridge. One Lancaster was lost. In the photograph is Lancaster Mk.I Special PB996/YZ-C minus nose or dorsal turret, flown by Squadron Leader C. C. Calder.

Lancaster X KB832 WL-F of 434 'Bluenose' Squadron RCAF blows up shortly after take off from Croft on 22 March 1945 for the daylight operation to Hildesheim. Flying Officer Horace Payne RCAF took off at 1055 hours but the Lancaster was caught by a sudden blast of wind, which took the bomber onto the grass. Payne tried to bring the aircraft back onto the runway but he over corrected and he then closed the throttles but he was unable to avoid racing across the airfield. A tyre burst and a collision occurred involving Lancaster X KB811 SE-T of 431 'Iroquois' Squadron RCAF before KB832 came to a halt near East Vince Moor farm. A fire started in the port engine and this spread rapidly. The crew managed to get clear and a general evacuation order was broadcast. At 1127 hours the bomb load exploded and the force of the blast removed the roof of the farmhouse and set fire to hay and nearby buildings. Incredibly, no one was injured but it was late afternoon before the airfield was declared fit for use. (George Kercher)

Dortmund (Harpenerwcg) oil plant from 19,000 feet on 24 March 1945 when 173 Lancasters and twelve Mosquitoes of 1, 6 and 8 Groups attacked this plant and the Mathias Stinnes plant at Bottrop. Three Lancasters were lost on the Dortmund raid.

A 22,000lb 'Grand Slam' loaded on Lancaster B.1 Special PD113/YZ-T of 617 Squadron at Woodhall Spa prior to the raid by twenty Lancasters on the U-boat shelter at the Valentin submarine works at Farge on the River Weser north of Bremen on 27 March 1945. The crew are Flying Officer E. W. Weaver, air bomber; Flying Officer R. P. Barry, rear gunner; Flight Lieutenant J. L. Sayer DFC, pilot; Flying Officer V. L. Johnson, flight engineer and Flying Officer F. E. Wittmer, navigator. The U-boat shelter was a huge stucture with a reinforced concerete roof 23 feet thick and was almost ready for use when 617 Squadron dropped twelve of the 22,000lb bombs, two of which penetrated the roof, bringing down thousands of tons of concretre rubble and rendering the shelter unusable. No aircraft were lost in the attack on Farge or on the raid on an oil-storage depot by ninety-five Lancasters of 5 Group. Lancasters dropped a total of forty-one 'Grand Slam' bombs operationally. (IWM)

Heligoland pictured from 17,000 feet on 18 April 1945 when 969 aircraft, 617 of them Lancasters, attacked the naval base, the airfield and the town on this small island. The bombing was accurate and the target areas were turned almost into crater-pitted moonscapes.

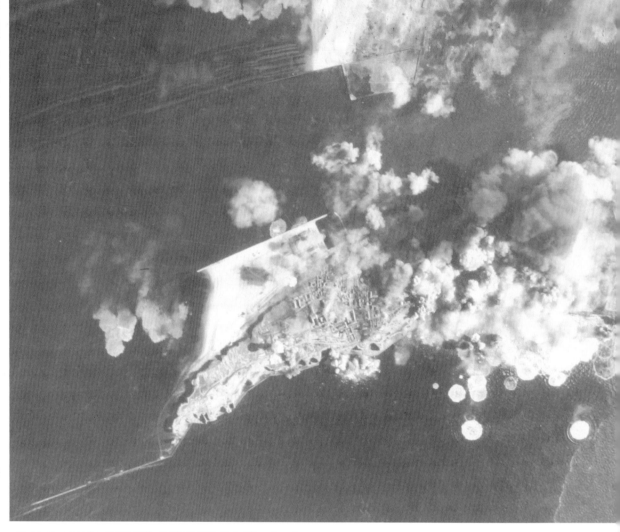

Lancasters en route over the Alps to Berchtesgaden on 25 April 1945. Hitler's home, referred to as the 'Chalet' by the RAF, was the target for 359 Lancaster heavy bombers and fourteen *Oboe* Mosquito and twenty-four Lancaster marker aircraft. Included in the mighty force were thirty-three Lancasters of 9 Squadron and 617 the 'Dam Busters', each carrying a 12,000lb *Tallboy* bomb.

Berchtesgaden from 18,000 feet on 25 April 1945. Those who bombed the 'Chalet' mostly missed. A mountain peak between the *Oboe* ground station and the aircraft had blocked out the bomb release signal. Since *Oboe* signals went line of sight and did not follow the curvature of the earth, the further the target, the higher one needed to be and the *Oboe* Mosquitoes flew at 36,000 feet because of the Alps. Crews heard the first two dots of the release signal and then nothing more. They were unable to drop and brought the markers back.

...npty ruins of Hamburg in May ...ltogether, Lancasters dropped ...,612 tons of bombs in 156,000 ...ties in the Second World War.
(IWM)

The crew of 'V for Victory' found their aircraft appropriately lettered for VE-Day in May 1945. They are reading the surrender news on an airfield near Rheim L–R: Flight Lieutenant M. F. Colvin (RAF), Flight Sergeant G. C. Prunster, of Geraldton, Western Australia; Flight Lieutenant R. W. Markham, of Melbou Flight Sergeant G. R. Goodard, of Perth; Flight Lieutenant R. G. Bligh, of Sydney, and Sergeant A. N. Maxwell (RAF).

er B.I R5868 *S-Sugar* of 467 Squadron RAAF at Kitzingen airfield, Germany on 7 May 1945 for the repatriation of British ex-PoWs during Operation *Exodus*.
which completed her 137th and final operational bombing sortie on 23 April 1945 to Flensburg, is now on permanent display at the RAF Museum, Hendon,
. Lancaster III ED888 PM-M *M for Mother* completed the most number of trips of any Lancaster – 140 in 103 and 576 Squadrons (the latter as PM-M *Mike*
and 103 Squadron again, May 1943 to December 1944 – in Bomber Command. (*IWM*)

PoWs wait to board Lancaster I ME455 LS-O of 15 Squadron for the flight home during Operation *Exodus*. Mildenhall's Lancasters, each carrying twenty-four
rried them home from Juvincourt near Rheims to Westcott and Wing between 10 May and 30 June 1945. (*via Harry Holmes*)

Ex-British PoWs file past Lancaster III PB935 F2-Z of 635 Squadron at Lübeck on 11 May 1945 during Operation *Exodus*. In the distance is a Gloster Meteor jet fighter. (*IWM*)

During Operation *Manna* 29 April to 7 May 1945 Lancasters flew 2,835 food sorties and PFF Mosquitoes made 124 sorties to 'mark' the dropping zones and Bomber Command delivered 6,672 tons of food to the starving Dutch people. (*IWM*)

most of whom were engine room personnel, after the second attack. Around 900 men were killed, drowned or suffocated, having been trapped on board in watertight compartments. Only 87 sailors were recovered from the ship by cutting through the double bottom from the outside. One Lancaster, of 9 Squadron, was severely damaged by flak and landed safely in Sweden with its crew unhurt. The Bomber Command ORS Report S.226 of 25 July 1945 said that, 'The bombing accuracy achieved in a series of *Tallboy* operations carried out by 9 and 617 Squadrons during the period December 1944 to March 1945 have been analyzed from plots. No. 9 Squadron are quipped with the Mk.XIV bombsight and 617 with the SABS Mk.IIA and consistently greater accuracy has been achieved by the latter squadron. All bombs falling more than 400 yards from the aiming point have been classified as gross errors. On this basis, one of the 69 bombs plotted for 617 Squadron and five of 50 bombs plotted for 9 Squadron have been counted as gross errors. The random errors of 617 Squadron are smaller than those of 9 Squadron and an overall estimate of the effectiveness of the two forces in achieving a given density at the aiming point is approximately 2:1 in favour of 617 Squadron ... the results of the two squadrons accordingy provide a comparison between the two sights. The proportion of gross errors with the Mk.XIV is greater than that with the SABS Mk IIA, in the order of 2:1 in favour of SABS. It must be pointed out, however, that this is only true in those operations in which the tactical freedom of the Mk.XIV or the necessity for a small and well-defined point of aim for synchronization with the SABS do not confer an advantage on the former sight. For instance, SABS IIA could not be used satisfactorily in a large-scale ground marking attack by night.'

22. *The Battle of Hamburg: Allied Bomber Forces Against A German City in 1943* by Martin Middlebrook (Penguin, 1980).
23. Sebald, op. cit.
24. Bomber Command Quarterly Review' No.11
25. *The Bomber Command War Diaries* by Martin Middlebrook and Chris Everitt (Midland, 1985).
26. Flight Sergeants Probert, McClune and Venning and Sergeant Bayliss all perished on this dreadful night. 'Ricky' Dyson was awarded the George Medal for his attempt to save the lives of the crew and he was presented with the award by King George VI at an investiture at Buckingham Palace when the war had ended.
27. Friedrich Reck, *Tagebuch eines Verzweifelten*.
28. Swales was born in Durban South Africa and he served first in the Army and was with the Eighth Army throughout the North African campaign. He transferred to the South African Air Force in June 1943 and trained as a pilot, being posted to England.
29. Art Green, Flying Officer Ed Dalik, navigator 2, Willie Mood, navigator 1 and Johnny Campbell had returned to Little Staughton before Hough did. Sergeant Denny Naylor, the flight engineer, who had baled out safely never returned to the squadron. Squadron Leader Grillage, who was probably hit by gunfire, as he was in line between the Me 262 and the port outer engine, did not survive.
30. The next day 56 Lancasters of 3 Group and including some 562 and 109 Squadron aircraft, returned to the Eifel and tried to bomb the Schwammenauel dam on the Roer. They were prevented from doing so by cloud cover at the target and only two aircraft bombed. Bombing of the Urft dam on 8 December

by 205 Lancasters of 5 Group, who were escorted by 39 Mustangs and 50 Spitfires of 11 Group, was affected by 9/10ths cloud and no results were seen. A Lancaster of 630 Squadron was lost. On 11 December the raid by 233 Lancasters of 5 Group and five Mosquitoes of 8 Group, who were escorted by 188 fighters, finally achieved hits on the Urft dam but no breach was made. This was despite 35 *Tallboys*, as well as the main force bombs, being aimed at it by 9 and 617 Squadrons. A Lancaster of 57 Squadron was lost. The series of raids did blast 13 feet off the top of the Urft dam but no large breach was ever made and the Germans were able to release large quantities of water whenever they wanted to impede American troop movements further downstream. Air Marshal Harris later commented: 'Many direct hits were in fact scored. This was not sufficient, although photographs showed that the top of the Urft dam was deeply chipped at three points. In one case the chip extended almost down to the water level, which at the time of reconnaissance was 13 feet from the top. The enemy evidently manipulated the water-level so as to avoid erosion of the dam and spillway.'

31. On 18/19 December 308 bombers attacked Danzig (Gdynia), Münster and Nuremberg. In the Gotenhafen and Danzig areas three crews of I./NJG 5 claimed all four Lancasters that failed to return from the raid on Danzig. Bad weather interfered again before operations resumed on 21/22 December when 475 heavies attacked Cologne, Bonn, Pölitz and Schneidemuhl. Three bombers failed to return from the raid on Pölitz. On 22/23 December 166 Lancasters and two Mosquitoes attacked Koblenz without loss while 106 aircraft of 4 Group raided the Bingen marshalling yards on the Rhine 30 miles south-west of Frankfurt. On Christmas Eve, 104 Lancasters of 3 Group bombed Hangelar airfield near Bonn, losing one aircraft. Ninety-seven Lancasters and five Mosquitoes attacked the marshalling yards at Cologne/Nippes. The nights of 25/26–27/28 December were much quieter with no main force operations on the 25/26th because of bad weather. On New Year's Eve 149 Lancasters and 17 Mosquitoes attacked the railway yards at Osterfeld. Three Lancasters failed to return, 2 claimed by Hauptmann Johannes Hager, *Staffelkapitän*, 6./NJG 1 in the Essen area. Twenty-eight Lancasters of 5 Group attacked cruisers in Oslo Fjord. One Lancaster was lost. Sixteen Halifaxes and 10 Lancasters laid mines in the Kattegat and Lancaster (PB894 of 630 Squadron) failed to return, shot down by Hauptmann Eduard Schröder of 3./NJG 3 into the sea. During December *Nachtjagd* flew 1,070 sorties and shot down 66 bombers.

32. On 1 January, 102 Lancasters and two Mosquitoes attacked the Dortmund-Ems Canal near Ladbergen, which the enemy had once more repaired. Two Lancasters were lost. One of them was a 9 Squadron aircraft piloted by Flying Officer R. F. H. Denton, which was hit by flak shortly after bombing and was set on fire. Flight Sergeant George Thompson, the 24 year old Scottish wireless operator, rescued both gunners from their burning turrets but suffered severe burns in doing so. The Lancaster crash-landed at Brussels and Thompson was rushed to hospital but he died three weeks later. The mid-upper gunner, Sergeant E. J. Potts, also died of his burns. Thompson, a former grocer's assistant, who did not become a wireless operator until 1944 and had only been on operations for two months before his death, was awarded a posthumous Victoria Cross for his courage. That night the main force attacked the

Mittelland Canal, rail yards at Vohwinkel and Dortmund. On 2/3 January 514 Lancasters and seven Mosquitoes bombed Nuremberg and 389 aircraft raided Ludwigshafen. Four Lancasters were lost from the Nuremberg force and one Halifax from the Ludwigshafen raid. Hauptmann Kurt-Heinz Weigel of 11./NJG 6 claimed two four-engined bombers west and south-east of Stuttgart for his 2nd and 3rd victories. Hauptmann Martin 'Tino' Becker *Kommandeur,* IV./NJG 6 claimed a Lancaster south of Mannheim, north of Bruchsal, and another Lancaster over Luxembourg for his 44th and 45th victories.

33. *'Musical Parramatta'* was devised for visual ground marking. In the event of the target area being obscured by 10/10ths cloud conditions, a sky marking technique consisting of similar coloured flares attached to parachutes for a slow descent and known as 'Wanganui' was used. Both were reputed to have originated from the choice of the Commanding Officer of 8 Group, AVM Don Bennett. As Parramatta is a place name in Australia and Wanganui a place name in New Zealand it would appear that there is an element of truth in the matter.

34. Tail warning radar (AGLT).

35. Of 645 Lancasters and 9 Mosquitoes dispatched, 11 Lancasters failed to return. Four more crashed in France. Despite the extensive damage sustained in the mid-air collision, ND968/G was subsequently repaired and returned to B-Flight, 460 Squadron RAAF. The aircraft survived the war, finally to be SOC on 4 October 1945. Lancaster I NN766 PM-R of 103 Squadron, which had left Elsham Wolds at 18.23 hours, was most probably the aircraft that collided with *O-Oboe.* The unfortunate aircraft flown by Flying Officer W. J. McArthur RCAF crash-dived into a hill near Hohrodberg (Haut-Rhin) during a snow storm about 23 miles SE of where the collision had taken place. The remains of the seven-man crew were not recovered for more than a week until the snow receded, and they were buried 25 metres from the crash site by a party of local people and a nun. Aircraft and crew were identified by the crew identity discs and parts of the aircraft wreck. After the war the crew of NN766 were reburied in the Münster Communal Cemetery, French Military Plot in a comrades grave, which the French community considered a great honour. At the crash site, a memorial has been placed in commemoration of the crew, six of whom were Canadians.

36. Thirty-one bombers were claimed destroyed by *Nachtjagd.* Hauptmann Hermann Greiner of 11./NJG 1 claimed three Lancasters over Hanover for his 43rd-45th victories. Two Lancasters were lost on a raid on a bottleneck in the German supply system in the Ardennes in a valley at Houffalize in Belgium.

37. The marker, Figgis was captured and taken prisoner and was returned after the end of the war.

38. Four Halifaxes and two Lancasters failed to return from the raid on Hanau and one Lancaster, which failed to return from the raid on Neuss, crashed in Belgium.

39. Frank Mouritz returned to Australia in July with the probability of starting a second tour as part of Tiger Force, the new name of 5 Group, bombing Japan. The Atom Bomb prevented this.

40. Stig Dagerman, *German Autumn,* 1988.

41. Hans Erich Nossack.

42. It was revealed later that the Lancaster was overloaded by 166lb.

43. During January-February 1945 *Nachtjagd* crews flew 1,820 sorties, claiming 302 victories – 117 in January and 185 in February – but *Nachtjagd* lost 94 aircraft and the majority of the crews flying them.

44. *Stab* and I./NJG 6 crews flying Ju 88s claimed nine Lancasters destroyed over and around Karlsruhe.

45. Five Lancasters crashed in the same area around the town of Bruchsal, NE of Karlsruhe on 2/3 February 1945 (three of 189 Squadron – PB848, flown by Flight Lieutenant N. B. Blain, crashed in a wood near Heidelsheim S of Bruchsal. All except rear-gunner KIA. Flight Sergeant Don Clement RCAF had a similar escape to Sergeant Dyson, being blown from his turret by an explosion, which was possibly caused when the Lancaster was hit by flak making a 2nd bomb run over the target with its bomb load still aboard. PB743, flown by Flight Lieutenant J. D. Davies, exploded on its bombing run over Weingarten, SW of Heidelsheim after dropping the 4,000-pounder and part of the load of incendiaries may have been hit by a *Schräge Musik* equipped night fighter. Flight Sergeant Les Cromarty DFM, rear-gunner, on his 2nd tour, was again the sole survivor when he was blown out of his turret and he landed by parachute. ME298/B of 463 Squadron came down at Unterowisheim nearby after being attacked by a night fighter and possibly being hit by flak over Karlsruhe. Flying Officer R. K. Oliver RAAF and four crew KIA. They are buried in the British and Commonwealth war cemetery at Durnbach, as are the six crew of PB840, believed shot down by Oberfeldwebel Heinrich Schmidt of 2./NJG 6. The 5th Lancaster was PB306 of 467 Squadron RAAF (shot down by Hauptmann Gerhard Friedrich at Karlsdorf) piloted by Flight Lieutenant N. S. C. Colley. All eight crew, average age 21, were KIA.

46. Leutnant Herbert Altner of 8./NJG 5 claimed three Lancasters over Stettin.

Chapter 12

All Clap Hands for the Walking Dead

We knew the time on target was between 10 and 10.30pm and joked that we'd catch the Germans just as they were coming out of the pubs. In hindsight I don't feel good about that but for the most part, we didn't think in terms of people being killed but of areas we had to hit. That was how things were in 1945.

Flight Sergeant John Aldridge

Stanley Harrison RAAF pedalled on his bicycle up to 460 Squadron RAAF 'B' Flight office at the front of one of the large hangars at Binbrook. It was the morning of 13 February 1945. The Australian pilot was unaware that it was the 13th of the month and would not worry about it. In any case he was not superstitious, at least not about the date. He could not know that he would be part of the BBC news in the early hours of the following day. But as he rode up from the Officers' Mess he realized that the weather was fine and that meant that they would be operating over Germany that night. Having checked that all his crew were fit for flying at 09.15 he reported this to Squadron Leader Bob Henderson DFC, 'B' Flight Commander. All the aircraft captains, or 'skippers', wcrc sitting around in the Flight Office talking shop or about any interesting happenings, personal or otherwise, in which Bob Henderson joined every now and then when something concerning the Flight, operations, the performance or operation of the aircraft was being discussed. At 10.00 Henderson went to the daily conference in the Squadron Commander's office. The three flight commanders, the navigation, bombing, wireless and gunnery leaders, were all present and while they reported their state of readiness, details of the 'Operations for Tonight' came through from Bomber Command via group and base headquarters. Harrison explains:

'At lunch in the mess Bob Henderson told me that we were flying that night in *J-Johnny* instead of our usual kite *T-Tommy* and that, as briefing was not until later

in the afternoon, we would have time to run-up the engines and check the aircraft. I contacted the crew in the sergeants' mess and told them to be at the locker room at 2 p.m. to take our gear out to the aircraft, to run it up and check it over. There we collected our Mae Wests. Jack Peacock, the wireless operator, took the kit bag of our leather flying helmets, Peter Squires, the flight engineer, took his bag of tools and on the way out to the aircraft we collected the eight .303 Browning machine guns for the turrets.

'After the crew bus had taken us to our aircraft dispersal area on the perimeter of the airfield, Peter and I gave it a thorough check over externally and internally, including starting up the four engines with a complete test in all phases of operation for each. When the starboard outer engine was run up, 'Curly', officially Flight Sergeant Tony Walker, tested his mid-upper gun turret for smooth, efficient rotation, elevation and depression of the guns. He counted into his intercom microphone as he did so, to test that the intercom was OK in all positions of the turret. Maurice Bellis, the bomb-aimer, tested the H_2S radar transmitter, as Max Spence, our navigator, was still at Navigation Section waiting for any "gen" that may have come through concerning times for navigators' briefing, etc. When the port outer engine was being run up, Jock Gilhooly, the rear-gunner, tested his turret in the same way as the mid-upper, while Jack tested the *Gee* radar receiver.

'After a thorough check of the cockpit controls and instruments, compasses, transmitters and intercom at all points, we left the bomb doors open ready for loading from the bomb trolleys and switched off the motors. Leaving our gear in the aircraft we returned to the Flight Office to learn that briefing was at 18.00 with a meal at 17.00 but the navigators' briefing was at 16.45. This was unusual as the navigators were normally briefed after the meal, before the main briefing, so I thought that maybe it was a very long trip, or a very involved route. The fuel load was 2,154 gallons – maximum load.

'While sitting in the ante room of the mess after our meal, a few whispers were going around about our target for tonight. The Russians were pushing westwards in the southern sector of the Eastern Front, so we looked at the map in the newspapers and my tip was Dresden. I mentioned this to one of the navigators and he blurted out, "Who told you?" The cat was out of the bag now but naturally I kept it quiet, sitting there thinking of the route we might fly and the heavily defended areas along the way.

'At about 17.40 I went over to the briefing room and drew the Aids Boxes, for use if we were shot down, and our flying rations. There was the usual moan when we had "Empire" chocolate, as it was the worst grade of chocolate available but it was remarkable how good it would taste after we left the target and settled down to the long tiring trip back. Then we would be trying to stay alert, when a natural winding down from the tension of the bombing run and general fatigue set in. We each received two small three-penny bars of chocolate, half a box of barley sugar sweets, or about six sweets each and two packets of chewing gum. Our Aids Boxes contained concentrated foods, a compass, rubber water bottle, some water purifying tablets and some Benzedrine tablets, which bucked you up if you needed a little extra to make a break for it, etc.

'We emptied our pockets and then put back only handkerchiefs, about £1 in money, an identity card and an Aids Box. The rest of the contents of our pockets – keys, letters, bus tickets and anything else – were placed in the bag that had contained our Aids Boxes with a label for each crewmember. Then all individual bags went into the big crew bag and the intelligence clerks locked this in a safe. This ensured that if we were shot down, there was nothing to tell the Germans where we came from, so they would be unable to identify our Squadron and its location. At least this was the theory. But some of our Squadron who were shot down and interrogated and later escaped back to England, said that the first thing the German interrogator said to them, after hearing that the crashed aircraft had our Squadron letters "AK" on it was, "How is your com-

manding officer, *Hewgie* Edwards VC?" (The Germans never could get their tongues around "Hughie"!)

'Maurie had his target map and we looked at the route on the big map at the front of the Briefing Room and the photos of the target area, its defences and known searchlight areas, as well as the heavily defended areas on or near our route. Times for sunrise, moonrise and moonset, as well as the phases of the moon, were all on the board. So were "phase of attack" times, "H" hour (the actual time of the start of the attack when the first phase commenced dropping their bombs), take-off time, total distance, bomb loads and ETA back at base. On another board was all the signals gen: the master bomber's call sign, together with those of the deputy master bomber, radio link and the VHF radio channel on which to receive them. Shortly before briefing was due to start, Max came in with his navigator's bag crammed full with maps, charts and instruments. In reply to my query of, "What do you think of it Max?" he made the dry wisecrack, "I wish Joe Stalin would get an air force of his own or come and fight on the Western Front if he wants our help like this!"

'The corniest crack of all was overheard from behind. "I guess there won't be many Jerries left in Dresden after tonight!" Similar wisecracks were being passed and general back-chat was being indulged in around the room while the crews all waited. Max told me that we were in the second phase, "H+2" to "H+4" and that we were on the lowest bombing height again. (There were four bombing heights, each 500 feet above the next, starting from our height and going up.) Then everyone was on their feet as the Squadron Commanding Officer entered, followed by the station CO and the base commander. We waited until they were all seated then we all sat down again but there was no talking now and the room was suddenly quiet as the Squadron CO, Squadron Leader "Mick" Cowan, walked to the front and started the briefing proper:

"Your target tonight is Dresden.[1] The attack is divided into three phases.[2] Here are your aircraft letters, phase times and bombing heights. First phase on target from "H" to "H+2 minutes". "*B-Beer*", Flight Lieutenant Marks."

'Flight Lieutenant Marks stood up. "All correct sir!" (Indicating that all his crew were present and ready to fly.)

"18,000 feet."

'This checking of the crews and allocation of the heights was repeated until all the aircraft in the first phase had been detailed.

'Second Phase on target from "H+2" to "H+4".

"*O-Oboe*, Flying Officer Whitmarsh."

"All correct sir!"

"19,000 feet."

"*J-Johnny*, Flying Officer Harrison."

'I was on my feet. "All correct sir!"

"18,000 feet."

'As I sat down there was a whispered comment from my friend Doug Creeper, who was sitting behind me: "Can't that kite of yours get any higher than that, Stan?"

'I did not bother to reply. Our aircraft, *J-Johnny*, was certainly not new, had completed more than 30 raids on Germany and was not the fastest in the Squadron but as I had pointed out to my crew, *Johnny* had developed a very good habit of coming back at the end of each trip.

'After all the crews had been allocated their bombing heights, the CO called for the various specialist leaders to give their briefing.

'The Flying Control Officer produced his blackboard. "The runway for take-off is "22" (i.e., the compass bearing was 220 degrees). "A" and "B" Flight aircraft will taxi round the perimeter track behind the control tower to this side of the runway, whilst "C" Flight aircraft will turn left from their dispersal areas and taxi to the other side of the runway. On a "green", taxi on to the runway and take off on the second "green". Watch the corner of the runway. It's soft on the grass there, so taxi slowly and keep on the asphalt!"

'We had heard most of this at every briefing since we joined the Squadron but there were some new crews and repetition did no harm considering the speed at which some clots taxied. A fully loaded Lanc had a maximum overall take-off weight of 84,000lb, so it took some distance to stop. This could lead to trouble when 23 aircraft had to taxi to the end of the runway and even with "C" Flight coming round from the other side, there would still be 15 of us following one another along that side.

'Foggo, as the Control Officer was affectionately known, then had his little joke. "The runway for return will be the long one (2,000 yards) but I cannot tell you at this stage from which end we will be landing you!" This raised a small laugh and we were thankful that the forecast was not for strong winds.

"The beacon will be flashing the usual "BK". Join the circuit at 2,000 feet and do not call up (for permission to land) until you are over the airfield! All three emergency airfields are fully serviceable."

'This was a very comforting thought in case we lost engines; brakes or the undercarriage would not lock down.

"When coming back over the East Coast, you must be at 6,000 feet, as the Dover belt of ack-ack guns are still in operation to guard against flying bombs. Do not exceed 250 mph." (This caused general laughter as the Lanc cruised at 180 mph.)

"Burn only your navigation lights and not your downward recognition light! Any questions?"

'As there were none, the CO called the "Met bloke" who had charts drawn showing where the weather fronts were located and another giving cloud amounts, heights of bases and tops for the whole of the route to the target and home again. He gave us the gen on the weather to be expected during the whole flight. Cloud was expected from the French coast in to the target, hopefully with some breaks near the target, to give a clear view on the bombing run.

"Weather here mainly clearing, with no cloud over England on return." (I hoped he was right this time, for we did not want another cloud base of 150 feet after a long trip like this one, with everyone tired and 23 aircraft having to find their way down through it to our airfield. One of these recently was enough for a very long time to come.)

"Icing level 3,000 feet, with Icing Index 'Moderate' to 'High' in cloud. Any questions?"

"How about contrails?"

"Only above 20,000 feet, so they won't worry you! Anything else?"

'The CO called on the Bombing Leader: "All aircraft are carrying the same load, one 2,000lb and eleven containers of incendiaries."[3]

"Bomb-aimers select and fuse bombs when the bomb line is crossed. After bombing, check immediately that all bombs have gone and if unable to get rid of any hang-ups there, do not jettison them on the track out of the target but keep them until you cross the jettison area in The Wash on your return." (Not long back some clot jettisoned a canister of incendiaries in the first leg of the route out of the target and gave every night fighter within 50 miles a clear signal of the route being flown from the target.)

"Set target pressure (estimated atmospheric pressure) as you enter the aircraft and use the Broadcast Bombing Wind, multiplied by 1.1."[4]

"The Signals Officer will give the time of this broadcast. All aircraft are carrying flashes. Captains, keep your aircraft straight and level while the red light is on and let us have some really good photos tonight."

'That sounded easy in the Briefing Room but with other aircraft, slipstream turbulence, not to mention searchlights and ack-ack, it was not quite as simple as that over the target and our camera had fogged up with condensation on our last three trips.

"Bomb-aimers obtain your pro-formas and bomb-stations for your aircraft from the Bombing Section after the briefing. Any questions?"

'The CO then called the Gunnery Leader: "Just a word to all gunners! Enemy night fighters are particularly active in this area, so keep an even sharper watch in your search pattern than usual." (Comforting news, I don't think but then he was not likely to tell them that there were no fighters about and that they could go to sleep, was he?)

"You all know your search plans. Cover all the sky, all the time. Load your guns while you are still in your dispersal area and do not unload or leave your turret until you are back in your dispersal area. Jerry may try an intruder raid with night fighters again and it could be tonight, so stay alert even when approaching base."

'The CO now called the Signals Leader: "R/T call signs of the master bomber, deputy master bomber and R/T link are 'Snodgrass 1, 2 and 3'. The main force bomber stream is 'Press On'. Channel 'C' on VHF and '1196'. Wireless operators listen out on your Marconi set on the wavelength shown on your 'flimsies', which are available at the back of the briefing room. Remember, skippers, if you cannot get the master bomber on VHF, tell your WOP to select '1196' and press button 'C'. Broadcast wind velocities will be broadcast at 00.15, 15 minutes before 'H' hour and will be the usual five-figure group preceded by 'X'. Aircraft on 'Darkie' watch on the return trip will be *G-George*, Flying Officer Dowling; *J-Johnny*, Flying Officer Harrison; and 'K2', Flying Officer Creeper. Do these captains know what you have to do?"

"Yes sir," we replied.

"On the return journey listen out on Channel D for any aircraft in trouble or lost. Very well, that's all. Any questions?"

'Now it was the turn of the Intelligence Officer, Squadron Leader Leatherdale and a First World War pilot, who was always worth hearing: "Your target tonight is the Old World city of Dresden. The attack is divided into two parts. 5 Group are opening the attack at 22.30, two hours before your 'H' hour, with a slightly different aiming point. You should see their fires still burning when you get there. Jerry is shifting all his government offices with staffs and records for the Eastern Front to Leipzig – raided by 4 Group last night – Dresden and Chemnitz. These three cities are roughly in a triangle. Dresden has not been attacked before as there were no targets there but now, with the 'Big City' being evacuated partly to Dresden and with

large concentrations of troops and equipment passing through to the Russian Front, the city is crammed full and needs disorganizing. As you can see from the target map, the city is fairly easy to identify and, on your bombing run from approximately north to south, you have several good pin-points to help you check your run.[5]

"Now for the route. Base to Reading, to Beachy Head, to the Rhine, keeping clear of Mainz to starboard. Then on until you pass just slightly starboard of Frankfurt. Frankfurt has a large searchlight area and some ack-ack guns, so keep clear and stay on track. Turn slightly north and then run up as though heading for Leipzig, or when you pass to port of that, as though the 'Big City' is your target. Just north of Leipzig, you head east and across through this searchlight belt and you may have quite a few lights put up there but there should be little or no flak. North of Dresden you have a turn of nearly 90 degrees, so watch out for other aircraft and so avoid collisions. You have a reasonably long run-up and, after bombing, you hold the same course until you have completed this short leg, then turn south-west towards Stuttgart and Nuremberg. Keep on track and pass south of these two places or you may have trouble. Then you head west, cross the Rhine on the south-east corner of France and keep clear of this area, where they are still active and getting too many of our aircraft. Cross the coast at Orford Ness at 6,000 feet at least and then lose height across The Wash to base.

"The defences of Dresden are not considerable but they may have brought back mobile flak guns from the Eastern Front, so the flak may be moderate but I doubt if you will find it heavy. *Oboe* Mosquitoes are marking the target at 'H-2' with a single red TI. Then the flares will go down and Pathfinders will drop their TIs. Red and green TIs cascading together will be used only if they can positively identify the Aiming Point. If there is cloud over the target, 'blind-marker' crews will use sky-markers, which will be green flares dripping red stars. Your order of preference for bombing will be: 1. master bomber's instructions. 2. Red and green TIs. 3. Sky-markers on the exact heading of 175 degrees True at 165 mph indicated airspeed. 4. H$_2$S run.

"Any questions?"

'The CO now walked out to the map, summarized the briefing and told us the heights at which to fly on each leg of the route:

"Phase times for return: First Phase, 10 minutes before ETA. Second Phase, on ETA. Third Phase, 10 minutes after ETA. Use Aldis lamps for taxiing out and taxi slowly, even on return, when you will have some daylight! Position yourselves on the circuit on your return and we will get you down much more quickly. Any questions? Have you anything to say sir?'' (This was addressed to the Station CO.)

"Yes. I just want to impress on you chaps the necessity to be very careful to keep a very keen lookout at all turning points and so avoid any risk of collisions!'' (Didn't he think we knew that? About 200 aircraft all heading for the same point within 6 minutes at the most, with no lights on, was enough to make anyone keep a very keen lookout! We could not guess that within two weeks he would be the one who would have a mid-air collision over France when the Met blokes "boobed" and we would have to climb through 15,000 feet of cloud. After the other aircraft crossed on top of him, wiping out all four of his propellers and his canopy, he dropped back down into the cloud and was the only survivor, losing the crew he had borrowed for the trip!)

"All right chaps, that is all. Have a good trip and hit it really hard."

'We all filed out to the locker room to change into our flying clothes. Jack and Maurie collected their pro-formas and flimsies on the way. Jock and Curly started their long job of getting dressed in electrically heated flying suits, socks and gloves, while Peter and I changed too. Max had gone back to the Navigation Section. It was a cold night on the ground and the Met bloke said that the temperature at 20,000 feet would be –25 degrees, which would not be as bad as the –45 degrees we had had once or twice. But it would still be quite cool so I put on my long wool and rayon underpants and long-sleeved singlet. As *J-Johnny* was not a cold kite, I did not put on my big hip-length socks but put on my usual pair of woollen socks and a pair of woollen knee-warmers before getting back into my trousers, then my flying boots. My shirt collar was left undone and tie loosened but left on, in case of diversion to another airfield on return. It would be awkward to go around without a collar and tie. I left the front collar stud in place, as there was a small compass built into the back of it, for use if I had to try to get back from Germany on the ground. I put on my once white silk scarf to keep the wool of the roll-neck pullover away from my neck, as it got very irritating after a few hours rubbing on the stubble of whiskers, and then a sleeveless pullover and the big rolled-neck one that came down over my hips, eliminating any draught between trouser top and battledress when seated. Then, with my torch and small-scale map, with the whole route on it, stuck into the top of my right boot and my flying rations down the left one, I was ready. I put "George", my fur

dog mascot, into my battle-jacket and then went to see how the rest of the crew were getting on. I carried my three pairs of gloves (silk, chamois leather and outer leather zippered gauntlets) and found Peter ready and waiting for me, similarly attired, except for all the gloves. John needed practically nothing extra, as he sat on top of the heater unit. Maurie had a few extras similar to Peter and also a big scarf, as it got draughty with his head down in the open-ended Perspex bubble while he was keeping a lookout for night fighters homing on to us from below.

'Curly and Jock were in their electrically heated suits and socks and now Curly pulled on the waterproof outer flying suit I had loaned him, as his issue buoyancy suit was too bulky to get him, and it, into his turret together. (No doubt it was Curly who was too bulky but this arrangement suited him very well.) Jock put on his big roll-neck sweater, a sheepskin vest (by courtesy of the Australian Comforts Fund through the hands of his skipper in the cause of another warm and happy gunner) and then his battledress jacket. Long knee-hip socks and heated flying boots completed their outfits, with their heated gloves.

'Max had not come in yet but would follow later so we went to get the crew bus out to the aircraft in the dispersal area. Many crews had the same idea and after finding the right bus in the darkness and telling the WAAF driver our aircraft letter, we piled into the back and waited until the thing was full to overflowing with other crews. We visited several other "B" Flight dispersals and wished the other skippers well.

"Have a good trip. Doug!"

"Same to you Stan; I bet I beat you home tonight!"

"So you ought to. You have a start on me. I'm in the second phase!"

'We arrived at our dispersal and again Peter and I went right around the aircraft, thoroughly checking for leaks, looking at the tyres for pressure and seeing that the aileron and rudder chocks had been removed. After checking inside again, we were ready to run-up and when everything was in order we switched off and climbed out for a final smoke, spit, swear, yarn and a "leak" before take-off. We had about half an hour to go and the boys on the ground crew took the wheel chocks away, as I would not be running up again, while I went over to the ground crew hut to sign the aircraft maintenance Form 700. I just took a quick look to see that it had been signed up by the various maintenance types and then signed it as taking the aircraft in satisfactory condition. The main thing was that the Flight Sergeant in charge of the aircraft said it was OK.

If he said it was OK, then you could bet your boots or your life that it was!

'Max arrived, got in and sorted all his gear out, with his charts, etc., in their right places. The Doc came round with his "wakey-wakey" tablets and Peter took charge of them, except for two each for Jock and Curly. We very rarely used them but it was handy to have them in case anyone felt really tired! They had an effect for about 4 hours and I wanted to know who took them and how often. Everyone now had their Mae Wests on and the rest of the crew had on their parachute harnesses, as their parachutes were stored separately near where they were stationed, while I sat on mine and strapped the harness on when I got into my seat at the controls. It was about 10 minutes before we were due to take-off so we all climbed aboard, with a final "See you in the morning about 6 o'clock" to the ground crew and their reply, "Right – have a good trip, Skip!"

'We sorted ourselves out in our various positions and started up the engines. We confirmed with Max that the Distant Reading compass was correct and then tested and left the oxygen turned on. With a thumbs up to the ground staff by torchlight, we were signalled out on to the perimeter track, having the radio on in case of a change of runway, etc. Maurie shone his Aldis signalling lamp on the edge of the asphalt about 50 yards ahead and, with engines just idling, we taxied slowly along. Peter kept a lookout on his side (starboard) and called the distance between the starboard wheel and the edge of the track and kept an eye on the brake pressure gauge. Jock kept the lookout behind to ensure that no one taxied into us from the rear. The Lanc was heavy to taxi with a full load but answered to the brakes and motors, although you could feel the weight on the corners. At the controls you felt that the air was its natural element and it "suffered" this crawling along the ground, only because it was necessary so that it could become airborne again.

'This taxiing took so long that we seemed to be taking an age to get to the take-off point but then everything took so long on these operations. We were about three-quarters of the way to the start of the runway and about half-way down a slight slope beside the bomb dump when I noticed a truck coming round on the track from the airfield controller's caravan and its lights suddenly disappeared behind something in front of us. I had Maurie shine his lamp directly ahead and there seemed to be a dark shape out there, probably an aircraft but no lights were visible. Then suddenly torches and lights shone from everywhere out in front, with frantic signals for me to stop. As if I needed to be signalled to stop! I had a fully loaded aircraft, some unidentified obstacle was blocking the perimeter track in front, and there was grass, probably soft, to port and a drop down to the entry to the bomb dump to starboard – where did they think I was counting on going?

'I turned on the landing light (which we never used for taxiing in case it got into the eyes of a pilot taking-off and we did not use it for landing either) and it revealed two aircraft ahead in an unfriendly embrace! Just what we did not want at this stage, a taxiing accident! Peter was already worrying me about the engines over-heating, as we had been taxiing downwind most of the time since leaving the dispersal. I warned the crew that there had been a taxiing accident and we might be late taking-off. Max was not amused as he would have to watch all his timing calculations very carefully now to see that we set course on time or, at the worst, try to make time on the way, which was not easy with a fully loaded aircraft. Jock was now shining his torch out the back to warn any aircraft behind us not to taxi into us – I knew that there were three following us.

'After a few minutes, which seemed a very long time, we were signalled to turn off the perimeter track on to the grass in order to pass the obstruction. How I would have liked to break radio silence to warn the others of the obstruction and to get confirmation that the grass was firm enough to take our weight without getting us bogged. But we really had no alternative. I could not go forward, I could not turn to starboard and the track behind was blocked by other aircraft waiting for me to show them that it was safe to turn to port, then swing wide to starboard round the trouble ahead.

'I became reconciled to having to risk getting bogged and I was convinced that the airfield control types out there, signalling to me to move, did not really know if I would get bogged or not but they also had no alternative to offer. Peter reminded me again that the motors were getting "bloody hot, Skip!" I bit his head off by telling him didn't I already know that and what did he want me to do about it? I couldn't turn into wind here and we had other problems at the moment!

"Tell me when the gauges get well into the 'red' just before they blow off!"

"They are into the 'red', Skip and I thought you should know that we haven't got very long before we have real trouble with them!"

'I realized that I was getting edgy and as I started to turn off the track I said, "Sorry, Pete but I don't like this going on to the grass caper after old Foggo's warning about the soft grass up at the corner of the runway."

"I don't like it either," he replied, "but it seems all right so far, Stan."

'We made our way slowly around the two aircraft to a clear section of perimeter track. I got an enthusiastic thumbs up signal in the light of a torch from a very relieved airfield control chap, who had solved one of his problems and, in a few minutes, would have only the taxiing accident to sort out. We had a clear run to the ACP's caravan and now the pre-take-off drill was done, with each item repeated aloud, so that Peter could check them all. Maurice came up out of his position in the nose for the take-off and sat beside Max. I flicked my lights to the ACP to indicate that I was ready and immediately he gave me the "green" from his signalling lamp, as all the aircraft from the other side of the perimeter track had taken off while we were sorting out our problem.

'We taxied out slowly, keeping as near to the end of the runway as possible in order to use every yard of it that we could for take-off. We rolled forward a short distance to straighten the tail wheel, then stopped again. The friction nut on the throttles was tightened firmly so that they would not work shut if my hands came off them for any reason. Gyro was set on "zero" and "unengaged", i.e. it was free to spin and to indicate any change in direction in the darkness up beyond the end of the two rows of runway lights.

'I opened the throttles to the gate (normal maximum power position) for the two inboard engines as Peter reported, "Fuel pumps on. All set for take-off!"

'The motors were not the only thing revved up, as the adrenaline was flowing and I always got a feeling of goose pimples with the sound of the Merlins at full throttle. The ACP flashed another "green" indicating that the runway was clear. I told the crew, "Righto, here we go!"

'With the throttles for the outboard engines nearly half opened and Peter holding the inboard throttles open, I released the brakes and pushed the control column as far forward as I could to get the tail up as quickly as possible. The aircraft had been vibrating with all this power on and the wheels locked with the brakes. Now it surged forward in spite of the full load. I corrected any tendency of the aircraft to swing with the thrust of the engines by using the starboard throttles. When we had the tail up and were heading straight along the runway, I took the outboard throttles to the "gate" also and called to Peter, "Full power through the gate!" He pushed all four throttles past the gate to the "emergency" position and locked the friction as tight as he could get it so that the throttles could not creep back when he took his hands off them.

"Full power locked on!" he reported.

'I felt the extra power as a thrust in my back. A quick glance at the gauges for revs and boost confirmed that all the engines were OK and, with both hands now on the control column, I concentrated on those two rows of lights between which we now raced. I held the aircraft down so that we were not bumped prematurely into the air as we went over a slight rise about three-quarters of the way down the runway. This would have us in the air in a poor flying attitude and one in which it took longer to build up speed. As we came to the end of the runway I eased back on the control column and we climbed away.

"Undercart up!"

'Peter repeated the order and selected "up". The red warning lights came on, then went out as the under-carriage became fully retracted. We had reached 135 mph, which was the minimum flying speed at which you could stay in the air with three engines and a full load. I always relaxed a little and breathed more easily once we had 135 on the clock. (Fourteen trips later I was very busy for a while at this stage, as I had to shut down the port outer engine due to a coolant leak at a height of 400 feet!) Now I asked Peter for 2,850 revs and +9 boost, which brought the throttles back to the normal "full power" position, at a height of 400 feet.

"Flaps up in easy stages."

'Peter repeated and complied, raising them five degrees at a time, while I re-trimmed the aircraft to accommodate these changes. A mistake made with this operation, with the flaps raised too quickly, would cause the aircraft to lose lift, then a stall and a crash could occur. With training and growing confidence between the two of us, I did not hesitate to call on Peter to operate the flaps on both take-off and landing. Although he had had no training as a pilot, he now had a good understanding of changes in conditions, which required slightly different operation of the flaps. A crew that understood what each had to do and cooperated so that it was done most efficiently was on its way to being a good crew and good crews had the best chance of surviving.

'With the flaps up and a climbing speed of 145–150 mph, I asked for "2,650 rpm and +7 boost". Peter repeated the details and brought the throttles back to our "climbing power" setting. We climbed on a head-ing of 270 degrees and shortly Max told me to turn back to base, then, when back over base, we set course on our first leg to Reading and we were on our way at last! Large bombing raids certainly took a long time to get under way and were not a case of "sit in the dispersal hut and scramble when the siren sounded" as in the Battle of Britain days for fighter boys. *Otto* and *Kari*, our two legendary German night fighter boys, who patrolled the northern and southern sectors of Germany, were probably sitting around waiting to hear where we were heading tonight.

'At 10,000 feet we lowered the engine revs to save both fuel and the engines and completed a check of the oxygen flowing to all of the crew, also checking the emergency intercom. On this run to Reading we kept a very sharp lookout for other aircraft as they climbed from the various airfields to join the main bomber stream, all heading for this first turning point. I tested the autopilot and after an initial "kick-up" "George" engaged, which I anticipated, settled down and functioned quite well. I then disengaged it and we continued our climb. At Reading we had the benefit of all the other aircraft still having their navigation lights on but I still had to dive a little to avoid one clot who turned without checking that we were there.

'We set course for Beachy Head and that bacon and eggs for tea seemed well down now and I nibbled some chocolate, interrupting Peter's log keeping to give him some. He answered with a thumbs up "thank you" before going back to his log and "gallons per hour used", etc. I called to each of the crew in turn to ask how things were in each position and to see if the gunners' heated gear was working OK. All replied "OK, no problems" and Maurie merely rolled over and went back to snoozing. His time for looking for fighters and later guiding us to the target had not yet arrived.

'After altering course slightly at Beachy Head we were out over the Channel. Here I got to thinking that the tension, although under control, was too high. I thought of offering a prayer for a safe return and wondered whether or not I might be a good leader and set an example to my crew. I was having trouble maintaining our required rate of climb, so I asked Peter for a slight increase of 50 rpm, which meant that he had to re-synchronize the four engines. If this was not done correctly, the sound of the engines developed a "beat", which seemed to go right through your head after a few minutes and the best way of doing this was to look along the line of the two propellers on each side. The "shadows" of the props appeared to move when they were out of sync and remained practically still when the engines were synchronized to the same rpm. A small thing really and I suppose I should not have let it get to me but in my book it was just tidy flying and one less thing to get on the nerves of skipper and crew.

'I switched off the external lighting master switch and the boys checked that the lights were all out. (Some chaps went over Germany with their lights on and a few of them even returned!) We were climbing again and

Jock now had on his "village inn", the automatic gun-laying turret. After he had adjusted the settings it worked well, giving warning beeps on the intercom when another aircraft came within range of its radar-scanning beam. The beeps got louder and more frequent as the other aircraft came closer, building up the tension until Jock identified it through the small infra-red telescope mounted near his gun-sight. All our aircraft were fitted with two infra-red flashing lights in the nose and these were visible in the rear-gunner's telescope. The rate of exchange in the frequency of the beeps is what I listened for and when there was little or no change it usually meant that another Lanc had drifted across our track and Jock would come through with "It's OK, Skip, it's one of ours".

'Maurie was now lying on his stomach with his head down in the Perspex bubble, keeping a lookout down below. Max gave me an ETA for the next turning point and then muttered some suitable comments about the Germans and the radar jamming in particular, as his *Gee* set had just become unusable because of the jamming signals obscuring everything else on the screen.

'I asked him about the H_2S airborne radar: "How is your Y-set?"

"OK so far," he replied and on we flew.

'Five minutes later Max was back on the intercom and very annoyed. The Y-set had packed up now and this was serious. We were over cloud, unable to see anything on the ground and had no means of establishing our exact position, with a long way to go to the target and back again, as well as keeping clear of those heavily defended areas mentioned at briefing.

'Jack had just received the first Broadcast Wind which he gave to Max, who commented, "I hope they're accurate tonight because we haven't got anything else."

'He was not the only one who had that hope. I quietly thought to myself what a big place Germany was to be flying over with no navigational gear, except a compass, a watch and a Broadcast Wind. It would be bad enough after the target, as I always said that we could get home by flying "west with a bit of north in it". But the route going in was going to be tricky if those Broadcast Winds were not accurate or if we missed them when they were broadcast.

"Jack," I said, "you will be careful not to miss those Broadcast Winds won't you?"

"That's for sure, Skip, you can count on it!"

'I quietly thought to myself, "Yes, I knew I could" and it was that feeling of complete confidence in each other, which had grown up through our training together that was so important now. As I thought about it I realized that I had the same confidence in the other crews in the

Squadron and in the other squadrons, who would be sending back their calculated details of the wind, as we had done on other trips. So of course the Broadcast Winds would be accurate. That is what made Bomber Command the force that it was.

"How's the heat tonight, Stan?" Jack was doing his usual thorough check of all his responsibilities, as well as making sure of receiving the Broadcast Winds and, I suspected at the time, was just making sure the Skipper was not brooding on the loss of the Y-set.

"OK, thanks, Jack!"

"All right with you, Max?" he asked, but Max was not really paying attention to the heating or anything else, except his navigational problems after the failure of his equipment.

"It's fine but if you have any spare heat you could try to unfreeze that scanner," he replied.

"No hope of that, I'm afraid," said Jack.

"Aye, what about the poor bloody frozen gunners?" Jock had joined in the talk. "It's all right for you lot with all your mod cons. Curly and I have got minus 23 degrees back here!"

"Isn't your electrical heating working, Jock?"

"Aye, it is, Skipper but it's still bloody cold!"

"Don't let your turret freeze up will you?" (I realized that it was quite a while since I had felt the slight swing of the nose of the aircraft caused by the rear turret being turned from one side to the other and then back again to check free movement.) Curly joined in. "No chance of that, Stan!"

"Good, Curly," I replied, smiling to myself at the immediate banding together of the two gunners against any implied criticism. A minute or two later I felt the nose swing slightly one way then the other as Jock checked his turret and I had another quiet smile to myself.

'We were lucky as we approached ETA Frankfurt as there was a break in the cloud ahead to port and we could see the searchlights. Max was pleased, as this put us bang on track, so we turned on ETA alongside Frankfurt. So far, so good and all was well.

'Maurie said, "I think we're going into those lights!"

'They always looked closer than they really were, particularly from his position out front. I did not know if he thought that I would fly straight into a group of searchlights, which were not defending our target, or if he was just getting a little on edge. We were right on track with not too much further to go and this was the turning-point that I was worried about when we lost the Y-set, as being only slightly off course would have put us right over the defences of Frankfurt.

"Nice work, Max! We hit that turning point right on the nose!"

"Good, Stan. Those winds must be spot on, thank heavens!"

"Blast the idiot!" Some clot had jettisoned his load of incendiaries. They were strung out, burning on the ground, marking our new course for every night fighter this side of Stuttgart to see! Thank heavens the clouds were moving across again so that they were being screened. Occasionally, another aircraft was seen near us and identified as friendly, either visually or by Jock through his infra-red telescope.

'Max now wanted a slight increase in our speed to make our next turning point on time, so Peter had to re-synchronize the engines, while still keeping a lookout on the starboard side. Occasionally we hit the slip-stream of another aircraft and this threw us around but it was a good sign as it meant that someone else was flying our course and we hoped that his navigation equipment was functioning correctly so he was right on track. It also meant that we were not the only aircraft on this area for the German radar-predicted flak guns to concentrate on, if there was a unit near here.

'Even when experienced many times, the effect of hitting the slipstream of a four-engined aircraft still caused the old heart to thump a bit. It was as though some giant hand had taken hold of the aircraft and twisted it one way and up or down at the same time. There was nothing you could do about it, except to push the control column forward and apply full opposite bank to avoid a possible stall and to level the wings. After a matter of a few seconds that felt like hours, the aircraft would dive through the area of affected air and return to normal feel and control again.

'As we sat there flying steadily on towards the target, I did not realize that the tension was gradually mounting until something very simple annoyed me, then I had a quiet talk to myself. "Relax, you silly goat. Things are under control!" The clip for the oxygen tube to my facemask had slipped off the strap of my parachute harness, so that the whole length of the tube was dangling from the facemask and was dragging it whenever I turned my head, which was nearly constantly at this stage of the trip. I had got annoyed at the fool of a way of securing it, as it would not stay in place but at the next try it remained fixed and all thoughts of animosity towards it and its inventor died without trace.

'I checked through the crew again with some casual remark to each of them and judged by their replies whether their oxygen supply was OK and for any signs that they were tensing up.

"Any icicles out the back, Jock?"

"No, not yet, Stan but it's none too warm, ye know!"

'He was all right and wide awake. "How are things on top Curly? Can you see anything?"

"No. Everything is quiet up here, Stan. Where are we now?" (Evidently my turn for a test!)

"Just running north of Leipzig, Curl."

"Leipzig. OK."

"Anything down there Maurie?"

"Yes. A heck of a lot of cloud but nothing else!"

"What petrol are we using at this rate, Peter?"

"About 185 miles per hour, Stan. I'll check on my tables if you like."

"No, that's OK, thanks. Is that a chink of light through the curtain there?"

"Whereabouts, Stan?"

'Instantly, Peter was searching the blackout curtain between the navigator's area and us for any sign of light. "It's all right, Pete, it's only a reflection from the Perspex in your bubble." (This bubble in the side window on the starboard side allowed Peter to look down and it had caught some stray light from outside and reflected it into our area.)

"What is our ETA at this last turning-point, Max?"

'After a while Max replied, "Well, it's hard to say as I'm only running on DR (Dead Reckoning) based on Broadcast Winds. I hope they're somewhere near accurate!"

"How do you think they are?"

"Not too bad so far, I think, Stan. Our ETA is 23.57."

"How does that make us for time?"

"About a minute late, so step it up a little, if you can."

"OK, Max, I'll try 170 but this kite is getting old now."

"Righto, Stan but we need a bit more speed."

"2,350 revs, thanks, Peter."

"2,350. Right, Stan."

'The revs were increased and I kept checking the airspeed to see if I could coax that extra 5 mph. In a newer aircraft I would have just put the nose down for 200 to 300 feet, then level out when we had 170 and slowly pick up the height again. *Johnny* was reluctant to go much over 17,000 feet and it would be a hard job to pick up the height that we had lost. After a while, with no increase in speed visible, I asked Peter for 2,400 revs and eased the nose forward slightly to gain that extra speed. As the speed increased I carefully kept it and coaxed *Johnny* back up again to approximately 17,500 feet. (The Lanc was very hard to accelerate by use of engines alone. Anything up to 300 revs increase had to

be used to get the extra speed. But then only 50 revs over the original was needed to hold it, so the easiest way to increase revs by the amount necessary to the hold speed and actually gain that speed was by losing height gently followed by slowly regaining the lost altitude.) "You can put the bomb sight on now, Maurie!"

"OK, Stan. Is 'George' right out?"

"Yes and has been for over an hour!" (Bombsight gyros needed time to settle and it was best to give them about half an hour.)

'Up ahead we could now see the bright patch on the clouds caused by a searchlight belt and we were thankful that the cloud was shielding us. There was nothing to do but search the sky for fighters and fly on and continue to search.

"What's that over there on the port bow?"

"Yes, there was something black there!"

'I searched for it by looking lightly away from where I thought it was, then I saw that it was another aircraft, which looked like a Lanc. "Curly, can you see that aircraft on the port bow, slightly up?"

'After a short wait, "Yes, it's another Lanc I think, Stan."

'The aircraft did not close in or move away and gradually I could make out the twin fins and rudders and the four Merlins. He was close enough but he was above us and headed our way. On we flew and I started to look for the time to turn at the last turning point before the target.

"There are some fighters about, Stan, I think," said Jock. "I've just seen two of their flares out here behind us." (small flares were used by the night fighters to indicate our route). "Try looking right back past the port rudder fin. I can just see the two tiny orbs of red light dropping slowly."

"Yes, you're right, Jock. Keep your eyes open for them now, the pair of you."

"Aye, I will!" Jock replied in his broad Scots accent.

"Yes, right," said Curly and our nervous system got another notch tighter.

"How's our ETA, Max?"

"Two minutes to run but we're still a bit late, so we have to turn early and 'cut the corner', OK?"

"Yes, OK, Max. What is the next course?"

"179, Stan – I'll tell you when to turn."

"179! Right, Max."

'I resumed searching from side to side and back again and repeated this again and again and again, as there were likely to be other aircraft making good this turning-point after some slight variation from their proper track.

Others might be going to cut the corner earlier than we were and could be coming across us.

"All right, start turning now, Stan."

"Turning on to 179! Thanks!" Making sure it was clear; we came round to 179. "Steering 179 now, Max."

"OK, Stan. I think we should just about be right on time at this speed! Twenty-one minutes to run to the target."

"Twenty-one! OK."

'As I looked ahead I saw a glow in the distance and realized that it was the glow of the fires started by the earlier attack by 5 Group. After all this flying we were at last getting near the target.[6]

"OK Max, I can see it ahead and there is a break in the clouds so should get a good run."

'Rather agitated, Max asked, "How far is it ahead?"

"Oh, quite some distance yet – about 15–20 minutes I would guess."

"Oh, righto. I thought you meant we were nearly there and that I had boobed and got us here too early!"

"Not likely with you worrying over our times all the way, Max!"

"This course will put us bang on target too! Turn on the VHF will you, Jack?"

"She's on, Skipper."

"OK, thanks." I selected channel C and after a few seconds the background noise told us that the set had warmed up and I left it turned on waiting for the master bomber to start broadcasting. A few more fighter flares were seen, so they knew where we were and everyone was now very wide awake and searching the sky intently. Jack received the Bombing Wind and, after Max converted it, passed it to Maurie.

"3-1-5, 25. Right, thanks, Max."

'Maurie set it into his bombsight. We were tracking nicely towards the target and suddenly a voice came on the headphones: "Snodgrass 1 to Snodgrass 2. Here is a time check. In twenty seconds it will be 00.15. 10 . . . 5, 4, 3, 2, 1. Now! Over."

"Snodgrass 2 to Snodgrass 1. Loud and clear. Out!"

'It was all so very British! Here we were running into the target in the heart of Germany after 4½ hours flying with no navigational aids and wondering how we were going to make it. Now, when we were at last in sight of the target, we were being greeted by a couple of typically English chaps with very English call signs, quietly checking that they had got the time right, down to the last second! Our reception was all right, so we did not have to worry about the other sets. The illuminating flares were going down now and they hung in the sky in

rows like gigantic yellow lanterns. More and more of them dropped and the whole sky in that area was lit up.

"Just hold it steady about there Skip and we should be right on it."

"OK, Maurie!"

"Curly and Jack, keep that search going. They're dropping more fighter flares. Are you in the astrodome Jack?"

"In the astrodome, Skipper!"

"Aye, I've got my eyes wide open, Skip."

"She's right, mate," replied Curly.

'The TIs were being dropped now and Maurie was satisfied with our track towards the target. "Yes, there go the TIs, Skipper. We're right on track!"

"How are we for time, Max?"

"Three and a half minutes to run."

"Fair enough!"

'The target was now obscured from my view, as it had passed under the line of the nose of the aircraft. Peter was busy pushing "Window" down the chute to confuse the German radar operators.

'Again a voice came loudly out of nowhere: "Snodgrass 1 to Press On. Bomb on the red and green TIs. Bomb on the red and green TIs. Out."

'This was repeated by the R/T link.

"The red and greens. OK, Skip," said Maurie. "Left! Left! Steady!" he chanted and I repeated and executed these instructions as he alone now guided the aircraft to the bomb release point.

"Steady!"

'I replied "Steady" as I tried to keep the aircraft straight and level while still watching out for other aircraft near us on our level, directly above and slightly ahead. The greatest danger over the target was not from searchlights, flak or fighters (who usually stayed clear of the area immediately over the target to give the flak gunners an "open go") but collisions or being bombed by an aircraft above us. I was watching another Lanc on my side that was slowly crossing our course slightly above us, when Peter pointed out one on his side also. I watched these two as we continued our run-in.

"Left! Left! Steady!" These were repeated and executed and Maurie's chant became, "Steady! Steady! Steady!" The aircraft on the starboard side had crossed OK and was now just clear of us but the one on the port side was going to be a nuisance. There were not many searchlights and little flak, thank goodness. A very bright searchlight came very close but at the last moment before catching us it swung away. There was no more noise than usual while the sounds of bombs exploding, as heard in Hollywood movies, proved that the producer had never been here! Exploding flak was usually seen but was only heard when it was very close and if you could smell the cordite as well it was time for a "damage report"!

"Steady! Steady! Left! Left! Steady!" chanted Maurie and I complied. "That aircraft is getting closer!"

"We might just make it, as the release point must be close."

"Steady! Bomb bay doors open!" I repeated and executed.

"Snodgrass 1 to Press On! Bomb the centre of the red and green TIs. Bomb the centre of the red and green TIs. Out."

"Did you get that, Maurie?" I switched off the VHF to cut out the R/T link's voice, which might have interfered with Maurie's instructions.

"Yes. Centre of red and greens," Maurie replied quickly.

"Steady! Steady! *Steady*!"

'I felt a slight bump, like someone kicking the wooden seat of a chair you are sitting in.

"Cookie gone! Incendiaries going," reported Maurie.

'The red camera light started to blink in front of me but I was more concerned with the aircraft that was coming from the port side and was now nearly above us. As his bomb bay doors were open, I turned away to starboard.

"Sorry Maurie!" I said. "Another photo gone west but he nearly bombed us!"

"OK, Skip, take it away."

'We had bombed at 18,000 feet, having lost our extra 500 feet running in from the last turning point. As we straightened up again I brought the rev levers up until we had 2,500 and, with nose down, we headed out of the target with 220 on the clock.

"179 is the course, Skip," Max came through, as though we were just leaving a practice bombing range.

"OK, Max. Are things quiet up there with you, Curly?"

"Yes, OK, Skip but I think there are fighters about as there's a lane in these searchlights."

"OK. Keep that search going well."

"Corkscrew port, go!"

'I heard the turret machine guns open up as Jock's call came through. With a warning of "Down port!" I threw everything into the corner, full port bank, full port rudder and control column forward. We heeled over and dived to port and as the speed built up we came out of it as I dragged back on the control column, calling to the gunners "Changing – up port!" With the build-up in speed we went up like a lift. Before we lost all this speed I called "Changing – up starboard!" Then, as we lost speed, "Changing – down star-

board!" As we started to dive again, Jock called, "Resume course, go! It's OK, Skip, he passed us by but he's disappeared up in the starboard beam so keep your eyes open for him, Curly."

"Starboard beam up. OK, Jock."

'We settled down again on our course, with everyone alert and searching intently.

"Next course is 2-1-5, Stan."

"OK, turning on to 2-1-5."

"All clear starboard, Stan," reported Peter. Aircraft that were visible in the glare over the target could not be seen now but we did see one or two that turned close to us. We settled on to the new course and, after a few minutes, I looked back to starboard and saw Dresden burning. While I watched, I saw a fire start in the air and there, against the target, appeared the perfect miniature outline of a Lanc. The port wing burned furiously and, after flying level for a few seconds, the aircraft heeled over and dived down as the wing fell off. We were too far away to see if any 'chutes came out. "One of our aircraft is missing." Max logged the time, height and position.

"Are you busy Max?"

"No, not for the moment."

"Well, you wanted to see a target."

"Righto, Stan."

'Max came out from behind his curtain and asked, "Where?"

'I pointed to the rear over my left shoulder where the yellow of the flares, the white of the incendiaries burning on the ground, the searchlights and the pin-point of light in the sky (from the flak at the stragglers from "last phase") could clearly be seen. Clouds of smoke rose thousands of feet into the air. With the last of the red and green TIs, it completed a Technicolor nightmare of Hell.

"Aagh! I never want to see that again," said Max. "I'll go back to my charts. You can keep that."

'But he stayed a bit longer to look hard at the scene, before disappearing back behind his curtain. I suppose it was an awful shock to suddenly be confronted with such a sight. I realized that the rest of us had become used to this type of scene, while Max had spent his time on each trip at his charts without knowing what was actually happening outside the aircraft and what it looked like. I never did find out what his thoughts about it really were but I suspected that he actually was a very sensitive type, who disliked being suddenly confronted with such a scene of destruction. I never knew anyone who really liked the job but I suppose there were some who did.

"It looks like we've done our job," remarked Peter.

"Yes," I replied. "I don't think we'll have to come back again . . . All right, now, let's see that none of those fighters jump us on the way home. Are you going down in your bubble, Maurie?!"

"Yes Stan. I'll give you a call when I want a rest from flying upside down."

(When he did I rolled the aircraft over until Curly could see down under us and called, "All clear, starboard", then I rolled it over on to the other wingtip and waited for his call, "All clear, port".)

"We're on the job too, Stan, you can count on it," said Jock.

"That's right, Stan," joined in Curly.

"Good, I'm glad to hear it. How long to our next turning-point, Max?"

"Not for quite a while yet, Stan. This is a long leg and I'll let you know in good time."

"Right, Max."

'I noted that, as usually happened, the crew tended to be informal in speaking to me, except during take-off and landing and when we were near the target area, when it became "skipper" or "Skip". I assumed this was an unconscious recognition of their reliance on me but that reliance was really on each other, so perhaps it was only a matter of naturally looking for a leader in times of stress and danger.

"Can I have the '1196' in for our 'Darkie' watch please, Jack.!"

"Yes. It's on now, Stan."

"Thanks."

'I thought back on the attack and the roles of the various participants. From the master bomber who often marked the Aiming Point from only 3,000 feet, to the marker crews from the Pathfinder Force, to the Flare Force aircraft and to the main force; a very complex machine of destruction. The Marker crews and Flare Force aircraft dropped their TIs and flares over the target, then turned away, flying around and rejoining the stream of main force aircraft coming into the target, then dropping their bombs on their second run through the target. Once through the target was enough for me but before not too many more trips we were selected as a Flare Force crew, finally joining the Pathfinders for the rest of the war.

'We flew on and on, making the next turning point and turning more westerly, now that we were past Nuremberg. Presently I saw a patch of light in the sky to port and wondered what searchlights they were, until it dawned on me that they were the lights on the shores of Lake Constance, Switzerland! I wondered what they thought of the war, apart from the money they were making. Being neutral certainly paid off, when you could be the world's clearing-house! I told Max and he was quite satisfied. We were slightly off track to the south but we were clear of Stuttgart so we waited until we were very close to the light before altering course to nearly due west, along the Swiss border towards France.

'I was tired and hungry, which was no wonder, as we had now been in the air over 9 hours. My last piece of chocolate tasted very good, poor quality or not and a cup of sergeants' mess tea from Peter's thermos tasted wonderful and helped get the eyes open again. I had "George" doing the work now but had my hand on the lever to disengage the autopilot the moment anything happened, so there was only a partial relaxation. Across the Rhine now, we altered course for England, losing height as we went so that our airspeed built up to 200 on the clock. If the Jerry fighters wanted us they would have to find us and catch us. My thoughts wandered. Dresden had certainly copped it but hang this supporting Joe Stalin and his boys – it was just too damn far. Helping Monty and his merry men was much more "the shot" that appealed now.[7]

Peter broke into my wandering thoughts to ask if I had changed the supercharger control down to "medium" as we had descended into that range. He was happy to know that I had and it was good to know that he was still right on the job, although like all of us he was now very tired.

'Halfway across France Max told me that his *Gee* set was working again. "We are only 15 miles off track, Stan but you had better alter 30 degrees to starboard to avoid that possible trouble spot they mentioned at briefing."

"Righto, Max. Altering 30 degrees to port. Now." (Trouble spot? Briefing? That all seemed days ago. I seemed to have been sitting in this seat for a week.) Only 15 miles off after more than 4 hours' navigating back from the target by dead reckoning and the Broadcast Winds, was a terrific effort and I congratulated Max, who merely uttered that "George", our dog mascot, must have really been looking after us.

'The French coast was crossed, then the Channel, through the fence of lights at Orford Ness, navigation lights "on" and nose down for base. As we approached I listened out and heard the various boys calling up as they reached home and I checked out who had arrived back safely. Our beacon flashing "BK" was a very welcome sight. There was no story book or Yankee film welcome, just, "*Johnny*, 1,500 feet" from the control tower. I knew that my call for permission to land had been heard in the debriefing room, where we would be posted up on the "Returned" board.

'It all happened very quickly now and after more than 9½ hours in the air I shook myself wide awake to make sure that nothing could go wrong in the last few minutes. We had permission to join the circuit. Maurie was out of the nose. I called "Downwind" and immediately Doug called me: "Keep in close, Stan, I'm right behind you."

"Right, Doug," I replied in strictly non-RAF R/T procedure.

'I flew a tight circuit on the ring of lights surrounding the circuit area, cut in close at the funnel, leading to the start of the runway, and wasted no time. Doug Creeper would have swung a little wider and turned into the funnel a little later than usual to give me time to get clear of the landing area so that he would not have to go around again. After nearly 10 hours in the air, having to waste time by flying round the circuit again was something no one wanted, particularly when we landed 23 aircraft in less than 33 minutes.

"*Johnny*. Funnels!"

"*Johnny*. Pancake!'"

"*Johnny*. Pancaking. Out. Full flaps. 2,850 revs."

'Peter complied. I managed to grease it on and Jock gave his greatest praise – complete silence! As soon as I touched down, Control called, "Keep rolling, *Johnny*".

"*Johnny* rolling," I replied, with a quiet smile to myself. I was not likely to stop in front of my mate and have him land on me, when we had just worked things so that we could both get down quickly. I suppose our talking between ourselves was not heard officially but they "officially" warned the aircraft that had just landed that another was landing immediately behind. At that time of the morning it was all a bit much for me.

'We arrived back at our dispersal and were greeted by the ground crew who were pleased to hear that we had no trouble with the aircraft and that there was no damage to it that we knew of. In the crew bus going back to the crew room we greeted other crews, talking tiredly about the trip and any trouble they may have had. Jack dumped his gear quickly and hurried to the debriefing room to put our name on the board and so reserve our place in the queue of crews waiting to be debriefed. The rest of us arrived shortly afterwards. By way of an informal report, the Squadron Commander asked me, "How was it, Stan? Much flak, any damage, good run to the target?"

"A pretty quiet trip, thanks, sir," I replied. "Only light flak and a few fighters about but I don't think we have any damage."

"Good – it was a long one and you will be looking for bed. Tell your crew to turn in straight away too."

"Right. Thanks, sir, I will."

'As I turned away I thought that there was something odd about that last remark but then one of the other skippers spoke to me and the thought went out of my head. As I headed for a cup of tea, the Doc was quietly running his eye over each of us without any fuss.

"How was it?" he asked.

"Not bad, Doc but it was a long one. Nine hours 45 in the air."

"Yes, a good night's sleep is what you need. Do you want anything?"

"No thanks Doc I have no trouble. I'm off to sleep as soon as my head hits the pillow. I just have to stay awake while 'Bags of Flak' rambles on over there." I indicated a table at which one of the crews was being interrogated by the WAAF Intelligence Officer, known to all as "Bags of Flak" due to her habit during the interview with returning crews of asking, "How was the target area? Bags of flak?"

'The Doc smiled, as he was in on all the jokes and sayings round the Squadron and knew what ops were like, having closed the rear door of the Flight Commander's aircraft five times, from the *inside*. "That's good. If there is anything when you wake up, just drop over and see me."

'The tea and biscuits tasted wonderful and Jock and Curly were arguing as usual over whose turn it was to have the tot of rum that I didn't drink, as well as the tot each had already had. Jock knew very well that it was Curly's turn but this was a harmless way to unwind a bit after the trip and the rest of us joined in with suitable comments, while silently cursing "Bags of Flak" for taking so long with each crew. At last it was our turn.

"What time did you bomb? What did you have in your bombsight?" she asked. (I would never forget her look of dismay and then disbelief when later, after a daylight raid on Cologne, with an Aiming Point near the cathedral, Maurie, who was bored stiff with this same question time after time, decided to liven things up by replying, "Two nuns and a priest!")

"Was there much flak?" (Someone must have told of her of her nickname.) "What did you think of the raid?"

"We had a quiet trip," I replied. "A very concentrated attack. One aircraft seen shot down shortly after we left the target."

"Anything else?"

"No, I think that's the lot, thanks." I signed the report and at last was on my way to breakfast. While eating my bacon and eggs I vaguely heard the CO say that he thought we might be on again that night but I was too tired to care or connect. I was only interested in a good long sleep. I said "Cheerio, see you later" to the others in the mess. No one was missing from the trip so we were all happy. I fell into bed at 07.45 but little did I know that I would be woken at 12.45 to be told that we were on the Battle Order for that night! After a late lunch, the whole routine, just complete, would be repeated. After another trip, of 9 hours 20 minutes in the air to Chemnitz,[8] I would fall into bed tomorrow morning, exhausted and with only one assurance that there was some limit to how often we were expected to be able to continue these operations. The Doc would tell me to get "a good, long sleep". When I replied, "Just like yesterday Doc?" he would quietly say, "No – if they try to put any of you who have flown these last two trips on a Battle Order for tonight, I will declare you medically unfit."

'Thank God for the Doc!'[9]

For most of the participating aircrew the Dresden raid of 13/14 February was another well executed and very efficient area bombing attack. Flight Sergeant Ray Base of 115 Squadron at Witchford, flight engineer on a Lancaster captained by Major Martin DFC SAAF was on his 20th operation.

'We took off at 21.45, taking Group Captain Reynolds as an observer. Bomb load consisted of one 4,000lb cookie and seven incendiary clusters, making a total of 7,820lb, plus 2,114 gallons of fuel to make the deep penetration raid and back. It was a very clear night with good visibility apart from the odd small cloud. We flew right down France, along by Stuttgart, up to within 50 miles of Berlin and then on to Dresden. The attack was on the old part of the city which was covered in snow. We arrived over the city about three-quarters through the raid, so things were well alight by then. The marking TIs were mostly red and green and showed up clearly among the fires. It was a very good attack, with the whole city burning, the streets being outlined in fire. Of the fires themselves, the burning buildings were very bright and around the outskirts were large dull red glows from the region of the railway station, gasworks and other industrial buildings. We experienced moderate flak over the target. As we left the target and turned on course for home we saw a Lancaster about 1,000 feet below silhouetted by the glow of the fires. I could see the Lanc's exhausts. Our mid-upper gunner then spotted a Ju 88 following the Lanc and then we saw a Ju 188 (clearly identified by its pointed wings) to the left and behind the Ju 88. There was a small cloud below and the three aircraft went into it and the cloud lit up with a large explosion, typical of a bomber blowing up. There were lots of searchlights over the Ruhr on our way back and very strong headwinds restricted our ground speed to 80 mph. We went down to 5,000 feet

over France to get more favourable winds. We got back with five minutes' fuel left – we drained all our tanks while in the circuit and all four fuel warning lights came on as we landed at 06.50 hours. Flight time was 9.05 hours.'[10]

As tons of explosives plummeted from the sky, an 800 degree C firestorm, similar to that created in Hamburg on 27/28 July 1943, tore through the heart of the Saxon capital, burning an estimated 25,000 to 40,000 Dresdeners alive. A prisoner on the Kleine Festung in Theresienstadt seventy kilometres away saw, from his cell window, the glowing red reflection above the burning city and heard the hollow thud of the bombs like hundredweight sacks being thrown into a cellar quite close to him. In the Altmarkt 6,865 corpses were burned on pyres by an SS detachment which had gained experience at Treblinka concentration camp.

Flight Sergeant John Aldridge of 49 Squadron who flew 33 operations as a Lancaster bomb-aimer between September 1944 and April 1945, and who took part in the 5 Group bombing of Dresden, recalls:

'The very next night Chemnitz was to be the target of a similar attack, 330 aircraft to make the first and 390 the second attack three hours later. In this case Harris at Bomber Command (probably under pressure from Bennett of the Pathfinder Group) decided that 8 Group's Pathfinders would carry out the marking for both attacks and we, in 5 Group, would carry out a separate attack on an oil plant at Rositz near Leipzig. However, with cloud cover and with 5 Group low level marking, 8 Group had to rely on sky marking and no concentration of bombing was achieved. I saw personal evidence of this as our (5 Group) withdrawal route linked up with the force returning from Chemnitz and I well remember the fires were scattered over 20 miles. Would Chemnitz have been a second Dresden if the same procedure as in that attack had been carried out?'

On the night of 20/21 February 514 Lancasters and 14 Mosquitoes set out for Dortmund, another 173 bombers raided Düsseldorf, 128 aircraft attacked Monheim and 154 Lancasters and 11 Mosquitoes attacked the Mittelland Canal. Including diversionary and minor operations aircraft, 1,283 sorties were flown. Twenty-two aircraft failed to return. Worst hit was the Dortmund force, which lost 14 Lancasters. These raids were followed on the night of 21/22 February by 1,110 sorties against Duisburg, Worms and the Mittelland Canal and another 27 aircraft were lost plus seven Lancasters crashed in France and Holland. The two consecutive nights, 20/21 and 21/22 February proved a profitable 24 hours for several German pilots[11] including Hauptmann Johannes Hager, *Staffelkapitän*, 6./NJG 1 who claimed two *Viermots*. *Bordfunker* Unteroffizier Walter Schneider who contributed to the last 13 of Hager's victories recalls:

'On 21 February we took off at 00.24 hours. I soon spotted a *Viermot*, which our pilot shot down after a short chase at 01.12 hours. On the outbound flight from Düsseldorf I managed to get hold of another one on my radar and this one was made to crash at 01.23 hours.[12] Later the same day, at 22.48 hours we again received orders to take-off. This time we had to fly in the direction of Duisburg. Soon we encountered the formation of bombers and we succeeded in shooting down six *Viermots* between 23.09 and 23.21 hours. By skilful use of the oblique cannon, my pilot was able to set the bombers on fire with short bursts into the engines. The crews thus had more time to safely bale out. After this exploit I was commissioned.'[13]

After shooting down the two Lancasters over Dortmund and returning to Gütersloh, Heinz-Wolfgang Schnaufer and his crew had a rest period until a *Werkstattflug* (air-test) was called at 18.15 hours for Bf 110 G9+EF. The flight lasted 21 minutes and the Messerschmitt was declared 'serviceable.' Leutnant Fritz Rumpelhardt, Schnaufer's radar operator, recalls:

'The late night sortie on 21 February 1945 was to become Schnaufer's most outstanding achievement in two-and-a-half years' service as a night fighter pilot. It was always a point of honour with him to be the first in the air after the order to scramble so that he could assess the situation and brief his squadron. Chance played quite an important part in the second operational sortie on 21 February. I was alone in the squadron mess having my supper, having missed the order "Heightened Preparedness", so when the order to scramble came the Major was ready but I was not. He did not mince his words about my apparent dilatoriness. In spite of the ensuing mad rush, the rest of the squadron was already airborne, on its way to Düsseldorf. By the time "EF" lifted off from the aerodrome it was 20.08 hours. Events now turned in our favour. Following the instructions received from Ground Control we believed that the others had reached the engagement area but we were somewhat puzzled when we could see neither bombers, nor night fighters nor, in fact, any anti-aircraft fire ahead of us. Schnaufer was debating whether to follow our present track when we suddenly noticed over to the North, probably in the Münster area, a lot of light anti-aircraft fire. Again this puzzled us. Guns of that calibre were effective up to 2,000 metres only, yet the British bombers usually flew between 3,500 and 6,000 metres over the Fatherland. Without further thought Schnaufer altered heading to the north-west to cut off the bombers returning home.

'At 2,500 metres we flew through a thin layer of cloud and our radar showed us several targets. Suddenly we were in a condition of "shroud," above us a thin layer of stratus through which the moon shone, giving us an opaque screen above which we could see clearly the black silhouettes of the bombers from quite a distance. Schnaufer closed upon a Lancaster flying along unsuspectingly slightly to our starboard at altitude 1,700 metres. We had been airborne just over half-an-hour. The Major closed with the target, left to right, from below and delivered the first attack with the two vertically mounted 20mm cannons, just behind him, in the cabin. He aimed between the two engines on the right-hand side. The fuel tanks were located there and this method brings the quickest results. The time was 20.44 hours. The right wing of the bomber was badly damaged; a huge flame illuminated the sky. The Lancaster held steady for a while, long enough to allow the crew to escape by parachute before it fell to earth and crashed.

'There followed attack after attack, the sky seemed to be full of bombers! Now the British crews knew we were there and began their violent manoeuvres, twisting and turning in an effort to escape us. Schnaufer had to follow all their corkscrew movements, to remain in a position under the bombers' wings where the return fire could not be brought to bear upon us yet ready, himself, to use the *Schräge Musik*. In one case we practically stood upon our wing tip whilst firing. Things became more difficult for us when we crossed the front line and the American anti-aircraft batteries opened up. Within a period of 19 hectic minutes we managed to shoot down seven bombers – without so much as a scratch – testimony to the Major's great skill and ability to get in quickly, line up his target and dive away quickly. Normally during this wild fighting I would hardly have had time to note the details thoroughly but because of the "shroud effect" the pilot did not need my assistance at the radar to guide him on to each target and I had more time than usual to observe the effects. Oberfeldwebel Wilhelm Gänsler[14], our gunner, gave great support as usual but even he could not help when we attacked our eighth Lancaster bomber. At the crucial moment we exhausted the ammunition to the upward-trained guns and as a result had the greatest difficulty in getting away from the concentrated fire from the bomber crew.

'We still had our four horizontally mounted cannons in the nose of our fighter but these too refused to function during our ninth attack and we had to stop chasing the bombers. On the way back to base we had to fly again over the American batteries and by now the Major was thoroughly weary, almost spent. I called, therefore, upon Dortmund to give us all possible assistance to clear us back to Gütersloh with all expediency and with this help Schnaufer greased our faithful G9+EF on to the ground. The night's work was done, we were back at base and it was just short of 22.00 hours. Once we had taxied in and shut down the engines, we sat in silence for a couple of minutes, thankful to have got through it and thought about the men who had gone down that night and hoped that they had managed to parachute to safety. Many years later I received a letter from an Englishman, Stanley Bridgeman. He had been a crewmember of Lancaster JO-Z of 463 Squadron shot down that night at 21.02 hours above Holland. All his crew had managed to escape by parachute. My prayers had been answered in part.'[15]

The second in a series of terrifying area-bombing raids on German cities, which had thus far escaped the bombing, went ahead on 23/24 February. Over 360 Lancasters and 13 Mosquitoes carried out the first and only area-bombing raid on Pforzheim, a city of 80,000 people, from only 8,000 feet and 1,825 tons of bombs were dropped in just over 20 minutes. More than 17,000 people were killed and 83 per cent of the town's built up area was destroyed in "a hurricane of fire and explosions". Ten Lancasters failed to return.[16]

Among the oil targets attacked in daylight during late February was the Alma Pluto benzol plant at Gelsenkirchen, which was bombed on two successive days on the 22nd (when Osterfeld was also bombed) and the 23rd, and a few days later, on 27 February. One Lancaster failed to return from the first of these raids and no Lancasters were lost on the second raid although a Halifax crashed in Holland where a Lancaster of 186 Squadron also put down in trouble. The crew dropped their load and made their usual quick exit from the heavily defended target area, the sky around them being filled with bursting shells. Some seconds later the Flight Engineer reported a loss of hydraulic power, which was serious as without hydraulics they would not be able to lower flaps or undercarriage. The pilot decided to lower both while hydraulics were still available and then try and land at an Allied base, as with flaps and undercarriage down

they would never make it back to Stradishall. Lying in the nose the bomb-aimer was the first to spot the emergency landing area. It was not ideal for a Lancaster as it was only a narrow and short stretch of metal planking but the pilot was considered one of the best and decided that he could get the aircraft down. They landed without mishap and taxied to the end of the strip. The Germans held the field and the pilot ordered the crew to man the guns. He wanted to fight it out rather than give up an intact Lancaster. Fortunately, the troops that came to meet them proved to be Royal Engineers.

The 27 February was a wintry day when, at around 15.00, Flight Lieutenant N. C. Cowley's crew in 186 Squadron made their approach to Gelsenkirchen. Cowley was an experienced pilot having flown at least 27 sorties. The target area was obvious from a long way off with the HE and incendiary bombs exploding on the ground and defending ack-ack shells bursting in the air all round the bombers. The air bomber recalled:

'It was our turn to go in. As Air Bomber it was my job to direct the pilot so that the target was lined up in the Sperry Bombsight. My bomb load consisted of a 4,000lb bomb and the remainder a mix of 1,000lb HE and incendiaries. The bombs were programmed to release in a set order – the streamlined bombs going first, followed by the clusters and, lastly, the cookie, the theory being that all the bombs would arrive on the ground at the same area. To my horror the cookie dropped almost immediately the release button was pressed. It soon caught up with the lighter bombs, scattering them all over the sky until one, and then, it seemed, all the rest, simply blew up. The aircraft was caught in the blast and disintegrated. Aircrew members are trained to react to emergencies, I am thankful for the drills, which, though boring at the time, proved their worth on this day. My first duty was to listen for instructions from the Captain but there was no response from the intercom to my request. My next duty was to jettison the escape hatch in the nose, absolutely vital if the cockpit crew were to escape. This was accomplished without difficulty but I was aware of the ground getting closer – we were diving almost vertically and on fire! At this point I fitted my parachute and dropped away from the aircraft. I came to on the ground, in great pain and very cold, and surrounded by German soldiers. My boots had gone – either in the descent or acquired by one of the Germans whilst I was still out cold. They patched my arm wound and took me to HQ where, to my great surprise, I met our Wireless Operator.' Cowley and four of the crew were killed, Flight Sergeants J. M. Young and H. G. Kimber being the only survivors.

Meanwhile, *Nachtjagd* had been planning a final large-scale offensive effort codenamed *Unternehmen* [Operation] *Gisela* an intruder operation over England. However only 142 Ju 88Gs could be committed to *Gisela*, which went ahead on 3/4 March, the 2,000th night of the war, when 234 bombers raided the Fischer-Tropsch synthetic oil plant at Kamen (the fourth raid on this target in eight days) and 222 aircraft attacked an aqueduct on the Dortmund-Ems Canal at Ladbergen. From these two raids, seven Lancasters were lost. Over England on the bombers' return the German intruders shot down 24 aircraft[17] but the German losses were higher.[18]

In March Bomber Command flew a record 53 day and night operations and as losses were still being felt at squadron level, some of these raids saw over 1,000 bombers taking part. On 11 March 1,079 aircraft, including 750 Lancasters, the largest number of aircraft sent to a target so far in the war, headed for the railway supply yards and railway lines at Essen in daylight to try to prevent the transfers of munitions and materials to the front. (Essen became the second largest bombing raid of the war when, the following day, 1,108 aircraft, including 748 Lancasters, set out to bomb Dortmund). The Essen raid was the last to this city which, despite being completely cloud covered, received 4,661 tons of bombs dropped accurately on *Oboe*-directed sky-markers.

Flight Lieutenant John Fern, a 25 year old pilot from Saskatchewan in 434 Squadron had lifted *Y-Yorker* off from Croft on their fifth operation. Except for Pilot Officer William Jones, the 37 year old flight engineer, who was from Liverpool, the crew were all RCAF commissioned officers and all were on their second tour. Approaching the target at 17,300 feet Fern and the 25 year old bomb-aimer, Tom Copeland from Ontario, guided their Lancaster into the Essen strike zones over the *Oboe*-directed sky markers. Copeland released the bomb load and about 33 seconds later they struck the railway yards. Copeland requested Fern to keep a straight course, as he wanted to "take a good picture". Immediately the Lancaster was hit by 88mm anti-aircraft shell. Everyone on board except for the rear-gunner, 25 year old Flying Officer Ben Marceau from Quebec, who was on his 47th op, were killed instantly. The shell that hit *Y-Yorker* also blew out the cockpit windows of the trailing Lancaster following about 100 feet behind and 50 feet above. *Y-Yorker* plunged on fire into the target area to crash near Margaretenhohe

where the wreckage of the doomed Lancaster was spread over a two-mile area.

The force of the explosion had blown Ben Marceau right out of his Frazer Nash rear turret. Severely wounded and unconscious, he fell from 17,300 feet to 2,000 feet amid heavy clouds before he came to and was able to open his parachute. Marceau landed very heavily in a field. Two Russian POWs forced to work in the field saw the Canadian land and they rushed over to him. Marceau was badly injured in the legs, shoulders, eye and face and they helped him by using his first aid kit to dress his wounds. Marceau gave them his two survival kits that he was carrying because he knew that capture was soon at hand as he could see three German soldiers running towards them. They searched him three times over for weapons or documents. The sergeant then took both survival kits away from the Russians and the other two German soldiers, who were about 15 years old, picked Marceau up and walked him about a kilometre back to their flak post, the sergeant kicking him in the legs from behind all the way. Fortunately, his heavy flying boots protected him. Marceau was exhausted and in severe pain and, as he sat himself down against a fence, the young German soldiers stayed at a distance as if frightened. Perhaps they sensed that the day of reckoning for Germany was near. Later, he was taken away in a truck and he vaguely recalled one of the soldiers trying to remove his wedding ring but before falling unconsciousness again he clinched his left hand so his ring could not be taken from him. Later that day he awoke only very briefly on an operating table in a hospital. Marceau was unconscious for five days and was then interrogated by a German officer who asked him what were the names of his crew were and where the other four crewmembers were. Marceau spent the next seven weeks in German and Belgian hospitals before being liberated in the Ruhr by American forces just five days before VE Day.[19]

On the night of 14/15 March when 244 Lancasters and 11 Mosquitoes attacked the Wintershall synthetic oil refinery at Lützkendorf near Leipzig, 18 Lancasters were lost. Also, 100 Group lost two Mosquitoes and two Fortress IIIs of 214 Squadron during *Jostle* radio countermeasure duties in support of the main force.[20] On 15/16 March, 267 bombers made an area attack on Hagen and another 257 Lancasters and eight Mosquitoes raided the Deurag oil refinery at Misburg. Six Lancasters and four Halifaxes failed to return from Hagen and four Lancasters were lost on the Misburg raid while a RCM B-17 was also lost. The following night 277 Lancasters and 16 Mosquitoes attacked

Nuremberg and 225 Lancasters and 11 Mosquitoes bombed the old cathedral city of Würzburg which contained little industry but was famous for its historic buildings. They dropped 1,127 tons of bombs with great accuracy in 17 minutes, destroying 89 per cent of the built up area and killing an estimated 4,000–5,000 people. During the night's operations 30 aircraft were lost, 24 of them Lancasters on the Nuremberg raid, mainly to German night fighters, which found the two bomber streams on the way to the target.[21] Bomber Command's tactics of deception and radio counter-measures had, by now, reached a fine perfection.[22]

On 20/21 March no less than three feint attacks took place in support of the main force attack on the synthetic oil refinery at Böhlen, just south of Leipzig, by 235 Lancasters and Mosquitoes. No amount of jamming could conceal the roar of 800 aircraft engines but the spoofs, diversionary attacks and countermeasures helped keep losses down to nine Lancasters.[23] On 21 March Bomber Command flew 497 sorties in raids on Rheine, Münster and Bremen for the loss of only five Lancasters and that same evening the heavies attacked refineries at Hamburg and Bochum.[24]

Next day raids on rail yards continued with daylight attacks on Hildesheim, Dülmen, Bremen and Nienburg. A Lancaster of 434 'Bluenose' RCAF, blew up shortly after take-off at 10.55 from Croft. Flying Officer H. Payne RCAF took off for Hildesheim but the Lancaster was caught by a sudden blast of wind, which took the bomber onto the grass. Payne tried to bring the aircraft back onto the runway but he over corrected and he then closed the throttles but he was unable to avoid racing across the airfield. A tyre burst and a collision occurred involving a Lancaster of 431 'Iroquois' Squadron RCAF, before the Lancaster came to a halt near East Vince Moor Farm. A fire started in the port engine and this spread rapidly. The crew managed to get clear and a general evacuation order was broadcast. Half an hour later the bomb load exploded and the force of the blast removed the roof of the farmhouse and set fire to hay and nearby buildings. Incredibly, no one was injured but it was late afternoon before the airfield was declared fit for use.[25]

Another area attack, which was carried out by Lancasters of 3 Group, was made on Bocholt. Minutes after the strike, crews looked back to see a pall of smoke 'black and ominous' rising to about 15,000 feet where once was a town. They also noticed a tremendous smoke screen stretching from Arnhem to Duisburg along the west bank of the Rhine, which was to cover troop movements, as a large-scale attack was pending.

On Saturday 23 March, 128 Lancasters attacked bridges at Bremen and Bad Oeynhausen and hit both of them, losing two of the Lancasters. At 15.30, 80 Lancasters bombed the little town of Wesel, which was an important troop centre behind the Rhine front in the area about to be attacked by the 21st Army Group massing for the Rhine crossings at dawn. It was an important point in the defensive system on the east bank of the Rhine and the Germans had not only turned it into a massively fortified position, with strong points, machine-gun nests and tank obstacles, but had concentrated troops and armour there for the expected British crossing. Once a town of 25,000 people, Wesel was already, because of its tactical importance, one of the most devastated places in Germany. In ten minutes, the roads, which had been cleared from the previous attacks were blocked and pitted with fresh craters. More than 400 tons of bombs were dropped on the troops and many strong points were destroyed. Five hours later, at 22.30 hours, only a short time before Field Marshal Sir Bernard Montgomery's zero hour, as the 1 Commando Brigade followed by the 51st Highland Division closed in, over 190 Lancasters followed it up with another attack, to complete the work of the afternoon. In exactly nine minutes, well over 1,000 tons of bombs went down on those troops who had crept back into the ruins to await the British commandos' attack. In all, more than 1,500 tons of bombs were dropped in the two attacks – a weight of bombs, which had already almost completely wiped out cities eight times the size of Wesel.[26]

Flying Officer John Rogers, a Queenslander and a cameraman attached to a RAF Film Production Unit, had a close-up view of the attack on Wesel. With their cameras peeping through the shuttered windows of a house facing Wesel across the Rhine, Rogers and other members of the Film Unit saw and filmed the Lancasters pounding the town into rubble. Besides being among the first cameramen to make a close-up ground record of an Allied air blitz against a German city, Rogers was the first RAAF man to cross the Rhine at ground level with the Allied armies. He and his colleagues had crossed a pontoon bridge a few hours after the bridgehead had been established and had come under machine-gun fire almost at once from a pocket of resisting Germans between the Film Unit vehicle and the Rhine. Wesel was taken with only 36 army casualties. In a message to Air Chief Marshal Sir Arthur Harris, Field Marshal Montgomery said, 'The bombing of Wesel last night was a masterpiece and a decisive factor in making possible our entry into that town before midnight.' The commandos who made the capture also sent a message congratulating the crews. The capture of Wesel, they said, cost them only a handful of men.

On 25 March Bomber Command flew 606 sorties against the main reinforcement routes into the Rhine battle area and Hanover, Münster and Osnabrück were heavily hit. Four bombers were lost (three to flak and one due to being struck by a bomb over the target). At Downham Market PB913, in 635 (PFF) Squadron, had been prepared as master marker aircraft for a raid on Osnabrück and the airfield controller scheduled it to take off first. However, the flight engineer, checking the aircraft, was not satisfied as the fuel gauges showed nil. The pilot, Squadron Leader George A. Thorne, who had crash-landed his ailing Lancaster near Woodbridge the previous October, anxious to go, checked the Form 700 with the ground crew and, noting that the aircraft was documented as fully serviceable, suggested that the fuel gauges had merely stuck. Just as the pilot was about to taxi out, the flight engineer, who had tapped the gauges in vain, reported that he would not be satisfied until the fuel had been checked. The engines were cut and the ground crew ordered to dipstick the tanks as a fuel check. They were found to be almost empty! Thorne, ordering the crew to follow, raced for the spare aircraft and hurriedly checked it over, but it was not fitted with VHF for the master bomber to instruct crews. Racing back to their original Lancaster, they taxied round to a bowser and ordered that the 2,154 gallons be put in immediately. It took 20 minutes or so. Meanwhile, the rest of the squadron had taken off, leaving the master bomber behind. Rarely did aircraft fly direct to their target, but, as in this case, went south first to complete the first leg of the journey in safety behind the Allied lines, to shorten the actual time over enemy territory. Thorne asked the navigator the chances of getting there on time if they cut across the heart of Germany. They were 50/50. At maximum speed they sped in a direct line to Osnabrück without opposition except for intensive flak as they crossed the Dortmund-Ems canal which, now such a regular target, was heavily defended. As Osnabrück approached below, so the main force hove into sight. No sooner had they marked than bombs were dropping. Thorne was awarded the DSO for marking the target.

In April *Nachtjagd* achieved 33 victories to take the arm's total claims for 1945 to 528 kills but the writing was on the wall. On Sunday 8 April, just over 230 Lancaster crews were briefed just after lunch for a raid on the oil refinery at Lützkendorf and 440 aircraft were

to bomb the shipyards at Hamburg. At Fulbeck a 49 Squadron crew were told by the CO that they were 'tour expired' since the signal he had received during briefing had reduced the number of operations required from 36 to 33. They were scrubbed from the operation and the reserve crew in *N-Nan* took their place. The rear-gunner, Roy Wilkins had completed about three trips less than the rest of the crew because of illness and, since the rear-gunner in the reserve crew had contracted ear trouble, Wilkins volunteered to take his place. The tour expired crew and Pollington went to see the crews off. Sitting on the grass waiting for *N-Nan* to swing onto the main runway they idly picked clover. Pollington picked three four-leafed clovers in succession! Laughingly, everyone said, '*You lucky bastard . . . it looks like your crew will get the chop tonight*'. Roy Wilkins gave them a thumbs up from his rear turret as *N-Nan* roared down the runway on what was a pleasant early spring evening. Later the tour expired crew went to the Hare and Hounds in Fulbeck village for a drink before rolling back into their hut. Although they had not had the pleasure of knowingly flying their last op, the feeling of having finished was nevertheless fantastic. Next morning Wilkins' bed was empty. They thought he might have landed elsewhere but nothing more was ever heard of him or the crew with which he was flying. The refinery was rendered inactive at a cost of six Lancasters and their crews.

Next day 40 Lancasters carried out the last raid on Hamburg when they raided oil-storage tanks, and 17 aircraft of 617 Squadron blasted the *U-boat* shelters in the already devastated city with 22,000lb *Grand Slam* and 12,000lb *Tallboy* bombs. Known as cookies by RAF crews, the 4,000lb, 8,000lb and 12,000lb blast bombs were dubbed 'Block Busters' by Fleet Street. *Grand Slam* bombs could reach a velocity of 1,000 feet per second (680 mph) when dropped from 20,000 feet.[27] Two Lancasters failed to return from the raid on Hamburg. That night 591 Lancasters and eight Mosquitoes visited Kiel and bombed the *Deutsche Werke* U-boat yards. Reconnaissance pilots had detected the pocket battleship *Admiral Scheer*, a sister ship of the *Graf Spee,* moored in the inner dockyard basin at Kiel two days earlier. Like the *Tirpitz*, the *Admiral Scheer* had been driven to Kiel when Gdynia was first threatened by the Russian Army and had previously played an important part in the defence and evacuation of German pockets of resistance on the Baltic coast. As the equivalent of an armoured cruiser with exceptionally powerful armament, the *Scheer* was still of great importance to the enemy, if only because Allied warships had to be kept in readiness to attack her if she left harbour. The attack was made in clear weather. Marking and bombing was extremely well concentrated around the aiming points and many crews reported a violent explosion. Sergeant F. Jenkins RAAF, an air bomber, saw an explosion fling debris many hundreds of feet into the air as his Lancaster arrived and, in the glow of the fires, he saw six ships around the *Scheer* amid dense clouds of smoke, through which came heavy AA fire. When the bombers left, the *Scheer* lay almost completely upside down in much the same position as Bomber Command had left the *Tirpitz*. The *Admiral Hipper* and the *Emden* were badly damaged. Three Lancasters were lost.[28] Germany now had only one pocket battleship left, the 12,000-ton *Lützow*, which shared the fate of the *Admiral Scheer* on the afternoon of 16 April when Lancasters arrived over Swinemünde with more 12,000lb bombs to leave the ship's stern resting on the bottom in shallow waters.

Further raids were made on the Engelsdorf and Mockau rail yards at Leipzig and rail yards in the northern part of Plauen. Seven Lancasters were lost on Leipzig where the eastern half of the yards were destroyed. On the night of 14/15 April, 500 Lancasters and 12 Mosquitoes took part in an operation against Potsdam just outside Berlin. Although Mosquito bombers of the Light Night Strike Force had attacked the Big City almost continually, this was the first time the *Reich* capital had been attacked by heavies since March 1944. One Lancaster was lost to an unidentified night fighter over the target. Maurice Bishop, pilot of *Winsome Winnie* of 218 'Gold Coast' Squadron at Chedburgh, recalls:

'This flight, which took 8 hours 55 minutes, was our most remembered. About an hour from the target my mid-upper gunner suddenly shouted, "Down skip!" I pushed the stick forward hard and saw another Lanc sliding over the top of us on a slightly different heading, same height. My gunner saw the exhaust flame just in time as it was closing in on us. The searchlight activity over Berlin was intense and we were just sliding past one that was fixed when it suddenly locked straight on to us and I was completely blinded. I started to change height, speed and direction, as taught, and went into a diving corkscrew, pulling out the bottom dive quite hard and throwing the old Lanc around by feel as I was still blinded by the searchlight. Then suddenly we were clear before the night fighters spotted us and we dropped our load on the target and came home OK.

'The next day down at dispersal the ground engineer said, "What were you up to last night?"

'I said, "Why?"

'He said, "Look at this" and he took me up the steps and showed me the upper wing between the fuselage and the starboard inner. The skin had a wrinkle in it. We must have pulled out of the dive with our full bomb load on board and the old Lanc had taken it under protest.'

An attack on Pilsen, on 16/17 April 1945, involved 222 Lancasters, one of which, MD733 of 463 Squadron flown by Flying Officer J. A Hagley RAAF of 463 Squadron, failed to return to England.

'Aircraft was on track on outward route and climbing at 03.10 hours, 7,200 feet, when suddenly in the light of a half moon an aircraft of unknown origin attacked the aircraft. The attack came from slightly to port in front, approximately 200 yards above, at 400–600 yards range. The aircraft received strikes on starboard inner, starboard mainplane, engineer's panel, starboard side of pilot's cockpit, oil supply to starboard outer, No. 1 tank on starboard – which was losing fuel, main fuselage above W/Op and navigator's compartment, plus the hydraulic and electrical systems. The aircraft was flooded with hydraulic oil. The strike on the starboard inner set it on fire, but this was feathered and the Graviner was applied successfully.

'Immediately prior to 463 being attacked, a Lancaster was seen flying on the port side above at 600 yards. A second or two after the sighting, the rear-gunner and air bomber heard machine gunning and almost simultaneously 463 was attacked. No tracer was seen. The aircraft, with its starboard inner on fire, dived to port to avoid revealing position of the bomber stream. After corkscrewing it was found that the starboard outer was losing oil rapidly, and it was then decided to set course for the English Channel via Juvincourt, the English Channel being the nearest jettison area for bombs. However, these good intentions were foiled, because height could not be maintained and thirteen 500 MC bombs were jettisoned safely at 03.25 hours. After jettison action had been taken, the aircraft was able to climb to 4,800 feet, at which height course was set for Juvincourt by aid of stars, as navigator's equipment was unserviceable.

'The flight engineer nursed the starboard outer, although for an hour this engine was not registering an oil pressure. Juvincourt eventually appeared 20 miles on the port side at 05.00 hours, when the starboard outer seized, imparting considerable vibration to the aircraft. The crew were then told by the captain to "put on parachutes and stand by". The rudder was then lashed with rope by the air bomber and flight engineer to assist the pilot. The 4,000lb HC was then jettisoned.

Aircraft was flown over Juvincourt at 2,500 feet, with starboard outer on fire and unable to feather it owing to lack of voltage, due to failure in electrical circuit. The aircraft was in danger of immediate explosion owing to the petrol still flowing to the nacelle by the windmilling action of the starboard outer. The order, "emergency, jump, jump, jump" was given and all the crew escaped.'

At 17.45 on 17 April, as Lancasters of 57 and 630 Squadrons were being bombed up at East Kirkby for the night raid on railways at Cham near the Czech border, two 1,000lb MC bombs for one of the Lancasters went up, causing sympathetic explosions. The airfield appeared to be a shambles and ambulances had to be called from other stations. Four airmen were killed and 14 injured and there were two civilian casualties, one of which was fatal. Next morning, after a survey in daylight of wrecked and toppled Lancasters, the station engineer officer reported five completely written off and 14 with varying degrees of damage. The No. 3 hangar, which was being used for storing incendiaries, was also severely damaged, as was Hagnaby Grange Farm.

The end came on 25 April with a raid by 482 aircraft on coastal batteries on the Friesian Island of Wangerooge and, in a fitting climax to bomber operations, on Hitler's mountain retreat at Berchtesgaden in the southeast corner of Germany. The Obersalzberg, a beautiful mountainous region, close to the Austrian border, was one that had long appealed to Hitler. Following the Munich Putsch and his imprisonment, Hitler had stayed in the Obersalzberg, writing part of *Mein Kampf* there. Royalties from the book's sale had enabled the German dictator to buy a house called the 'Berghof'. After coming to power the building had been rebuilt on a lavish scale, the best-known addition was the dramatically named 'Eagle's Nest', a tea-house that had been built on Kehlstein Mountain apparently as an isolated conference building. Hitler's home, referred to, as the 'Chalet' by the RAF, was the target for 359 Lancaster heavy bombers and fourteen *Oboe* Mosquito and 24 Lancaster marker aircraft. Included in the mighty force were 33 Lancasters, of 9 Squadron and 617 the 'Dam Busters', each carrying a potentially devastating 12,000lb *Tallboy* bomb in their long, rakish bomb bay. For once, the BBC was permitted to announce the raid while it was in progress. At least 126 P-51 Mustangs of 11 Group RAF, and 98 P-51s from two American fighter groups, provided escort relays along the route, a round trip of 1,400 miles.[29]

In the summer of 1940 11 Group's few squadrons of Spitfires and Hurricanes had held Hermann Goering's legions at bay, a defeat that had put in motion the gradual fall from grace for the rotund *Reichsmarschall*. By 1945 his beloved *Luftwaffe* existed in name only and he no longer had the ear of his *Führer*, who was safely tucked up in his bunker in Berlin while Goering now had to find shelter in one of the air-raid tunnels under the remote mountain fortress.

Pete Keillor, a US 78th Fighter Group Thunderbolt pilot at Duxford, had the honour of leading the Group on the escort mission for the Lancasters. He guessed – wrongly – that the 'British bomber guys' wanted to fly in daylight 'once' so they loaded 'two bunches with 8,000lb bombs' and sent them down to Berchtesgaden. 'Maybe they thought they'd catch Hitler there' he mused. In fact, ever since D-Day and on many days since, RAF Bomber Command relinquished their nocturnal role and mounted many pulverizing raids in the daylight hours. The Mustangs flew on over the sea and crossed into Belgium at 06.30 hours but they missed the planned rendezvous with the Lancasters over Luxembourg, as Pete Keillor recalls:

'I reported in over the continent and ground control told me that my bombers were an hour ahead of where they were supposed to be. I put on extra power and finally caught up with them and escorted them to the target. I started counting them and saw that they were the wrong bunch. [They were the 16 Lancasters of 617 Squadron]. If I remember right there were a 110 in the first bunch and 88 in the second and the second was ours. American bombers all had tail markings so you could tell which was which, but the Lancasters were just a bunch of planes, not even in real formation. So, after they'd dropped their bombs [on Hitler's "Chalet" and the local *SS* guard barracks] I left them and hurried back to pick up the others. Sure enough we found them and escorted them in and out. That was the prettiest scenery I ever flew over. It was perfectly clear – you could see forever – and we followed the north side of the Alps for hundreds of miles. Steep mountains went down to lakes in the valleys and it sure made you want to see it from the ground.'[30]

Those who bombed the 'Chalet' mostly missed[31] but the Berghof sustained much blast damage as a result of the bombs and the *Tallboys*.

Pilot Officer L. Knight on his first operation and his crew in 625 Squadron were about to be reported as missing from this operation when, two hours overdue, he landed safely back at Kelstern with two engines out of action. Only 53 bombers attacked their primary target but at the SS barracks one building and several others were damaged. Six of the 3,500 who had sheltered in the air-raid tunnels were killed. Goering was not one of them but he was captured later and received his judgement at Nuremberg, but a lethal suicide pill prevented his execution for war crimes. Soon after the raid, the US 3rd Infantry Division won the race to occupy Berchtesgaden and share in the spoils of victory. Bomber Command's last bombing operations were flown that night when 119 Lancasters and Mosquitoes, directed by the master bomber, Wing Commander Maurice A. Smith DFC, attacked oil storage depots at Tonsberg in southern Norway and U-boat fuel storage tanks at Vallo in Oslo Fjord. Operation orders for attacks on Heligoland on the 26th and 27th were each cancelled in turn. Yet, the war was not over for the bomber crews. Four days later Operation *Manna* began, as the Lancaster squadrons began dropping food and not bombs.[32]

With the Germans at the brink of defeat, thousands of people in the western and north-western provinces of the Netherlands, which were still in German hands, were without food. Parts of the country had been under German blockade and 20,000 men, women and children had died of starvation during a very short period and the survivors were in a desperate plight. Dutch railwaymen had gone on strike in protest against German demands and, as a result, there was no distribution of food. Townsfolk went foraging in the country and thousands camped in fields in search of food. Five slung panniers, each capable of carrying 70 sacks containing flour, yeast, powdered egg, dried milk, peas, beans, tins of meat and bacon, tea, sugar, pepper and special vitamin chocolate, were fitted into the Lancaster bomb bays. Orders were issued for each squadron to drop the panniers in their allotted area, which they would find 'marked' by PFF Mosquitoes after liaison with the Dutch authorities and the underground movement.[33] Only the bedridden appeared to be confined to their homes as the Lancasters flew over to drop their loads and there was a sea of hands waving handkerchiefs and flags to greet the RAF bombers while even some German gunners standing by their anti-aircraft guns waved solemnly in acquiescence.

The authorities tried to keep the drop zones clear but there were a few incidents. A Lancaster of 186 Squadron, which was briefed to drop five large panniers each on Waalhaven aerodrome near Rotterdam, dropped three packages, by which time crowds had swarmed across the field and they could not risk dropping the others. Another Lancaster could not get all its packages away because the bomb doors had been damaged by small-arms fire. Back over Stradishall the pilot found that he could not lower the undercarriage. While 'jinking' his aircraft to jolt the wheels down, a package

fell, strewing tea, sugar and tins over the countryside to the north of Stradishall which caused something of a race between villagers and the RAF recovery party. Finally the pilot flew to Woodbridge and landed safely on the long runway. Next day two bags from an aircraft above hit one of this squadron's Lancasters, fortunately without causing damage. The drops continued for several days. Crews reported that, on a number of houses, messages had been whitewashed – 'Thanks RAF' and 'Good Luck Tommy'. Many crews gave their own sweet rations and their aircrew issue, wrapped up and tied by string to handkerchiefs or pieces of linen to make a parachute. They flung them from the open windows of their Lancasters with notes saying, *Ver Het Kinde* – 'For The Children'. The sweets became a free for all! Stones marked out 'TABAC' and a whip round of the cigarette ration was organized and it was dropped at the location the next day. A target indicator in the Rotterdam area fell by a house and set it on fire. One pannier dropped in a lake, but later crews reported rowing boats going out to salvage the contents. During the operation one Lancaster, after dropping 284 sacks, got into trouble over the North Sea on the return journey. A short in a microphone heater caused a fire in the rear turret and exploded rounds of ammunition. The pilot was able to land at Oulton without injury to any of the crew. During Operation *Manna* from 29 April to 7 May a total of 6,684 tons of food were dropped in 3,156 sorties by Lancasters and 145 flown in Mosquitoes.

Maurice Bishop, pilot of *Winsome Winnie* of 218 'Gold Coast' Squadron, recalls: 'On 30 April we did our first food drop on Operation *Manna* to Rotterdam and 2 May to The Hague, both marvellous low flying, 250 feet. The "*Thanks*" messages on the roofs with towels and sheets I will always remember.'

The last operational order of the war for offensive action by Lancasters was issued on the morning of 3 May when 427 (Lion) Squadron at Leeming was instructed to detail nine aircraft to lay mines in the Kattegat that night. At 22.30 the Lancasters started out and eight had taken off when a general order suspending all operations was received. They were contacted by radio, recalled and they landed with their mines. At Skipton-on-Swale 424 (Tiger) Squadron already had eight aircraft airborne when the recall was received, with instructions to fly locally for four hours to lessen their fuel and so reduce their load for landing.

EXODUS Operation Order No. 1 was issued on 2 May. Two days later Lancasters were landing at

Brussels and Juvincourt to repatriate prisoners-of-war from Germany. Westcott was the main reception base and there were many touching scenes as soldiers, sailors and airmen jumped out of the Lancasters on to British soil for the first time for several years in some cases. Every effort was made to provide a welcome and military bands played the Lancasters in. At one reception station the response was measured in the rate of rations consumed in one day – 15,000 cups of tea and half a ton of cakes. EXODUS continued during VE Day, celebrated on 8 May, and was followed by Operation *Dodge,* the repatriation of Eighth Army soldiers from Bari in Italy. Most Lancaster units, not on repatriation duty, were stood down on VE Day. At Middleton St George, a Canadian Lancaster station, a pipe-band marched round followed 'by the station personnel in various stages of intoxication'. Anyone rash enough to be properly dressed had his tie clipped off while others had the 'wingtips' of their luxuriant moustaches trimmed too. Tragically, one Lancaster loaded with 25 passengers and a crew of six got into trouble soon after take-off from Juvincourt and it appears that the passengers were told to take up station at the rear of the aircraft. This upset the flying trim and the pilot lost control. The Lancaster dived into the ground near Roye-Ami and all the occupants were killed. Apart from that tragedy, 74,000 ex-POWs were brought safely home in Lancasters up to 28 May when the final evacuation was carried out.

Maurice Butt, a pilot in 149 Squadron recalls: 'VE Day, 8 May, found many hundreds of RAF and other recently liberated prisoners of war on the tarmac at Brussels Airport, awaiting transport back to England. The boys of Bomber Command gave up their celebration leave to come and get us out and we piled into the Lancs, the most excited "bombloads" ever carried. I was lucky, being the first on our plane and scrambled forward to the bomb-aimer's station; spotting everything approaching, after about half an hour, there were the white cliffs of Dover. At that moment, the front gunner handed me his helmet. Incredibly, Winston Churchill was speaking from the House of Commons, announcing the victory news and I could hear it quite clearly on the earphones.'

With one eye on the peace, Churchill tried to distance himself from the bombing of German cities. He declared that, 'The destruction of Dresden remains a serious query against the conduct of Allied bombing'. This was the same Winston S. Churchill who, on 22 June 1941, had said. 'We shall bomb Germany by day as well as night in ever-increasing measure, casting upon them

month by month a heavier discharge of bombs and making the German people taste and gulp each month a sharper dose of the miseries they have showered upon mankind.' Many others tried to denigrate the efforts of Bomber Command and its leaders, notably 'Bomber' Harris but they have nothing to be ashamed of. The real pioneering achievements in bomb warfare – Guernica, Warsaw, Belgrade, Rotterdam – were the work of the Germans. As early as August 1942, when the vanguard of the German Sixth Army had reached the Volga and not a few were dreaming of settling down after the war on an estate in the cherry orchards beside the quiet Don, the city of Stalingrad, then swollen (like Dresden later) by an influx of refugees, was under assault from 1,200 bombers. And, that during this raid alone, which caused elation among the German troops stationed on the opposite bank, 40,000 people lost their lives.[34]

Sergeant Frank W. Tasker, a Lancaster mid-upper gunner in 622 Squadron says: 'The most successful of our nightly operational flights and the ones that I remember so well were those on Dresden and Chemnitz. Since World War II some Germans have complained about those raids having taken place. Have they conveniently forgotten, how for the first TWO YEARS of the war, the *Luftwaffe* was bombing London (where I lived) and elsewhere in UK day and night! Have they also forgotten the V-1 flying bombs and V-2 rockets they were still indiscriminately sending to kill innocent women and children in England? Surely they haven't also forgotten about the gas chambers they used!'

Flight Sergeant John Aldridge recalls: 'Afterwards, when I read criticism of the bombing, I did wonder what I'd been a part of but at the time it was just a job we had to do.'

'I never spent much time wondering what was going on down below' recalled Rod Rodley. 'I eased my conscience feeling that the Germans must do what we'd been doing, which was to evacuate non-participants. I never pictured what a bomb could do to a human frame. I'd done my duty, which was to take a load of high explosive to an aiming point laid down by those in authority above me, whom I trusted. If I'd been an imaginative character I might have wondered exactly what happened when those bombs hit but I merely hoped that I was hitting a factory or machine tools or something of that ilk. The only way I could have got a picture of the effect of bomb attack on people was to go to the East End of London. I had no great desire to do that. I was not troubled in my conscience because we were fighting a very ruthless enemy. We all knew this. Our families were home behind us and we were rather like a crusader with his sword in front of them. My thoughts at the time were that I have a family and a bigger family – the public – and I was going to do my damnedest to stop the Germans coming across. If you go into war you've got to win it, and if you are too weak you suffer the trials and tribulations of being a slave race. Some of our intelligentsia are writing in the peace and warmth of their homes about how wicked the bombing campaign was. They don't realize that they wouldn't have had that freedom to do so if we had not had 55,000 aircrew who lost their lives for their sake.'[35]

> My brief sweet life is over,
> my eyes no longer see,
> No summer walks, no Christmas
> trees, no pretty girls for me,
> I've got the chop, I've had it, my
> nightly ops are done,
> Yet in a hundred years from now,
> I'll still be twenty-one.[36]

For thousands of Bomber Command aircrew, the war was never over. Their daily hell would follow many of them to their graves.

Leave them their glory.

Notes

1. Dresden was targeted as part of a series of particularly heavy raids on German cities in Operation *Thunderclap* with a view to causing as much destruction, confusion and mayhem as possible. The other cities were Berlin, Chemnitz and Leipzig which, like Dresden, were vital communications and supply centres for the Eastern Front. *Thunderclap* had been under consideration for several months and was to be implemented only when the military situation in Germany was critical. The campaign was to have started with an American raid on Dresden on 13 February but bad weather over Europe prevented any US involvement until the 14th. Dresden was to be bombed in two RAF assaults three hours apart, the first by 244 Lancasters and the second by 529 more.

2. 1 Group, of which 460 Squadron was one, would be in the second phase. Two hundred and forty-four Lancasters of 5 Group were to commence the attack at 22.15 hours on 13 February, using its own Pathfinder technique to mark the target. This was a combination of two Lancaster Squadrons – 83 and 97 – to illuminate the target and one Mosquito Squadron (627) to visually mark the aiming point with Target Indicators from low level. The aiming point was to be a sports stadium in the centre of the city, situated near the lines of railway and river which would serve as a pointer to the Stadium for the marker force, especially since it was anticipated that visibility might not be too good. A second attack was timed for 01.30 hours on the 14th by another 529 aircraft of 1, 3, 6 and 8 Groups, with 8 Group providing standard Pathfinder marking. Calculations were that a delay of three hours would allow the fires to get a grip on the sector (provided the first attack was successful) and fire brigades from other cities would concentrate fighting the fires. In this second attack target mark-

ing was to be carried out by 8 Pathfinder Group. The bombing technique to be carried out by the main 5 Group Lancaster Force was known as the Sector type, which had been developed by 5 Group in area attacks. This meant that each aircraft headed up to the aiming point on a different heading – in the case of the Dresden attack from about due south to about due east, each with differing delays for bomb release after picking up the aiming point on the bombsight. This meant that the bombing covered a wedge-shaped sector, resulting in a great number of fires being started over the whole sector, since a great proportion of the bomb load consisted of incendiaries. Finally, 450 B-17s of the US 8th Air Force were to attack Dresden shortly after 12.00 on 14 February. To assist the night operations of Bomber Command (a force of 344 Halifaxes was to attack an oil plant at Böhlen near Leipzig at the same time as the first attack) various 'spoof' attacks were to be made by Mosquitoes on Dortmund, Magdeburg and Hanover. In addition to the above, routing and feints were to be carried out by the main forces to reduce night fighter reaction to a minimum. In the case of the 5 Group attack the outward route consisted of no less than eight legs with feints towards the Ruhr, Kassel, Magdeburg and Berlin using 'Window' at the same time.

3. Each container held 150 4lb incendiary bombs.

4. These settings were for the bombsight, with the 'multiplied by 1.1' to prevent any German radio interception operator from making any sense of our broadcast and so be unable to substitute a false message.

5. See note 1.

6. When the illuminator force of the Pathfinders arrived over Dresden cloud cover was 9 to 10/10ths up to about 9,500 feet. The marker force of Mosquitoes found the cloud base was at about 2,500 feet. The cloud was not too thick and the flares illuminated the city for the markers who placed their red TIs very accurately on the aiming point. At 22.13 hours, 244 Lancasters, controlled throughout by the master bomber, commenced the attack and it was completed by 22.31 hours. More than 800 tons of bombs were dropped. By the time of the second attack cloud cover had cleared to 3 to 7/10ths but despite this the master bomber could not identify the aiming point, due to the huge conflagrations and smoke and a decision was made to concentrate bombing on areas not affected. An area was marked by the Pathfinders both to the left and to the right to assist in concentrating the bombing and good concentration was achieved. In all, 529 Lancasters dropped more than 1,800 tons of bombs. So great were the conflagrations, caused by the firestorms created in the great heat generated in the first attack, that crews in the second attack reported the glow was visible 200 miles from the target.

7. In all, during the two RAF raids 1,478 tons of HE and 1,182 tons of incendiaries were dropped. In the third attack 316 of the 450 B-17s of the 8th Air Force dispatched, attacked Dresden shortly after 12.00 on 14 February, dropping 771 tons of bombs. (The Americans bombed Dresden again on 15 February and on 2 March). RAF Bomber Command casualties were six Lancasters lost with two more crashed in France and one in England. An 800 degree C firestorm tore through the heart of the Saxon capital, burning thousands of Dresdeners alive. In a firestorm similar to that created in Hamburg on 27/28 July 1943, an estimated 25,000 to 40,000 Germans died in Dresden. (At Böhlen the weather was bad and the bombing scattered).

8. The 14/15 February raid on Chemnitz, again in two phases, cost eight Lancasters and five Halifaxes.

9. 460 Squadron RAAF flew more Lancaster sorties (5,700) than any other squadron and, as a consequence, suffered the highest Lancaster losses in 1 Group (140 + 31 in accidents).

10. Flight Sergeant Base had witnessed the demise of the only Lancaster claimed shot down by night fighters. Just six Lancasters were lost from the 796 Lancasters and 9 Mosquitoes dispatched. Major Hans Leickhardt, *Kommandeur* of II./NJG 5 was probably the only *Nachtjäger* to make contact with the Dresden force; he shot down two Lancasters.

11. Major Heinz-Wolfgang Schnaufer, *Kommodore*, NJG 4 took off from Gütersloh at 01.05 hours in Bf 110C G9+MD. Employing *Schräge Musik* attacks delivered below the bombers in an *Einsatz (*sortie) lasting 2 hours 9 minutes, he shot down two Lancasters at about 11,000 feet WSW of Mönchengladbach-SW of Roermond.to take his score to 109. Hauptmann Adolf Breves of IV./NJG 1 took off from Düsseldorf airfield at 02.13 hours on 21 February in his Bf 110 and claimed three aircraft in the Ruhr area to take his score to 16.

12. Fourteen Lancasters were lost on Dortmund. Düsseldorf cost four Halifaxes and one Lancaster. Monheim resulted in the loss of two Halifaxes. Mittelland Canal was w/o loss. In total 22 aircraft failed to return.

13. On 21/22 February German ground control identified the course and height of the bomber stream heading for Worms and, before the heavies reached their target, succeeded in infiltrating 15 *Spitzenbesatzungen* of NJG 6 into the bomber stream in the area of Mannheim-Worms. No jamming of their *SN-2* sets was experienced and neither were any Mosquitoes encountered. Eight *Nachtjagd* crews claimed 21 bombers destroyed in the target area. Hauptmann Breves claimed two more *Viermots* in a 50-minute sortie in the Ruhr area as his 17th and 18th and final victories of the war. Oberfeldwebel Günther Bahr of 1./NJG 6, flying Bf 110G 2Z+IH with Feldwebel Rehmer as *Bordfunker* and Unteroffizier Riediger as *Bordschütze* shot down seven Lancasters of the Worms force on their bombing run to the target in quick succession. Hauptmann Johannes Hager's six *Viermots* were his 40th-45th *Abschüsse* (all but six of his 45 claims were later confirmed) and he was awarded the *Ritterkreuz*. Hauptmann Heinz Rökker, *Ritterkreuzträger* and *Staffelkapitän* of 2./NJG 2 also destroyed six (56th-61st kills); five of his *Abschüsse* were of the Mittelland Canal force. Rökker ended the war with 63 *Nachtjagd Abschüsse* (including 55 *Viermots* and 1 Mosquito) + 1 day victory in 161 sorties with NJG 2.

14. Gänsler, an experienced *Bordschütze* who had formidable night-vision, had previously flown with Oberleutnant Ludwig Becker and had shared in 17 kills with him. He was awarded the *Ritterkreuz*.

15. Lancaster I NG329 JO-Z of 463 Squadron was MIA at Gravenhorst. Schnaufer's final 15 victories came in 1945, nine of them in one 24-hour period on 21 February, to take his grand total to 121 bombers in 130 sorties (114 of his kills were four-engined Stirlings, Halifaxes and Lancasters) and he was decorated with the *Ritterkreuz* with Oak Leaves, Swords and Diamonds. Leutnant Fritz Rumpelhardt took part in 100 of these successful attacks and Oberfeldwebel Gänsler in 98. Rumpelhardt was the most successful *Bordfunker* in *Nachtjagd* being credited with 100 *Abschussbeteiligungen*, or 'contributions to claims'. Schnaufer died in a motor car accident in France on 31 July 1950.

16. Bomber Command's last Victoria Cross of the war was awarded for an action this night. The master bomber was Captain Edwin Swales DFC SAAF. A German fighter twice attacked his Lancaster over the target. Swales could not hear the evasion directions given by his gunners because he was broadcasting his own instructions to the main force. Two engines and the rear turret of the Lancaster were put out of action. Swales continued to control bombing until the end of the raid and must take some credit for the accuracy of the attack. He set out on the return flight but encountered turbulent cloud and ordered his crew to bale out. This they all did successfully but Swales had no opportunity to leave the aircraft and he was killed when it crashed. He is buried at the Leopold War Cemetery at Limburg in Belgium.

17. Thirteen Halifaxes, nine Lancasters, one Mosquito and one Fortress III.

18. Altogether, 33 Ju 88G night intruders were lost during *Gisela*. Five German aircraft crashed on British soil and eight other crews were reported missing. Three more crews perished in crashes on German territory. Six crews baled out due to lack of fuel and 11 crashed on landing.

19. Rick Thomson, The Nanton Lancaster Society. The other crewmembers KIA apart from Fern, Copeland and Jones were Flight Lieutenant George Rowe DFC, navigator (22) from Ontario; Flying Officer Joe Latremouille, WOp/AG (22) also from Ontario and Flying Officer Gibson Scott, MUG, (26) from BC, Canada. Two other Lancasters were shot down on the Essen raid with all crews lost. Two Lancasters failed to return from the raid on Dortmund the next day.

20. Hauptmann Martin 'Tino' Becker of *Stab* IV./NJG 6 and his *Funker* Unteroffizier Karl-Ludwig Johanssen in a Ju 88G-6 claimed nine bombers, the highest score by a German night fighter crew in any single night. Becker shot down six Lancasters of the Lützkendorf force. After expending his last ammunition on the sixth Lancaster he positioned his Ju 88G to the side of two more Lancasters and finally a Fortress III, piloted by Flight Lieutenant Norman Rix DFC, and Unteroffizier Karl-Ludwig Johanssen manning the twin rear facing machine guns, shot each one down in turn. Johanssen's three victims counted towards the grand total of his pilot so the B-17 was Becker's 57th official victory. Johanssen was awarded the *Ritterkreuz* two days later. Becker's score at the end of the war was 58 night victories. A second Fortress III flown by Flight Lieutenant Johnny Wynne DFC flew at around 24,000 feet while the Lancs flew towards the target at 20,000 feet. For the homeward trip the Lancs and the Forts were to fly at 3,000 feet above sea level to make it difficult for the German night fighters to locate and attack them. Wynne's Fortress was within half an hour's flying time of the Rhine when his aircraft was hit and he flew 80 miles with the No. 2 engine on fire and the fuel tank, which by now was half full, expected to explode at any time. He was 60 miles from the Rhine where the land, south-west of the river, was occupied by the Allied armies. Unfortunately, strong winds had caused the main force to fly further south and east of the planned track and the Fortress had been hit 25 miles east of the position recorded in Flying Officer Dudley Heal DFM, the 1st Navigator's log. The No. 2 engine gradually disintegrated but Wynne was sure that they had, by now, reached the safety of French territory. Wynne ordered his crew to bale out. All

nine men vacated the aircraft in less than five minutes. Wynne managed to keep airborne but by the time he was ready to leave, baling out was no longer an option, he was far too low and the aircraft refused to climb. Incredibly, the flames died down and finally the engine fire went out. Wynne somehow managed to reach England where he crash-landed at Bassingbourn in Cambridgeshire. Five of the nine men never returned. The 2nd navigator, who had broken his ankle, was hospitalized. Dudley Heal became a POW. The rest of the crew were rounded up, put in a school basement and later they were hauled into the street by a lynch mob. Four were murdered in cold blood; the fifth was free for a day and, after giving himself up, was beaten by a mob before being murdered by Gert Biedermann, a 15 year old *Hitler Youth,* who shot him in the head. Biedermann, who had dug the bodies of his mother and five brothers and sisters from the rubble after the bombing of Pforzheim, was later tried, found guilty and sentenced to 15 years imprisonment. See *Confounding the Reich* by Martin W. Bowman (Pen & Sword, 2004).

21. Oberleutnant Erich Jung, *Staffelkapitän* 5./NJG 2 in Ju 88G-6 4R+AN with his *Funker* Feldwebel Walter Heidenreich and flight mechanic Oberfeldwebel Hans Reinnagel, destroyed eight Lancasters, some by Jung with his *Schräge Musik* and some with his forward-firing guns. Heidenreich, who had taken part in 12 kills with Oberleutnant Günter Köberich, who had been killed in an American raid on the airfield at Quakenbrück in April 1944, shot down the 3rd victim, which took Jung's personal score to 28 kills. Hauptmann Wilhelm 'Wim' Johnen, *Kommandeur* of III./NJG 6 claimed his 32nd and final victory of the war, a Lancaster SE of Würzburg.

22. On the night of 17/18 March when there was no main force activity, a sweep by 66 Lancasters and 29 Halifaxes was made over Northern France to draw German fighters into the air and formations of Mosquito bombers carrying cookies visited targets in Germany. On 18/19 March 324 aircraft carried out an area bombing raid on Witten, the force losing eight aircraft including six Halifaxes. Meanwhile, 277 Lancasters and eight Mosquitoes carried out an area raid on Hanau and just one Lancaster was lost. On 19 March 79 Lancasters attacked the Consolidation Benzol plant at Gelsenkirchen without loss. Benzol plants in Germany were attacked on successive days and nights, 17, 17/18 and 18 March.

23. *Nachtjäger* claimed 11 Lancasters shot down. Three of the missing aircraft this night were shot down SW and W of Kassel by Hauptmann Johannes Hager, *Staffelkapitän* of 6./NJG 1 flying a Bf 110G-4, his 40th-42nd and final victories of the war. (Hager had a total score of 48 *Abschüsse*.)

24. One hundred and seventy-eight aircraft carried out an accurate attack on the rail yards at Rheine and the surrounding town area for the loss of one Lancaster. Some 160 Lancasters raided the railway yards at Münster and a railway viaduct nearby for the loss of three bombers. Another 133 Lancasters and six Mosquitoes headed for Bremen and accurately bombed the Deutsche Vacuum oil refinery without loss. Twenty Lancasters of 617 Squadron attacked the Arbergen rail-bridge just outside Bremen and destroyed two piers of the bridge for the loss of one Lancaster. On the Bremen raid Lancaster B.I (Special) PD117 of 617 Squadron was hit by flak from the railway-mounted flak battery 2./902, the aircraft exploding with tremendous force with its full bomb load on hitting the ground at Okel, south of Bremen, leaving a crater 40 metres wide. Only small frag-

ments were found of the aircraft and its five-man crew, who are all commemorated on the Runnymede Memorial for the Missing of the RAF. The B.1 Special Lancaster had a crew of five instead of the usual seven. One hundred and fifty-one Lancasters and eight Mosquitoes raided the Deutsche Erdölwerke refinery at Hamburg and 131 Lancasters and 12 Mosquitoes a Benzol plant at Bochum. Five Lancasters were lost, four of them from the Hamburg force and a RCM Fortress, which was supporting the Bochum force, also failed to return. Hauptmann Dieter Schmidt, commander of the 7th *Staffel* NJG 1 achieved his 40th and final kill; a Lancaster near Cologne (probably NG466 AR-Y of 460 Squadron RAAF – five of the crew KIA). Hauptmann Kraft of 12./NJG 1 claimed a Lancaster near Bochum, for his 51st *Abschuss*.

25. Two hundred and twenty-seven Lancasters and eight Mosquitoes raided Hildesheim for the loss of four Lancasters. One hundred and thirty Halifaxes, Lancasters and Mosquitoes bombed Dülmen in an area attack without loss and 124 Halifaxes, Lancasters and Mosquitoes raided targets at Dorsten, again without loss. Another 102 Lancasters of 5 Group, in two forces, attacked bridges at Bremen and Nienburg without loss and the bridge at Nienburg was destroyed.

26. One hundred and ninety-five Lancasters and 12 Mosquitoes carried out the last raid on Wesel without loss.

27. Some 41 *Grand Slam* bombs were delivered before the end of the war in Europe.

28. They were claimed shot down by Leutnant Arnold Döring and Hauptmann von Tesmar of IV./NJG 3 and Hauptmann Heinz Ferger of III./NJG 2.

29. *Barnes Wallis' Bombs: Tallboy, Dambuster & Grand Slam* by Stephen Flower (Tempus, 2004).

30. *Wandering Through World War II* by Pete Keillor (Privately published, 2003).

31. A mountain peak between the *Oboe* ground station and the aircraft had blocked out the bomb release signal. Since *Oboe* signals went line of sight and did not follow the curvature of the earth, the further the target, the higher one needed to be and the *Oboe* Mosquitoes flew at 36,000 feet because of the Alps. Crews heard the first two dots of the release signal and then nothing more. They were unable to drop and brought the markers back.

32. As early as 24 February, a Lancaster of 115 Squadron had been on detachment at Netheravon for experiments in dropping provisions. In early April tests were made at Witchford for loading containers in the two types of bomb bays with which Lancasters were fitted. By 6 April practice drops were made and next day Major R. P. Martin gave a demonstration drop to officers of Bomber Command Headquarters assembled at nearby Lacey Green.

33. PFF Mosquitoes made 124 sorties to 'mark' the dropping zones.

34. *On The Natural History of Destruction* by W. G. Sebald.

35. By the end of the war no less than 73,741 casualties were sustained by Bomber Command of which 55,500 aircrew had been KIA or flying accidents, or died on the ground or while prisoners of war. It is a casualty rate that compares with the worst slaughters in the First World War trenches. Operational bomber losses were 8,655 aircraft and another 1,600 were lost in accidents and write-offs. Approximately 125,000 aircrew served in the front line OTU and OCUs of the Command and nearly 60 per cent of them became casualties. In addition,

almost 9,900 more were shot down and made POWs to spend one, two or more years in squalid, desolate *Oflags* and *Stalags* in *Axis* held territory. Over 8,000 more were wounded aboard aircraft on operational sorties. Bomber Command flew almost

390,000 sorties, the greatest percentage of them by Avro Lancasters, Handley Page Halifaxes and Wellingtons. Theirs of course were the highest casualties.

36. *Requiem for a Rear Gunner* by Sergeant R. W. Gilbert.

RAF Bomber Command Battle Order 5 June 1944

Squadron	Station	Aircraft	Command
7	Oakington	Lancaster BI/III	Bomber
9	Bardney	Lancaster BI/III	Bomber
12	Wickenby	Lancaster BI/III	Bomber
15	Mildenhall	Lancaster BI/III	Bomber
35 'Madras Presidency'	Graveley	Lancaster BI/III	Bomber
44 'Rhodesia'	Dunholme Lodge	Lancaster BI/III	Bomber
49	Fiskerton	Lancaster BI/III	Bomber
50	Skellingthorpe	Lancaster BI/III	Bomber
57	East Kirkby	Lancaster BI/III	Bomber
61	Skellingthorpe	Lancaster BI/III	Bomber
75 RNZAF	Mepal	Lancaster BI/III	Bomber
83	Coningsby	Lancaster BI/III	Bomber
97 'Straits Settlements'	Coningsby	Lancaster BI/III	Bomber
100	Grimsby	Lancaster BI/III	Bomber
101	Ludford Magna	Lancaster BI/III	Bomber
103	Elsham Wolds	Lancaster BI/III	Bomber
106	Metheringham	Lancaster BI/III	Bomber
115	Witchford	Lancaster BI/III	Bomber
156 'East India'	Upwood	Lancaster BI/III	Bomber
166	Kirmington	Lancaster BI/III	Bomber
207	Spilsby	Lancaster BI/III	Bomber
300 *'Masovian'*	Faldingworth	Lancaster BI/III	Bomber
405 'Vancouver' RCAF	Gransden Lodge	Lancaster BIII	8 Group PFF Bomber Cmd
408 'Goose' RCAF	Linton-on-Ouse	Lancaster BII	6 Group Bomber Command
419 'Moose' RCAF	Middleton St George	Lancaster BX	6 Group Bomber Command
428 'Ghost' RCAF	Middleton St George	Lancaster BX	6 Group Bomber Command
460 RAAF	Binbrook	Lancaster BI/III	Bomber
463 RAAF	Waddington	Lancaster BI/III	Bomber
467 RAAF	Waddington	Lancaster BIII	Bomber
514	Waterbeach	Lancaster BI/III	Bomber
550	North Killingholme	Lancaster BI/III	Bomber

Squadron	Station	Aircraft	Command
576	Elsham Wolds	Lancaster BI/III	Bomber
582	Little Staughton	Lancaster BI/III	Bomber
617 'Dam Busters'	Woodhall Spa	Lancaster BI/III	Bomber
619	Dunholme Lodge	Lancaster BI/III	Bomber
622	Mildenhall	Lancaster BI/III	Bomber
625	Kelstern	Lancaster BI/III	Bomber
626	Wickenby	Lancaster BI/III	Bomber
630	East Kirkby	Lancaster BI/III	Bomber
635	Downham Market	Lancaster BI/III	Bomber

Operation *Chastise* – Dams Raid 16/17 May 1943

617 Squadron, RAF Scampton, Lincolnshire. 5 Group.
Primary targets: Möhne, Eder and Sorpe dams.
Secondary targets; Schweim, Ennerpe and Dieml dams.

Aircraft	Captain	Target	Remarks
ED932 *G-George*	Wing Commander Guy Gibson DSO DFC	Möhne/Eder	Released mine at Möhne
ED864 *B-Beer*	Flight Lieutenant David Astell DFC	Möhne	Shot down en route to the dam
ED887 *A-Apple*	Squadron Leader Melvyn 'Dinghy' Young DFC	Möhne	Hit Möhne Dam. Lost off Dutch coast on return
ED906 *J-Johnny*	Flight Lieutenant David J. H. Maltby DFC	Möhne	Hit the Möhne Dam
ED925 *M-Mother*	Flight Lieutenant John V. 'Hoppy' Hopgood DFC*	Möhne	Lost at the Möhne Dam
ED929 *L-Love*	Flight Lieutenant Dave J. Shannon DFC RAAF	Möhne/Eder	Released mine at Eder
ED937 *Z-Zebra*	Squadron Leader Henry E. Maudslay DFC	Möhne	Lost after hit by blast of his own bomb
ED909 *P-Popsie*	Flight Lieutenant Mick Martin DFC RAAF	Möhne	Released mine at Möhne Dam
ED912 *N-Nuts*	Flight Lieutenant L. E. S. Knight RAAF	Möhne/Eder	Breached the Eder Dam
ED865 *S-Sugar*	Pilot Officer Lewis J. Burpee DFM RCAF	Sorpe	Lost on outward flight
ED934 *K-King*	Flight Sergeant Vernon W. Byers RCAF	Sorpe	Lost on outward flight
ED936 H	Pilot Officer Geoff Rice	Sorpe	Hit the sea before crossing enemy coast. Aborted
ED921 *W-William*	Flight Lieutenant J. Les Munro RNZAF	Sorpe	Hit by flak on outward flight. Aborted
ED924 *Y-Yorker*	Flight Sergeant Cyril T. Anderson	Diemel/Sorpe	Did not bomb
ED927 *E-Edward*	Flight Lieutenant Robert N. G. Barlow DFC RAAF	Sorpe	Lost on outward flight
ED918 *F-Freddy*	Flight Sergeant Ken W. Brown RCAF	Sorpe	Released mine at Dam wall
ED923 *T-Tommy*	Flight Lieutenant Joe C. McCarthy DFC RCAF	Sorpe	Released mine at Dam wall
ED886 *O-Orange*	Flight Sergeant W. C. Townsend	Ennerpe	Released mine at Dam wall
ED910 *C-Charlie*	Pilot Officer Warner Ottley	Lister	Lost en route to the dam

Bomber Command Lancaster Aircrew Victoria Cross Recipients

	Squadron A/c	Action/Award
Nettleton, Acting Squadron Leader John Dering, pilot	44 Lancaster	17.4.42 28,4.42
Gibson, Acting Wing Commander Guy Penrose DSO* DFC* pilot	617 Lancaster	16/17.5.43 28.5.43
Reid, Acting Flight Lieutenant William RAFVR pilot	61 Lancaster	3/4.11.43 14.12.43
Cheshire, Wing Commander Geoffrey Leonard DSO* DFC RAFVR pilot	617 Lancaster	8.9.44
Thompson, Flight Sergeant George RAFVR, WOp	9 Lancaster	1.1.45 20.2.45*
Palmer, Acting Squadron Leader Robert Anthony Maurice DFC RAFVR pilot	109 Lancaster	23.12.44 23.4.45*
Swales, Captain Edwin DFC SAAF, 'master bomber'	582 Lancaster	23/24.2.45 24.4.45*
Bazalgette, Acting Squadron Leader Ian Willoughby DFC RAFVR 'master bomber'	635 Lancaster	4.8.44 17.8.45*
Jackson, Sergeant (later Warrant Officer) Norman Cyril RAFVR flight engineer	106 Lancaster	26/27.4.44 26.10.45
Mynarski, Pilot Officer Andrew Charles RCAF mid-upper gunner	419 Lancaster	12/13.6.44 11.10.46*

*Posthumous award

Bomber Command Battle Order – Units Operating Lancasters (less training units) 18 April 1945

Unit	Location	Type
1 Group HQ Bawtry		
12	Wickenby	Lancaster I, III
100	Elsham Wolds	Lancaster I, III
101	Ludford Magna	Lancaster I, III
103	Elsham Wolds	Lancaster I, III
150	Hemswell	Lancaster I, III
153	Scampton	Lancaster I, III
166	Kirmington	Lancaster I. III
170	Hemswell	Lancaster I, III
300 *'Masovian'*	Faldingworth	Lancaster I, III
460 (RAAF)	Binbrook	Lancaster I, III
550	North Killingholme	Lancaster I. III
576	Fiskerton	Lancaster I, III
625	Scampton	Lancaster I, III
626	Wickenby	Lancaster I, III
No. 3 Group HQ Exning		
15	Mildenhall	Lancaster I, III
75 (RNZAF)	Mepal	Lancaster I, III
90	Tuddenham	Lancaster I, III
115	Witchford	Lancaster I, III
138	Tuddenham	Lancaster 1. III
149 'East India'	Methwold	Lancaster I, III
186	Stradishall	Lancaster I, III
195	Wratting Common	Lancaster I, III
218 'Gold Coast'	Chedburgh	Lancaster I, III
514	Waterbeach	Lancaster I, III
622	Mildenhall	Lancaster I, III

Unit	Location	Type
No. 5 Group HQ Swinderby		
9	Bardney	Lancaster I, III
44 (Rhodesia)	Spilsby	Lancaster I, III
49	Syerston	Lancaster I, III
50	Skellingthorpe	Lancaster I, III
57	East Kirkby	Lancaster I, III
61	Skellingthorpe	Lancaster I, III
83 (PFF)	Coningsby	Lancaster I, III On loan from 8 Group
97 'Straits Settlements' (PFF)	Coningsby	Lancaster I, III On loan from 8 Group
106	Metheringham	Lancaster I, III
189	Bardney	Lancaster I, III
207	Spilsby	Lancaster I, III
227	Strubby	Lancaster I, III
463 (RAAF)	Waddington	Lancaster I, III
467 (RAAF)	Waddington	Lancaster I, III
617 'Dam Busters'	Woodhall Spa	Lancaster I, III Special Operations
619	Strubby	Lancaster I. III
630	East Kirkby	Lancaster I, III
No. 6 Group (RCAF) HQ Allerton		
419 'Moose' (RCAF)	Middleton St George	Lancaster X
420 'Snowy Owl' (RCAF)	Tholthorpe	Halifax/Lancaster X, I (3)
424 'Tiger' (RCAF)	Skipton-on-Swale	Lancaster I, III
427 'Lion' (RCAF)	Leeming	Lancaster I, III
428 'Ghost' (RCAF)	Middleton St George	Lancaster X
429 'Bison' (RCAF)	Leeming	Lancaster I, III
431 'Iroquois' (RCAF)	Croft	Lancaster X
433 'Porcupine' (RCAF)	Skipton-on-Swale	Lancaster I, III
434 'Bluenose' (RCAF)	Croft	Lancaster X
No. 8 Group (PFF) HQ Huntingdon		
7	Oakington	Lancaster I, III
35 'Madras Presidency'	Graveley	Lancaster I, III
83	Coningsby	Lancaster I, III Detached to 5 Group
97	Coningsby	Lancaster I, III Detached to 5 Group
156	Upwood	Lancaster I, III
405 'Vancouver'	Gransden Lodge	Lancaster I, III
582	Little Staughton	Lancaster I, III
635	Downham Market	Lancaster I, III

Appendix 5

Comparative Heavy Bomber Sorties and Casualties

Aircraft	Sorties	Lost (percentage of sorties)	Operational crashes (percentage of sorties)
Lancaster	156,192	3,431 (2.20)	246 (0.6)
Halifax	82,773	1,884 (2.28)	199 (0.24)
Wellington	47,409	1,386 (2.92)	341 (0.72)
Stirling	18,440	625 (3.39)	59 (0.32)
Hampden	16,541	424 (2.56)	209 (1.26)
Whitley	9,858	317 (3.22)	141 (1.43)
Manchester	1,269	64 (5.04)	12 (0.95)

Index